The Bell Tower and Beyond

The Bell Tower and Beyond

Reflections on Learning and Living

David Emory Shi

Illustrations by J. Ronald Boozer

Edited by Judith T. Bainbridge

University of South Carolina Press

Published in Columbia, South Carolina, by the
University of South Carolina Press

Manufactured in the United States of America

06 05 04 03 02 5 4 3 2 1

Library of Congress Cataloging-in-Publication Data

Shi, David E.

The bell tower and beyond : reflections on learning and living / David Emory Shi ; illustrations by J. Ronald Boozer ; edited by Judith T. Bainbridge.

p. cm.

ISBN 1-57003-466-4

1. United States—Civilization. 2. United States—History. 3. United States—Biography. 4. Education, Higher—United States—Philosophy. 5. Creative writing—Philosophy. 6. Southern States—History. 7. Shi, David E. I. Bainbridge, Judith T. (Judith Townsend) II. Title.

E169.1 .S5556 2002

973—dc21 2002000864

For Gordon Williams Blackwell
President, Furman University
1965–1976
and
John Edwin Johns
President, Furman University
1976–1994

Contents

Illustrations

Acknowledgments

Books may have individual authors, but they in fact are group projects. This compilation of speeches, columns, and reviews has benefited greatly from the contributions of others.

Judy Bainbridge's editorial insights and discriminating judgments were immensely helpful. My former Furman classmate, Ron Boozer, now a Charlotte architect, produced the evocative drawings of the Furman campus. Furman staff member John Roberts provided essential research support, and Alex Moore at the University of South Carolina Press shepherded the manuscript through the production process. I am also grateful to the *Greenville News,* the *Atlanta Journal-Constitution,* the *Charlotte Observer,* the *Christian Science Monitor,* the *Fort Lauderdale Sun-Sentinel,* the *Philadelphia Daily News,* the *Philadelphia Inquirer,* the *Providence Journal,* the *Raleigh News and Observer,* the *Tampa Tribune,* the *Virginian-Pilot,* and the *Washington Times* for publishing these essays in earlier forms.

This book is dedicated to two former Furman presidents whose leadership and friendship I cherish. Through their actions and their lives, they have affirmed the value of liberal learning and helped Furman gain its rightful place among the nation's finest private colleges.

Preface

I lead a double life. Although trained to be a professor and paid to be a college president, I yearn to be a full-time writer. Prose ambushed me at an early age. Words, I discovered, have power and beauty, as well as an elusive precision. To select the right words and craft compelling sentences requires intense concentration. Yet the subtle nuances of language offer immense pleasure. For a bookish child growing up in Atlanta, writing offered the self-delighting inventiveness of a linguistic game.

Over the years, the quest for perfect words has become a passion verging on an obsession. Writing unleashes our inventiveness and frees us from the sludge of the trivial. Words and sentences, if well chosen, can become levers for social betterment. As playwright Tom Stoppard once observed, "I don't think writers are sacred, but words are. They deserve respect. If you get the right ones in the right order, you can nudge the world a little."

The private process of converting perceptions into prose lubricates our imagination. Words enable us to express unspoken sources of insight: memory and observation, emotion and thought. In sum, writing is so seductive because it is the most powerful medium for corralling ideas, interpreting our chaotic surroundings and random encounters, and exploring the connections between past and present, self and society.

Speeches were the original form of writing, and I deliver lots of them. College presidents are notorious for their podium platitudes and highfalutin harangues. In fact, as some wag once observed, presidents tend to be one of two types: the historians or the ministers—those with a long memory and those with a long message. I was trained as a historian yet yearn to be a minister. As a result, my audiences pay a dear price. They may not be any wiser after one of my speeches, but they are much older.

The speeches included in this collection represent an important tradition in American higher education: the ceremonial rituals that serve as the sinews of our sense of community. Colleges are bound together not by accident but by shared values and goals that must be perennially refreshed and *enacted.* Ceremonial rituals help remind us what we are about and where we are headed—together. Ezra Pound once spoke of people "gathering a live tradition from the air," but as he well knew, traditions in fact are not so easily grasped or renewed. Convocations, inaugurations, commencement exercises, dedications of new buildings, and the annual meetings of academic honor societies provide opportunities for campus communities to reflect together on their shared commitment to learning and service (such academic events might be called "pompous circumstances").

Liberal learning at its best is a collective experience. It requires space and time to be together, to share knowledge, and to nurture common values amid striking differences of background, temperament, and custom. After all, as the poet William Butler Yeats once asked, "How but in courtesy and ceremony / are innocence and beauty born?" By being ceremonial together, we celebrate and make manifest our conviction that we pursue liberal learning collegially, and we keep alive our faith in learning as a dialogue.

The newspaper columns collected here represent a tantalizing privilege: the freedom to write about anything. Several years ago, when asked to become a regular essayist on topics of my own choosing, I could not resist the opportunity. Such journalistic freedom, limited only by weekly deadlines and rigid word limits, has enabled me to pause and reflect at the intersection of learning and living—describing the distinctive nature of higher education, exploring the mysteries of everyday experience, indulging my love for history, and, in general, trying to make sense of the world we inhabit.

Writing columns and book reviews has not only allowed me to learn more about interesting topics; it has also provoked self-discovery. The crucible of composition helps refine one's ideas and feelings. Of course, writing for the public also serves as a vehicle for one's vanity. Like all columnists, I harbor the childish premise that what interests me will fascinate others.

Since 1994 I have had the honor of serving as president of Furman University. The opportunity to work with bright students, talented professors, and dedicated staff and alumni is a rare privilege. Yet the life of a college or university president is also quite demanding. It involves long hours and endless meetings. Weekends are workdays, and crises erupt with regularity. As the *New York Times* recently pointed out, a successful college presidency requires "the skills of God, on a good day." I cannot imagine a more diverse array of responsibilities and activities than those performed by a college president: scholar, politician, visionary, counselor, minister, judge, architect, accountant, investor, athletics booster, surrogate parent, public speaker, civic leader, event planner, crisis manager, and fund-raiser. Leading a university requires the skill of a politician, the patience of Job, the thick skin of an elephant, and the stomach of a goat.

In recent years, the relentless emphasis on raising money and maintaining the good will of diverse constituencies has engendered a conspicuous timidity in many college presidents. Few campus leaders seem willing to discuss in public or in print subjects outside the realm of higher education. Who can blame them? The public arena has become so contentious and volatile, so factional and strident, that campus leaders need to be cautious. Presidents are expected to generate publicity but avoid controversy.

I have enjoyed the luxury of serving under a board of trustees that encourages my journalistic endeavors and tolerates my eccentricities. The trustees also recognize that while a college must guard its independence, it must also remain connected with the needs and activities of a changing society. Campuses and communities have good works to pursue together. In this respect, higher education is a civic as well as intellectual enterprise. Colleges must nurture a willingness to do and be good in an imperfect world. This commitment to learning as an active engagement with society animates my outlook as president and as essayist.

Unburdened by great expectations, the fugitive pieces collected here represent the most relaxed and relaxing form of writing. By definition, a newspaper column embodies a brief narrative on a particular topic, usually marinated with the author's own personal observations and opinions, and occasionally blessed with an unexpected coherence and compressed immediacy. To be sure, such succinct narratives lack the depth to be conclusive. "One short choppy wave after another" is the phrase Virginia Woolf used to characterize her own essays and book reviews. Yet the flexibility afforded by open-ended journalism is exhilarating. In an age of ferocious specialization, I relish being a quirky generalist.

If there is a common theme or tendency in this miscellany of speeches and columns, it is my interest in the past, in people, and in the process of becoming educated. As a professor, president, writer, and historian, I frequently think about how we live and how we should live, all the while trying to avoid any imperious moralism in dealing with such matters. These meandering meditations are intended to be instructive and entertaining, provocative and even redemptive—for both author and reader. As Samuel Johnson recognized in the eighteenth century, the only purpose of writing is "to enable readers to enjoy life or better endure it."

Part 1

The Academic World

A Precious Inheritance

Inaugural Address

| *April 19, 1995*

It is custom that brings us here today. It is tradition that binds us together. We have gathered on this radiant spring day to renew a common purpose, affirm a faith, and begin a new era in Furman's long and distinguished history.

Like the majestic trees that grace this campus, Furman has deep roots and extensive branches. It is now almost two centuries old.

Today's ceremony involves much more than the investiture of a new president. It also reminds us that this university is a "precious inheritance" bequeathed to us to protect and nurture. The legacy we inherit from generations past is indescribable yet still tangible; it embodies all the lives, energies, and resources that have been devoted to the university over the last 169 years.

Today, therefore, we would do well to remember our anchoring principles and lofty intentions. From its inception, this institution has assumed that intellectual inquiry and spiritual reflection can thrive together. The Latin motto on the university seal declares that Furman exists "for Christ and for learning."

Over the years, Furman has broadened its mission and revised its programs—and it has been blessed by the presence of female students since its merger with the Greenville Woman's College in 1933.

Yet despite undergoing many changes since 1826, Furman has remained a college whose animating purpose is to fashion graduates quick of mind and generous of soul.

Four years ago, Furman and the South Carolina Baptist Convention entered into a prolonged debate over the governance of the university. That debate ended a year later with a mutual agreement to sever all legal and financial ties. As a result, we are now in control of our own identity and have the opportunity to shape our own destiny.

Furman's newly independent status, however, does not mean that it is now rudderless in a secular sea. The ideals of liberal learning, civic virtue, and social responsibility remain firmly in place and give direction to all that we do. As the world careens toward the end of a century and the start of a new millennium, this university will continue to provide an ecumenical setting that encourages students, faculty, and staff to grow in faith as they grow in knowledge.

Such a reaffirmation of our historic purposes helps to anchor our vision of Furman's future. While justifiably proud of the university's past accomplishments, we need to challenge ourselves to improve every aspect of what we do.

In elevating our ambitions, however, we must avoid the temptation to imitate schools with more prestigious names and smaller hearts. Hear me well: we will continue to traverse our *own* path to excellence.

For us, however, excellence is not a destination or a goal, not simply a higher ranking in *U.S. News and World Report* to be coveted, reached, celebrated, and forgotten. Instead, excellence at Furman involves the very spirit in which we do things.

Several months ago, in preparing a speech for the New England Society of Charleston, I reread Henry David Thoreau's account of a trip that he and his brother took in a homemade boat down the Concord and Merrimack Rivers. His observations bristle with revelations about the spirit of excellence.

At one point, Thoreau describes visiting Williams College, nestled among the Berkshire Mountains in western Massachusetts. "It would be no small advantage," he declares in passing, "if every college were thus located at the base of a mountain."

Thoreau did not explain what advantages a college would derive from such a location. But I think I know what he meant. Furman, too, rests at the base of a noble mountain. Every day the imposing stature of the Blue Ridge admonishes us to strive for more than the merely adequate; it goads us to raise our sights, to stretch ourselves to the very limit of our potential.

Doing so will require wise and sometimes painful choices. Those choices will succeed to the extent that our facts are correct, our priorities clear, and our convictions firm.

Where does Furman want to go from here? What will be our distinguishing emphases and attributes? Where do we focus our attention, and how do we best allocate our resources?

Furman will continue to be an inviting crossroads where character and characters, architecture and landscape intersect; a place of beauty and benevolence where young people are encouraged to develop a personal style and design a way of life; a college where history, civility, and concerns of the spirit and social justice still matter; a learning community where students are more intoxicated by ideas and relationships than by alcohol.

At the same time, Furman University, like American society itself, is going to be more cosmopolitan in its outlook, more diverse in its composition, more international in its interests, and more sophisticated about the implications of technology than in the past.

Perhaps the most exciting development at Furman in coming years will involve our approach to liberal learning itself. Although people often talk about a liberal arts education as if it were a static enterprise unchanged since ancient times, its meaning and its structure have in fact evolved with a changing society. Over the years, new fields of study and new modes of learning have been admitted into the liberal arts curriculum with great benefit.

Furman has become an exemplar of a new type of liberal arts college. While our curriculum remains grounded in the traditional humanities, arts, and science disciplines, we also recognize that selected preprofessional programs can effectively complement the liberal arts and be of great service to the larger community.

At the same time, Furman has become especially committed to active forms of learning, both inside and outside the classroom. An old proverb, variously attributed to the Chinese or the Sioux Indians, expresses the benefits of such engaged learning:

Tell me and I forget;
Show me and I remember;
Involve me and I understand.

Like this proverb, Furman stresses that liberal learning is not simply a spectator sport—nor is it limited to the conventional classroom. We want our students to do more than passively memorize facts and theories. We encourage them to analyze, synthesize, and evaluate information, to pose questions, challenge assumptions, form hypotheses, conduct their own research and experiments, and present their findings to others.

This interactive, problem-solving approach to learning is helping Furman breach the walls of the ivory tower stereotype. It also gives our students greater responsibility for their own education, sharpens their self-confidence, and hones their leadership and communication skills.

Furman's ability to sustain such an innovative approach to learning is threatened by the same turbulent forces that are buffeting all colleges. The continuing decline in federal and state support for higher education and the soaring costs of new periodicals and books, computers and scientific equipment, increased financial aid, and expanded student services, are straining college budgets everywhere.

Because the next few years in our enterprise will be financially challenging, our fortitude in focusing on what really matters must be all the stronger if we hope to cement Furman's place among the very best colleges in the United States.

Yet there are some encouraging developments that make me very optimistic about Furman's future. The applications for next year's freshman class have set an all-time record in number and quality. Financial support from the Greenville community and from our extended alumni family is at record levels. We thus have the luxury of focusing on more than mere survival; our challenge is to determine at what level we will excel.

Visitors often comment about the stunning beauty of Furman's campus. To be sure, we take justified pride in the quality of our grounds and facilities. But in fact this university's greatest asset is its people. I have been amazed at the talent and the dedication of the folks populating this campus. The students have been incredibly warm and gracious. They continually lift our spirits and give us confidence in the future. We feel fortunate to associate with them.

We feel equally fortunate to work with such a gifted faculty and staff who perform the real work of the university. They have repeatedly enlarged my vision and stimulated my imagination.

As we begin this journey together, I solicit the patience, cooperation, and insights of all members of the Furman family.

In 1977 Robert Penn Warren, one of this country's most distinguished writers, published a novel titled *A Place to Come To.* Although it deals with Vanderbilt University, his alma mater, its essential theme is equally relevant to our purposes at Furman.

Warren uses evocative prose to describe the perennial human need for lasting relationships, for developing a sense of rootedness in a place of lasting significance. He recognizes that it takes a great deal of history to make a great university.

Like all colleges, Furman still has some history to overcome, but it has much more history to celebrate. Furman, you see, is not only a special place to come *to,* as Robert Penn Warren phrased it; it is a special place to come *from* as well. I can testify to that fact. My own enduring experiences at this college are an indelible part of my life, my convictions, my view of the past, and my hopes for the future.

Many of you, I am sure, feel the same sense of indebtedness to this university. We work, learn, play, and occasionally struggle in this place—and in the process its spirit and texture affect our thoughts and memories for the rest of our lives.

It is not only a campus where knowledge is shared; it is a common ground where our very sense of self and our need for community and for spiritual purpose are awakened and nourished.

In coming years I hope that we will continue to communicate honestly and humanely with one another, that our relationships with one another will deepen, and that we will continue to rejoice together, struggle together, and delight in each other.

By doing so we can ensure that Furman remains a university congenial in its differences, compassionate and fair in its actions, tenacious and bold in its commitment to an education of the highest quality.

So as you leave this auditorium, please carry with you some of the excitement I feel for Furman's present and its future. And take with you as well some appreciation for the proven ability of this university to liberate young people without casting them adrift. It is indeed a precious inheritance.

The River of Time

Address to Alumni Volunteers

| *April 14, 1997*

When I used to work for a living, I taught history. What makes history so endlessly fascinating is that it constitutes an endless series of stories. The stories concern people making choices and dealing with circumstances they often do not understand and cannot control. History's oldest duty is the preservation of such stories. As we grow older, we measure our past by the narrative fragments that we keep in memory.

Our lives in fact turn on the pivot of memory, and we express and interpret our memories through the crafting of stories. The root of the word *history* is story, and as such it recognizes our human impulse to fashion our historical selves into stories. We are all practicing historians. As we go through life, we represent ourselves to others through our life story.

As we age, our attention focuses more and more on the past. We savor the events and experiences, the people and relationships, that enhanced our lives.

So we inhabit the past as we live *in* the present. What we are today is an inheritance of the past. Like a rock formation, our lives are the accumulation of our past activities, representing layer upon layer of past moments that have formed the basis of who we are and what we embody. What we remember, what we stress as significant, and what we omit from our storied past define our present.

As we grow and mature, the story changes. We stress different events as having been decisive in affecting our life course, and as we do so, we give those events new meanings.

All this is said by way of introduction to the fact that this university is responsible for some of the most memorable stories that we include in recounting our life histories.

This campus is an imaginative location as well as a physical setting. The buildings, trees, fountains, and lakes have a remarkable power to evoke time and place, to dislodge

memories of colorful characters who graced the hallways and offices, and to resurrect stories of relationships that remain timeless in their significance.

Even though we view our pasts through different lenses, we all see in our memories of Furman a visual landscape that glistens with warm memories, recollections of shared friendships, shared residence, shared struggles, and shared joys.

Two weeks ago a freshman hall invited me to join them for pizza in the dormitory, and we ended up telling Furman stories to one another. As we sat on the floor enjoying each other's fellowship, one of the students asked me how I had decided to come to Furman as a student.

The question provoked a rush of nostalgia, for I have a sprawling set of Furman memories that I carry around like an overstuffed suitcase. As I explained to the freshmen, Furman for me was like love, a place I fell into—almost by accident.

As a high school senior in Atlanta, I went with a friend on a tour of college campuses. I wanted to visit Wake Forest and Davidson, and he wanted to visit Furman and Davidson.

We went to Wake Forest and Davidson first, then stopped by Furman on the way home. No sooner did we drive through the front gate and see the fountains shooting skyward than I knew this was the place for me. It was love at first sight.

And once I enrolled as a freshman, Furman began to form me into a new person. It was here that caring people helped me learn to see life through my own eyes. To be sure, Furman is much different from the place I first visited in 1968. As I walked across the campus this week, I noticed with new awareness the evidence of change. New buildings, new students, new professors.

But when you think about it, colleges are places of constant change. Like rivers, indeed like time itself, colleges are always in motion, however placid they might appear. For a college to resist change would mean a slow death sentence. Our loyalty is thus not to a place that never changes but to an institution that must change for future generations of students and professors, just as it has done for us.

When we think about it, we would not have it any other way. After all, change has always been a part of Furman's distinctive development. If this were not so, we would be located in Edgefield, where the Furman Academy was located before the Civil War, or at the old campus in downtown Greenville.

But, of course, in another sense Furman does not change. Like a river, the various classes of students keep moving through and changing this channel of learning, yet it remains Furman University.

In the midst of new buildings and arenas and playing fields, Furman remains a place filled with remarkable people motivated by high ideals and demanding standards, a place inspired by a palpable spiritual power. It remains a place where students develop a profound sense of belonging to a community of learners and seekers, an unpretentious place where young people can grow and express themselves freely, where people know and care about each other and are known and cared for by them, a place where students are persons rather than numbers.

Such a college of character is worth having, worth saving, worth enhancing, and worth strengthening.

I want to share with you the remarkable story of Rose Forgione, a graduate of the class of 1948. A native of New York, she majored in biology at Furman. She went on to earn a master's degree from Columbia University and then taught at Duke and the University of Vermont. She never married.

Nor, to our knowledge, did she ever return to Furman. She died last spring, and a few weeks ago we learned that she left her entire estate to Furman. The real story behind her bequest is not its extraordinary size, though at $2.4 million it is certainly historic. Nor is it the fact that the bequest was a surprise.

The real story is twofold: Miss Forgione's love for Furman transcended both time and distance—and I believe that is true for all of us. The other part of her story is that every seemingly routine contact Furman made with her and her brother Louis, class of 1949, was of utmost importance. Those contacts included telephone calls from classmates to solicit her annual gift of one hundred dollars and occasional letters and publications from our alumni office.

In other words, when you do volunteer work for Furman, you are helping to encourage more Rose Forgiones.

As you reflect on your own relationship to Furman, ask yourself, as Miss Forgione surely did, what matters most to you about Furman and the mission of this special place.

Which stories remain etched in your memory?

Is it the beauty of this corner of God's earth? Is it the quality of the teaching and learning that goes on here? Is it the people? Is it the influence Furman has had on your life? Or is it all these things?

Whatever your answer, I trust you will understand a basic truth: this is your university, to cherish and nurture, to remember and describe, where you are, and at whatever time in life you find yourself.

And if you continue to cherish and nurture this university, future generations of young people will have the privilege to know her as you do.

Our sense of belonging to a place, like the process of translating memories into stories, is never finished. Nor should it be.

A Holy Place

The Dedication of the Charles E. Daniel Chapel

| *April 6, 1997*

In the twenty-eighth chapter of the book of Genesis, Jacob declares: "How awesome is this place! This is none other than the house of God, and this is the gate of heaven" (Gen. 28:16–17).

It is with a similar sense of reverential awe that we gather together in the fullness of spring to dedicate this holy place.

Saint John tells us that the word became flesh and dwelt among us. Today we might say that the word has become brick and wood and steel, and it summons us to a sanctuary whose acoustics are so keen that one can almost hear the whisper of God in a child's ear.

A new building bespeaks what we value and what we embody. It is altogether fitting that the Charles Ezra Daniel Memorial Chapel sits astride the Furman mall and represents the fourth point on our educational compass—with the Herman Lay Physical Activities Center to the south, the James B. Duke Library to the west, and McAlister Auditorium to the north. These four buildings testify to Furman's long-standing commitment to nurture the whole person: the intellectual, physical, spiritual, and artistic.

As for this new chapel, no building on the campus has been more keenly anticipated or so long in coming. Fifty years ago, in March of 1947, Furman's president John Plyler told the board of trustees that "it seems almost unthinkable that we have gone almost 121 years without a building resembling a church on . . . campus."

Yet the unthinkable was true. At the original Furman campus in downtown Greenville, chapel services were conducted in Judson Alumni Hall. At Greenville Woman's College, students attended chapel in the auditorium in the Ramsay Fine Arts Building.

President Plyler ensured that a chapel appeared in the original plan developed in the early 1950s for the new Furman campus, but a lack of funds kept such a building

only a dream until Homozel Mickel Daniel's magnificent bequest in 1993. Almost thirty years earlier, "Mickie" Daniel had confided to President Gordon Blackwell that she was leaving money in her will for Furman to build a chapel in honor of her husband.

The wait may well have been providential. Never has there been a more appropriate time; never has there been a greater need for a clearly identified place of worship, a serene and sacred space at the very crossroads of the campus.

In the aftermath of Furman's traumatic separation from the South Carolina Baptist Convention in 1992, some observers predicted that Furman would quickly abandon its Christian heritage and embrace the secularism so common at many liberal arts colleges of national stature. They were wrong. Religious conviction, activity, and debate are flourishing as never before, and the university remains steadfast in its commitment to bring the human in contact with the divine.

For it remains true, as Richard Furman wrote in 1768, that "learning is an excellent Handmaid for Grace."

Now 171 years old, Furman continues to be an ecumenical fellowship of learners, a liberal arts college that bears insistent witness to its religious heritage. This new chapel will bolster such a mission.

Chapels help us encounter God's grace. We enter them with open minds and receptive hearts, for they offer a place of refuge from the chaos and corruptions of the world, a place to sit and listen for the voice of God, a place to interrogate the soul and learn from its cries and whispers. To be sure, we pilgrims cannot grasp or control the sacred; it is impalpable. We can only sense its presence and feel its uplifting power.

The Daniel Chapel provides an insistent witness to our need for a more transcendent appreciation of what really matters. We live in an age gorged on the trivial yet hungry for meaning. By reminding us of God's presence in our lives, this chapel will help raise our aspirations.

Indeed, that is why chapels are usually vertical in form. Like an exclamation mark, their tall steeples and steep roofs punctuate our intentions and disrupt our complacency. In the process a chapel offers comfort and assurance, challenge and judgment, hope and benediction. The Daniel Chapel's holy aura reminds us that we did not create ourselves and that the search for truth and meaning is best pursued in a spirit of communion and humility.

In its purest sense, religion is not an escape from reality but an insight into reality and all that surrounds it. Faith does not provide easy answers to the unknowable or unwanted; it is what we do and who we are in the face of the unknowable and the unwanted.

To those who helped build this chapel, including those who gave countless hours as volunteers, and to Mrs. Daniel who funded it and Charlie Daniel who inspired it, we owe a great debt for creating a place of simple elegance that is easy to find and hard to leave.

For as the psalmist declares, "Behold how pleasant it is when brethren dwell in fellowship!" (Psalms 133:1).

A New Approach to Liberal Learning

| *September 7, 1998*

Many of the six hundred private liberal arts colleges in the United States are becoming victims of their own myths. The prevailing public image of such schools remains that of an ivory tower isolated from the real world and its practical concerns, a serene sanctuary of higher learning where bright students prepare for graduate or professional school—and have little interest in or affinity for practical concerns or the business world.

To be sure, there is nothing inherently wrong with such an image: for almost three centuries, liberal arts colleges have excelled at helping young people learn to think critically and broadly while nurturing in them a sense of lifelong curiosity and civic virtue. By exposing students to all the major disciplines, liberal learning provides both the breadth of cultural knowledge and a level of intellectual sophistication necessary to help young people assume leadership roles in a society of growing technological complexity and moral ambiguity.

Now, however, such traditional notions are under siege. Students are understandably concerned about paying for an expensive private education and then supporting themselves after graduation. They and their parents are demanding more job-specific training. Many students are voting with their feet, migrating from the traditional liberal arts disciplines and small private colleges to more narrowly focused preprofessional and technical programs and large public universities.

To their credit, many small colleges are responding to such new realities with innovative new programs and emphases. A number of them are demonstrating that their liberal arts foundations can be enriched by incorporating experiential forms of learning. In the process, they are breaking down the false barriers between liberal learning and the worlds of work and daily life. With the philosopher Alfred North Whitehead, such colleges recognize that "if education is not useful, what is it?"

At Wheaton College in Massachusetts, for example, students are required to complete at least one internship before graduating. Wheaton has developed a network of eight hundred organizations—businesses, government agencies, hospitals, museums, social service agencies and other types of organizations—to provide such internship opportunities.

At Kalamazoo College in Michigan, 85 percent of the 1,250 students complete at least one internship before graduating. Each year, students participate in more than 400 internships in 25 states and a dozen countries. An equal number of students at Lafayette College in Pennsylvania serve as interns each year.

Claremont McKenna College in southern California offers numerous "practicum modules" that organize students into small teams to work with local corporations or government agencies on actual projects. Explains one of the Claremont McKenna professors: the program seeks to make "the student an active learner instead of a passive learner. It involves a very different view of the world, of education" than that undergirding conventional classroom instruction.

At Furman, approximately one half of the 2,600 students hold career-related internships, teaching fellowships, or undergraduate research fellowships each year. Some 150 of these students benefit from $2,500 stipends provided by the university to support such experiential learning opportunities.

An emphasis on applied learning opportunities permeates the academic experience at Furman. Political science majors hold internships with government agencies in Washington, D.C., and with law firms across the South; premedical students intern with hospitals and medical schools around the country; biochemistry majors conduct research at the Centers for Disease Control in Atlanta and the Naval Research Laboratory in Washington, D.C.; economics majors work in marketing, accounting, and human resources positions; and art majors help advertising agencies with graphic design projects. An endowed internship program enables students to pursue such experiential learning opportunities abroad.

Participation in internships or research projects often ignites a passion for learning too often lacking in conventional classroom environments. By putting into practice the ideas and theories learned in classrooms and textbooks, students take greater responsibility for their own education—and assume greater risks. Their professors serve more as mentors and partners than as the conventional omniscient teacher, facilitating and guiding more than instructing.

Such applied forms of liberal learning help students discover more about themselves and their abilities. Working as an intern in a hospital, law firm, or bank, or as a research assistant for a biologist or historian often helps confirm—or deflect—a student's postgraduate plans. Students involved in such *applied* liberal arts opportunities also develop greater self-confidence and sharpen communication skills that give them a definite advantage when they enter graduate school or the work force. And there is another advantage: many students receive permanent job offers from their host agencies as a result of their intern experiences.

Liberal learning at its best is not passive—nor is it limited to the conventional classroom or pristine campus. Numerous studies demonstrate that greater student involvement in the educational process—at every level—translates into more meaningful and enduring learning.

Students in this dynamic technological society must do more than memorize facts and theories. They must be encouraged to analyze, synthesize and evaluate information, pose questions, challenge assumptions, form hypotheses, conduct their own research and experiments, apply and test their knowledge in real world situations, and present their findings to others.

Engaged learning thus holds the promise of invigorating academic life, dismantling the ivory tower stereotype, and fostering a new educational philosophy that will enable liberal arts colleges to reassert their relevance to modern life. Those colleges reluctant to integrate real life experiences into their educational programs would do well to recall the advice of the Greek dramatist Sophocles: "One must learn by doing the thing, for though you think you know it—you have no certainty until you try."

Graduation Agony

| *May 31, 1998*

It is commencement season again at high schools and colleges across the country, and platitudes are in full bloom. Amid the pomp and circumstance of these great public rituals, seniors are being mercilessly subjected to speeches larded with tired clichés and boring bromides.

Few graduation addresses are memorable; most are painfully predictable. Speakers can be counted upon to alert students that graduation is not an ending but a beginning, that the world is at their feet, and that their future is ahead of them. The graduates are also encouraged to make the world a better place, to remain intellectually curious, and to contribute to their alma mater. The prevailing formula for a commencement speech involves pointing with pride, viewing with alarm, closing with hope—and wishing folks "Godspeed," whatever that means. In the end, the graduates are urged to "go forth"—as if they had any choice about the matter.

I still have vivid memories of my own college graduation—even thirty years later. My classmates and I reveled in the energy and excitement of the event and basked in our collective sense of accomplishment and pride. But our most powerful feeling was the mounting fear that the commencement speech would never end.

Someone once compared a graduation speaker to a corpse at an old-fashioned Irish wake. You are needed to have the party, but no one expects you to say much of importance.

Yet I have heard some excellent commencement speakers. They usually share a refreshing lack of solemnity. They also recognize that a commencement address does not need to be eternal to be memorable. After all, most of the graduates are more concerned with grabbing a diploma and getting out of their medieval robes than reflecting on their metaphysical condition and listening to a stranger tell them how to live the rest of their lives.

There are commencement speakers who do not conform to the stereotype. For example, novelist Stephen King told seniors at the University of Maine that if "you turn up forty years old, drunk and maudlin at alumni parties, talking about how great everything was when you were in school, man, you are one sick puppy." A little irreverence at a graduation ceremony can help relieve the emotional tension. To wit: Jeff Danzinger, editorial cartoonist for the *Christian Science Monitor,* informed Middlebury College graduates that life "is, after all, essentially a joke. If you don't think so, look at the hats you're wearing." In a similar vein, columnist Russell Baker told Connecticut College graduates that the best advice he could give people going out into the real world was "Don't do it. I have been out there. It is a mess. . . . Whatever you do, do not go forth."

Alistair Cooke, the distinguished British-born writer and commentator, alerted graduates of Smith College to the importance of generational relations. No career is "more urgent for a little while to come," he stressed, "than the career of tolerating your parents," for "it will soon give way to the even more challenging occupation of tolerating your children."

Several years ago people began circulating over the Internet an unconventional commencement address supposedly delivered by the novelist Kurt Vonnegut. He advised graduates to wear sunscreen, keep their old love letters, and discard their old bank statements. He also told them to "accept certain inalienable truths: Prices will rise. Politicians will philander. You, too, will get old. And when you do, you'll fantasize that when you were young, prices were reasonable, politicians were noble, and children respected their elders." As it turned out, Vonnegut did not write the speech. It was instead the creation of a Chicago newspaper columnist. Whoever the author, however, its wit and candor provided a welcome respite from the stereotypical commencement address.

But leave it to Yogi Berra, former catcher for the New York Yankees, to lampoon the advice-giving tradition of graduation speakers with his own distinctive malapropisms. A few years ago he gave Michigan State graduates the following advice: "First, never give up, because it's never over till it's over. Second, during the years ahead, when you come to a fork in the road, take it. Third, don't always follow the crowd, because nobody goes there anymore. Fourth, stay alert. You can observe a lot by watching. Fifth, and last, remember that whatever you do in life, ninety percent of it is half mental."

To all graduates, past and present, Godspeed (it means good fortune).

Welcome, President Barker!

| *January 23, 2000*

The Clemson faithful—including my orange-bleeding father-in-law—are still basking in the glow of a turnaround football season. But they should be even more excited about the arrival of Jim Barker, their dynamic new president.

Barker, who seems much younger than his fifty-two years, is an architect by training and a leader by nature. He has served as dean of the architecture school at Mississippi State and at Clemson. Most recently, he has been dean of the new College of Architecture, Arts and Humanities. As a Clemson graduate, he promises to bring much-needed stability and continuity to his new office. He also is bringing a lot of energy and excitement to the Clemson community.

I have enjoyed getting to know Jim Barker and look forward to working with him to enhance the quality of higher education in the Upstate. At a recent luncheon meeting, I alerted him that being a university president is one of the most demanding yet fulfilling careers imaginable.

The life of a college president is a world without weekends, a life always on call or on stage. The pace is frenetic; the atmosphere is organized chaos. No job is more diverse. One minute you are wrestling with new curricular proposals or helping to recruit top students and professors, and the next you are analyzing how better to invest the university's endowment. Today's agenda might involve selling real estate or meeting with architects and contractors to discuss a new building project.

Almost every day or night there is an athletic contest or cultural event to attend on campus or a speech to deliver off campus. There are staff meetings, faculty meetings, and informal gatherings with students to attend, irate phone calls from parents and alumni to answer (fire the coach, stupid!), and queries from the media to address. Trips to Columbia to buttonhole legislators or the governor occur almost weekly. And of course there is money—lots of money—to be raised.

A university president's daily routine often mirrors that of a dentist: it entails an endless series of half-hour meetings, most of which are filled with excruciating pain.

New presidents who think they already know everything are in for trouble. My own state of mind over these past six years has progressed from cocksure ignorance to thoughtful uncertainty. I warned President Barker to gird himself for an endless series of appearances at civic clubs and IPTAY meetings. He will learn to hate the sight of chicken and green beans.

On a more serious note, what Jim Barker needs most to be successful is a more steadfast commitment to Clemson from the people and politicians of this state. In recent years, government funding of higher education has improved. And last year the state legislature devoted much of the new bond bill to long-overdue construction and renovation on public college and university campuses.

Such efforts are to be applauded. But Clemson continues to struggle with inadequate financial resources for an institution of its quality and potential. As a major research university, it has distinctive requirements for expensive equipment and competitive faculty salaries. Professors in many disciplines at Clemson are paid much less than their counterparts at other land-grant universities. To the extent that legislative funding for Clemson's demonstrated needs increases, the entire state will benefit.

One of the major responsibilities of a new college president is to help members of the campus community reaffirm their values, replenish their energy and commitment, and develop an animating vision of what their institution can become.

Jim Barker is already hard at work fulfilling such responsibilities. With our help, he can implement his dazzling vision for Clemson in this new century. So, President Barker, welcome to your new presidential duties. Hasten slowly—and pack your Rolaids.

Joab Lesesne

Wisdom with a Smile

| *September 17, 2000*

In an age with few heroes, it becomes even more important to honor those who stand above the crowd. Furman University recently had the privilege of bestowing an honorary doctoral degree upon Joab Lesesne, the retired president of Wofford College. He had served as Wofford's president for twenty-eight years. And he served it well—with a special genius that everyone observed yet no one can define.

Joe Lesesne was raised on a college campus. His father, a Wofford graduate, was president of Erskine College. After graduating from Erskine, the younger Lesesne went on to earn his M.A. and Ph.D. degrees in history from the University of South Carolina. He began his career at Wofford in 1964 as an assistant professor of history, and he soon distinguished himself in the classroom. Lesesne was a memorable teacher who made the past shine with interest and significance.

Professor Lesesne was appointed assistant dean in 1967. Soon thereafter, he implemented the college's interim term, a four-week winter learning program that has become an indispensable part of a Wofford education. He later became director of development and then dean of the college. In 1972, at the ripe age of thirty-four, he was named Wofford's ninth president. Lesesne quickly realized that going from the faculty to the presidency meant abandoning righteousness for pragmatism.

As a resolute champion of the distinctive virtues of residential liberal arts colleges, Lesesne led Wofford through a remarkable era of progress, change, and achievement. The college's endowment soared during his long tenure, new buildings were constructed, and he helped attract a stronger, more diverse faculty and student body. Along the way, President Lesesne displayed extraordinary composure and resilience. Hard to surprise and even harder to shock, he showed the magnanimity of a saint in dealing with complaints and crises.

President Lesesne became a leader of national prominence within the higher education community. He was the first southerner to chair the board of the National Association of Independent Colleges and Universities, and he headed the council of presidents of South Carolina's private colleges. In addition, he is a retired major general in the South Carolina Army National Guard, and he continues to chair the South Carolina Commission on Natural Resources.

Yet the real value of a career can sometimes be better gauged by a person's character than by a public portfolio. Joe Lesesne is a warm man with a big heart; he has no enemies—even among those who disagree with him. Known for his casual intensity and refreshing humility, he loves to tell stories and to catch fish.

For almost thirty years as a college president, Joe Lesesne manifested unshaken nerve, rescuing wit, and, above all, a love for Wofford that has never waned. He had a special affection for students. He teased them, entertained them, inspired them, and guided them. They responded with equal affection.

It has been invigorating for those of us still learning how to be a college president to associate with such a wise colleague. I cannot imagine anyone more effective at helping the people of this state appreciate the important role played by Wofford and the other private liberal arts colleges. Joe Lesesne is one of those refreshing people who prefers to grin rather than scowl, banter rather than pontificate. He has been a wonderful mentor.

In his compassionate awareness of others, in his instinctive respect for them, in his declared willingness to help, in his courtesy, tolerance, and gentleness, Joe Lesesne demonstrated that the highest intelligence is at its most fertile and expressive when allied to the deepest humanity. As to all of these traits, he has provided us the great gift of his example. Blessed are those who perform good works and earn our respect and admiration. Thanks, Joe.

Francis Wesley Bonner

Legendary Administrator

| *October 14, 1993*

When Frank Bonner accepted a position in the English Department at Furman in 1949, he planned to stay a year or two and then move on to teach Chaucer at a more prestigious university. Instead, he stayed at Furman thirty-eight years—as both teacher and administrator. As the chief academic officer under three presidents, he had a profound effect on Furman's educational program.

President John Plyler recognized Bonner's administrative skills soon after he arrived on campus and appointed him dean of the men's college in 1953, the year that ground was broken on the new campus. Soon Bonner was involved in planning the campus, and he was put in charge of equipping the new buildings and supervising the move to the campus.

In 1961—the year the move was completed—he was named dean of the university, and a few years later his title was changed to vice president and dean. In 1972 President Gordon Blackwell recognized Bonner's extraordinary service to Furman by appointing him vice president and provost, and he continued in that position during President Johns's administration. For almost three decades, the "Bonner style" shaped the university's academic program.

To disagree with Frank Bonner was to risk disintegrating, burned and wrinkled, beneath the torch of his wrath. When he was aroused, his carriage would stiffen, his complexion redden, his jaw set, and he would foam and snort like a mastiff. Those who say that his bark was worse than his bite have never been bitten by him. When told that someone had complained that he rubbed people's fur the wrong way, Frank replied: "Let the cats turn around!"

His overpowering public image reminds one of Benjamin Jowett, the nineteenth-century head of Oxford's Balliol College, who would occasionally call his dons together

to invite their opinions on a matter of importance. At the end of the meeting, Jowett would announce: "The vote is twenty to one. I see we are deadlocked."

Similarly, Dr. Bonner ruled the academic roost at Furman. Yet his imperious style was both greatly exaggerated and greatly appreciated. His shrewd administrative skill, wise counsel, and forthright convictions have benefited us all over the years.

Frank Bonner believed that a strong faculty was the first prerequisite for a strong educational institution, so he set about to find the most highly qualified teachers in every discipline and persuade them to come to Furman. He visited the best graduate schools to recruit bright young scholars, and he also raided other college faculties. His remarkable success as a recruiter is demonstrated by the fact that he hired most of the senior professors now teaching at Furman. Under his leadership, Furman's faculty grew from 82 to 152, and the number with doctorates increased from 34 to 86 percent.

In 1973 Dr. Bonner's greatest wish came true when Furman was granted a chapter of Phi Beta Kappa in recognition of its improved educational program.

Frank Bonner also served as acting president after John Plyler retired in 1964 until Gordon Blackwell arrived in 1965. During that time he made three major decisions that had far-reaching consequences for Furman: he signed the federal nondiscrimination forms, he arranged for the integration of African American students into the student body, and he secured a federal grant for the completion of the science building.

He also made numerous contributions to intercollegiate athletics by serving as faculty chairman of athletics at Furman and by providing wise leadership in the Southern Conference and the NCAA.

Although we could list many other accomplishments, it seems sufficient to say that Frank Bonner never wavered in his defense of academic freedom nor in his support of academic standards nor in his belief in liberal arts education. For these and many other reasons, Furman University is a much finer university today than it was when he came here more than forty years ago.

John Crabtree

Dean Extraordinaire

| *January 12, 1994*

Everything goes downstream in time, except for a few special people who lie anchored like rocks in the bed of a river. As John Crabtree has demonstrated, there is a certain kind of greatness that comes from remaining at the heart of a great institution for a prolonged period. Almost two years ago, when John announced his decision to retire, someone justifiably asked why. He replied that it was time for him to step aside "in favor of a less experienced and less able person." I am living testimony to the truth of this explanation. He has been a hard act to follow. Dr. Crabtree is far too magisterial a figure to talk seriously about, but this occasion demands it.

Just as there is no training for being born, there is none for being a college administrator. It is a vocation filled with blessings and cursing; and if at times a dean treads in the sun and walks with giants, even more often he must make his way through the slough of despond.

As a high school student in Raleigh, North Carolina, John Crabtree initially trained for a career in music. He was a frequent soloist with church and school choruses and dreamed of becoming an opera singer. But one day in 1945—as he sat looking out over the Pacific from the deck of an aircraft carrier—he came to the conclusion that he would be better suited to an academic life and decided to be a college teacher. Looking back now, we know that the decision he made that day was providentially blessed, for he affected the lives of thousands of Furman students and greatly enriched the life of this institution, which he served for thirty-six years with extraordinary distinction.

John Crabtree came to Furman in 1957 from the University of North Carolina at Chapel Hill, where he was finishing work on his Ph.D. in English literature. He brought with him a reservoir of easily summoned knowledge and a certain courtly eloquence redolent of English ways that set him apart from his peers. ("Ah, England," says George Orwell, "a nation of snobbery and privilege, ruled largely by the old and silly.")

Professor Crabtree soon acquired a reputation for being a luminous teacher who inspired students to love literature and all of the arts, and his Shakespeare class became one of the most popular courses on campus.

John transformed his classroom into a stage, and there he held sway with theatrical panache and matchless authority. In his distinctive tenor voice, rich, resonant, and hauntingly cadenced, he conveyed to his students an unrelenting excitement, almost a giddiness, at the encounter with a Shakespearean text. He knew that Shakespeare was no dated genius. The bard shared the halfness and imperfection of humanity and wrote the text for modern life. With a thespian's flair and fervor, John lifted the superlative power and beauty of Shakespeare's words off the printed page, words of fire, clothed in power and rammed with life and texture. For many years he also directed Furman's distinguished study-abroad program in Stratford-upon-Avon, where students attended and analyzed productions of the Royal Shakespeare Company.

Like most good-hearted souls, John had not planned to go into college administration, but he accepted an appointment as assistant dean for academic affairs in 1965. Over the next twenty-eight years he held a series of important positions, including dean of students, chairman of the English department, and vice president for academic affairs and dean.

A truly vigorous mind seeks problems as salt seeks water. Its possessor refuses to accept the status quo and tenaciously assaults complacency. Shakespeare knew this very well. In *Henry IV, Part 1,* Prince Hal describes Percy as a Hotspur who "kills me some six of seven dozen Scots at a breakfast, washes his hands, and says to his wife, 'Fie upon this quiet life! I want work!'"

The man we honor today, though a peaceable sort, solved administrative problems and pursued academic excellence in the same aggressive way. As chief academic officer from 1982 to 1993, John encouraged departments to seek and hire the most highly qualified teachers. He promoted excellent teaching by increasing faculty salaries and providing generous support for travel, research, and other forms of professional development.

During his tenure as vice president and dean, the faculty grew from 169 to 199, the number of women on the faculty almost doubled, the percentage of faculty with doctorates increased from 83 to 91 percent, and average faculty salaries increased by 80 percent.

Dean Crabtree strengthened the curriculum by supporting the addition of new courses and programs in many areas, including international studies and Asian studies, and by approving the creation of eleven new majors. With his help, the departments of art and music flourished, and other departments—such as chemistry, psychology, and political science—gained national recognition.

Although John Crabtree himself knew little about computers and even disdained the use of a typewriter, he believed strongly that all departments should have up-to-date scientific and electronic equipment. To this end he supported the installation of the campus computer network and provided computer equipment for a majority of the faculty.

Such tangible accomplishments are indeed impressive. But of far greater importance is the substance of this man, what he is, what he stands for, exemplifying virtues, honoring commitments, fulfilling responsibilities, defending principles. As an articulate spokesman for a liberal arts education, John ably represented Furman on many important public occasions. He brought to the position of vice president and dean an eloquence, a sense of refinement, and an appreciation for beauty that set a new standard for those who follow him in that office.

William E. Leverette Jr.

Exemplary Teacher

| *June 22, 2000*

In the Prologue to the *Canterbury Tales,* Chaucer's Clerk of Oxenford was lean and wore threadbare clothes because he used all the money given him by loving friends to buy books and thereby continue his studies. Like most faculty members from the Middle Ages to the present, his passion was for learning and ideas rather than for material pleasures.

In Chaucer's memorable words: "Gladly wolde he lerne and gladly teche."

The Clerk viewed teaching as a calling rather than a career, a calling that often offers mastery but rarely fame, applause, or wealth. Its chief reward is inherent in its tasks.

William E. Leverette Jr. is an example of such a teacher. As a Furman professor, he helped enrich and sustain the university's tradition of excellence in teaching and his steadfast commitment to liberal learning.

One of Bill Leverette's favorite historical subjects is Henry Adams, the descendant of two presidents who became a brooding writer and professor of history at Harvard. At one point in his famous autobiography, Adams notes that "a teacher affects eternity; he can never tell when his influence stops." Similarly, Bill Leverette's influence on his students continues to reverberate through our lives. He certainly has cast a spell on me.

During freshman orientation each year, I have the privilege of giving a speech to the new students and their parents. At one point in those remarks, I lapse into personal reflection and tell them that the most precious aspect of any college is the voice of an inspiring teacher, and I go on to say that one such inspiring voice for me was that of a history professor named Bill Leverette who retired several years ago.

He was a man of ideas who also possessed a full and gracious heart. Dr. Leverette was the first professor I came to know well as a person. That is, he shared himself as well as his knowledge and his wisdom. He extended to me the hospitality of his home as well as his study. We cut wood together, played golf and laughed together, and we enjoyed strenuous discussions about politics past and present. In the process Bill Leverette became an advisor about life, a confidante, a friend. And under his tutelage I began to experience what a liberal education in its ideal sense can be.

Professor Leverette told us not simply about the past but about life as he understood it: an often lonely yet exciting and ultimately historical business. Along the way he added dashes of irony, wit, humility, and the dignity that comes from facing, if not necessarily resolving, some of life's terrible ambiguities. How bracing it was to be in the company of this teacher for whom scholarship was a heroic enterprise. How beneficial to be challenged to become a better writer, a clearer thinker, and a more tenacious defender of one's own assumptions and conclusions.

In honoring Bill Leverette, then, we pay tribute not simply to an individual but also to the notion of teaching as a calling, to the animating premises of liberal learning, and to the rewards of history as a field of inquiry. Both in class and in his office, on a hike or on the golf course, Bill impressed upon us that the past, like the present, is filled with surprise and unpredictability, with hard-pressed people making difficult choices on the basis of inadequate information, with struggle, dream, accomplishment, and tragedy.

But his own words do a much better job of conveying his values and virtues. Almost twenty years ago Bill crafted an engaging essay for the *Furman Magazine* about his lifelong interest in the Vanderbilt Agrarians, that eccentric group of writers and professors who sought to defy the premises of modern industrial capitalism.

At one point in the essay Bill discards his scholarly perspective and discusses his own passion for history. He writes:

> I do not believe that many scholarly types enter their specialty for purely intellectual reasons. One has emotions and loyalties. That is certainly the case with me. My concern with history is a concern with self, with loved ones, friends, colleagues, students, ideas of value, with objects I like, with pleasures I want to keep enjoying. . . . That is what history is all about, behind the abstract-sounding

> generalizations, a systematic inquiry into the dreams and hopes people have been capable of, and what was good or bad, practical or foolish in their value.

Professor Leverette, in teaching us history as he knew it, helped us learn more about life—and ourselves.

Robert McNamara

Overcoming the Odds

| *October 26, 1997*

The greatest benefit of working at Furman is the opportunity to associate with so many dedicated professors and talented students. One of the most interesting among our two hundred faculty members is Dr. Robert McNamara, an assistant professor of sociology who has just published his ninth book, *Beating the Odds: Crime, Poverty, and Life in the Inner City.*

It is an unusual project for a professor because Dr. McNamara uses his own disadvantaged life history to explore some of the major social problems of our age—poverty, dysfunctional families, divorce, foster care, delinquency, gang violence, and street crime—and to give hope to those dealing with similar problems.

Born in New Haven, Connecticut, in 1960, Bob McNamara was the youngest of four brawling boys. They and their parents lived a hand-to-mouth existence in the poorest and most violent section of the city. Bob's Irish father was a stern autocrat, an alcoholic, and a compulsive gambler. Fired from one job after another, he projected his own frustrations onto his family. In "our house," McNamara recalls in *Beating the Odds,* "sentiment or emotions other than anger and aggressiveness were not tolerated."

The McNamara clan formed "a dirty, unkempt, and unruly" household punctuated by brutal confrontations between father and sons. Food was scarce, and "there were few options except to steal what I could from other people's homes, from pharmacies, and local grocery stores."

McNamara's parents divorced when he was ten years old, and he was passed back and forth between them. Eventually, however, his mother grew tired of providing for his needs, and she began paying other people to take him into their homes.

Over the next few years McNamara was farmed out to nineteen different families, most of whom took him in solely to gain a cheap laborer. Exploited at every turn and possessing one pair of pants and three shirts, he quickly realized that being "a foster child is one of the most frightening things that could ever happen to a young person."

Bob often ran away from these "foster" families and lived on the streets. At age twelve he became the only white member of an African American gang known as the Black Cobras. School provided the only pleasant and stable outlet from his family turmoil. He enjoyed sports and delighted in reading, but many of his teachers labeled him a failure. One of them declared that he would "never go anywhere in life," telling him, "The best you can hope for is to find a well-paying factory job somewhere. You do not have what it takes to go to college."

Fortunately, however, another teacher saw in him real promise and nurtured his academic talents. She wrote in his high school annual: "To Bob McNamara, a diamond in the rough." Likewise, one of his football coaches recognized his potential and became his first supportive foster parent.

These positive role models helped Bob change the trajectory of his life. He began taking classes at the local community college while working at two jobs. His academic success led him to enroll in the state university, commuting sixty miles each way in order to attend classes. In the process of working with an inspiring professor, he developed a passion for issues relating to criminal justice. His stellar grades helped gain him a scholarship to the graduate school at Yale.

Beating the Odds lives up to its title: it offers an illuminating and poignant account of a wayward young life redeemed. In detailing the realities of life among America's underclass, it makes for sobering as well as captivating reading. And it offers inspiration to those of us who spend our days influencing young people in their educational development. To go from a street gang to Yale University to the faculty at Furman gives new meaning to the American Dream.

Greg Mason

A Study in Hope and Resilience

| *April 12, 1998*

On October 30, 1997, Greg Mason, then a Furman freshman, was riding in a car with four other students when a drunk driver plowed into them. The impact of the collision catapulted Greg into the front windshield; he suffered massive facial trauma, an open skull fracture, and third-degree burns.

When a rescue team cut Greg from the wreckage, the Riverside High School graduate had no vital signs. Paramedics restored his breathing and transported him to the hospital, where doctors told his parents, Pam and Tim, that their only child would probably not survive the night. Yet in the face of the bleak odds, the physicians—like the Masons —clung to hope and "never, never, never, gave up on Greg," says Pam. "Everyone, the paramedics, trauma nurses, neurosurgeons, specialists, and intensive care personnel at Greenville Memorial were incredible. They saved my son's life."

Greg, who was in a deep coma, defied the odds. A few days after the accident, he underwent extensive brain surgery to close his head wounds. The surgery was successful, but Greg remained unconscious. He finally emerged from the coma thirty days later.

While Greg slowly regained consciousness, his friends maintained a vigil outside the intensive care unit. As the days passed and the support network grew, Greg's father began sending weekly e-mail notes to update friends and relatives on Greg's condition. Each message was signed, "Keep praying. Pam and Tim."

Since the accident, Greg has endured eighteen more surgical procedures to repair and reshape his face and head. Although his cognitive skills remain sharp, he has had to relearn the most basic physical actions, from swallowing to speaking. Upon his release from the hospital in April 1998, the Masons were advised to place Greg in a nursing home because of his many medical needs. Medical officials also told them that their son's goal of returning to Furman was unrealistic.

"We were told to not have any expectations for Greg," says Pam. But Greg and his parents were resolute. "He told me that he would return to Furman. 'That is where I belong. I'm supposed to be there,'" his mother recalls.

Through intense physical therapy, Greg made slow but steady progress. Last summer, he returned to classes at Furman. He has enrolled in at least one class each term and has targeted May of 2003 for graduation. Confined to a wheelchair, Greg is legally blind and is deaf in one ear. But he can move his legs, his speech is improving, and he hopes to walk one day. A freshman hall has "adopted" him, taking him to football games and parties.

His mother is always by his side. She accompanies Greg to class, takes notes for him, and records all lectures. She helps him with his homework and take-home tests and jokes that computer science (Greg's major) is one of her least-favorite subjects.

"I told him I never wanted to go back to college," she explains, smiling at Greg during a break between classes. "I'm too old for this."

"You're not old, Mom," Greg replies. "You're lovingly antique."

Supported by a caring circle of friends and family members, the Masons draw their remarkable strength and inspiration from one another. Their son's resilience, determination, and lack of self-pity amaze his parents.

"He's gone through all of this (surgery, physical therapy, and recovery) without crying, without whining. He works so hard," says Pam.

When asked about his parents' role in his recovery, Greg struggles to express his appreciation. "Nothing that we do," Pam insists, touching her son's hand, "will ever be as hard as what he does."

The Masons embody the invisible yet redemptive reality of hope. Their sense of hope is not simply optimism. Rather, it is the certainty that the challenges of life, however perplexing or mysterious, warrant our best efforts, regardless of how they turn out.

"We are saved by hope," said Saint Paul to the Romans. There is no medicine as potent as hope, no tonic so powerful as the will to live.

The Timmons Family Legacy

| *January 17, 1998*

All colleges and universities, whether public or private, depend upon the support of generous individuals for their continued survival and improvement. Indeed, the United States has the greatest ethic of private philanthropy in the world.

A tangible example of such philanthropy is Furman's Timmons Arena. The new facility is a dream come true for thousands of Furman supporters who have long desired an on-campus facility for basketball games, concerts, and other recreational and entertainment activities.

It was made possible by three Greenville siblings: Jean Timmons Pelham, Charles Timmons, and Bill Timmons.

Jean and Bill attended Furman, and the entire Timmons family has been a pillar of support to the university for many years. In fact, the family connection with Furman goes back to the turn of the century, when William Sr. and his brother, Charles, attended the university. Charles's name is inscribed at the base of the World War I memorial on campus, honoring those alumni killed in the conflict.

This influential family warrants a chapter in the history of Greenville. But one member, Bill Timmons, has, with tenacious courage and quiet leadership, made not only Furman but this community as a whole a better place to live and work.

For forty years Bill has served as the chairman of Canal Insurance Company. He has also been a founding director of Southern Bank and Trust and Carolina First, president of the Sertoma Club, and a leader of the chamber of commerce.

Born in Greenville in 1924, Timmons left college to join the Army Air Corps during World War II. He flew B-24 and B-29 bombers and later became a pilot instructor.

Just weeks before his discharge in 1945, the twenty-one-year-old Timmons contracted polio and was sent to the Army-Navy Hospital in Hot Springs, Arkansas. He spent the next two years in intensive and often painful rehabilitation.

Connie Jackson, a nurse in Hot Springs, met Bill and was charmed by his positive outlook and vigorous spirit. The two began dating and later married.

Through sheer grit and determination, Bill rose to the challenge of his physical misfortune. He had entered the hospital on a stretcher and was told he would probably never walk again. Two years later, having progressed from a wheelchair to crutches and a long-leg brace, he emerged, walking upright with the help of a cane and in the company of the vivacious Connie, with whom he would later have eight children.

Bill returned to Greenville and, along with many other veterans, enrolled at Furman. Just a year into his studies, tragedy struck again when his father was killed in an automobile accident. Bill felt compelled to drop out of college to help manage the family business, Canal Insurance Company, with the help of his younger brother, Charles. Ably assisted by dedicated employees, the two novice businessmen set Canal on the path to becoming one of the nation's largest companies specializing in insuring trucks and their cargo, taxicabs, and buses.

In the process, the Timmons family helped shape Greenville's civic and cultural life in a self-effacing way. "Over the years," Buck Mickel recalls, "the Timmonses have always been very generous with their finances and their personal service on behalf of this community. Yet they have never allowed any publicity, preferring to stay in the background."

Today, Bill is the patriarch of an ever-growing Timmons clan (he has twenty-two grandchildren). Now in his fifth term as a member of the Furman board of trustees, including past service as chairman and vice chairman, he has provided distinguished leadership to the university. He and his family take special interest in funding scholarships, maintaining the beauty of the campus, and supporting its athletic teams.

Bill is a warm-hearted man of stoic integrity. He loves life and he loves people. Nothing pleases him more than to be surrounded by his platoon of grandchildren. They nourish his radiant cheerfulness. His broad smile, an attribute common to the entire Timmons family, radiates warmth and hope. And his tranquil dignity, robust spirit, and moral gravity inspire those around him. He has known the worst yet never complained; he has gone about his good works with humility and grace; and he has shown how even the unwanted event can be given a constructive turn.

At a time when cosmetic celebrities garner more attention than substantive heroes, we would do well to follow the soul-stiffening example of Bill Timmons. He has experienced the ordeal as well as the triumph of the human spirit. How fitting it is that the new arena ensures that Bill, Charlie, and Jean, as well as the Timmons family name, will forever be remembered at Furman.

Letting Go

| *August 31, 1997*

The Shi household seems rather vacant these days. Last week we took our older child to North Carolina to begin his freshman year in college. Before we left Greenville, I realized that the process of moving into his dorm room and greeting roommates and their families would be so chaotic that some important things would not get said. So I wrote a fatherly, Fred MacMurray–type letter in advance, which I left on our son's dormitory bed. It reads in part:

Dear Jason:

Please tolerate one last paternal sermon. In other words, keep reading—and don't let the clichés you are about to encounter get you down.

As you begin the greatest adventure in your life, you need to know several things. The most important is this: we are very proud of you as you start your college career.

To be sure, it is terribly hard for us to let you go, but it is time for you to be on your own—and you are ready. Perhaps the most important thing that parents can teach their children is how to get along without them. What you are, what you do, and thereby what you become depends on what you believe about yourself. In this regard Mom and I have great confidence in you, and that gives us considerable comfort as we head back to Greenville. You have the ability, commitment, and common sense to excel in your schoolwork—and your life.

You will soon discover that college is not simply a high school with higher standards. It is an entirely new way of exercising your mind, and, of course, an entirely new way of living and dealing with people—including yourself.

Beginning today you are as free as you will likely ever be again. You will be able to think, do, and act as you please. No one will tell you to go to bed or get up, to make your bed or do your homework. How you handle your new freedom is likely to affect you for the rest of your life.

You will discover, for instance, that intelligent young people do not always behave in intelligent ways. Indeed, the most common mistake that freshmen make is to become intoxicated by their new freedom. Caught up in the festive distractions and temptations of college life, they quickly get behind in their schoolwork, and before they know it, they are in a deep hole.

So by all means get off to a good start. Set aside study time each day—and when you study, really concentrate. (Remember what I used to say about hitting a baseball during your Little League days: FOCUS!)

Although you have worked hard to prepare yourself for the experience of college, you are not totally ready—no one is. You will be confronted with many new ideas, exciting activities, interesting people, and tough choices.

College is great fun, but it is not painless. You will have some discouraging times. Although surrounded by people, you will experience bouts of loneliness. And you will encounter roommate problems, academic problems, and financial problems. Learning to deal with such problems is the mark of an educated and mature person.

Be smart—and think twice before you make decisions or do things. Mom and I want you to be bold in what you stand for and careful in what you fall for. In other words, hold on to the values you have developed and don't get sucked into the "anything goes" culture of campus life. Character is much easier kept than recovered. "Always do right," as Mark Twain suggests. "This will gratify some people and astonish the rest."

If you make your selections wisely, if you realize early on that your self-esteem does not depend on how much you drink or smoke or party late into the night, if you realize the benefits of not majoring in minor things, then you will thrive in your new setting.

Enough of my lecturing. Suffice it to say that God adores freshmen. So go forth and prosper. We love you—every minute of the day. Although we will be separated by many miles, you will never be far from our thoughts.

Love,
Dad

P.S. If you have any extra spending money, please send it home.

War and Remembrance

| *November 11, 1998*

Today is Veterans Day. Yet only a few Americans will participate in memorial services, and even fewer are aware of the holiday's origins or its rituals. What a pity! We would do well to remember those who served and died to preserve our peace, freedoms, and prosperity.

Veterans Day dates back to the eleventh hour of the eleventh day of the eleventh month in 1918, when the Armistice was signed, ending World War I. To honor the 116,000 servicemen who died in the war, President Woodrow Wilson declared that November 11 should thereafter be recognized as Armistice Day. In 1938 Congress voted to make Armistice Day a federal holiday, and in 1954 the holiday was renamed Veterans Day to recognize the veterans of all wars.

This Veterans Day has a special significance at Furman. In 1921, three years after the Armistice was signed, Furman and Greenville paid tribute to the university's World War I veterans in a moving ceremony that unveiled a memorial statue of a doughboy. The copper soldier was one of numerous similar statues erected across the country to honor veterans of World War I. The Doughboy depicts a soldier rushing into battle, wielding a grenade in one hand and a rifle in the other.

The term *doughboy* was used by European soldiers to describe their American allies. The U.S. troops arrived in France from a training base in Texas that was known for its white adobe soil. The soil often discolored their uniforms, giving them a "doughboy" appearance.

When the Furman Doughboy was first dedicated, hundreds of area residents turned out at the old campus in downtown Greenville. A bugler played taps as Mrs. T. J. Lyons, the mother of a Furman student who died in France during the war, gently loosened the fastening of the American flag that shrouded the statue.

An article in the July 1921 issue of the *Furman Bulletin* reported that the "handsome statue with splashes of molten gold and the youthful figure of an American Doughboy in France, preserved in lasting metal and stone, stood revealed to the eyes of the expectant throng." When the statue was uncovered, "applause broke forth. Tears filled the eyes of beholders and ex-service men wept as they saw the figure, so life-like, emerge."

Five hundred and forty Furman men, almost the entire student body of the then all-male college, volunteered for service during the Great War. Six of them died during the war—Pvt. Thomas J. Lyons Jr., Pvt. Otis Brodie, Lt. John H. David (the first South Carolina officer killed in action), Lt. Charles S. Gardner (who, though seriously wounded, refused to be removed from the battle), Sgt. Charles E. Timmons Jr. (who "went to death beyond the call of duty, while aiding men from another company"), and Cpl. Talmadge W. Gerrald (who gave his life trying to save a wounded comrade). Their names are inscribed at the base of the Doughboy.

Since that dedication day, the Furman Doughboy has become one of the university's most enduring landmarks. When Furman moved to its current location, so did the Doughboy. It was erected near the south end of the lake in 1957 and is one of the few surviving remnants of the old campus.

Over the last forty years, the Doughboy has lost its luster. The weather has taken its toll, and on two occasions it has been vandalized by Citadel cadets. So a few months ago, the Doughboy was removed from its concrete pedestal and transported to Jeff

Monnick's studio in Columbia. Monnick, the chief conservator of the South Carolina State Museum, spent three months cleaning the corroded doughboy figure, replacing its discolored copper, plugging several bullet holes, and reinforcing its internal framing.

This Veterans Day, Furman University will honor the forty-two million people who served in the military since the Revolutionary War and also celebrate the return of the Doughboy. It will remember those who gave what Abraham Lincoln called "the last full measure of devotion" in the nation's hour of need.

Lincoln spoke for the entire nation, then and since, when he wrote a letter to the mother of five sons lost on the field of battle during the Civil War: "I cannot refrain from tendering to you the thanks of the Republic they died to save. I pray that our heavenly father may assuage the anguish of your bereavement, and leave you only the cherished memory of the loved and lost, and the solemn pride that must be yours to have laid so costly a sacrifice upon the altar of freedom."

On Becoming Paladins

| *October 3, 1999*

What is a Paladin? A freshman from California asked me this question last week. Many folks new to the Greenville area ask the same question. The short answer is a knight on horseback. The long answer, however, is more complicated—and more interesting.

The first person to label Furman athletes paladins was a colorful Greenville sportswriter named Carter "Scoop" Latimer. In 1927 he described Furman's basketball team as "paladins of the court." Thereafter, the nickname was used for the basketball players. Yet until 1961, Furman's other athletic teams used different names. The baseball team was known as the Hornets, the football team the Purple Hurricane, and the track team the Roadrunners.

In 1961, however, the student body voted to make Paladins the official nickname for all the school's intercollegiate athletic teams. A student volunteered to play the role of knight at football games, and Mrs. R. P. McAbee of Piedmont loaned a beautiful white horse for him to ride. Each time the team scores, the Paladin rides down the sidelines.

The desire to adopt a single symbol for the athletic teams mirrored the reason for constructing the "new" campus, which officially opened in the fall of 1958: the need to combine all-male Furman University and the separate Woman's College on one campus. The male students arrived in 1958, but most women did not move onto campus until 1961. As the sports editor of the student newspaper explained that year, "It would seem that the time has come for definite steps to be taken to unify the teams under one symbol. The University itself is in the process of unifying, and it seems only natural for the athletic teams to follow."

The students fastened on the name Paladins for several reasons. The term dates back to the medieval period, when paladins were the most courageous and virtuous knights at the court of Charlemagne, the emperor of the Holy Roman Empire during the early

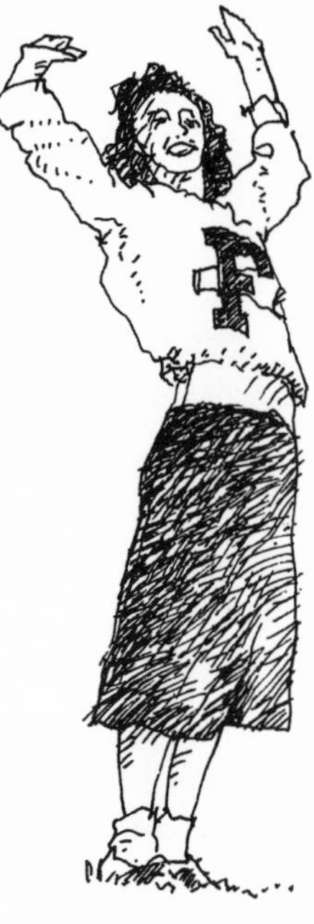

ninth century. The emperor's paladins wore a purple plume atop their helmets and typically rode white stallions. They exhibited an insatiable appetite for battle and displayed intense loyalty to the empire and the emperor. As a Furman student noted, the Paladins nickname thus provided "a tangible symbol, colors of purple and white, and is easily adaptable to a fight song." It also was unique. No other college used the term for its athletic teams (there is a high school in Paramus, New Jersey, that has adopted the Paladins moniker).

But what many people today do not realize is that there was a contemporary reason for the popularity of the term *paladin* among the Furman students. In 1961 one of the most successful television shows was "Have Gun, Will Travel." Its star, Richard Boone, played the role of Paladin, a dapper cowboy gunfighter-for-hire who also happened to be a Renaissance man—well-educated, multilingual, and virtuous to a fault. The half-hour show aired on Saturdays, at 9:30 p.m., just before another popular western, "Gunsmoke."

Whatever the historical origins of Furman's adoption of the name Paladins, we hope that our students continue to live up to its dictionary description: valorous persons "of outstanding worth or quality who are firm in support of some cause or objective." Go Paladins!

Warren Wilson College

An Ethic of Work and Learning

| *April 29, 2001*

There are more than three thousand institutions of higher learning in the United States. They come in all shapes and sizes, and they pursue quite different missions. The diversity of American higher education is one of its greatest strengths.

One of the most distinctive American colleges is located near Asheville, North Carolina. Nestled in the Swannanoa Valley, Warren Wilson College is one of just a handful of colleges nationwide that require every student to hold a part-time campus job. And the jobs include much more than filing, answering phones, or running errands. The 750 students at Warren Wilson mow the grass, fix the plumbing, and operate tractors and bulldozers, chain saws and trucks. They tend the college fields and organic gardens, harvest the crops, and maintain herds of pigs and cattle. In fact, other than a few licensed tradesmen, it is the students who perform almost all of the physical labor needed to operate the college. They collect the trash, paint buildings, and serve as electricians and security officers. They also coordinate the college's web page and help produce many of the college publications.

An often-recounted joke among the students at Warren Wilson College is that the letters *WWC* do not simply represent the school's initials. They stand for "We Work Constantly." Juniors and seniors tend to land the most desirable campus work assignments, such as managing the three-hundred-acre organic farm, but every student worker is paid the same—about $2,500 a year, which is credited toward room and board.

"Work and service help prepare you for what it takes to build a community, to be a member rather than just a spectator in your own village," says Ian Robertson, the "dean of work" at WWC. A native of England whose college major was pig husbandry, Robertson joined the private liberal arts college in 1980 as the supervisor of the campus garden.

"Work also builds pride among the students," he says." They take ownership in Warren Wilson because they have a stake in the school and are not just passing through for four years."

The major religious denominations founded many such "work" colleges during the nineteenth and early twentieth centuries, including Furman and Davidson. The colleges were intended to give students from impoverished, mostly rural, backgrounds a chance to earn a degree in exchange for their labor. However, as economic conditions improved and endowments grew, many such colleges abandoned their mandatory work programs. Now, however, there seems to be renewed interest in work-centered colleges. Their holistic educational philosophy appeals to a growing number of students (and their parents).

Warren Wilson College was initially called the Asheville Farm School, founded in 1895. In 1942 it was renamed for Warren Hugh Wilson, a prominent Presbyterian missionary who focused on improving rural life.

The college has no football team and no fraternities or sororities. Students focus instead on music, creative writing, contra dancing and outdoor recreation such as cycling, hiking, rock climbing, and kayaking. In addition to working fifteen hours a week, WWC students are also required to participate in some form of community service. The result is what the college calls the triad, a character-building blend of academics, labor, and service that helps students develop a strong work ethic and an engaged sense of social responsibility.

At first glance, Warren Wilson looks like a typical small liberal arts college. Its stone and wood buildings and walkways are graced by beautiful grounds. With its mountain backdrop, the campus is one of the most scenic in the nation. But a closer inspection reveals the true character and distinctive texture and charm of WWC. Students in this outdoor rustic setting dress in casual work clothes, and environmental studies is the most popular major. The college's president, Douglas Orr, trained as a geographer and is an accomplished bluegrass musician, as is his wife, Darcy.

Warren Wilson celebrates it distinctiveness. As its admissions material proclaims, "We're not for everyone, but then maybe you're not everyone."

Part 2

Writing and Reading

The Fate of Books in a Digital Age

Phi Beta Kappa Address, Davidson College

| *March 9, 1999*

Let me begin by expressing my congratulations to the new members of Phi Beta Kappa for your distinguished achievements. You and your parents should cherish what this event represents.

I will never forget my own induction ceremony into Phi Beta Kappa—the atmosphere was electric with excitement, the parents were bursting with pride, and the student initiates were justifiably proud. But the most evident emotion was the absolute dread that the speech would never end.

In that regard, I promise not to keep you more than an hour or two. You may not be any wiser after one of my speeches, but you will be a great deal older.

I begin with a question: What are the implications of the much-ballyhooed digital revolution for the culture of books?

I was prompted to think about this topic when I encountered a provocative statement by the Canadian writer Robert Fulford. He announced that the traditional book is in danger of becoming "an outdated shrine, a place only for occasional worship."

The dwindling interest in books and serious reading raises an obvious question: As we spend more and more time "online," shifting our attention from book to screen, tactile to digital, are we abandoning some of the basic premises and processes of liberal learning?

After all, the most important transmitters of our knowledge and our reflections have been *books.* Books have formed the core of civilized life, the juncture where facts and feelings meet. For centuries, books have provided a primary source of pleasure, inspiration, and instruction at every level of our cultural life. Ever since Julius Caesar ordered written scrolls cut into individual pages and bound together, we have become a page-turning species.

Yet now we are told that the bound book has become a doomed technology, a mere curiosity of bygone days. The dean of the architecture school at MIT, for example, predicts that books in the twenty-first century will be irrelevant "except to those addicted to the look and feel of tree flakes encased in dead cow."

I must confess that I am such an addict. I love books made of wood pulp and leather. Even though I spend much of my working day in front of a computer screen, manipulating a twitching cursor, I remain devoted to books.

I buy them, borrow them, loan them, and give them away. I read them, review them, write them, collect them, stumble over them, think about them, even dream about them.

Books make for pleasing company. They are quiet, accessible, and patient. They offer consolation and excitement. They do not whine or call during the dinner hour, nor do they carry grudges. They suffer interruptions with grace and are eminently portable. They accompany you to lunch or to the bathroom or to the beach, and in the process they provide wise counsel and welcome companionship.

Of course, books are more than a source of intellectual interest; they can also become objects of art and affection. In our house, in fact, books furnish the rooms. Whole populations of volumes have migrated into every crevice and cranny. They line the shelves to overflowing and sit in untidy stacks on tables or in corners.

On occasion, provoked by a fleeting sense of order and proportion, I assault the sprawling piles. As if selecting lambs for sacrifice, I gather up the most exposed and under-appreciated books and donate them to a local school or library. Yet no sooner do I winnow the volumes than the craving for more reasserts itself.

Such is the fate of the bibliophile. Like an alcoholic attracted to a liquor store, I cannot pass a bookshop without going in. Once inside these alluring bazaars, I stroll the aisles, lingering here and there, pulling one book and then another off the shelves, scanning the table of contents with ravishing eyes, seduced by the crisp new pages and firm bindings. There is something almost sensuous in the feel and heft of a new book. The aroma of paper, glue, leather, and ink excites the senses.

My passion for books over other pleasures puts me in distinguished company. When the ancient Roman orator Cicero met Cleopatra, he asked not for a night of love but whether the queen of the Nile would lend him some volumes from the legendary library at Alexandria.

Similarly, Erasmus, the great sixteenth-century Christian humanist, confessed, "When I get a little money, I buy books; and, if any is left, I buy food and clothes." Erasmus knew that the silent wisdom contained in books and the cocooned pleasures of reading supersede more superficial pursuits. Books have formed the core of civilized life, the juncture where facts and feelings meet, the bundle of pages in which we wrap truth, hope, and dread. The narrative tradition embedded in books has shaped how we explain, how we teach, how we entertain ourselves.

Yet while voracious in my taste for reading, I have not gone so far as the English woman who ate an entire New Testament, day by day, between two sides of bread and butter. She did so as a remedy for fits.

Books can indeed be therapeutic. Of all the forms of human relaxation, reading is the most dignified way to redeem time and solace the soul. Books can help educate and channel our ambitions, upset our prejudices, and disturb our complacency. They can also liberate us from the sludge of the trivial.

Yet of all the gifts that literature delivers, the capacity of reading to connect us with others is the one most often overlooked and undervalued. Books can liberate us from the provincialism of our selves. They transport us away from home and our workaday routines into a realm of new experiences, challenging ideas, and interesting people. In the process of capturing our imagination, books help dramatize our days and enrich our sense of the joys of being human.

But I am being too general. Let me use the ballast of a concrete example to suggest why I am so enamored of books and the opportunity they provide to expand and inform our sense of human community.

One of my favorite authors is the late Eudora Welty, the genteel Mississippi native who wrote with poetic precision and sympathetic curiosity about the people of the Mississippi Delta. "What I do in writing of any character," she once explained, "is to try to enter into the mind, heart, and skin of a human being who is not myself."

Such an objective echoes what colleges such as Davidson and Furman are aspiring to do. We, too, are trying to help young people develop an empathetic outlook that enables them to better understand and appreciate the diversity of the human spectacle.

Eudora Welty's writings help us imagine being different. In the process of immersing readers in the folkways and myths, manners and mores of the area known as the Yazoo Trace, she makes the strange familiar and the familiar seem strange. Her luminous prose is seasoned with authentic details and saturated with the tang and scent of the Delta.

Consider this arresting description from a bittersweet love story titled "At the Landing": "The river went by immeasurable under the sky, moving and dimly catching and snagging itself, freeing itself without effort, heavy with its great waves of drift, deep with stirring fish." There is no straining in such observant prose. Like an impressionist painter, Welty stipples her narratives with delicate ironies and astute observations, all of them as striking as a needle point.

She often uses humor to bring her characters alive, as in this passage from *Delta Wedding:* "His hands took her by the hair and pulled her up like a turnip. On top of the water he looked at her intently, his eyelashes thorny and dripping at her. . . . 'I couldn't believe you wouldn't come right up,' says Roy suddenly, 'I thought girls floated.'"

Welty's narrative art reveals how literature can transform the mundane into the magical and invest ordinary lives with unexpected dignity. Her writings not only offer information; they reward our attention by giving language to dream, story to memory, empathy to reflection. How this occurs, how the process of reading compelling fiction affects our psyche, remains a mystery, but this much is sure: the honing of our rational capacities and social awareness depends upon the narrative imagining contained in such stories.

Narratives give time a shape and direction—and so we invent, tell, listen to, and read stories in order to understand what and where we have been, to make sense of lives unfolding in time. In the process of conveying stories in words, we sharpen our capacity to imagine being different, to enter into the lives and experiences of others.

By reflecting while we read, we also compose stories of our own in an effort to explain ourselves to ourselves and to others. Story reading and storytelling are thus our chief means of understanding the past and imagining the future, of seeing and appreciating differences among people.

In the end, however, the act of reading forces us to undertake the most difficult feat of all: to think on our own.

Yet in this multimedia age and this frenetic era of diminished leisure, the habit of reading bound books is dying. The frenzied pace of our wired and wireless world often denies us the time to engage a serious book. People much prefer the less strenuous pleasures of television and video. Most Americans born after 1970 are image-oriented rather than text-oriented. They spend more time and mental energy looking at pictures than the printed word. This is a development of ominous consequences, since a culture rooted in images is consigned to shallowness.

So where does this leave us as readers? The fate of books and of reading has become the subject of some very sophisticated discussion of late. Let me cite just two prominent participants in this cultural debate.

In 1993 Richard Lanham, an English professor at UCLA, published a stimulating book titled *The Electronic Word* in which he hailed the impact of new circuit-driven technologies, proclaiming that electronic media will transform "the arts and letters into one activity as never before." Words printed on paper, Lanham contends, are static and inert, trapped in a formal arrangement assigned them by some anonymous staff member at a publishing house. To liberate texts from such artificial constraints, Lanham believes, they must be digitized, downloaded, and then displayed and enlivened through hypertextual media.

In other words, unlike conventional printed text that is organized in linear fashion, hypertext is non-sequential writing made up of blocks of prose that can be selected and combined by the reader in multiple ways. Such improvised hypertexts, Lanham claims, will soon displace the tradition of linear writing. They will democratize literature by enabling the user to manipulate the text rather than remain dependent upon what another author has decided and written.

Lanham represents a postmodern sensibility that resents the traditional authority exercised by a book's author and resists the fixed boundaries implied by a book's bindings. He is a self-described revolutionary who wants to overthrow the author and empower the reader by replacing bound books with multimedia technologies. The latest new computer tools and video technologies, he argues, can liberate the individual from the tyranny of the printed book, the constraints of printed text, and the hierarchical domination of the author.

Lanham relishes hypertext's interactive and open-ended qualities. A hypertext novel is modeled after the varied possibilities of video games. Just as users manipulate video games according to their individual preferences and abilities, a reader of hypertext navigates through the novel, selecting among an infinite array of plot and action options. There are no endings predetermined by authors. The reader controls the text; the original author becomes irrelevant. Such hyperfiction has no beginning or end. The reader chooses where to enter and exit a story and determines the fates of the characters.

This is heady stuff. To be sure, the notion of every reader being a creative writer through the medium of multiform hypertext is alluring. Yet Lanham goes too far in dismissing authors and books. His postmodern perspective has provoked many earnest critics, none more passionate than Sven Birkerts, a professor who teaches at Mount Holyoke College. He has steadfastly resisted the imperial presumptions and anarchic possibilities of computer-generated fiction.

In 1994 Birkerts published a collection of powerful essays titled *The Gutenberg Elegies*. Birkerts believes we are at a crucial turning point in the development of civilization. Never before has the life of the mind in America been more threatened. We are living in a state of intellectual emergency—a crisis caused by our naïve willingness to embrace new "televisual" technologies at the expense of the traditional book.

For Birkerts, the postmodern world so eagerly embraced by Lanham and others offers us in fact a Faustian bargain in which we sell our souls in exchange for a "digital future." The well-read person is disappearing, Birkerts declares. We are now surrounded by technopunks who can retrieve whole libraries of information with a keystroke and who chill out by watching MTV, but who cannot appreciate the sophisticated talents of Jane Austen or Henry James.

"As the world hurtles on," Birkerts laments, "the old act of slowly reading a serious book becomes an elegiac exercise. As we ponder that act, profound questions must arise about our avowedly humanistic values, about spiritual versus material concerns, and about subjectivity itself."

Birkerts beautifully describes the solitary act of reading: the sensations of it, the passion and fascination of it, the way a novel or biography captures you in its imaginative web long after you've finished the final page. By emphasizing the humanistic contributions of conventional books, Birkerts provides a lover's insight into the romance of reading. He correctly notes that while we have mastered the science of processing and communicating mountains of *information,* we have not yet figured out how to process and deliver *wisdom* at the speed of light.

In this regard we would do well to remember Woody Allen's boast that he had taken a speed-reading course and had just completed Tolstoy's *War and Peace* in two hours. When asked what he had learned from the novel, he replied: "It's about Russia."

For Birkerts, the traditional book is sacred. He dismisses hypertext as visually seductive but ultimately anarchic and boring. And he insists that the medium through which words are conveyed changes their essence. As he explains, the "tree hiked to and seen is not the tree driven to and seen, even though it is the same tree."

What Birkerts sees at stake is nothing less than the tradition of Western humanism. He claims that "our entire collective subjective history—the soul of our societal body—is encoded in print. . . . If a person turns from print . . . then what happens to that person's sense of culture and continuity?"

Birkerts is a compelling defender of the printed book. Like a true believer listening to a tent revivalist, I found myself at times nodding and swaying in agreement as I read *The Gutenberg Elegies.*

I, too, believe in the sanctity of aesthetic experience and in the ability of reading to help us achieve some profound connection with other human beings, however slight and fleeting. Yet while sympathetic with Birkerts's anxiety for the fate of the book, I do not share his apocalyptic panic in the face of our wired world. As his jeremiad unfolds, he subverts his argument by dismissing all forms of electronic media.

Here is a typical statement from *The Gutenberg Elegies:* "[Circuit and screen] are *entirely* inhospitable to the more subjective materials that have always been the stuff of art. That is to say, they are antithetical to inwardness."

In the end, I found Birkerts's argument arresting but not convincing. Just as the pencil has survived the typewriter, books will survive in our digital world. They may even flourish on the flickering screen as readily as they did on the printed page. As both a theoretical and a practical matter, those of us concerned about the fate of the book need to engage rather than dismiss the digital revolution and its magical implications. Like it or not, it is the communications technology of the future. The convergence of the Internet with the instantaneous transmission and retrieval of digital text is an epochal event. But it is by no means a disastrous event.

Yes, reading text on a screen rather than a printed page may provoke different responses from the reader, but such responses may not necessarily be demonic or destructive. In coming years bound books and electronic books will exist side by side, just like home stereos and Walkmans do today, and they will probably come to complement one another in beneficial ways.

So, my friends, the choice we face is not simply between computer screen and printed page—our predicament is much more threatening: namely, between a future in which serious reading has a meaningful impact on our culture and one in which it does not. That we are faced with this choice has little to do with whether a book is in print or pixel form, and everything to do with the nature of well-established mass media such as radio, television, and film, and the commercialized mass culture these media have engendered.

These mesmerizing forms of passive entertainment have immersed us in the trivial and the ephemeral. As a result, fewer and fewer people find sustained reading sufficiently stimulating, and, as a consequence, the verbal scores and rhetorical abilities of young people are steadily declining. Virtual reality and digital graphics encourage us to bypass writing and even language altogether. Our multimedia mania has led us to view printed words as primitive substitutes for dazzling graphics and video.

The number of Americans who engage in regular reading is steadily declining. Some 15 percent of American adults are functionally illiterate, and as many as 40 percent have only minimal reading skills. The illiteracy rate in the United States is three times higher than that in supposedly backward Russia.

But how can this be, you ask? Bookstores seem to be doing a thriving business. Yet only 10 percent of the population reads 70 percent of the books published in the United States, and the majority of adults never read for pleasure. Close reading and deep thinking are demanding activities, and most people would rather watch television or play a video game or surf the Net.

If we do not sustain a commitment to reflective reading, then it matters little whether the books of the future are printed or electronic. Our capacity to form critical opinions and make informed decisions will continue to diminish.

Let me end these remarks with an avuncular plea for you to turn off the television, cell phone, and computer and pick up a book, in any of its forms. The habit of reading will keep you humble, invigorated, and informed. It will expand your horizons, and it will keep you thinking when all of your other faculties are diminished.

Other than marital bliss and wine, learning is perhaps the only source of satisfaction that improves with age. As the British writer Thomas Carlyle recognized, "What we become [in life] depends on what we read after all of the professors have finished with us. The greatest college of all is a collection of books." Happy reading!

Pleasures of the Essay

| *November 28, 1999*

Labels classify and perplex. I have been asked if I enjoy being a "journalist." The label disturbs me. After all, journalists are not well respected these days. Come to think of it: they have never been well respected. As the acid-tongued writer Ambrose Bierce announced in 1878, "nobody in the United States has ever been hanged for killing a journalist. Public opinion will not permit it."

In recent surveys ranking the reputation of various professions, journalists fall below telemarketers and used-car salesmen—and well below college presidents! So call me a writer, call me a columnist, but please don't call me a journalist.

In fact, essayist might be the best description of my role as biweekly opinion writer. That is the right label for what I am trying to do. Three years ago *Greenville News* editorial page editor Tom Inman invited me to write essays about whatever I wanted. Who could turn down such an opportunity?

Much of the pleasure of essay writing derives from its open-ended quality. By definition, an essay embodies a brief narrative on any particular topic, usually flavored with the author's own personal observations and opinions. The magisterial eighteenth-century writer Samuel Johnson called the essay a "loose sally of the mind" and "an irregular undigested piece" of prose.

An essay tries to make sense out of the chaos surrounding us. It also offers the perfect forum for a writer in middle age, for an essay is the fruit of ripened experience and seasoned observation.

Essays enable writers to discuss ideas—or at least mull them over—without becoming embroiled in the furor of contemporary political debates and cultural wars. Unlike journalists, essayists are not preoccupied with the breaking news of the day. Instead we parade our own interests and interrogate our own ignorance. Like cats purring to please themselves, we are hopelessly undisciplined and self-centered; we presume that anything of interest to us will be enthralling to others. We pontificate about all sorts of idiosyncratic topics, and in the process of reflecting on the minutiae of everyday life, we inflict our thoughts upon innocent readers. In sum, essayists are wordy amateurs delighted by little excursions of the mind.

Michel de Montaigne, a reflective sixteenth-century French lawyer, was the father of the modern essay. In 1571, about the time Shakespeare was starting school in England, Montaigne retired at age thirty-eight to his family estate in southern France. To stimulate his thinking, he began writing what he called *essais,* or meandering "attempts" to capture in words "what I know."

Montaigne's essays provide a seductive mixture of personal revelation, wide reading, and acute observation. He was candidly egotistical yet modest and unpretentious, profoundly wise yet constantly protesting his ignorance, learned yet careless, forgetful, and inconsistent. Above all, he was capacious in his interests. No subject eluded his grasp. He wrote about sadness, liars, fear, prayer, humility, education, children, aging, idleness, the pleasures of scratching, and a thousand other topics. Yet whatever his theme, he displayed a remarkable consistency of tone and temperament, a quick eye for the telling detail, and an appreciation for life as a form of theater and self-fashioning. In the process, he sprinkled his reflections with nuggets of epigrammatic insight. ("No wind is right for a seaman with no predetermined harbor." "On the loftiest throne in the world we are still sitting on our own rump." "Since we cannot attain to greatness, let us have our revenge by railing at it.") And he mastered the fine art of using words to inform and persuade pleasurably.

Montaigne confessed that he wrote essays in an effort to understand himself and his world. He strove to sustain the reflective values of a humane culture. His motto was etched in a beam above his study. It reads: "Nihil humani alieni mihi puto." Loosely translated, it means, "Nothing human is alien to me."

Such an all-encompassing credo remains relevant to the essayist today. What shall I write about tomorrow? Ah, the world awaits . . .

A Passion for Poetry

| *November 1, 1998*

Like most bookish boys, I enjoyed writing from an early age. For a time, around age thirteen or so, I even aspired to be a poet. After school I would hole up in my bedroom and try to transform my observations, thoughts, and feelings into quatrains and sonnets. (I quite self-consciously used a fountain pen to express the seriousness of the enterprise.)

Poetry was an exhilarating endeavor for an ungainly teenager, and I naively began to imagine myself becoming a celebrated bohemian living in New York's Greenwich Village or the Left Bank of Paris.

The only problem with this adolescent fantasy was that I wrote awful poems that grew more terrible with time. My rhymes were passable, but too often I left my meter running. My elegies were not poignant; they were pathetic. Even my efforts at free verse were constrained by mediocrity. I knew I was in trouble when my sister, normally a quite sympathetic sibling, recommended that I focus on blank verse—literally. Of course, a paucity of talent has not kept others from writing poetry. Ogden Nash once declared that he would "rather be a great bad poet than a good bad poet." In my case, however, I was neither good bad nor great bad but simply bad.

So, about the time I started wearing braces on my teeth, I gave up any hope of becoming a bard and decided that my inability to express myself in a few words meant that I should focus instead on becoming a lawyer. That, too, would prove to be another dead end, but that is another story. Suffice it to say that poetry for me was the first of several roads not taken.

Yet while remaining devoid of poetic talent, I have sustained a love of poetry. Part of its allure is its difficulty. Writing a poem is much more challenging than writing a fortnightly newspaper column because it places such a stern premium on compression and economy. As the most concentrated form of expression, it involves the art of selecting words with their utmost meaning and combining them in extraordinary ways so that they have an enduring effect. As Emily Dickinson stresses, "a Word that breathes distinctly / Has not the power to die."

Poetry's exacting demand for linguistic precision helps explain why few poems are perfect. Unlike prose, poetry offers no room for error. A poet must be a virtuoso of diction who calibrates the exact valence of each word selected. Each word carries such great weight because every word must be the right one. Such fierce discrimination makes the successful choice all the more fulfilling. The Irish poet William Butler Yeats recognized the subtle perfectionism of his craft when he observed that "the correction of prose is endless, [whereas] a poem comes right with a click like a closing box."

A successful poem not only employs precise and pungent words in powerful combinations; in the process it uses elements of wit and surprise, passion and rhythm, metaphor and imagery to embody complex emotions and provoke strong feelings. In making the commonplace compelling and the mundane meaningful, poetry illuminates and affirms our humanity and expands our horizons.

One example of poetry's beguiling brevity will have to stand for many. In one of her last poems, Emily Dickinson declares that

> *To make a prairie it takes a clover and one bee,*
> *One clover, and a bee,*
> *And revery.*
> *The revery alone will do,*
> *If bees are few.*

Such austerely beautiful poetry offers us a refreshing respite from our clamorous routine. Poems provide new insights into our own experiences and our particular selves, and even some tentative answers to the large questions involving our identity and our fate. As William Carlos Williams recognizes in "Asphodel, That Greeny Flower," poems often provide salvation as well as sustenance, yet few people read them. People "die miserably every day / for lack / of what is found there."

Looking Backward into the New Millennium

A Book Review

| *January 1, 1998*

As we come to the end of a tired century and prepare to start a new millennium, where are we headed and what compass will we use to stay on course?

This question animates Neil Postman's new book, *Building a Bridge to the Eighteenth Century: How the Past Can Improve Our Future.* The title suggests his answer. Postman believes that we should retrieve the "good ideas" espoused by Enlightenment humanists such as Voltaire, Rousseau, Jefferson, and Franklin.

In particular, Postman celebrates the ways in which leading eighteenth-century thinkers both embraced and questioned the pervasive faith in scientific progress that characterized their age. Excited by the thrill of discovery, they garnered hope and vitality from the notion of scientific advance while at the same time recognized its limitations and pitfalls. Like Postman, the Enlightenment rationalists revolted against prevailing orthodoxy and inherited superstitions. Many of them questioned the widespread assumption that technological innovations necessarily fostered moral and social improvements, and they believed that there was a transcendent purpose to existence, a divine source of meaning embedded in life's mystery.

For almost thirty years, Postman, chair of New York University's department of culture and communications, has been an articulate and impassioned skeptic. A self-described "enemy of this century," he resembles Rousseau and Thoreau in his relentless questioning of the presumed benefits of modern technology. He wants to infuse our "technoculture" with humane values and long-range concerns.

In provocative books such as *Amusing Ourselves to Death* (1985), *Technopoly* (1992), and *The End of Education* (1995), Postman has highlighted the dangers of a television-absorbed society and a naive embrace of technology and educational fads. In the process, he has steadfastly appealed for a more reflective approach to cultural change. *Building a Bridge to the Eighteenth Century* is meant "for those who are still searching for a way to confront the future, a way that faces reality as it is, that is connected to a humane tradition, that provides sane authority and meaningful purpose."

Postman fears that we are becoming tools of our tools. He proudly confesses that he does not use a computer; he writes with pen and paper. To him, the Internet is a "mere distraction." He refuses to use e-mail or voice mail. Yet he insists that he is not "anti-technology." Instead he strives to avoid being "tyrannized" by the relentless march of electronic media. Like Franklin, Jefferson, and Voltaire, he stresses, we should take greater care in thinking through the broader implications of new technology and constantly ask what costs and benefits derive from new gadgets.

For example, Postman notes that automobiles have improved personal mobility and accelerated economic growth but in the process have "poisoned our air, choked our cities with traffic," and degraded the natural environment. More immediately, he asks if we have paused to consider the corrosive effects of computer dependency on our "psychic habits, social relations, and, most certainly, in our political institutions, especially electoral politics."

Postman acknowledges that the computer revolution has provided an almost limitless supply of information. The problem yet to be addressed, however, "is how to transform information into knowledge, and how to transform knowledge into wisdom."

Amid our digital age, Postman fears for our freedom and our humane sensibilities. The mind-numbing and manipulative effects of multimedia culture threaten independent thinking. Our only hope, he asserts, is for parents and teachers to instill in children "the cultivation of a skeptical outlook based on reason." Engendering such critical thinking will be crucial to protecting individual liberty and democratic processes.

Postman also highlights the need for children to be exposed to religion. Any person claiming to be educated, he insists, must appreciate the role played by religion in the formation of culture. It simply is not possible, he concludes, for an educated person to avoid asking questions about why we are on this planet and for what purpose.

Postman's brisk critique of contemporary trends and his urgent appeal for a commonsense skepticism make for compelling reading. His prose is witty and combative, lucid and self-revealing. If at times his provocative proposals seem quixotic, one cannot help but admire his range of interests and his moral stamina—as well as his dogged integrity. In this sense, Postman resembles the eighteenth-century thinkers whose ideas and ideals he seeks to resurrect. Not bad company.

A Love of Sacred Music

A Book Review

| *December 12, 1999*

I love music. It entertains and inspires. It also puzzles me. I wish I better understood its peculiar dynamics and its mysterious appeal. Like a teenager engaged in a first romance, I am greatly stirred by a passion I cannot fully comprehend.

I cannot remember my life without music. Our father loved to sing to us—even in foreign languages. At an early age I dutifully learned to play the trumpet, then the French horn, and later the guitar. I know, I know: I should have started with the piano if I ever hoped to master music theory. But we did not own one, and my circle of callow male friends viewed piano playing as a girl thing. We had not yet heard of Horowitz or Serkin or Van Cliburn—or even Billy Joel!

I have never been more than a mediocre musician, but I have remained an unabashed music lover—especially in December. Amid this holiday season we are graced with an abundance of cantatas, oratorios, and choral performances. I relish the opportunity to hear sacred music performed well.

Music and religion are linked in a complex embrace. Martin Luther described liturgical music as "a noble, wholesome, and cheerful creation of God" capable of providing a conduit to the divine. "Next to the Word of God," he declared, "music deserves the highest praise." Sermons occasionally leave us drowsy and dulled; sacred music never fails to excite and exalt us. No one leaves a performance of Handel's *Messiah* or Bach's *St. Matthew Passion* or Gregorian chants unmoved. After the first performance of the *Messiah* in 1743, one of Handel's patrons told the composer that he had produced some "noble entertainment." Handel was not flattered. "My Lord," he replied, "I should be sorry if I only entertained them. I wished to make them better."

What is it about such expressive music that suggests the presence of the divine and generates such powerful spiritual feelings? How does music transport us to a world of delighted imagining?

In response to such profound questions, Dr. Albert Blackwell, a professor of religion at Furman and an accomplished musician, has written a sophisticated new book titled *The Sacred in Music.* From the start he recognizes the difficulty of his task. How does one express in words the ineffable effects of music? The spontaneity of feelings aroused by organized sounds defies simple analysis and verbal expression. We do an injustice to the peculiar power of music when we try to capture its essence in mere words.

Yet Blackwell believes that the sacramental effects of music can be articulated with confidence if not with absolute precision. He contends that "religion and music are complementary resources for interpreting our lives." Sacred music, he adds, manifests a transcendent power capable of promoting religious reflection and commitment. It speaks both to our minds and our emotions. As Beethoven insisted, music derives its distinctive appeal from being "the mediator between intellectual and sensuous life."

Many people find that, of all the performing arts, music has the most power to affect our souls by expressing God's majesty and our own frailty. Saint Augustine recognized as much when he recalled his own conversion experience: "The tears flowed from me when I heard your hymns and canticles, for the sweet singing of your Church moved me deeply. The music surged in my ears, truth seeped into my heart, and my feelings of devotion overflowed, so that the tears streamed down. But they were tears of gladness."

More specifically, Blackwell contends, sacred music prepares people for worship by quieting the frenzied pace and psychic worries that mark our days. "Be still and know that I am God," says the psalmist, and reverential music helps to still our restless lives, suspend our rational calculations, and make us receptive to spiritual emotion. A state of repose invites reflection. "The first condition of right thought is right sensation," the poet T. S. Eliot observed. "If you have seen and felt truly, then if God has given you the power, you may be able to think rightly."

Blackwell also argues that sacred music helps us proclaim and celebrate shared beliefs. As a traditional hymn asserts,

The hymns thy people raise,
the psalms and anthems strong,
hint at the glorious praise
of thy eternal song.

Performing or listening to sacred music promotes a sense of healing and harmony. In this regard, Blackwell believes with Handel "that beauty, and in particular the beauty of music, can help to save a fallen world." Hallelujah!

Part 3

Contemporary Culture

What Happened to the Simple Life?

| *May 14, 2000*

During the early 1980s I wrote a book titled *The Simple Life: Plain Living and High Thinking in American Culture.* It traces the ideal of simpler living from the colonial period to the modern era, focusing on different groups and individuals and their efforts to define and sustain a good life.

One of the most thought-provoking of those individuals was Henry David Thoreau, the Massachusetts philosopher, poet, and naturalist who engaged in a famous experiment in plain living and high thinking at Walden Pond during the 1840s.

I recently read that one of the best-selling audiotapes is Thoreau's famous *Walden,* his famous account of his stay at Walden Pond. This revelation provoked a festival of ironic images. Imagine, for example, frazzled commuters listening to Thoreau rhapsodize about life in the woods and preach the virtues of simplicity and self-reliance while they themselves rush in quiet desperation through bumper-to-bumper traffic to get to their workplace.

Yet perhaps Thoreau would take solace in the fact that Americans today still find his message compelling—even if vicariously. He provokes us to think about what a simpler life might currently entail.

Although he was an eccentric man and contentious thinker, Thoreau is an irresistible writer; to read him is to be wrenched away from our customary world and delivered into a place we fear as much as we need. Many of his essential ideas remain relevant to our own clumsy efforts to pursue happiness.

Judging from what we read in the newspapers and watch on television these days, the prevailing notion of happiness seems to be acquisitive and self-indulgent. In recent years we have witnessed not only the resurgence of the economy but also the revival of the distinctively American faith in endless abundance as the key to personal fulfillment and national purpose.

Michelob beer commercials tell us that "you can have it all," and many Americans are grabbing all the gusto from life they can. We live amid a powerful consumer culture that nourishes the conviction that more money and newer things are necessary ingredients of the good life. We are taught that to buy and to possess is to be happy and that every one of our needs can be met, every anxiety relieved, every want satisfied, by the spending of money or the acquisition of status symbols. This passion for possessions has been a frequent theme in our popular culture.

One of the hit songs of the 1980s, performed by Madonna, includes the chorus: "Don't you know that we are living in a material world, and I am a material girl?" She then adds:

They can beg and they can plead
but they can't see the light
'cause the boy with the cold, hard cash
is always Mr. Right.

In the process of such pervasive consumerism, personal bankruptcies have soared during the 1980s and 1990s because people are buying more than they can afford or need.

The unabashedly materialistic notion of the good life that envelops America in the 1990s has imposed severe psychological and physical demands. Underneath the seeming attractions of life in the fast lane is the disturbing fact that the three most frequently prescribed drugs in this country are an ulcer medication, a hypertension reliever, and a tranquilizer. Stress has become one of the nation's leading public health concerns. The director of behavioral medicine at the University of Louisville recently observed that "our mode of life itself, the way we live, is emerging as today's principal cause of illness."

The excessive concern for money and things has been accompanied by clogged calendars. In the corporate or professional workplace, more and more people arrive at work early and stay late. Today the typical corporate executive works three hours longer each week than in 1979, and he or she takes 20 percent fewer vacation days. The American Medical Association reports that the average white-collar worker gets sixty to ninety minutes less sleep each night than needed.

All of us, it seems, are constantly complaining about how busy and how tired we are. Of course, many people thrive as busy executives and professionals. They find an intrinsic satisfaction in high-pressure, high-stakes careers and thrive on the stress of competition and the adrenaline it generates. And they are quite content with life in the fast lane. Others decide to sacrifice personal and familial simplicity in order to serve humanity in one of the helping professions.

But for those who despair because their calendars are too crowded, their lives and homes too cluttered, their commuting too draining, and their self-image distressingly shallow, let us turn back to Thoreau to see how he might help.

Why might people be reading Thoreau now? It may be because many feel as if they lead lives of what he called "quiet desperation." A survey conducted in 1997 by the Merck Foundation reveals that 82 percent of Americans agreed that they buy and consume far more than they need, and 86 percent said that their children were "too focused on buying and consuming things."

A more recent survey reports that "voluntary simplicity" is one of the leading social trends of the 1990s. Almost 50 percent of adult Americans claim that they have taken steps in the last year to simplify their lives.

Simplicity workshops are popping up across the country. In recent years five books about leading simpler lives have been best-sellers. There is now a simplicity home page on the World Wide Web, and television programs have been devoted to the subject.

There is now a national newsletter titled *The Simple Life,* published in Seattle by Janet Luhrs. She explains that simplicity "is all about deliberately slowing down, finding the time and space to live in the moment, to really experience life."

Those attracted by this ideal of simplicity are seeking to lead lives that are outwardly more simple and inwardly more rich. They have recognized that there is more to life than increasing its speed.

Indeed, economists have begun to use the term *downshifting* to describe the growing trend whereby people are consciously seeking to slow down and simplify their lives.

For people feeling rushed, stressed, harried, for those who are frustrated that they can never seem to get enough done and that time is always running out, Thoreau deserves

reconsidering. He offers a tonic alternative to lives worn down from life in the fast lane. "Why should we," he asks in *Walden,* "live with such hurry and waste of life?" He repeatedly urges his readers to "simplify, simplify, simplify!"

Yet too many readers of *Walden* continue to be confused by the practical implications of Thoreau's message and his example. Understanding *Walden* as a whole is a hopeless task. Thoreau condenses complex ideas into pithy epigrams, four or five to a paragraph. The density of his thoughts, his self-conscious use of paradox and hyperbole, and his often sanctimonious tone provoke dozens of different readings.

In the popular imagination, Thoreau remains the mythic hermit preaching the necessity of wilderness isolation and primitive self-sufficiency. Most people assume that he turned his back on human society and retreated to the primeval woods where he sat on a log and ate nuts and berries. A deeper understanding of Thoreau, however, requires taking his words seriously but not always literally. He once confessed his weakness for using exaggerated language. "You must," he said, "speak loudly to those who will not listen."

By looking at what Thoreau did as well as what he said, one discovers that his philosophy of living was in fact quite different from the stereotypic image most of us have of him.

He was a remarkably hard-working and self-reliant man, a pencil maker, a professional surveyor, and a carpenter. His bivouac at Walden Pond lasted only twenty-six months. His cabin was just a mile or so from town, within earshot of the Concord church bells, and so close to the Lincoln highway that he could smell the pipe smoke of passing travelers. Thoreau hardly led the life of a hermit while camping out at Walden Pond.

By his own accounting, he had "more visitors while I lived in the woods than any other period of my life." Almost every Saturday his mother and sisters walked to the pond to bring him something special to eat. And he kept in touch with social life in Concord by reading the newspaper and by making forays into town. "Every day or two," he remarks in *Walden,* "I strolled to the village to hear some of the gossip which is incessantly going on there."

In other words, Thoreau was not an isolated primitivist but a commuter of sorts himself, a falcon-eyed suburban sojourner who, like so many of us, led one life and fancied at times that he led another.

Born in Concord in 1817, Henry David Thoreau was a slight, wiry young man with a droopy nose, rebellious spirit, tart personality, and keen mind. His father was a pencil maker, and his mother ran a boardinghouse. Henry attended Concord Academy, and in 1833, at age sixteen, he enrolled at Harvard to study classics and Eastern languages.

After graduating in 1837, Thoreau returned to Concord, where he taught school with his brother for a while, then worked as a day laborer. In 1841 he moved in with Ralph Waldo Emerson and his family. In exchange for his room and board, Thoreau worked as a handyman, tended the garden, tutored Emerson's son, and took frequent walks with his host.

In 1845 Thoreau accepted Emerson's offer to let him build a cabin on some of his land along Walden Pond. He borrowed an ax—which he conscientiously returned with a sharper edge—cleared the site, and then he built a cozy cabin of boards and brick, inserted two used glass windows and a fireplace, shingled the roof and walls, and stocked the interior with a bed, desk, chair, and books. His new dwelling cost exactly $28.12. (He was a good accountant.)

Thoreau moved in to his cabin on July 4, Independence Day, and he immediately set out to discover how many of the so-called necessities of life he could do without in order to experience the wonders of nature and the joys of self-culture. He wanted to conduct an experiment in living according to Emersonian principles of individualism, simplicity, and self-reliance.

"I went to the woods," he declared, "because I wished to live deliberately, to front only the essential facts of life, and to see if I could learn what it had to teach, and not, when I came to die, discover that I had not lived." Thoreau viewed his venture in the woods not as a permanent escape but as a temporary retreat. He wanted to gain a more mature understanding of the good life and a more penetrating sense of his own self and his larger society.

His purpose, he said, was to "entertain the true problems of life," to "live deeply and suck out all the marrow of life, to live so sturdily and Spartan-like as to put to rout all that was not life."

While living at Walden Pond, Thoreau grew beans, kept a journal, and meticulously recorded what he observed around the pond and during his daily hikes. He would often, as he wrote, sit in the dooryard of his cabin "from sunrise to noon, rapt in a reverie, amidst the pines and hickories and sumacs, in undisturbed solitude and stillness, while the birds sang around or flitted noiseless through the house."

In writing *Walden* Thoreau wrestled with two questions that remain immensely relevant: "How much is enough?" and "How do I know what I want?" At one point he writes that too many of his neighbors "live meanly, like ants." They were so busy pursuing their workaday concerns that they lost sight of higher priorities such as faith, family, community, and reflection. Their health and sanity, he observes, were being "frittered away by [meaningless] detail." To them, he proclaims: "Simplicity, simplicity, simplicity! I say, let our affairs be as two or three, and not a hundred or a thousand."

In such passages, Thoreau recognizes that there are basically two ways to get by in the world. The first is to increase one's income; the other is to reduce one's desires and therefore one's expenses. We are rich, he explains, in proportion to the number of things we can afford to do without. Thoreau urges us to slow down and take time to reflect on who we are, where we are, what we are doing, what we enjoy, what we value, what we love, and what we really want to accomplish.

Through his textured descriptions of his observations and ruminations, Thoreau helps us see the beauty of a rose-colored sunset that warms the horizon of our concerns; he helps us experience the sense of wonder provoked by a discovery in nature; he shares with us the death of a close friend or relative. Each of these commonplace occurrences impresses us with a significance that cannot be expressed in words, something we can appreciate but not fully understand.

In *Walden* Thoreau reveals how possible and important it is to snatch the eternal significance out of the fleeting and the commonplace events of our days. This, we learn, is the great magic trick of human existence.

In 1847, after two years of life in the woods, Thoreau sold his cabin to Emerson's Irish gardener and returned to Concord. His experience at Walden Pond had provided him with a chance to reflect upon life and to pursue his activities as a naturalist, but, as he confesses, a "civilized man must at length pine there." Thoreau still found in himself "an instinct toward a higher, or, as it is named, spiritual life, and another toward a primitive rank and savage one, and I reverence them both."

Satisfying both instincts, however, required that he live not in permanent isolation at Walden Pond but in what he calls a "border life," commuting between primitivism and civilization. That way he could combine what he calls "the hardiness of the savages with the intellectualness of the civilized man."

Thoreau thus discovered that a good life could be led best not situated in the wild or in the city, but in what he calls "partially cultivated country" like the village of Concord. While always appreciating the virtues of solitude, Thoreau had come to appreciate the virtues of companionship.

His friends and his family, he realized, provided him with much-needed emotional warmth. "Think of the consummate folly of attempting to go away from here," he wrote in his journal. "Here are all the friends I ever had or shall have, and as friendly as ever. A man dwells in his native valley like an acorn in its cap. Here, of course, is all that you love, all that you expect, all that you are."

Thoreau later published *Walden* (1854) not in order to convince everyone to abandon their factory jobs and city homes and build isolated cabins in the forest but instead to show the benefits of living in tune with the inner life of nature and at peace with the sense of our own integrity. "I would not have anyone adopt my mode of living on my account," he stresses. "I would have each one be very careful to find out and pursue his own way." Thoreau urges people to simplify their lives but to do so in their own way. Each person must clear a personal path to salvation.

So for those harried commuters who despair because their calendars are too crowded, their lives and homes too cluttered, their work too demeaning and their commuting too draining, Thoreau's notion of the good life provides a balm of insight.

His ethic of simpler living remains relevant. It can practiced in cities and suburbs, townhouses and condominiums; yes, even in law firms, medical clinics, banks, and brokerage houses. A simpler life's basic requirement is not a rural homestead or a monastic regimen or a faddish preference for L. L. Bean boots, trail mix, and alfalfa sprouts.

The primary requirement is a deliberate ordering of personal priorities so as to distinguish between the necessary and superfluous, useful and wasteful, beautiful and vulgar. Knowing the difference between personal trappings and personal traps is the key to mastering the fine art of simple living.

Still, you might ask, how does one apply such an ethic to daily life? Unfortunately, there is no magic formula or checklist to follow in making such decisions. It is not that simple or easy because it is not, after all, a single idea.

There is no simple life as such, only a variety of patterns of living that are apparently simpler than those that prevail at any given moment. This means that the degree of simplification is ultimately a matter for each person to establish. It is impossible to say that this or that possession or activity is universally expendable and should be discarded.

Money or possessions or activities in themselves do not corrupt simplicity, but the love of money, the craving of possessions, the lure of conformity, and the prison of activities do. Until you make peace with yourself, you will never be content with what you have.

Perhaps Thoreau's most valuable message is how to live comfortably with our most valuable companion, ourselves. There can be no genuine simplicity in the relationships of life, no genuine simplicity in the manner of living, if we are not at heart honest with ourselves. If we are to lead more contented, more fulfilling, and more creative lives, it is crucial to distinguish between our desires and our needs—and it is equally crucial for us to live more deliberately than we do.

Many of us drift through our days, propelled by the weekly routine and by the larger social whirl, unaware that we may have lost sight of our own priorities. This is the essence of simplicity—to live with full awareness of our choices and to confront each day with passion. This means becoming a more conscious and conscientious consumer, not only of things but also of time and commitments. Simplicity can offer a way out of the complexities, hypocrisies, and the passion to possess and display that we all suffer from. But it is a narrow and tortuous path to follow.

Yet genuinely simple life, that middle way between excess and deprivation, is difficult to achieve and even harder to maintain. "'Tis a gift to be simple," says the Shaker hymn, and it indeed requires the gift of God's grace to provide us the fortitude and imagination to sustain a regimen of enlightened restraint in the midst of our modern culture's conspicuous consumption ethic.

Deliberate simplicity is not a destination; it is the attitude and means by which we travel. Its success depends upon the strength of our spiritual commitment and the quality of our self-esteem.

If you are hesitant to change the trajectory of your life in its direction, then perhaps you need to ask with the poet Adrienne Rich, "With whom do you believe your lot is cast? From where does your strength come?"

Reflections on the Verge of Autumn

| *October 4, 1998*

Have you noticed? The sun is setting earlier, and there is a subtle chill in the evening air. Bright green foliage is slowly fading to tawny russet; some leaves—mostly dogwoods—have withered and begun to drop. "As imperceptibly as grief / The summer lapsed away," wrote Emily Dickinson. Fall is sneaking up on us. Are you ready?

Last week a freshman from Florida confessed that she had never experienced a "real" fall while growing up in the Sunshine State. I assured her that she is in for a treat. Autumn is my favorite time of the year (spring would be number one were it not for hay fever). The fall season has many virtues. Its arrival makes most of us more attractive by forcing us to put more clothes on. Moreover, just as the cooler weather makes dogs frisky, it also helps us feel more robust—and it stimulates our appetites. The cool weather, I have decided, triggers some primeval appetite sensor that prompts us to stock up on calories just as the squirrels are busily stockpiling acorns.

The balsam freshness of an autumn breeze reminds us how extraordinary the ordinary always is. Our surroundings seem more intense—azure skies, sparkling sun and dappled shade, rich colors and pungent smells, even the air itself, at last swept free of summer's stifling humidity. I especially relish this transitional period when everything is poised for the new season. With still warm days yet cool nights, we stand between two extremes, perched on the edge of change, a territory ripe for poetic insight. The German writer Goethe once declared that "beginnings are always delightful; the threshold is the place to pause."

Such seasonal turning points give variety to the routine of our days and prompt us to reflect upon ourselves and our blessings. On the cusp of autumn, a wind of anticipation is in the air. Without realizing it, we mentally begin preparing ourselves for change. We imagine cooler weather, shorter days, and the gorgeous palette of fall colors: scarlets and golds, oranges and umbers.

By putting us in a reflective mood, autumn summons up memories of youthful activities and simple pleasures. As a child, I loved to play football games in the backyard with neighborhood kids, then afterward sit together on the cool grass, talking and joking about anything and everything. Each November my brother and I would rake the fallen leaves into huge mountains that we would leap onto and bury ourselves in. As a college student at Furman, I relished autumn walks around the lake or strenuous hikes in the nearby mountains. On our return from Caesar's Head, we would buy crisp apples and freshly pressed cider.

Autumnal activities prompt us to think about what really matters. Our lives derive much of their meaning by their participation in a time not measured by clocks and watches, days and weeks, but by the recurrent turning of the seasons. If spring is the season of birth and renewal, fall is the season of maturation and reflection. Cooler weather leads us to appreciate our good fortune and good friendships. Days of thanksgiving are ahead.

Yet there is also something poignant amid the new season's sweetness. Autumn represents, after all, the sunset of the year, when the natural world repeats the annual ritual of growing old and shedding its youth. In her poem titled "God's World," Edna St.

Vincent Millay imagines the gleaming hues of autumnal woods below gray skies and morning mists. They "ache and sag," she declares, "and all but cry with colour!" Millay knew that nothing evokes our sense of mortality like the onset of fall.

Last week one of the nightly news programs reported that some 22 percent of Americans are depressed by the arrival of autumn because it represents to them the end of the year, a prelude to winter, and, in many respects, the end of life. Yet there is something serenely reassuring about the way in which the natural world handles the life-and-death rhythms of the year. As the poet May Sarton observes, "I think of trees and how they simply let go, let fall the riches of a season, how without grief (it seems) they can let go and go deep into their roots for renewal and sleep."

Likewise, we, too, should appreciate rather than regret the turning of nature's cycles. We, too, should learn to "let go" of our gregarious summer pursuits and turn inward for nourishment.

So do not curse the looming darkness. Embrace the new season and the eternal rebirth that it promises. Do not view autumn as simply a rude doorway into dreaded winter; rejoice in the colorful tapestry and distinctive possibilities of the coming season. Get outside. Take a hike. Grab a rake (and some gloves). Buy some books. Count your blessings. To everything there is a season. This fall offers us redeeming work and nature's wonder. Enjoy.

Leadership Is for Lovers

| *March 1, 1998*

A reader called me last week to ask that I write a column about the *L* word. I asked if that meant liberalism. Or Lipinski the skater, perhaps? Or Lewinsky the intern? "No," she explained, "I mean leadership. It's one of the most discussed and least understood topics in the world."

It is also one of the most important topics. Organizations desperately seek better leadership. They want leaders who are committed to excellence, are unafraid of change, and have the resilience to adapt their organizations to the dramatic changes affecting the economy and society. And they need leaders of pristine integrity committed to trustworthiness and high moral standards.

The current social environment requires a new type of organizational leadership. The old-style view was individualistic and hierarchical. It said: "I'm the boss and I have all the answers, I don't make mistakes, and no one may question my authority."

Today we live in a much more complex society where individual rights, democratic processes, and shared governance are paramount. As a result, leaders can no longer view their role as that of a cowboy roping a steer and dragging the organization where they want it to go. Modern leadership is inspirational and conversational. It requires getting everyone involved and excited about the future by creating an atmosphere of ferment, innovation, and freedom.

The best leaders, it seems to me, are those who inspire people to perform rather than simply order them to do so. As Dwight Eisenhower once said, modern leadership is "persuasion and conciliation and education and patience." He then put a piece of a string on a table and said, "Pull it, and it will follow anywhere you wish. Push it, and it will go nowhere at all."

There are many key attributes of great leaders, but an indispensable quality is love. Leaders need to have a passionate devotion to their organization and its future. When I address Furman freshmen each fall, I tell them that one of the most important things they will do is to discover what they love and surrender themselves fully to it.

The great leader need not have a beautiful face, a resonant voice, a brawny physique, or an elegant facility with words. Such charisma may be desirable, but it is not required. Leaders succeed to the extent that they have an abiding commitment to what they are doing and the organization they are serving. "Find a leader who loves his business," explains Warren Buffet, the investment genius, and the organization will have a much better chance of success.

Such leaders project an infectious "can-do" spirit. There is an old Texas saying that "you can't light a fire with a wet match." The world is moved by people who are enthusiastic. They can lift organizations and help people exceed their own expectations. Impassioned leadership helps common people do uncommon things.

Inertia is the rust corroding organizational effectiveness. Too many organizations follow the Paul Masson theory of leadership: "We will deal with no problem before its time." Loving leaders root out such complacency.

In this sense leadership is for lovers, for people who love their country, their alma mater, their organization, their work. The best leaders are inspiring because they are themselves inspired by a higher purpose, devoted to a transcendent cause, and passionate in their attachments. People want to follow leaders who are exemplary, who insist upon quality, who help us define and achieve ambitious goals.

Leaders who love what they are doing display a contagious self-confidence, an unwarranted optimism and incurable idealism that animates others to undertake demanding tasks. In short, compelling leaders empower and liberate. They create an environment in which people are encouraged to be creative leaders themselves, to bond together as teams or groups or volunteers, to solve problems or meet challenges too big for any individual.

So, yes, leadership is for lovers—for people with a disciplined passion informed by a desire to build and serve. Schools can teach it, books can describe it, and organizations can foster it. But only as individuals can we embrace and embody it. We do not so much need great leaders as we need leaders who can arouse the greatness in us. As the Gospel of Mark declares, "Whosoever of you shall be the chiefest, shall be servant of all."

Going to the Dogs

| *May 26, 1998*

A recent trip to a pet store prompted me to reflect upon our national passion for animals. People were buying everything from gourmet food to jeweled collars to wool sweaters for their pets. These doting animal lovers are not alone. Americans own about 240 million pets. Our spending on pet supplies and food is soaring, from about $4 billion annually twenty years ago to about $17 billion today.

But these statistics hardly convey the emotional investment we make in our pets. Consider these examples: Among people who have pictures in their wallets, nearly half of them carry pet snapshots, while only 2 percent have photos of their mothers-in-law. (Of course, I carry both!)

More than half of the fifty-four million dog owners buy Christmas gifts for Fido or Fluffy. Some people even purchase "get well" cards for their pets after being at the vet. The most popular reads: "Sorry to hear you got fixed."

As for me, I went to the dogs early in life. From the time I was a toddler, I have always enjoyed canine friends. To be sure, not all dogs are loving and lovable. But those of my experience have been the embodiment of loyalty, courage, and forgiveness.

Our current dog is a frolicking young yellow lab named Shasta (we also have two aloof cats and a surly iguana). When I return from the office each evening, Shasta greets me in a frenzy of comical affection.

She behaves like a jack-in-the-box, hopping up and down on all fours, ecstatic at the prospect of a reunion with her human friends. I usually respond in kind, not really hopping so much any more—I have a bad knee—but showering the dog with demonstrative hugs and saccharine praise. My wife, Susan, often watches in bemused disbelief as I cavort like a child with my four-legged playmate. But as I remind her, the great thing about dogs is that you can act foolish around them and get away with it.

For me, dogs are ideal companions because they never display any bitterness or pretensions and are endlessly forgiving. They exude a wholehearted acceptance of life; they greet each moment with interest and energy. Their zest for life is exhilarating.

The consistency of dogged devotion is also appealing. Whatever my mood or degree of exhaustion at the end of a day, I can count on Shasta offering an ecstatic greeting as if I were a long lost friend. Shasta yanks me out of my self-absorption. Her effusive welcome is always the same, rain or shine; her reservoir of love is unlimited.

The craving to be appreciated is one of our most basic desires, and canines readily accommodate our needs. When you're at the end of your leash or feel hounded at work, a dog's affection can be immensely therapeutic.

Occasionally, I may be in the doghouse with my wife or children, but I am always on good terms with our retriever. Pets also help lower our blood pressure, increase survival rates of heart attack victims, enliven the outlook of the elderly, reduce doctor visits, and lift the spirits of the disabled and the mentally ill.

While providing such benefits, dogs make few demands. All they require is food, affection, an occasional grooming, and a willingness to throw their favorite toy until one's arm collapses.

The simple needs of dogs reveal the futility of our own overcomplicated lives. Dogs also remind us of age-old virtues such as simplicity, acceptance, caring, cooperation, and trust. As an African proverb explains, if people lived up to the reputation of a dog, they would be saints.

So if you are looking for companionship, love, and entertainment, turn off the television and visit the humane society kennels. They have four-legged orphans eager to be adopted. In fact, they will greet you with open paws.

Is Anybody Happy?

| *May 27, 2001*

Is everybody happy? Or rather, is *anybody* happy?

Ever since Thomas Jefferson asserted that the pursuit of happiness is our inalienable right, Americans have been feverishly stalking the good life. But happiness is an elusive goal. Despite our economic success and technological advances, we ache with melancholy and loneliness.

Signs of *un*happiness abound. Rates of clinical depression have been doubling every ten years. Divorce has become more common than marriage. Everyone, it seems, is complaining of overwork and stress, insomnia and anxiety. Sufferers are flocking to pharmacies for relief. The three most frequently prescribed drugs are an ulcer medication, a hypertension reliever, and a tranquilizer.

We covet happiness, we yearn for it, but what is it? Is it something we find or something we create? Is it a function of what we *have* or what we *do,* or how much we *earn,* or what we *accomplish*?

Through the centuries, people have offered quite different definitions of happiness. "All you need for happiness," said Daniel Boone, "is a good gun, a good horse, and a good wife"—in that order. In a similar vein of male chauvinism, the satirist H. L. Mencken asserted that "the only really happy folk are married women and single men."

With the passage of time, however, the pursuit of happiness has become more focused on self-gratification. "Don't worry, be happy!" the jazz singer Bobby McFerrin crooned in 1989, and more than ten million people bought the record. Even more embraced the song's simple formula for happiness.

Every age has its illusions. Ours has been that happiness is synonymous with smiling yellow happy-face decals and "Have a nice day" greetings. Happiness is presumed to be as readily available as a prescription medicine or a do-it-yourself video. One company hawking "feel good" tapes claims that the curative cassettes will enable the purchaser to "wake up every day, completely happy, eager to live."

According to hucksters, we can also achieve happiness by eating less or eating more, by undergoing liposuction or cosmetic surgery or a hair implant. We can take Prozac or St. John's wort or rub ourselves with crystals or follow the teachings of L. Ron Hubbard or hire a personal fitness trainer.

Many people assume that more money will bring them happiness, only to discover that wealth does not bring a greater sense of well-being. A recent study of one hundred multimillionaires reveals that rich people are no happier than the rest of us. Between 1957 and 1990, per capita income in America more than doubled, yet, as psychologist David Myers notes in *The Pursuit of Happiness,* the number of Americans who reported being "very happy" has remained constant.

What especially complicates the pursuit of happiness is its relative nature. We don't want simply to be happy in our own right. We want to be happier than *other* people, which is extraordinarily difficult, since we assume they are happier than they really are.

No matter how satisfied we are with our salaries and possessions, there is always someone else who seems to be doing better. This annoying disparity goads us to earn more and buy more. Breaking the grip of such self-defeating envy is one of the keys to a happier life. "I should say," observes a character in Michael Frayn's novel *A Landing on the Sun,* "that happiness is being where one is and not wanting to be anywhere else."

So what is to be done? First, we need to recognize that there are no shortcuts to genuine happiness, no "quick-fix" therapies or drugs to bring lasting fulfillment.

Second, some people are naturally unhappy. Their body chemistry or doleful disposition leads them to embrace cynicism and melancholy. Brooding animates their days. They wear marks of woe and furrowed brows like badges of honor.

Third, happiness is not synonymous with pleasure. It is instead a deeper emotion that originates from within. Recent psychological studies conclude that enduring gratification cannot be gained by direct effort; instead it is a byproduct of how we live.

Happiness, like Carl Sandburg's fog, creeps into our lives on little cat feet. It results from a sense of mental and moral contentment with who we are, what we value, and how we invest our time and resources for purposes beyond ourselves. Thomas Jefferson equated happiness with the living of a socially virtuous and useful life. "It is neither wealth nor splendor, but tranquility and occupation [meaningful work]," Jefferson said, "which give happiness."

Jefferson recognized that the happiest people are those who find joy in the commonplace nourishments of daily living. They relish their friendships, families, work, faith, pets, and hobbies. And they are not bedeviled by the urge to get something more, something new, something better. As the writer Edith Wharton insisted, "If only we'd stop trying to be happy, we could have a pretty good time."

America's Car Culture

| *July 9, 2000*

Soaring gas prices have angered people, but no one seems to be driving less. Like Granny in Jan and Dean's popular 1964 song "The Little Old Lady from Pasadena," we cannot keep our foot off the accelerator. We are crazy about our cars—and always have been. "The American," William Faulkner lamented in 1948, "really loves nothing but his automobile." His sardonic observation retains its force over a half century later.

There are now more than two hundred million cars in the United States. In Los Angeles there are more cars than people. Some families spend more on their monthly car payments than on their home mortgage. We dream of cars as we dream of lovers—they express our fantasies; they fulfill our desires. Our intense love affair with cars began as soon as they were invented.

Since its first appearance in the 1890s, the automobile has embodied deep-seated cultural and emotional values that have become an integral part of the American Dream. All of the romantic mythology associated with the frontier experience has been transferred to the car culture. The pursuit of happiness on the open road rolls along on four wheels. Americans have always cherished personal freedom and mobility, rugged individualism and masculine force, and the advent of the horseless carriage combined all these qualities and more.

The automobile traveled faster than the speed of reason; it promised to make everyone a pathfinder to a better life. It was the vehicle of personal democracy, acting as a social leveling force, granting more and more people a wide range of personal choices—where to travel, where to work and live, where to seek personal pleasure and social recreation. As a journalist explains, the automobile is the "handiest tool ever devised for the pursuit of that unholy, unwholesome, all-American trinity of sex, speed and status."

A century ago, automobiles were viewed as friends of the environment; they were much cleaner than horses. In 1900, for example, New York City horses deposited more than 2.5 million pounds of manure and 60,000 gallons of urine on the streets. Some 15,000 dead horses also had to be removed from the city streets each year. The motorcar promised to eliminate such animal waste.

The car also offered a quantum leap in power. In 1901 *Motor World* magazine highlighted the subconscious appeal of the motorcar by alluding to its horselike qualities: "To take control of this materialized energy, to draw the reins over this monster with its steel muscles and fiery heart—there is something in the idea which appeals to an almost universal sense, the love of power."

But it was one thing to rhapsodize about the individual freedom offered by the horseless carriage when there were a few thousand of them spread across the nation; it is quite another matter when there are 200 million of them. In 1911 a horse and buggy paced through Los Angeles at eleven miles per hour; in the year 2000 an automobile makes the rush-hour trip averaging four miles per hour. American drivers are stuck in traffic for eight *billion* hours a year. College graduates entering the workforce in the summer of 2000 will spend four years of their lives behind the wheel.

Yet despite congested traffic, road rage, polluted air, and rising gas prices, Americans have not changed their driving or car-ownership patterns. Suburban commuters have resolutely stayed in their vehicles rather than join car pools or use public transportation. Teens continue to fill high school parking lots with automobiles. And the Sunday driver remains a peculiarly American phenomenon.

America's love affair with the car has matured into a marriage—and an addiction. We refuse to consider other transportation options. As a popular bumper sticker resolutely declares, "You'll Get Me out of My Car When You Pry My Cold Dead Foot from the Accelerator."

The automobile retains its firm hold over our psyche because it continues to represent a metaphor for what Americans have always prized: the seductive ideal of private freedom, personal mobility, and empowered spontaneity. Our solution to rush-hour gridlock is not to demand public transportation but to transform our immobile automobile into a temporary office, bank, restaurant, bathroom, and stereo system. We talk on the phone, eat meals, don makeup, cash checks, and listen to music and audiobooks.

A company that records audiobooks reports that two of its most popular selections among commuters are Henry David Thoreau's *Walden* and Mark Twain's *Huckleberry Finn*. An interstate highway is not exactly a path to Walden Pond, nor does a BMW much resemble Huck's raft, but Americans remain firmly committed to the open road—even if only in our imaginations.

The Classics Stage a Comeback

| *February 12, 1999*

A miracle is occurring in classrooms across the United States. Greek and Latin, two ancient languages thought to be long dead and suffering from rigor mortis, are witnessing a remarkable resurrection.

The American Classical League reports that the number of elementary school students learning Latin has quadrupled during the 1990s. Interest in Greek, while not as widespread, is also growing. The number of high school students taking the National Latin Exam achievement test has risen from 9,000 in 1978 to more than 100,000 this year. In the past two years, the number of college students opting for Latin has increased by 25 percent.

At Furman the number of freshmen taking the Latin placement test has almost doubled over the last four years, and there has been a 150 percent increase in the number of students taking introductory Greek. To be sure, Spanish remains by far the most popular foreign language at Furman and across the United States, but the growing interest in Latin and Greek is stunning.

What gives? Why would classical languages and literature witness such renewed interest? Some observers suggest that young people today are especially intrigued by mythology. Television shows such as "Hercules: The Legendary Journeys" and "Xena: Warrior Princess" attract huge audiences and cultlike devotion. The virtues embodied in such campy superheroes are self-evident. As the narrator explains at the beginning of "Xena," a "land in turmoil cried out for a hero. A mighty princess forged in the heat of battle—her courage will change the world." True to form, the fire-breathing, wall-walking, leather-corseted Xena and her plucky sidekick Gabrielle wander the countryside "in the golden age of myth," battling injustice and barbarians. In the process, they combine the themes of Greek mythology with the melodrama of the World Wrestling Federation and the hip dialogue of "Melrose Place"—an unbeatable combination.

Others who see a connection between popular culture and the revived interest in the classics credit Robin Williams's performance in the movie *Dead Poet's Society.* He plays a charismatic English teacher who inspires students with his impassioned commitment to literature, his theatrical energy, and his animating credo: *Carpe Diem* (Seize the day), not to be confused with *Fac ut gaudeam* (Make my day).

Ironically, part of Latin's appeal to students is its distinctive difficulty. One of this year's Christmas catalogs offers a sweatshirt that reads: "Si Hoc Legere Scis Nimium Eruditionis Habes," which means, "If you can read this, you're overeducated." Likewise, in a Latin classroom in California, a sign says: "Rise above the vulgar crowd, take Latin." Yet students soon learn that Latin is not so alien from English. In fact, of the nearly one million words in the English language, some 600,000 are derived from Latin. The percentage of Latin derivatives is even higher in French and Spanish.

Consider as well the many Latin phrases that we regularly use, such as alma mater, status quo, de facto, vice versa, and et cetera, et cetera. Ergo, many parents see Latin as the best linguistic preparation for their children. It is a language whose highly disciplined grammar and sentence structure enable people to express ideas with great precision and nuance. In the process, it helps students enrich their vocabulary and hone their ability to think logically and express themselves clearly. A British study reveals that seven-year-olds who take Latin perform better than their peers in spelling, grammar, history, and European languages. And in the United States, students who have studied Latin score an average of 150 points better on SAT tests and have higher grades than other students.

So there seems to be a quid pro quo at work here. Students are gaining tangible benefits in exchange for their study of Latin. They are also learning to adapt Latin to modern expressions. A high school recently voted to change its motto from English to

Latin. The results were surprising. The English motto was "I hear, I see, I learn." The Latin version came out as "Audio, Video, Disco." (They decided to stick with the English version.)

Amid this Christmas season, I summon up my own meager knowledge of Latin to wish you the best: *Adeste fidelis, Pax vobiscum,* and *Die dulci fruere* (Have a nice day). And do not be surprised if you hear a teenager working at Hardee's ask a customer, "Frictos cum ista cupisma?" (You want fries with that?).

Deliver Us from Evil

| *May 27, 1998*

The headlines of late have been scarred with perplexing tragedies. Every week, it seems, we confront another shocking report of people intentionally inflicting pain and destruction on the innocent.

The church bombing in Illinois and the shooting at the Oregon school cafeteria are only the latest of many such horrifying events. Last week a Florida man killed his four-year-old son, murdered three police officers, and shot himself. Last month, in Jonesboro, Arkansas, two children randomly killed a teacher and four schoolmates. Back in December we learned of the grisly mayhem outside a school in West Paducah, Kentucky, when a "bright but aloof" fourteen-year-old opened fire on fellow students as they knelt at a prayer service before school started. Three girls were killed, and five other students were critically wounded.

Commentators have provided many explanations for these senseless events: broken homes with abusive or absent parents; children suffering from serious mental disturbances, economic hardship, alienation, or boredom; gratuitous violence on television shows and in movies and video games; and easy access to guns.

Such factors have undoubtedly influenced these terrible events, but taken together they never congeal into an inclusive explanation. Nor do such interpretations adequately explain other horrific acts of violence such as the Oklahoma City bombing, the Unabomber killings, or the perennial scourge of psychopathic serial killers.

There are, to be sure, no easy answers, but what is usually missing from the media analyses of these atrocities is an awareness that evil still flourishes in this supposedly enlightened world—and that the potential for evildoing lurks within each of us, even the young. Understanding our propensity for malicious destructiveness requires going beyond sociology and psychology into the realms of metaphysics and theology. And ultimately it requires us to reassert the legitimacy of moral responsibility.

For most of American history, Satan the evil tempter was a pervasive presence in people's lives. The philosopher-poet Ralph Waldo Emerson declared that "there is a capacity of virtue in us, and there is a capacity of vice to make your blood creep." Yet this broad notion of personal sin has largely receded from our everyday vocabulary, and in the process we have lost an important moral marker.

Earlier generations of Americans took for granted the persistence of evil in the human psyche. In his novel *Billy Budd, Sailor,* Herman Melville wrestles with the "mystery of iniquity." At one point he characterizes petty officer Claggart as having "the mania of an evil nature, not engendered by vicious training or corrupting books or licentious living, but born with him and innate, in short 'a depravity according to nature.'"

Melville's phrasing derived from the Bible. In the Judeo-Christian tradition, evil is not a function of ignorance, poverty, or broken families. Nor is it a state of mind or a moral inconvenience. Instead it is a malevolent thread woven into the very fabric of our being.

Today, however, people rarely discuss unsettling concepts such as depravity or sin or wickedness. We live in a therapeutic age, which assumes that every felt need can be met, every anxiety relieved, every problem remedied—by more money, more therapy, or more medicine. In such an environment, we do not feel comfortable invoking a word like *evil.* Instead we refer to doers of evil as "misguided" or "deranged" or "disadvantaged." Evil's most beguiling deceit is to persuade us that it does not exist.

Evil is not an illusion or a state of mind to be wished or prescribed away. It is not a matter of taste or fashion, like or dislike. Instead it is an exaggerated and twisted form of the congenital sinfulness manifested by the human species: rich and poor, sophisticated and illiterate, conservative and liberal. "If the Bible is about anything," writes Peter Gomes, the chaplain at Harvard, "it is about the subtle, ruthless, remorseless persistence of evil."

The concept of demonic tendencies and temptations, however, is not limited to the biblical tradition. It buttresses all major religions. Whether named Satan, as in the Bible and the Koran, or Mara, in Buddhist scripture, the tempter is a malignant, belligerent force of human nature that must be vigilantly combated.

We will never know why evil exists. It simply is. But its mystery should not paralyze or intimidate us. On the contrary, our recognition of its insidious power should provoke us to action. Mother Teresa confessed that when she first saw lepers, she recognized in herself a demonic "little Hitler" who wanted to obliterate them. Instead, she embraced them. Virtues such as decency, courage, honesty, and compassion remain our best weapons against the potential evil within. We need a strong will in order to do good, but it is even more necessary for us not to do evil. As Paul urged the Romans, "Be not overcome of evil, but overcome evil with good."

The Decline of Fatherhood

| *June 21, 1998*

Father's Day features lots of new ties and golf balls, fishing rods and tennis rackets, weed eaters and nose-hair trimmers. Although the idea of a special day honoring dads originated when retailers lobbied for another national holiday to help boost gift sales, such commercial motives should not diminish the legitimacy of honoring fatherhood. It is a cause for celebration and concern, now more than ever, for fathers are an endangered species. More than a third of all American children are growing up without fathers in their home.

The sharp decline of fatherhood is one of the most devastating social trends of our time. Between 1960 and 1990, the percentage of children living apart from their biological fathers more than doubled, from 17 percent to 36 percent. The growing absence of fathers has been an important factor associated with the most disquieting social ills of the 1990s: crime and delinquency, premature sexuality and out-of-wedlock births to teenagers, declining educational achievement, child neglect and abuse, teen violence and suicide, and, perhaps most damaging, the rising number of women and children mired in poverty. No other social group is so poor or stays poor longer than single-parent families.

While we rejoice at examples of a child from a single-parent home achieving success, the overall trends are distressing. Of course, statistical correlations do not necessarily prove causal connections, but unmarried mothers are the fastest growing segment of the poor. Child abuse is higher among children in female-headed, single-parent households than in conventional two-parent households. Among those children born in 1980, 31 percent of whites and 59 percent of blacks will spend their childhood years with only one parent. On average, a child raised by a single parent (usually the mother) is twice as likely to drop out of high school, 2.5 times as likely to become a teen mother, and 1.4 times as likely to be an idle young adult—out of work and out of school.

Anthropologists tell us that a sense of fatherly responsibility is an acquired rather than an inherited social role. Human cultures have employed sanctions and rewards to encourage parental responsibility in males and to constrain their sexual energy. The institution of marriage, of course, is the primary way by which a society sanctifies the long-term relationship of parents. As the great cultural anthropologist Margaret Mead observed, there is no society in the world where men will stay married for very long unless culturally required to do so.

The good news is that there are signs of improvement. The divorce rate has dropped from 50 to 40 percent during the 1990s, and teen pregnancy, which soared during the 1980s, has steadily declined in recent years. The Save Our Sons organization in Greenville is an example of many grassroots efforts to revive a sense of paternal responsibility. The strong economy has also helped promote more stable families. And in 1994 the National Fatherhood Initiative convened its first National Summit on Fatherhood. Vice President Al Gore provided the keynote address, thereby giving the issue the spotlight of national attention.

But more can be done to reinvigorate the institution of marriage as an essential social institution. Employers, for example, could be more sensitive to the disruptive effects on marriage of transferring employees to another city or state. They could also be more generous and equitable concerning paternal leave policies. Leaders of the entertainment industry—especially producers of television shows and movies—could do much to revitalize the stature of fatherhood through choosing more socially responsible themes, characters, and plots.

Public policy issues also need to be addressed. Congress is now considering a bill to end the IRS "marriage penalty" and increase the value of the tax exemption for dependent children. A welfare system that unwittingly provides monetary incentives for mothers to avoid marriage and work is at last being reformed.

These are just a few suggestions among many that warrant attention. In the end, it seems, fatherhood will be revived not simply by passing laws but by instilling in young men a sense of paternal responsibility before they become parents. America's children—and their fathers—deserve no less.

The White-Collar Sweatshop

| *August 13, 2001*

Feeling overworked and demoralized? You have plenty of company.

A recent Roper poll finds that job satisfaction is at its lowest ebb since the organization began its surveys. As corporate profits and stock prices have plummeted in recent months, people are working longer and harder—for less pay, fewer benefits, and fading job security.

Something has to give. Fatigued by their round-the-clock regimen and fast-forward pace, people are arriving at work with their enthusiasm gone, energy spent, and creativity stunted. New York management consultant Robert Swain reports that "everybody is exhausted, and nobody really thinks things are going to get better."

The deterioration of the white-collar workplace began in the 1980s when hostile takeovers and colossal mergers led many companies to adopt a "slash-and-burn" approach to cutting expenses and positions. Over the past twenty years, some 45 million employees have been laid off—at least once.

Those who have managed to keep their jobs have faced rising expectations and disturbing uncertainties. Executives and professionals now work four hours longer each week than in 1979, and they take 20 percent fewer vacation days. As the Lexus commercial boasts, "Sure, We Take Vacations. They're Called Lunch Breaks."

The breakneck combination of overwork and frenetic leisure leaves no time for true relaxation. Hurtling from meeting to meeting, project to project, cell phone to laptop, we ignore our children and neglect our spouses. Burnout is rampant.

Our morale grows stale even as our work grows more intense. A sense of melancholy overwhelms us as we trudge through the relentless routine of our workaday world.

Longer working hours and greater stress also degrade our health. The American Medical Association reports that the average white-collar worker gets sixty to ninety minutes less sleep each night than needed. Job dissatisfaction—not cholesterol, smoking, or lack of exercise—is the surest predictor of heart trouble.

Of course, since the colonial era, Americans have embraced a dedicated work ethic. But it is racing out of control. New technologies have made work a 24/7 activity. People are shackled to their jobs, skipping lunch hours and taking laptops, beepers, Palm Pilots, and cell phones home at night. In *White-Collar Sweatshop,* author Jill Fraser quotes a manager at a large financial services firm who reported that "she had been so overloaded and understaffed that she had been forced to work through the entire night before her wedding."

On average, Americans work 350 hours more per year than Europeans. For many people, the 37-hour workweek has become a fond memory. The average workweek for professionals in the United States is now 47 hours. Over 25 million Americans work more than 50 hours per week, and another 11 million spend over 60 hours on the job.

Such frenzied schedules help explain the surge of work-related disorders. Stress accounts for almost 90 percent of all primary-care physician visits. One estimate claims that work-related stress cost the economy over $200 billion last year.

Some people seem to thrive amid the longer hours and constant pressure. Their compulsive personalities require the constant stimulation of such high-octane careers. A Gallup Poll reports that 44 percent of Americans call themselves workaholics who willingly put in insanely long hours—and often brag about it.

Some use work as a refuge from the chaos and conflicts of home life. Others have become addicted to what one journalist calls "we need the money" careers. These "work to spend" Americans are convinced that they must generate more and more income to support their increasingly expensive habits. "You get trapped by big houses, big cars, the lifestyle, the nice vacation," admits a senior manager at Intel.

Some exhausted workers, however, are seeking a way out of the "white-collar sweatshop." Polls show that 20 percent of salaried employees have exchanged fewer working hours for lower salaries. These "downshifters" are seeking a better balance between their work and their personal lives, and they are asking employers about part-time and flex-time options.

To be sure, restoring balance to work lives careening out of control is easier said than done. Busyness has become our business. To slow down seems impossible. But there are always options, however painful they might seem. Rearranging our priorities and redefining goals requires a courageous conversation with our selves as well as our bosses.

We need to spend our days as carefully as we spend our dollars. After all, time is our most precious possession. It is life itself.

Senior Citizens in Cyberspace

| *February 4, 2001*

Amid all the hype associated with the Internet revolution is a development of surprising scope and significance: the fastest growing group of computer users is not children or young adult members of Generation X. It is senior citizens.

Older Americans are embracing the Internet with the enthusiasm of teenagers. Millions of retirees are booting up, logging on, and surfing the Web. The number of older citizens going on line is expected to increase from about fourteen million today to twenty-seven million by 2003. Seniors are online more hours per week at home than any other age group. In light of such trends, new retirement communities are wiring their centers and installing computers with Internet access.

To many seniors, though, the Internet is more than a hobby or an inexpensive way to keep in touch with their children and grandchildren. For seniors who may be lonely, isolated, or limited in their mobility by health problems, a computer and the Internet offer an enticing window to a new world that is both interactive and enlightening. Seniors can join online book clubs, participate in discussion groups, read hometown newspapers, reconnect with military units or college friends, learn about medical issues and prescription medicines, take college courses, and make new acquaintances.

Entrepreneurs are creating websites to attract older consumers. One of the most popular sites is SeniorNet.com, which hosts chat rooms and more than four hundred discussion groups with forty-five book clubs. Members may participate in virtual walking clubs or in discussions covering such topics as genealogy, cooking, World War II, gardening, pets, and politics.

SeniorNet has more than thirty-eight thousand members, publishes a quarterly newsletter, offers discounts on computer-related products and services, holds national and regional conferences, and collaborates in research on older adults and technology. It also operates learning centers that offer low-cost computer instruction. In 1997 the organization operated ninety learning centers around the country. None had a waiting list. Now there are more than two hundred centers, and almost all have waiting lists of four hundred or more.

The Furman University Learning in Retirement (FULIR) program offers several computer courses each term—fall, winter, and spring. These popular courses are almost always full and range from Beginning Computers for the Terrified to various advanced-level courses.

Such demand for computer instruction among the chronologically advanced is only going to increase. Advances in technology that favor older Web users, such as larger screens and arthritic-friendly mouses and touchpads, are rapidly closing the digital divide between the older and younger generations.

Of course, the Internet can never replace a personal visit or a warm hug. But it can help reignite a passion for learning and interaction. "The Web has the potential to transform the entire experience of aging," says Hugh O'Connor, director of the American Association of Retired Persons (AARP) Research Information Center. "We are just starting to understand the implications, but it's already clear that the Internet can stimulate independent living among the elderly."

To be sure, many older Americans initially balk at the expense and complexity of computers. Some of them suffer from "computer psychosis," a fear of new technologies. I know this from experience. Several years ago I encouraged my parents, both in their seventies, to get a computer. They emphatically refused, saying that they had absolutely no interest in such modern gadgets. Undeterred by their resistance, I brazenly took a computer to their house, connected it, and then paid a Furman student to begin tutoring them in its use.

Within a month, they were addicted. Hour after hour, day after day, they were online, exploring the infinite resources of the Web, unleashing a barrage of e-mail messages to family and friends, and playing computer games into the wee hours of the morning. Soon, my father, a retired advertising executive, decided he needed more processing speed, so he bought a more powerful PC system, complete with speakers and CD hookup. The only downside to my parents being octogenarian computer geeks is that they are so often online that it is impossible to reach them by phone.

So if you are senior citizen who spends most of the day watching television, get off the couch and onto the computer. Get connected! A whole new world of ideas and connections awaits in cyberspace to excite your curiosity, boost your spirits, and extend your life. Happy surfing.

Haunting Realism

The Art of Andrew Wyeth

| *June 29, 1997*

Andrew Wyeth and Greenville have had a close relationship for over a decade. In the 1980s Arthur and Holly Magill owned twenty-six Wyeth paintings and over two hundred drawings, most of which were on display at the County Museum of Art. The Magill collection has since been sold and relocated to Japan, but local interest in Wyeth remains high. Indeed, last summer's Wyeth exhibition set all-time attendance records.

What is it about Wyeth's art that generates such interest? His fans would no doubt offer different answers, but to me Wyeth's distinctive power comes from the haunting realism that envelops his canvases. Whether depicting an object, a dwelling, or a person, he portrays scenes and subjects that are at once familiar yet disquieting. His precise drawing lures you into a recognizable world, but it is in fact a stranger world than first imagined.

Wyeth is not satisfied with merely copying what he sees. He wants to dig beneath appearances and reveal more than the obvious. "You can have the technique and paint the object," he explains, "but that doesn't mean you get down to the juice of it all. It's what's inside you, the way you translate the object—and that's pure emotion."

Working with fierce energy and dedicated haste, Wyeth infuses his art with his own emotions and with powerful symbols. In other words, he presents a personal representation of his observed world, not simply a recorded one. His realism is expressive rather than simply imitative. And it derives its peculiar potency from the tension between the delicate precision of his rendering and the power of the emotions he conveys.

Wyeth shows us the artistic benefit of knowing and cherishing particular places. He finds his subjects nearby, in the scenes and characters around his home in the historic Brandywine Valley near Chadds Ford, Pennsylvania, and near his summer retreat on the coast of Maine. A man steeped in local and family history, Wyeth's eighty-year life turns on the axis of memory. His art seems timeless, belonging neither to the past nor the present but to an arrested moment seized and transformed by his own fertile imagination.

Wyeth's evident passion for his surroundings and their heritage remind us that you cannot be neutral about a place where you have lived so long and to which you have given such significance. "I don't love the Brandywine Valley because it's scenic, or because it's beautiful," he stresses. "I love it the way you love your mother. I love it because I was born here, because I live here.

The people Wyeth portrays are especially mesmerizing. Women and men, young and old, black and white, they are stripped of mere prettiness and any hint of sentimentality. For some unexplained reason, Wyeth prefers to depict people who are emotionally flawed. "Every damn person I paint," he explains, "goes mentally off. It's a drama that's really shaken me."

Wyeth's human subjects project a thought-burdened intensity that entices extended scrutiny and empathy. Their life-battered faces, creased with experience and frozen in thought, provoke insights that reside beneath surface appearances. In this regard, I suspect that much of Wyeth's popularity results from his distinctive skill to invest ordinary, unappreciated folk with a strange dignity that transcends their circumstances.

One of the recurring motifs of Wyeth's portraits is that his subjects rarely look directly at the viewer. Instead they are depicted from the rear or looking down or aslant, expressing a wistful weariness or an anxiety ennobled by fortitude. They seem to share Wyeth's own preoccupation with past dreams and personal reflection. "I don't like people looking at me," he once observed. "I want to be left alone with my thoughts."

If the mark of great artists is their ability to capture our imagination after we leave the museum, then Wyeth qualifies for greatness. He is one of those rare artists whose work, no matter how familiar, always seems fresh and provocative.

Part 4

Greenville and Greenvillians

Nathanael Greene

Greenville's Namesake

| *February 20, 2000*

There are more than two dozen communities in the United States named Greenville. South Carolina's happens to be the largest. Many people assume that the city was so named because of the area's verdant foliage. In fact, however, the South Carolina General Assembly named the new county in 1786 in honor of Revolutionary War hero Nathanael Greene.

A Rhode Island Quaker, Greene led the American army in the Carolinas during the Revolution. When George Washington named Greene commander of the Southern Department in 1780, the American war effort in the South was floundering. The British enjoyed undisputed control of Georgia and South Carolina and were threatening to invade North Carolina. Within two years, however, Greene's ragtag force had stalemated more than eight thousand British troops in the Carolinas and Georgia.

As the son of pacifist Quakers, Greene was an unlikely military genius. Born in 1742, he grew up in a household that denounced war and viewed formal education with suspicion. His parents were strict Quakers who believed that "worldly learning" undermined piety. Young Nathanael had to whet his appetite for military life by secretly acquiring books about warfare and tactics. In 1773 Nathanael was "read out" of the local Quaker meeting for attending a militia gathering.

When the first shots of the Revolution were fired at Lexington and Concord in 1775, the Rhode Island legislature created its own army and made Greene the commander. He quickly impressed George Washington with his leadership, intelligence, and courage. Within a year, the commander-in-chief was telling key political figures that Greene was his best general. Greene distinguished himself at the battles of Trenton, Brandywine, and Germantown, and he was with Washington at Valley Forge.

When Greene took command of the poorly equipped southern army late in 1780, he discovered that morale was low and discipline lacking. He took out a personal loan to secure needed military supplies—including food, clothing, and weapons. Sizing up the situation, he realized that his small army of sixteen hundred men was no match for the veteran British forces under Lord Charles Cornwallis. So he adopted a hit-and-run strategy. A man of infinite patience, skilled at managing men and saving supplies, aggressive but not rash, Greene was perfectly suited to a war of delay and attrition.

Greene boldly split his army, hoping to force Cornwallis to do the same. He sent a detachment led by Virginian Daniel Morgan to bolster local militia in upstate South Carolina, while he moved his main force to the Pee Dee River near Cheraw. The ruse worked. Morgan lured the confused British troops into a hectic chase across rough terrain. When the Redcoats cornered the Patriots in an open meadow near Cowpens, the exhausted British fell victim to superior marksmen and horsemen, and Morgan's men delivered "a devil of a whipping."

Morgan's victorious troops rejoined Greene's main force, and the Americans retreated into North Carolina, drawing a vengeful Cornwallis behind them. Greene wanted to extend the British supply lines and gradually wear them down. Cornwallis marveled at his foe's abilities. He admitted that he never felt "secure when encamped in his neighborhood. He is vigilant, enterprising, and full of resources."

On March 15, 1781, Greene's army engaged the British at the Battle of Guilford Court House. In the end, the Patriots retreated, but the Redcoats sustained higher casualties. Exhausted and hungry, Cornwallis's troops limped to the port of Wilmington.

Greene, meanwhile, led his fifteen hundred men south to engage the eight thousand British soldiers still scattered across South Carolina. During the spring and summer of 1781, his army lost three battles but kept wearing down the British. As he explained, "We fight, get beat, rise, and fight again." By late 1781, the British still clung to Charleston and Savannah, but the countryside belonged to the Americans. In December 1782, the British evacuated both cities, and a peace treaty was signed the following year.

After the war, Greene and his family settled at Mulberry Grove plantation near Savannah. Regrettably, the last years of his life were a constant struggle. Unwilling to use slaves, Greene could not find enough help to manage his fields, and he became mired in debt. On June 19, 1786, he developed a fearful headache (probably sunstroke) and died. He was only forty-four.

The entire nation mourned. A few weeks later, when the South Carolina legislature "ordained a county by the name of Greeneville," it honored the general who had won the war in the South. Let us remember for whom we are named.

Buck Mickel

Fanfare for an Uncommon Man

| *August 9, 1998*

"When a sage dies," says the Talmud, "all are his kin." The rabbis meant by this that everyone should mourn the passing of a wise leader. Likewise, the sudden death of Buck Mickel stunned all of Greenville and left a huge void of leadership in this community.

Buck's multifaceted career defies brief summary. As the dynamic president of Daniel Construction Company, he oversaw the construction of major projects around the world, from a pharmaceutical plant in Ireland to an airport in Saudi Arabia to the Hyatt hotel in downtown Greenville, among many others. In the process he transformed Daniel Construction Company into an international giant and orchestrated its merger with Fluor Corporation in 1977.

Yet Buck was much more than a successful corporate executive. He was also a generous philanthropist, a creative entrepreneur, an enlightened champion of higher education, a civic visionary, and a devoted husband, father, and grandfather. He served as an inspiring mentor to countless people: those who worked for Fluor Daniel; those in the community who collaborated with Buck on major projects such as the Bi-Lo Center, the Peace Center, and the year-round Governor's School for the Arts; and the directors of two dozen national corporations on whose boards Buck served. For these reasons and many more, we cannot pay too large a tribute to this self-effacing man whose feisty spirit would have dared the devil.

Neither flamboyant nor eccentric, but a pillar of common sense and integrity, Buck Mickel was the moving force behind most of the major projects and improvements in the Upstate over the last forty years. He possessed not only an immense capacity for service but also a touch of genius that everyone recognized and no one can define. He was a rare combination of strength of purpose, power of concentration, and self-discipline with grace and charm. Simply being near him lifted one's spirits and bolstered one's confidence. He was a dynamo of energy, ideas, and, above all, action. His credo was encapsulated in a simple maxim: "Do what you'll say you'll do and then some."

Mickel harbored a restless determination to build a better community for the benefit of all. In the process he manifested the "can-do" spirit that has come to epitomize Greenville. A robust man with an engaging smile, firm handshake, ready wit, and endless stories, he was a delightful companion and an inspiring presence. To work with Buck Mickel on a project was to be in the presence of a vital force, a singular personality, and a tireless agent for progress. Retirement and rest were not in his vocabulary.

In the months before his untimely death, Mickel had focused his concern on the need for this community to cultivate future generations of leaders capable of transcending their own institutional loyalties and personal ambitions so as to foster the general welfare. He worried that Greenville's dramatic growth and influx of newcomers was eroding our ability to envision and shape a compelling future. This concern crystallized when Buck helped form the Greater Greenville Forum, a new organization intended to address local issues and nurture in its members a keener sense of civic responsibility. Buck hoped that such a leadership forum would help get key people—especially among a younger generation of leaders—more involved in the discussion of community issues and inspire them to get things done rather than allow inertia and special interests to determine our fate.

Buck Mickel is no longer with us, but he remains a vivid presence in our thoughts. Like an ultimatum, he forbids us to fall short of our potential. He remains a formidable example, goading us to strive, to improve, to build, and never to yield to indifference. The endowment he bequeathed to us is an enduring legacy: a zest for life, a life of service, and a love of humankind. He will be remembered and admired for the exuberant man he was no less than for all that he achieved on behalf of this community. May such be said for all of us.

Max Heller

Community Servant

| *May 10, 1998*

Furman University's annual Founders Day convocation celebrates our heritage and recognizes those who have helped enhance the Furman experience and the Greenville community.

Max Heller is one of these people. His rise to prominence in Greenville parallels Furman's own emergence from a small sectarian college to an independent, nationally prominent liberal arts institution.

Heller's remarkable life story is worth repeating. It begins in 1937 in Vienna, when the eighteen-year-old Austrian met five charming young women from Greenville who were touring Europe. Seven months later, when Nazi troops were taking over his homeland and terrorizing the Jews, Max wrote to one of the Greenville girls, Mary Mills, and asked her to help him escape to the United States. She eagerly agreed to sponsor Heller and his sister and reported that she also had found him a job.

Penniless and knowing little English, Max arrived in Greenville in August 1938 and began work an hour later as a stock boy sweeping floors in the Piedmont Shirt Company. The next day a coworker told him to report to the front office because "a judge wants to see you." Heller feared the worst. "When I heard that a judge wanted to see me I was terrified," he recalled. "I thought he was going to send me back to Austria."

At the front office, Heller was greeted by Judge John Plyler. He was a "stately, handsome man" who extended his hand and welcomed the young immigrant to Greenville. He "offered to help me learn to speak English and told me that he had just been named president of Furman University."

At that moment, Heller remembered, "I knew I had found a home in Greenville. It was then that I learned the great lesson that a simple act of kindness can mean so very much."

It wasn't long before the enterprising young man had become vice president of the shirt company. In the meantime, Max's parents had also escaped Nazi oppression and had come to America, as had the lovely young woman who was to be his bride.

Trude and Max married in 1942. They lost ninety members of their families during the Holocaust, but in Greenville they quickly established a new life together. By 1948 Max had started a company of his own, Maxon Shirt Company, which grew into a major textile enterprise.

Max also became actively involved in his adopted community, and twenty years after founding his company, he sold it to devote himself full time to serving Greenville, his state, and his synagogue. During his two distinguished terms as mayor, he led the way in revitalizing downtown Greenville. He also served as president of the chamber of commerce and as chair of the state development board.

Through the years, Max and Trude, who has been a community leader in her own right, have been very involved with Furman. Max has been a longtime member of our advisory council and a special friend of the Collegiate Educational Service Corps, an organization that enrolls more than fifteen hundred students who serve as volunteers in some seventy-five social service agencies in Greenville County. "The Service Corps is what is so wonderful about Furman," Heller explains. "It embraces the community. Furman reaches out to people. It is inclusive."

In 1975 Furman awarded Max an honorary doctor of laws degree, and in 1984 Trude received the Mary Mildred Sullivan Award for noble and humanitarian service. In recent years they have established several scholarships at Furman, one of which is named for Mary Mills Roberson, the woman who helped Max escape to America.

Max and Trude exude a love of life, of people, and of giving to their community that deserves recognition and emulation. They are an inspiration to those of us lucky enough to have lived in this country all of our lives—and perhaps take our good fortune for granted. "My wife and I," Max says, "had a terrible experience [under the Nazis] and you can come out of that two ways: bitter or more appreciative of life."

For those who believe it is better to light a candle than curse the darkness, Max Heller provides a bright model of a life well lived. We all can benefit from his outstanding example.

Embracing the Homeless

| *January 12, 1997*

Minor incidents are often charged with moral significance. A case in point occurred a few weeks ago at the First Presbyterian Church in Greenville. As the parishioners arrived for the morning worship service, a young homeless man, unwashed and disheveled, dressed in cast-off clothes, wandered into the sanctuary. After the service he was warmly greeted by members of the congregation as well as by the associate minister, who inquired if he could be of any help. The hobo shook his head and left the building.

Later that day the associate minister was driving down Main Street and saw the young transient on the sidewalk. The associate minister stopped his car, got out, and again asked the stranger if he could be of any assistance. At that point the sojourner made an awkward confession: "I'm homeless only for today and for a good purpose. Actually, I'm a Furman University student. Our sociology class is doing field research, assuming the role of homeless people in order to experience what life on the streets is really like." The student went on to explain that he had attended the affluent church that morning expecting to be scorned and shunned, only to be embraced as one of God's children.

This incident offers encouraging evidence that people are practicing the principles their faith professes. Like most religions, the Christian faith urges believers to be open and hospitable to strangers. The Bible repeatedly asserts that all people, regardless of race, creed, socioeconomic condition, or hygiene are deserving of dignity and care. Centuries ago God heard the cry of homeless people and delivered them out of oppression in Egypt. In turn, they were instructed to love strangers, for "you were [once] strangers in Egypt." Jesus, who himself often had "nowhere to lay his head," ministered with unrelenting compassion to the poor and vulnerable and urged people to help "the least" of those in the community. In being so hospitable to the "homeless" Furman student, the members of First Presbyterian Church seized an opportunity to put into practice the compassion of the living Lord: "I was a stranger and you welcomed me."

This incident also reminds us not to take the plight of the homeless for granted. On any given night, more than half a million people sleep on the sidewalks and in the alleyways of American towns and cities. Indeed, the sight of homeless people has become so familiar that it has lost much of its power to provoke reflection or prick concern. Yet the statistics are startling. The number of homeless people in Greenville has increased more than fourfold since 1990. Six years ago local officials estimated the homeless population at 100. This year, a one-night street count put the number at 450.

The profile of the homeless in Greenville is changing. Eddie Guthrie, chaplain at the Salvation Army in Greenville, reports that most of the people seeking relief at the shelter just four years ago were unemployed men between the ages of forty and sixty who had a history of drug or alcohol abuse. Today, more than half of the people temporarily housed at the center are employed. Guthrie is also counting more young people and women among the homeless. Most of the Greenville homeless are natives of the area; a third are made up of families.

Dr. Robert McNamara, a sociology professor at Furman who is completing a comprehensive study of the homeless in Greenville, says the fastest growing groups among the homeless population are women, children, and the working poor earning minimum wage. "Housing costs take up so much income," he explains. "Oftentimes they're faced with either eating or having a place to stay."

There are several homeless shelters in Greenville: the Rescue Mission, Salvation Army, Place of Hope (United Ministries), Shepherd's Gate, and Home for New Beginnings. Dr. McNamara notes that there will always be a need for more beds and shelters for the homeless. But in general, he observes, Greenville does a good job of sheltering the homeless compared to other cities.

The welcoming behavior of the congregation at First Presbyterian Church reinforces this perception. Still, one wonders if the healing voice of such Christian charity is the norm or the exception. Do all congregations open their doors and their hearts to the homeless and the unloved? If not, they need to remember that a church is intended to be a sanctuary as well as a place of worship.

Tackling the Illiteracy Problem

| *September 6, 1999*

Another school year has begun, and young people across the Upstate are exchanging summer jobs and television programs for new homework assignments. Each day they tote backpacks filled with books of all shapes, sizes, and colors. Some students grumble and groan about having to read such textbooks. But they should consider themselves lucky. At least they know how to read.

Unfortunately, one out of every five residents of Greenville County is functionally illiterate—unable to complete a job application, read a menu, write a check, or help with a child's homework. Such a high illiteracy rate helps explain why South Carolina has one of the lowest high school graduation rates in the nation. On a more basic level, the nation's prisons are filled with individuals who can barely read. Sixty percent of all inmates are illiterate. Eighty-three percent of the juveniles in detention have few reading skills. And 90 percent of the prisoners on death row are illiterate.

Yet there is an agency in Greenville that is attacking the problem. The Greenville Literacy Association (GLA) provides one-on-one tutoring for students and teaches basic reading, writing, speaking, and math skills to adults. It also offers English as a Second Language (ESL) instruction to the rising number of immigrants moving into the Upstate. More than two thousand people benefit from the services at the GLA each year, and more than five hundred citizens volunteer as tutors. They bear inspiring witness to the empowerment that literacy provides. If people improve their reading skills, they can get better jobs, take better care of their families, be less likely to be involved in drugs and crime, and enjoy the delights of reading for pleasure.

Take for example the story of Lynn Futtrell. A school dropout, she arrived at the literacy association in 1987 unable to read on the third-grade level. Three years later she completed the adult education program at Greenville Tech and earned her GED. In 1997 she graduated from Clemson with a degree in special education. Today, she is a successful teacher and literacy volunteer leading a productive life.

Or consider the story of Barbara Kamieniecki. In 1981 she and her husband and two young children escaped from Communist Poland. They arrived in America knowing no English. Through the GLA tutoring program and through her own tenacious desire to succeed, she became proficient in speaking and reading English and now is a valued employee at Furman. Her older son just graduated from Furman, and her younger son will be a senior next year.

Such success stories are only two of many. Whether it is being able to read the Bible, pass a driver's test, order a meal, or read a letter from a grandchild, literacy is a fundamental skill, perhaps the most important skill a person can develop. Abraham Lincoln had little formal schooling (little was available on the Kentucky-Indiana frontier), yet he became a prominent lawyer because he developed a passion for books. Reading builds a love for learning and in the process opens the mind to all sorts of creativity. A book, a story, a dream, a promising future—literacy is the best gift we can give to our children and our community.

GLA is working to ensure that every Greenville County resident who wants to learn to read and write will have that opportunity free of charge. To do so, the association has embarked upon a bold plan to take literacy outreach to the communities. Adults needing assistance in their reading skills are more likely to attend classes in their local communities. Working in conjunction with other community agencies and the school district, branches have been opened in Simpsonville, Greer, and North Greenville, and others are under development in West Greenville.

This new outreach program, however, is expensive. While the GLA receives generous support from the United Way, it is seeking an endowment to finance its new outreach effort. They have gotten off to a fast start. More than $1.5 million of their $2 million goal has been pledged. With your help they can reach their goal and in the process help improve the lives of many in our community.

Charles Hard Townes

Distinguished Native Son

| *July 11, 1999*

Who is Greenville's most distinguished native? A strong case could be made for Dr. Charles H. Townes. In fact, a new book titled *1,000 Years, 1,000 People: The Men and Women Who Charted the Course of History for the Last Millennium* lists Townes as one of the thousand most important people in the world over the past thousand years. Others listed include Martin Luther, Christopher Columbus, and William Shakespeare. Among those deemed not quite important enough to be among the top thousand were John Kennedy, Ronald Reagan, and Bill Gates.

To be sure, such rosters are highly subjective, but the inclusion of Townes seems warranted. He is a Nobel Prize–winning physicist who invented the maser and the laser.

Born in 1915, Charles Hard Townes grew up on the outskirts of Greenville on a twenty-acre farm near what is now St. Francis Hospital. His father, Henry Keith Townes, was an attorney and gentleman farmer whose homestead included a large garden, fruit trees, and several cows, chickens, and ducks. Such an environment, Charles remembers, encouraged him "to pay attention to the natural world, work with machinery, and know how to solve practical problems and fix things innovatively." Townes attributes much of his success to his beginnings in Greenville, "a place of well-established sensibilities and rhythms" that offered a "reassuring stability."

Charlie Townes knew from an early age that he wanted to become a scientist. A precociously bright and inventive boy, he enrolled at Furman University as a sixteen-year-old freshman. Both his parents had graduated from Furman, as did his two brothers. While excelling in his studies, Townes also competed on the swim team and played trumpet in the marching band. In 1935 he graduated summa cum laude with majors in physics and foreign languages. He recalls that Furman gave him "an excellent and broad experience." Professor Hiden Cox "made physics both fascinating exploration and rigorous logic. He also knew when to allow students to explore, and when to nudge them along the right path."

After graduating from Furman, Townes earned a master's degree at Duke University. He then enrolled in the doctoral program at the California Institute of Technology. "Cal Tech," he remembers, "was then at the top of the physics world." Three years later, a newly doctored Townes headed across country to New York, where he began work for Bell Labs, the research division of AT&T. In early 1941, with the prospect of war looming on the horizon, Townes began designing radar systems for American bombers.

After the war, Townes joined the physics department at Columbia University. In 1951, while sitting on a park bench, he conceived the idea for what would become the laser (Light Amplified by Stimulated Emission of Radiation). He realized that an amplified emission of optical light could produce an intense beam of energy powerful enough to cut steel and precise enough to measure exact distances or perform surgery. Seven years later, Townes published a paper detailing the theory behind the laser and how it could be produced. Initially, many physicists dismissed his ideas as impractical. But he would prove them wrong. Like Jacob with the angel, he wrestled tirelessly with the problem until it blessed him with a solution.

After winning Guggenheim and Fulbright fellowships, Townes became provost of MIT in 1961. While continuing his research on lasers, he also served as the senior advisor to President Kennedy's Apollo space program that eventually landed men on the moon. In 1964 he was awarded the Nobel Prize for his contributions to the invention of lasers. Joining him in Sweden to receive the award was Martin Luther King Jr., who received the Nobel Peace Prize.

Three years later Townes moved to the University of California at Berkeley and shifted his research from lasers to astrophysics. Although now officially retired, he remains at the top of his field. He continues to supervise graduate students and is playing a major role in the development of a super telescope. And in 1999 he published a captivating book titled *How the Laser Happened: Adventures of a Scientist.* In its conclusion, he testifies that his life has been immeasurably enriched by science: "its awesomeness, connectedness, and the beauty of all its dimensions."

Townes is a gracious man who at age eighty-four is remarkably active and alert. As an interpreter of celestial miracles and molecular mysteries, he has explored the unknown with tenacity and humility. All of humanity has benefited from his efforts. Next time you are having laser surgery, using a laser printer, watching kids play laser tag, or listening to reports of laser beams in space, you can take pride in the fact that a Greenville boy made them all possible.

John Broadus Watson

Behaviorist from Travelers Rest

| *July 25, 1999*

Few Greenville natives have achieved greater stature or excited more scandal than John Broadus Watson. Born in Travelers Rest in 1878, he became one of the most celebrated psychologists of the twentieth century. Some rank him as second in importance only to Sigmund Freud.

Textbooks often refer to Watson as the "father of behaviorism"—a school of thought that believes most human behavior is environmentally determined. Watson's own personal behavior was anything but conventional. Dr. Charles Brewer, a distinguished Furman professor who has carefully studied Watson's life, calls him "the misbehaving behaviorist."

Watson was the fourth of six children born to Emma Roe and Pickens Butler Watson. Emma was a pious woman opposed to drinking, dancing, and smoking. Her husband had different tastes. He was a hard-drinking brawler who engaged in a series of extramarital affairs that led him to abandon his family in 1891.

In the aftermath of his father's departure, young John spiraled out of control. He rebelled against his teachers and his mother. He picked fights with other children and was twice arrested for minor offenses. Yet after graduating from Greenville High School at age sixteen, he seemed to have righted himself and gained admission to Furman.

As a college student, Watson did not excel academically. Furman professors described him as being a lazy loner with a brilliant intellect who was very inconsistent in his classroom performance. Watson later recalled that one of his Furman teachers, Prof. Gordon B. Moore, introduced him to psychology and inspired him to fulfill his intellectual potential.

After graduation from Furman, Watson taught at a one-room school in Pickens County. But his outspoken atheism outraged many parents, and after one year of teaching, he left what he considered to be the overly conservative South and began graduate study in experimental psychology at the University of Chicago. Watson flourished in his new environment, and at age twenty-five he was the youngest person ever to earn a Ph.D. at the university.

Watson taught at Chicago for five years before being appointed professor and director of the psychological laboratory at the Johns Hopkins University in Baltimore, where his theories and experiments made him a celebrity. He believed that psychology should be the science of objective behavior, discarding all references to subjective thoughts, feelings, and motivations. For Watson, only that which was observable was important. The goal of psychology, he thought, should be to predict a behavioral response given a particular stimulus.

In 1915 Watson was elected president of the American Psychological Association. Articles on the brilliant and handsome scientist appeared regularly in the national press. In turn, he contributed articles to popular magazines like *Collier's* and *Good Housekeeping.* Watson claimed that he could take any infant and use behaviorist techniques to make "him a doctor, lawyer, artist, merchant-chief and, yes, even beggar-man and thief, regardless of his talents, penchants, tendencies, abilities, vocations and race of his ancestors."

By 1920 Watson had become one of the most important psychologists in the world. Then a personal scandal nearly ruined him. Like his wayward father, Watson was unfaithful to his wife. He carried on several affairs during their seventeen-year marriage. His most publicized liaison was with Rosalie Rayner, a young graduate student at Johns Hopkins who belonged to one of Baltimore's most prominent families. Mrs. Watson discovered love letters from her husband to Rayner that were eventually published in newspapers across the country. The day after the Watsons were divorced, forty-two-year-old John married twenty-one-year-old Rayner. University officials requested Watson's resignation.

Watson's academic career was over. So he took his theories on behaviorism and applied them as an executive with the J. Walter Thompson Advertising Agency. Watson earned a fortune in business. He continued to publish important books on psychology—*Behaviorism* (1924) and *The Psychological Care of Infant and Child* (1928)—but by the 1930s his main interest had shifted to advertising, and he ended his scholarly pursuits.

During his retirement, Watson built a working farm in Connecticut and spent his time caring for animals and maintaining a workshop. Shortly before his death in 1958, he gathered all of his unpublished works and slowly burned each piece one by one. When his secretary protested the loss to posterity and to history, Watson only replied: "When you're dead, you're all dead."

In 1957, the year before his death, the American Psychological Association paid him the following tribute: "To Dr. John B. Watson, whose work has been one of the vital determinants of the form and substance of modern psychology. He initiated a revolution in psychological thought." In 1984 he was inducted into the South Carolina Hall of Science and Technology.

Part 5

The South

The South and Its Heritage

| *January 26, 1997*

The heated debate about the Confederate battle flag reminds us of the peculiar potency of the southern heritage—and its mythology. In William Faulkner's *Absalom, Absalom!* Canadian Shreve McCannon asks Mississippian Quentin Compson in their Harvard dormitory room: "Tell about the South. What's it like there. What do they do there. Why do they live there?"

The nuances and the complexities of the questions paralyze Quentin. Capturing the essence of southern culture in a few words remains a daunting challenge. Over the years, southerners and non-southerners have made countless efforts to understand this storied region and explain why it engenders such loyalty from its children and such criticism from its neighbors. Faulkner himself confessed that he "would never live long enough to exhaust" the subject.

Part of the difficulty is that there are in fact many Souths. Virginia is quite different from Louisiana; Greenville is distinct from Charleston. In addition, the historical experiences and prevailing folkways of whites, blacks, Creoles, Native Americans, and Hispanics differ markedly. Obviously, white southerners and black southerners view the region and its heritage from distinct and often contrasting perspectives. But despite such cultural and racial variety, there is also one South of myth and memory that still exerts a powerful hold on public perceptions.

Some distinguishing characteristics are easy to document. Sociologists tell us that southerners have been and remain more conservative, more religious, more patriotic, more rooted in place, more gracious and hospitable, and more resistant to change than other Americans. Southerners also drink more iced tea, eat more chicken and barbecue, consume more fast food and Twinkies, own more pickup trucks, guns and rifles, attend more NASCAR races and wrestling matches, are more prone to violence, and watch more daytime soap operas than other Americans.

But these are attributes rather than essences, symptoms rather than causes of southern distinctiveness. By far the most common explanation for the unique features of the southern experience is "the war." The South is the only American region (other than Indian territory) to have been a separate nation, to have suffered military defeat on its own soil, and to have experienced military occupation and political reconstruction by a former enemy. When asked why the South had produced such a disproportionate number of great writers, the Mississippi novelist Walker Percy replied: "Because we got beat." Yet if military defeat alone were a sufficient catalyst for great writers, Italy would have been the literary center of the world for centuries.

Perhaps the emphasis should not be on the defeat of the Confederacy itself but the persistent defensiveness embedded in the southern experience. As a minority region promoting a minority worldview, the white South has long found itself the target of criticism and abuse—much of it justified. The sense of being a besieged region has in turn helped unify diverse southerners behind a tenacious defense of old values and traditions.

During the 1920s, for example, the irreverent Baltimore satirist H. L. Mencken repeatedly dismissed the South as being a backwater region awash in vicious racism and shallow piety. The South, he insisted, lacked any serious intellectual and cultural life. He called it the "bunghole of the United States, a cesspool of Baptists, a miasma of Methodism, snake charmers, phony real-estate operations, and syphilitic evangelists."

Such venomous attacks prompted a spirited defense of traditional white southern values by the group of poets, critics, and philosophers known as the Nashville Agrarians. Likewise, during the 1950s and 1960s, the southern way of life built on white supremacy found itself on the defensive in its efforts to preserve segregation against the federal courts and the justice department.

Having lost the segregation fight and not yet resolved its deeply embedded racial tensions, many southerners now find themselves in the throes of an identity crisis. The region is fast losing many of its defining qualities in the midst of unprecedented economic development and the relentless influx of people, businesses, and venture capital.

In many respects the South is now indistinguishable from the rest of the nation thanks to the homogenizing effects of suburban sprawl. Yet those who claim that the "Americanization of Dixie" has leached all the historic distinctiveness from the region need to spend some time outside Atlanta, Charlotte, Dallas, and Fairfax County, Virginia. And they need to listen to those who insist that the battle flag remain atop the state house in Columbia.

What continues to make the South distinctive is the persistence of its own sense of distinctiveness. In Dixie, old times are not forgotten. The legacy of remembrance, the tension between old and new, guilt and innocence, pride and shame, still resonates through many minds in the midst of the dramatic changes reshaping the landscape of southern life.

Southerners do not simply live in the present and dream of the future. We are forever glancing backward in the process of moving forward, acknowledging that our common history lives on as an influential character in the ongoing drama of our lives. Whether loved or hated, the historic South remains a prominent thread in the fabric of our being. As Faulkner recognizes in *Intruder in the Dust,* "The past isn't dead. It's not even past."

Yet unless we loosen the grip of a nostalgic past upon our present consciousness we will not be able to resolve the thorny issues or direct the powerful forces that are going to shape the future of this beloved region. We should cherish the past and recognize its continuing role in our lives, but not be enslaved by it.

The Palmetto State

Past and Present

| *September 28, 1997*

Greenville is rapidly becoming a community of newcomers. People from across the country and around the world are settling in the Upstate, attracted here by new job prospects, the attractive quality of living, and the fabled hospitality of southerners.

The immigrants bring with them a wealth of talents and energy, but they often know little about the heritage of South Carolina. A case in point: last week a newcomer asked why the palmetto is the state tree rather than the yellow pine, the white oak, or the magnolia.

The palmetto tree emerged in South Carolina folklore during the Revolutionary War. On May 31, 1776, a powerful British fleet lay siege to the port of Charleston, then the richest city in North America. An uncompleted fort on Sullivan's Island was all that stood between the British flotilla and the city. Hurriedly fashioned out of palmetto logs, sand, and marsh clay, Fort Sullivan sheltered some 425 patriot militia under the command of Col. William Moultrie. They were short of ammunition but long on courage. When asked if he could defend the "slaughter pen" of a fort, Moultrie replied: "Yes I can."

As the battle began on June 28, the tide turned early against the British. None of the English captains was familiar with the tricky shallows and crosscurrents of Charleston harbor. Low tide prevented most of them from bringing their warships close enough to the fort to take advantage of their superior firepower. In addition, several ships ran aground on the shoal where Fort Sumter now sits. Most of the seven thousand British shells that struck the fort on Sullivan's Island were absorbed by the soft, spongy palmetto logs.

In the meantime, the Americans unleashed a well-aimed barrage that disabled much of the British fleet. Lord William Campbell, South Carolina's royal governor, was aboard the British flagship, the *Bristol,* and was hit by an oak splinter that later proved mortal.

A splinter also wounded the British commodore, tearing off his pants and leaving "his posteriors quite bare."

The *Acteon,* one of the newest and finest warships in the British navy, ran aground during the battle. As the crew abandoned ship, they set it ablaze, and, so the story goes, American observers on Fort Sullivan noted that the smoke plume formed the shape of a palmetto tree.

With every ship damaged and having suffered more than two hundred killed and wounded, the British fleet retired in disarray. "This will not be believed when it is first reported in England," wrote the British surgeon. "I can scarcely believe what I myself saw that day—a day to me one of the most distressing of my life."

The Battle of Sullivan's Island was the first decisive American victory of the war. As such it gave added credibility to the Declaration of Independence, issued six days later. The battle also saved the city of Charleston. It would be three more years before the British tried again to take the valuable port.

The little log fort on Sullivan's Island was renamed Fort Moultrie in honor of its victorious commander, who would later serve two terms as governor, and the palmetto tree thereafter became the state emblem. It was added to the state seal and the state flag, and in 1939 the state legislature named it the official state tree.

In light of the continuing influx of newcomers into South Carolina, the palmetto tree takes on fresh significance as a state symbol. The spongy qualities of the tree suggest the absorptive qualities that South Carolina has displayed in accommodating thousands of diverse newcomers.

Now, if you want to know how the shag became the Palmetto State's official dance, you will have to ask someone else—someone with a sense of rhythm.

C. Vann Woodward

Interpreter of the New South

| *February 6, 2000*

The South recently lost an insightful interpreter and loving critic. C. Vann Woodward, the most eminent and influential authority on southern history, died December 17, 1999, at age ninety-one. A native of Arkansas, the son of a school principal and a Latin teacher, he was educated at Emory, Columbia, and UNC–Chapel Hill. After serving in the navy during World War II, he taught at Georgia Tech, Johns Hopkins, and the University of Virginia before joining the Yale history department in 1961. He retired from Yale in 1977.

Woodward received every major award and form of recognition the academic community can offer. He was elected president of the Southern Historical Association, the Organization of American Historians, and the American Historical Association.

Over the long span of his distinguished career, he produced some of the most important works of southern history. His *Origins of the New South, 1877–1913* won the Bancroft Prize in 1952, and he received the 1982 Pulitzer Prize for *Mary Chesnut's Civil War.* His other major works include *Tom Watson: Agrarian Rebel (1938), Reunion and Reaction: The Compromise of 1877 and the End of Reconstruction* (1951), *The Strange Career of Jim Crow* (1955), *The Burden of Southern History* (1960), *Thinking Back: The Perils of Writing History* (1986), and *The Future of the Past* (1989).

Yet Woodward cannot be defined as simply a teacher and scholar. He was an articulate voice for progressive social change who punctured many of the romantic myths and illusions enshrouding southerners' views of the past. In the process, he told us much about the racial tensions that have shaped and burdened the South's development.

Take, for example, his best-selling book, *The Strange Career of Jim Crow.* It is a compilation of lectures written after the Supreme Court's landmark decision to integrate the public schools in 1954. Woodward emphasized that legally mandated racial segregation in the South was not a long-standing and inviolable tradition, as its apologists claimed. It was a relatively new phenomenon.

For more than a decade after the end of the Civil War, Woodward argued, blacks and whites in many southern states often mingled in public places without incident. It was not until the late 1880s that the rigid system of legal and political segregation became pervasive. Laws appeared in state after state requiring racially separate schools, restaurants, hospitals, orphanages, parks, railroad cars, and even public restrooms. To Woodward, the fact that widespread legal segregation emerged only at the end of the century was of great significance to Americans confronting court-ordered integration in 1954. A prejudicial system of segregation that had been cobbled together in a few years, he stressed, could be more readily and peacefully dismantled.

While Woodward's optimism about a quick ending of segregation proved to be misplaced, his underlying message about the enduring effects of history in shaping the present proved to be poignantly accurate. He repeatedly highlighted the South's history of defeat, poverty, and racism as defining the essence of southernness.

As a son of the South, Woodward felt a keen sense of guilt for its persistent violence and bigotry. While candidly recognizing his native region's "enduring value," he repeatedly urged his fellow southerners to confront their peculiar racial heritage and embrace the compromises needed to bridge their social divide. As he declared in 1964, "It would be a tragic decision to make intransigence and desperate adherence to a discredited code the test of southern loyalty." His observation still rings true.

Jefferson Davis

Flawed Leader

| *November 5, 2000*

Poor Jefferson Davis. In the popular imagination, he is known simply as the earnest man who led the Confederacy to defeat and destruction. Yet as William J. Cooper Jr. demonstrates in a superb new biography of the Confederate leader, Davis spent most of his life as a loyal American soldier and statesman who might well have become president of the United States—had his beloved Mississippi not seceded.

Jefferson Davis was born in a Kentucky log cabin and raised on a Mississippi farm. In 1824 he enrolled at the U.S. Military Academy, where he was a mediocre cadet who chafed at rules and restrictions; he compiled more demerits than plaudits. After graduating from West Point, he spent the next seven years in various army posts in the Old Northwest. In 1835 Davis married the daughter of his commander, Col. Zachary Taylor, against her father's wishes, and left the army to become a cotton planter in Mississippi. His bride died of malaria three months later. For ten lonely years thereafter, a heartbroken Davis developed Brierfield, a plantation near Vicksburg given to him by his older brother.

During the 1840s, Davis became a prominent states' rights Democrat and an ardent proponent of the unrestricted expansion of slavery into the territories. He was elected to the U.S. Congress in 1845. That same year he married Varina Howell of Natchez, a charming woman half his age. After their first meeting, Howell wrote her mother: "Would you believe it, he is refined and cultivated and yet . . . a Democrat." She recognized that Davis was a self-righteous man of "uncertain temper" and mulish obstinacy who assumed that "everybody agrees with him." Yet she admired his self-confident refinement, wide and deep reading, and "winning manner of asserting himself."

Davis was a lean, erect man with an angular face—high cheekbones, hollow jaws, dark, deep-set piercing eyes, thin lips, square chin, and prominent nose. Chronic health problems—dyspepsia and neuralgia—made him appear haggard and careworn.

Davis resigned his House seat in 1846 to take command of a Mississippi regiment in the Mexican War. After returning home a wounded war hero, he served with distinction in the Senate and as secretary of war under Franklin Pierce. In 1857 he reentered the Senate, where he focused on the right to extend slavery into the Kansas and Nebraska territories. He confessed that he was "dogmatic and dictatorial" about such issues, yet when the secession crisis unfolded, he was no fire-eater; he hated the thought of leaving the Union. Nevertheless, on January 21, 1861, having learned that Mississippi had formally seceded, Davis resigned his seat in the United States Senate. It was, he said, "the saddest day of my life." Less than three weeks later, he was named president of the Confederacy.

President Davis was a hard worker, ardent patriot, and capable military strategist, but he had fatal flaws of capacity and judgment, which Cooper meticulously documents. Davis was dogmatic in his defense of slavery, intolerant of criticism, ignorant of public finance, and incapable of managing his feuding generals, most of whom were incompetent. Perhaps worst of all, Davis could not inspire public enthusiasm or accept political compromise.

As the war ground on, Davis struggled in vain to deal with the starvation, dissension, and desertions plaguing the quixotic Confederate war effort. In the end, as federal troops closed in on him, he hoped to escape to Texas and mount a guerrilla resistance movement. But he and Varina were captured in south Georgia in May 1865.

Davis was charged with treason and imprisoned in Fortress Monroe, Virginia. He suffered many humiliations while a prisoner but remained defiant. He refused to request a pardon, demanding instead a trial to vindicate his actions and express his fervent belief that the South had a constitutional right to secede. After his release in May 1867, he rejoined his family in Canada, traveled in Europe, struggled as an insurance executive, lived off the charity of supporters, wrote his memoirs, and died unreconstructed in 1889.

William Cooper, a distinguished professor at Louisiana State University, has succeeded in bringing Davis back to life in all of his complexity and subtleties. Based on a wealth of primary sources and stippled with color, texture, and detail, his definitive new biography gives lavish attention to Davis's career before and after the Civil War. It also provides compelling insights into the spirited Varina Davis.

In his last public address before he died, Jefferson Davis advised southerners that the "past is dead." He told the ardent defenders of the Old South to "bury its dead, its hopes and aspirations; before you lies the future—a future full of golden promise." It was good advice then—and now.

The Big Chill
Cooling the South

| *September 6, 1998*

Thank God for Willis Carrier. We owe the inventor of air-conditioning a special tribute. Not only has his remarkable idea enhanced the quality of our lives, it has also been the primary factor in transforming the South since the end of World War II.

The sultry climate has been one of the most powerful forces influencing southern history. A long growing season made the region ideal for intensive agricultural development, and this in turn led eighteenth-century colonists to rationalize the use of human slavery. Likewise, the stifling heat has shaped many of the region's folkways, from the rhythms of daily life and the design of homes to the distinctive drawl of southern speech patterns and the supposed indolence and short tempers of the residents.

All this—and more—began to change with the development of air-conditioning. In 1902 a young New York engineer named Willis Haviland Carrier designed an "apparatus for treating air" for a Brooklyn printing company. His invention used chilled coils to cool the air and lower the humidity.

Four years later, two southern engineers, Stuart Cramer and I. H. Hardeman, coined the term *air-conditioning* when they installed a Carrier cooling system at the Chronicle Cotton Mills in Belmont, North Carolina.

Thereafter, air-conditioning systems—bulky and expensive—were incorporated in many other industrial locations: mills, factories, breweries, and bakeries. Not until the 1920s, however, did air-conditioning begin to be adapted for more public uses.

In 1922 Carrier invented a centrifugal compressor that facilitated much smaller cooling units and thereby initiated what came to be known as "comfort cooling." By the 1930s, movie theaters, department stores, office buildings, banks, restaurants, railroad cars, and hotels in the South began to be air-conditioned. But it was not until the 1950s that cooled air became widespread in the South.

In 1951 inexpensive window units were invented, and soon thousands of homes featured dripping, humming metal boxes hanging out bedroom windows. My siblings and I in Atlanta were so dazzled by our first window unit that we showed it to our friends as if it were an exotic attraction at a carnival.

Today, more than 90 percent of southern homes and businesses have air-conditioning, and the effects have been profound. Mortality rates have dropped, and economic activity has soared. Working conditions have improved along with productivity. The lure of cooler southern living began to attract millions of folks from other regions. During the 1960s, for the first time since the Civil War, more people moved into the South than out.

In the next decade, twice as many arrived as left. What were once stagnant communities have blossomed into thriving metropolises and cosmopolitan cities, all made possible by cooled air. As a resident of Houston declared in July during the record Texas heat wave, "Without Freon, we'd be dead."

Of course, there have been trade-offs. Air-conditioning has made summers more bearable, but the texture of southern life has also changed, not always for the better. Air-conditioning transformed residential architecture in the South. Suburban split-level ranch homes replaced two-storied Victorian homes with wraparound porches. Ceilings were lowered, windows reduced in size, and long central halls eliminated. Sleeping porches were converted into sunrooms, and front porches disappeared in favor of rear patios.

Even more significant has been the social impact of air-conditioning. Along with the nearly universal ownership of televisions, the spreading availability of air-conditioning has reduced neighborly interaction and made us a more private society. The tradition of families gathering on front porches or lawns on hot summer nights, sitting in rockers or swings, sipping lemonade or tea, listening to cicadas and tree frogs, telling stories and greeting neighbors, has faded from view.

"When I was growing up," one of my neighbors remembers, "all of the families on the street would sit on their front porches, just like Aunt Bee and Sheriff Taylor in Mayberry. But now people stay inside and often folks don't even know their neighbors, much less speak to them."

Perhaps southern neighborliness has been a victim of air-conditioning. But front porches are making a comeback. And the region's warm hospitality may simply have found new—and cooler—outlets. You still see it displayed in shopping malls and grocery stores, coliseums and office towers. Family reunions and church homecomings have moved inside, but their social importance has not diminished. A few revivalists still rely on tents, but many more have moved to air-conditioned quarters. Friendliness does not require perspiration to make it sincere.

So we southerners owe Willis Carrier a debt of thanks. Many of us would not be here without him.

Kudzu

The Weed That Ate Dixie

| *March 5, 2000*

Folks in the Upstate are understandably concerned about the effects of uncontrolled growth—suburban sprawl, traffic congestion, air pollution, and loss of green space. But no one is discussing a suffocating form of vegetable growth that threatens to choke us all: kudzu. In a few weeks, warm spring days will revive the dormant plant from its winter slumber, and its legumelike runners will resume their incessant advance, spreading in all directions, striking terror into landowners and newcomers alike.

Kudzu was initially embraced rather than feared. It first appeared in the United States in 1876. It was one of several ornamental plants in the Japanese Pavilion at the Centennial Exposition in Philadelphia. In Japan and China, people made medicinal tea from kudzu roots and used it to treat a variety of ailments, from hangovers to dysentery. The stems provided a fiber that was used in making cloth and paper. By the turn of the century, southerners were planting kudzu as a shade vine on arbors and porches.

During the Great Depression, kudzu became pervasive in the South. In 1933 the Soil Conservation Service provided eighty-four million kudzu seedlings to landowners throughout the region. Civilian Conservation Corps workers planted the kudzu on public lands, and the government paid farmers to grow the bean vine on their property. The planting program was intended to provide a protein-rich source of animal feed and a means of erosion control. Years of overplanting cotton and neglecting the land had rutted the southern landscape and washed much of the topsoil into the Gulf of Mexico. Kudzu promised a quick and easy solution. "Cotton isn't king in the South anymore. Kudzu is king," declared one enraptured Georgia farmer.

The planting scheme worked better than expected. Too well, in fact. Not only did kudzu fill in the region's red-clay gullies, banks, and ditches; its fast-growing tendrils engulfed trees and telephone poles, railroad tracks, fences, and signs. Farmhouses, tractors, barns, and abandoned cars were soon swallowed up by the "vine that ate Dixie." There were even reports of slow-footed hikers being strangled by rogue vines.

In 1953 the U.S. Department of Agriculture declared that kudzu had become a menace to society and should no longer be used as a cover crop. Researchers shifted their focus from propagation to eradication, and federal agencies spent billions of dollars trying to kill the "noxious weed."

But still it grew—and still it grows. Today, kudzu covers almost 8 million acres—more than 11,000 square miles. And it is grabbing another 120,000 acres every year. A single vine can grow more than a foot a day. And kudzu is virtually drought-proof. Because its roots can reach down as far as ten feet, it needs little surface moisture to thrive in the warm soil. Hardy and relentless, kudzu has become the greatest imperialist of the plant kingdom, advancing on all fronts to acquire more territory. The desperate situation calls for desperate measures. In 1994 a Georgia legislator introduced a bill making it a crime for a property owner to allow kudzu to spread to a neighbor's land.

Whether for good or ill, the ubiquitous vitality of kudzu has helped the "green menace" become a celebrated feature of southern folklore. The late James Dickey wrote a poem titled "Kudzu" that evokes its grasping terrors:

Japan invades, Far Eastern vines,
Run from the clay banks they are
Supposed to keep from eroding,
Up telephone poles,
Which rear, half out of leafage,
As though they would shriek,
Like things smothered by their own
Green, mindless, unkillable ghosts.
In Georgia, the legend says
That you must close your windows
At night to keep it out of the house.

Other southerners are less solemn about the voracious vine. Several communities host annual kudzu festivals that feature Kudzu Queens. Members of a Georgia militia group dub themselves kudzu commandos. Kudzu is the name of a southern rock and roll band and a popular restaurant in Tryon, North Carolina. A few years ago, a film titled *Kurse of the Kudzu Kreature* appeared, and cartoonist Doug Marlette has for years produced a popular comic strip called *Kudzu*. A regional book service named itself Kudzu to reflect its motto: "We cover the South."

Kudzu, however, is no laughing matter. Rise up, defenders of the South! Grab your hoes and summon your goats and cattle. We must smite the alien invader before it wreaks havoc on all that is good about our traditional way of life. And besides, fighting kudzu is better than fighting each other, which we seem to be doing a lot of lately.

Part 6

America Past and Present

A Tangled Fabric

| *April 24, 1997*

The study of the past is a source of endless fascination, in part because history is a dynamic process of discovery. It is never static, never complete. Our sense of the past is constantly being revised to accommodate new evidence and new perspectives.

One of the most interesting topics of historical research and revision in recent years has involved the relations between Indians and Anglo-European-African settlers during the colonial period. Scholars known as ethnohistorians have combined the disciplines of anthropology, archaeology, sociology, and history to describe the complex exchange of folkways and social practices that transformed both Native Americans and transatlantic immigrants. In the process, these scholars have punctured many stereotypes.

For example, Indians did not comprise a monolithic group. Hundreds of different tribes lived in North America, and they spoke different languages, practiced different customs and economies, and often fought with one another over land, hunting rights, and captives.

The European settlers and their African slaves were equally diverse. The eleven million people who crossed the Atlantic before 1820 came from many different countries, regions, and social classes, and they brought with them quite different motives. Many of the newcomers were either indentured servants or slaves, and England transported some fifty thousand convicted felons to North America, most of them to Maryland or Virginia (inside the Beltway?).

Yet for all of their diversity, the peoples of the Old and New Worlds were in daily contact throughout the colonial era and exercised a profound effect upon one another. Despite the impression given by movies and television shows, Native Americans spent far more time living and working with the colonists than they did fighting them.

And far more Indians were killed by infectious diseases than by muskets. Millions of Indians succumbed to smallpox and measles. Whole tribes disappeared. Yet, however much they were exploited or decimated by disease, the Indians were not simply passive victims; they were active agents of resistance and accommodation in the face of changing circumstances. They adjusted to new conditions and circumstances and, where possible, asserted a measure of control over their shared society.

In addition to a thriving trade exchanging European technology for Indian products, a fascinating ecological exchange occurred as the result of Anglo-European-African settlement in the New World. Before 1492, Europeans had not encountered corn, potatoes, and many kinds of beans (kidney, lima, snap, and others). Christopher Columbus returned to Spain with a handful of corn kernels, and within a few years corn had become a staple crop throughout Europe. The white potato that we commonly call Irish actually migrated from South America to Europe and only reached North America with the Scots-Irish immigrants of the 1700s.

Indians shared other new foods with the Europeans—peanuts, peppers, pineapples, avocados, tomatoes, squash, pumpkins, cacao (the source of chocolate), and chicle (for chewing gum). These new foods enriched the diets of the European and African settlers and helped extend their lives. At the same time, the Indians discovered new meats—chicken, pork, and beef—brought over from Europe and new grains—wheat, barley, and oats.

The borders between Indian and colonial cultures were thus permeable rather than rigid. A considerable number of Indians and Europeans crossed over and became members of the other's society. Thousands of Indians were converted to Christianity, and many white traders lived in Indian villages and married Indian women. Sir William Johnson, the British superintendent for Indian affairs just prior to the Revolution, lived for fifteen years with a Mohawk woman, fathered Mohawk children, wore Mohawk clothes, and participated in their tribal dances.

Many others engaged in similar cross-cultural migrations. The result was a series of new hybrid social groups, different from what had existed both in North America and the Old World. Native Americans, Anglo-Europeans, and Africans intermingled daily during the colonial era and in the process learned and adapted from one another's cultural heritage—often in ways only vaguely understood at the time. Such multicultural exchanges remind us that our past was more complex than we often assume—filled with surprise and unpredictability, with people determined to shape their fate, with stories of struggle and tragedy but also cooperation and coexistence, stories that warrant our attention and respect.

George Washington's Rules of Civility

| *January 3, 1999*

The first month of the year is called January in honor of the two-faced god Janus, who could see in two directions at the same time. Likewise, the New Year prompts us to look back and look ahead and to make resolutions for improvement.

Yet after a few weeks of trying to improve ourselves, most of us admit failure. We resemble the man who embarked on a crusade to reduce his weight and recorded his "progress":

1995: I will get my weight down below 180.
1996: I will watch my calories until I get below 190.
1997: I will follow my new diet religiously until I get below 200.
1998: I will try to develop a realistic attitude about my weight.

For him and for us, bad habits are dreadfully persistent.

Yet regardless of our failures, most of us continue the perennial effort to better ourselves. Those long on resolve but short on personal objectives for 1999 may want to turn to our Founding Father for inspiration. In the 1740s a teenaged George Washington carefully transcribed into a notebook 110 "Rules for Civility," compiled by French Jesuits in the year 1595.

For the rest of his life, Washington carried the list of maxims with him and strove to embody the deceptively simple principles and rules of conduct. There is a newly published version edited by Richard Brookhiser, called *Rules of Civility: The 110 Precepts that Guided Our First President in War and Peace.*

Washington's self-improvement list seems especially appropriate for our own uncivil culture. His guide to conduct includes the following:

Rule 1: "Every action done in company [public] ought to be done with some sign of respect to those that are present."

Rule 2: "When in company, put not your hands to any part of the body not usually discovered." (This seems especially appropriate for baseball players.)

Rule 22: "Show not yourself glad at the misfortune of another though he were your enemy."

Rule 45: "In reproving [someone else] show no sign of choler, but do it with all sweetness and mildness."

Rule 49: "Use no reproachful language against any one, neither curse nor revile."

Rule 56: "Associate yourself with men of good quality if you esteem your own reputation; for 'tis better to be alone than in bad company."

Rule 73: "Think before you speak."

Rule 82: "Undertake not what you cannot perform but be careful to keep your promise."

Rule 88: "Be not tedious in public speaking, make not many digressions, nor repeat often the same statements." (In other words, don't talk like a college president.)

Such good manners and basic courtesies, Washington and other members of his generation taught, are the necessary attributes of citizens in a republic. As President John Adams wrote his son and future president, John Quincy, "Treat the world with modesty, decency, and respect."

The simple civilities that Washington tried to practice remain relevant at the beginning of the twenty-first century. Goodness knows, modern American life could benefit from greater self-control and a revival of basic courtesies. All around us we see insolence and vulgarity run amok. From attack politics to abusive language, from provoked fistfights on television shows to rising incidents of road rage—all are ugly symptoms of the culture of incivility that corrodes our sense of community.

So as you set about adopting your own resolutions, consider George Washington's emphasis on controlling our selfish inclinations and showing respect for those around us. As he stresses in rule 110, "Labor to keep alive in your breast that little spark of celestial fire called conscience."

Restoring Civility to Congress

| *May 4, 1997*

In recent months Congress has seemed more like a circus than our highest legislative body. House members have unleashed obscenities, called each other liars and fascists, engaged in shoving matches, and passed measures denying speaking privileges to colleagues.

To be sure, Congress has always been an arena for rancorous rhetoric and partisan feuds. Before the first Congress met, John Adams predicted that its members would make more noise than sense and display more meanness than greatness.

Yet rarely, if ever, has such venomous behavior in the Congress been so pervasive. A Democratic senator recently left the Senate chamber muttering: "I'd like to take an Uzi in there and spray the place."

Such incidents prompt me to suggest a facetious interpretation: congressional behavior began its decline into boorishness and incivility when the ritual of dueling went out of favor in the mid-nineteenth century.

The prospect of mortal combat, the advocates of dueling argued, encouraged gentlemen to exercise greater care in their use of language and in their relations with others. As the author of *The Art of Dueling* observed in 1836, "the loss of a few lives is a mere trifle, when compared with the benefits resulting to Society at large." A dueling society, Americans assumed in the early nineteenth century, was a polite society.

An elaborate series of strict rules and procedures emerged to govern duels, and scores of politicians participated. Duels were usually provoked by a personal insult or a slur against one's wife or mistress. In 1807, for example, Gen. James Wilkinson prompted a duel with Virginia congressman John Randolph by calling him a "prevaricating, base, calumniating scoundrel, poltroon and coward." Ten years later, Thomas Hart Benton, the future senator, killed a young lawyer who had resented being called a puppy.

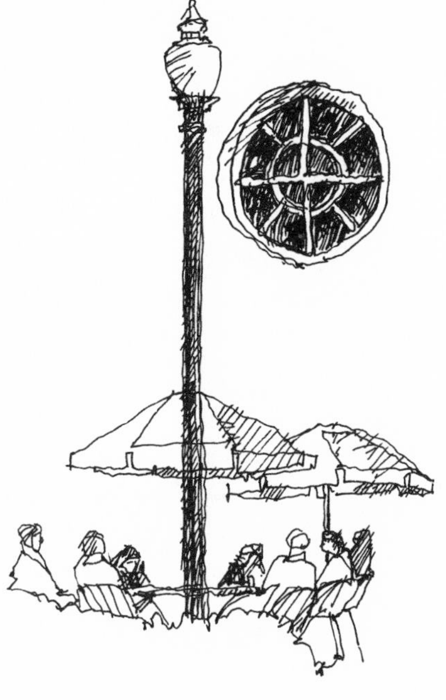

Etiquette required that the duel must occur within forty-eight hours of the challenge—to minimize target practice and to allow for mediation by third parties. Often, the dispute was resolved before shots were fired. If negotiations failed, the contest was usually scheduled at dawn in a secluded spot. After the seconds urged one last effort at reconciliation, the contestants faced each other, usually ten to fifty paces apart. The more grievous the insult, the closer the distance. In 1819 two incensed politicians unleashed shotgun blasts at four paces.

If both shots missed, the disputants could either declare the issue resolved or reload and try again. If your bullet struck home, a dueling manual explained, you should "express regret" before leaving the scene. If hit by a bullet, "treat the matter coolly." And if the wound proved mortal, "go off with as good a grace as possible."

Dueling was most common in the South, a fact that gave rise to the observation that southerners will be polite until they are angry enough to kill you. Sometimes honor took precedence over survival. The night before his duel with Secretary of State Henry Clay in 1826, lifelong bachelor John Randolph resolved "to receive without returning Clay's fire. He continued, "Nothing shall induce me to harm a hair of his head. I will not make his wife a widow, or his children orphans. Their tears would be shed over his grave, but when the sod of Virginia rests on my bosom there is not in this wide world one individual to pay his tribute upon me."

True to his word, Randolph fired into a stump behind Clay, while Clay's shot missed as well. Clay asked for a second round. His next shot pierced the gown Randolph was wearing. Randolph then fired into the air, declaring, "I would not fire at you, Mr. Clay." The two men then shook hands, and their quarrel ended.

Of course, dueling was a terrible practice that deservedly went out of fashion. Yet today, when unrestrained rudeness and rancor prevail in the halls of Congress, one wonders if the politicians might benefit from instituting a dueling option—not with real guns but with water pistols or meringue pies at ten paces. It might help relieve the tension and demonstrate how silly and degrading their behavior has become. Or better yet, the mutually offensive politicos might simply retire to a remote area, far from the House or Senate. The key word is *retire.*

Martin Luther King Jr. and the Civil Rights Movement

| *January 14, 2001*

The annual celebration of Martin Luther King Jr.'s birthdate continues to arouse excitement or outrage as people honor his accomplishments and debate his foibles. Yet it is also an opportunity for us to remember the crucial role he played in fostering a civil rights movement that continues to transform American society. King first emerged as a leader of national prominence in 1955. As the twenty-six-year-old minister of the Dexter Avenue Baptist Church in Montgomery, Alabama, he agreed to lead a citywide boycott against the municipal bus system.

Like many other southern cities, Montgomery had a local ordinance that required blacks to sit in the back of buses and to give up their seat to whites. The boycott was triggered by the arrest of Rosa Parks, a middle-aged black seamstress and long-time critic of segregation who served as secretary of the local NAACP chapter. Tired after a long day's work, she boarded a city bus on December 1. Several stops later, the bus driver ordered her to stand so that a white rider could take her seat. She refused. The driver stopped the bus and warned Parks that he was "going to have you arrested." She replied, "You may do so." Parks later explained that she wanted to discover "once and for all what rights I had as a human being and a citizen." And besides, she added, "my feet hurt."

Word of Parks's arrest raced through the African American community. By midnight, black leaders decided to organize a massive boycott of the bus system. E. D. Nixon, a railroad porter, union leader, and former president of the state and local NAACP, had been looking for the right moment to organize a mass protest, and the arrest of Parks, a beloved community leader, provided the needed catalyst. While Nixon phoned area ministers to enlist their support, student and faculty volunteers from Alabama State

University stayed up all night to produce thirty-five thousand flyers denouncing the arrest and urging support for the boycott.

On December 5, the successful first day of the bus boycott, representatives of churches, neighborhood organizations, and political clubs met to assess the situation. After heated debate, they all agreed to endorse the boycott and formed the Montgomery Improvement Association to coordinate the mass protest. The group elected the untested King to serve as its president.

Born in Atlanta, the grandson of a slave and the son of a prominent minister, King was intelligent, courageous, and charismatic. He was also an eloquent and passionate speaker. Drawing upon the Bible, the writings of Henry David Thoreau, and the teachings of Mahatma Gandhi, he had developed a philosophy of nonviolent civil disobedience. Rosa Parks's refusal to turn over her bus seat was a perfect example of such nonviolent resistance.

On the night of December 5, King addressed a mass meeting at a downtown church. Thousands of blacks attended, crowding the church and spilling outside. King delivered a riveting speech. He first expressed the frustration of his listeners who had been "intimidated, humiliated, and oppressed because of the sheer fact that they were Negroes." But now they were fighting back. King explained that "there comes a time when people get tired of being trampled over by the iron feet of oppression."

The huge audience began shouting "yes" in unison and stomping their feet in approval. Once they quieted down, King continued, assuring the public, "We are not here advocating violence. We have overcome that." The only weapon they would use would be the "weapon of protest." King concluded by urging his listeners to remember their Christian principles as they continued the boycott. "If you protest courageously, and yet with dignity and Christian love, future historians will say, 'There lived a great people—a black people—who injected new meaning and dignity into the veins of civilization.'"

The Montgomery boycott achieved stunning solidarity. Ridership on the bus system plummeted. Blacks organized car pools, used black-owned taxis, or hitchhiked to work or to shop. A few rode horses or mules. Many white supporters provided rides. Such an unprecedented mass protest infuriated many whites. Policemen harassed and ticketed black car pools, and white thugs assaulted hitchhikers.

During the boycott, King was arrested twice and threatened often. A few weeks after the boycott began, someone threw a bomb onto the porch of King's parsonage. Upon learning of the incident, he hurried home to find his wife, Coretta, and their infant daughter unharmed. In the street, however, hundreds of vengeful blacks, some of them armed, were threatening to assault whites. King urged the angry bystanders to attack hate with love: "We must love our white brothers no matter what they do to us." His remarkable magnanimity defused the volatile situation and led the crowd to disperse.

The Montgomery bus boycott had lasted almost a year when the Supreme Court ruled that the city's segregated bus ordinance was unconstitutional. A few weeks later, on December 21, 1956, Dr. King and the Rev. Glen Smiley, a white minister, shared the front seat of a bus.

But the boycott accomplished much more than ensuring equality of treatment on Montgomery's sixty-four buses. It revealed to blacks across the country the power and potential of nonviolent resistance. For thousands of African Americans, hope replaced resignation; action supplanted passivity.

The successful boycott also catapulted young Dr. King into a position of national leadership of the Civil Rights movement that would earn him the Nobel Peace Prize in 1964. In Montgomery, King, Parks, Nixon, and others showed that deeply embedded social evils could be engaged, resisted, and transformed through moral tenacity and loving opposition.

Yes, King's birthdate is worth remembering—and his extraordinary achievements are worth honoring.

Abraham Lincoln

Pragmatic President

| *February 12, 2001*

February 12 is Abraham Lincoln's birthday. It used to be a day of national celebration and remembrance. No more. With each passing year, his birthday attracts less notice. Likewise, public awareness of Lincoln and his achievements has reached a low ebb. A recent survey of high school students revealed that fewer than half could identify Lincoln as the author of the Gettysburg Address.

Interest in Lincoln was much more exuberant in April 1865 when he visited Richmond, the occupied Confederate capital. Arriving at the wharf, he was greeted by a group of African American workers. One of them recognized the Union leader and shouted, "Bless the Lord, there is the great Messiah! Glory, Hallelujah." They then rushed up to Lincoln and knelt at his feet. The embarrassed president implored them to restrain themselves.

Lincoln may not garner such unbridled reverence today, but he certainly deserves remembrance as perhaps our greatest—and certainly our most enigmatic—president. What special qualities helped the hayseed lawyer win the 1860 presidential election, preserve the Union, and end slavery?

One of Lincoln's most endearing attributes was his unpretentious humanity. Born in 1809 in a Kentucky log cabin, and raised on the Indiana and Illinois frontier, the "great commoner" was a self-made man driven by restless ambition. Tall and lanky, homely and gawky, he worked as a rail-splitter, farmhand, carpenter, butcher, ferryman, storekeeper, postmaster, and surveyor before becoming a self-educated attorney.

Elected to the Illinois legislature in 1834, Lincoln served four terms, distinguishing himself by his honesty and courage. Early on, he displayed a rare ability to deflect criticism and generate sympathy through his folksy storytelling and self-deprecating humor. In 1858, when someone suggested that he might one day move into the White House,

Lincoln scoffed: "Just think of such a sucker [the common slang for an Illinois native] as me as President."

Lincoln also developed an effective blend of moral idealism and political realism. During the 1850s he denounced "the monstrous injustice" of slavery and earnestly opposed its extension into the new territories of Kansas and Nebraska. But his keen awareness of the practical limits of public opinion and constitutional law kept him from advocating immediate abolition in the southern states. Before 1862 he never questioned the right of people to own slaves in those states where it was legal. Such principled pragmatism infuriated militant abolitionists, then and since, but Lincoln believed that a democratic republic requires balancing ideals with realities. Moral passion, he acknowledged, "has helped us," but ultimately it must give way to "cold, calculating, unimpassioned reason."

Still another distinctive attribute of Lincoln as leader was his humility and flexibility. He was not afraid to admit a mistake or to change his mind. When the Civil War erupted, for instance, he confessed that he was poorly prepared to lead the nation into such a massive conflict; as a one-term Congressman, he had little knowledge of military strategy or government administration. Yet he was eager to surround himself with talented, outspoken lieutenants whose contrary views helped educate and mature the inexperienced president.

Likewise, the profound challenges and harrowing traumas of the "terrible war" transformed and elevated Lincoln. He grew into greatness. His law partner, William Herndon, said that Lincoln "grandly rose up" to meet the stern demands of a nation in peril. As commander in chief, Lincoln displayed a courageous decisiveness. He was willing to do whatever necessary to "subdue the enemy" and preserve the Union: making compromises to keep the Republican party from fragmenting and the border states from seceding, instituting an unpopular military draft and martial law, limiting free speech and habeas corpus, liberating slaves under Confederate control, and enlisting blacks in the Union military. Such actions resulted in an unprecedented expansion of presidential authority.

Finally, Lincoln was a master of political rhetoric. He knew full well the power of carefully chosen words to inspire courage and sacrifice. Even though he had little formal schooling, he sustained a lifelong passion for reading. He especially loved Shakespeare, the Bible, and the Declaration of Independence. Such sources taught him the virtues of taut, simple, direct prose. He strove to keep his speeches short and pithy so as to invest each phrase with exceptional force and clarity.

The result was a distinctive style of expression that embodied both Lincoln's own democratic ideals and those of the fractured nation. The final sentence of his second inaugural address retains a potent immediacy that reminds us of his peculiar greatness and of American ideals not yet fully achieved: "With malice toward none, with charity for all, with firmness in the right, as God gives us to see the right, let us strive on to finish the work that we are in, to bind up the nation's wounds, to care for him who shall have borne the battle, and for his widow and orphan, to do all which may achieve a just and lasting peace among ourselves, and with all nations."

The First Impeachment

| *January 26, 1999*

The chaotic partisanship evident among both parties in the impeachment of President Bill Clinton seems tame when compared to the trial of President Andrew Johnson in 1868. The participants in that first presidential impeachment were quite explicit and unapologetic about their political purposes. As the prominent Massachusetts senator Charles Sumner declared, "Impeachment is a political proceeding before a political body with a political purpose."

Andrew Johnson was an accidental president with an unusual background. Born in 1808 near Raleigh, he never attended school but had a zest for learning and developed an intense ambition to surmount the poverty of his youth.

At age fourteen Johnson was apprenticed to a tailor who taught him to read, and after brief stints with tailors in Laurens and Greenville, South Carolina, he decided to seek his fortune in the mountains of eastern Tennessee. In 1826 the penniless wayfarer began walking west from Raleigh and several weeks later arrived in Greeneville, Tennessee.

Johnson found work in the village tailor shop and soon had his own thriving clothing store. He married a woman who taught him to write, and over the years he grew quite prosperous, acquiring several slaves in the process.

Politics, however, became Johnson's passion. Beginning in the 1830s, he emerged as one of the leading Jacksonian Democrats. A bitter critic of the "swaggering" planter aristocracy "who are too lazy and proud to work," Johnson was a fervent populist who promoted free land for the poor, defended slavery, and promoted white supremacy. A notoriously stubborn man, he became a self-righteous, hot-tempered orator who enjoyed strong drink and employed abusive language to belittle his opponents. His fiery speeches and firm principles helped him win election as mayor, congressman, governor, and senator.

Like many other whites living in mountainous east Tennessee, Johnson ardently believed in the Union. In 1861 he was the only southern senator in a Confederate state to vote against secession, leading critics to denounce him as a "traitor" to the region. Yet his devotion to the Union did not include opposition to slavery. He hated the Confederacy because he hated the planter elite. "Damn the Negroes," Johnson bellowed to a friend during the war, "I am fighting those traitorous aristocrats, their masters."

Abraham Lincoln selected Johnson as his running mate in 1864 solely for political reasons. He and his advisers thought that the addition of a southern Democrat and Unionist would strengthen the Republican ticket in the face of northern impatience with the war effort.

The strategy worked and Lincoln was reelected, but Johnson did not get off to a good start as the nation's new vice president. On the morning of Lincoln's inauguration, he was not feeling well, so he drank some whiskey—too much, as it turned out. As he delivered his speech at the ceremony in the Senate chamber, it quickly became evident that he was inebriated. A New York newspaper reported the next day that Johnson was "a drunken boor."

Six weeks later, in April 1865, John Wilkes Booth shot Lincoln and elevated Johnson to the White House. At that time, with the long Civil War drawing to a close, Republicans controlled both houses of Congress. Led by the so-called radical faction, including Sumner, Benjamin Wade, and Thaddeus Stevens, they hoped Johnson would endorse their efforts to use military force to "reconstruct" the defeated South from top to bottom. "Johnson, we have faith in you," said Wade of Ohio.

But Wade and his radical colleagues were soon disappointed. They wanted former Confederates tried for treason and demanded civil rights and voting privileges, and confiscated farmland for the freed slaves.

Johnson, however, thwarted their efforts. He promoted the quick restoration of southern state governments without involving Congress. He issued wholesale pardons to former Confederate leaders, and he fired army generals who promoted rigid enforcement of the Reconstruction acts passed by Congress. At the same time, he insisted that the South was a "white man's country" and ordered black families evicted from formerly white-owned land on which they had been settled by federal troops.

Such actions outraged the radicals. "Is there no way to arrest the insane course of the president in Washington?" asked Thaddeus Stevens of Pennsylvania. Unfazed by such opposition, Johnson vetoed twenty-nine bills passed by the Republican Congress, including a civil rights bill, and he opposed ratification of the Fourteenth Amendment, which extended full legal protection to all citizens.

Johnson was a man of limited ability and narrow vision. He lacked Lincoln's resilience and pragmatism. In the process of promoting his lenient southern strategy, Johnson allowed his temper to get the better of his judgment. He castigated the radicals as "factious, domineering, tyrannical" traitors who constituted "a gang of cormorants and bloodsuckers who have been fattening upon the country." By 1867 newspapers were reporting that the differences between Johnson and the Republicans were irreconcilable.

The Republicans first tried to impeach Johnson in 1867, alleging a variety of flimsy charges, none of which represented an indictable crime. The head of the Secret Service, for example, shared rumors about an alleged presidential affair with a woman seeking pardons for former Confederates. Johnson was also accused of public drunkenness, and one Congressman even tried to implicate him in the assassination of Lincoln. After listening to the hodgepodge of charges, a House member from Iowa concluded: "While the President has been guilty of many great follies and wickedness," it was better to "submit to two years of misrule . . . than subject the country, its institutions and its credits to the shock of an impeachment."

Thwarted in their impeachment efforts, Republican radicals next tried to use legislation to neutralize the president. In 1867 they passed several dubious laws that shifted power from the president to Congress. One of these measures, the Tenure of Office Act, prohibited presidents from dismissing their own cabinet members.

When Johnson decided to provoke a showdown by firing his disloyal secretary of war, Edwin M. Stanton, on February 21, 1868, the radicals immediately called for his impeachment. They were so irate, said the secretary of the navy, that they would have impeached Johnson "had he been accused of stepping on a dog's tail." Horace Greeley, the editor of the *New York Tribune,* declared that Johnson had become "an aching tooth in the national jaw, a screeching infant in a crowded lecture room." There could "be no peace or comfort till he is out" of office.

The impeachment debate in the House was clamorous and vicious. One congressman said Johnson had dragged the robes of his office through the "filth of treason." Another denounced the president as "an ungrateful, despicable, besotted traitorous man—an incubus." Still another called Johnson's advisers "the worst men that ever crawled like filthy reptiles at the footstool of power." On February 24, 1868, the House passed eleven articles of impeachment by a party-line vote of 126 to 47.

The Senate trial was a great spectacle before a packed gallery. Witnesses were called, speeches made, and rules of order debated. Johnson wanted to plead his case in person, but his attorneys refused, fearing that his short temper might erupt and hurt his cause. The president thereupon worked behind the scenes to win over undecided Republican senators, offering them a variety of political incentives.

As the weeks passed, the trial grew tedious. Senators slept during the proceedings, spectators passed out in the unventilated room, and poor acoustics prompted repeated cries of "We can't hear." Debate eventually focused on Stanton's removal, the most substantive impeachment charge. Johnson's lawyers argued that Lincoln, not Johnson, had appointed Stanton, so the Tenure of Office Act did not apply to him. At the same time, they claimed (correctly, as it turned out) that the law was unconstitutional.

As the five-week trial ended and the voting began in May 1868, the Senate Republicans could afford only six defections from their ranks to ensure the two-thirds majority needed to convict. In the end, seven moderate Republicans and all twelve Democrats voted to acquit. The renegade Republicans offered two primary reasons for their controversial votes: they feared damage to the separation of powers if Johnson were removed, and they were assured by Johnson's attorneys that he would stop obstructing congressional policy in the South.

In a moment of high drama, the deciding vote was cast by Edmund Ross, a first-term Kansas Republican who in the days leading up to the verdict was "hunted like a fox" by both sides. He insisted that his decision was an act of courage based on principled constitutional scruples: "If the president must step down upon insufficient proofs and from partisan considerations, the office of president would be degraded" and "ever after subordinated to the legislative will." Years later, John F. Kennedy was so inspired by Ross's dissenting vote that he featured him in his Pulitzer Prize–winning book, *Profiles in Courage.*

Historians have since discovered that Ross was not so principled: he demanded several political favors from Johnson in exchange for his vote. Whatever his motives, Ross's defection infuriated those promoting impeachment. One of his constituents fired off a bitter telegram: "Kansas repudiates you as she does all perjurers and skunks."

Although the Senate failed to remove Johnson, the trial crippled his already-weak presidency. During the remaining ten months of his term, he initiated no other clashes with Congress. In 1868 Johnson sought the Democratic presidential nomination but lost to New York governor Horatio Seymour, who then lost to Republican Ulysses Grant in the general election. A bitter Johnson refused to attend Grant's inauguration. His final act as president was to issue a pardon to former Confederate president Jefferson Davis.

In 1874, after failed bids for the Senate and the House, Johnson won a measure of vindication with election to the Senate, the only former president ever to do so, but he died just a few months later. He was buried with a copy of the Constitution tucked under his head.

As for the impeachment trial, only two weeks after it ended, a Boston newspaper reported that people were amazed at how quickly "the whole subject of impeachment seems to have been thrown into the background and dwarfed in importance" by other events. May we be so lucky in 1999.

Cecilia Beaux

Forgotten Artist

| *March 25, 2001*

Who is America's greatest female painter? Most people would name either Mary Cassatt or Georgia O'Keefe. Some would dismiss the question as condescending, since a painter's greatness should not be defined by gender. Yet the distinctive challenges facing women artists justify distinctive appreciation for their fortitude and talent.

Certainly that was the case a century ago, when the leaders of the American art community, all of them male, asserted that the nation's best female artist was Cecilia Beaux. In 1899 William Merritt Chase proclaimed that Beaux was "not only the greatest living woman painter, but the best that has ever lived." Her portraits won numerous gold medals at exhibitions in the United States and in Europe, and her talented brush was in great demand among the nation's social and political elite. By 1916 a critic could assert, "Miss Beaux as an American painter has no rivals at all." Six years later, when the *New York Times* conducted a survey to name the "twelve greatest American women," Cecilia Beaux headed a list that included Jane Addams and Edith Wharton.

Yet Beaux is little known today except among art historians and connoisseurs. How is it possible for such a revered painter to disappear as though she never existed? The answer tells much about the mercurial quality of artistic reputations.

Born in 1855, Cecilia Beaux grew up in a West Philadelphia household of talented women. Her mother died twelve days after giving birth, and her distraught French father fled to Provence, leaving behind his infant daughter and her sister to be raised by their widowed grandmother and two aunts amid pinched gentility. Cecilia was raised in an atmosphere of strict moral rectitude, cultural vitality, and hard work.

Beaux was educated at home and then spent two years at a Philadelphia finishing school. By the age of sixteen, she had decided to turn her talent for drawing into a career. To generate income, she first painted portraits of children on ceramic plates to be hung on parlor walls. By the 1880s, however, Beaux was able to begin taking formal art lessons. But her guardians insisted that she work with a private instructor so as to avoid being exposed to the "coarse" behavior and vulgar language of male students—as well as nude models. In 1883 she opened a studio in Philadelphia and produced her first major canvas, a stunning portrait of her sister and nephew. It won first prize at the Pennsylvania Academy of the Fine Arts and later drew keen attention at exhibitions in New York and Paris. This precocious success led to more study in Paris that greatly broadened Beaux's horizons and deepened her sophistication.

Beaux returned to Philadelphia in 1889, and soon thereafter her reputation as a portrait painter of the wealthy and famous soared. Her works were widely exhibited and praised, and her connections in the art world grew ever more extensive. In 1895 she became the first woman instructor at the Pennsylvania Academy, and the next year, after a triumphant exhibition at the Paris Salon, she was elected to the Société Nationale des Beaux-Arts. In 1901 she was invited to the White House to paint a portrait of Mrs. Theodore Roosevelt and her daughter. She was elected to the National Academy of Design in 1902. Yale and the University of Pennsylvania awarded her honorary degrees.

Beaux's sumptuous portraits resemble those of the more celebrated John Singer Sargent. But where Sargent was self-consciously theatrical, Beaux was more reserved—a technician rather than a performer with a brush. She abhorred ostentation and theatricality. Where Sargent assaulted the canvas with panache and cleverness, she labored over her subject's composition and treatment in an effort to capture the "weight of personality." She once told a friend: "I never do anything easily."

For all of Cecilia Beaux's obvious talent and success, however, her reputation quickly faded after her death in 1943. Her focus on portraiture did not help sustain her stature. Art critics and historians prefer painters with wider interests. In addition, her emphasis on patrician men and sheltered women and children has alienated many art critics. Even more important in explaining Beaux's declining stature is her resistance to changing artistic fashions. Unlike her rival Philadelphian, Mary Cassatt, she did not align herself with impressionism or any other "rebel" movement. Beaux shunned the avant-garde and sought to join the art world aristocracy. She once dismissed cubism as "egotistical, insane, insincere and ugly."

Such artistic conservatism has grated on art historians and critics. Equally disturbing to such modern sensibilities is that Beaux doubted that women painters would ever display the creative power of a Rubens or Michelangelo. "To produce a great painting," she insisted, "requires a certain objectivity which is rare in women." But Beaux also stressed that, in the end, "success is sexless." Her own success in defying the conventions of her time and excelling within a male-dominated profession deserves renewed attention and acclaim.

Gurus of Cornflakes

| *September 19, 1999*

A century ago, Dr. John Harvey Kellogg of Battle Creek, Michigan, transformed the nation's breakfast habits. In the process, he became a millionaire fitness guru for America's rich and powerful—and the inspiration for a recent movie, *The Road to Wellville,* which took great liberties with historical truth.

Born in 1852, Kellogg was the seventh of fifteen children, five of whom died in childhood. Such pervasive disease and death helped convince the Kellogg family to embrace the new Seventh Day Adventist Church, founded by Sister Ellen White in 1863 in Battle Creek. Adventists believed that the imminent second coming of Christ made it imperative for them to organize their daily lives around their faith. This included avoiding coffee, alcohol, tobacco, meat, and "rich foods."

To promote her beliefs, Sister White founded a health spa and later hired the twenty-four-year-old Kellogg to run what came to be called the Battle Creek Sanitarium. He was a freshly trained physician and ardent Adventist who feared that the human race was decaying through physical and moral degeneracy. To him, sickness usually resulted from a moral failing. Kellogg therefore preached the benefits of proper diet, adequate rest and exercise, fresh air, and commonsense dress (no corsets!). His dietary advice was straightforward: "Eat what the monkey eats—simple food and not too much of it."

Like Sister White, Kellogg found human sexuality disgusting and prescribed nearly total abstinence, even for his married patients. Any sexual activity, he believed, could lead to a long list of disorders, ranging from heart disease to insanity. After marrying in 1879, Kellogg and his wife, Ella, slept in separate beds and never had children of their own. Instead, during their long marriage, they adopted forty-two impoverished youngsters, most of whom had been victims of abuse or neglect.

Under Kellogg's charismatic leadership, the Battle Creek Sanitarium prospered. By the early twentieth century, it employed eighteen hundred staff members, hosted thirteen hundred guests at a time, and had become internationally famous as a place of refuge and recovery for the sick and neurotic, the underweight and overweight. The guests included many celebrities: actress Sarah Bernhardt, three-time presidential candidate William Jennings Bryan, polar explorer Adm. Richard Byrd, Dale Carnegie, Amelia Earhart, Thomas Edison, Henry Ford, and retailers S. S. Kresge and J. C. Penney.

Dr. Kellogg prescribed unusual remedies. He believed everyone should start the day with an enema. He made underweight patients lie in bed with weights on their stomachs and eat twenty-six meals a day, and he required patients with high blood pressure to eat ten to fourteen pounds of grapes a day.

Dr. Kellogg also touted the benefits of eating bran. Convinced that dry, brittle food strengthened teeth and helped suppress sexual desires, he prescribed large amounts of zwieback (twice-baked bread). When one of his patients broke a tooth on his zwieback and asked for ten dollars in compensation, Kellogg and his brother William began looking for a softer breakfast alternative. The result was cornflakes.

Soon the brothers began marketing Toasted Corn Flakes as a ready-to-eat cereal that would suppress sexual desires and promote healthy bodies. In their first year they sold 100,000 pounds of cereal. But their business success generated controversy. Sister White was furious that Dr. Kellogg had embraced commercialism. Their dispute took an unexpected twist when Kellogg discovered that Sister White was secretly eating chicken in violation of her vegetarian beliefs. In the end, Sister White accused Kellogg of blasphemy and excommunicated him from the Adventist faith in 1907.

Kellogg, however, continued to thrive as head of the sanitarium and, even more important, as a cornflake entrepreneur. Competitors in the cereal industry cropped up, including Kellogg's own patient C. W. Post (Post Toasties, Raisin Bran, etc.). But worst of all for Kellogg, his brother William, eager to widen their product's appeal, added sugar to the flakes. This horrified Dr. Kellogg, who believed that sugar reversed the cereal's sex-suppressing effects. The two brothers sued each other and eventually parted ways. In 1906 Will founded the Battle Creek Toasted Corn Flake Company, which later became the Kellogg Company. The rest, as they say, is history. Today, the Kellogg Company—with sales of more than $6.7 billion last year—is the world's leading producer of cereal and convenience foods.

And what of Dr. Kellogg? He eventually retired to Florida, where he lived to the ripe age of ninety-two.

The Scopes Trial Revisited

| *August 6, 2000*

Seventy-five years ago the "trial of the century" occurred in the small town of Dayton, Tennessee. Like many historical events, the prosecution of twenty-four-year-old John T. Scopes for violating a new state law prohibiting the teaching of evolution has become enshrouded in myths. Most people derive their perceptions of the Scopes trial from *Inherit the Wind,* the enduring play (1955) and movie (1960) that was more dramatic than authentic. It portrayed Scopes as the heroic victim of fanatical fundamentalists eager to impose biblical literalism upon America's youth. *Inherit the Wind* also implied that the fundamentalist movement was killed in the process of Scopes being convicted.

But as historian Edward Larson reveals in his Pulitzer Prize–winning book, *Summer for the Gods,* the facts surrounding the famous case differ from the prevailing images of it. For example, the trial was staged from the start. No sooner had the Tennessee legislature passed an antievolution statute than the American Civil Liberties Union (ACLU) offered to defend the first teacher who defied it.

The civic leaders of Dayton, eager to bring attention and cash to their decaying mining town, sought to capitalize on the ACLU's offer. They asked Scopes to let them prosecute him for the good of the community. He was cordially "arrested" before heading off for a tennis match, and the planned spectacle was on.

On July 13, the opening day of the trial, Dayton swarmed with hundreds of curiosity seekers and a mob of reporters from across the nation. Radio networks provided live coverage of the proceedings.

The two stars of the show were William Jennings Bryan and Clarence Darrow. The sixty-five-year-old Bryan volunteered his services to the state's prosecution team. A three-time Democratic nominee for president, he had the prestige and eloquence to lead the fundamentalist crusade. The sixty-seven-year-old Darrow was Bryan's polar opposite. A renowned Chicago trial lawyer, he was a militant agnostic who believed that most of the world's evils had been caused by organized religion. Brilliant and quick-witted, Darrow literally forced himself upon the defense team in his effort to prevent "bigots and ignoramuses" from controlling public education.

Bryan and the prosecutors initially stressed that the case had nothing to do with religion; the state legislature had the authority to exclude any subject from the curriculum of the public schools because the legislators represented the will of the majority. Darrow countered that the antievolution statute was illegal because it mandated a particular religious perspective that violated academic freedom and the separation of church and state.

When the judge refused to allow scientific experts to testify about the "truth" of evolutionary theory, it appeared that the trial was over. But Scopes's defense team had one last card to play. They called the celebrated Bryan as a witness for their side. In the trial's most dramatic confrontation, Darrow forced Bryan to admit his ignorance of science and to confess that he did not always accept the Bible as literal truth. Having achieved his primary purpose—to humiliate the godlike Bryan—Darrow offered to save time by asking the jury to find the defendant guilty. He knew they would do so anyway, and he hoped to win the case on appeal to the U.S. Supreme Court. In the end, Scopes was convicted and fined one hundred dollars. Darrow, however, was denied his effort to appeal the case to the Supreme Court when the Tennessee appellate court, while upholding the antievolution statute, overturned the ruling on a technicality regarding the fine.

Despite the prevailing view today that Darrow had lost the case but won the battle against Bryan and old-time religion, no one in 1925 saw the Scopes trial as a triumph for the defense or a defeat for fundamentalism. In fact, the antievolution forces actually went on the offensive after the Scopes trial. State legislatures and school boards throughout the South banned the teaching of evolution. By 1930 only 30 percent of public high schools across the country still taught evolution.

Today, religious groups are pressuring school boards to include Bible-based theories of human origins in the curriculum. A 1993 Gallup poll showed that 47 percent of adults favor creationism over evolution and 35 percent agree the Bible should be taken literally. Last year the Kansas Board of Education voted to drop evolution as a required topic in biology classes. The battle that began in Dayton persists. It endures, says Larson, precisely because it embodies "the characteristically American struggle between individual liberty and majoritarian democracy." And, he might have added, the ongoing struggle between science and religion, knowledge and faith.

Hawaii

We Stole Her Fair and Square

| *July 9, 2000*

Aloha! Our family is enjoying a Polynesian vacation amid pineapples and palms, leis and luaus, daring surfers and graceful hula dancers. It is our first visit to the fiftieth state, and the "land of paradise" has lived up to its fabled reputation. Hawaii is truly an exotic place of spectacular beauty and extraordinary hospitality—punctuated by high prices. Bathed in sunshine and cooled by gentle trade winds, the islands feature rich red soil, lush green plants, and gaily-colored flowers; cloud-crowned volcanic peaks and secluded waterfalls; and, of course, coral beaches shaded by towering palms and laved by white surf and turquoise water.

Hawaii's unique ecosystem includes no snakes. The primary pests are the six million tourists who invade the archipelago each year. Like locusts, we converge from all corners of the globe, swarm into the airports, clog the highways, and invade the beach resorts, flip-flopping our way along the shore at Waikiki and Maui, oblivious to the impact we are having on the state's fragile environment. The Polynesian paradise is quickly turning into the world's playground.

Hawaii has always had an ambivalent relationship with the outside world. When Capt. James Cook, the English naval adventurer, accidentally discovered the islands in 1778 while searching for Asia, a perpetual transaction began between the Polynesian natives and Western entrepreneurs. The Hawaiians killed Cook when he returned a year later, but by then the Englishman had set in motion a cultural exchange that would change the islands forever. Not only did the English introduce goats, pigs, pumpkins, melons, and onions; they also left behind smallpox and venereal diseases that ravaged the Polynesians. By 1890 the native population had plummeted from more than 500,000 to 40,000.

During the early nineteenth century, the Sandwich Islands, as Captain Cook had labeled them in honor of his patron, the Earl of Sandwich, became a popular way station for whalers and traders of all nations. The American invasion of Hawaii was led by Christian missionaries, who began converting the "heathen" natives and sinning sailors in 1820. By the mid-nineteenth century, Americans in Hawaii had shifted their interest from piety to profits. The ferocious demand for cane sugar in California enticed investors to develop large plantations in the islands. In 1875 the American planters convinced Congress to allow Hawaiian sugar to enter the country duty free. Twelve years later, this trade agreement was amended to grant the United States exclusive right to a naval base at Pearl Harbor, outside of Honolulu. These agreements sparked a boom in sugar growing, and Americans came to dominate the economy. In 1887 the Americans forced Hawaii's king to create a constitutional government. This "Bayonet Constitution" weakened the monarchy and strengthened the political clout of the American landowners.

Hawaii's political climate changed dramatically when the king's courageous sister, Queen Liliuokalani, ascended the throne in 1891 and tried to restore Hawaiian sovereignty. The sugar planters responded by organizing a revolt in 1893. The American ambassador in Honolulu used marines to support the rebels and afterward declared that the islands were to be a U.S. protectorate. As he reported to Washington, "The Hawaiian pear is now fully ripe, and this is the golden hour of the United States to pluck it." Within a month, a delegation representing the new American-controlled Hawaiian government visited Washington and signed an annexation treaty.

But the new American president, Grover Cleveland, refused to recognize the treaty and sent a special commissioner to investigate the political situation in Hawaii. The commissioner declared that the American businessmen who had staged the coup had acted improperly. President Cleveland then sought to restore the queen to her throne, but the American rebels resisted. On July 4, 1894, they proclaimed the Republic of Hawaii and called for annexation to America as soon as possible.

There matters remained until William McKinley became president in 1897. Unlike Cleveland, he encouraged Congress to annex Hawaii. A joint resolution by the House and the Senate passed by simple majorities in both houses, and Hawaii was annexed to the United States in the summer of 1898. A little more than sixty years later, in 1959, Hawaii became the fiftieth state.

In 1993 President Bill Clinton signed a congressional resolution formally apologizing to the Hawaiian people for the way in which the American government had interfered in its political life. This month marks the 102nd anniversary of Hawaii's annexation. It is a day marked here more by ambivalence than celebration, as native Hawaiians, now representing only 21 percent of the state's population, grow increasingly concerned about the erosion of their traditional culture and the degradation of their environment. As a local journalist observes, "Pick up any local newspaper in Hawaii and you will read about some beloved beach, some ancestral landmark, some pristine wilderness threatened by development, industry and sheer overpeopling."

What transformations will the next hundred years bring to this island paradise? No one knows for sure, but the traditional Hawaiian welcome of leis and alohas may turn into "no trespassing" signs. Who could blame them? Aloha.

The Greatest Generation

| *May 30, 1999*

I agree with Tom Brokaw: the Americans born in the prosperous twenties and raised during the hardscrabble thirties represent our "greatest generation." Of course, I am biased—my parents are members of that generation. As young adults, they joined millions of others in helping the Allies win a war and defeat fascism.

They emerged from the war mature beyond their years, sobered and disciplined by their experiences, yet upbeat and confident about their prospects. As a group, their patriotism and devotion to God and community have been unmatched by any generation to succeed them. Many of them have seen the best and worst that life has to offer. As Franklin Roosevelt declared, this generation had "a rendezvous with destiny."

Recent movies such as *Saving Private Ryan* and best-selling books—Brokaw's *The Greatest Generation* and Stephen E. Ambrose's *Citizen Soldiers*—are placing a renewed focus on this age group, now in their twilight years. They deserve the attention and the acclaim.

Ambrose, one of America's most gifted historians, notes that it "was a splendid generation, those men and women who fought World War II and then led us through the next forty years. They had unique opportunities and they measured up. They did it, in part, because of what they learned in the war. The value of teamwork. The need for initiative and willingness to accept responsibility. The necessity of discipline. The benefits of deferred gratification. Most of all, a sense of national unity and shared experience."

Yet for all of their accomplishments, the members of this generation remain exceptionally modest when compared to younger folk. Perhaps no one in the Upstate better embodies the spirit of this generation than Joseph A. de Francesco.

This native of France, known for his quick wit and sterling integrity, was awarded an honorary doctor of humanities degree by Furman University. He enrolled at Furman in the fall of 1938 as an exchange student but left after one year to enlist in the armed forces defending his homeland at the start of World War II.

Captured by the German army in early 1940, he escaped and made his way to Algiers, where he rejoined the French army after the Allied landings in North Africa. He went on to serve with both the Free French and United States Armies. In 1943 he joined the Office of Strategic Services and later served as an aide to Gen. Dwight Eisenhower.

In 1944 de Francesco was selected to participate in the secret Jedburgh operation. This elite group of three hundred French, American, and British commandos derived its name from guerrilla bands in the Jedburgh region of twelfth-century Scotland. As D-Day approached in June 1944, the "Jedburghs" parachuted into France. Their mission was to disrupt German military communications and transportation and to lead the French resistance forces in support of the Allied landings. Working in three-man teams, the Jedburghs carried out more than one hundred operations. De Francesco's own team helped delay a German division headed to defend the Normandy beachhead. Twenty-two of the French Jedburghs were captured by the Nazis and shot as spies. "We were told during our training that 75 percent of us would not make it back," says de Francesco. But more than 250 did survive. We had remarkable success."

The Jedburghs were one of the first "special forces" and today are among the most highly decorated of all World War II combat units. Many Jedburghs went on to become generals, ambassadors, and top business executives.

For his efforts during the war, de Francesco received the Bronze Star from the United States and the Croix de Guerre from the French government. In 1994, when he led a contingent of surviving Jedburghs to France to commemorate the fiftieth anniversary of D-Day, he was awarded the French Legion of Honor.

After the war, de Francesco pursued a successful international career in the shoe industry. Upon his retirement, he and his wife returned to South Carolina and settled in Woodruff, where he has worked with Habitat for Humanity, adult literacy programs, and other community endeavors. For his efforts on behalf of Rotary International's Youth Exchange Program, which helps high school students travel to other countries for a year of study, he has been named a Paul Harris Fellow, the organization's highest honor. He has also taught courses in the Furman University Learning in Retirement Program.

Like so many members of his generation, Joseph de Francesco is an ordinary man blessed with extraordinary character, a simple man whose life has been elevated by greatness, a decent man who knows the meaning of personal responsibility, a courageous man who realizes that freedom often requires defending.

The Mighty Eighth

| *October 23, 2000*

Of the sixteen million Americans who served in uniform during the Second World War, fewer than six million remain alive. The survivors represent an invaluable historical resource. I recently had the opportunity to chat with several veterans of the Eighth Air Force. Their story is more compelling than any John Grisham novel or Hollywood script.

Organized in Savannah, Georgia, in 1942, the Mighty Eighth received a mission so unconventional that many deemed it suicidal. From bases in England, the American fliers were to launch long-range bombing missions against Germany's war industries, striking heavily fortified weapons-manufacturing plants, oil refineries, and railroads. The attacks would occur during daylight hours, when the targets could be readily identified and civilian casualties kept to a minimum.

The British airmen, whose previous attempts at daylight bombing had failed miserably, scoffed at this Yankee idea. The skilled German fighter pilots, they said, would cut down the Americans before they could reach their target.

But Gen. Ira Eaker, the resolute Texan who commanded the Eighth, dismissed such concerns. He was convinced that the newly designed B-17 Flying Fortress could fend off Luftwaffe attacks with its nine .50-caliber machine guns. The B-17, he claimed, could also absorb a lot of punishment and keep flying.

Eaker and the Mighty Eighth would prove their critics wrong—but at a high price. In 1943 the Eighth began massive bombing raids on German targets. The casualties were staggering. Because American fighter planes did not have enough fuel to escort the B-17s all the way to the targets, the slow-flying bombers were easy prey for the Luftwaffe.

Of an estimated 200,000 aviators and crewmen who flew with the Eighth, 28,000 were shot down and captured, and another 26,000 lost their lives. No other U.S. military command suffered a higher casualty rate. In the spring of 1944, the Eighth's losses were reduced when long-range P-51 Mustang fighters arrived to escort them to their targets and back.

Dr. John Johns, president emeritus of Furman University, flew thirty-five missions as a member of the Eighth. He and his fellow crew members were keenly aware of the risks; they knew that luck would determine their fate. "I was certainly a lot more superstitious then than I am now," says Johns, who flew his first mission on June 21, 1944, a raid over Berlin. "You wanted to keep doing the same thing while your luck was holding out. During my time as a navigator, I also became more religious."

Bud Porter, a retired General Motors employee living in Hilton Head, flew nine missions with the Eighth as a ball turret gunner. His plane was shot down over Hamburg, but the crew managed to coax the B-17 to a crash landing in Belgium, then under Allied control.

Porter, a native of Newark, New Jersey, vividly recalls the frequent bad weather and the immensity of the bombing effort. "It was like taking off into soup. But once you got above the clouds it was beautiful. As the turret gunner on the bottom of the plane, I would look out and see the sky filled with hundreds of planes. Sometimes the stream of planes would stretch three hundred miles. It was a magnificent sight that I will never forget."

Porter and Johns noted the difficulties of coordinating such a huge stream of bombers through to their targets amid bad weather, mechanical and electronic failures, fighter attacks, smoke screens, antiaircraft artillery defenses, and human errors. It was a wonder that more were not lost.

The veterans highlighted how young the men were—the average age was twenty-three—and the grueling rhythms of their daily regimen. The flight crews would awaken at two in the morning, take off at dawn, and reach the targets over Germany at midday. They would return to the base by late afternoon.

The Eighth included many celebrities. Actor Jimmy Stewart flew twenty combat missions. Clark Gable participated in five missions before Hitler put a bounty on his head that led his commanders—against his wishes—to reassign the film star to noncombat duty.

By disrupting Germany's war economy and transportation system, the Eighth Air Force played a vital role in defeating the Nazis. The group's heroic contributions are highlighted at the Mighty Eighth Air Force Heritage Museum outside of Savannah, Georgia.

Eleanor Roosevelt

Model of Independence

| *August 8, 1999*

Hillary Clinton's bid for a New York Senate seat recalls another politically active first lady, Eleanor Roosevelt. Like Mrs. Clinton, Eleanor Roosevelt was a bold personality and independent thinker.

Unlike Hillary, Eleanor Roosevelt was a real New Yorker. Born in 1884, the niece of Theodore Roosevelt, she grew up in the privileged world of the social elite. Her aloof mother, Anna, died of diphtheria when Eleanor was eight, and only two years later her father died of alcohol abuse. Orphaned at age ten, and plagued by insecurity and shyness, Eleanor went to live with her grandmother in upstate New York. At age fifteen she enrolled in a prestigious finishing school in England. After returning to Manhattan, she participated in the debutante season and began a courtship with her distant cousin Franklin, a handsome, ambitious Harvard graduate. They married in 1905. Over the next ten years or so, she bore six children, one of whom died in infancy. "My family filled my life," she recalled.

Disaster struck in 1918 when Eleanor discovered that Franklin, then serving as assistant secretary of the navy, was engaged in an affair with Lucy Mercer, her friend and social secretary. "The bottom dropped out of my own particular world," Eleanor remembered. "I faced myself, my surroundings, my world honestly for the first time." Still struggling with her own self-esteem, she offered Franklin a divorce. He declined, in part because his imperious mother threatened to disinherit him. A penitent Franklin promised to end his relationship with Mercer (he did not).

Eleanor, then thirty-four, accepted her husband's apologies and decided to continue the marriage, but under new conditions. She now felt free to develop her own personal identity and emotional liberty, and she embarked on a lifetime of social service and political activism. They both realized that their shared goals for the country could be best served through what became an unconventional partnership. What it lacked in personal intimacy it made up for in mutual respect. "There is no experience from which you can't learn something," Eleanor later wrote. "And the purpose of life, after all, is to live it, to taste experience to the utmost, to reach out eagerly and without fear for newer and richer experience."

During the 1920s, Eleanor taught school, managed a business, coordinated political campaigns, chaired investigative committees, and became a respected lobbyist. She championed an array of progressive social causes: affordable housing, child labor regulations, a minimum wage, and civil rights for blacks. At one point the Ku Klux Klan became so concerned about Eleanor's criticism that it offered a reward to any member who would kidnap her.

When Franklin contracted polio in 1921 and became a paraplegic, Eleanor supervised his rehabilitation and bolstered his spirits and political ambitions. She had enormous energy. Compassionate without being maudlin, more stoical than sentimental, she exuded warmth and sincerity, and she challenged the complacency of the affluent. "No woman," observed a friend, "has ever so comforted the distressed or so distressed the comfortable." A Maine fisherman described her endearing qualities: "She ain't stuck up, she ain't dressed up, and she ain't afraid to talk."

After Franklin's election as president in 1932, Eleanor redefined the role of first lady to include a politically prominent role for herself. Franklin was the politician, Eleanor explained; she was the agitator. She was the first woman to address a national political convention, to write a nationally syndicated daily column, and to hold regular press conferences. She crisscrossed the nation during the Great Depression, visiting with migrant workers, coal miners, farmers, blacks, and others hardest hit by the economic crisis. Journalists dubbed her Eleanor Everywhere. Franklin said she served as his "eyes and ears," as well as his conscience. In her travels, Eleanor defied local segregation ordinances, supported women's causes, highlighted the plight of unemployed youth, and implored Americans to live up to their humanitarian ideals.

After Franklin's death in 1945 in Warm Springs, Georgia (with Lucy Mercer at his side), Eleanor continued to play a prominent role in public affairs. As a leading member of the American delegation to the United Nations, she drafted the Declaration of

Human Rights for the U.N. in 1948. At her death in 1962 she was widely recognized as the century's most influential woman. Hillary Clinton claims Eleanor Roosevelt as her heroine. Certainly she can learn from Eleanor's own discovery that it "takes courage to love, but pain through love is the purifying fire which those who live generously know."

The Glorious Fourth

| *July 4, 1997*

Amid the fun and fireworks of America's favorite summer holiday, let us pause to reflect upon the original purpose of Independence Day. Some history is in order. On July 2, 1776, the Second Continental Congress resolved "that these United Colonies are, and of right ought to be, free and independent States, and they are absolved from all allegiance to the British Crown."

This historic action prompted John Adams to predict in a letter to his wife, Abigail, that future generations would remember July 2, 1776, as their "day of deliverance." People would celebrate the occasion with "solemn acts of devotion to God Almighty" and with "pomp and parade, with shows, games, sports, guns, bells, bonfires and Illuminations [fireworks] from one end of this continent to the other, from this time forward, forever more."

Adams got everything right but the date. Americans fastened not upon July 2 but July 4 as their Independence Day. To be sure, it was on the fourth that Congress formally adopted the Declaration of Independence, but the colonies by then had been officially independent for two days. The Declaration of Independence, drafted by Thomas Jefferson, was not read in public until July 8 and was not copied onto parchment and signed by the delegates until August 2. In fact, the last of the fifty-six delegates to sign the document, Thomas McKean of Delaware, waited until 1777 to do so!

July 4 became our Independence Day by accident. In 1777 Congress forgot about any acknowledgment of the first anniversary of independence until July 3, when it was too late to honor July 2. As a consequence, the Fourth won by default.

In 1777, in the midst of the Revolutionary War, the patriots of Boston marked the first full year of independence with great gusto. At dawn ships in Boston harbor fired a "grand salute" to the new day. In the afternoon a prominent minister preached a patriotic sermon to the state legislature. Afterward, Gov. John Hancock proposed thirteen

toasts from the balcony of the statehouse, one for each of the new states. Similar activities occurred throughout the new nation.

As time passed, however, Independence Day celebrations have focused more on entertainment and recreation than remembrance. By 1811 Benjamin Rush, a prominent Philadelphian and signer of the Declaration of Independence, could complain to John Adams that the Fourth of July festivities in his city had neglected to recall their original purpose: "Scarcely a word was said of the solicitude and labors and fears and sorrows and sleepless nights of the men who projected, composed, defended, and subscribed the Declaration of Independence." Another observer lamented that Americans had become so preoccupied with their "private concerns" that they failed to recall, must less appreciate, the historic significance of Independence Day. "The memorable days of our Revolutionary history," sighed a Charlestonian, "do not now bring with them . . . those lively feelings [of patriotism] which they formerly did."

During the 1830s a British observer witnessed his first July 4 celebration in New York and mused: "The Americans may have great reason to be proud of this day, and of the deeds of their forefathers, but why do they get so confoundedly drunk?"

Why indeed. On this Independence Day, let us enjoy the fellowship of family and friends. But in between the roar of powerboats, the sizzle of grilling hamburgers, the fizz released by pulled pop-tops, and the crackle of fireworks, let us also remember that this day is not simply a celebration of ourselves but of our past, and of the sacrifices of others on behalf of the liberties we now hold dear but so often take for granted.

A French Apostle of Liberty

| *June 17, 2001*

Almost every state in America has a town named Fayetteville or a county named Fayette. But few people realize why those place names are so prevalent. They all were named in honor of an adventurous Frenchman: Marie Joseph Paul Yves Roch Gilbert du Motier, better known as the Marquis de Lafayette.

He was only twenty years old and an orphan when he sailed to America to offer his services to George Washington. Lafayette had heard about the American Revolution at a dinner party, and he immediately resolved to help the struggling colonies.

Born in 1757 to a noble family, Lafayette lost both his parents before he was thirteen. His father was killed by the British in the Seven Years' War, and the young Lafayette yearned to become a soldier himself. "I was crazy to wear a uniform," he remembered. And he wanted revenge against the British. So in 1777 Lafayette used part of a substantial inheritance to outfit a ship. Leaving behind his pregnant wife and year-old daughter, and knowing no English, he set sail for Philadelphia. Upon his arrival, the Continental Congress appointed him major general (he refused payment for his services).

Young Lafayette had little military experience but limitless energy and conviction. The red-headed romantic was intoxicated by a love of liberty and driven by what Thomas Jefferson later called "a canine appetite for fame." Gen. George Washington found Lafayette captivating. He wrote to Congress that the young Frenchman "possesses a large share of bravery and military ardor." At the Battle of Brandywine, Lafayette was shot in the leg. After recovering, he joined Washington's threadbare army for the brutal winter at Valley Forge. There he earned the nickname "The Soldier's Friend" for sharing the troops' privations and relentlessly foraging for provisions. He returned to France in 1779 to enlist greater French support for the American rebellion and brought back a fresh commitment of soldiers, weapons, and cash for the cause. As one of Washington's division commanders, he played a vital role in the entrapment of Gen. Charles Cornwallis and the British army at the decisive Battle of Yorktown.

Having helped America gain its independence, Lafayette returned to France in 1781, a "hero in two worlds." For the rest of his life, the democratic aristocrat remained an incessant champion of liberty. He promoted independence for Greece, Italy, and Poland, and he played a leading role in the early stages of the French Revolution.

In 1789, after an enraged crowd stormed the Bastille in Paris and released its prisoners, Lafayette sent George Washington the key to the jail as a souvenir. Lafayette then drafted a French bill of rights inspired by Jefferson's Declaration of Independence. But his moderate stance irritated the more radical French revolutionaries. In 1792 he fell afoul of the Jacobins when he tried to protect the royal family from execution. The Assembly denounced him as a traitor, and he fled to Belgium, where an Austrian patrol captured him. While imprisoned in an Austrian dungeon, Lafayette learned that many of his relatives were guillotined in Paris during the Reign of Terror. His despondent wife and daughters traveled to Vienna to beg for his release but only gained permission to join Lafayette in his cell. After Napoleon Bonaparte defeated the Austrians in 1797, Lafayette and his family gained their release. Back in France, Lafayette eventually became a leading member of the Chamber of Deputies. At La Grange, his French estate (for which La Grange, Georgia, is named), he hosted freedom fighters from around the world.

Throughout his turbulent life, Lafayette maintained an intense affection for the United States. He carried on a regular correspondence with George Washington, James Madison, and Thomas Jefferson, and he named his first son George Washington and a daughter Virginia.

In 1824 President James Monroe and the Congress invited Lafayette to visit the United States in anticipation of the fiftieth anniversary of the Revolution. After his triumphal arrival in New York City, the theatrical Lafayette spent nineteen months visiting all twenty-four states, drawing huge crowds, and delivering rousing speeches. He dined in the White House with President Monroe and visited Jefferson at Monticello. In Columbia he toured South Carolina College (now the University of South Carolina). In Tennessee he was greeted by Gen. Andrew Jackson, the hero of the Battle of New Orleans.

The Marquis de Lafayette died on May 20, 1834, at the age of seventy-six. His coffin was covered with earth from the battlefield at Bunker Hill that he had brought back with him in 1825. The American flag has flown over Lafayette's grave ever since. A new flag is raised every July 4. His name continues to symbolize an audacious commitment to freedom. He was indeed an apostle of liberty. Vive Lafayette!

John Brown

Martyr or Madman?

| *November 18, 2001*

The terrorists who crashed into the World Trade Center and the Pentagon were convinced they were messengers from God engaged in a holy war. Such fanaticism is not unique to Islam. Virtually all religions have spawned violent zealots willing to die—and kill—for their beliefs.

John Brown, for example, believed that God had appointed him "a special agent of death" to "break the jaws of the wicked" and eliminate the "wicked curse of slavery." Born in Connecticut in 1800 and raised on the Ohio frontier, Brown grew up in an intensely reverent Christian household. His parents were ardent opponents of slavery, and young John inherited both their fervent religious beliefs and their antislavery convictions. A confirmed Calvinist, he was convinced that a righteous and angry God demanded strict obedience and exacted stern punishment.

Brown struggled all his life to find a successful calling. He worked as a tanner, shepherd, and farmer, served as an itinerant minister, speculated in real estate, and traded in cattle, but never prospered enough to end his chronic indebtedness. Burdened by frustration at his business failures, Brown increasingly identified his suffering with that of the slaves. He developed an intense desire to punish slaveholders for their wickedness.

In 1837, when Brown learned that an antislavery editor had been killed by a mob in Illinois, he stood up in his Ohio church and declared: "Here before God, in the presence of these witnesses, I consecrate my life to the destruction of slavery." By mid-century, Brown had come to view himself as a latter-day Moses. God had dispatched him to free the slaves and lead them to the promised land.

It was on the plains of Kansas that John Brown initiated his campaign for racial justice. Slavery had been prohibited in the new territories of Kansas and Nebraska, but in

1854 Congress passed a law allowing the settlers of each territory to vote on the issue. Throughout 1854 and 1855 Kansas became a battleground between pro- and antislavery settlers. Brown called on volunteers to join him in a "secret mission." On the night of May 23, 1856, he rode with four of his sons and three others into a proslavery village along Pottawatomie Creek in southeastern Kansas. Brown's self-appointed vigilantes of virtue dragged five men from their cabins and hacked them to death with broadswords in front of their screaming families.

What came to be called the Pottawatomie Massacre ignited guerrilla warfare in Kansas. On August 30, Missouri "border ruffians" raided the antislavery settlement at Osawatomie. They looted and burned houses, and shot John Brown's son Frederick through the heart. The elder Brown, who barely escaped, looked back at the burning village being devastated by "Satan's legions" and muttered, "God sees it." He then swore to his surviving sons and followers: "I have only a short time to live—only one death to die, and I will die fighting for the cause."

In October 1859 fugitive John Brown sent shock waves across the United States when he and twenty followers, including five blacks, seized the federal arsenal at Harper's Ferry, Virginia. He intended to arm slaves in the area and spark a slave insurrection throughout the South. But his plans were foiled when townsfolk discovered the raiders and alerted the militia. Brown and his men holed up in the fire engine house, where they were surrounded.

Colonel Robert E. Lee and his aide, Lieutenant J. E. B. Stuart, arrived with a force of marines that stormed the engine house. A young officer found Brown kneeling with his rifle cocked. Before the pious patriarch could fire, the marine thrust his sword forward, striking Brown's belt buckle with such force that it bent the blade back on itself. He then used the hilt to beat Brown unconscious. The siege was over. Brown's men had killed four people and wounded nine. Of their own group, ten died (including two of Brown's sons) and seven were captured.

The wounded Brown was convicted of treason on October 31. At his sentencing he delivered an emotional speech: "Now, if it is deemed necessary that I should forfeit my life for the furtherance of the ends of justice . . . I say, let it be done." On December 2,

1859, Brown donned black pants, a black coat, and a black hat, then climbed into a wagon and sat on a coffin as he rode to the gallows. He died "with unflinching firmness," believing that slavery would be ended only through "very much bloodshed."

Although Brown had failed in his effort to start a slave revolt, he had become a martyr for the antislavery cause in the North. As the editor of a Pittsburgh newspaper proclaimed, "While millions of prayers went up for the old martyr yesterday, so millions of curses were uttered against the hellish system which so mercilessly and ferociously cried out for his blood." Brown's desperate actions panicked the slaveholding South. Militia companies were called out to patrol the streets in every major city and town.

Was John Brown a bloodthirsty madman or a principled militant doing God's bidding? Opinions continue to differ about the murderous idealist. Conclusions regarding his enigmatic personality remain hidden in the folds of history, heaven, and hell.

Today, religious belief remains a powerful catalyst for violence in the name of justice. John Brown has many modern counterparts who attack the innocent in order to remedy the alleged evils of society. Like Brown, these pious terrorists assault the complexities of injustice with the terrible certitude of violence. A nation of laws cannot endorse such murderous idealism. Abraham Lincoln spoke for many when he observed after Brown's execution: "We cannot object [to his hanging] even though he agreed with us in thinking slavery wrong. That cannot excuse violence, bloodshed, and treason."

Invading Afghanistan

| *October 21, 2001*

Afghanistan may be a forbidding land of steep mountains and barren plateaus, but it has also been a place of immense strategic importance for thousands of years. It has served as the enticing crossroads of central Asia, connecting India with Iran, Russia with China. As a gateway between Europe and Asia, it has lured hosts of adventurers, missionaries, and invaders: Persians and Uzbeks, Tajiks and Greeks, Mongols and Russians. During the nineteenth century, the British decided that their continuing control of India, the jewel of their empire, depended upon their subduing the warring nomadic tribes of Afghanistan. The catastrophic British experience in the rugged land offers important lessons for the allied coalition against Osama bin Laden and his Taliban hosts.

In late 1838 the Army of the Indus, comprising 16,500 British, Indian, and Afghan troops, set out from Lahore, in what is now Pakistan, to invade Afghanistan. Their purpose was to establish a bulwark against the southward advance of an increasingly ambitious Russia. Traveling with the army were 38,000 servants and family members. Opposing the British and Indians were Afghans led by a charismatic Pushtun tribal leader named Dost Mohammad. He had assumed control of the throne in Kabul in 1826. In July 1839 the British won a decisive victory. Dost Mohammad and a few loyal followers were exiled to India, and the British installed a puppet ruler named Shah Shujah. Believing the country sufficiently subdued by their use of bribes and bayonets, the British sent most of their solders back to India. But the various Afghan tribes never accepted the authority of the new king or his British protectors. Resentment festered, and in late 1841 the Afghans staged a general uprising. British officials were killed and dismembered, and the British-Indian army was surrounded.

On January 1, 1842, the British negotiated a capitulation agreement that promised a safe withdrawal from Kabul and through the mountain passes to the British garrison at Jalalabad, some ninety miles away. The Afghans insisted, however, that several soldiers be kept behind as hostages to ensure that the British force lived up to its promise to leave. On January 6, the demoralized British and Indians began their hasty retreat eastward through the snowbound passes. The week-long trek was an unmitigated disaster. Afghan tribesmen repeatedly ambushed the fleeing invaders as they groped their way along the high-walled canyons. Others among the retreating army died from exposure and exhaustion. Those who surrendered or were wounded were killed. The besieged British troops made their last stand at a place called Gandamak. Hopelessly outnumbered and armed with only twenty muskets and forty bullets, the sixty-five soldiers were slaughtered.

Of the 4,500 British and Indian troops and 12,000 civilians—men, women, and children—who left Kabul, only one man, an army doctor wounded by an Afghan knife, made it out of the country to Jalalabad. Only a few others, nine children, eight women, and two men, were taken back to Kabul as prisoners. In his poem "The Young British Soldier," Rudyard Kipling conveyed with chilling precision the pitiless ferocity of the Afghans:

When you're wounded and left
On Afghanistan's plains,
And the women come out
To cut up your remains
Just roll on your rifle
And blow out your brains,
And go to your Gawd
Like a soldier.

When word of the humiliating debacle in Afghanistan reached London, the government immediately ordered a new expeditionary force to the region. In the fall of 1842, this new British army entered Kabul long enough to rescue the British hostages and prisoners and burn the city center. They left behind a seething resentment of foreign intervention that has lasted to this day. Although British and Russian invaders would repeatedly return to Afghanistan, the Afghans take great pride in the fact that they have never been conquered by a non-Islamic power. Their tenacity, resourcefulness, and zealotry have made them formidable opponents in their own land.

Desperately poor Afghanistan remains a strategic place, but for new reasons: it has become the crossroads of international terrorism. President Bush has warned that rooting out the al Qaida terrorists and the Taliban who give them sanctuary will be a nasty business. The fighting will be unconventional; the Taliban have shown little interest in the etiquette of war outlined in the Geneva Convention. Prolonged ground combat will test the fortitude of the American people. The allied coalition has assembled the forces to prevail in Afghanistan. Do we have the will to endure a protracted conflict? Will we have the insight to avoid the errors of previous interventions in Afghanistan? Only time will tell. But the fact that the leaders of the United States and Great Britain are wrestling openly with these questions is encouraging. As British Prime Minister Tony Blair stressed, "We will act with reason and resolve"—and a close reading of history, one hopes.

The Election of 1876

| *November 18, 2001*

Commentators keep saying the nation has never experienced such a protracted presidential stalemate as that between Al Gore and George Bush. In fact, however, the bitterly contested presidential election of 1876 makes what is going on this year seem like a minor disagreement.

In 1876 Republican Rutherford B. Hayes campaigned against the New York Democrat Samuel J. Tilden. As the voting began on November 7, Hayes, a Union war hero then serving his third term as Ohio's governor, predicted that Tilden, a wealthy corporate lawyer and reform governor of New York, would win the election.

The early returns showed Tilden ahead in New York, New Jersey, Connecticut, Indiana, and all of the southern states. By midnight Hayes had resigned himself to defeat "after a very close contest." He consoled his wife, Lucy, and went to bed. He awoke to read newspaper headlines declaring Tilden the victor.

Yet while Hayes had slumbered, Republican Party leaders had hatched a plan to snatch victory from the jaws of defeat and in the process plunge the nation into a protracted crisis. Although Tilden won more than a quarter million more votes overall than Hayes, the Republican strategists knew that their candidate could claim the presidency if he could win back the electoral votes in Florida, Louisiana, and South Carolina—all closely contested states still dominated by Republican regimes reinforced by federal troops. In the early morning hours of November 8, Republican leaders sent telegraph messages to their allies on the official canvassing boards in the three key southern states, ordering them to challenge the initial election returns. Later that day a phalanx of "visiting statesmen" from both parties headed south to try to influence the final tallies.

In each of the three southern states, there was widespread evidence of bribery, forgery, and intimidation. Republicans argued that white Democrats had coerced black Republicans into not voting. Democrats countered that the Republicans used federal troops to ensure high participation by black voters, some of whom voted more than once. Both parties accused the other of stuffing ballot boxes. The governor of Louisiana revealed that he was willing to "sell" his state's electoral votes for $200,000.

In the end, the Republican-controlled election boards invalidated thousands of "fraudulent" Democratic votes, declared Hayes the winner in each of the three contested states, and appointed Hayes's supporters as the official electors. Local Democrats filed their own set of rival returns and put forward their own slate of electors. Americans now confronted an unprecedented dilemma: each party claimed victory in the contested states, and each accused the other of fraud. It fell to Congress to decide who would win the electoral votes of Florida, Louisiana, and South Carolina—and thus win the presidency. Yet the Democrats controlled the House, and the Republicans controlled the Senate. Neither body would allow the other the responsibility to certify the electors.

The confusing situation grew more chaotic and riotous as the weeks passed. Someone fired a bullet into Hayes's house in Columbus. Newspaper editorials expressed concern about growing civil unrest. The *Albany Argus* saw "the prospect of war on every street and on very highway of the land" if Hayes were given the presidency.

Finally, as the New Year arrived with no resolution, Congress created a bipartisan electoral commission to decide the matter. The fifteen-member commission was composed of five senators, five representatives, and five Supreme Court justices. They included seven Republicans, seven Democrats, and Justice David Davis, an independent thought to be pro-Democratic.

However, just days before the commission was to meet, shortsighted Democrats in the Illinois legislature elected Davis to the U.S. Senate, requiring him to resign from the electoral commission. The appointment of Davis's replacement, Justice Joseph P. Bradley, gave the GOP a slim 8-7 edge on the commission.

In early February the commission, by a strict party-line vote, recommended to the House that all the contested electoral votes be awarded to Hayes. Democrats in the House threatened to filibuster.

A greater crisis was averted through a series of secret meetings at which Republican and Democratic officials struck an informal bargain. The Republicans promised that Hayes, if named president, would withdraw the last federal troops from the southern states, letting their Republican governments collapse. In return, the Democrats would adopt the electoral commission's recommendation. A magnanimous Governor Tilden urged the Congress to endorse the recommendation.

On March 2, just two days before the scheduled inauguration, the House voted to accept the commission's report and declared Hayes the new president by an electoral vote of 185 to 184. The so-called Compromise of 1877 brought an end to federally enforced Reconstruction and ultimately permitted the return of white supremacist rule in the South.

The disputed election of 1876 dogged Hayes, an honest man, the remainder of his days. His critics often referred to him as His Fraudulency. Hayes honored his commitment to serve only one term as president and retired to Ohio in 1881.

Hayes penned in his diary what he hoped the nation would learn from his controversial election: "All thoughtful people are brought to consider the imperfect machinery provided for electing the President. No doubt we shall, warned by this danger, provide, by amendments of the Constitution, or by proper legislation, against a recurrence of the danger."

Perhaps this time we will follow Hayes's advice.

Christmas Musings

| *December 21, 1997*

Amid this Christmas season many of us find ourselves torn between conflicting interests. While recognizing that Christmas is intended to be a holy day celebrating the birth of Jesus, we are preoccupied with buying presents or imagining what Santa will bring us.

Christmas, however, has long been associated with contrasting activities. In ancient times it was a prolonged festival known as Saturnalia, a boisterous and licentious secular event celebrating the end of the harvest season, the arrival of the winter solstice, and the start of a new year. It took on a Christian connotation in the fourth century, when Pope Julian I established December 25 as the date to honor the birth of Christ. The date was chosen in an attempt to co-opt Saturnalia activities.

In the seventeenth century, New England Puritans tried to suppress Christmas revelry by fining people who engaged in "feasting" or abstained from work. They insisted that any celebration of the Lord's birth was without biblical sanction. In their view, Christmas was a relic of paganism and popery.

The Puritans also wanted to avoid transplanting to the New World the gluttony, drunkenness, dancing, gambling, and mass begging that characterized the Christmas season in Europe. The Reverend Cotton Mather abhorred the "abominable things" that took place in conjunction with Christmas. He and others especially disliked the practice of wassailing, when gangs of drunken youths would besiege the homes of the wealthy, demanding food, drink, and money—or else. One wassail song made blunt threats:

We've come here to claim our right . . .
And if you don't open your door,
We will lay you flat upon the floor.

So much for the Christmas spirit! (The southern colonies, by the way, maintained the pagan Christmas traditions without apology.)

As time passed, the Puritans lost out to the partyers, and raucous Christmas celebrations became commonplace in American society. One almanac included a bit of Christmas doggerel that highlights popular priorities:

Christmas is come, hang on the pot,
Let spits turn round, and ovens be hot;
Beef, pork , and poultry, now provide,
To feast thy neighbors at this tide;
Then wash it all down with good wine and beer,
And so with mirth conclude the YEAR.

Often the celebrants became so rambunctious that they threatened civil order. Shopkeepers barred their doors, and wealthy folk hired armed guards to protect their property. In 1828 officials in New York City established the first professional police force after a season of particularly violent Christmas brawls.

During the 1820s, the perennial chaos associated with Christmas prompted efforts by the social and political elite to reform the holiday tradition. Clement Clarke Moore, the wealthy son of New York's Episcopal bishop, led the crusade. With his popular 1822 poem, "A Visit from Saint Nicholas" (also called "The Night before Christmas"), Moore initiated the idea of a jolly, sleigh-riding night visitor who brought gifts to children at Christmastime. Newspaper editors and retailers joined in the effort to transform Christmas into a family-oriented holiday centered on gifts. By 1908 a trade publication could announce that "Christmas is the merchant's harvest time, and it is up to him to garner in as big a crop of dollars as he can."

Although rambunctious activity and drunken marauding continued during Christmases throughout the nineteenth century, the occasion slowly began to center on children and the home. By midcentury, Santa Claus had become a common figure in stories and advertisements. At the same time, people redoubled their efforts to infuse Christmas with more explicit religious overtones. For churchgoers, biblical stories about the gifts of the Wise Men, the baby Jesus, the Holy Family, and the benedictions of angels provided captivating symbols around which to organize a feast of familial gift giving.

Likewise, the most familiar Christmas hymns were composed or updated during the nineteenth century to consecrate the occasion.

By the closing decades of the nineteenth century, the tension between Christmas reverence and retailing was firmly in place. As a magazine editorial declared in 1887, "Let us get back to first principles. What is Christmas for? Not to enrich the shopkeepers." Nine years later a convention of ministers was called in New York City to discuss how to deflect the "extravagant expenditure" of Christmas into "more spiritual and scriptural channels."

So the tensions we feel this Christmas between piety and indulgence, reverence and consumerism, are not new to the American scene. Putting "Christ back in Christmas" is an old objective. The fact that it has proven so difficult does not make it any less imperative. Let us recall that the only gifts Jesus wanted were our devotion to God and our love for others. Merry Christ-mas!

"Auld Lang Syne"

| *December 31, 2000*

With the exception of "Happy Birthday," it is probably the most recognizable song in the English-speaking world. But every December 31, when millions raise their glass, link arms, and toast the New Year, few will actually know the words to "Auld Lang Syne." Fewer still are familiar with its colorful author.

"Auld Lang Syne" was first published in 1796, and researchers think at least half of the verses were written by Robert Burns. The son of a tenant farmer, Burns never claimed full credit for the song, confessing that he transcribed part of it "from an old man's singing." Literary historians continue to debate whether Burns is Scotland's greatest poet, but all agree he was the most romantic and sentimental.

The phrase *auld lang syne* means "from long ago." Like many of Burns's works, the song celebrates long-remembered friendships and loves, the joys of the past, and, of course, imbibing in the "cup of kindness."

"Auld Lang Syne" was one of more than one thousand poems and songs that Burns authored during his short life of thirty-seven years. His works have been translated into more languages than any other poet, except Shakespeare.

Many of Burns's phrases have become part of our common expression. How often, while reading the morning paper, have we pondered "man's inhumanity to man," or resigned ourselves to the truth that "no man can tether time or tide," or steeled ourselves with the resolve to "do or die"?

Burns toiled most of his life as a tenant farmer and tax collector. In 1786, however, he published a volume titled *Poems, Chiefly in the Scottish Dialect.* It was an immediate success, hailed by simple country folk and sophisticated critics alike. Flushed with his sudden fame, the twenty-six-year-old Burns set out for Edinburgh, where he was celebrated by the city's elite.

Burns's songs and ballads provide earthy accounts of eating, drinking, and carousing. The poet was a literal romantic who constantly crossed the bounds of acceptable behavior. He fathered fifteen children, six out of wedlock. To his credit, though, the "Ploughman Poet" accepted paternal responsibility for all of his children, and he provided them with financial support.

Burns described himself as a "miserable dupe to love." He added that "God knows I am no saint. I have a whole host of follies and sins to answer for." Yet people loved him despite his excesses. His lover and later wife, Jean Armour, once lamented, "Poor Rob—he should have two wives."

Women forgave Burns's wandering eye in part because he was so charming and affectionate. A Scottish woman declared that "no man's conversation ever carried her so off her feet" as that of Burns. He showered women with poetry, songs, and soul-baring letters. He relished their company, once announcing that the "sweetest hours that e'er I spent are spent among the lasses."

In 1789 Burns secured a post as a tax collector and moved to Dumfries in 1791, where he lived until his death. He produced the bulk of his poetry during the final twelve years of life. Some of his detractors claimed the poet died of venereal disease, but most scholars believe he died of heart disease exacerbated by the hard manual labor he undertook as a youth. More than ten thousand people clogged the streets of Dumfries to mourn Burns's death. His popularity has grown ever since.

So this New Year's Eve, as you are toasting the coming year, raise a glass to Robert Burns and learn the words to "Auld Lang Syne." You will impress your friends.

Should auld acquaintance be forgot,
And never brought to mind?
Should auld acquaintance be forgot,
And auld lang syne?

For auld lang syne, my dear
For auld lang syne,
We'll take a cup o' kindness yet,
For auld lang syne!

And surely ye'll be your pint-stop [pay for your drink],
And surely I'll be mine;
And we'll take a cup o' kindness yet,
For auld lang syne.

We twa hae run about the braes [hillsides],
And pou'd [pulled] the gowans [daisies] fine;
But we've wander'd mony a weary foot,
Sin auld lang syne.

And there's a hand, my trusty fiere,
And gie's a hand o' thine,
And we'll take a right guid-willie waught [goodwill drink],
For auld lang syne.

ing as a consultant to business, he formerly served in various federal agencies in such positions as personnel director, employment and employee relations supervisor, and training and development specialist. Dr. Short has published articles in *Management Review, Resource, MSU Business Topics, Personnel Journal, Public Administration Review,* and *Training and Development Journal.*

William P. Smith, DBA (Arizona State University), is an assistant professor of management at Hofstra University. He is a member of the Academy of Management and local chapters of the American Society of Personnel Administration and American Society of Training and Development. His professional interests focus on temporary employment and employee turnover and absenteeism.

Carol L. Stamm, PhD (University of Wisconsin, Madison), is assistant vice president for academic affairs at Western Michigan University. Her research interests include inventory control, quality control, and measurement theory. She has numerous publications in a variety of journals.

Sherry E. Sullivan, PhD (Ohio State University), is associate professor of management at Bowling Green State University. She has published more than 20 articles, including ones that appeared in the *Journal of Management, Journal of Applied Psychology,* and *Career Development Quarterly.* Her research interests include stress management, career transitions, and compensation systems.

James M. Todd, PhD (University of Texas), is professor of management at Fogelman College of Business and Economics, Memphis State University. He is the author of several cases. In addition, he served as president of the Southern Management Association.

Jerry L. Wall, PhD, SPHR (University of Missouri, Columbia), is director of the Center for Business and Economic Research and professor of management at Northeast Louisiana University. He holds senior-level accreditations in both personnel research and training and development from the Personnel Accreditation Institute. He has consulted extensively in both the public and private sector, is the author of numerous articles, papers, and books, and has served as president of the Midwest Society for Human Resources and Industrial Relations.

Alice H. Walton, PhD (Iowa State University), an assistant professor in the College of Business Administration at the University of Mercy, specializes in human resource management and organizational behavior. Dr. Walton is also coprincipal of a human resource management consulting firm and a business focusing on the placement of individuals with disabilities. She is also a member of the Academy of Management, American Psychological Association, American Society of Training and Development, and the Society for Human Resource Management.

John P. Wanous, PhD (Yale University), is professor of management in the College of Business at Ohio State University, where he teaches organizational behavior and human resource management at the undergraduate, masters, and doctoral levels. His research has focused on realistic recruitment processes (RJPs). He is a fellow of the American Psychological Association.

Edward G. Wertheim, PhD (Yeshiva University), teaches organizational behavior and human resources management at the College of Business Administration, Northeastern University, at Boston, Massachusetts. He has published widely in the areas of performance appraisal, career development, and organizational behavior issues in high-technology management.

Dianne H.B. Welsh, PhD (University of Nebraska, Lincoln), is an assistant professor of management at Eastern Washington University in Spokane. She teaches organizational behavior, human resource management, and organization theory and management. Her research interests include reward systems, international applications of behavior management, and ethics. Her most recent publication is entitled, "Managing Russian factory Workers: The Impact of U.S.-Based Behavioral and Participative Techniques," which appeared in *Academy of Management Journal.*

Elizabeth C. Wesman, PhD (Cornell University), is an assistant professor of personnel and industrial relations at the School of Management, Syracuse University. Her research interests are in the area of employment discrimination and international labor relations. She has published articles on sexual harassment, comparable worth, and the study of unions as organizations.

Roy H. Williams, PhD (University of Alabama, Tuscaloosa), is professor of management information systems and decision science in the Fogelman College of Business and Economics at Memphis State University. He has taught for many years in the fields of management, production and operations management, and statistics, with special emphasis on use of computers to enhance the several areas of interest. He has been active in consulting and case development for executive MBA programs. He is a member of DSI and the American Statistical Association.

Floyd G. Willoughby, PhD (Michigan State University), teaches strategic management, human resources management courses, and a research course at the undergraduate and graduate levels. He does research in the area of competitive positioning and implications for human resources planning and management. He actively consults with medium-sized, high-technology business in the Metropolitan Detroit area.

Kenneth M. York, PhD (Bowling Green State University), is associate professor of management and chairman of the department of management and marketing at the School of Business Administration, Oakland University. He has published research on the application of behavior and quantitative decision theory to evaluating incidents of possible sexual harassment in the workplace. He develops and makes extensive use of experiential learning exercises in his organizational behavior and human resource management courses.

OTHER CONTRIBUTORS

James Ball
Robert S. Burns
Curtis Campbell
Karen Baretta Chandler
Kendra Clausen
Byron Curtis
V. Carol Danehower
Toni A. Denton
Linda Dudgeon
Wendy Eager
Felicia A. Finston
Cliff Hodge
John Konica
Penny Richards
Right Associates, Inc.
Pamela Stevens
Mike Struth
John C. Sulzer
Robert R. Taylor
Janet Taynor
James R. Terborg
John P. Wanous
Robert L. Williams
American Association of Retired Persons
Assessment Designs, Inc.
Executive Enterprises, Inc.
University of Southern California
West Publishing Company
John Wiley & Sons, Inc.

Contents

Introduction

Any textbook can provide an extensive overview of the human resource management function. Here I provide a brief discussion so you have a bit of background about the key role played by those who participate in human resource management activities. In the world of managers there are three key variables: people, things, and data. The most difficult of the three factors to manage is people, and yet people have the greatest impact upon an organization's success or failure.

Human Resource Management (HRM) is the profession that attempts to develop programs, policies, procedures and activities to promote the satisfaction of both individual and organizational goals, objectives, and needs. Who is involved in the broad domain of HRM? The group includes executives, managers, line supervisors, staff supervisors, and personnel professionals. The person engaged in HRM activities does not have to be a personnel professional! This fact makes a book of this type critically important. A supervisor or manager may be engaged in interviews, performance appraisal, training and development decisions or other HRM activities. In addition, the book attempts to bridge the gap between textbook theory and real world experience.

My own background of having worked several years before I pursued a college education and my experience as a student who worked full time while going to school in the evenings led to my need to create a book that brings the real world to the student. On too many occasions the professor taught the textbook but never related theory to practice. This book provides a series of experiences designed to help you understand better the management of people at work. The media used include cases, incident cases, role-playing exercises, cost-benefit, field, and in-basket exercises. The section of the book that introduces each medium will explain what it is, why it was chosen, and how to use it. A variety of experiences is provided to involve you in real-world problems and, thus, help you gain an understanding of people at work. Some of you will be introduced to personnel work through these media. Most will already have been exposed to the literature and research of personnel. Many of you have had experiences at work that will help you deal with the exercises. However, realize that even as I write this book new case law is being written, new court cases are being heard and new HRM situations are coming to the attention of the public. Emerging issues include violence in the workplace, treatment of employees who contract AIDS, discrimination on the basis of employee lifestyle, and additional guidance related to employee surveillance issues.[1]

Most of the topics that are usually considered as part of personnel or managing people at work are treated herein. Cases or exercises are included about such topics as employment (manpower), planning, recruiting people, and selecting applicants. Experiences also are given about orienting and assigning people to jobs, developing careers, and evaluating employees' performance. Some cases or exercises deal with developing managers, compensating people for their work, training, providing safe working conditions, and coping with unions. Other cases and exercises deal with difficult employees, minority employment, leadership and supervision, and evaluation of the effectiveness of the personnel program.

People work for many different kinds of organizations; therefore, many different kinds of examples are given. The settings include small, medium, and large organizations from many places in the United States and abroad. The settings are in business, government, hospitals, universities, and symphony orchestras. Some cases depict good personnel practices; others depict poor personnel practices. Rarely is there just one factor to be considered. Most often there are one or more major factors and some secondary factors.

In doing these exercises, which simulate real life, you may often feel you don't have all the information you'd like to have before making a decision. Actually, there are many real-life situations where there isn't sufficient time or money to acquire enough information. Sometimes the information isn't available. You often may wish to state what additional information you would *like* to have; however, based on what you know now and what you can reasonably infer, you can make your decisions accordingly.

Most of the situations presented here are disguised; nevertheless, all are based on real situations. Few organizations like to reveal real situations. Cases are designed not to illustrate optimum conditions but to serve as learning mechanisms that will allow you to distill your experience, the theories you have learned, and the research you have carried out and to apply them to a given situation.

WHAT IS HUMAN RESOURCE MANAGEMENT?

There are many definitions of Human Resource Management (HRM). One I like best is offered by George T. Milkovich and John W. Boudreau (1994). In their very successful textbook, these authors define human resource management as "a series of integrated decisions about the employment relationship that influences the effectiveness

---

[1] Recent census data reveals that in five states, homicide is the leading cause of death in the workplace. Case law with regard to interpretations of the Americans with Disabilities Act and employees with AIDS will occur and a body of case law will exist in the area of employer obligations with regard to employee surveillance.

of employees and organizations." The definition is an important one, in that it reflects the evolution of human resources management as we know it today from the old welfare departments of the early 1900s.

Shortly after the turn of the century, the development of the managerial school of thought known as **Scientific Management** came into vogue. Scientific management emphasized the importance of hiring employees who had the skills, knowledge, and abilities for the machinery in use. Matching the worker to the machine and providing financial incentives was the means to greater productivity. Decisions about what to do and how to do the work came from management. HRM functions were performed by the higher-ranking people. Around the second decade of the century and until about 1930, very basic personnel functions (e.g., screening, recordkeeping, and payroll) were performed by personnel departments. The role of personnel departments expanded significantly over the next 40 years. The **Hawthorne Experiments** of the late 1920s provided a powerful impetus for change. The experiments done at the old Hawthorne Works in New York State led to the conclusion that satisfied workers can be productive workers. In essence, monetary rewards *and* non-monetary rewards positively impact performance.

The expanding role of labor unions and flurry of new laws during the period of the 1930s through the 1970s led to the creation of two specialized departments within the human resources management function: labor relations and personnel administration. Evidence of expansion of the HRM role in organizations could be seen in terms of the personnel departments' involvement in staffing, training, development, compensation, placement, union relations, contract negotiation, and grievance handling, among other activities.

During the last quarter century the world has shrunk and the personnel administration role has taken on a new name and ever-broadening responsibilities. Human resource management is much more than a name change. HRM as a name recognizes people as a resource and asset to the firm. Employees are recognized as the difference between success and failure in the competitive environment of our ever-shrinking world.

The past 10 years have provided new challenges and heightened the focus of old challenges to the organizations of the 1990s and beyond. Noe et al. (1994) identify global, quality, technology and structure, and social challenges that must be addressed if an organization is to be successful. These authors note "that we are in the midst of a global restructuring of the world's markets." As U.S. companies expand into these international markets, they must better prepare employees for the challenge international assignments represent. This preparation must include preparing the family for the separation involved or transition to living abroad and assisting the employee to understand the culture better (e.g., time, goal, social orientation).

Total quality management or continuous quality improvement are just two of the names given to a commitment to quality, an identification of the customer(s), knowledge of what the customer(s) want, and meeting or exceeding the customers' service and product needs. Quality has become a way of life for many firms; firms that are driven by a customer-focused obsession that always has employees seeking ways to improve on existing processes and results. Employee expertise is utilized and decisions are based on fact. The **Malcolm Baldrige National Quality Award** represents tangible recognition for those organizations that lead the way in quality achievements. Colleges and universities, often led by their business schools or schools of engineering, are integrating quality issues into their curriculum and forming quality councils to address improvement in their own processes.

Technology and structure are very important variables in the success equation. We appear to have created a new world overnight, given the rapid change in technology and its impact upon everything we do. To match the new ways of doing business that have moved us from reliance on main frame computers familiar to a relative few trained experts to the world of networks in every office and personal computers on every desk, new organizational structures have evolved. Instead of traditional organizations with lines and boxes, we see self-managed work teams visually represented as pizzas with pepperoni inside. Inside, in truth, are the people with the needed skill sets to accomplish the goals related to their particular mission. For business schools and for human resource management, that means assuring that an employee has good human relations, teamwork, leadership, and related qualitative skills.

The social challenge faced by U.S. companies is reflected in anticipated and current changes in the workforce, labor market composition, skill needs, employee values, legal compliance, and ethical issues. The shift in the demand and supply for labor across key industries (e.g., health, manufacturing, service), preparation of the new labor force, aging of the current workforce, possible changes in work ethic and related values are all elements that will keep HRM folks working overtime. In addition, local ordinance, state statutes, and federal legislation is promulgated on what seems to be a daily basis. HRM professionals must ensure that the companies have the right people with the right skills, knowledge, ability, and values needed for the 21st century.

In summary, nearly everything we do, see, and hear is touched by the human resource function. If something touches a person's life, it touches the work that person performs. For example, as organizations consider the movement of today's employee from one location to another, equal consideration must be given to the "trailing spouse." This is a particularly important issue where an overseas assignment is involved. However, needs and career interests of the spouse must be considered for a domestic move as well. Increasingly, the employer is faced with families that involve dual careers.

One reads in the newspaper about violence in the workplace. As an example, the tragic situation that occurred at the Royal Oak Post Office a few years ago, where a terminated postal worker returned to the premises and took the lives of several people then turned the weapon on himself. A news headline for the nation, but a review of the facts indicates that this tragedy had within it many human resource management issues. This book exposes you to some of the issues a person in HRM faces. It is intentionally a potpourri of issues intended to get your feet wet, so to speak.

References

Milkovich, G. T.; and Boudreau, J. W. *Human Resource Management,* Burr Ridge, IL: Irwin, 1994, p. 804.

Noe, R. A.; Hollenbeck, J. R.; Gerhart, B., and Wright, P. M., *Human Resource Management: Gaining a Competitive Advantage,* Burr Ridge, IL: Irwin, 1994, p. 786.

Part 1

Cases in Human Resource Management

A case is a description of an administrative situation and usually includes information about the setting of the situation. This information includes such things as geographic location, organization size, and business or sector. Often, the case describes the background of the key factors involved in the experience. Finally, the case describes the happenings in the administrative situation.

PURPOSES OF CASES

The purposes of analyzing cases in personnel include the following:

1. To improve the decision-making ability of managers or potential managers group. Many management experts believe that decision making is at the core of effective management. The cases treated herein are centered on the person at work. The role to be played by the analyst can be that of a supervisor of persons or a personnel specialist.

2. In addition to developing managerial abilities, such as more effective decision making, the case method is designed to expose management students to the environment of managerial decision making and to develop facilitative attitudes useful for effective decision making. Thus, cases present to the analysts situations that require them to make decisions and take risks under time pressure and with uncertainty surrounding the decision. The student must make a choice by discussion time. He or she often may feel that there is inadequate information provided in a case for making an optimal decision. This is also true in much managerial decision making. There is information the decision maker would like to have, but it is not available, or there is no time to get it, or it would be too costly to acquire. The decision maker must make a decision based on the limited information available. Because cases are necessarily short and lack some information, they help to provide students with the situations for developing facilitative attitudes.

3. Another major purpose in using cases is to provide the opportunity to apply research findings and theoretical explanations to real situations and test their applicability. Frequently, one may have learned cognitively what a research study found or have understood what a theorist said about why people behave the way they do. But the ultimate purpose of managerial training is to improve managerial behavior and, thus, it is hoped, improve the satisfaction and development of the employees, the organization's performance, and the manager's satisfaction and success. If management students cannot apply these findings to real situations, they may have been taught a body of knowledge that is interesting and intellectually challenging, such as a study of optics might be to a clergyman or chemistry to a social worker; but this knowledge is not likely to contribute significantly to the students' successful careers. Unless students can apply the research and theory accurately and insightfully to simulations of reality, such as cases and exercises, it is not likely they will be able to do so in the real problem situation.

STRUCTURING CASE ANALYSES

There are many ways of analyzing cases and discussing them. To be most effective, all members of the class or discussion group must contribute something. This moves the learning situation away from the one-way communication method, or lecture. Lectures, no matter how brilliantly done, involve only a few human faculties. If care is not taken, the lecturing process degenerates into the sounds being emitted from the lecturer's mouth, traveling through the air, and scarcely pausing in the receiver's brain, before passing into the pencil-taken notes. In case discussions, each discussant delivers his or her thoughts, reacts to others' thoughts, and defends his or her own. The discussant, thus, is using brain, mouth, eyes, ears, and probably hands to convey the message. This is how learning is accelerated or enriched, or both.

One useful technique is to structure the discussion, at least to some extent. If the discussion jumps from point to point, it may be difficult for many discussants to follow. One model for structuring these cases is the following:

Step One

Clearly define the major and secondary problems involved in the case. These problems can be classified by such topics as personnel activity—for example, selection, evaluation, and compensation. Stating and agreeing on the topics and rank ordering of them sets the agenda of discussion. This is not always easy to do. Because of differences in the discussants' backgrounds, there will be varying interpretations of the data. Moreover, not all the information in the case is essential or even useful in understanding the situation. In a real-work situation, the supervisor (manager, administrator, and the like) is flooded with clues and information. The effective supervisor must separate the relevant from the irrelevant and focus on the former.

Step Two

Develop a model of the cause of the problem (or success). There are many possible relations that influence the results. These factors include:

1. *Individual factors:* The cause might be in the perception, motivation, abilities, or attitudes of the persons in the case.

2. *Dyadic factors:* The significant factor can be the relationship between two crucial actors in the case, such as superior–subordinate.

3. *Small group factors:* The work-group interrelationships might be the paramount factor influencing such problems as restriction of output or success of the football team.

4. *Intergroup activities:* The cause of the problems can be systematic differences in several groups who must interact: salespeople and production managers, doctors and nurses, unions and managements.

5. *Environmental factors:* There may be factors in the work environment that are crucial—time pressures, economic factors, governmental pressures and so forth—that lead to the results described. So, too, in a case you must arrange the data, the variable, and so forth into a model of the situation. In some cases, the ages of the people may be vital information—for example, when evaluating future pension costs or management succession. In other situations, it may be interesting, but not crucial, to know ages. The race of an applicant may be important in a firm under affirmative action pressure. On the other hand, it may be totally irrelevant to the analysis of a health and safety case.

Step Three

Consider alternative solutions to the problem or explain the successful experience: Once you have defined your problem and modeled the relationships, the next step is to consider a reasonable number of solutions—the more the better. However, one usually cannot consider a large number because of time pressures and the limited ability of most people to compare a large number of alternatives. Most of us eliminate from serious consideration those solutions that seem least likely to solve the problem quickly and expeditiously. Three or four alternatives are systematically compared factor by factor.

Step Four

Choose and implement a solution: The analyst chooses a solution and is prepared to defend that choice. The analyst also plans how she or he would make it work. Thus, if the solution is to fire a person, several things must be considered to make sure the choice was the right one and one that is workable. For example, when the firing should be done, how it should be done, and by whom it should be done must be considered, as well as clearing the matter with superiors.

There are many analytical structures to which cases can be fitted. The structure just described has proved to be a useful one.

STUDENT PREPARATION FOR CASES

A few hints may help you prepare good case analyses. First, read the case, underlining important points and making rough notes of what you think are the key problems and their causes. Do some preliminary thinking about solutions. If you have the opportunity, discuss your ideas with others in the class. Then lay the case aside for a while.

Second, return to the case later and reread it. Make added notes. Where there is not enough information, make reasonable assumptions and state them. Remember, in your proposed solution, that what you suggest being done might affect others. Make sure you don't solve a problem in one department and cause one in another. Write up your first draft report now. Put the case down again.

Third, return to the case later and make sure it says all you want to say and the way you want to say it.

This approach will help you begin to develop your analytical abilities. First, you will learn to separate the important information from the less important. Next, you will begin to apply the research and theories you have learned to the problems. Then, you will begin to increase your repertoire of solutions and analyze them rationally and logically, computing the trade-offs. Finally, you will remember to anticipate the implementation problems.

CATEGORIZING CASES

The cases are given in the next section of this book. It has been customary to classify cases by topics, and this has been done here. If a case is classified under Orientation, you can be sure that this is a major focus of the case. However, it may not be the only focus of the case. The cases are realistic; rarely are they single problems or singly caused problems. Look for all the personnel and human aspects that seem relevant. *A key point: Beware—Instructors disagree about the importance of having discussion questions included at the end of a case so do NOT focus exclusively on the discussion questions and miss the big picture. This is known as "missing the forest for the trees." The questions are placed at the end of the case or item to stimulate your thinking, not to provide you with the key HRM concept/issue or to direct you to the learning item's "solution."*

Section A

Introduction to Human Resource Management

1 *Too Personal for the Personnel?**

"Were you sexually or physically abused as a child?"

"When did you first have sexual intercourse?"

"Define love. What is your experience of being loved? Of loving another?"

"Have you fathered unwanted pregnancies? Explain. Has your partner had an abortion(s)? Explain."

"What would make you primitively and joyously happy?"

These questions were asked of employees who attended the *Leadership and Management* and *Team Building* courses offered by the firm of Fritz and Friends Management Consulting. A General Accounting Office (GAO) investigation revealed the information provided below. The management consulting firm was suggested by Timothy Castle, former director of railroad safety. Castle had met John Fritz, head of Fritz and Friends, when Castle participated in Fritz courses. The training provided was done under contracts that did not require Fritz and Friends to compete with other firms. The firm was used from 1989 to 1993. During that period the firm was paid $167,185 plus the costs of materials and other expenses for eight courses.

The Water and Air Traffic Safety Agency (WATSA) is a fine organization that has as its responsibility the safety and protection of ships that play the various ports of America's internal waterways. On the waterways, this consists of assuring the safe

*This is a disguised case. The names of people and agencies have been changed but the information provided is accurate.

passage of trawlers, tugboats, ferries, and tankers. The WATSA, though, has broad responsibilities of all manner of traffic safety. It is the WATSA's responsibility to investigate the cause of grisly plane crashes, train wrecks, trucking disasters, pipeline explosions, and, as noted earlier, shipping accidents.

The WATSA culture is a very conservative one, so it came as a big surprise recently when *The Washington Post* reported that the agency was sending employees to "Men's Awareness Workshop," training seminars where they responded to some very very sensitive personal questions, including those listed previously.

Employee reaction to the training courses varied dramatically. One WATSA employee, who took two Fritz courses in Washington and a week-long course in Florida, said, "I thought it was a great course. It was all how you went into it." However, not everyone loved the Fritz courses. Many did object to the content of the program. One of those individuals was Rep. John D. Dingell (D–Mich), who asked the GAO to investigate. Others viewed the training as abusive, brainwashing, bizarre, and humiliating. Forte told the GAO one participant was called a "slime bucket" by Fritz during a "feedback" session. The WATSA said it is looking to hire an outside auditor to figure out what happened. In the meantime, Fritz and Friends has been cut out of the curriculum.

Discussion Question

Identify the human resource management issues in this case. How could the problems you identified have been avoided?

---

*2 Economic Security Agency (A)**

The flashbulbs exploded simultaneously as the last body bag was zipped and loaded into the medical examiner's van. Dr. Joseph Spellman, chief medical examiner, a 25-year veteran of the examiner's office, had thought he'd seen it all until this one. Police did their best to maintain crowd control but it was virtually impossible. The people on the sidewalk pushed forward to get a peek at the sensational scene before them. The scene on the sidewalk in front of the Economic Security Agency Building was one of body bags and bedlam. There stood Dr. Spellman, microphones thrust in his face, and reporters from KYW, WCAU, WIP, WPIX, and any other radio and TV folks who could hold a microphone or videocam fired questions at him in rapid succession. He felt like he was at a shark feeding frenzy and he was fresh meat.

---

*The names and places used in this case are, for obvious reasons, fictitious but the events described are real. Unfortunately, similar events occur with increasing regularity in today's workplace.

THE SETTING

Philadelphia is known to some outsiders as the City of Brotherly Love and to others as home of the most ill-mannered fans in pro sports. The locals have a different perspective about Philadelphia. They think the city gets rich from the center city parking tickets the police write. Employees come to their jobs by public transportation because of the high cost of parking in the center city area, very expensive parking tickets, and the high propensity of city fathers to have a private firm boot or tow cars away.

Actually, Philadelphia is a great historic place with a rich past: Old Swedes Church, Independence Hall, the Liberty Bell, and many other landmarks. Even moviegoers have fond memories of Rocky Balboa and his triumphant run up the steps of the Philadelphia Art Museum where Balboa's statue formerly reposed. Despite the tragic Move violence from several years ago, the city is not viewed as one that is particularly violent. The workers at the Economic Service Agency (ESA) were to learn that violence can occur in the workplace—a violence that can touch both the innocent and the accused.

No one would think of the Economic Service Agency as an organization where employees take their life in their hands by simply coming to work every day. The stress and strain of the job, the demands that recently acquired technology places, and a perception that many of the supervisors do not care about their subordinates, may be the cause of low morale, lack of loyalty, and possible fits of anger by employees. Sometimes, if you put too many people into too tight a space and ask them to excel both in terms of the quality of work and quantity of work, a backlash results. And so it was at the ESA.

The administrative offices of the Economic Service Agency's Mid-Atlantic Region are located in Philadelphia's north central section of the city. The 400 North Broad Street location is a large, gray four-story building that blends in so well with its surrounding that the average pedestrian walks past it every day before he or she realizes what it is. Across the street are the *Philadelphia Inquirer* and *Philadelphia Daily News* buildings. These are the major daily newspapers for the metropolitan Philadelphia area. State government buildings are just a stone throw away. Office buildings line both sides of Broad Street for several miles without a break.

THE OFFICE

When one arrives at the building, it becomes clear there are very few private offices. Only the highest-ranking officials at the ESA have an office. Most workspaces are really small cubicles. The majority of the employees sit at a desk in open areas. A view from the doorway after one steps from the elevator reveals many, many rows of desks neatly aligned one after another. People add a personal touch to give their own area some individualism. Flowers, decorations, cartoons—anything a creative mind can think of serves the purpose. All employees have telephones, but supervisors have the ability to have someone monitor a subordinate's telephone calls.

Private calls are made from a bank of telephones in the hallway on each floor. The ESA managers put in place an employee surveillance system. The agency took its lead from many corporations that have installed electronic listening devices and observation posts. There was a concern that employees not abuse telephone privileges nor fail to give a full day's work for a full day's pay. The employees were aware that electronic surveillance monitoring was occurring. However, knowing and liking it were two different things.

BACKGROUND

Sixty-five percent of the employees at ESA were women. Forty-five percent of the employees were African-American. All of the employees live in the metropolitan area. The City of Philadelphia, Camden, and nearby suburbs represent the home area for 95 percent of the employees. The typical employee is a high school graduate who later pursued college courses at a community college. Several of the professionals and managers joined ESA right out of college. Until the last two years, few of the employees were computer literate. A major training effort and attempt to improve employee motivation was launched in late 1991 so people would be ready for rapid technological change.

Most of the employees here have worked for ESA at this location for a minimum of 15 years. Few have advanced very far from their entry-level position. The employees routinely get a step in pay grade after prescribed periods of time in rank. The computer technology has now replaced many workers' old manual systems and stop-gap methods used by employees to rationalize the system of papers processed for a variety of purposes.

A very small percentage of the ESA professionals and managers act in a customer service capacity. These individuals handle inquiries about their social service accounts. Most of the queries are handled by mail. The vast majority of the requests for information have to do with a need to update and verify the amount contributed to Social Security, years of service that counts toward Social Security and the amount and kind of Social Security benefits available to the individual. The people at ESA handle an unbelievable amount of paper. Their task is to make sure that the right information gets into the right file for each individual, where claims are filed or where changes are being made in a person's contribution or employment status.

For years, the people had multiple manual systems to handle the large volume of paperwork. Since 1982, however, the administration has worked to develop a computer system that could accurately handle the information recorded for the hundreds of thousands of people processed through the Philadelphia office. The system is continually be revised and upgraded because the ESA had bought a specific package from a major computer software company and later tried to customize the software so the ESA's unique needs could be addressed by the computer system. In 1991, a meeting of the information systems people, managers, professionals, and clerks led to a decision to scrap the old computer system and start again. Many of the clerks were ambivalent about the decision, because they did not want to learn another system;

but they also knew that the old system had many flaws. A new system came on-line in 1992. The new system required major efforts on the part of the employees to master it. To those who did understand how it worked and what (data) must be entered, the change to the new computer hardware and software made life easier. Others found the change to be traumatic.

Economic Security Agency (B)

"If you value your sorry life, you had better get out of my face! I am tired of you picking on me. I was here before you came here. I will be here after you leave. Simply put, I am going to leave your pitiful a-- behind. You think you are hot stuff. You are nothing to the people in this unit who can make you look good or make you look bad," Nate Randall told his supervisor, Delores Thomas. Delores turned to walk away. After a few steps, Nate mumbled something to himself but not loud enough for her to hear him. "What did you say?" Delores asked. She said, "Repeat what you said, so I can have grounds to get you suspended or fired. It would be my pleasure. I do not have to deal with your insubordination."

What followed was a screaming and cursing match that required the intervention of several employees. Nate was sent home. He left vowing "to get even with her and others who took her side of the argument . . ." This was the third time in a month that he and his supervisor had been feuding. After each incident, Nate got angry and threatened retaliation against Delores and anyone else who happened to be in the area. Also, it was the third time in that same period that Nate had lost money from his paycheck for his actions.

THE CO-WORKERS

Delores Thomas was a 1960 graduate of West Philadelphia High School. In high school, she was very popular, liked the night life, and hung out with a fast crowd. She never married. Her first and only employer has been the Economic Security Agency. Thirty-three years later she is still there doing what she has been doing since her graduation. She is now entering her 34th year. Delores attended Community College of Philadelphia, where she worked on an associate of science degree with a major in general business. An opportunity to work lots of overtime and substantially increase her earnings led to her giving up her educational pursuits. Although Ms. Thomas completed 54 credit hours and needs only 9 credit hours to finish her program, she never went back. She has committed herself to doing her job well and working well with the people around her. Delores has developed a reputation as a hard-working, personable, and caring person who helps others improve themselves. Her rise to a GS-11 has been steady but slow. Nate was the one and only difficult personnel problem that she had not resolved to her satisfaction.

Nate Randall was also a 1960 graduate of West Philadelphia High School. He and Delores traveled in the same crowd, although they never seemed to care for one another. He, too, liked the nightlife. After high school, Nate entered Lincoln University, where he earned a bachelor's degree in education. Nate joined ESA after he completed his degree requirements. He came to SSA as a GS-7. Nate later attained a level GS-11 but, because of personal problems that affected his work performance, Nate was demoted to GS-7. The demotion was the least of several disciplinary alternatives. However Nate blamed others for not supporting him in his time of trouble. He refused to attribute the disciplinary action to his own performance. These problems occurred in 1988 about the time of his divorce and failure to gain custody of his three children. He quickly transformed himself from a positive, happy, and productive employee to one who became sullen and angry. Over the previous three years, his performance had been in sharp decline and he had become much more belligerent.

Discussion Question

After this last incident, Delores tried to decide what to do about Nate. He seemed unwilling to accept responsibility for what has happened in his work life. She had listened to his threats and was concerned about him and about his state of mind. What should she do next, she wondered?

Economic Security Agency (C)

Delores was concerned about Nate. After the last incident, Delores met with Nate and attempted to clear the air. She prepared an agenda and followed the agenda. The result was a stormy meeting. Given his previous outbursts and no apparent remorse or willingness to change his behavior, Delores took the next formal step. Delores acted on the behavior of Nate by requesting and receiving approval for his suspension. The suspension was to last for several days. Delores had carefully documented the problems that she had had with Nate. However, Nate decided to appeal the suspension. The suspension was then delayed until the employee-management team could hear the grievance. The team consisted of two employees and a representative from the Employee Relations Division.

On the day of the hearing before the employee-management team, Delores stepped off the elevator to find Nate waiting for her there. He said to her, "Got a minute? You know the hearing will take place shortly. I want you to go easy on me in there. You provoked me by the comments you made."

Delores responded, "Nate, I have to tell these people the truth. The problem that we are having is not new, it is serious and it frightens me. You have been going downhill for nearly three years now. When will it stop? When will you turn your life around?"

Nate could not restrain himself, "Look, you arrogant, power hungry S.O.B.! I tried the soft approach. Now I am going to tell you what I really wanted to say in the first place. You play ball with me or I will put sugar in the tank of that Lexus you love so damn much. If that's not enough, somebody better keep an eye on that house of yours. There just might be a fire with you in it!"

Delores walked away. She could not believe her ears. This guy had really gone off the deep end. Before the hearing, she went to Mr. Eldridge Coleman, her boss, to inform him of the exchange. Eldridge called in Nate to get his side of the story. Nate denied ever having met with Delores and he vehemently denied making any threats to her. At the hearing, however, he was officially reprimanded for his previous behavior.

Discussion Question

What should Mr. Coleman do? What are the issues of concern to him and for the ESA?

Economic Security Agency (D)

Nate continued to be a disruptive influence in Delores Thomas's section. Despite the hearing and disciplinary action, this troublesome personnel problem did not go away. Rather than discipline him, the department manager, Paul Johnson, talked Delores into agreeing to transfer Nate to another section. Delores agreed to remove any reference to this previous incident with Joe from his personnel file. Finally, Nate transferred to another section.

Joseph Cooper had been section chief for four years. Although he was a veteran of 15 years with the agency and four years as section chief, he had not had a "headache" like Nate Randall. In less than six months, Nate had made his presence felt. He always seemed to be in trouble. Joseph was still angry with Delores for not leveling with him about the problem employee that Nate had been. Had he known about these problems, Joseph would not have agreed to Nate's transfer. Now, Joseph had to meet Nate to discuss his most recent improper work behavior.

THE MEETING

The meeting with Joe started off well but quickly degenerated into a shouting match. Nate told Joseph that he was racist. "That was the cause of the whole problem," Nate said. Joseph said that his being black and Nate's being white had nothing to do with Nate's poor performance. The name calling began and before long things got ugly.

Nate was pushing the wrong guy when he tried to loud-talk Joseph and boss Joseph around. Before long, the two were rolling on the floor flailing away at each other, and the secretary was calling security to come quickly to get the two of them apart. When security arrived, both men were bruised and battered. Neither would back off. Threats of violence were made by both men. The security guards were advised to hold these two men until Mr. Coleman could get there. When he arrived, he listened briefly to the details of what happened. Coleman was seriously concerned about the state of mind of both men but, since it was Nate who started the trouble, he made a decision to send Nate home. He told Nate not to return until he had undergone psychiatric evaluation. He gave Nate the name of the company's psychiatrist, then asked the security people to escort Nate from the premises. After Nate left, Mr. Coleman spoke briefly to Joseph, then returned to his office. Nate had previously received several verbal and written reprimands from his supervisors and had been warned, after Delores Thomas's allegations, that violent behavior would not be tolerated.

Discussion Questions

Examine the events that occurred in this portion of the case from a human resource management perspective. What issues come to mind? Evaluate Mr. Coleman's handling of the Joseph Cooper and Nate Randall situation. How would you have handled this matter?

Economic Security Agency (E)

The employee–management grievance committee's decision was rendered two weeks after a hearing. The decision to suspend Nate Randall without pay was upheld in a 3-0 vote. Nate was uncharacteristically quiet when informed of the grievance committee's decision. Now that the decision was upheld, the disciplinary action could be carried out. Nate cleared off his desk, packed away a few things, and gave some papers to a colleague. When he left the premises at the end of the day he nodded in the direction of Joseph Cooper, whose office was situated near Nate's. Joseph was surprised and perplexed to see a big grin on his face.

At the end of Nate's suspension he did not report to work. No one was able to reach him for several days. Many of his co-workers became alarmed, because he was not one to simply disappear. Also, some of his peers knew that he had gone through a nasty divorce and custody fight for his children. In order to pay his child support payments and mortgage, Nate *had* to work.

On the morning of January 14, Nate quietly stepped off the elevator. He was wearing an overcoat. The temperature outside was a warm 52 degrees F. Several people spoke to him but he did not answer. He headed straight for his work area. Without a single word, he pulled out an AK-47 from under his heavy coat and opened fire.

He then turned and walked to Mr. Coleman's office. He opened fire on Mr. Coleman from point blank range. He calmly walked to Joseph Cooper's office and opened fire, killing Joseph and wounding the section secretary. Afterward, he walked along the corridor, randomly shooting at anyone who came near him. A SWAT team was called to the scene. When they arrived they found Coleman, Cooper, and a fellow supervisor dead, and several employees were badly wounded. They found Nate Randall on a flight of stairs between the third and fourth floor, sitting in a pool of blood. He had taken his own life. Apparently, he had used a .357 magnum to kill himself. The entire tragic incident occurred in a matter of minutes.

When Philadelphia police obtained a warrant to search Nate Randall's home they found a note and lots of mail. The mail was piled on a table in the kitchen. Some of it had not been opened. The police learned from his mail that Nate had accumulated a great deal of debt. His telephone had been disconnected. He was in arrears on child support payments, and the automobile dealer was preparing to repossess his car. A note was found. It indicated that he had been distraught over the divorce and his inability to see his children on a regular basis. Problems at work and the suspension that followed compounded the situation. In the bedroom, the police found a folder that contained a collection of newspaper clippings. The clippings were news accounts of violent crimes that had occurred over the past year. These accounts covered homicides that had occurred in a wide variety of settings. There were incidents from colleges and universities, corporations, and post office facilities. One article mentioned the fact that James Fox, a noted criminologist at Northeastern University, discovered 411 incidents in which an employee killed an employer or vice versa.

Discussion Question

Review the events described in this case. What are the relevant issues? What could management have done to avoid the violent event that occurred?

3 Phoenix Department of Human Services

"Man, I am really scared! I couldn't believe my ears when Ronnie told me that Jack died of AIDS. Rumor has it that he caught it from his old lady. She supposedly hooked up with a dude that was heavy into drugs . . ."

It was quite a shock for everyone to learn of Jack's death. Two months have gone by since his passing, yet his co-workers were still trying to come to grips with Jack's death and its cause. Employees were particularly fearful because of the nature of their jobs at the department. The department provides a community-based program that offers residential, vocational, counseling, and other specialized services for the mentally disabled. A major component of the program is to allow clients to retain their dignity. One means of accomplishing this objective is to permit them as much autonomy as possible. One step in that direction is to permit clients to live in a community setting.

The staff members face many diverse situations. Employees receive training in "passive defense skills to enable them (the staff members) to deal with violent and/or aggressive clients in a nonabusive manner." Evidence of violence was shown, including "numerous incidents involving biting, scratching, throwing of objects, hitting, violent outbursts, and pinching by the clients."

As publicity regarding AIDS increased, and when more employees became aware that Jack died of AIDS, the agency, effective January 20, 1989, required its staff members to complete an AIDS antibody screening test.

Requirement

In this situation, is mandatory AIDS testing legally defensible? Why or why not? Explain.

---

4 St. Peter's Community Healthcare System (A)

In recent years, St. Peter's has expanded facilities and programs to broaden its role in healthcare delivery. The Father Winfred Robinson, SJ, Pavilion—a building expansion project that opened in 1994—enhanced ambulatory care and provided an organized center for inpatient critical care services. The Eugene M. Miller Center also opened in 1994 to respond to the unmet community need for substance abuse and teenage mental health services.

In addition, recent campus activities have included the construction of the 97,000 square foot Fathers of Healing Office Building, the development of on-site radiation therapy services, an updated pediatric unit, additional parking space, renovation for additional labor and delivery rooms, an updated pediatric unit and additional parking space. Specific ambulatory initiatives implemented at Fathers of Healing include a system of five ambulatory centers and physician practice assistance programs.

These investments have helped position St. Peters as a progressive provider of services for residents of North Oakland County.

HIRING OF TEE SHIELDS

Tyrone (Tee) Shields visited St. Peter's personnel office in 1991. He was interviewed and hired after he successfully completed all tests and his screening interview was excellent. Shields was informed that employees at St. Peter's were required to be properly groomed. Specfically, regardless of position at the hospital, the employee must satisfy a clean-shaven grooming code. On June 7, 1991, Shields began work at the hospital as a medical records clerk. He was assigned to the hospital's pharmacy where his work was exemplary.

After 75 days, Shields began to think about the conclusion of his probation period. He reviewed his performance and interactions with others, including his supervisor, Mark Croft. He and Mark were scheduled to meet to discuss Tee's performance and whether Tee would qualify for employment as a regular employee. The 90-day probation period had been uneventful and Shields believed that he had done his job well. Aside from Mark's jokes about that "growth on his face" and gentle reminders that he needed to "get a shave" or "get rid of that beard," Tee had received nothing but praise.

The meeting seemed to go really well until Mark informed Tee that he would not continue Tee's employment. Tee was floored! When he asked why, Mark simply got quiet and refused to say. Tee was persistent. Finally, Mark admitted that Tee's work was fine but because of his involvement with the public, Mark had to enforce the hospital's clean-shaven grooming code. He said he was simply getting too many complaints from the hospital's administrator, Glenn Thomas. Thomas strongly supported the hospital's dress and grooming code and saw no reason to make *any* exceptions. Thomas felt that beards were not appropriate. In fact, all of the hospital's employees who dealt with the public were expected to conform to a dress code. These employees were to be appropriately attired and properly groomed. Good grooming meant that no one who had contact with the public could wear a beard. Thomas had explained to all supervisory personnel, including Mark Croft and members of the personnel office, that he had read an important article on the subject. The research on customers' preferences, buying habits, and reactions to other people's attire indicated to him that people tend to trust clean-shaven men more than bearded men. Not long after the article was shared with other members of the executive team, the clean-shaven grooming code was written and implemented. Shields said that he was aware of Mr. Thomas's feeling about beards. Shields noted that he kept his beard trim and it was a small beard. However, he mentioned that he did try to remove his beard but when he did so he developed a very bad rash. A visit to his doctor revealed that he had a skin condition called pseudofolli-culitis barbae (PFB), that his doctor said affects a high percentage of black males. The skin condition occurs when shaved hair curls back and pierces the skin. The result is skin inflammation, which sometimes leads to abscesses. The solution to the problem, according to Tee, is not to shave. Despite Tee's explanations and protestations, he was terminated.

Tee had quite a surprise for the hospital. He wasted little time running to a top employee-rights attorney. The attorney took the case on a contingency basis and filed briefs in Michigan's civil court. What did Tee complain about? He charged the company with discrimination. He believed that, although all employees who had contact with the public were obligated to obey the rule, the rule discriminated against blacks. Tee said he had asked his supervisor if he noticed anything different about many blacks in sports. He noted that several black basketball and baseball players had the condition. They, too, suffered from PFB. Tee, through his attorney, argued that, because the condition is especially prevalent among blacks, a rule calling for the dismissal or failure to hire those who grow a beard has a more negative effect on blacks. The attorney noted that PFB affects between 45 percent and 85 percent of all black males who shave. Further, Shields's attorney argued, that

Mark's doctors had instructed him to grow a beard as a means of curing the PFB problem.

The hospital rebuttal was that the rule was lawful because (1) it was applied equally to all employees who had contact with the public and (2) it was a business necessity. Customers, the hospital claimed, are distrustful of employees who have beards or goatees. Because of the competitive nature of the medical business, a hospital must respond to the needs and wants of the patient. The good-grooming policy is evidence (to the patient) of courteous, motivated, and disciplined employees. Finally, the hospital's lawyer cited from case law to justify its "no beard" rule. In at least one instance, a federal court recognized a similar rule to be a legitimate business necessity.

Discussion Questions

1. Can a rule that is informed uniformly in regard to employees be deemed illegal? If yes, why? If no, why not?
2. Does the hospital have the right to impose a grooming policy, one that includes a no beard rule, on its employees?
3. If you were the judge in this case, would the hospital's business necessity defense succeed or fail? Why?

St. Peter's Community Healthcare System (B)

Bruce Beecher swiveled in his office chair and glared at his unused ashtray. "I'd like to kill somebody," he growled. "They just had to go through with the ban on smoking . . ." Bruce was not a happy camper!

Beecher, a 10-year employee at the hospital, enjoyed working with the public and helping people. So, it was no surprise that he decided to leave his old job at an auto supply company to join St. Peter's. His years of going to school and Oakland Community College had paid off in his earning his associate degree in medical records administration. He worked as a receptionist at one of only two centrally located hospital reception areas. He assisted and guided folks to their destination in what was perceived to be a very confusing maze.

Many employees surrendered early to the hospital's new ban on smoking in private offices. The ban would be one of the county's strictest bans on workplace smoking ever put into effect. Discussions among human resource management professionals suggested that other organizations would be watching to see how well the ban worked.

On Friday, Beecher was into his sixth nerve-jangling day without nicotine. He had decided to kick his two-pack-a-day habit, rather than to leave his desk and his telephone to smoke.

Bruce felt that he had a real dilemma. Having smoked for over 20 years, he knew it would be difficult to quit. Also, he knew that if he left his desk very often, people needing directions to various departments would be on their own. "It would cost me dearly to leave," he said.

Fellow employee Linda Copeland wasn't about to give up her cigarettes. She smoked and fumed in the hospital's sterile new $800 smoking room, complete with a fancy ventilation system. Despite the new no smoking ban, the hospital decided to provide smoking rooms. Each room meets stringent ventilation requirements and can be used only for smoking.

Discussion Questions

1. Do companies have a right to not hire people who smoke or restrict employee's smoking on the organization's premises?
2. What rights do smokers have?

---

5 Paradise Valley Hospital

Karen Vogel, 41, is a registered nurse (RN) who works full-time as operating room supervisor at St. Vincent's Hospital. In the short time (one year) that she has been at the 104-bed hospital, she has come to really enjoy her work. St. Vincent's Hospital holds American Hospital Association (AHA) membership and has Joint Commission of Accreditation of Hospitals (JCAH) approval. It is a general medical and surgical institution that employs 362 people (excluding medical and dental interns as well as residents or other trainees). During the previous 12 months, the hospital admitted 4,040 patients. The occupancy rate is 72.1 percent, and most patients come for a short-term stay of less than 30 days.

Karen still gets angry when she thinks about her unceremonious dumping at Paradise Valley Hospital. On practically a daily basis she had thought about suing her former employer for firing her unjustly. In the Paradise Valley employee handbook, Karen noticed a list of three categories of employees. Paradise Valley's book listed her as a "permanent employee."

At Paradise Valley, Karen had risen to the position of director of nursing. Getting to the top job in nursing was not a simple process. Her 16 years of hard work and dedication at Paradise Valley had paid off. Along the way she had worked each shift, worked many double shifts, and served in a number of wards. In addition, Karen had worked her way up through the various supervisory levels. She had served as shift supervisor, operating room supervisor, and head nurse.

Karen was viewed as an exceptional nurse. She seemed to possess just the right amount of interpersonal skills to go along with her technical competence. Over the years she had observed the many mistakes made by her predecessor, Joyce Kinicki. The knowledge gained from this vicarious learning experience had served her well. Despite her good performance evaluations and apparent success in the job, Karen found the director of nursing job to be too demanding. After 18 months in the job, she understood why Joyce often drank her lunch.

Karen's position on the Paradise Valley Hospital staff required a great deal of adjustment. Although the job seemed overwhelming at times, Paradise Valley was similar to St. Vincent's Hospital but (from Karen's perspective) with two important differences: (1) The former was larger and (2) unlike St. Vincent's, was managed by an incompetent administrator. While the second point is subjective and open to question, there can be no doubt about the first point. Paradise Valley Hospital is a 611-bed, not-for-profit hospital that admits an average of 24,686 people annually. It is an AHA member and has JCAH accreditation. This general medical and surgical hospital has an occupancy rate of 81.6 percent, employs 2,147 people (excluding certain interns, residents, and other trainees), and over half its patients are hospitalized for less than 30 days.

Paradise Valley Hospital is a large, bustling institution that caters to the needs of a rapidly growing population. The hospital serves a large Phoenix suburb of over 100,000 people. Nearly three years ago, the hospital received permission to undertake an expansion program. The result, after approval by the zoning board, was a badly needed, new 100-bed wing and additional office space for hospital staff. Unfortunately for Karen, the completion of the new wing occurred nearly one year after she was fired. Exhibit 1 offers a partial organizational chart.

Limited space was one of many problems the former director of nursing faced. Her most difficult problem, however, was her boss, Julian Anderson. Anderson had come to Paradise Valley Hospital 25 years ago. Now he serves as the hospital's chief executive officer. Over the years he had developed a systematic approach to handling any administrative problem that arose. He firmly believed that if you let a problem alone long enough it would go away. Julian believed in his philosophy and practiced it. The result: problems became larger, not smaller. Paradise Valley Hospital's bigger facility and larger census no longer functioned well under the direction of a laissez-faire manager who had become obsolete.

Anderson's problems often became problems to be handled by the director of nursing. Karen learned how good Julian was at throwing problems and issues back in the laps of those who made him aware of the problem. As relates to the nursing staff, Karen had to solve major problems: (1) state and nationwide surveys as well as informal discussions indicate that job satisfaction is low among nurses; (2) the demand for nurses' services are such that nurses are highly mobile; (3) despite the fact that continuing education is so essential, the hospital does not support or encourage nurses who seek educational opportunities while working; (4) understaffing and outdated hospital policies lead to large amounts of overtime, reduced professional efficiency, burdensome paperwork, and an inefficient use of nursing skills, as well as scheduling inflexibility; (5) a very limited fringe benefit package for nurses exists; (6) nurses' salaries are not competitive with those offered by Phoenix, Scottsdale, Glendale, and Mesa hospitals; and (7) all of the previous problems lead to low effectiveness of patient service, low morale of the nursing personnel, as well as high turnover. Although Anderson was told about these problems, nothing was done.

EXHIBIT 1 Paradise Valley Hospital Partial Chart

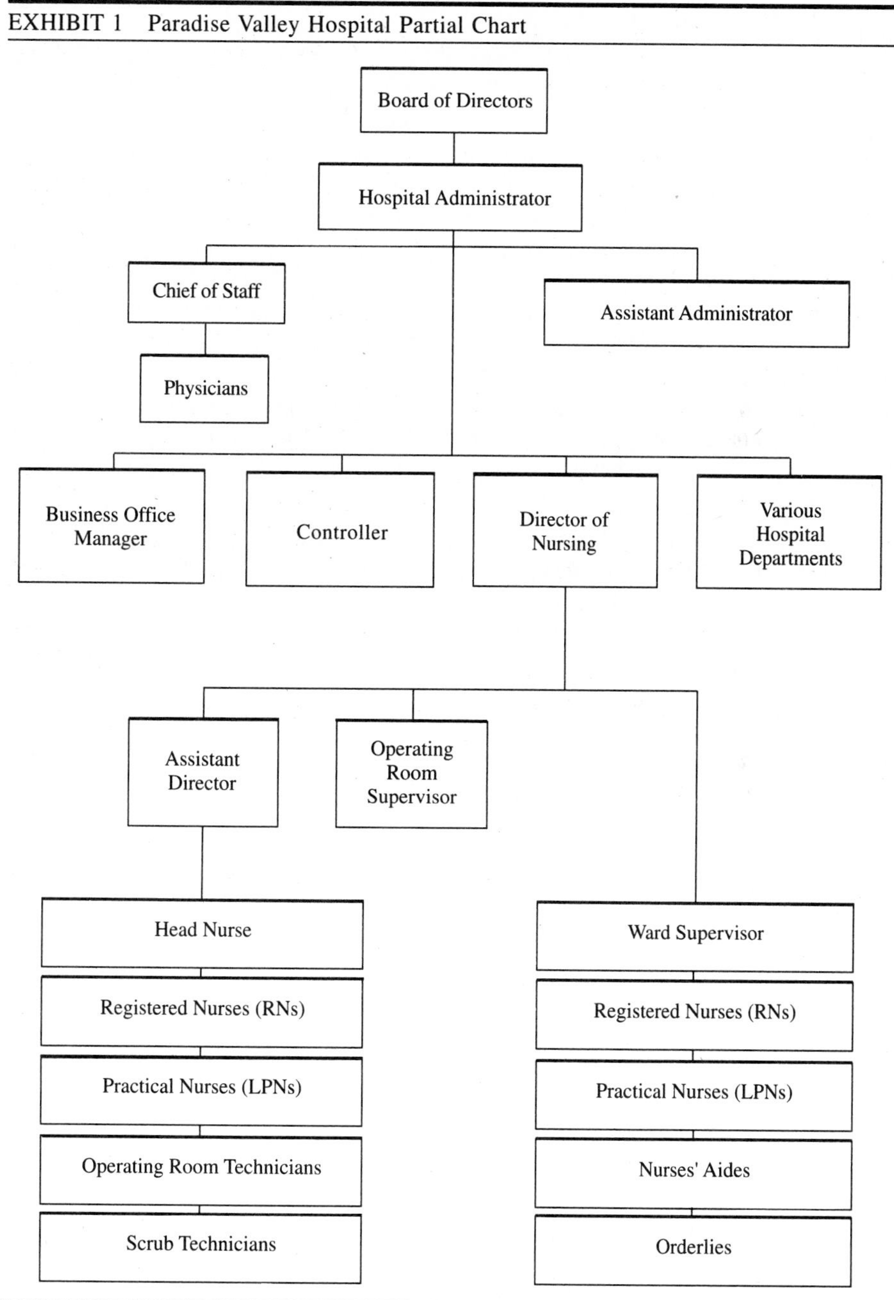

About two weeks before her dismissal, Karen and Julian met in his office.

Karen

Mr. Anderson, I have received your appraisal of my work.

Julian

In a little over 18 months you seem to have mastered a very difficult job. I could not expect anyone to do better.

Karen

If my performance is so great, why don't you listen to me when I tell you about staffing and other problems?

Julian

I *do* listen to you!

Karen

You're right, you listen, but you never seem willing or able to take my advice, or follow my suggestions, or help solve problems we discuss. I need support—not resistance.

Julian

Are you telling me how to do my job! As director of nursing, it is your job to solve nursing problems, not mine.

Karen

It's a little late for that. Realistically, I know you have a lot of pressure on you, but so do I. For the past six months, I have tried to do my job realizing that things would not change.

Julian

You can think what you want. The hospital's paying you well to do your job. Do your job or let somebody else do it!

Karen

I am going to do just that. Let me go back to my old job as operating room supervisor, and I will gladly let someone else have the headaches.

Julian

No problem. By next week we'll have your replacement. I have just the person for the job.

In less than two weeks Karen was replaced. Julian selected someone who would do everything he asked without questioning his decisions. Karen did not get what she expected. Instead of a demotion to the job she requested, she received a "pink slip." According to Julian, "no suitable positions were available." Prior to leaving the hospital, Karen was given an exit interview by Cyprian Devine, the hospital's vice president of personnel. Although the vice president was cordial and took care to record Karen's answers to each question, the interview went well as long as Cyprian was able to stick to her list of questions. When Karen asked about the *real* reason for her dismissal and the availability of the job she had requested, Cyprian was quite evasive. A frustrated and disappointed Karen Vogel left the vice president's office. She was convinced that Julian Anderson had had her fired for no good reason.

Discussion Questions

1. What are the major problems?
2. How would you describe Julian Anderson?
3. How effective do you feel Karen was as director of nursing?
4. Did Paradise Valley Hospital have the right to discharge Karen Vogel?
5. What legal action might Karen take? Would you recommend that she take legal action? Why or why not?

---

6 Dynamic Airlines, Inc.

Dynamic Airlines, Inc., is a small regional airline company that has served the small towns of Arizona for years. The airline, based at Sky Harbor Airport in Phoenix, flies from there to such places as Winslow, Flagstaff, Yuma, Gila Bend, Bullhead City, and the Grand Canyon. Some of its planes are small propeller-driven planes that are 15 years old, others are newer small jet-propelled aircraft.

The company has maintained a good reputation for reliable, courteous service at reasonable prices. In recent years, the most difficult problem has been the battle to keep prices down. Although the airline has virtually maintained a monopoly in the areas it serves, keeping prices down has been a difficult task. The cost of fuel, air fleet, and labor costs have all risen sharply.

Arizona is a state with many geographical contrasts. The diversity can be seen in the red rock beauty of Sedona, the big city atmosphere of Phoenix, and the picturesque desert landscape of Casa Grande. Flagstaff, for example, is located at an elevation of nearly 7,000 feet above sea level while Phoenix is only 1,100 feet above sea level. Many of the winter trips to such places as Flagstaff, home of Northern Arizona University, contained a measure of excitement. Temperatures there were often much, much colder than those in the desert towns such as Phoenix. Often, there was snow and plenty of wind. Pilots really had to know how to handle the company's small planes in rugged weather.

Recently a Dynamic Airlines employee was overheard telling another employee at the ticket counter in Sky Harbor:

> I can't believe it! Not Captain Jody Foster! Are you putting me on? He's the best at flying in the tricky wind currents and bad weather. You know that Jody has been flying for us for 27 years. Now they want him to retire at age 60. I tell you, after reading about the Age Discrimination in Employment Act, I know that our management is in trouble. No one, under that law, can be forced to retire at some mandatory age. I have looked into this issue for years. We should not forget that recent court decisions suggest that people who are willing and able to work cannot be discriminated against. That law says that no one can be forced to retire because of age.

Pilots are a critical resource at the airline. Often they get the pilot who wants to get his or her flying experience so he or she can qualify to fly planes for the major airlines. So, Dynamic is a good starting place. Lately though, a number of more experienced pilots, all 60 or over, have been looking for a commercial airline that would hire them. They contend that, in such areas as Winslow or Flagstaff during the winter, their experience makes them uniquely qualified to cope with unforeseen circumstances and to handle crises effectively.

Discussion Questions

1. What do you think about the experienced pilots' contention that they are uniquely qualified?
2. To what extent do laws, such as the Age Discrimination in Employment Act (as amended in 1986), protect these pilots?

---

*7 Harassment or a Misunderstanding: The Case of Amanda Stein**

"I've got to do something; these comments are really bothering me. I don't want to disrupt the group or create a big problem. I just want the comments to stop."

Amanda Stein, associate product support engineer at Xicom Corporation, was discussing a work situation with Joan Parnell, a colleague from another department one day after work. "Frank [Frank Villa, her boss] has been making these remarks ever since I began working here. This is beginning to affect my work, and I have to figure out a way to get it to stop. But I have to be very careful; otherwise, I could end up creating a lot of problems for a lot of people, including myself."

XICOM CORPORATION'S CUSTOMER SERVICE ORGANIZATION

Stein joined Xicom in July 1988, soon after graduating from Northeastern University with a bachelors of science in electrical engineering. Originally from Sharon, Massachusetts, she was the only woman in Villa's 13-person group.

Xicom Corporation specializes in networking systems technologies. Founded in 1962, Xicom has since become a leader in the data communications industry. After specialization in modern production and sales for over 15 years, Xicom

---

*This case was prepared by Edward G. Wertheim, Northeastern University.

expanded its line of products to become a total systems company. Its major competitors today are Digital Equipment Corporation, AT&T, IBM, and General DataComm.

All customer problem calls are received at the customer service center, and approximately 150 support engineers work to solve the many problems that customers have with their Xicom equipment. Lead support engineers work with development engineers to solve these problems in the shortest amount of time possible.

THE NETWORK MANAGEMENT GROUP

Customer service is split into four groups, each dealing with a specific communications product area. Frank Villa is project manager for the network management group. Villa, 35, recently divorced and the father of three was born and raised in Caracas, Venezuela and received bachelor's and masters degrees in electrical engineering as well as an MBA from SUNY-Albany.

The network management group relied heavily on team meetings and frequent interactions. Group members were expected to share information quickly and easily. Social outings outside of work were common with most of the group participating.

"This is a good group," Amanda reflected. "Frank seems to have a solid rapport with everyone; we want him to succeed."

Stein seemed to have gained respect quickly from her co-workers. After three months on the job, she became the lead technical support engineer in the company for the 860 Network Management System.

"You know I thought this job was over my head, but I've done it, in large part because of the support I got from Frank and the group. It wasn't just in the beginning, either. I have to admit that Frank continues to give me challenging projects and to support me.

"I thought it would bother me to be the only woman in the group, but I have been treated wonderfully; for the most part I am treated professionally and am respected. I couldn't have succeeded without the support I got. I am seen as the expert on the 860; I am the main contact with service and development for all customer problems."

CONFLICT IN THE OFFICE

In September 1989, Stein asked Villa for three days of personal time for the Jewish holidays. Stein had not accumulated any vacation time at that point and felt that personal time was a reasonable request.

Amanda

> Frank, I'd like to use some of my personal time for the Jewish holidays.

Frank

> I've never understood why in this country we have to all adjust our schedules for such a small minority. You know if you would just see the light and believe in Jesus, we wouldn't have this problem. (laughing)

Amanda

I am Jewish, and we have our own set of beliefs. So, can I take the time off?

Frank

Well, I guess so. Is your boyfriend from your tribe, too? He must be pretty wealthy then, huh?! (laughing)

"I was stunned by his comments," Amanda remembers thinking. "I wasn't really sure if he was joking or serious. Perhaps I have had a sheltered background, but I had never heard anything like that. I didn't say anything at the time, but the comments began to eat at me over the next few weeks."

Amanda

Frank, I'd like to discuss the incident that happened when I asked for time off.

Frank

What's the problem, Amanda? You got your time off, didn't you?

Amanda

Yes, Frank, but your comments about my religion were out of line.

Frank

I was just joking around, Amanda. I didn't mean to offend you; I'm sorry if what I did bothered you. I admire your people.

Amanda

I understand that you didn't mean to offend, but comments like that make me feel very uncomfortable and affect my work. To be an effective team, I think we need to be sensitive to issues like this.

Frank

You are absolutely right, Amanda. But there is a lot of kidding around here; people tell a lot of jokes and often they involve ethnics or races. I hear a lot of jokes about Hispanics but it doesn't bother me. In fact I tell jokes about Hispanics. We have a great group, Amanda. No one has complained about this. You know, you have told some jokes around here I never thought I would hear a woman tell. We probably have the best group here and joking is a part of what keeps morale so high here. We could all go around making sure we don't say anything that could possibly offend anyone and it wouldn't be much fun working around here.

Amanda

Frank, you have never heard me tell a joke at the expense of an ethnic group or race, and it may not bother you but it bothers me when people tell any ethnic jokes.

Frank

Again, I am sorry if I offended you, but I think you are being too sensitive. You might need a thicker skin to make it in this engineering environment you're in. I think you have been successful in part due to your ability to take it and give it right back. Most women would have shriveled up around here but you haven't. You're certainly going to have a lot worse happen to you, Amanda.

"I knew I really hadn't gotten through," Amanda told Joan. "Perhaps it is a cultural issue. And Frank did make some points I was already aware of. Maybe I am being too sensitive. Even so, I basically think that Frank just doesn't see that this behavior is unacceptable in this culture; at least I would like to think so.

"You know, Joan," Amanda continued, "I really like Frank, and I am pleased about his promotion to project manager. I honestly want to help him."

"Have you thought about going to the affirmative action office?" Joan suggested. "Maybe she can give you some suggestions about what to do."

"I thought about it, especially when the little comments continued, and I realized this wasn't really joking; but I still would rather not go that route. They would have to notify Frank's boss [Bob Humphrey] and I don't want to get into that. You know what can happen. Plus in the workshop we attended last fall, we covered the formal procedure for dealing with sexual harassment; but I'm not sure this is harassment and, even it is, I would rather solve this on my own. And nothing really has happened to me; I certainly can't point to any concrete harm that has been done to me; I have progressed as fast as I could. I keep thinking that I am going to deal with a lot worse than this and handle it myself; I've got to solve this myself."

"I take it the problem continues?" Joan asked.

"Nothing happened for a while, but then recently Frank started again and this time in front of other people. He told jokes about women, blacks, Hispanics, as well as Jews, all of which make me feel embarrassed and uncomfortable. I wondered if it was only me, so I talked with some of the guys in the group, but they told me that this was the way Frank is and not to take it personally."

TROUBLE AT THE GROUP MEETING

"The last straw came at a group meeting last week. We had our regular group meeting, except that this time Bob [Bob Humphrey, Villa's boss] was there. Villa was questioning me on a customer service contract issue."

Frank

Are the salespeople aware of the new contract offerings?

Amanda

Yes, but I don't feel that marketing is adequately stressing to the sales force the extra revenues that can be made from this type of contract program. The commissions just aren't high enough for sales to want to put the effort into selling them. The salesmen are afraid to push extra fees on customers who have already spent hundreds of thousands of dollars on equipment.

Frank

(laughing) Money, money, is that all you people ever think of? Why are you people so cheap? (others laughed)

Amanda

I'm sorry, but I think this issue is important. Let's take this off-line.

"At that point, I realized that whatever I had tried up to now was inadequate. I wanted to give him the benefit of the doubt, but this incident was in front of everybody. Nothing I have tried has worked. I expected Humphrey to say something then, but he didn't. I have given more thought to going to see EEO but I still feel and think it is too risky."

"Then, the next day Bob Humphrey stopped in and asked to speak with me."

Bob

> Amanda, you looked a bit shaken by Frank's comment; I could see how you took it, but I don't think he meant it the way you took it. I don't think he understands that a comment like that could bother anyone. This is all pretty new to him. You know he wrote a pretty glowing performance appraisal for you. He doesn't mean anything malicious. Your group is right on target for the quarter, and I just wouldn't let something like this get to you. I've put Frank under a lot of pressure; this is his first real managerial position and he's doing pretty well, all things considered. When the quarter is over, I'll talk to Frank about this, if you want me to.

"So that's where I stand, Joan. I don't know what to do. Bob is saying 'Don't rock the boat.' And I don't want to. I also didn't want Bob involved and still don't. But I can't let this go on any more."

Section B

Job Analysis and Human Resource Planning

8 *Morgan's**

A COMPREHENSIVE HUMAN RESOURCE MANAGEMENT CASE

Morgan's is a growing (and now major) retail store in Nashville, Tennessee. The store sells a wide range of medium to high-priced consumer items. While its reputation was built on the sale of clothing for men and women, Morgan's now sells children's clothing and a large assortment of nonclothing items, including jewelry, cosmetics, and even some furniture.

The owner and president, Joyce Morgan, is the daughter of the store's founder. She has an MBA from the University of Tennessee (six years ago) and has worked for the store for 10 years. She has been president since her father retired three years ago.

Joyce Morgan has been pleased with the rapid growth of the store in recent years. Sales have increased 200 percent over the past five years, and profits have grown commensurately. Unfortunately, this kind of growth usually leads to problems as well as benefits. For example, it has become increasingly difficult to control orders and inventories. More than ever before, the store seems to be either out of stock or overstocked on certain items. And, as one might expect, this explosive growth has led to some key human resource problems. The human resource challenges are the focus of the present case.

Employment at Morgan's has grown from 102 to 214 in the past five years. Of these 214 employees, 196 are within the retail operations. This unit of the company includes the director of retail operations, four managers (each in charge of a different

---

*This case was prepared by Professor Ronald W. Clement, Murray State University.

retail line), and 20 retail supervisors who manage the 171 sales associates (formerly called "salesclerks"). The remaining 18 employees include three managers of "support" units (who report to the president) and their staffs. One support unit is the human resource department, which includes the manager and three employees. The manager, Bill Goode, has been with the company for 20 years and has been in charge of the HR unit for the past 10. He has no formal education in human resource management except for a series of one-week seminars he attended eight years ago at UT. He was selected to be the HR manager because of his knowledge of company operations and his ability to get along with people. Bill is a former retail supervisor. It's worth noting that his department handles not only "personnel" duties but also any other company matters (e.g., public relations) that do not clearly fall under one of the other units.

The most obvious human resource challenges faced by this growing retail organization lie primarily in the areas of hiring, training, performance evaluation, and compensation. Consider the area of retail supervision. Of the 20 retail supervisors, 13 have been hired within the past 18 months. Although part of this hiring effort was due to the growth of the company itself, another part is related to a high level of dissatisfaction among the retail supervisors. Those who have left (and a few who remain) have complained at various times about the following issues:

1. "Insufficient pay" compared to what they think they can get elsewhere.
2. A "lack of company support" (e.g., money, time) in learning how to manage their areas.
3. An "unmotivated" sales force.

The director of retail operations, Jerry Clark, disagrees with these statements. He believes that the retail supervisors themselves are the real problem. He has mentioned to Joyce Morgan several times that the HR unit selects (from within as well as from the outside) unqualified people to be retail supervisors.

There seems to be some validity to Clark's viewpoint. For example, the company's job descriptions, including those for the position of retail supervisor, are woefully out of date. In fact, there is some doubt that they ever were any good. Further, supervisory positions are filled from within whenever possible, and the more senior employees are given first choice (unless they are clearly not fit for the job). Outside recruiting relies almost exclusively on newspaper ads and employee referrals. The selection process consists of a very simple, one-page application blank, brief interviews with the manager of human resources and the relevant manager in retail operations, and a physical exam. The director of retail operations makes the final hiring decision based on the feedback he receives from this process.

Training of retail supervisors is strictly on-the-job. Newly hired supervisors spend their first day with a member of the HR unit to become oriented to the company (e.g., philosophy, hours, pay, benefits). Then the new supervisor "tags along" with an experienced supervisor for one full week. By the second week, the new supervisor is in charge of an area. The procedure for a new supervisor promoted from within is similar except that the "orientation" session is briefer.

Evaluation of retail supervisors is based on a graphic rating scale developed about five years ago by Bill Goode. The four retail managers rate each of their five retail supervisors once per year on 10 dimensions. The dimensions include dependability, knowledge of work, quality of work, getting along with others, and so forth. Each of these is rated on a five-point scale, running from very poor through average to very good. Although this rating technique is used primarily for determination of pay increases, all four retail managers also claim to spend a fair amount of time each year discussing other issues important to their retail supervisors.

The compensation system at Morgan's is not as systematic and thorough as it should be. For example, a new retail supervisor's initial pay is based on a comparison of his or her qualifications in comparison with those of current supervisors. Key "qualifications" looked at include education, experience, knowledge of store operations, and so forth. Future increases in pay are based largely on the results of the performance evaluations described above. However, Bill Goode occasionally recommends an "appropriate" general increase when he feels that the pay increases for a certain category of employees (including retail supervisors) have not kept up with inflation.

Questions for Case Teams

Assume you are a team of consultants called in by Joyce Morgan to help her examine the effectiveness of the company's human resource system. She is especially concerned about that system's impact on her retail supervisors and the individuals to whom they report. Focus specifically on that concern. Ask any questions about other "facts" you need to know, but try to raise these questions during class so others will be aware of the new information. Remember the recommendations for organizational change need to consider political issues.

Team 1 What procedure would you recommend to Joyce Morgan for the development of accurate job descriptions for retail supervisors?

Team 2 How should Joyce Morgan go about developing a human resource plan for the retail supervision area of the company?

Team 3 What approach would you recommend to Joyce Morgan for the recruitment of retail supervisors?

Team 4 How should Morgan's go about selecting individuals to be retail supervisors? What would you suggest to Joyce Morgan?

Team 5 Recommend an effective approach to the training of retail supervisors at Morgan's. How would you go about determining the topics to be covered in this training?

Team 6 How can Morgan's develop an effective performance appraisal system for retail supervisors? Describe the system you would recommend to Joyce Morgan.

Team 7 How can Morgan's go about developing an effective pay system for retail supervisors?

Instructions to Presenters

1. Use visual aids with key words or data to allow your audience to easily follow your presentation. In addition to your visual aids, you should provide your instructor with a one-page outline of your presentation.
2. The presentation should not exceed 25 minutes, with another 25 for class discussion afterward.
3. Grading will be based on your ability to apply human resource management concepts and also on the organization and clarity of your presentation.
4. Finally, each team member must submit a paper—basically a report to Joyce Morgan. You may rely at least partly on the text and the class notes for the presentation and the paper, but you must also use at least five other sources (and these must be cited within the paper).

Instructions to Audience Members

You are expected to get involved. Be prepared to direct questions to the presenters. You absolutely must read and analyze the case before class.

*9 Monongahela Mittens Manufacturing**

Monongahela Mittens Manufacturing (MMM) is a medium-sized manufacturing facility that produces high-quality gloves and mittens. Its product line consists of three basic models: a driving glove (Model 101), a dress glove (Model 102), and a ski mitten (Model 103). There is a strong seasonal demand for this ski product; 70 percent of all sales occur in the four-month period from November through February. The marketing and manufacturing departments have arrived at the following production schedule (Table 1) for the next fiscal year and have asked for your comments. This schedule minimizes inventory costs, a major consideration of the firm.

As a human resources manager, one of your tasks is manpower planning. This involves calculating how many people will be necessary for the firm to meet its production plans, and instituting plans and programs to insure that they will be available. There are certain assumptions you must make, based on information gathered from the industrial engineering department and your own department's records. The following pieces of information concern things that cannot be changed in the short run.

1. Standard Labor Hours. The total standard labor hours needed to produce each unit (pair) are:

*This case was prepared by Professor Marian M. Extejt, John Carroll University.

Model	*Hours*
101	0.33
102	0.33
103	0.40

2. Standard workday. The union contract defines a standard workday as eight hours. Any overtime is paid at 150 percent of standard wages.

3. Time loss. Absenteeism varies by quarter.

Quarter	*Percent of Actual Hours Lost*
1	2.5%
2	1.0
3	1.5
4	2.0

4. Wage Rate. The current average wage rate is $6.50/hour. Fringe benefits costs equal 15 percent of salary costs. All employees receive fringe benefits.

5. Production Schedule. The total annual demand for products is:

TABLE 1 Production Schedule for FY 1985 (one unit = one pair)

Model	*Quarter 1 (July–Sept.)*	*Quarter 2 (Oct.–Dec.)*	*Quarter 3 (Jan.–Mar.)*	*Quarter 4 (April–June)*	*Total*
101	5,551	3,629	4,296	9,180	22,656
102	5,551	3,629	4,296	9,180	22,656
103	16,653	13,131	8,400	29,784	67,968
Total	27,755	20,389	16,992	48,144	113,280

Model	*Number of Units*
101	22,656
102	22,656
103	67,968

The maximum number of units that can be produced in any one quarter is:

Model	Number of Units
101	9,200
102	9,200
103	30,000

The following pieces of information concern things that can be changed in the short run. You can manipulate these items, but consider the costs as well as the benefits of doing so.

1. Productivity. People do not or cannot produce at 100 percent efficiency. The standard hour figures given for production assume that a person is working continually and, therefore, do not reflect what is really going on. At this point, your department has measured productivity at 82 percent. Without the introduction of new technology or machinery, it is your best guess that productivity could be improved a maximum of 4 percent.

2. Staffing levels. Currently 21 people are engaged in the production process. The skills and abilities of all labor are interchangeable. Additional persons are not difficult to obtain, but hiring, training, and layoff costs do exist.

Discussion Questions

1. If current staffing levels are maintained, are there enough employees available to allow MMM to achieve its production schedule? If not, how many additional personnel are required? What alternatives does MMM have to secure these personnel?
2. If there are too many persons during any one production quarter, what alternatives does MMM have to deal with the surplus? Be sure to consider both the costs and benefits associated with each of these alternatives.
3. What effect will improving productivity have on staffing levels?
4. Can you suggest any shifts in production from one quarter to another that would help smooth out staffing requirements?

*10 Smiths of Smithville**

A very somber group left the October 1989 executive meeting of Smiths of Smithville. The long expected decision to downsize with a major reorganization and staffing reductions was confirmed by President Franklin Smith, Jr. The results from the

*Case was prepared by Professor Elmer H. Burack. Copyright © Elmer H. Burack, 1992.

three-year-old *Project Turnaround* were pronounced "largely a failure." The Fiber and Fabrics divisions (see Exhibit 1) were to sustain the major thrust of the organizational and staffing changes since the old-line (fine) Furniture Division was quite

EXHIBIT 1 Partial Corporate Organization Chart

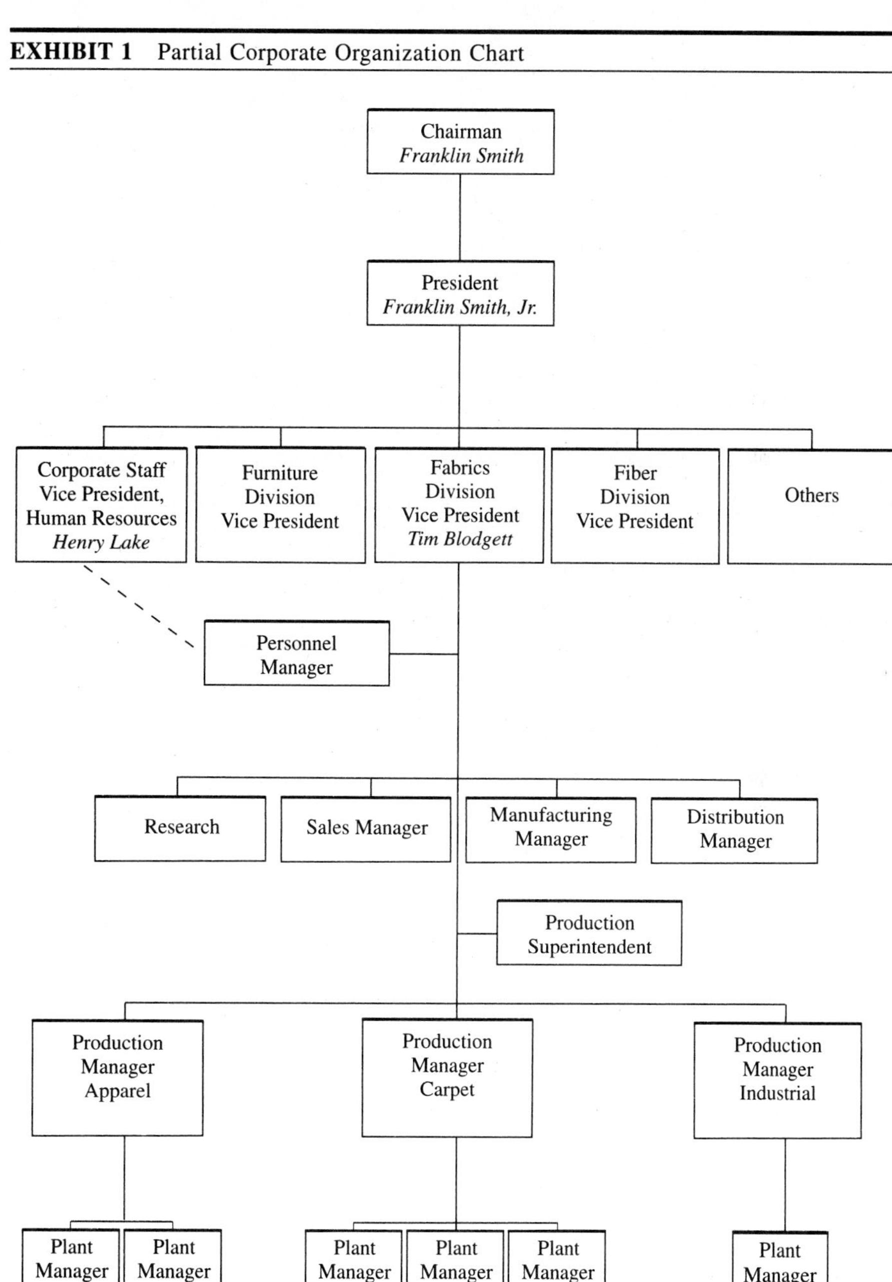

small and relatively stable. The managerial group was to be reduced by 25 percent and the workforce by 10 percent. It was also announced that: the current vice president for Fiber Division was taking early retirement; and that the two divisions, Fibers and Fabrics, would be consolidated under the current 39-year-old Fabrics' Division vice president, Tim Blodget (see Exhibit 2). Tim in consultation with the VP for human resource, Henry Lake, was to present a "short list" of recommended managerial and workforce personnel for termination.

In sum, they would have to trim 35 managers from the current group of 140 and 90 workers from the current workforce of 900. Chairman Franklin Smith and his son, President Franklin Smith, Jr., concurred on the guidelines issued to both Tom and Henry:

1. Since the last major staffing reductions two years ago affected mostly hourly people and since most people eligible for early retirement had already made their decisions, this cut was to focus importantly on managerial personnel.
2. Any termination involving an employer over 50 years of age and 20 years of service was to be reviewed by President Smith prior to any action being taken.
3. Seniority, though important and to be considered, was not to be the primary criterion for determining exclusions from the "short list"—primary emphasis was to be placed on performance and long run potential.
4. Women and minority people were not to be separated more aggressively than other employees.

EXHIBIT 2 The Downsized Organization

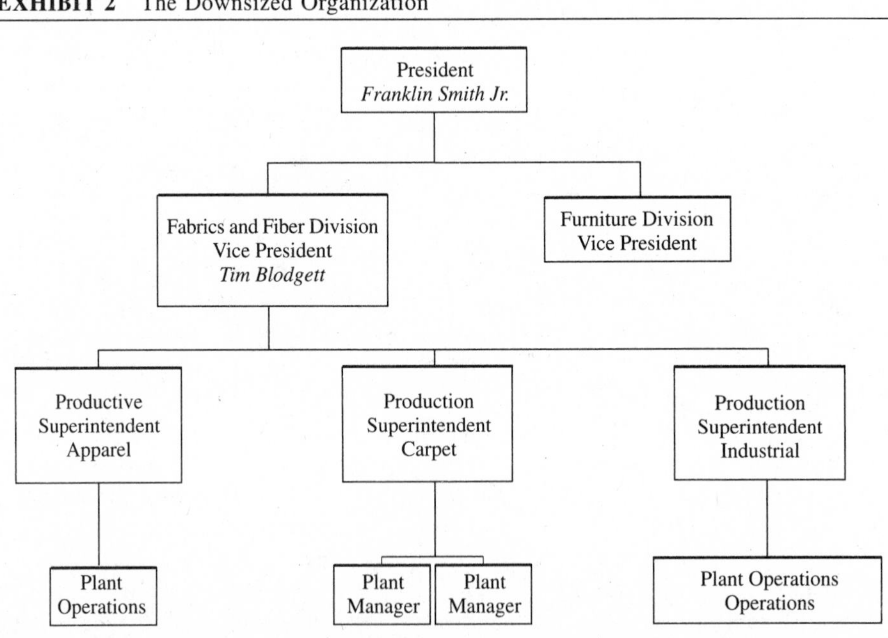

BACKGROUND

Smiths of Smithville was founded in 1938 as a fine furniture manufacturer in a small South Carolina town. Over the years, because of company growth, a new executive facility and administrative complex was constructed and located in a small town to make it proximate to people from several neighboring towns. The company became such an important factor in area employment and influence that the town was renamed Smithville in honor of the founder Franklin Smith. When his son, Franklin Smith, Jr., came into the business and moved into an officer's position in the early 70s, Smith Furniture was officially renamed Smiths of Smithville. Both Franklin Smith an his son attended top-flight business programs at Southeastern schools and, thus, from the beginning, formal education and a degree were stressed for all managerial personnel. Under Franklin Smith, Jr., who took over in 1978, formal education and the MBA often served as passports for mobility and promotion. Not surprisingly there was an educational diffusion effect, which influenced educational systems and the educational plans of the area's labor supply. By 1975 all new plant employees had at least completed high school and many had community college certificates. Largely due to the more recent influence of Franklin Smith, Jr., the character of the company changed radically over the 1970–85 period. Most sales growth resulted from acquisitions of fiber and fabric companies and the development of new products and markets. Fibers for wearing apparel and cloth products for furniture rapidly gave way to products designed for the automotive industry (interiors and trunk), tourist trade (fabrics for shipboard furniture plus carpeting), and the airline industry (seat and cabin fabrics and carpets). When Japanese automotive manufacturers established facilities in Ohio, Tennessee, California, and elsewhere, Smiths of Smithsville sought to penetrate these fast-growing markets too. When clothing manufacturers shifted to leisure-time wear, Smith products were prominent in their new wearing apparel. Company sales peaked at $1 billion in 1983.

ORGANIZATION CLIMATE

Smith employees in the past were enthusiastic regarding their employment. Excellent employee relations, a generous benefit program, regular awards for quality, and the use of Smith's products in nationally featured excursion ship, plane, car, and clothing advertising all contributed to employee company identification and a feeling of being a part of the "Smith Family."

The Smith family aggressively sought to make company employment rewarding and productive. Generous pay and fringe benefit packages, plus numerous career growth opportunities due to the rapid expansion of the company, maintained the attractiveness and stimulation of company employment. Also, company officials readily used the term *positive climate* to describe the culture. Company picnics, tuition programs, and a bottom-up/grow-your-own philosophy were examples of the company's numerous activities, creating golden handcuffs of employment and thereby loyalty and commitment. Most employees, if asked, would say that "If you make it through the tenth year and you're reasonably productive, you are largely assured that Smiths will always have a place for you." Thus, both management and employees envisioned a reciprocal *"agreement"* involving mutual benefits.

CORPORATE DECLINE

Though the company sustained two consecutive no profit years (1986, 1987), major losses in 1988, and no profit improvement in 1989, the trail of financial difficulties were said to date back to the late 1970s. One senior plant manager neatly summarized their problems:

> We simply grew too fast and then couldn't handle the rapidly growing organization that resulted. The furniture company became essentially a fiber and fabrics company. A two plant operation became a seven plant enterprise with almost 1,500 employees and a billion dollars in sales. We didn't have to consolidate. Sloppy staffing and lack of controls quickly transformed us into an overmanaged poorly communicating organization. Different plants set up different performance appraisal systems. Also, there was a heavy bias toward rating people's performance as *superior,* which was never corrected. Performance, quality, and even new product development suffered as a result.

Quality and the lack of creative product development were interrelated. Newer product applications required higher quality and delivery standards. New fibers and fabrics had to be developed to meet these stringent demands. In addition, German, Japanese, and various Pacific Rim countries started producing top-notch products at lower prices. The company was completely unprepared for these marketing dynamics. Additionally, over a period of perhaps 10 years, competitive pressures became even more intensive as new high-strength materials, new colors, just-in-time delivery arrangements and further elevation in quality levels took place. In late 1984, the vice president for human resources finally received authorization to hire an outside consulting firm. The consultants were to conduct a general management systems audit and counsel with various senior managers. One of the highlights from their report is presented in Exhibit 3. A major consideration in the selecting the consulting firm was the fact that it had a "total quality subgroup," which indoctrinated well with the *total quality management* concepts of Deming, Juran, and others. Exhibit 3, based on Deming's 14 quality initiatives, is an example of their orientation (this summary exhibit is supported by highly detailed analyses too extensive to include here).

Discussion Questions

The following questions are enumerated to assure full coverage in your commentary. Since the questions are interrelated, it is preferred that you treat these in a comprehensive way. Be sure to approach these from the strategic perspective of human resource management.

EXHIBIT 3 The Fourteen Points: Calibrating Progress Towards TQM in a New Paradigm Mode

Ratings

1	*2*	*3*	*4*	*5*
Classical approach; business as usual; individualistic and competitive; top-down leadership.		*Progress widely recognized, differences noted; new actions with regularity.*		*Clear, well established; consistent; embedded in culture.*

The Points	*Rating*	*Documentation*
1. Create constancy of purpose for product/service improvement.	1 (2) 3 4 5	____________
2. Adapt the new TQM/QVS philosophy	1 2 3 (4) 5	____________
3. Cease dependence on continuing surveillance/mass inspection.	1 2 (3) 4 5	____________
4. End practice of awarding business based on price alone.	1 2 (3) 4 5	____________
5. Continuing improvement: Q-V-S; production/distribution.	(1) 2 3 4 5	____________
6. Institute organization wide training to update competencies appropriate to TQM.	1 (2) 3 4 5	____________
7. Leadership: supportive, visionary	(1) 2 3 4 5	____________
8. Positive learning environment; people learn from mistakes; individual improvement, involvement and adaptation stressed.	1 2 (3) 4 5	____________
9. Teamwork, mutual staff-line support and cooperation; balance individual and group effort.	1 (2) 3 4 5	____________
10. Positive symbols and signs identifying a QVS culture with which all can identify.	1 2 3 (4) 5	____________
11. Clear organizational and operational goals uniting effectiveness and efficiency, short and long term.	(1) 2 3 4 5	____________

EXHIBIT 3: *(concluded)*

12. Individual identification with product/service; pride of workmanship; supervision, system, and materials congruent with TQM/QVS.	1 ② 3 4 5	________
13. Institutionalize training education as basic strategies.	1 2 3 4 ⑤	________
14. Organize for instituting a total TQM effort including a top management team, a critical mass of knowledgeable people throughout the organization and continuing means to nourish the quality culture.	1 ② 3 4 5	________

1. Assume the role of a human resource consultant conversant with strategic business and human resource matters. Develop a brief executive summary, say one or two paragraphs, of what you feel this company situations entails.
2. What are the major issues confronting the company and the priorities which might be assigned to these, and the rationale for your selections?
3. Provide representative groups of strategic human resource matters from question 2 and suggest how these might be tackled. Use whatever models and at least four perspectives which seem appropriate to your approach, but be sure and reference the source of these.
4. What are some important examples of research projects to be launched by the vice president of human resources regarding issues or questions for which appropriate data or information are not likely to exist at present?

*11 Downsizing the Organization**

Alpha Gamma Company is a multidivision company serving worldwide consumer and technical markets. Annual sales are in excess of $1 billion. Its history dates back well over 100 years, during which time it has had a centralized authority structure and paternalism in terms of its culture.

The company has been quite successful and profitable over the years. However, sales dropped 8 percent in 1980 from the previous year. While sales and net profits both rose somewhat in 1981, 1982 showed a reduction in total sales, with the company operating at a significant loss, due primarily to the severe impact of the 1981–82 recession.

*This case was prepared by Professor Cliff Harrison, Concordia College.

The year 1982 was troublesome in other ways, with the company becoming the target for an unfriendly takeover by another corporation. As a defense strategy, the company was forced to sell off one of its most profitable businesses, since that business was what the unfriendly suitor was after. This action effectively warded off the takeover bid.

While successfully blocking the 1982 takeover attempt, the company was facing new challenges. The newly appointed chairman and chief executive officer was moving to a philosophy of decentralization, which led to a corporate restructuring of the organization. This, coupled with the divestiture of a major division and the state of the economy, was producing a surplus of employees at the headquarters level. With one less business to service (the divested division), and fewer corporate services needed by the decentralized divisions, the company was faced with the need to reduce its staff of headquarters, managers, professionals, and other support personnel.

The decision was made to reduce overhead costs significantly, including payroll expenses. With corporate overhead now too high for operating divisions to absorb, the chairman decided that significant cost reductions would be required, although no specific dollar or headcount objectives were mandated. Each department head was charged with the task of determining where personnel, programs, or other costs could be cut. Lists of employees who could be "surplused" were drawn up, along with the plan for other cost reductions. These plans were discussed with the CEO and, in cases where the plans were not rigorous enough, further negotiations and pressures were applied to increase them to a level satisfactory to the chairman.

The initial program called for reduction of the corporate headquarters staffs by 150 employees, including clerical. The initial list of 150 employees to be terminated was carefully reviewed. The employee files and performance data were scrutinized by the human resources chief and internal law department to reduce, as much as possible, the risks of discrimination complaints and litigation.

Following considerable debate among the senior managers about the use of external outplacement services, it was decided that outplacement services would be provided by using internal human resources professionals, rather than engaging an external outplacement consulting firm. Consistent with its historical paternalistic culture, there was considerable concern for the surplus employees, especially those with long service and being more senior in age. It was anticipated that these employees would experience severe termination trauma and would need carefully planned and orchestrated assistance.

When the staff reduction plans were complete and the reduction date established, group meetings were held with key managers by human resources professionals to train them in how to handle the termination interviews. Each manager was given a script to follow in conducting the interviews so inappropriate statements would be avoided as much as possible. A packet of materials for each employee to be terminated was provided during these briefings.

Final selection of employees to be terminated was done by department heads, with careful oversight by the CEO and human resources director. It was the department head who later conducted the terminations, rather than the immediate supervisors. Final decisions on which employees would go were made by the department heads. Selection was made principally by selecting those who were incumbents of positions being eliminated and by the selective judgments of department managers. Performance was a lesser factor, due to the lack of objective performance data. Seniority was indicated as a factor when it related to newer employees.

There was heated debate over how much notice employees should be given prior to termination day. Due to the concern that there could be disruption, rebellion, and possible destruction, especially in data processing areas, it was decided that the day of notice would also be the last day worked. The best the human resources chief could do was to get agreement to move the termination date to midweek, rather than Friday. This meant that terminated employees could begin work with the human resources counselors immediately, rather than having to agonize over a weekend without any constructive work being initiated. While the human resources executive believed that the employees were mature and loyal enough to handle advance notice in an appropriate manner, he was not able to convince top management of that. This appears to be in conflict with the indicated paternalistic nature of the organization.

The severance formula was 3 percent of annual salary multiplied by years of service (a $40,000-a-year employee with 20 years of service would have received $24,000, paid out as salary continuation). Minimum amount of severance was four weeks' pay. Benefits—health, dental, and life insurance—were kept in force for the duration of the severance payment period. The period of payment also was counted as time worked for pension calculation purposes. By the time the termination date arrived, a career counseling center and placement center had been established (in the headquarters facility, but with a separate entrance). Internal counseling, desk space, telephone usage, word processing, and printing of résumés was provided for those who wished to take advantage of the centers' services. About 70 percent of those discharged did use the centers. In addition, the company wrote to 500 employers in the area, advising them of the staff reduction and of the types of employees who were available for other positions. Considerable response was received, which resulted in many employees being hired from this activity. The company also paid for résumés to be put on a regional computerized job bank utilized by subscribing organizations.

Following the staff reduction, the chairman held a series of group meetings with remaining headquarters employees to discuss what was done and to provide the reasons for the action. No other formal efforts were made to assess the impact of the staff reduction on the remaining organization or on steps taken to overcome the negative consequences. The managers interviewed during this study stated that the impact was very negative on morale, on employee loyalty and commitment, and on productivity. This condition continued for a number of months, employees being obsessed by the fear that the "other shoe" would drop and that they might be next to be terminated. Their concerns turned out to be accurate; about nine months later, the second reduction was decided upon. Fifty more headquarters employees were to be dismissed.

Discussion Questions

1. Assess the conditions that led to the retrenchment decision. What alternative strategies could have been employed to reduce or eliminate the staff reduction?
2. What effect would you expect the reduction to have on those being terminated?
3. Discuss how the employees to be terminated were selected. What would you have done differently? What potential risks do you see?
4. What are the advantages of an in-company outplacement program versus using an external consulting firm?
5. What are the positive and negative consequences of the firm's strategy of giving no advance notice to the selected employees?
6. What impact do you believe the staff reduction will have on the remaining organization? What actions could the company take to minimize negative impact of such a reduction?
7. How adequate and appropriate was the company's severance package and other assistance provided?
8. What steps would you take to plan and implement the second staff reduction? What specific things would you do differently from the first cutback?

---

*12 Job Descriptions at HITEK**

INTRODUCTION

Jennifer Hill was excited about joining HITEK Information Services after receiving her MBA. Her job involved examining compensation practice, and her first assignment was to review HITEK's job descriptions. She was to document her work and to make recommended changes, which would include the reduction of the more than 600 job descriptions.

BACKGROUND

To its stockholders and the rest of the outside world, HITEK is a highly profitable, highly aggressive company in the computer business. In addition to its numerous government contracts, it provides software and hardware to businesses and individuals. From its inception in the late 1960s, it maintained its position on the leading

---

*Reprinted by permission from *Personnel and Human Resource Management* by Randall Schuler, Stuart Youngblood, and Vanda Huber.

edge by remaining flexible and adaptable to the turbulent environment in which it operated. It is a people-intensive organization that relies enormously on its human resources; therefore, it is in HITEK's best interest to establish policies and procedures that nurture productivity and enhance the satisfaction of its employees. A memo from the president to HITEK employees that exemplifies this approach appears as Exhibit 1.

Because the computer industry is growing at an incredible pace, opportunities for placement are abundant and the competition for high-quality human resources is tremendous. HITEK had grown about 30 percent in the last three years, and its management knows that, just as easily as it attracted new employees, it could lose them. Its turnover rate is about average for its industry.

HITEK remains relatively small at 1,000 employees and it prides itself on its "small company culture." This culture is maintained partly by the use of a computer memo system that can put any employee in touch with anyone at HITEK and by the utilization of open office spaces—with no doors, in many cases. The relatively flat organizational structure (see Exhibit 2) and the easy accessibility of all corporate levels also promotes an open-door policy. All-in-all, employees enjoy working for HITEK, and management is in touch with the organization's "pulse."

With the notable exception of the human resources department (HRD), there are few rules at HITEK. Work in a department is often shared by all levels of employees, and positions are redefined to match the specific skills, abilities, and interests of the incumbent. Overqualified and overachieving individuals are often hired, but then are promoted rapidly. Nothing is written down, and, if newcomers want to know why something is done a certain way, they must ask the person(s) who created the procedure. There is extensive horizontal linkage between departments, perpetuating the blurring of distinction between departments.

EXHIBIT 1 O'Hara's Computer Memo to Employees

Subject: Share a Thought Luncheons

To: All Employees

From: Billy O'Hara

Date: July 31

HITEK has always been a company whose employees contribute innovative and creative ideas. For this to continue, our environment needs to be one where employees are comfortable expressing their ideas.

The Share a Thought Luncheon that I introduced in the recent issue of our newsletter is one avenue for you to informally share an idea or a concept. This time is intended to be an informal session with Andy Simms, Joe Feldon, and me.

Our first luncheon is scheduled for August 13. To join us, just drop me a brief summary of your idea. You will receive additional details as the luncheon date approaches.

I welcome your ideas and look forward to some interesting "brainstorming" sessions.

EXHIBIT 2 HITEK's Organizational Chart

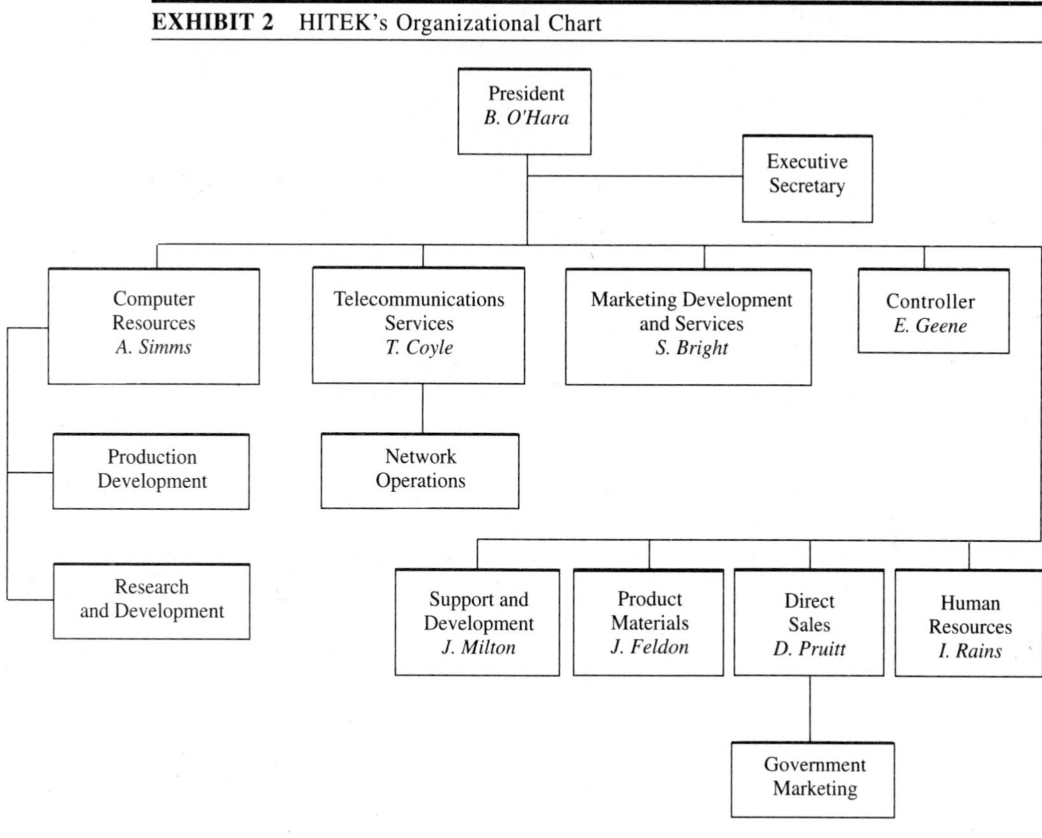

THE HUMAN RESOURCES DEPARTMENT

The HRD stands in stark contrast to the rest of HITEK. About 30 people are employed in HRD, including the support staff members or about one human resource employee per 33 HITEK employees. As can be seen in Exhibit 3, in addition to the vice president for human resources, there are managers of (1) compensation and benefits, (2) human relations, (3) employment, (4) training and development, and (5) the fitness center. On average, four people report to each of these managers, including one person, such as the compensation analyst, who is expected to hold a professional degree.

The vice president for human resources, Isabel Rains, rules the department with an *iron fist.* HRD employees are careful to mold their ideas to match Rains's perspective. When newcomers suggest changes, they are told that "this is the way things have always been done," because "it's our culture." Most of the HRD functions are bound by written rules and standard operating procedures. HRD employees know their job descriptions well and there is little overlap in duties.

With the exception of one recruiter, all 12 of the incumbents whose positions are represented in Exhibit 3 are women. Only half of them have degrees in industrial relations or human resources management, and only a fourth have related experience with another company. Most of them have been promoted from clerical positions. In fact, some employees view the vice presidency (of HRD) as a "gift" given to Isabel, a former executive secretary, the day after she received her bachelor's degree at a local college, rather than a position of authority and expertise. Connie Yarro's background is in library work, and, although the other four managers have HRM degrees, their only experience is in college internships—with HITEK. Their subordinates found their way to human resources through various channels, from fashion merchandising to secretarial work.

In other departments, it is widely believed that professional degrees and related experiences lead to expertise. Mentoring, whereby a senior employee helps socialize a newcomer into the company and arranges experiences to increase the newcomer's skills and competencies—and hence his or her confidence—is common. But because none of the HRD employees can be considered a senior employee, mentoring is minimal. Consequently, HRD employees tend to be defensive and secretive in dealings with employees in other departments, perhaps as a result of their insecurity.

The major reward systems of the company are not linked to the human resources department. Even the company's annual employee recognition dinner is perceived as a reward from Billy O'Hara, not from HRD. Thus, the HRD is perceived as an ineffectual group of clerical employees.

One incident that conveyed the HRD's image to Jennifer Hill occurred during her second week on the job. While preparing a job description with Dave Pruitt, Jennifer explained that she would submit the job description to Janet Voris for final approval. Dave became confused and asked, "But Janet is only a clerical person; why would she be involved?"

EXHIBIT 3 The Structure of the Human Resource Department

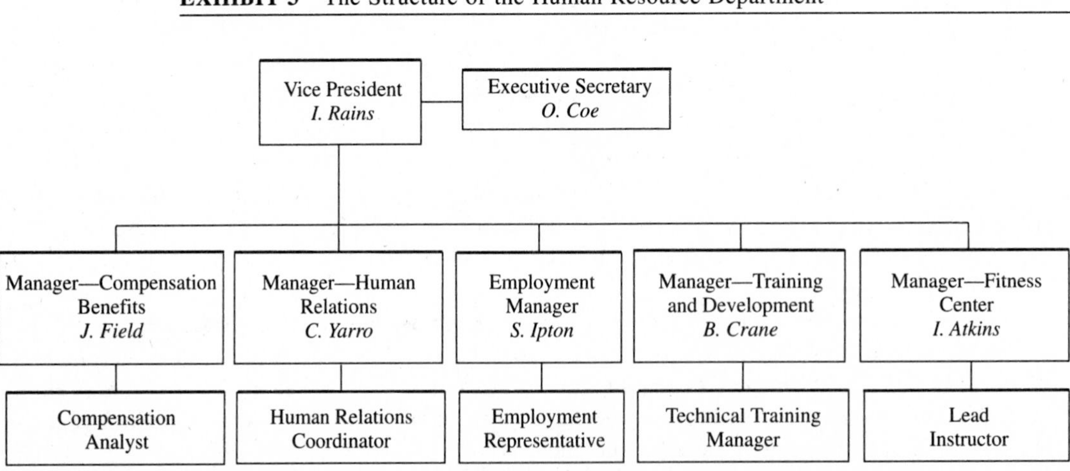

JENNIFER HILL'S DUTIES

At HITEK, the pool of job descriptions had grown almost daily as newcomers were hired, but many of the old job descriptions were not discarded even when obsolete. Other job descriptions needed updating. Because the job descriptions, particularly those representing benchmark positions, were going to be important in HITEK's hiring and revised compensation program, Jennifer knew she would have to do a careful job of determining what changes were needed. She also felt that it would be beneficial to HITEK and to the HRD if she could help managers understand other ways in which the job descriptions could be used.

Jennifer spent some time thinking about how to proceed. She considered the uses of the job descriptions and what steps she would need to take to accomplish all that was expected of her. Support from within the HRD was scarce, because other employees were busy gathering materials for the annual review of HITEK's hiring, promotion, and development practices conducted by the Equal Employment Opportunity Commission.

After six harried months on the job and much frustration, Jennifer had revised all of the descriptions that were still needed (an example of "old" and "new" job descriptions appear as Exhibits 4 and 5). She also was beginning to develop some strong opinions about how the HRD functioned at HITEK and what needed to be done to improve its effectiveness and its image. She decided to arrange a confidential lunch with Billy O'Hara.

EXHIBIT 4 An "Old" Job Description

Associate Programmer

Basic objective	Perform coding, testing, and documentation of programs, under the supervision of a project leader.
Specific tasks	Perform coding, debugging, and testing of a program when given general program specifications. Develop documentation of the program. Assist in the implemetation and training of the users in the usage of the system. Report to the manager, management information services, as requested.
Job qualifications	Minimum: (*a*) BA/BS degree in relevant field or equivalent experience/knowledge; (*b*) programming knowledge in FORTRAN; (*c*) good working knowledge of business and financial applications. Desirable: (*a*) computer programming experience in a time-sharing environment; (*b*) some training or education in COBOL, PL1, or assembler languages.

EXHIBIT 5 A "New" Job Description

Associate Programmer

General statement of duties	Perform coding, debugging, testing, and documentation of software under the supervision of a technical superior. Involves some use of independent judgment.
Supervision received	Works under close supervision of a technical superior or department manager.
Supervision exercised	No supervisory duties required.
Examples of duties	(Any one position may not include all the duties listed, nor do listed examples include all duties that may be found in positions of this class.) Confers with analysts, supervisors, and/or representatives of the departments to clarify software intent and programming requirements. Performs coding, debugging, and testing of software when given program specifications for a particular task or problem. Writes documentation of the program. Seeks advice and assistance from supervisor when problems outside of realm of understanding arise. Communicates any program specification deficiencies back to supervisor. Reports ideas concerning design and development back to supervisor. Assists in the implementation of the system and training of end users. Provides some support and assistance to users. Develops product knowledge and personal expertise and proficiency in system usage. Assumes progressively complex and independent duties as experience permits. Performs all duties in accordance with corporate and departmental standards.
Minimum qualifications	Education: BA/BS degree in relevant field or equivalent experience/ knowledge in computer science, math, or other closely related field. Experience: No prior computer programming work experience necessary. Knowledge, skills, and abilities: Ability to exercise initiative and sound judgment. Knowledge of a structural language. Working knowledge in operating systems. Ability to maintain open working relationship with supervisor. Logic and problem-solving skills. Develop system flowcharting skills.
Desirable qualifications	Exposure to BASIC, FORTRAN, or PASCAL. Some training in general accounting practices and controls; effective written and oral communcation skills.

Discussion Questions

1. What are the goals of HITEK? What are the goals of the human resources department? Why does the conflict create problems for HITEK?
2. Organization members can draw from several bases of power, such as referent power or reward power. Is the human resources department powerful? Why is it important for HITEK to maintain a professional competent human resources function?
3. Jobs change frequently at HITEK. Shouldn't the HRD simply discontinue the practice of job analysis and stop writing job descriptions?
4. What steps should Jennifer Hill take in performing the tasks assigned to her? How do your answers to the earlier questions affect your answer?
5. Is the new job description (Exhibit 5) better than the old one (Exhibit 4)? Why or why not?
6. What should Jennifer suggest to the president concerning the image and operation of the HRD?

Section C

EEO, Affirmative Action, and Reverse Discrimination

13 Majestic Hotel: Just a Phone Call Away

Ron and Kathy Tracy were rather tired from their long cross-country drive from Toledo, Ohio, to Las Vegas, Nevada. Although they both felt worn out, they were excited about the rare opportunity for the two of them to have a holiday just for two. After many hours on the road, they looked forward to their stay at the Adams Mark Hotel in downtown St. Louis. The hotel, one of their favorites, is located within a stone's throw of St. Louis's famous Arch, the "Gateway to the West."

After a few more hours' drive they arrived in St. Louis. They unpacked, grabbed a quick bite to eat, then took a brief stroll over to Busch Stadium to see the home of the baseball Cardinals. Despite the fact that Ron traveled by wheelchair, nothing held the couple back from taking walks and doing other things together. Ron proved the old adage that people with disabilities could do anything a person without disabilities could do.

On their return from the ballpark, Ron remembered that they needed to call ahead to confirm hotel reservations for their next stop. The Tracys hoped to get an early start, then drive west to Denver. So, before they went to bed, Ron called the Majestic Hotel in Denver. The conversation follows:

Ron

Reservations desk, please.

This is Jean, how may I help you?

Ron

I would like to confirm that we have a reservation there tomorrow for a room that is wheelchair accessible.

Jean

Sir, there are wheelchair accessible rooms available for tomorrow, but I am unable to guarantee your reservation.

Ron

I don't understand. You say you have wheelchair accessible rooms but cannot guarantee them? Is my request for a nonsmoking, single, king-sized bed a problem?

Jean

Yes sir, that is a problem. We cannot guarantee that there will be rooms with king-sized beds available for those physically disabled individuals who have a nonsmoking preference. We have a limited number of rooms with king-sized beds set aside for nonsmoking guests. If guests with disabilities decide to stay an additional day, we may not be able to accommodate them. Our computerized reservation system assigns the designated rooms for future guests on the basis that people using the rooms will vacate those rooms in accordance with the reservation request they made prior to coming to the hotel or, where possible, to the reservation made upon arrival.

Ron

I am still confused. People not needing wheelchair-accessible rooms can also encounter situations where people decide to stay a day longer. Are those with disabilities treated the same way?

Jean

I am sorry. I can definitely tell you by telephone that we have your reservation. That is not a problem. What I cannot do is give you a 100 percent guarantee that a wheelchair-accessible room will be available. There is a possibility that a wheelchair-accessible room with twin beds will be available. Nearly all of our wheelchair-accessible rooms are in the twin-bed configuration. That's about it.

After talking with Jean at Majestic, Ron decided to call a larger, more expensive hotel chain in Denver. Finally, he requested and received a wheelchair-accessible room that met all of his specifications at the downtown Denver Embassy Suites Hotel. Ron and Kathy would have to pay more for their accommodations at the Embassy Suites than they would have had to pay as Majestic. Their trip had gotten off to a rotten start!

Discussion Questions

1. What rights do guests with a need for wheelchair-accessible rooms have?
2. What responsibility does a hotel have to respond to the needs of those who need to be accommodated?

---

*14 EEO and AIDS: A Right to Know**

Service supervisor Ellen Leary didn't need to be a doctor to know that Jim Fleermond, a fifth-year service rep, didn't look well. She was sure it had something to do with his many recent requests for time off to see his doctor.

"You feeling all right, Jim?" she asked when she met him at the water fountain.

"Why, did I do something wrong?" he asked defensively.

* Reprinted with permission from THE EEO REVIEW, #248, September 1987.

"Not at all, you're doing fine," she assured him. "Just asking."

In the following weeks, Vic Marconi, service supervisor in another unit, approached her. "How's Jim Fleermond?" he inquired.

"Okay . . . well, not okay, I guess. He has to see his doctor all the time. Why do you ask?"

"I heard he hangs out with a gay crowd. One of them just died of AIDS, and another has been diagnosed positive. I thought you'd want to know."

"Oh!" Leary was stunned. "I . . . thanks for telling me, Vic."

When Fleermond asked her for time off to see his doctor again, she used the opportunity to confirm her suspicions.

"I'd like to say yes, Jim, but you're asking for a lot of time off these days," she said. "It would help me to know what this is all about."

"I don't have to tell you," he retorted.

"I've stretched the rules for you more than once," she said firmly. "If you want more time, I want to know the reason."

"You won't tell anyone?" Fleermond said anxiously.

"Anything you tell me is confidential," said Leary.

Fleermond acknowledged that he had been diagnosed as having ARC—AIDS-related complex.

Leary was saddened to hear her suspicions confirmed. She consulted with the medical department to see if she needed to take any special measures for Fleermond or other employees. But they said no special steps were necessary.

At the next staff meeting, Vic Marconi asked her, "Whatever happened with Fleermond? Was there anything to those rumors?"

Leaning toward him, she said quietly, "Don't spread it around, Vic, but you were right. The poor guy has ARC."

"What a rotten break," Marconi sighed.

Within two weeks, Leary's department began to have morale problems. She no longer saw Fleermond chatting with co-workers. And he suddenly had a lot of space around him. He seemed to be isolated from other employees. Then she heard that several employees would not use the water fountain. She explained to them that it was perfectly safe, but got nowhere. "I'm not going to take a chance of getting AIDS," one of them said. Poor Fleermond, she reflected. He now has to cope with unfriendly co-workers in addition to his illness.

Finally, Fleermond resigned. She expressed her sympathy and well wishes—but was relieved at his departure.

To Leary, it seemed that a difficult problem had been resolved for her—until she was informed by personnel that Fleermond had filed suit against the company, claiming constructive discharge (being forced to resign), discrimination because of handicap (AIDS), and invasion of privacy.

Discussion Questions

1. What, if anything, did management do wrong in this case?
2. Do you think the lawsuit against the firm will be successful? Why or why not?

*15 Affirmative Action and Whom to Hire**

Mr. Green, vice president of personnel, of the Hackney Paper Box Company has to make a decision on whom to hire to be personnel manager for a 125-employee Hackney box plant located in Philadelphia, Pennsylvania.

The company affirmative action office has strongly advised him to hire a young black woman, June Triss, who has applied. But Mr. Green believes a young white male applicant, Bob Young, to be better qualified for this specific job. Mr. Green has narrowed the field to these two. Hackney Paper Box Company has 47 small plants, each with a white male personnel manager. There are no other management-level personnel employees in the company except at corporate headquarters, where there are 10 management-level white male employees. Of Hackney's approximately 1,000 management-level employees, only six are black, two are Mexican-American, and six are female. Prior to 1964 no management-level persons were from any minority group and there were no females in management.

Mr. Green's evaluation and summary of the qualifications of the two applicants are as follows:

I. June Triss
   a. Extremely intelligent but seemed to lack common sense.
   b. Master's degree in industrial relations from Cornell, a magna cum laude graduate.
   c. Three years' experience as an assistant personnel manager at a leading nonunion department store; no union relations experience.
   d. Mediocre references from Cornell and the department store.
   e. Ambitious—told the plant manager she would have his job in three years.
   f. Poor personality—informed Mr. Green she was interviewing Hackney, not Hackney interviewing her.
   g. The members of the management group in Philadelphia did not seem to like her.
   h. She has stated that she would sue the company for discrimination if she did not get the job.

II. Bob Young
   a. Three years of college as a personnel major but forced to transfer for economic reasons to a small liberal arts college in his hometown. He received a degree in history and graduated in the middle third of his class.
   b. Five years' experience as assistant personnel manager in a 500-employee unionized paper box plant.

---

*This case was prepared by Professor James C. Hodgetts of Memphis State University and is intended to be used as a teaching device rather than to show correct or incorrect methods of operation.

c. Good references from his college and excellent references from the paper box plant.
d. Excellent personality—Mr. Green and all members of management with whom he talked at Philadelphia liked him.
e. Not very aggressive—Mr. Green doubted if he would ever progress very far in the company but believed he would be an excellent plant personnel manager.

Both Triss and Young had answered an advertisement in the *New York Times.* The advertisement set minimum qualifications of a college degree and three years' experience as an assistant personnel manager. The advertisement did not say what kind of experience as an assistant personnel manager and did not say union relations experience was necessary.

All of the Philadelphia managers were white males. The personnel department at Philadelphia consisted of the manager and a secretary. The plant manager and production superintendent had experience dealing with the union but this was primarily the job of the personnel manager.

Mr. Green has to make a decision this week so the new personnel manager can spend some time with the retiring personnel manager before he leaves.

Discussion Question

What should Mr. Green decide? Why? Carefully explain.

---

16 Mutual Consent*

BACKGROUND

Bambinos' Sauce Company was founded in New York City in 1942 by Lorenzo and Contassina Bambino, recent immigrants from Italy. Using a decades-old family recipe, their sauces became an immediate hit in the greater New York area. Over the years the product line was expanded, the company grew to over 500 employees, and its products were in demand by restaurants and specialty stores throughout the mid-Atlantic region.

TRUEHARDT'S EXPERIENCE AT BAMBINOS'

Carole Truehardt had taken a job as an outside sales representative for the company on graduating from college in 1985. Carole was a vivacious and friendly person, who loved meeting people and going out and having fun. Customers seemed to enjoy her personality and sense of humor, for she quickly became one of the top sales

* 1992, David M. Leuser, PhD, Plymouth State College of the University System of New Hampshire.

reps in the state of New Jersey. This was quite an accomplishment in a regional industry where the sales force was dominated by men. While there were occasional rumors after company social functions that she could be "quite a partier," her consistent sales record and outgoing nature made her generally popular in the patriarchal, family run organization.

However, Carole was beginning to experience some dissatisfaction with her current position. After seven years on the job, she remained in essentially the same entry-level sales position into which she had been hired. Granted, the company had moved her around through a variety of territories, and it always paid her expense vouchers without question. For that matter, her salary plus commissions gave her an income as high as some men who worked several levels above her in the organization.

Yet she couldn't seem to land a real promotion. Several of the men who had joined the organization after her were now in a variety of supervisory and managerial positions. She had begun applying for promotion in earnest four years ago, but her boss, Carmine Giovanni, had consistently dissuaded her. He claimed that she was "too valuable to the company" in her current position. At one point, about three years ago, Giovanni had given her a significant raise and a slight increase in responsibility. She was put in charge of training for all new sales representatives in the greater New York City area. Oddly enough, one of the first recruits that she trained was her boss's nephew, Antonio.

While she really did enjoy her work, she wanted a career, not just a job! She began to think that she might stand a better chance of promotion outside the marketing organization. Then she saw the job listing in the company newsletter: Assistant Vice President for Public Relations. Among other things, the listing stated "Industry understanding a prerequisite, good interpersonal skills a must, marketing experience a plus."

THE APPLICATION

Carole immediately polished up her résumé and sent off a three-page letter of application to Enrico Bambino, the vice president for public relations. About two weeks later, Bambino called Carole at her home on a Sunday evening. He explained that he was considering her for the position, though there were several other men who looked better than her on paper. Carole asked for an opportunity to prove herself. Bambino reminded her that there were no female junior executives (nor executives, for that matter) at Bambino Sauce Company, and never had been. However, he indicated that he was aware of her reputation in the marketing organization, and he agreed to interview on that basis. He made arrangements for her to visit with him at the executive offices in New York City on Friday afternoon.

THE INTERVIEW

Carole arrived early for the interview and was ushered into Mr. Bambinos' office shortly thereafter. On her introduction, she extended her arm to shake Mr. Bambinos' hand. Bambino smiled and shook her hand, then immediately clasped his left hand about hers as well. Looking deeply in her eyes, he commented: "You are even more beautiful than they said you were." Carole blushed, and asked if they could get on with the interview. Bambino agreed, on the condition that she call him "Enri," rather than Mr. Bambino.

The interview went quite well. Carole felt that she had impressed Mr. Bambino with her knowledge of the industry as well as the values and preferences of their customers. For his part, Bambino was impressed with her charm and personality. He asked her to accompany him to dinner so they could continue their conversation in a more intimate atmosphere. Carole readily agreed, and they went off to eat at one of the finest Italian restaurants in New York City.

During dinner, Bambino began to discuss his passion for fine wines. Carole was impressed with his broad knowledge and apparent worldliness. He introduced her to the fine points of the many rare wines.

After dinner, he invited Carole over to his suite to show her his collection of rare wines. Carole was flattered, and responded: "Of course I'd love to, but won't your wife be upset if I come unexpectedly?"

Bambino explained that he and his family live on an estate in Connecticut, but that for the last three months he had been maintaining a suite in the city "for those nights when I have to work late or the traffic's just impossible." He said his wife and kids liked it that way, because he wasn't grumpy when he got home anymore.

When they arrived at the suite, Carole was impressed with its size and the fine quality of its furnishings. But Bambinos' wine collection, covering a whole wall in the sitting room, was the most impressive thing. Bambino allowed her to sample several wines that were each over 75 years old. Carole felt very warm and comfortable.

When Bambino dimmed the lights, turned on the CD player, and asked her to dance, she wasn't quite sure how to respond. "But what would your wife think? Perhaps we shouldn't . . ."

"Oh hush, my dear," said Bambino as he placed his hand over her mouth and gently helped her to her feet. "She understands."

Carole doesn't remember a whole lot after that. The next morning, she awoke in the bedroom alone. There was a note taped to the mirror.

> Carole,
>
> Thanks for a lovely evening. We really ought to do it again sometime. Sorry I had to leave early, but I've got a 7:00 meeting. Take your time, I won't be back in town until Monday.
>
> Just submit your expense voucher to my secretary and I'll take care of everything.
>
> Affectionately,
>
> Enri

THE OUTCOME

Throughout the next week, Carole pondered the events of the past Friday. She was sure that she had made a good impression, though she felt funny about how things had ended up. After all, she really didn't want that to happen. But she had had a wonderful time with Enri, and she felt that she had an excellent shot at the promotion.

Another week passed and Carole still hadn't heard anything from Bambino. She was thinking about calling him, but didn't want to appear to pushy. One evening she was at the Rigoletto, a posh Philadelphia restaurant, waiting for the arrival of the owner, Roberto Rigoletto. Roberto was one of her best customers. Carole felt especially close to Roberto. He had been her first big contract back in 1986 and a regular and loyal customer ever since then. He had sort of taken her under his wing and taught her most of what she knew about the industry. In addition, he had referred her to a number of additional restaurants in the area, resulting in a significant and long-lasting boost in sales.

As Carole waited, she thumbed through the evening paper. When she got to the business pages, she couldn't believe what she saw. In the section on "People in the News" she read that Antonio Giovanni had just been promoted to the position of assistant vice president for public relations at Bambinos' Sauce Company, after three years of experience in sales in the New York City area.

Just then, Roberto arrived. He could see that Carole was upset, and asked her to explain what was wrong. As Carole told him the story, he began to clench his fists. But when she told him what happened Friday evening, his face turned red and his eyes bulged. Suddenly he interrupted her: "You are my girl!" he shouted, and stormed out of the restaurant.

The next day Carole phoned her boss and explained what had happened. She told him that Bambino had raped her, but that she would spare the company the threat of a scandal if she were promoted immediately to the vacant position of regional sales manager for the Philadelphia area.

Giovanni replied that the promotion was not his business, and, for that matter, it was not hers either. He indicated that he had spoken to Enrico Bambino shortly after her interview when Bambino had called him for a reference. Giovanni warned Carole that the Bambino family did not react well to threats and advised her to let the matter drop.

The following night, as she was watching the evening news, Carole had another shock. Robert Rigoletto, the prominent young Philadelphia restaurant owner, had been arrested at a posh New York restaurant, where he was alleged to have shot an executive from the Bambinos' Sauce Company five times in the chest. Enrico Bambino, age 48, who had been dining with a young female companion, was listed in critical condition.

Discussion Questions

1. What are the significant management problems in this case? Who is potentially or actually impacted by them?
2. In what ways does the Civil Rights Act of 1991 make the company even more vulnerable to Carole's charges?
3. Explain who should do what now, and why.

17 Meritor Savings Bank v. Vinson

A former Meritor Savings Bank employee, Michelle Vinson, brought suit against the bank and her supervisor, a vice president there. She alleged that the vice president and manager of one of Meritor's branches, Sidney Taylor, demanded sexual favors from her.

Ms. Vinson first met Mr. Taylor in 1974. On that occasion, she asked him if she might obtain employment at the bank. Mr. Taylor gave her an application, which she completed and returned the next day. Later that same day Mr. Taylor called to inform Michelle that she had been hired. Taylor served as supervisor of Vinson when she began her employment as a teller-trainee. She was later promoted to teller, head teller, and assistant branch manager. All information available indicates that her advancement was based on merit alone. In September of 1978, Vinson informed her supervisor (Taylor) that she was taking sick leave for an indefinite period. On November 1, 1978, the bank discharged her for excessive use of that leave.

According to Vinson, she had "constantly been subjected to sexual harassment" by Taylor. At trial, she testified that, when she was hired and during her probationary period as a teller-trainee, Taylor treated her in a fatherly way and made no sexual advances. Shortly thereafter, however, he invited her to dinner and, during the course of the meal, suggested that they go to a motel to have sexual relations. At first she refused, but out of what she described as fear of losing her job she eventually agreed. Vinson says that Taylor thereafter made repeated demands on her for sexual favors, usually at the branch, both during and after business hours. She estimated that over the next several years she had intercourse with him some 40 to 50 times. In addition, Vinson testified that Taylor fondled her in front of other employees, followed her into the women's rest room when she went there alone, exposed himself to her, and even forcibly raped her on several occasions. These activities stopped after 1977, she stated, when she began and continued a relationship with a young man.

Vinson also claimed that Taylor touched and fondled other women employees of the bank, and she sought to call witnesses to support this charge. However, although some supporting testimony was admitted, the court did not allow her "to present wholesale evidence" of a pattern and practice relating to sexual advances to other female employees. She was instructed that she might well be able to present such evidence in rebuttal. Despite the alleged repeated sexual advances, Vinson acknowledged that she was afraid of Taylor and, therefore, never reported his harassment to any of his supervisors and never attempted to use the bank's complaint procedure.

Taylor denied all charges made by Vinson. He denied allegations of sexual activity. He said that he never fondled her, never made suggestive remarks to her, never engaged in sexual intercourse with her, and never asked her to do so. He claimed that the sexual harassment accusations were the result of a business-related dispute. The bank also denied Vinson's allegations and asserted that the bank was not aware of any sexual harassment by Taylor. The bank claimed it did not know and could not have known, given that the former employee made no complaint to Taylor's supervisors or through the grievance process.

Requirement

Carefully examine the facts presented in this case, study Title VII of the Civil Rights Act of 1964, and review the EEOC Guidelines on Sexual Harassment before you answer the questions posed below. ***Do not*** research the *Meritor Savings Bank, FSB* v. *Michelle Vinson et al.*; to do so defeats the purpose of this intellectual exercise.

Discussion Questions

1. Is the behavior described "illegal sexual harassment"?
2. Identify and discuss the factors you considered in responding to the first question.

---

18 And Justice for All (A)

During the late 1970s, Americans began to read about reverse discrimination cases. In a legal brief submitted, whites were declaring that their rights were being trampled on when minority individuals were designated to be "underprivileged," "economically disadvantaged," or any of the other labels used to describe individuals who were members of protected groups who were underrepresented in the nation's most prestigious schools.

Two landmark cases on this subject are *DeFunis[r]* v. *University of Washington Law School* (1971) *and Bakke* v. *Board of Regents and University of California (Davis)* (1978). In the former case, DeFunis, a white male, was denied admission to the University of Washington Law School while a number of minority applicants were admitted. The facts of the case reveal that Mr. DeFunis had somewhat higher Law School Admission Test (LSAT) scores and, in some instances, higher grade point averages than some of the minority students who were admitted. DeFunis brought suit against the school. However, when the case reached the U.S. Supreme Court, the court declared the case moot because DeFunis had been admitted since the case began winding its way through the legal system and he was now about to graduate.

The reverse discrimination issue did not go away simply because the court refused to rule on the *DeFunis* case. Later came the *Bakke* case. Allan Bakke, a white male, was a former engineer who applied to the medical school at the University of California (Davis). He was denied admission, in part, because of a dual admission program operated by the university. According to court documents, the 100 seats available each year to medical students were divided so that 20 of them were set aside for "economically disadvantaged." The 20 students selected were not directly compared to the whites in the 80-seat category. Bakke learned, with the help of certain anonymous university employees, that he had higher Medical College Admission Test (MCAT) scores than some of the minority group members accepted in the special category. In both these cases, attorneys for the whites who filed the lawsuits argued that the grades earned and the standardized test scores should be either the primary basis or the sole basis of the selection process. Skin color or membership in a particular group, in their judgment, should not influence the process. Whites, in effect, are harmed by a process that is influenced by such vital national goals as need for diversity of student body and the need to overcome centuries-old problems of racism.

Discussion Questions

1. Which are the most appropriate factors to consider in making graduate and professional school admission decisions? Explain.
2. Do you agree with the school's argument or the plaintiffs' arguments regarding the admission process?

And Justice for All (B)

Recent reports indicate that the Office of Civil Rights of the Department of Education is holding compliance reviews at Harvard and the University of California at Los Angeles to check for violations of the Civil Rights Act of 1964. Certain groups of students perceive that they are not being treated fairly. They are—or are perceived to be—too smart.

The University of California at Berkeley is a most obvious case in point. At this popular, prestigious institution, they simply do not have the space to accept most of its would-be students. For the fall of 1989, the school had 3,500 freshman places and 21,301 applicants! Competition for those spots, therefore, is extremely intense. Berkeley, however, has been extremely aggressive and successful in recruiting minority students. Berkeley's student body is now 48.5 percent white—giving whites less representation on campus than in the population of the state as a whole.

Berkeley has a convoluted, complex set of policies that are designed to avoid racism. However, Berkeley could change the ethnic mix of the student body more by relying strictly on grades and standardized test scores to determine admission.

But, Asian-Americans are complaining that they are *not* getting a fair deal in admission to top-level colleges. One controversial study released in 1989 provides support for their contention. The school's academic senate found no systematic bias against Asian-Americans but suggested admissions policies may have kept out an estimated 18 to 50 well-qualified Asian students in each of the years between 1981 and 1987. By traditional standards of academic merit, Asian-Americans seem to have justifiable case. In fact, the Berkeley chancellor apologized and promised to correct the problem. One concern of the school, however, is that more than 25 percent of the entering class will be Asian-Americans, although the minority makes up only 7 percent of California's population. The rejected Asian-Americans feel that test scores and grades should "speak loudest."

Discussion Questions

1. Which are the most appropriate factors to consider in making graduate and professional school admission decisions in light of the information presented in this section? Explain.
2. Do you agree with the argument of the school or plaintiff regarding the admission process?

---

*19 Forest Park Corporation (B)**

Bob Pelzer, manager of employment planning, almost swallowed his morning doughnut whole. The headline seemed to jump off the page—FOREST PARK MUST ACT TO CURB BIAS. The article continued with the story that the U.S. District Court had ordered Forest Park to start implementation of Judge Paul Kimble's plan to end practices of racial discrimination on hiring and promotion. He was just turning to the continuation on page 8 when his secretary buzzed to say that his boss, the director of employee relations, was on the phone. No point in putting it off. He picked up the receiver. "Dick, I was just reading the news; what does it all mean?"

Dick

I'll give it to you straight, Bob—we're in big trouble. Not only do we have to locate the managers for the textile expansion, but now we've got to get the EEOC people off our backs, too. I'd appreciate your input on this problem. Got any ideas?

Bob

I haven't had time to think about it, Dick. I haven't even finished the article in the paper. Have you got details on this mess?

---

*This case was prepared by Professor George E. Stevens, Kent State University, and Professor R. Penny Marquette, University of Akron. The case is disguised for obvious reasons.

Dick

You'll have a copy of the Atlanta EEOC report on your desk in an hour. I'm afraid you're going to have to think fast. We knew they were coming down, but I checked with the plant manager and the new personnel director, and I was assured that everything was in order—now this! After the review last week, I flew down to check things out personally and you wouldn't believe the things the old personnel director did down there! Applications "misplaced," selected jobs designated for minorities only, people promoted over other people regardless of seniority . . .

Bob

It was *that* bad?

Dick

I'm afraid so. It's all said and done now. We have a new personnel director, and we've simply got to get on the right track. The president was on the phone first thing this morning, and he's asking some tough questions. I need answers—fast. That's where you come in. I need to know exactly how we go about selecting, developing, transferring, and promoting people at all levels, including professionals and managers. Prepare a report and get it to me by 12:00 tomorrow. I'm going to meet with the president at 3:00 tomorrow and that'll give me some time to study it.

Bob

Okay, Dick, you'll have the report in plenty of time.

Bob hung up the phone and sat back. Why, he wondered, did things always seem to happen at the worst possible time? The corporation was just beginning to expand its involvement in the textile industry. To meet the company's needs, Bob was working on a program to speed up hiring. His biggest headache was trying to find approximately 75 lower-range and middle managers. Now he'd have to stop working on the textile expansion and start worrying about equal opportunity.

Bob had come to Forest Park 10 years ago after earning his degree. He had developed a strong interest in corporate staffing systems and had held an internship one summer working closely with the human resource systems coordinator of a medium-sized firm. This experience had helped him land the job at Forest Park, and his interest and willingness to work resulted in rapid promotions. Now Bob is manager of employment planning. About the time he joined the company, it entered into a period of moderate but continuing growth. His internship experience had been with a company of 6,000 employees. When he joined Forest Park 8,000 people were employed, 2,500 in the headquarters building. That number had since grown to 12,000 workers, 7,500 of whom worked away from headquarters at 16 other domestic locations. The diversification into textiles would swell the employee ranks and number of subsidiaries even further.

Only once in the past 10 years had Bob considered the possibility that the company's hiring and promotion policies might be discriminatory. He had been working with Pamela Gillis, the corporation's former EEO manager, and she had given him a special attrition report on female and black professionals at headquarters. On the surface it appeared that the company's policies were nondiscriminatory, but closer inspection of the records revealed a clear trend. Both blacks and women were paid slightly less than male Caucasian professionals with comparable qualifications and tended to receive consistently lower performance ratings compared with white male peers. There seemed to be a critical three-year period during which these individuals decided whether to leave or stay. The report made the corporation look like a stone wall for women and minority professionals. They worked for a few years, got nowhere, and left. Bob had hoped to work on these hiring and promotion issues with Pamela. Even though she seemed in too big a hurry, she did a good job. Unfortunately, after one particularly upsetting incident, Pamela also gave up on the company and left.

A young woman who identified herself as a university graduate with a major in accounting had applied for a job at the headquarters office. The receptionist gave her a clerical application to complete and, even after the woman questioned the appropriateness of the form—there was no place to list college degrees, just high schools and technical schools—the receptionist simply assured her, "Don't worry about it, just do the best you can."

The woman was interviewed, took typing and shorthand tests, and was offered a stenographer's job. Through it all, she never said a word in protest. Then came the notice from the Human Relations Commission that she had filed a complaint. Boy, he remembered, did we pay for that one! Here she was, a degreed accountant with a 3.5 grade point average and two years of experience, and we try to make a clerk out of her.

The knock on the door brought him back to the present. It was his secretary with Judge Kimble's plan. Sifting through the inevitable legal jargon, Bob outlined the essential requirements for the remedial program:

1. A listing would be made of all affected minority class members showing name, date of hire, and dates of all promotions with job classifications.

2. Assurances would be made that the qualifications required of affected class members for transfer or promotion would not exceed the qualifications of the least-qualified white male currently or previously employed in the job in question.

3. Assurances would be made that affected class members would be provided training by the company, sufficient to ensure a fair opportunity to be successful in their new jobs. Should an affected class member show unsatisfactory performance after a reasonable amount of counseling and training, the employee would be returned to the previous position or to a position mutually agreed upon by the company and the worker, with no loss of pay.

4. Guarantees would be provided to ensure that each member of the affected class would receive individual counseling to ensure a thorough understanding of his or her opportunities under the remedial plan.

5. The plan would be implemented unilaterally, regardless of union agreement, although the plan should be discussed with the union in an attempt to reach an understanding and solicit its help in correcting the situation.

6. The completed plan must be submitted to the Equal Employment Opportunity Commission and be in operation by 30 days after EEOC's approval.

Bob carefully studied his outline, wondering aloud how he could possibly meet, the many requirements. He had enough problems getting the managers for the text operation, and Dick already had told him that a reasonable percentage of these people should come from minority categories. Where was he supposed to find the people?

In all honesty, he had to admit that a big part of the problem was the inadequacy of the existing personnel planning staffing system. Entry-level professionals were generally found in campus interviews by recruiting department staff. Beyond entry level, however, the system was a mess. Bob maintained a manual card file covering the whole company, but the cards were usually out of date and invariably incomplete. When departments had openings, they frequently suggested people to fill the new slots or promotions, and their recommendations were frequently acted on. Members of the recruiting department had contact with people at headquarters who might be good candidates for promotion, but these sources excluded people working at 16 other U.S. locations.

Bob leaned back in his chair and closed his eyes. The present personnel planning system would never meet the demands of the company for internal growth. The EEOC problem just aggravated the situation. The first step was done—identifying the problem. What, he asked himself, should I do now?

Discussion Questions

1. What problems does the corporation face in terms of staffing?
2. How would you evaluate Bob's performance as the corporation's staffing manager?
3. What alternatives are available for *(a)* attracting the staff necessary for the new textile expansion and *(b)* meeting the Affirmative Action requirements?
4. Which alternative do you consider best? Why?
5. Based on the details of Judge Kimble's plan, in what ways would it have been costly (or more profitable) for the company to have developed a sound equal opportunity plan of its own and enforced it?

---

*20 "Fair Is Fair," Isn't It?**

Sitting at his desk on the afternoon of August 10, Dean Bob Frederick was perplexed by the recent turn of events involving the university central administration, his administrative secretary, and himself. The dean re-read the memorandum from the personnel director, which specified "remedial action" to be taken in disciplining Laura Adams, his administrative secretary. He knew he had implicated himself by writing the memo defending Laura and even more so by initially allowing her to take a class during working hours, a violation of university regulations. But if the university permitted minority employees to enroll in courses during working hours,

---

*This case was prepared by Professors Thomas R. Miller, Robert R. Taylor, and V. Carol Danehower, all of Memphis State University.

why shouldn't Laura be allowed to do so? He knew that she was very perplexed with the present circumstances and was worried about keeping her job and maintaining her reputation at the university. He also knew Laura felt the decision was not fair, since she had secured her supervisor's permission to take the class and now was being punished. As Dean Frederick pondered his next action, he wondered how this little incident had gotten out of hand. With all his other job pressures, he certainly could do without this additional burden.

BACKGROUND

Dr. Bob Frederick is dean of the college of business at Southmont State University, a comprehensive university of about 20,000 students located in a medium-sized city in the Southeast. Dr. Frederick, in his fourth year as dean, supervises over 100 faculty members and 20 administrative staff in the college. In the dean's office, are four classified employees: Laura Adams, his administrative secretary, a secretary, and two clerk-typists.

Laura, the most senior employee, has worked in the college for almost 10 years and is regarded by the dean and others as an excellent employee. She knows the job well, has fine skills, and is a valuable asset to the dean's staff. For almost seven years she has been working on a bachelor of business administration degree, taking two courses per semester, including summers, in addition to her full-time position in the dean's office. Although her progress has been slow, Laura has maintained almost continuous enrollment at considerable personal sacrifice, and she was now approaching the end of her program. In fact, she planned to complete her last two courses in the summer term and graduate at the August commencement. Indeed, it was her desire to complete the degree this summer (before degree requirements changed in the fall, which added a calculus course to the program) that had led up to the current problem. The degree program requirements under which Laura entered the university were "expiring" at the end of the summer term.

Southmont State has a long established policy of supporting the continuing education of university employees. This policy included in-service training programs as well as college credit courses for employees seeking undergraduate degrees. For those pursuing college credit through formal university classes, the institution has adopted detailed regulations under its Employee Education Program, which specify:

1. Classes must be taken outside normal university working hours (normal working hours include meal breaks).

2. Exceptions will be considered only if the employee is within six credit hours of graduation and a required course is not available outside normal working hours. If an exception is approved for the employee to attend class during working hours, class time will be charged against the employee's annual leave at 150 percent of the length of the class period, (i.e., one would be charged 90 minutes of leave for attending a 60-minute class). (*Note:* It was generally known that these were rarely approved.)

3. Enrollment in or the attendance of classes during normal working hours, without an exception approved by the president of the university or the vice president of business and finance, will be considered sufficient grounds for termination of university employment.

Also, the university offers limited financial support to full-time employees with at least six months of service for enrollment in job-related college courses. Under the Staff Scholarship Program, the university will pay the tuition for a maximum of six semester hours of coursework on proper application, recommendation by their supervisors, and approval of the president. Explicit in the program guidelines is the statement that supervisors, in recommending staff scholarships, must give employee job performance and university goals highest priority.

Laura Adams has participated in the Staff Scholarship Program since she has been enrolled at Southmont and has always had the support of her supervisors. For this summer, Laura had received $330 from the scholarship fund for two three-credit courses costing $165 per course.

The two summer courses in which she was enrolled were industrial marketing (offered at night) and international marketing (offered from 10:50 AM to 12:30 PM on Monday through Friday). Although Laura was generally aware of the prohibition against course attendance during working hours, the day course was necessary for her graduation and was not offered at an alternate time. Also, when she had discussed the situation with Dean Frederick, he told her that, under the circumstances, it was all right for her to take this course during the day, provided she would make up the lost time resulting from class attendance (eight and one-third hours per week). He also was aware of Laura's desire to complete the degree in the summer term to avoid taking additional courses to satisfy new degree requirements, which took effect in the fall semester.

Laura was not completely comfortable with being absent from the office from 10:50 until 12:30 during the five-week term of the international marketing course, even though she did have Dean Frederick's approval. However, since she forfeited her one-hour lunch period each day, she was absent from her work only about 40 minutes longer than normal and was making up this time. Also, she was aware that at least one other employee in the college was taking a course during working hours under the scholarship program. Indeed, Laura recalled a piece in a university publication, *Southmont Insights,* about black employees completing their degrees under a program permitting them to enroll in courses during the work day. Thus, she felt she should not be overly concerned about taking one course for five weeks in the middle of the day. If it is fair for one person to be off during the normal work period, why shouldn't it be fair for another? she thought.

THE STAFF ENROLLMENT AUDIT

During a routine audit of staff course enrollment by the personnel department at Southmont State, Laura Adams's name appeared on the roll of the international marketing class. Laura was called to the personnel department to meet with Agnes Johnson, benefits manager, on August 1.

Laura told Ms. Johnson that she was familiar with the Staff Scholarship Program and was aware that it did not normally permit class enrollment during regular working hours. When asked if she had been granted an exception, Laura replied that she had Dean Frederick's permission to take this course, although she did not have it in writing. Laura inquired if this requirement applied to all employees, given her knowledge of the minority secretary who was enrolled in a daytime class. Ms. Johnson replied that it applied to all employees except those allowed this privilege under the Black Staff Scholarship Program, a part of the university's mandated desegregation agreement in the *Powell* v. *Morgan* suit (see Appendix A). Laura also indicated she knew that the procedure required use of annual leave at one and a half times the class period even if an exception had been approved. In view of the circumstances, Ms. Johnson suggested that Ms. Adams secure a statement from Dean Frederick explaining what had happened.

On August 2, Laura delivered to Ms. Johnson a memorandum from Dean Frederick, which included the following points:

1. Ms. Adams had his permission to enroll in the international marketing course in the 10:50 to 12:30 period.
2. She agreed to make up her lost time from class attendance by using her lunch hour plus extra time after work.
3. This course was the only available course that would fit in her degree program.
4. Since she was so near the completion of her degree program, the dean felt it important she finish in August, since she would have faced additional requirements if her program extended into the fall.
5. Laura is sorry for the inconvenience this caused the university and is agreeable to being charged 150 percent of the class-period time against her annual leave.

Ms. Johnson forwarded Dean Frederick's memo to Mr. Alex Farrell, director of personnel, to whom the apparent violation had been directed for action.

THE CENTRAL ADMINISTRATION'S RESPONSE

Alex Farrell reviewed the information he had received on the infraction, including the copy of Ms. Adams's staff scholarship application, the notes from Agnes Johnson's meeting with Laura, the memo from Dean Frederick, and the telephone conversations with the dean. After considerable thought, Farrell wrote a memo to the vice president for business and finance, Lawrence Sheffield, outlining the issue and his recommendation for action:

1. Ms. Adams had been a long-term and valued employee who had been working on a degree for about seven years.

2. A clear violation of a university procedure had occurred, but he did not feel the termination of Ms. Adams was warranted.

3. Her annual leave should be charged at the 150 percent rate for lost time. Dean Frederick's office would need to submit corrected time and leave records for this period.

4. Ms. Adams was to repay the $165 to the staff scholarship fund.

5. Since Ms. Adams violated a university procedure and was aware of this, she should receive a written reprimand from Jerry Forrest, the academic vice president (Dean Frederick's superior).

On August 8, Lawrence Sheffield replied to Alex Farrell that he concurred with his recommendation and that Mr. Farrell should notify Dean Frederick of the appropriate remedial action to be implemented.

THE DEAN'S DILEMMA

When Dean Frederick received the August 10 memorandum from Alex Farrell that outlined the action to be taken against Laura Adams, he was disturbed. He somewhat understood the position taken by the central administration in the case, since he recognized the problems that could result in a large organization if personnel procedures were not observed. He knew bureaucracies had to have rules, but he believed the punishment was unduly harsh with the requirement that Laura pay back the course tuition and receive a written reprimand from the academic vice president. Were they trying to make a example of her? Perhaps more importantly, was it right for her to be disciplined so harshly for this violation of the staff scholarship procedure while other employees on campus, because of their race, were eligible for time away during normal working hours to attend class? In fact, he remembered reading about this in a recent *Southmont Insights* publication. He looked on the coffee table in his office, picked up the magazine, and scanned the reference to the Black Staff Scholarship Program:

> The Black Staff Scholarship Program, which permits black employees with at least two years of college to attend classes during regular working hours so degrees may be completed in a more timely manner, has produced two graduates, with three more due to graduate this December.

Although he was well aware that Southmont had a strong commitment to affirmative action, this situation troubled him. After all, "fair is fair," he thought. Laura was upset about the action taken against her and did not feel it was just. She had even talked about seeing a lawyer to file a reverse discrimination charge against the university, especially if the university tried to terminate her. Dean Frederick didn't think the decision was just, either. The dean knew he had contributed to Laura's "delinquency," and he felt some responsibility for this. She had relied on his approval of her enrollment. He certainly had to consider his obligation to her, and her work as a valued staff member? Shouldn't he be willing to take some of the heat for the problem he helped create?

Maybe, should he appeal the action recommended by the personnel director and approved by the vice president of business and finance? Possibly he could get a concession on the formal reprimand, since Laura seemed especially hurt by the potential damage to her fine record. The dean did not want to lose the support of a highly valued employee, but he also was reluctant to challenge Lawrence Sheffield, a powerful campus administrator, or his own boss, Jerry Forrest. Even though he wasn't comfortable with Sheffield's decision, Dean Frederick wasn't sure he could change anything if he tried. With the economy weakening and the state budget tightening, he knew that he would have some tough budgetary battles to fight in the near future. He would need the support of both Sheffield and Forrest in these negotiations. Maybe this was a fight he should not pick.

Dean Frederick also understood the need for Southmont's affirmative action program, brought about by the long history of underrepresentation of minority employment in state institutions of higher education. But should the remedies that address past discrimination result in inequitable treatment of present employees? He had wrestled with this issue many times himself. He also was aware that the courts had not clearly decided the matter in trying to balance the merits of the positions of both parties (see Appendix B).

It seemed to him that this situation had gotten completely out of hand. Certainly, he had underestimated the consequences of approving Laura's request to take the class, a decision which he had made without a great deal of thought. Although it was true that a rule had been broken, this had now become a "federal case." As he reflected on these considerations and pondered what he should do, he hoped to find a solution that would satisfactorily address these issues. Or was this seeking the impossible? He wondered.

APPENDIX A

Note on Court-Ordered Desegregation Settlement Affecting Southmont State University

In ruling on a 1968 civil rights lawsuit (*Powell* v. *Morgan*) filed initially against another public university in the state, the federal judge rendered a decision that ordered desegregation at all public higher education institutions in the state. In 1984, following the court's determination that inadequate progress had been made in dismantling the racially dual system of higher education, plaintiffs and defendants proposed a "stipulation of settlement" to the court. The negotiated stipulation of settlement had the concurrence of plaintiffs, defendant state officials, and the NAACP Legal Defense Fund, but was not accepted by the Civil Rights Division of the Department of Justice which, objected to the proposal's use of numerical goals and quotas and the absence of a "victim specificity" standard (which required that evidence of racial discrimination against an individual be established before a remedy can be provided that person).

After reviewing the proposal and hearing oral arguments, the judge signed the agreement over the objections of the Justice Department. In explaining the justification for the remedies of the settlement, the judge stated:

> The ultimate goal is *not* an ideal ratio of mix of black and white students or faculty. The goal is a state system of higher education in tax-supported colleges and universities in which race is irrelevant and in which equal protection and equal application of the law is a reality. On the road to achieving this state of color-blindness, there must be color-consciousness to overcome the residual effect of past color-based desegregation. The proposed settlement decree is not illegal, and it offers promise of more effective remedies in attacking a seemingly Gordian problem.

The lengthy stipulation of settlement contained 13 sections, one of which provided the foundation for the Black Scholarship Program at Southmont State University:

> Public higher education institutions will, within 120 days, request adequate funding through the budgetary process to institute a staff development program to enable black staff members to obtain advanced degrees and become eligible for positions of higher salary and higher rank within all institutions of higher education in the state.

As implemented by state institutions, the Black Scholarship Program provided special funding for staff development, which included release time from work, conference attendance, course enrollment opportunities, training seminar participation, internships, and the like.

To administer all actions specified in the stipulation of settlement, the court identified a desegregation monitoring committee, which would establish procedures for monitoring and reporting progression the desegregation of public institutions under the court order. The committee had reviewed and approved Southmont's specific program.

APPENDIX B

Note on Preferential Selection or Reverse Discrimination and U.S. Supreme Court Decisions

Title VII, Section 703A, of the 1964 Civil Rights Act states:

> It shall be unlawful employment practice for an employer (1) to fail or refuse to hire or to discharge any individual or otherwise to discriminate against any individual with respect to his compensation, terms, conditions, or privileges of employment because of such individual's race, color, religion, sex, or national origin.

Although the act provided a legal foundation for addressing discriminatory practices of employers, the rather general language of the act has resulted in varying interpretations by employers, employees, unions, federal enforcement agencies, and even the courts.

The implementation of equal opportunity has resulted in the development of affirmative action plans by many employers which, require them to establish goals and implement policies and procedures to assure employment opportunities for protected groups underrepresented in the workforce. In some cases, employers have initiated programs that provide preferential treatment for underrepresented, protected groups to attempt to fulfill EEO obligations and commitments.

The legality of preferential selection in support of affirmative action programs is highly controverisal. The courts have not provided broad, clear guidelines on this issue, having tended to rule, instead, on relatively narrow grounds.

The U.S. Supreme Court has upheld preferential treatment of minorities when a union and company have voluntarily agreed to an affirmative action plan giving preference to blacks for admission to a training program (*Kaiser Aluminum* v. *Weber, 1979*). However, in a case involving the layoff of white teachers with more seniority than black faculty (to achieve a specified racial composition), the Supreme Court ruled the affirmative action layoff plan of the school board and the teachers' union unlawfully violated the rights of white teachers (*Wygart* v. *Jackson Board of Education, 1986*). In a recent case, the City of Birmingham and some black firefighters agreed to a consent decree, which specified an affirmative action program to hire and promote firefighters. A group of white firefighters filed a racial discrimination suite charging reverse discrimination. In a five to four vote, the Supreme Court ruled that the white firefighters could raise a court challenge to the affirmative action decree (*Martin* v. *Wilks, 1989*). However, the 1991 Civil Rights Act (CRA) revised the court's decision by greatly restricting legal challenges to consent decrees. The CRA prevents challenges from parties to the suit who could have objected before the consent decree is entered or from those whose interests were represented by parties to the suit.

It should be apparent that the legality of the preferential treatment programs is a complex and rather confusing matter. In ruling on cases brought before them, the courts have considered the evidence of a history of discrimination by the employer, whether a voluntary affirmative action program had been agreed to by the union or employees and the employer, whether the challenged practice was the result of a court-ordered action, the severity of the impact of a preferential treatment on a nonminority party, and other issues. No doubt, the changing composition of the U.S. Supreme Court and forthcoming decisions on related cases will further define public policy in this evolving area of civil rights laws.

21 Federal Fabrics*

Federal Fabrics is a medium-sized, family owned, nonunion company employing approximately 80 individuals. The company manufactures fabric, which it sells to upholsterers. Federal Fabrics is fortunate to have landed a large contract with a leading producer of office furniture. This will require adding a sales correspondent, a production supervisor, and 15 employees for a third shift.

*This case was prepared by Professor Alice H. Walton, University of Detroit Mercy.

Federal Fabrics had never seen the need for formalized human resource policies in the company's "family environment." However, management recognized that the company was growing and, to effectively use its people as well as void costly employment litigation, the managers felt it was time to professionalize the HR function. Therefore, Federal Fabrics had recently hired its first full-time human resources director, Chris Sanchez.

One of Ms. Sanchez's first duties was to recruit and select the new sales correspondent, supervisor, and production employees as soon as possible. She began by examining the job descriptions for these jobs. She determined that the job descriptions were written approximately 10 years ago and were developed by asking the best-performing incumbent in each area to write their own job description. See Exhibit 1 for a copy of these job descriptions.

Ms. Sanchez launched her recruiting efforts by placing ads in newspapers and trade journals and contacting the local business colleges. She had the applicants complete the company's application blank (see Exhibit 2). She then set up interviews with the best candidates.

Ms. Sanchez's first interview was with Mr. Grant Perna. He was applying for the production supervisor's position. His credentials appeared very solid. He had extensive experience in related fields and has been a supervisor for five years. When Ms. Sanchez asked about his availability to work overtime, he informed her that overtime should be no problem as long as he was able to attend an Alcoholics Anonymous meeting at least once a week.

Her second interview was with Mr. Robert Taylor. He was applying for the sales correspondent's position. When Mr. Taylor walked in for his interview, Ms. Sanchez noticed that he was blind and used a walking cane. During the interview, Mr. Taylor told of his previous experience in customer service and indicated that this opportunity excited him because of the sales advancement opportunities.

One of the interviews for the production employees job was with Ms. Felicia Miller. Ms. Miller was recently laid off from her job as a production worker at a local company. Ms. Miller walks with a slightly noticeable limp. Ms. Sanchez asked Ms. Miller what was wrong with her leg, to which Ms. Sanchez said she was injured in her previous job and has an artificial limb.

Another candidate for one of the production jobs is Mr. Carl Jenkins. Mr. Jenkins is currently employed at a fabric manufacturer in a nearby state. His work experience seems right in line with what the company needs. He indicated that the reason he wanted this job was so he could be closer to his mother, who had recently been diagnosed with Alzheimer's disease.

EXHIBIT 1: Job Descriptions

Production Supervisor

- Supervises and coordinates activities of workers.
- Trains employees in work methods and procedures.
- Inspects products to verify conformance to specifications.

EXHIBIT 1: *Continued*

- Directs setup and adjustments of machines.

General Laborer

- Measures width of rolls of material.
- Identifies rolls with color-code card.
- Weighs rolls before and after coating processes.
- Conveys rolls of material, engraved printing or embossing rolls, and drums of daub and print color to and from machine, using dollies.
- Lifts rolls to letoff rack and windup racks, using hoist.
- Joins ends of material rolls with automatic sewing machine or tape.
- Observes material at windup rack and notifies operator of processing defects.
- Starts rolls onto core.
- Changes knives.
- Threads material into machine.
- Scrapes and cleans equipment.
- Removes scraps.
- Sweeps area.
- Keeps supply of rags and roll cores.

Sales Correspondent

- Compiles data pertinent to manufacture of special products for customers.
- Reads correspondence from customers to determine needs of customer not met by standard products.
- Confers with engineering department to ascertain feasibility of designing special equipment.
- Confers with production personnel to determine feasibility of fabrication and to obtain estimate of cost and production time.
- Corresponds with customer to inform of production progress and costs.

EXHIBIT 2 Federal Fabric Application Blank

Name: ______________________ Phone No. ______________________
Address: ______________________

____

Person to Contact in an Emergency: ______________________
Phone: ______________

Education:

Degree	School

Job Experience (list most recent first) :

1. Job Title: ______________ Length of Employment: ________

Duties:

EXHIBIT 2: *Continued*

Average Number of Days Absent per Month:
Did You Experience Any Work-Related Injuries? Yes/No
If Yes, please list.

What Restrictions Does This Injury Place on You?

2. Job Title: ______________ Length of Employment: ________
Duties:

Average Number of Days Absent per Month: ________________
Did You Experience Any Work-Related Injuries? Yes/No
If Yes, please list.

What Restrictions Does This Injury Place on You?

Military Experience: ______________________________

Special Skills and Abilities: ______________________________

Have You Ever Filed for Workers' Compensation? Yes/No

Do You Have Any Disabilities? If Yes, please list.

What Special Accommodations Would You Require to Perform the Job?

For EEO Purpose Only:

Sex:		Race:		Date of Birth:
	Male		White	
	Female		African American	____/____/____
			Asian	
			Native American	
			Hispanic	
			Other: ________	

22 Cooper Brothers Department Store (A)

The Cooper Brothers Department Store opened its doors in 1863. The dedication, capital, and sweat equity of a large German-American family that came to this country in 1842 made the store a reality. The store, originally a spacious general store located behind and near the old Reading Terminal, had a citywide reputation for knowledgeable sales people, high-quality merchandise, outstanding service, customer orientation, well-made clothes, and a "no questions asked" money back guarantee. The company has a slogan, *"No sale is final until the customer is completely satisfied."* Today, the company occupies a prime location at Eighth and Market Street. The store employee population exceeds 2,000 and the orientation toward its people remains to this day.

"A proud store with a proud heritage of 120 years of great service to the customer. A customer that is always right," Pat Wilson remarked to Carole Harvey.

"What I want to know is when is the employee right?" Pat asked. "It's too bad that Mr. Walker refused to accept the recommendation of Bobbie's supervisor, Mr. Holmes."

The conversation between the two counter clerks at the prestigious and venerable old-line department store resulted from Mr. Carl Walker, the general store manager's order to fire Bobbie Edwards. Bobbie had been with the store for nearly three months. She was terminated just three days short of the end of her probationary period. Bobbie was a model employee, who performed her job with a smile, knew her inventory, was reliable, and worked any day or evening schedule the store managers assigned her. Invariably, such schedules did not give her the equivalent of a full day's work.

DISCUSSION ABOUT BOBBIE EDWARDS

"William, I don't want to hear another word about how good a worker Bobbie Edwards was. I *know* what she could do! The issue is her appearance. What to do with an employee who weighs so much was the question," Mr. Walker said.

"Carl, don't 'William' me. Don't go 'formal' on me now. We both know that a person's weight is *no*t an appropriate basis nor is it a legal basis, in my judgment, for terminating an employee. It's just not fair," Bill White shot back. "Bobbie did do the job and did it well! Her weight may be something that she cannot control. What if there is a physiological explanation? It is possible that her weight condition should be treated as a disability. I am not sure. Do you think the feds or state civil rights commission would come down on us as a result of the firing?" Bill asked.

"There is no federal law that protects fat people. Obesity is not a disability, has not been a disability and will not become a recognized disability any time soon," Carl claimed. "I talked to Roger Harmon in employee relations about this situation. He said that there have been a few lawsuits but there is no federal law, and he didn't know of any state civil rights act provision that covered a company's ability to fire a 5′3″, 329-pound woman. The term used to describe Bobbie's condition is *morbid obesity.* I had Roger look into this. We owe it to our customers to provide folks who present a good appearance. I did not want the store to lose business. We did face the risk of losing business since the customers won't want to be served by someone like Bobbie."

Discussion Questions

1. What are the issues in this case?
2. Does Cooper Brothers Department Store have a legal basis for discharging Bobbie because of her weight?

Cooper Brothers Department Store (B)

The Cooper Brothers Department Store has had its theft problems in recent years. The department store has allowed for shrinkage. Shrinkage refers to damaged or soiled goods and theft. Merchandise handled by customers routinely causes some damage. Such merchandise must be reduced in price or discarded. Both company employees and shoppers are responsible for incidents of theft. For many years, the company routinely required polygraph examinations, or "lie detectors" as they are commonly called. However, recent laws have outlawed the use of these tests by other organizations than security, military, and government agencies. As a result, Cooper Brothers has been contracted with a company to administer honesty tests. These tests are paper and pencil tests that have as their basis old psychological tests developed in the 1930s.

Theft of merchandise, however, is not the only concern the department store has. The management wishes to monitor the performance of employees and to assure that company resources are not being wasted. During the past year, approval has been given for the installation of several electronic monitoring devices. Employees are not aware that their calls are being monitored nor do they realize that hidden cameras are recording their behavior on the job.

THE MEETING

Delores Thomas, store manager of the large, modern Cooper Brothers store in Troy, Michigan, called a meeting. Department managers, buyers, and administrative supervisors of the Cooper Brothers Department Store were required to attend a special meeting. At the meeting the attendees learned that the store was about to step up significantly its monitoring of employee and customer behavior. Specifically, the store manager was concerned about pilferage and about inappropriate or illegal behavior on the part of employees as well as abuse of privileges. Ms. Thomas cited the loss of expensive merchandise from certain departments, increases in damaged and soiled merchandise leading to large markdowns, and she was very upset about the recent arrests of employees for possession and selling of illegal substances (marijuana and cocaine) on the premises. Finally, she noted the higher telephone bills. She attributed the increase to personal long distance calls being made on the store's WATS line.

The store manager said that electronic monitoring in the workplace is very common. Ms. Thomas is surprised that she had not thought about using this approach for employees. Within 30 days, Ms. Thomas announced, there would be electronic or video monitoring by Cooper Brothers in bathrooms, locker rooms, and dressing areas. In addition, monitoring of telephone calls and electronic computer systems would be initiated. As needed and where applicable, she said, the department store will screen employee files, including electronic work files, electronic mail, network messages, and voice mail.

Discussion Questions

1. What are the issues in this case?
2. Does an employer have a right to engage in electronic monitoring?

Cooper Brothers Department Store (C)

Irv Thompson had no idea that a simple dress code would cause so much trouble! If Shirley Johnson hadn't come to work in those tight pants there probably wouldn't have been a dress code. Irv, as manager of the Birmingham Cooper Brothers store reflected on the turmoil that had surfaced over the past several weeks.

The counter clerks at Cooper Brothers are not particularly well paid. In fact, few of the people who serve the customers and take their orders are employed on a full-time basis. However, these individuals take pride in what they do, represent the store well, and make every effort to meet the needs of the customer. Despite their wages, these employees tend to dress well, presenting an excellent appearance to the customers they serve. On occasion, however, an employee would wear an outfit not deemed appropriate for job. Women who wore pants that fit much too snugly or clothes better suited for a night out on the town, rather than a business environment, were examples of the most common complaints heard by supervisors and managers. Each incident was handled on an ad hoc basis by the supervisor who had jurisdiction over the activities of a particular employee. This approach resulted in different disciplinary responses to the similar indiscretions. Some employees received an informal warning, others were verbally warned, some were sent home and still others were suspended. The store management decided to create a dress code so similar violations could be handled in a similar fashion. In addition, it was believed that a dress code would avoid the improper dress problem in the first place.

COOPER BROTHERS
NEW DRESS CODE

Effective January 1, 1994, the management requires that all female employees dress appropriately when they report to work. Specifically, female employees will no longer be permitted to wear pants while on duty. The acceptable options are dresses or skirts. *There will be NO exceptions to the new policy.*

Irv Thompson, Store Manager

During the meeting several questions were asked by those in attendance. Irv Thompson and Roger Harmon tried their best to answer the questions. Folks wanted to know if tank tops or shorts would be permitted. Others asked whether the policy applied to people who are not in view of the customer. One manager wanted to know whether the wearing of shorts would be permissible if the job worked was a hot uncomfortable one. Another wanted to know whether similar dress codes were devised for men. "It appears that women are the only ones affected by the dress code," the manager said.

All went well for exactly one month. Diane Carter, hair stylist, worked in the Birmingham store's beauty salon. Her supervisor called her into her office to remind her of the new dress code. Diane told her, "I have been working here eight years. In all of that time I have never worn tight pants and I don't intend to start now." She was immediately given a verbal warning. Within a week a written warning followed. After the second week of notification, Diane received a suspension notice. Again she refused to wear a dress or skirt. The supervisor fired her on the spot. Afterwards, she was interviewed by the local radio and television media. Ms. Carter said that she had "no regrets" about her decision. "I feel very strongly about the issue, and hopefully it will never happen to others."

Discussion Questions

1. Discuss the issues this case raises. Should this dress code be upheld?
2. What factors should company representatives consider when creating a dress code for the employees?

Section D

Staffing, Entry, Orientation, and Placement

23 Lansdowne Township Fire Department: No Place for a Woman

"Heck, how do these people know whether I can be a firefighter or not? If I can bench press 285 pounds and do a knee bend with 485 pounds this ain't about the stereotype of some puny woman. I'll put my biceps up against a lot of so-called macho men. I figure if I can clean-and-jerk 450 pounds, lift 1,220 pounds, and win matches in tae kwon do, I can be a firefighter! *Nobody* can tell me otherwise. They just don't want a woman in the fire department. I think when you have 77 positions and no woman qualifies in the history of the town, you have to figure the women applicants are *not* the problem! All they could tell me is that 'I didn't score high enough' on the department's physical test."[1]

Shirley VanArsdale may have felt that she qualified, but Fire Chief Robert Reich did not agree. He didn't care about her winning a powerlifting championship. Also, what she could do in terms of body building, weightlifting, and workout regimen meant little to him. What was important to him was whether this candidate or any other could score high enough to pass all parts of the firefighters' examination. Although Chief Reich refused to reveal her actual test scores, he did say, "She had the same opportunity everybody else had."

This township of 50,500 people has never had a female firefighter during the department's 20-year history. It is a fact that no one can explain, not even Fire Chief

[1] This is not a doctor's examination. The applicant is required to engage in tasks (e.g., rope climbing, running, sit-ups, carrying heavy objects, handle a fire hose, and so on).

Reich. The fire chief noted that, out of the 200 people taking the December test, only the top 10 finishers would be hired. He remarked, "It is a difficult but color- and gender-blind test. It's no one's fault that only 5 percent of the applicants can be hired!"

APPLICANT'S VIEW

Shirley VanArsdale, who is five feet, five inches tall, says she believes that she did well on the portion of the test that required her to scramble onto and across a ladder ledge. In the sit-up test, she was required to do at least 30 of them, but she did an additional 12. VanArsdale did not feel she performed well in the sledgehammer swinging test, however, but she says the problem was ill-fitting firefighting apparel not arm strength. Shirley explained that the firefighting coat was too big (it billowed out when she looked down hindering her vision) and the gloves she was provided were of different sizes—large and extra large. These two factors, she claimed, made it difficult to see what she was swinging at.

VanArsdale said she was hampered in several tests, including tests that seem to have no relationship to the duties of a firefighter. VanArsdale's bottom line: "I know the test is difficult and I know the competition is keen." Not all men can do this job and the same applies to women. I think I can do it."

Shirley has decided that she will either file a complaint with the state's civil rights division or talk to one of the local attorneys to see if one of them might take her case on a contingency basis.

AN OBSERVATION

Nearly all fire departments, with the possible exception of certain volunteer ones, require the applicant to pass written and physical examinations. There usually are many more applicants than positions available so the hiring process is a very competitive one. It should be noted that the physical test tends to be the major stumbling block for many of the female applicants. The percentage of female firefighters remains small. The National Fire Protection Association reports that 6,200 of 188,000 career firefighters are women. A look at a couple of the more progressive cities that seek a diverse group of firefighters reinforces this point. Chicago has 66 women in a force of 4,200 and Seattle has 74 women on a 988-person force.

---

24 Professional Leasing Services, Inc. (A)

Professional Leasing Services, Inc. (PLS), was incorporated in 1979 in Wilmington, Delaware. The firm is located in Tempe, Arizona, but Delaware's incorporation laws are deemed by many to be the best in the country for the business owner. Over the past 10 years the firm has achieved many of the original objectives established by its first owners. The company's profit picture looks great. Everything in the company's plans points to a bright future in a booming business. In fact, plans were being made to negotiate contracts with several key professional people so as to repudiate the stereotype of temporary agencies and to better serve companies who could not afford regular high-level employees in certain job classifications. This recent strategy has meant marketing of the idea that PLS can reduce labor costs by having companies pay a higher direct compensation cost but no indirect compensation cost for leased employees. Specifically, as much as 40 percent of the total compensation dollar consists of so-called fringe benefits. Theoretically, the hiring companies, as leasing clients, would not have to pay benefit costs.

In recent years, PLS has moved far beyond its initial business of offering to companies only secretarial and clerical workers. Former and current chief financial officers, hospital administrators, computer software experts, accountants, personnel directors, and other professionals and managers have been added to the company over the past three years. Profit picture aside, however, there may be a "fly in the ointment." The company has been so profit driven that it has failed to acknowledge one important employee-related problem. While the clients that utilize the services of Professional Leasing Service seem happy with the arrangement, the PLS employees have difficulty with the leasing concept. Traditionally, employees have some stability and, when they perform well for an employer, have an opportunity for upward mobility. Clients appear less likely to hire the PLS employees, so such immediate reward is not evident. Second, the PLS employees, appear less driven to act on the basis of company loyalty, since they feel that their very existence is so tenuous. PLS compensates its people well but pay doesn't seem to affect the loyalty/retention issue.

Requirement

Identify the advantages and disadvantages to clients, the leasing company and those employed of participating in a leasing arrangement.

Professional Leasing Services, Inc. (B)

The owner and principal stockholder of PLS, Byron Scott, has owned and sold a number of businesses. One business that is near and dear to Mr. Scott's heart is the Arizona Light Manufacturing Company of Scottsdale. The business, as the name implies, does light manufacturing work. Most recently, ALMC has provided Motorola Company with needed parts for the government products division. Byron has held onto Arizona Light Manufacturing because it was the first company he bought and operated. It has a sentimental value to him. He has nursed it along. The company's

TABLE 1 Equal Opportunity Report—Company Data

Job Categories	*Male*	*Female*	*White*	*Hispanic*	*American Indian, Alaskan Native*	*Asian/ Pacific Islander*	*Black/ non-Hispanic*	*Underutilization or Concentration?*
Officials and manager	158	42	140	16	9	1	0	
Professionals	237	241	432	29	17	0	0	
Technicians	47	50	27	54	9	1	8	
Sales workers	35	7	40	1	0	0	1	
Office and clerical	8	43	22	23	3	0	7	
Craft workers	28	12	22	8	5	2	3	
Operatives	472	502	275	543	99	1	56	
Laborers	657	343	762	219	10	0	9	
Service workers	33	16	13	16	8	1	11	
All categories	1,675	1,256	1,733	909	160	6	95	

legal counsel has been informed of a pending lawsuit that concerns the upward mobility and representation of members of protected classes as covered by Title VII of the 1964 Civil Rights Act. Arizona Light Manufacturing and Professional Leasing have both maintained the required EEO-1 Report as required by law. This report contains workforce composition data for each of nine job categories (as specified by the Equal Employment Opportunity Commission). The job categories range from that of officials and managers to service workers.

Arizona Light Manufacturing and Professional Leasing merged two years ago. Workforce composition data are presented in Table 1.

Note: These data represent an analysis of selected EEO-1 data. An analysis of relevant labor pool data is provided in Table 2.

TABLE 2 Relevant Labor Pool Data

Male	*Female*	*White*	*Hispanic*	*American Indian*	*Asian*	*Black*
51%	49%	63%	18%	13%	4%	2%

Discussion Questions

1. Identify those job classes (if any) that exhibit underutilization.
2. Identify those job classes (if any) that exhibit concentration.

25 Buena Vista Plant (A)

Forest Park Corporation's management has benefited greatly from its decision to acquire the Buena Vista textile plant in Macon, Georgia.[1] The decision to rescue the unprofitable plant was a good one. After the acquisition in 1976, the plant was modernized; new, capable managers were attracted to the plant, and the labor force expanded. By 1981, despite the extensive capital outlays, the plant was operating well into the black.

BACKGROUND

The Buena Vista plant had fallen on hard times before it became a subsidiary of Forest Park Corporation. The plant, which opened in 1955, was a major employer

[1] All names are disguised.

for 20 years. Unfortunately, things turned sour in the late 1970s, when the area suffered a mild recession at a time when foreign competition began to undercut domestic textile manufacturers. These events had a dramatic impact on the Buena Vista plant, because it had aging equipment, used outdated production methods, and had no investment capital.

The town of Macon suffered along with the textile plant. The plant's decline and other area company layoffs led to a dramatically higher unemployment rate. The city fathers were happy to learn of Forest Park's interest in the plant. The Chamber of Commerce, city officials, and local business leaders did everything possible to make the acquisition look attractive. And, they were rewarded for their efforts. Since the revitalization of the Buena Vista plant, the city's unemployment rate has fallen from a high of 12 percent to its present low of 4.5 percent. In addition, new industry has been attracted to the area. Over the past three years, there has been a housing boom as people flock to the area in search of better job opportunities.

THE PERSONNEL DEPARTMENT

Al Logan came to the plant in 1957 when he was fresh out of college. When Al joined Buena Vista, there was no personnel department. As the plant's personnel director, he virtually created the department from scratch. Before Forest Park took over, he had a department consisting of one other person, Cheryl Giffhorn, his secretary. He now has a new assistant, John Turner. John has been a willing pupil. His previous experience was as a textile worker. He has no college degree or specialized training in personnel. In the three years that he has worked in personnel, he has lived up to all of Al's expectations. Cheryl has been with Al for 14 years. As a secretary, friend, and confidante, she is absolutely indispensable. In fact, she is more of a personnel paraprofessional than a secretary.

During Al's years as a personnel director, he had made good use of his intelligence, willingness to work long hours, and his interest in personnel. He often regretted that he had majored in marketing, rather than in personnel. He knew that he needed to keep up with these new laws and regulations on health and safety, labor relations, equal employment opportunity, pensions, age discrimination, and sexual harassment, but he had more or less relied on directives from headquarters and help from employee relations specialists. Al had always feared that his failure would come back to haunt him.

Back in 1979, Al discovered that he had a staffing problem. Specifically, a large number of textile workers and textile supervisors were needed to meet human resources requirements for the plant's expansion. With assistance from headquarters, he was able to recruit the necessary personnel. Specialists from headquarters personnel set up a special assessment center program for textile supervisors. The program took a great deal of his people's time at first, but once assessor training was completed, everything ran smoothly. The assessment center included a personal interview, an analysis of a management case, a group exercise, and an in-basket simulation. These tests were decided on after the behavioral traits and skills needed for the jobs were ascertained. Workers in the plant seemed to really like the assessment center idea. Some claimed it was a more objective way of selecting supervisors than the good-old-boy method based on who fished, hunted, or played tennis together. (People who participated in the centers, however, could only be chosen by their supervisors.) The employee relations people from headquarters claimed the assessment center program would meet Equal Employment Opportunity Commission (EEOC) requirements. According to them, validity studies of assessment ratings at IBM, Sohio, Caterpiller Tractor, and AT&T all support the use of the assessment centers. Although Al knew little about such programs, if this one didn't meet all legal requirements, he felt it wouldn't be his fault.

The textile worker jobs were not filled on the basis of an assessment center. Such a procedure was judged to be too expensive. Instead, Al decided to use a psychomotor aptitude test. At first, he tried a finger dexterity test, but the preliminary validation results were not good. He had failed to find a strong relationship between scores on the test and each employee's job performance. A testing expert reviewed the data and confirmed Al's findings. The correlation between performance and test scores was only +0.48. The testing expert offered his own explanation for the modest correlation. He believed the finger dexterity test to be better suited for machinists, radio repairers, plumbers, and business machine operators. As a result of this discussion and job analysis of selected jobs, Al decided to try a manual dexterity test. Manual dexterity usually involves coordination with arm and eye and more gross movements than those involved in finger dexterity. Over the past two years, the personnel department has administered the Minnesota Rate of Manipulation Test.

THE TESTING PROGRAM

One evening after everyone in the department had left, Al thought about a recent discussion with John. John had told him that a Professor Sanchez had led a discussion about the Uniform Guidelines on Employee Selection Procedures. According to this professor, the guidelines required organizations with more than 100 employees to make adverse impact determinations at least once a year.

Al realized that he planned on using the manual dexterity test for selection purposes. Although two years have gone by, no validation study has been undertaken. The last validation study was for the old finger dexterity test. Since John volunteered to do the adverse impact determination and validation study, Al didn't oppose the idea. He wasn't convinced, however, that this was necessary.

John gathered data for all those textile workers who took the test. These workers were hired regardless of their test scores. After examining the personnel files, John identified 217 cases for analysis. (The data found in Table 1 are a representative subsample of those data.) John used the Pearson product-moment correlation

TABLE 1

Employee	*Sex*	*Race**	*Age*	*Test Score*	*Performance Rating*
1	M	S	35	36	90
2	M	W	32	44	95
3	F	S	44	50	95
4	M	B	42	49	93
5	F	B	36	46	89
6	M	W	33	52	94
7	M	W	45	50	92
8	M	S	48	50	93
9	F	B	34	42	83
10	F	B	46	44	89
11	F	S	30	40	87
12	F	S	39	48	95
13	F	B	31	47	90
14	M	W	49	39	80
15	F	S	47	48	92
16	F	W	40	38	79
17	M	S	44	38	80
18	M	W	33	36	72
19	F	S	43	46	89
20	M	S	36	48	92
21	F	W	22	46	89
22	M	B	28	32	70
23	F	B	19	48	94
24	M	B	23	48	94
25	M	B	27	36	74
26	F	W	18	46	85
27	F	W	26	44	79
28	M	S	21	50	95
29	M	B	23	34	70
30	F	W	28	44	83

Sex: M=Male; F=Female. Race: S=Spanish surnamed; W=White; B=Black. Age: Age at time of employment.
*No Native Americans applied.

coefficient[2] to validate the manual dexterity text. He wanted to use the predictive validity approach described in his personnel textbook. He hoped to examine the relationship between test scores and employee performance rating.

---

[2] This method is discussed in a number of statistical textbooks. See, for example, J.P. Guilford and Benjamin Fruchter, *Fundamental Statistics in Psychology and Education,* 5th ed. (New York: McGraw-Hill, 1973), pp. 79–98.

Discussion Questions

1. Are there possible negative outcomes for individuals and organizations when assessment centers are used?
2. Do you agree or disagree with John that an adverse impact determination should have been made sooner? Why?
3. What kind of relationship did John find between scores on the test and the performance rating?
4. Was there evidence of differential validity?
5. Assuming that a cutoff score for hiring of 41 was established, would use of this test have led to evidence of adverse impact?
6. Given the validity results you found, would you recommend use of this test as a selection device? If so, how would you use it?

Buena Vista Plant (B)

The plant personnel department at Buena Vista is extremely small.[1] Although the workforce it serves has increased dramatically, only three people handle all personnel matters. The last person to join the department, John Turner, did so in 1978. As the newest member of the department, John was the most knowledgeable about government regulations, laws, and court cases that impact personnel activities. Because John was relatively new to the department, he had little influence on Al Logan. Al also seemed a bit threatened by the fact that John was completing requirements for a degree in business administration. Much of what John knew about personnel administration he learned in classes at Emory University. He transferred into the personnel office from an assembly line job in the plant.

Cheryl Giffhorn is, in Al's eyes, the most valuable person in the personnel department. She has been his eyes, ears, and right-hand "man." As a friend and confidante, she has been absolutely indispensable. Cheryl has responsibility for prescreening nonexempt and hourly applicants, testing, and recordkeeping related to staffing and employee health. At present, she is deeply involved in preparing a report of the incidence of brown lung disease (byssinosis), chronic bronchitis, and emphysema—diseases all attributable to exposure to cotton dust. (These diseases are not now a problem at the plant, but the reports are required by OSHA.)

Al likes the personnel director. He likes working with people, and, in the early years, his job as personnel director was easy. Al saw his job as one of keeping things running smoothly, helping with morale, and solving employee problems. He enjoys getting out on the shop floor where the people are. Al is proud of being chairman of the United Fund Drive, a Rotarian, and a member of the Chamber of Commerce.

---

[1] All names are disguised.

Recently, he has found little time for the civic activities that he likes. Each year, like clockwork, he has found himself beating back attempts by the Amalgamated Clothing and Textile Workers and other unions to organize the workers. This task is getting harder and more time consuming each year. Last week, Al talked to a consultant who wanted to be paid for telling him how to keep unions out. According to Al, his biggest problem is government interference. Every personnel activity seemed to involve some law or government regulation. He knew that he needed to keep up with these new laws on health and safety, equal employment opportunity, pensions, compensation, and labor relations. His duties as personnel director of a larger workforce seem to leave him little time to keep up with recent amendments and court decisions.

One duty that has bugged him the most is his role in the grievance procedure. Employees complained about not having any assurance that they would be treated fairly, so the grievance procedure was developed by a committee representing employees at all company levels. The procedure seemed like a good idea at first, because it eliminated a complaint workers had, and it took away one union bargaining advantage. The problem was that more grievances were being filed and more grievances were going beyond the first and second steps. Grievances at the higher levels required Al's involvement, and he resented having to waste his time listening to petty complaints about wage discrimination, subjective performance evaluations, and being passed over for promotions. Now, a couple of these people had filed complaints with the EEOC and the Department of Labor.

THE NEW ADDITIONS

In January of 1981, two new lines were opened in the personnel department. Al now had authorization to add two new members to the department—one as an assistant personnel director and a second as a personnel assistant. Both jobs were for college-educated, trained professionals. Shortly after receipt of the job requisitions, a list of internal candidates arrived from headquarters. After examining the list (which included the name of John Turner), Al agreed to examine the records of five candidates for each job. By February, he had interviewed the top three candidates. Al selected Kathy Morris as the new assistant personnel director and Bill Benjamin became the new personnel assistant. (See Exhibit 1.) John, the heir apparent to the job, was not too pleased with Al's selection of Kathy as assistant personnel director.

Kathy had impressive credentials—she had a bachelor's degree from Delaware State College and an MBA from Golden Gate University. She had held a number of personnel positions during her six years with the company. Among her experiences were assignments as assistant personnel director at Spring Garden Research Facility, work in training, recruiting, and the EEOC office at its headquarters, as well as assignments at the Bristol, Tennessee, and Lexington, Kentucky, plants. Her performance, in all cases, was rated excellent. Bill Benjamin, the new personnel assistant, had only been with the company two years. He had majored in personnel administration at the University of Georgia. He spent his first year in the labor relations

EXHIBIT 1 Organization Chart for Buena Vista's Personnel Department

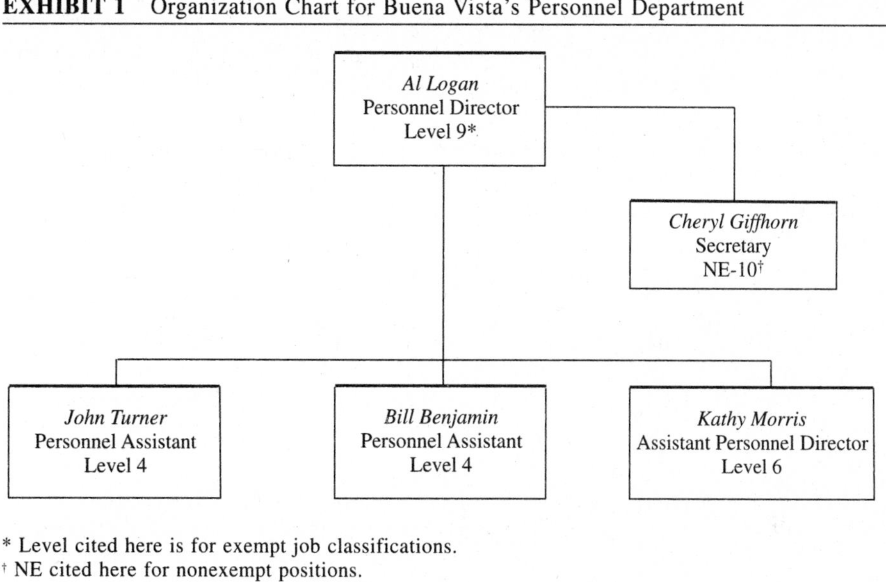

* Level cited here is for exempt job classifications.
† NE cited here for nonexempt positions.

department assisting others with collective bargaining. In his second year, he worked in the wage and salary department and took on special assignments for the director of employee relations. This is his first plant assignment.

THE TROUBLE WITH KATHY

It didn't take long for Al to realize that Kathy would be a problem. After only three months on the job, she started causing problems. She was a know-it-all. Every personnel policy was illegal. Or she disagreed with it. Al had to stop her from trying to change everything he'd ever written. Kathy fought him about the need to validate the assessment center. She claimed there was adverse impact on blacks. Kathy fought about company policy concerning pregnant women taking a leave without pay at the end of their second trimester. And she demanded that the disability policy be so written that pregnancy could be treated the same as any other disability. Well, Al had had enough. They were going to meet and have it out.

THE MEETING

"Mr. Logan, you wanted to talk to me?"

"Yes, Kathy, come in and sit down. This conversation is just between us. What I have on my mind needs being said."

"That sounds ominous; what is this all about?"

"Kathy, you have challenged our policies, disagreed with me on the handling of certain grievances, and, in general, have made a nuisance of yourself. What you are doing borders on insubordination, and I called you in to verbally reprimand you for your action."

"I am sorry you feel that way, Mr. Logan. My intent was to help you and to help the department. Some of our policies were written 10 or more years ago. As John suggested to you, some may not be consistent with current regulations, court decisions, and agency guidelines. For example, the plant policy on disability treats pregnancy differently than it treats other disabilities. In addition, policy here requires pregnant women, regardless of their health or nature of their jobs, to accept a leave of absence at the end of their second trimester. I don't believe that this policy treats women fairly."

"Kathy, do you know whether the policy is legal? If you know about anything that makes the policy illegal, then I will make a change; otherwise, back off."

"The legality of the policy is questionable at best, although I can't cite a specific regulation or law. But let me mention another problem area. I applaud your development of the textile supervisor assessment center, but my data on selection rates indicate a problem. While 70 percent of the whites participating in the assessment center are picked for promotion, only 52 percent of the black assessees are chosen. I think the EEOC and other agencies would question this difference. Plus, we have not done a validation study."

"You have the answer for everything, Kathy. Actually, I hear you challenging a lot of things, but I don't see anything supporting your position. As for the EEOC, when its representatives schedule a compliance review, then I'll do what they want—within reason. Now, since you have an answer for everything else, what do you think of our decision to fire Jeffrey Clement for moonlighting?"

"To be honest, Mr. Logan, I think you are making a big mistake. I believe there is precedent for firing an employee for holding two full-time jobs. Typically, the employee must make a choice. After reading the supervisor's report, however, I am concerned that the supervisor thinks Jeffrey is working two jobs. The supervisor has no proof, and the subordinate refuses to incriminate himself. I don't think we can force the guy, even under the threat of discharge, to admit this rule violation."

"Kathy, I think we have a difference of opinion over these policies. Maybe I am too close to them since I had to create them, but I want you to bring me something definitive—court cases, regulations, laws, and so on—rather than disagree openly with me. I have not kept up, and I know it. If you show me why change is needed, we'll make the change."

"Okay. Right or wrong, I have charged full speed without documentation or evidence to support my position. All through school and most of my previous jobs, I have been pretty independent. I'll work harder at being a better team player."

"Well, Kathy, it's just about time for a shift change. Let's see if we can get to the Coke machine before the mad rush makes that impossible. Treats on the big spender. And, by the way, please call me Al."

Discussion Questions

1. How would you describe Al?
2. What problems do you see in the personnel department?
3. Should John, the heir apparent, have been promoted? Why or why not?
4. What is the cause of the problems between Al and Kathy?
5. Examine each of the policy issues Kathy raises. Is she correct?
6. How would you describe Kathy?

---

26 Marcus A. Foster Medical Center (A)

The Marcus A. Foster Medical Center is located on Mt. Airy Avenue in the Germantown section of Philadelphia, not far from the original "stomping grounds" of the now famous Dr. Bill Cosby. The center, one of three such centers located strategically around the city, is named after another important black Philadelphian, the late Dr. Marcus A. Foster. Foster served as superintendent of schools in Philadelphia and later in Oakland, California. The center is nationally known for the treatment of and research on children's illnesses, including sudden infant mortality syndrome (crib death).

One early morning in June 1988, Margie Stoker got a "wake up call" from her supervisor, Paul Adams. Hearing from Paul at 6:30 AM was not a good sign. Margie is an assistant administrator at Marcus A. Foster Medical Center. She has worked with Paul for four years. Paul, since taking over as administrator, has worked hard to place the medical center on a sound financial basis. That task was not an easy one since most of the medical center's patients came from the surrounding community. This section of Philadelphia consists of working-class people who, out of necessity, live on a week-to-week basis. Large families are the rule and jobs are often hard to find. Many of the jobs found require limited skills, pay little, and offer little security. Benefits for employees are sparse.

An hour and a half after Margie's call from Paul, she sat in a staff meeting. Stella Harvey and Bob Bryan, both assistant administrators, were there. Paul wanted some answers. He made it clear that the center had a pressing problem that had to be resolved now! He explained how frustrated he had become. Robert Grayson, the center's controller and chief financial officer, told him about the large number of uncollectible hospital bills. The post office was returning bills addressed to former patients. These individuals had received treatment in the hospital's emergency room. The bills came back stamped "Return to sender—incorrect address." On average, the post office returned 48 such bills each week. These bills represented 11 percent of those mailed. Grayson speculated that the cause of the problem was either incomplete or inaccurate histories on the emergency room registration forms. He believed these problems led to incorrect mailing addresses. Sometimes, the name that appeared on the report was correct, but the street address was incorrect; sometimes, numbers were not transcribed carefully. Grayson set the hospital losses at $3,744 per week or $194,688 per year. As Grayson explained, these figures assume an average charge of about $78 a visit. He mentioned that there are wide variations in per-patient costs. The cause: treatments vary from treating a cut finger, bee stings, to overcoming broken bones, bad falls, or acute appendicitis. Severe injuries and sickness become inpatient visits rather than emergency room (e.g., a gunshot wound, stroke, or heart attack). It is not uncommon to write off two-thirds of the emergency room treatment costs but Grayson was concerned that poor recordkeeping may be costing the center a great deal more.

Paul and John were considering several options. One idea was to conduct a traditional training program. This program would emphasize the importance of the report to the medical center and teach the clerks how to fill out the report completely and accurately. A second thought was to replace the clerks. The clerks earn about $208 per week and have been at the medical center an average of three years. A third option considered is to conduct a systems analysis that would show why the clerks' performances were below standard.

There had to be an economical solution that would guarantee improved on-the-job performance and reduce the number of uncollectibles. Robert Grayson suggested two other alternatives. The center should only treat those who can show proof of their ability to pay (unless the situation is "life-threatening"). As a last resort, if all other bottom-line solutions fail, Robert says to close the emergency room. Stella commented that the clerks may not be the problem. Bob said he hoped the medical center would never close the emergency room. After the meeting, Paul told them that he wanted solutions to the problem "yesterday." They all wondered what the center should do.

Discussion Questions

1. What are the problems in this case?
2. What action(s) should the medical center staff take?

Marcus A. Foster Medical Center (B)

As John put down the phone, he recalled the actions taken to overcome the collections problem. He thought that he finally had the emergency room out of his hair. The phone call suggested otherwise. He had just finished talking to Stella Harvey, the medical center's director of nursing, and with the center's risk management officer, Marjorie Murphy. Stella informed John that she had just fired Mrs. Betty Frink. Betty has worked as a nurse at the medical center since 1987.

Mrs. Frink is an active 63-year-old widow, who by all accounts is in excellent health. Her co-workers described her as "sharp as a tack, good with patients, and a hard worker." However, Stella says Betty has one small problem. In taking medical histories from patients she simply doesn't always listen or she fails to list information regarding allergies to certain medications on the registration form. She had been fortunate in the past. Doctors and other nurses prevented at least three previous near disasters where she obtained the medical history. These patients might have died or become seriously ill if given certain medications not noted on the chart. In a recent scare, a staff nurse gave a sulfa drug to a distressed patient who had a bladder infection. The patient returned to the hospital three hours later looking bloated and suffering from respiratory problems. The patient claimed he had told Betty that he was allergic to sulfa drugs. This fact was not listed on the chart. After each near miss Betty received counseling. John remembered that about seven months ago Stella had mentioned "a problem with Betty" but Stella did not elaborate at that time. He gave Stella's comment little thought and did not explore with her the nature of Betty's problem. Now John wishes that he had probed more deeply into the situation.

Margie Stoker, the assistant administrator, met with Betty for her exit interview before Betty left the center. Margie asked Betty the usual questions about her experiences with the center. Margie explained the medical center's policies and told Betty that the medical center would quickly issue a check to her. The check would cover pay for regular hours, severance, and earned vacation. Betty did not know that Margie and Stella had reached an important agreement. Since Betty was a senior citizen, the hospital would not challenge her claim for unemployment compensation if she applied. In fact, Stella wished that Betty had had the opportunity to resign. Rather than make that offer she decided to end the termination interview without adding a new complication.

Discussion Questions

1. Was the decision to fire Betty an appropriate one?
2. How should this situation have been handled? Explain your answer carefully.

Marcus A. Foster Medical Center (C)

Paul Adams stared blankly out the window. He and the top administrators had just concluded a stormy staff meeting. The staff disagreed loudly when he came to the "Cynthia Hamilton problem." Bob and Stella believe Paul made the wrong decision. Robert sided with Paul in his decision regarding Hamilton. Ms. Hamilton applied recently for the position of switchboard operator. Over the years, Paul had handled a number of unusual personnel situations but this one required all the resources at his command.

About a week ago, Cynthia Hamilton showed up at the medical center's personnel office. Normally, a walk-in candidate attracts little attention from anyone on the hospital staff but this was not so for Cynthia. Cynthia and her dog came in together. On reporting to the personnel office, she stated her desire to apply for the position of switchboard operator. The position, she learned from a friend, was advertised in the *Philadelphia Daily News.* Cynthia informed the personnel receptionist, Ms. Helen Porter, that she was fully qualified for the position. The skeptical receptionist called Paul on the phone to explain the situation. Paul, after meeting with Cynthia briefly, confirmed that Cynthia was legally blind. He refused to have her tested for the job and he saw no need to interview her. He took personal responsibility for the rejection of her application. He felt bad about going over Margie Stoker's head on this one. As personnel director, the decision was Margie's to make. However, Paul felt certain that only a sighted person could operate the switchboard and hospital emergency signals.

Cynthia did not say a word. She immediately left the premises. Now, Cynthia's quick, silent departure is causing Paul some anxiety. Was this a test case of some kind? He acted swiftly and decisively. He couldn't imagine that anyone with significant vision loss could do the job. Also, he felt that if she could do the job, the medical center would have to pay for some tremendously expensive accommodations. Rather than be saddled with that cost, he'd rather not hire her. Margie later gave him a piece of her mind about making "personnel decisions." Although he thinks he can smooth Margie's ruffled feathers, something about this one continues to gnaw at him.

Discussion Questions

1. What are the problems in this case?
2. Tell what actions you would take in solving these problems and avoiding the problems in the future.

---

27 John Young Enterprises

John Young is owner and chief executive officer of John Young Enterprises, Cleveland, Ohio. John Young Enterprises (JYE) is a small firm that provides security guards and other protective services. It has been in business for 23 years. JYE has grown rapidly from a 5-man, rather loose-knit informal group into today's 486-employee company. JYE's major thrust is in the area of providing security guards for department stores, shopping malls, and a number of businesses in downtown Cleveland. In addition to this work, JYE furnishes security guard assistance for special events, such as athletic events, rock concerts, and musical programs. The most glamorous aspect of the business is its role as bodyguards to certain celebrities. In recent months, the firm provided protection for Bill Cosby, Barbara Streisand, Rod Stewart, Dollie Parton, Muhammad Ali, and former President Jimmy Carter.

John Young has thoroughly enjoyed watching his firm grow and prosper. He and his brother James (both former police officers) thought that they could carve out a niche for themselves by starting a security service. John and James had diligently saved money from their pay. John conceived the idea while attending a basketball game in Fort Wayne, Indiana. The old Fort Wayne Pistons played at the Coliseum there. He had traveled to Defiance, Ohio, to see his younger brother, Leroy. It was Leroy's idea to go to Fort Wayne. Leroy's only disappointment is his own son's disinterest in the business. Arthur is in medical school. Paul worked for the firm for five years and then quit. James's boys—Ted, Mathew, and Charles—tried the firm but have long since left it. Ted joined an architectural firm, Mathew is a stockbroker, and Charles is a drifter, living off the land. The family nicknamed him "Odd Job." At last report, he was living in Portland.

THE PROBLEM

When John hung up the phone, the words that he had heard fully registered. He was being sued, but he did not know whether to first call a personnel specialist or an attorney. No one had ever sued him over the use of lie detectors for preemployment purposes. During his 10 years as a police officer he had never heard of anyone filing a complaint against the department over its requirement that police recruit applicants pass a lie detector test. He remembered that written tests caused several problems, so he did not rely on them. John believes military or police experience, good character, the absence of a criminal record, and being at least 21 years of age are the significant factors to consider.

James Hamilton, the attorney, had spoken on behalf of his client, David Raskin. David had been rejected for the position of armed prison guard. The basic reason for the decision was the polygraphist's judgment that Raskin had given a number of deceptive responses to the questions asked. The questions asked on the examination are shown in Exhibit 1.

Hamilton raised a number of objections. First, he claimed that lie detector tests are misnomers. That is, they don't measure whether someone lies. At best they measure physiological reactions. Such reactions, he believed, could be caused by nerves as well as by various medical conditions. According to some research studies, the accuracy rate is only 50 percent—with a built-in bias against the truthful or honest person. In fact, Hamilton cited a report by the American Civil Liberties Union (ACLU) that termed lie detector tests "a form of 20th-century witchcraft." He also questioned the ability of unqualified polygraphists to interpret the results. His final comment to Young was a quote Hamilton attributed to former President Nixon: "Listen, I don't know anything about polygraphs, and I don't know how accurate they are. But I do know that they'll scare the hell out of people." Young turned these ideas over in his

EXHIBIT 1 Security Officer Polygraph Examination

Arrangements

At your request, *David W. Raskin* (applicant) was administered a polygraph examination on *August 6, 1984* (date,) for the purpose of verifying the applicant's employment application data and background information.

Procedure

Standard polygraph procedure was employed throughout the entire examination.

Questions Reviewed during Examination

Relevant issues pertaining to this examination were reviewed with the applicant as indicated by test questions and responses below.

1. Have you ever represented yourself to be anyone other than yourself?
2. Did you knowingly omit requested information from your questionnaire?
3. Did you submit information on your questionnaire which you know to be false?
4. Did you deliberately lie to your oral board?
5. Have you listed all of your regular employment?
6. Have you deliberately concealed any of your past employment?
7. Have you been asked to resign from any place of employment?
8. Have you ever been dismissed from any place of employment?
9. Have you ever quit a job because you thought you were going to be fired?
10. Have you deliberately concealed the true reason for leaving previous jobs?
11. Have you stolen any property from previous employers?
12. Have you stolen any money from previous employers?

---

1. Have you ever had any property repossessed?
2. Have you ever had any bills turned over to a collection agency?
3. Have you ever intentionally written a bad check?
4. Have you ever deliberately falsified any credit application?
5. Have you ever had any gambling debts?
6. Have you ever concealed any financial obligations you presently have?
7. Are you presently delinquent in payments on any financial obligations you have?
8. Have you ever had a court action taken against you in financial matters?

---

1. Have you ever used any form of narcotics without a legally signed doctor's prescription?
2. Have you ever smoked marijuana?
3. Have you ever illegally purchased any form of narcotics?
4. Have you ever illegally sold any form of narcotics?
5. Have you transported, or had in your possession, any form of illegal narcotics?
6. To your knowledge, do any of your relatives use narcotics illegally?

EXHIBIT 1 *(continued)*

7. To your knowledge, do any of your friends or associates use narcotics illegally?
8. Have you ever experimented with any narcotics (heroin, cocaine, morphine, opium)?
9. Have you ever experimented with any dangerous drugs (barbituates, amphetamines, speed)?
10. Have you ever experimented with hallucinogens (LSD, peyote, mescaline)?
11. Have you ever smoked hashish?

---

1. Have you ever completed a homosexual act with a male/female?
2. Have you ever solicited a homosexual act with a male/female?
3. Do you feel you have homosexual tendencies?
4. Have you ever accepted pay for the commission of any sex act?
5. Have you ever knowingly had sexual relations with a minor female/male?
6. Have you ever sexually molested a child?
7. Have you ever sexually exhibited yourself in public?
8. Have you ever been a party to an illegal abortion?

---

1. Other than what you have listed, have you ever been hospitalized?
2. Have you deliberately given false information about your physical or mental condition?
3. Have you ever had a nervous breakdown?
4. Have you ever had a mental breakdown?
5. Do you feel you have a drinking problem?
6. Have you ever been treated for alcoholism?
7. Have you ever been a patient in a mental institution?
8. Have you ever received psychiatric care or treatment?
9. Have you ever attempted to commit suicide?
10. Do you wear contact lenses?
11. Do you need contact lenses to correct your vision?
12. Did you wear contact lenses when you took your physical examination?

---

1. Have you ever been a member of the Communist party?
2. Have you ever been a member of any militant organization?
3. Have you ever participated in any demonstration or riot?
4. Have you made application for membership at the order or request of any militant organization?
5. Have you ever engaged in any serious criminal act?
6. Have you ever committed any serious undetected crime?
7. Have you ever accompanied other people while they engaged in any serious criminal act?

EXHIBIT 1 *(concluded)*

8. Other than what you have listed, have you ever been arrested?
9. Would the police solve any crimes if you told them all you know about a certain incident?

Conclusion

After careful analysis of the applicant's polygraphs and based on the physiological reactions indicated, it is the opinion of this examiner that:

____*a.* This applicant has told substantially the complete truth during the examination.

____*b.* Applicant has not told the complete truth and declined to give any information which may resolve deceptive responses.

____*c.* Applicant did not tell the complete truth but did give the following information regarding:

____*d.* Examination was inconclusive due to emotional and physiological inadequacies and is not rescheduled for testing.

____*e.* Results on this examination are inconclusive. Subject is scheduled to be retested on:

Respectfully submitted,

____

Polygraphist

mind. He was concerned about adverse publicity and a lost lawsuit. He did know that he never coerced applicants or employees into taking the polygraph. All polygraph takers complete the same form. (See Exhibit 2.)

As Young thought about the polygraph problem, something else connected in his mind. This was the second personnel headache he had confronted this month. Bobby Scofield had complained bitterly about his inability to review his personnel file. Bobby left the office screaming about his right to privacy and access to employment records. Young had asked Cheryl Miller, his assistant, to look into the matter. When she reported back to him she cited four federal laws: the Privacy Act of 1974, the Family Education Rights and Privacy Act, Fair Credit and Reporting Act, and the Freedom of Information Act. He wasn't convinced that these federal laws hindered him in any way. He could not believe that the federal government would meddle with a company's personnel file policies and procedures.

When Cheryl reported to John about the federal statutes, she also mentioned something that she felt was most important concerning the Bobby Scofield incident. Bobby had applied for a supervisory position at a firm near his home in Akron. (Although he liked working for John Young Enterprises, he had grown tired of the bumper-to-bumper commute to Cleveland each day.) Everything was going fine until the

EXHIBIT 2 Polygraph Consent Form

John Young Enterprises

I do hereby give my consent to a pre-employment polygraph examination (more commonly known as lie detector) to be administered by Joseph W. Spelman, certified polygrapher, on (date) August 6, 1984. I have been made aware that polygraph attachments must be made to my body and do give my consent to having the necessary attachments made. I understand that the examination is to be concerned with (subject of exam) the validity of my work history statements, conduct in previous positions and certain disqualifying personal behavior. and the only questions that will be asked me during any portion of the examination will be discussed with me and approved by me prior to the test. I understand that an audio tape-recording is being made of the entire test, including my discussions with the examiner before and after the actual testing, and that I may obtain a copy of that recording, at my own expense, at any time within three months from the present date. I hereby authorize the examiner to communicate the results of the examination to the requestor: John Young Enterprises.

(Witness)

(Witness)

David W. Raskin
(Signature of Respondent)

Akron company called JYE to verify his employment. Bobby assumed the firm would state dates of employment and last position held. To Bobby's chagrin, other information was provided. Salary history, promotional recommendations, performance appraisal data, and information on disciplinary matters was shared with the prospective employer. The release of these sensitive data without his permission and his inability to clarify or challenge the accuracy of information on disciplinary matters is what angered Bobby. According to Cheryl, Bobby claimed that other companies, such as IBM, allow employees to see their records and to change their records when inaccuracies are discovered.

John leaned back in his chair and wondered about these problems. He pondered his next move, but he also wondered what he might do to avoid these types of problems in the future.

Discussion Questions

1. Evaluate John Young Enterprises' use of the polygraph. What are the legal implications of utilizing polygraph examinations as a selection device?
2. Which state or federal laws provide guidance on the legal use of the polygraph?
3. Do employees have a right to read and copy the contents of their personnel file? Explain and support your answer.
4. Do employees have the right to deny third parties access to information related to their present or previous employment? Explain.

Section E

Career Management, Evaluation, and Training

28 Forest Park Corporation (A)*

During the past 10 years, Forest Park Corporation has grown from a small, relatively obscure chemical company into a diversified multinational corporation, with net sales topping $2 billion. Net earnings and stockholders' equity have improved markedly during the period. Over the 10-year span, the number of employees has increased from 13,000 to 27,000. The company has diversified into leather goods, medical instruments, pharmaceuticals, plastics, textiles, and various chemical products. Furthermore, as dramatic as this growth has been, Forest Park expects the trend to continue for at least five more years.

To a large extent, the success of Forest Park can be attributed to Don Rogers, Forest Park's director of employee relations. A neatly dressed, athletic-looking man of 46, Don had come to Forest Park 21 years ago and began with the company immediately after earning his MBA at Washington University. He was considered an outstanding problem solver; his biggest asset, his talent at solving complex problems, had won him recognition, increased responsibility, and rapid promotion. Everyone knew that it was his staffing, development, and training programs that had enabled the company to survive and flourish during 10 years of rapid growing pains. Since becoming director, however, staffing and development were no longer his major responsibility. He now was responsible for the big picture. This morning's employee relations managers meeting made it pretty clear that he'd better get involved in staffing and development again—and fast.

---

* This case was prepared by Professor George E. Stevens of Kent State University and R. Penny Marquette of the University of Akron.

Don sat gazing thoughtfully out the window of his office on the 20th floor. A tugboat churned up the Mississippi River, passing within shouting distance of Saint Louis's Gateway Arch. In his hand was Cathie Stango's file, thrust there a minute ago by Bob Pelzer, manager of employee planning. The file had been the central exhibit at the morning's weekly meeting with the professional employee relations staff.

Don had initiated the weekly meetings, and, in the past, they'd been extremely productive. Those who attended the meetings are listed in the partial organization chart (see Exhibit 1). New ideas were frequently generated, enabling the employee relations group to better serve the needs of the organization. This morning's meeting had not been productive. Bob had blown his stack right there in front of everyone. Don had always thought of Bob as a level-headed professional. Either he'd been wrong, or the situation was really serious.

A knock at the door quickly brought Don back to the present.

"Come in. . . . Yes, Karen?"

"Don, Bob stopped by just now and left this envelope for you."

"Thanks, Karen; that's all for now." Don opened the envelope and found a long handwritten note. He hoped it would explain this morning's outburst. He began reading.

> Don, I'm sorry I blew up at this morning's meeting, but we have a serious problem. We pride ourselves on recruiting the best people we can, and, over the past few years, we've had lots of employees involved in our tuition aid program. The program has permitted many of them to earn bachelor's and master's degrees going to school at night. Only dedicated, highly motivated people are successful in earning degrees while working full time. It's a tremendous strain on the employee, his manager, and his family. It isn't exactly cheap for the company, either. Last year we spent $200,000 on tuition aid. In most regards, the money has been well spent, but, in too many cases, there's no payoff for the company and it's our own fault.
>
> Cathie Stango quit the company today. As far as I'm concerned, it was the straw that broke the camel's back. She's been a member of the general bookkeeping department for nine years, working as a clerk. Her goal was to become an accountant in one of the accounting or finance departments. She's earned straight As at the University of Missouri, and it's been a whole year since she got her bachelor's in accounting, yet no one has promoted her!
>
> I'm supposed to be responsible for the manpower planning system, and I didn't know about her. The system simply doesn't contain a method for identifying all the people in the organization who are promotable. Right now we're relying on four sources to identify potential talent: (1) We are conducting interviews with the recruiting department staff, initiated by employees. These interviews are exploratory in nature, designed to find out about the employees' interests and qualifications. (2) The computer system theoretically provides us the name, location, present job, and educational background of each employee. Unfortunately, lots of people are missed because the data are often incomplete or out of date. (3) Departments that have openings may suggest the names of people they know about who are promotable. Obviously, this is a narrow and usually inequitable source of information. (4) We often have had contact with good candidates through our own activities. The problem here is that most of these contacts are at headquarters, excluding people located at our other 16 domestic locations.

> The point I'm trying to make is that we know about the jobs, but we don't know where the candidates are. This problem is especially infuriating where tuition aid participants are concerned because of our investment in their education. If we can't find a solution quickly, we should just discontinue the program. It's been in operation for 10 years now and it simply hasn't paid off.

Rogers reread the memo. The story seemed even more difficult to believe when he examined Cathie's file. Her performance was consistently rated superior to outstanding, her attendance record was excellent, her potential for promotion was rated high. It had taken her eight years of night school and summer school to acquire her accounting degree, and the company had paid for every penny of it. Now she was gone, doubtless bitter toward the company for not promoting her, and the company had lost a large dollar investment in her education. Where, he asked himself, had the company failed?

He reached for the phone and dialed Bob. "Bob, this is Don. I've read your memo and you're right. This is serious. How many more cases are there like this one? . . . 22 this year! You'd better bring me the details on all the employees who've left. I'd like to have them and any other supporting information you can provide. I'll be meeting with the vice presidents at 4:00 PM today and I'd like to present them with a strategy to overcome this problem." (Exhibit 2 is a copy of Cathie Stango's Employee Evaluation form; Exhibit 3 gives information on employees who had received tuition aid but had left the company because they had not been promoted.)

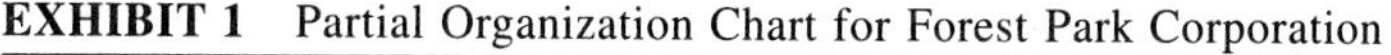

EXHIBIT 1 Partial Organization Chart for Forest Park Corporation

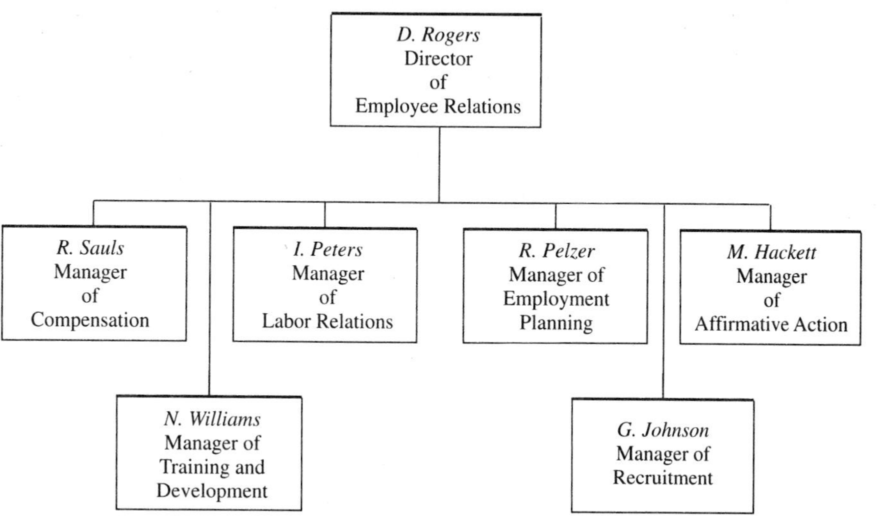

EXHIBIT 2

PERIODIC EMPLOYEE EVALUATION FORM

Name Catherine Stango

Position BookKeeping Clerk III

Department General BookKeeping

	Poor						Outstanding
Attendance	1	2	3	4	5	6	(7)
Attitude	1	2	3	4	5	6	(7)
Productivity	1	2	3	4	5	(6)	7
Promotability	1	2	3	4	5	6	(7)
Leadership Quality	1	2	3	4	(5)	6	7
Ability to Learn New Jobs and Tasks	1	2	3	4	5	(6)	7

Comments:
Cathie has just completed her bachelor's degree in accounting. As much as I hate to lose her, I can't recommend her too highly for promotion.

Employee's Signature Catherine Stango Date 1/4/82

Supervisor's Signature James Freeman Date 1/2/82

ROUTING: Original - Employee's File Personnel Department
Pink - Departmental File
Yellow - Employee

EXHIBIT 3 Participants Who Left

Name	*Minority Classification*	*Job Classification and Department where Employed*	*Degree Earned*	*Our Equivalent for the New Job Taken outside Forest Park (if known)*
1. Selma White	Female	Administration/secretary III	BS, management	Management trainee
2. George Sayer	n.a.*	Data processing/programmer I	MS, data processing	Programmer IV
3. Sondra Dreft	Female	Marketing research/clerk typist III	BS, statistics	Market analyst I
4. Manuel Diaz	Spanish-American	Maintenance/janitor III	BS, data processing	Programmer I
5. Roger Ernst	Black	Payroll/bookkeeping clerk II	BS, chemical engineering	Chemist
6. Rita Little	Black/female	Data processing/receptionist	Proficiency certificate—keypunch operator I	Keypunch operator I
7. Linda Arthur	Female	Marketing research/secretary II	BS, mathematics	Unknown
8. Samuel Brown	n.a.*	Data processing/programmer IV	MBA	Systems analyst II
9. John Smiley	n.a.*	Retail marketing/commission salesman	MBA	Assistant to the director of marketing—division level
10. Lee Arrowsmith	Native American	Transportation/vehicle maintenance worker III	BS	Unknown
11. Livingston Cooper	Black	Data processing/keypunch operator I	Proficiency certificate—computer operator	Computer operator II

EXHIBIT 3 *Concluded*

Name	*Minority Classification*	*Job Classification and Department where Employed*	*Degree Earned*	*Our Equivalent for the New Job Taken outside Forest Park (if known)*
12. Sarah Elims	Female	Steno pool/clerk typist II	Proficiency certificate—typing and shorthand	Secretary II
13. Roberta Dicks	Female	Marketing research/secretary II	BS, marketing	Unknown
14. Jose Rodriguez	Spanish-American	Generic drugs research/lab technician II	BS, accounting	Staff accountant
15. Lloyd Sanders	Black	Receiving/shipping clerk I	BS, management	Unknown
16. Gloria Atlas	Black/female	Data processing/clerk typist I	BS, data processing	Programmer I
17. Arlene Dailey	Female	Cafeteria/food service clerk II	Proficiency certificate—typing and shorthand	Secretary III
18. Carol Singleton	Female	Marketing research/market analyst I	MS, statistics	Market analyst III
19. Jack Grinlin	n.a.*	Mail room/general clerk III	BS, management	Mail room supervisor
20. Ada Winston	Female	Accounts payable/bookkeeping clerk II	BS, accounting	Staff accountant
21. Sally Donner	Black/female	Legal/general clerk III	BS, home economics	Dietician
22. Lester Ridgeway	n.a.*	Advertising/general clerk II	Proficiency certificate—laboratory technology	Unknown
23. Catherine Stango	Female	General bookkeeping/bookkeeping clerk IV	BS, accounting	Staff accountant

* n.a. means not applicable.

Discussion Questions

1. What are the key problems?
2. How would you rate Bob's performance?
3. Should the tuition aid program be discontinued?
4. Devise a plan to identify promotable people and insure that promotions are filled, from within, in an equitable fashion, whenever possible.
5. Do the data in the appendix indicate any special problems needing attention? What can be done about them?

*29 Performance Appraisal: The Case of the Second Evaluation**

Marcus Singh is an economist in the city of Rock Falls Department of Human Resources and Economic Development. He is 40 years old and has worked for the city of Rock Falls for the past 10 years. During that time, Marcus has been perceived by his supervisors as being an above-average performer, although no formal evaluations have ever been done in his department. About 10 months ago he was transferred from the department's industrial development unit to the newly formed Office of Research and Evaluation. Other employees also were transferred as part of an overall reorganization in the department. The organizational chart for the department is depicted in Exhibit 1.

Out of concern for equal employment opportunity, the department director, Victor Popelmill, recently issued a directive to all of the unit heads to formally evaluate the performance of their subordinates. Attached to his memorandum was a copy of a new performance appraisal form to be used in conducting the evaluations. Garth Fryer, head of the Office of Research and Evaluation, decided to allow his subordinates to have some input in the evaluation process. (In addition to Garth Fryer, the Office of Research and Evaluation was comprised of two researchers, Marcus Singh and Jason Taft, and one secretary, Connie Millar.) He told both of his researchers to complete a self-appraisal and a peer appraisal for the other researcher. After reviewing both the peer and self-appraisals, Garth completed the final and official appraisal of each researcher. Before sending the appraisal forms to Mr. Popelmill's office, Mr. Fryer met with each employee individually for the purpose of reviewing and explaining his ratings to the employee. Each employee signed his evaluation and indicated that he agreed with the ratings.

---

* Prepared by Professor James G. Pesek and Dean Joseph P. Grunenwald, both of Clarion University of Pennsylvania.

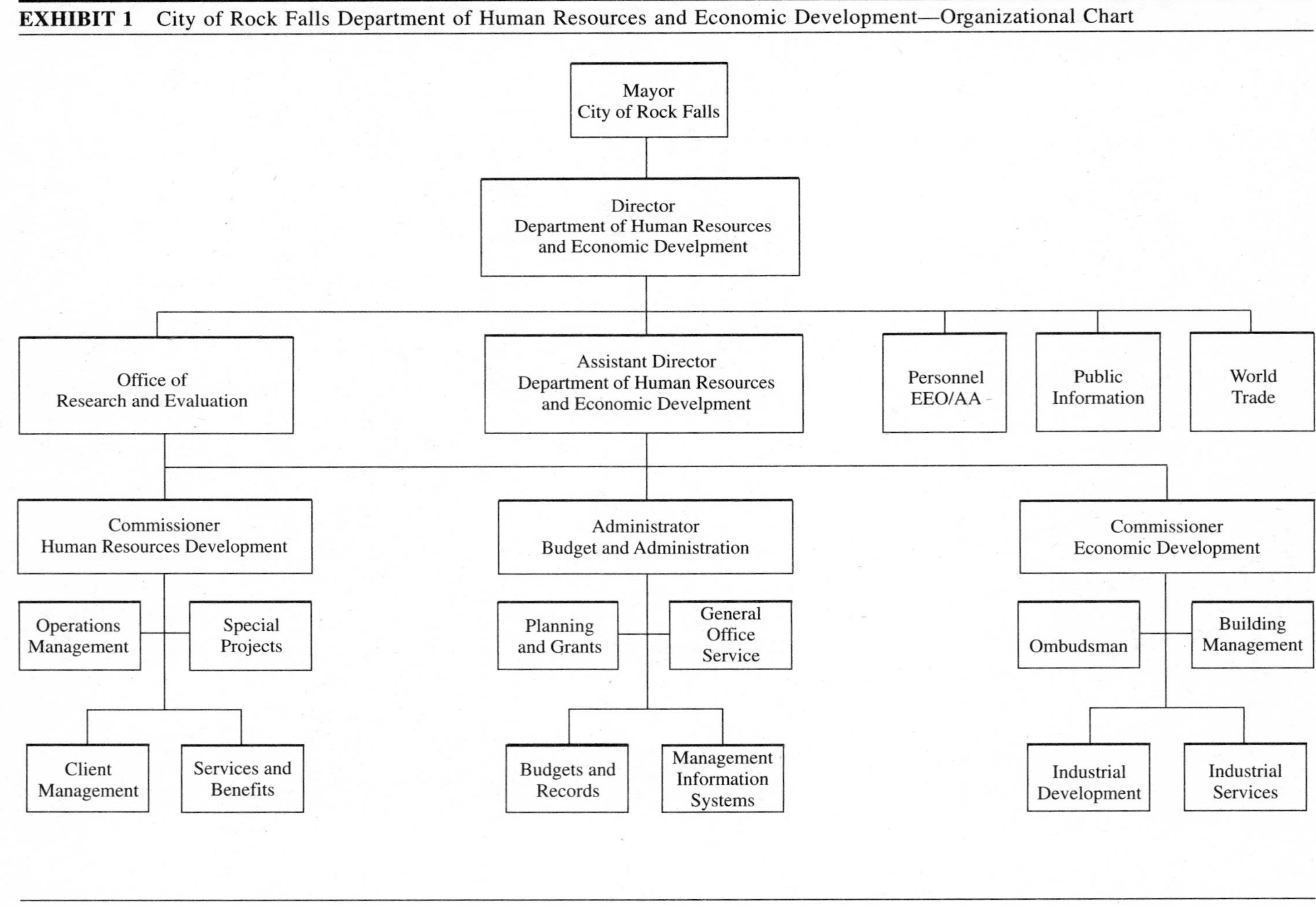

EXHIBIT 1 City of Rock Falls Department of Human Resources and Economic Development—Organizational Chart

EXHIBIT 2 Employee Evaluation Form

Employee Name: Marcus Singh Date: October 4, 1985

Job Title: Economist/Researcher

Please indicate your evaluation of the employee in each category by placing a check mark ( ) in the approp block.

	Outstanding	Good	Satisfactory	Fair	Unsatisfactory
KNOWLEDGE OF JOB Assess overall knowledge of duties and responsibilities of current job.	☑	☐	☐	☐	☐
QUANTITY OF WORK Assess the volume of work under normal conditions.	☐	☑	☐	☐	☐
QUALITY OF WORK Assess the neatness, accuracy, & effectiveness of work.	☐	☑	☐	☐	☐
COOPERATION Assess ability & willingness to work with peers, superiors, & subordinates.	☐	☑	☐	☐	☐
INITIATIVE Assess willingness to seek greater responsibilities & knowledge. Self-starting.	☐	☑	☐	☐	☐
ATTENDANCE Assess reliability with respect to attendance habits.	☑	☐	☐	☐	☐
ATTITUDE Assess disposition & level of enthusiasm. Desire to excel.	☑	☐	☐	☐	☐
JUDGMENT Assess ability to make logical decisions.	☐	☑	☐	☐	☐

Comments on Ratings: Valuable employee!

Supervisor's Signature: *Garth Fryer* Date: *Oct. 4, 1985*

Department: Office of Research and Evaluation

Employee's Signature: *Marcus Singh*

Does the employee agree with this evaluation? _X_ Yes ___ No

EXHIBIT 3 Employee Evaluation Form

Employee Name: Marcus Singh **Date:** October 18, 1985

Job Title: Economist/Researcher

Please indicate your evaluation of the employee in each category by placing a check mark ( ) in the appropriate block.

	Outstanding	Good	Satisfactory	Fair	Unsatisfactory
KNOWLEDGE OF JOB Assess overall knowledge of duties and responsibilities of current job.	☐	☑	☐	☐	☐
QUANTITY OF WORK Assess the volume of work under normal conditions.	☐	☐	☑	☐	☐
QUALITY OF WORK Assess the neatness, accuracy, & effectiveness of work.	☐	☐	☑	☐	☐
COOPERATION Assess ability & willingness to work with peers, superiors, & subordinates.	☐	☐	☑	☐	☐
INITIATIVE Assess willingness to seek greater responsibilities & knowledge. Self-starting.	☐	☐	☑	☐	☐
ATTENDANCE Assess reliability with respect to attendance habits.	☐	☑	☐	☐	☐
ATTITUDE Assess disposition & level of enthusiasm. Desire to excel.	☐	☑	☐	☐	☐
JUDGMENT Assess ability to make logical decisions.	☐	☐	☑	☐	☐

Comments on Ratings: Marcus needs to increase the quantity of his work to receive higher ratings. Also, he should take a greater initiative in his job.

Supervisor's Signature: Garth Fryer **Date:** Oct. 18, 1985

Department: Office of Research and Evaluation

Employee's Signature: Marcus Singh

Does the employee agree with this evaluation? ____ Yes X No

About one week after submitting the evaluations to the department director, Mr. Fryer received a memorandum from Mr. Popelmill stating that his evaluations of subordinates were unacceptable. Mr. Fryer was not the only unit head to receive this memorandum. In fact, all unit heads received the same note. On close examination of the completed appraisal forms from the various departments, the director noticed that not one employee was given a "fair" or "satisfactory" mark in any category. In fact, the vast majority of the employees were rated as outstanding in every category. Mr. Popelmill felt that his unit heads were too lenient, and his purpose was to have the department heads redo the evaluations in a more objective and critical manner.

Garth Fryer explained the director's request to his subordinates and proceeded to ask them to redo their self- and peer appraisals with the idea of being more objective this time. Once again, after reviewing his subordinate's appraisals, Garth formulated his ratings and discussed them individually with each employee.

Mr. Singh was not pleased at all when he found out that his supervisor had rated him one level lower on each category. (Compare Exhibit 2 and Exhibit 3.) Although Marcus signed the second evaluation form, he clearly indicated on the form that he did not agree with the evaluation. Jason Taft, the other researcher in the Office of Research and Evaluation, received all outstanding ratings on his second evaluation. Like Mr. Singh, Jason has a master's degree in economics, but has been working for the city of Rock Falls for less than two years and is only 24 years old. Mr. Taft also worked closely with Garth Fryer before being transferred to his new assignment 10 months ago. Recently, the mayor of the city received a letter from the regional director of a major government agency praising Mr. Taft's and Mr. Fryer's outstanding research. Although Jason and Garth are white and Marcus is a naturalized U.S. citizen from India, Marcus's working relationship with them and others in the department was good. On some occasions, though, he found himself in awkward disagreements with his co-workers in areas where he held strong opinions.

After Mr. Singh and Mr. Taft had signed the evaluations, Garth forwarded them to Mr. Popelmill's office, where they were eventually added to the employee's permanent file. When pay raises were awarded in the department three weeks later, Marcus Singh did not receive a merit raise for the next year. He was told that it was due to his less than outstanding evaluation. He did, however, receive a general increase of $500, which all employees received regardless of their performance evaluation.

Mr. Singh has refused to speak one word to Mr. Fryer since they discussed the evaluation, corresponding only through Ms. Millar or in writing. Marcus has become demotivated and has complained bitterly to his colleagues about his unfair ratings. While Marcus reports to work at 8:00 AM sharply and does not leave until 5:00 PM each day, he has been observed to spend a lot of time reading newspapers and books while at work.

Discussion Questions

1. What is the problem in this case? Who is to blame?
2. How would you have reacted if you were Marcus Singh?

3. How could this problem been avoided?
4. Critically evaluate the rating form used in this case.
5. What can be done to motivate Mr. Singh?

30 Performance Evaluation at Western Savings*

Charlene Brown has been a senior teller in the commercial loan department, at the main office of Western Savings and Loan Bank, for the past three years. Charlene and Darla Johnson, supervisor of the department, are both black and very good friends. Darla recently has learned that she is soon to be promoted to loan officer and has indicated to Charlene that she may be selected to replace her as supervisor of the department.

Terri Burke, who is white, has been a senior teller at one of Western Saving's branch offices for the past five years. Because she had a college degree, longer experience as a commercial loan teller, excellent rapport with co-workers, supervisory and managerial personnel, and customers, and because she exhibited desirable leadership qualities, she was selected to replace Darla as supervisor of the commercial loan department at the main office.

When Terri arrived at the main office she was introduced by Darla to her staff, which consisted of four senior tellers and one unfilled position. Darla began to show Terri all of the duties she was expected to fulfill as the new department supervisor. Terri immediately realized that many of the procedures she was familiar with at her branch office were handled differently at the main office, so she proceeded to learn the new procedures.

After a few days in her new position, Terri noticed that Charlene was not very friendly nor cooperative when she (Terri) asked questions concerning procedures. Terri talked to Darla about Charlene's attitude and was informed that Charlene had been hoping to be promoted to department supervisor, and she was angry that someone from one of the branch offices had been promoted over her. Terri was concerned about how well Charlene would accept her as a supervisor.

Over the next few weeks Terri noticed that at times Charlene would be joking with the other senior tellers, until she came around. Charlene would then stalk off with a scowl on her face, and the other tellers would look like children caught stealing cookies from the cookie jar. Terri was convinced that Charlene was trying to stir up resentment against her. Terri also learned that Charlene felt that she (Terri) wasn't qualified to be supervisor, because she was always asking questions about how certain things were done in the department. (Terri had been forced to ask questions about

---

* Prepared by Willie E. Hopkins and Shirley A. Hopkins, Colorado State University. This case is based on a supervisor's actual experiences; therefore, all names are fictitious.

transactions, because the procedures at the main office were different from her experience at the branch office. Charlene interpreted Terri's inquiries as lack of *knowledge and* incompetence, instead of adapting to new procedures.) Charlene had been pointing this out to the other tellers, causing them to challenge Terri's authority. Terri felt that Charlene was determined to make her look incompetent so she would be demoted and Charlene would be promoted to the position "she deserved," that of departmental supervisor.

Terri began to note that Charlene had several unacceptable habits. Charlene was consistently late for work, she had difficulties balancing her teller drawer, and she consistently made errors in figuring interest due on the commercial loans. Terri felt it was important that she talk with Charlene about these problems. Since Terri was inexperienced in these supervisory responsibilities, she talked to the operations manager, Mr. Tunston, about how she should proceed in this matter. Mr. Tunston told Terri that Charlene was a difficult employee, and several supervisors had had problems with her. He recommended that Terri document in Charlene's personnel file the content of their conversation and what the result was.

After her talk with Mr. Tunston, Terri took Charlene's personnel file with her to study. She was amazed! Mr. Tunston had told her that Charlene was a problem employee, yet all of her performance evaluations were quite high. She had received above-average raises, there were no problems documented in her file, and she had been promoted after short periods in her new assignments. Terri didn't understand the large discrepancy between what Mr. Tunston had told her about Charlene and the information she read in Charlene's personnel file. Nevertheless, she proceeded with plans to talk with Charlene.

Terri called Charlene into the conference room the next day. Terri was very nervous; she wanted to handle this well. She didn't have a problem with Charlene being black, Terri's husband was black; she just wanted to understand Charlene and hopefully diffuse the tension between them. Terri began to explain to Charlene that her consistent tardiness and teller errors were not an acceptable performance. She asked Charlene whether there were problems that she could help her with. Charlene was visibly angry but she refused to open up to Terri; she just said that she would do better. Terri tried to show Charlene that she was concerned and wanted to help, but Charlene was intent on not showing any signs of vulnerability. Terri ended the meeting and documented the event as Mr. Tunston had advised her.

A few more weeks passed and Charlene's performance had not improved at all. It was nearing the date for Charlene's performance evaluation. Terri was troubled. She did not want to be unfair to Charlene. She knew that Charlene's personnel file depicted her as a model employee, with the exception of her documented meeting of a few weeks ago. Terri decided that she could not give Charlene an extremely poor evaluation with such little supporting documentation, so she gave her an average evaluation. She mentioned Charlene's poor performance in the comment section, and recommended a small raise. Mr. Tunston supported Terri's evaluation and the raise. Terri was then faced with presenting the performance evaluation to Charlene; she was nervous again.

A one-word description of Charlene's response to the evaluation would be indifference. Terri was concerned because the other senior tellers were showing signs of sympathy with Charlene and greater signs of uncooperativeness toward her. Terri knew that something had to be done about the situation. She talked with a friend, Tina, in personnel and asked for her advice. Tina was well versed in equal employment opportunity laws. She warned Terri to carefully document all conferences and problems with Charlene to protect herself and the bank against any possible discrimination suit. Tina told Terri that a possible problem existed because incidences of poor performance had not been documented in Charlene's personnel file. Tina advised Terri to continue to document any problems she had with Charlene, and, if she could convince the operations manager to allow her to place Charlene on probation, to find out from him how it would need to be handled.

Terri began to carefully document all of Charlene's errors. She still wondered why prior performance evaluations indicated that Charlene had been such a model employee until she became her supervisor, and she began to research Charlene's history at the bank in hopes of finding out just what was going on. She researched Charlene's progress from her beginnings as a new loan clerk through operations, to new accounts, and finally a promotion to her present position. Terri found out that Charlene had been a problem employee from day one. It became obvious that her previous supervisors were intimidated by the fact that Charlene was black and they were worried about being accused of racial discrimination; so they gave Charlene good reviews and promoted her to get her "out of their hair," until finally Charlene was moved on to senior teller under Darla. The consensus was that, since Darla was also black, Charlene would finally quit causing them problems. This was true until Darla was promoted and Terri, unsuspecting, walked into the problem. Now Terri was forced to handle the problem no one wanted to face: Charlene was incompetent, and there was no documented evidence of this fact.

Several months passed, with the status quo in commercial loans, until Mr. Ring, the assistant operations manager, received a phone call from a preferred customer. Charlene had sent the customer a bill for his loan interest due, and he was calling to tell Mr. Ring that the bill was $620 short. Mr. Ring hung up the phone and immediately called Terri to his office. Terri was not surprised, and reminded Mr. Ring of the times she had told him about Charlene's errors. Mr. Ring had always told Terri that Charlene was so nice, that she must just be having a bad day. Mr. Ring rubbed his chin and admitted that perhaps he had been wrong. Terri asked whether he would be willing to support her in placing Charlene on probation. He thought for a few seconds and said yes.

Terri carefully documented the terms of the probation. Charlene was to work in foreign exchange for two months and she was not to be late nor have excessive transaction errors. If she violated her probation she was to be terminated. Charlene was called into the conference room and Terri presented the probation terms. Terri told Charlene that she had tried everything else, and, since Charlene persisted in her behavior, drastic measures were required. Charlene seemed a little more concerned than usual, but still refused to talk openly with Terri. The next day Charlene moved over to the foreign exchange position and a new teller, Rachel, took over Charlene's responsibilities.

The days passed, and, in spite of Charlene's efforts to meet her probation terms, she continued to make errors. However, Charlene seemed more willing to communicate with Terri, and actually asked for her assistance a time or two; but it was obvious that she was in a job that she was just not able to perform well. Two weeks before Charlene's probation was over, Mr. Tunston retired and an operations manager was brought to the main office from one of the branches. The new operations manager, Jean, had been the operations supervisor who was responsible for hiring Charlene three years earlier.

Jean walked into the main office early Monday morning. Charlene walked in shortly after Jean's arrival and, as Charlene saw Jean, a smile flashed across her face; she ran up to Jean and gave her a hug. Later that morning Terri went over to talk to Jean. Terri was apprehensive because she had witnessed the reunion of Jean and Charlene earlier that morning. Terri proceeded to fill Jean in on her department's current status. As she started to leave, Terri sat back down and began to tell Jean about the problems with Charlene. Jean's expression changed; she listened intently to the events of the last year unfolding. When Terri told Jean that Charlene had already violated her probation and would be terminated at the end of the next two weeks, Jean showed signs of concern. Jean told Terri that she didn't want Charlene to be terminated, that she could handle Charlene. Jean said she was going to take Charlene off of probation and talk to her. Terri protested, but Jean was determined to have her way.

Terri was totally disheartened. She had worked for over a year to manage this difficult problem and Jean destroyed everything in one day. Terri also knew that it would be even more difficult to interact with her staff, especially Charlene, now that Jean had undermined her authority. Terri dreaded coming to work the next day. When she arrived, Charlene was back at work in commercial loans and she was even in early. Charlene gave Terri a sneering smile and forced out a "good morning" when she walked into the department. Terri hoped things would not be as bad as she expected, but within a week Charlene was back to her old ways. Terri talked to Jean about Charlene's work, even Mr. Ring talked to Jean about the interest error, but Jean was confident that Charlene could be turned around by her efforts.

Jean continued to talk to Charlene, but her work performance and attitude deteriorated further. After two months of this situation, Jean finally admitted to Terri that perhaps she had been wrong about Charlene. During this time Mr. Ring had been promoted to vice president and moved to an office upstairs. Several more months passed and Charlene continued to make more and more errors. Jean was finally exasperated; she called Terri over to her desk. Jean told Terri that the only way to handle the problem was to get Charlene out of the main office. Jean said she knew of a promotion that would be available on the floater staff. The floater staff was composed of senior tellers who were supposed to be self-motivated and who could be sent to branch offices to cover vacations and leaves of branch personnel.

Jean said that she was going to recommend Charlene for this position. Terri protested and said she didn't think that was the way to handle the problem. Jean said it was the only way. Terri refused to sign the recommendation. So Jean decided to sign it herself. Charlene was delighted. She was sure she would be a supervisor in no time at all. Charlene was finally gone. Terri found that her staff began to work together better. It was even easier to come to work. However, word got back to the main office that Charlene was a disaster at the branches. Mr. Ring heard of the problems and asked Terri why she had recommended Charlene for the promotion. Terri told Mr. Ring that she hadn't recommended Charlene, and she told him about her discussion with Jean. He was very serious and walked away with a strange look on his face. A week later Jean was fired. According to the grapevine, Charlene is still raising havoc at the branches. Terri later left the bank to move to a different state and has since began a new career. But she has never forgotten the years of trials with Charlene.

Discussion Questions

1. What mistakes did management make in this case?
2. How could these problems have been avoided?
3. What can be done to avoid these problems in the future?

*31 A Training and Development Problem at Sumerson Manufacturing**

George Lewis began working for the Sumerson Manufacturing Company as a human resources department trainee a few days after he received his MBA degree in management from a large midwestern university. After a one-year training program he served two years as assistant director of training and development in one of Sumerson's large machining and assembly plants. He was promoted to plant director of training and development, in which capacity he served for approximately four years. When this assignment ended George was transferred to corporate headquarters as staff assistant to the corporate director of training and development. The corporate director was scheduled for retirement in 25 months. George hoped to become the next corporate director of training and development but knew this was very much dependent on how well he handled his first major assignment.

Sumerson was planning to open a new plant in 16 months. The new plant was to hire approximately 4,000 employees within three years. However, only one of eight production lines was to go into operation when the plant opened. The other seven would be phased in during the following three years. Construction of the new plant had just started in a small town of 10,000 persons 18 miles south of Memphis, Tennessee. The plant would be very similar to the plant in which George had been director of training and development. George was asked to submit a plan for training the personnel for the new plant. He was given four months to do the job.

---

* This case was prepared by Professor James C. Hodgetts of the Fogelman College of Business and Economics at Memphis State University as a basis for class discussion.

Top management had made the decision that personnel from its other 21 plants would be transferred to fill all second-level and higher-management positions. For most of these employees this would be a promotion. Also, most nonmanagement employees in the company would be offered jobs in the new plant but few were expected to accept. All frontline management must be trained by Sumerson, not hired "off-the-street."

George had 16 months, including his planning time, to decide how to train a workforce of approximately 450 new employees. About 55 to 60 management employees would be transferred to the new plant when it opened. He also had to make plans for training personnel for the expansion of the plant to 4,000 employees by the project's full operations date.

He was not sure what he should do, as this was the first time the company had ever built and staffed a new plant. There was no past experience on which way to go. He decided his first task was to identify his major problems.

Discussion Questions

1. In general, what training must take place prior to the opening of the new plant in 16 months?
2. What training must take place between the time the plant opens and all eight production lines are in operation?
3. How many frontline supervisors had to be trained?
4. How were they to be trained?
5. How many nonmanagement employees had to be trained?
6. In what skill areas must they be trained?
7. How were they to be trained?

---

*32 The Role of Training in Support of the Team Management Concept: A Case Study of Logan Aluminum, Inc.**

Objective of the Case Study

The primary objective of this case study of Logan Aluminum was to describe in detail the role and responsibilities of training professionals in a functioning team management organization. In order to determine that role and relate it to the larger organization, it was necessary to gain an overall understanding of Logan Aluminum, including the historical development of the mill, the physical facility, the management philosophy,

* This case was prepared by Patricia Brelsford, College of Notre Dame of Maryland.

organization structures, the management team, and the employees, as well as the training team. This case study has been developed using these broad categories as the basic areas of description.

THE ORGANIZATION

Logan Aluminum was constructed by ARCO Aluminum (ARCO), a division of the Atlantic Richfield Company, to be one of the most modern automated aluminum rolling mill facilities in the world. The mill was also to have an innovative management concept, which came to be known as the Logan Team Concept. Construction of the mill began in February 1981 and was completed late in 1983. Logan was the only new aluminum rolling mill with a hot rolling line to be built in the United States in nearly 20 years. Over $465 million was initially spent on the mill. Shortly after the mill began operations early in 1984, ARCO announced plans to divest itself of some of its metals businesses. The Logan mill was among those to be sold. Alcan Aluminum, Ltd., of Canada and Alcan Aluminum Corporation–USA, known as Alcan, signed a letter of intent to buy the ARCO facilities, including the Logan plant. However, the United States Justice Department opposed the sale on antitrust grounds. It's primary concern was the perceived potential for lack of competitiveness in the marketplace.

After several months of discussions, the sale was completed in January 1985, with an agreement that allowed Alcan to buy the other ARCO facilities but only 40 percent of the Logan mill. ARCO retained 60 percent of Logan. Under the government consent decree, neither ARCO nor Alcan was allowed to know anything about the manufacturing or marketing activities of the other. Since Logan is jointly owned, the solution was to establish the Logan facility as a separate corporation with its own president and board of directors. This is how Logan Aluminum was born.

THE PHYSICAL FACILITY

Logan Aluminum is located on a 900-acre site in Logan County, Kentucky. The scenic rolling countryside is in southwestern Kentucky approximately eight miles north of Russellville, Kentucky, a community of 7,000. The mill has 21 acres or over 1 million square feet under roof. The manufacturing facility includes the four distinct process areas of melt and cast, hot rolling, cold rolling, and finishing, along with a central maintenance area. The mill is connected by a walkway to the reception area and offices. Engineers, technician, unit managers, and team leaders have offices located in each functional area of the mill. An additional building, initially used as construction headquarters, houses the training center, the credit union, and company newsletter offices.

Logan is highly automated, with advanced manufacturing capability. Its state-of-the-art rolling technology makes it the world's most modern rolling mill. Metal rolls through at 6,000 feet per minute. Advanced computerized systems are necessary to help maintain the rigid quality standards required by customer markets as diverse as beverage containers, household foil, and building, automotive, consumer, and distributor products. With an initial annual capacity of 400 million pounds, the Logan Aluminum complex was designed for expansion to a 1 billion pound annual capacity.

MANAGEMENT PHILOSOPHY

The team management philosophy was an integral part of the overall planning for Logan Aluminum. Although ARCO had progressive management approaches for a long time, the startup of a new facility offered the opportunity to expand and refine that philosophy. The current manager of human resources, Mike Harris, was employed at another ARCO facility but was asked in late 1981 to work on a project to find out what was available in terms of progressive human resources concepts and principles.

After looking across the country and talking with a number of consultants familiar with progressive organizations, a consultant was selected to work with ARCO. Over the next two years, the planning group spent time, according to Harris, just thinking about what it wanted to create in terms of an organizational environment or organizational climate, how we wanted to treat our people, what our expectations were for people, and designing systems to be able to achieve the level of involvement that we were looking at.

The reason for ARCO's interest in the team management idea for Logan had two aspects, according to Harris. The first was the involvement of individuals at the corporate level who were supportive of the effort and had a conceptual understanding of what they wanted Logan to become. Their approach was that, if something was out there beneficial to them competitively and also helpful to people in having a sense of ownership and a better feeling about work in general, then they should do it. The other major influence was Atlantic Richfield Company's progressive management. It looked for opportunities to do progressive things. According to Harris, building a new plant offered an opportunity to avoid making many of the mistakes that had traditionally been made in terms of managing people.

What has emerged from the early planning and evolved over the first four years of startup has come to be known as the Logan Team Concept. The Logan Team Concept is reflected as a management philosophy throughout the organization from its publications and its public company image to its treatment of employees and its day-to-day work operations. Logan company literature says, "Logan is an idea. New levels of productivity. A new kind of workplace. A dedication to quality. A fundamental concern for people." In terms of company image, Logan managers are fond of talking about the team concept and making such statements as, "We pay people for what they know, not for what they do." Employees are not "employees" but "team members." The atmosphere is egalitarian, with no reserved parking or executive dining rooms, and with an all-salaried workforce. The focus is on being a team player and on everyone's being a vital member of the team. In the daily work operations, the team management philosophy is most evident in the area of job design.

The Logan Team Concept is defined in company literature as "A management philosophy that organizationally structures jobs in ways that permit people to work in teams, giving individual team members greater interaction with their co-workers and greater responsibility for a broader scope of work." As opposed to the classical approach to job design that identifies the individual job as the basic unit for performing work and breaks down the job into small, easily learned, repetitive tasks, the team approach defines the team as the basic unit for performing work. Each team is given a whole task to perform and all team members are encouraged to learn the skills necessary to perform all aspects of the team's work and they are rewarded for doing so. This approach emphasizes cross-training, learning new skills, and increasing each team member's skills in the total team task. Teams are relatively self-managed and autonomous but interdependent.

According to Logan's orientation manual, the team philosophy of job design views operating personnel in much the same way that most organizations view their managerial personnel. They are considered a resource; one that makes what they are able to do when the need arises more important than what they are actually doing.

ORGANIZATIONAL STRUCTURES

In addition to the overall management philosophy, formal structures within the organization facilitate the implementation and operation of the Logan Team Concept. These structures include the organization chart, operational procedures, and the framework for team functioning known as the Star Concept.

Logan Aluminum's organization chart is relatively flat for what is in essence a corporation separate from its joint owners. Even when compared to a traditional manufacturing facility, the five levels of president, president's staff, business unit managers, team leaders, and team members show broad spans of control and few "intermediary" positions between production and management. The business units function almost as separate small businesses, with their own technical and support staffs as well as operational teams. The objective of this approach is to bring the professional expertise to the problem site, rather than taking the problem to the professional site. Technical staffs can include engineers, metallurgists, technicians, and chemists as appropriate for the functional area. In addition to providing technical expertise within their own areas, the technical staff members also serve as resources for other functional areas.

Since the team is considered the basic unit for performing work, the team leader role is very critical. The individual in this position is responsible for coordination across functions and across shifts of operation as well as for the effective performance of the team itself. The long-range goal of Logan Aluminum to move to self-managing teams also makes the team leader role one that changes over time as teams mature and assume more responsibility for their own management.

Overall, the current organization chart at Logan Aluminum reflects a formal structure designed to facilitate its team management approach. However, management recognized early in the process that formal structure alone was not enough to make the concept work effectively. As a result, operational procedures were designed to accommodate the goal of team management as well. Operational procedures include a broad spectrum of activities that relate to the day-to-day work of producing aluminum. They include such aspects as job design, the organization's people perspective, how skilled employees are, how people are paid, accountability systems, scheduling time for team meetings and other participation activities, and the kind of information people have about work processes and costs.

Job design, as described earlier, revolves around the team as the basic unit for performing work. The team completes a whole task within a functional area, such as melt and cast or hot rolling. It is expected that team members develop the skills necessary to perform all jobs within their team's area of responsibility. The people perspective of Logan Aluminum also has been discussed. Viewing individual team members as valuable resources implies trust, mutual respect, and open communication in all aspects of operation.

The question of how skilled employees are has received a great deal of attention at Logan Aluminum. In the early stages of planning for the new ARCO facility, an important part of the decision-making process included site location. The decision to build a technologically sophisticated aluminum rolling mill in the middle of farmland in rural southwestern Kentucky brought with it the inevitable challenge of recruiting and developing a workforce capable of dealing with both the new technology and the different management philosophy. Part of the attraction of the site included the availability of a fairly homogeneous potential workforce with a strong work ethic and close ties to the region. There was also an absence of strong union sentiment even though most other area manufacturers were unionized.

The negative aspect of the location was that it would be rare to find a employee who had any experience in the aluminum industry. According to one business unit manager, however, this was a conscious choice on the part of ARCO. The company felt that the only place to get people with aluminum experience was from traditional organizations that would quickly put ARCO in very traditional patterns. The decision was made to sacrifice the short-term gains of hiring experience workers for the overall long-term benefit of being able to create a culture that would facilitate the development of the team management concept. According to a team member, that was a "pretty brave move when you consider that you started with people that called aluminum 'tin.'"

The strategy used to recruit potential employees included a number of aspects. Among the first ARCO and construction company employees to arrive at Logan were those in human resources and training. Such a large-scale construction project required hiring a large number of laborers and staff to assist during the building phase. The systems for recruiting new employees for the mill was developed at this time and with some modifications still exists.

The primary consideration in hiring was to determine those applicants who were best suited to work in a team management environment. For the applicant, the employment process involved a number of steps. The first step after referral from the state employment service was to attend a half-day prehire orientation session, which gave an overview of the organization, the team concept, and company expectations of employees. Those applicants who were still interested after this initial session completed an application and were screened in the assessment center. The assessment center included various types of testing, exercises, and simulations rated by observers. If the applicant "made it" through the center, he or she was considered for employment and was referred for additional interviews. On being hired, the employee attended a two and a half day posthire orientation, after which the necessary technical training began. Throughout the entire process, preference was given to Logan County residents, with secondary preference given to those from immediately surrounding areas.

Because of the lack of technical expertise in producing aluminum, a great deal of time was spent on technical training—some of it without the benefit of equipment that was not yet in place and running. One team member described the startup of the Hot Mill's rolling line as follows:

> I'd give anything for some kind of film to show the hot line when they first started it. No one knew a damn thing about what was going on—nobody knew nothing. It was the funniest sight. Both teams were together. There was about 25 of us at the time. Engineers were everywhere. The whole team would go to the back of the mill to Preheat. It [the aluminum] would go through the line and maybe make it through the Reverse Mill; and if it did, they would look just like the Keystone Kops running down the aisle to watch it go through. Most of the time it didn't. But whatever might happen, when it was ready to try it again, all 25 would head back to Preheat. I mean this went on 16 hours a day. I ain't kiddin'. There were times I would just stop and look and just burst out laughing. I mean I got down on the floor laughing. But you know, we were learning. That's the way you gotta learn—watching all these mistakes. Finally, one day a few people had enough sense to say, "Let's just stand here in case it makes it and we'll be here if we're needed on the line." There wasn't a day that I didn't go home wore out—but laughing.

Even with some training and experience, there was a great deal to learn about what to expect in a brand-new facility. The same team member described the following incident:

> Everybody was scared to hit a "stop" button—scared to death of a stop button. I was standing at the coiler one day as a sheet was going through the line and it didn't come down right for the coiler to pick it up. The sheet went straight out through the mill and right up through the aisles and down through the racks where the coils are stored. I was standing there watching. I would look at this one and this one would look at me with a "what do we do now" expression. Before it got the Cold Mill, I finally hit the stop button.

The skill level of employees is an integral part of the team concept. Ongoing training to increase and enhance employee skills has been an important aspect of Logan Aluminum's operations, particularly since skill level is so closely linked to how people are paid.

Employees at Logan Aluminum have been told from the beginning that they would be paid "for what they knew," rather than just for what they did. In theory, as team members mastered additional skills, they would be rewarded with additional compensation. Team members worked on a system that included seven levels through which operating technicians could progress as they developed new skills.

In reality, many of the early promotions were based on seniority, with an average time of approximately six months in grade. This situation was remedied by the development of a comprehensive pay and progression plan in 1986, which specified the requisite skills for each level and how they were to be demonstrated and measured. This plan has helped structure the pay for performance aspect of team management.

Accountability systems are an important control element in any organization. They are particularly important in team management organizations, which are sometimes viewed as having fewer controls or less accountability. Many of Logan Aluminum's accountability systems focus on the team as the basic unit not only in meeting production goals but also in such areas as a peer review system for performance appraisal and a statistical process control system for monitoring of product quality. Underlying the need for accountability, particularly to owners for bottom-line production figures, is management's acknowledgment that the team concept has contributed to a very favorable learning curve for Logan Aluminum when compared to other startup facilities.

Logan Aluminum is a continuous process operation, which makes scheduling very critical. The mill has three shifts, with most team members working rotating shifts. To provide the time for team meetings and other participation activities, team members report to work and are paid for one-half hour of team meeting prior to the beginning of their shifts. Team meetings are very important for communication, particularly for Logan Aluminum, since there are approximately 100 people in the mill during any given shift for an average of about four people per acre. Time and compensation, often at overtime rates, also are provided for team activities, such as team building sessions that involve the whole team. Team leaders and team members have the flexibility to send individuals to technical training sessions and offsite meetings, because cross-training allows other team members to assume different tasks within the team.

Information about work processes and costs is widely available to individuals at Logan Aluminum. Since team members work toward mastery of all tasks within the team, they have a broad understanding of work processes. They also must coordinate with other teams and other functional areas of the mill. The use of statistical process control enables them to see how they are performing. A display in the hallway between the mill and the administrative building has charts showing various types of production figures. In addition, a formal quarterly communications meeting is scheduled at various times throughout the shifts to enable all employees to attend. At this meeting, the president and other members of the management team share information on production costs, markets, outlook, and so on, and respond to employee questions. A number of plantwide committees, including a trust committee, also exist to facilitate communication.

The organization's operational structure provides the framework for team management at Logan Aluminum, but the heart of the team functioning is based on the "Star Concept." This concept defines the team boundaries and outlines the responsibilities each team has for its own operation (see Exhibit 1). A graphic illustration of the Star Concept is presented as follows:

EXHIBIT 1 Logan Star Concept

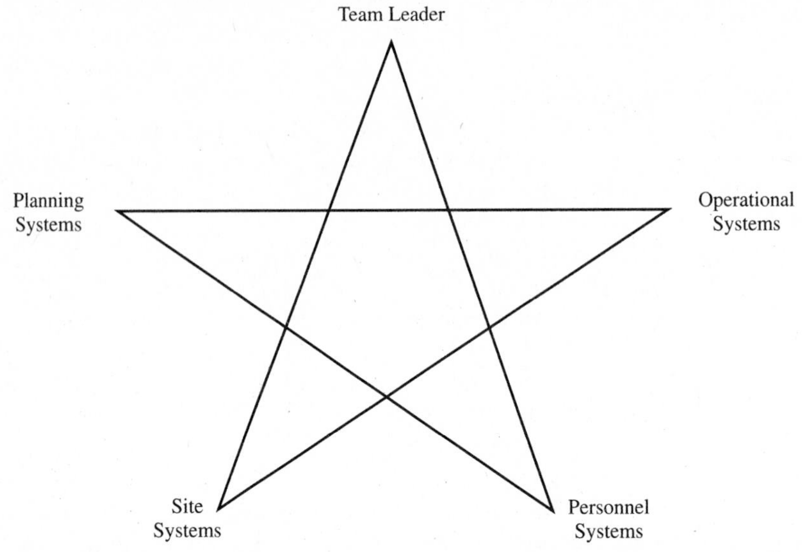

The team leader has defined areas of responsibility and such tasks as running team meetings, coordinating with other teams, completing performance appraisals, conflict resolution, and so on, depending on the maturity of the team. Newer or less-developed teams may require the team leader to perform more of the management responsibilities of a traditional first-line supervisor, while, with a more mature team, the appropriate role might be that of a coach, mentor, or resource person.

The role of other team members may change at various times to include responsibilities for performing needed tasks in the area of operational systems, personnel systems, site systems, or planning systems. The team members themselves decide where employees will work, provided they have received training in the skilled area to which they are assigned. Operational systems would include such tasks as operating the equipment, quality control, and routine preventive maintenance. As an example of the efficiency of self-managed teams, approximately 90 percent of routine maintenance of machines at Logan Aluminum is performed within the teams by operating technicians.

The other three points of the star—personnel systems, site systems, and planning systems—are those where similar employees in traditional organizations would have less active involvement unless they were specifically assigned to the task through a job description. Personnel systems might include selecting and training new team members, developing and conducting peer appraisals of team members, and liaison with a companywide committee concerned with review of personnel policies and procedures. Site systems involves all aspects related to the work site, especially housekeeping and safety. Safety concerns are always an issue and are particularly important at Logan, because of the type of machinery used and also the heavy use of forklift trucks and overhead cranes to move the metal and supplies. Planning systems are a very important aspect of team functioning. The team must keep accurate records, schedule and obtain necessary supplies, and project personnel needs to plan effectively to meet production goals without compromising the ability of the next shift to be able to meet its objectives.

The full implementation of the Star Concept at Logan Aluminum has not been completed. Different teams are at different levels of development. Some teams adopted the system early in plant startup and are nearing maturity, while other teams are in the early stages of implementation.

Logan's approach initially was to encourage use of the Star Concept but not to force it until the team and team leader were ready to take the necessary steps to use it. More recently, however, management has seen the need to take a more active role and has basically dictated that the Star Concepts would be implemented. Some team members observed that this "traditional" approach was not well received by team members. Yet they also commented that, as the concept has developed within the team and they saw and experienced the benefits of using it, most team members have accepted the change. One team member commented that "more structure is needed to give you flexibility and freedom." This sentiment has been echoed throughout all levels of the organization. One business unit manager described the need for boundaries and the role of the Star Concept in helping to provide a common direction for team members:

The real advantage of the Star Concept is that you have a focal point in the team to lead in certain directions. The points of the star correspond to the tasks of functions of management. You are trying to get people to develop some depth of knowledge in one of those areas—like personnel, for example. This gives them a better understanding of why certain decisions are made. That kind of structure puts more flexibility in the team and also helps develop an attitude that focuses more on business needs than on individual needs. The idea is for people to manage the place as if it were their own.

A great deal of time and effort was expended to develop the appropriate organizational structures to enhance the development of the team concept at Logan Aluminum. This was a necessary part of the process. Equally as important to the implementation of team management has been the management team itself.

THE MANAGEMENT TEAM

Logan Aluminum, though jointly owned, is managed as a separate corporate entity with its own board of directors and president. The board of directors is made up of three ARCO representatives, two Alcan representatives, and two representatives from other organizations. The president of Logan Aluminum had been a vice president of technology for ARCO Metals Company. The plant manager came from Alcan, the treasurer/controller from Alcan, and the human resources manager from ARCO. These three managers report directly to the president. There are three levels below these

EXHIBIT 2 Organization Chart

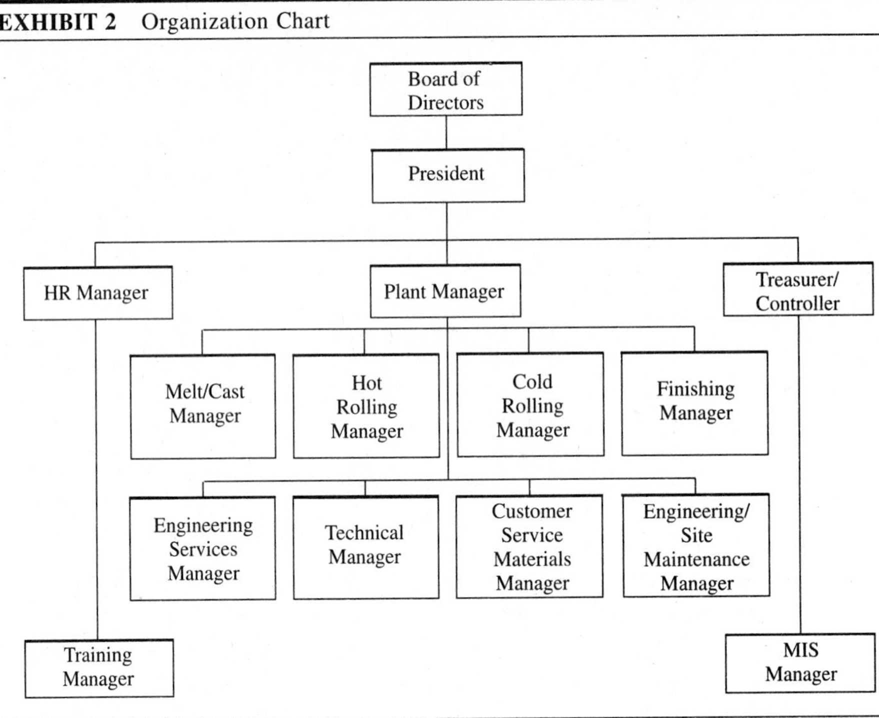

managers, including business unit managers, team leaders, and team members. An abbreviated organized chart for the management team at Logan Aluminum is illustrated in Exhibit 2.

Since ARCO was the major force behind the development of Logan Aluminum as a team concept facility, there was some question about the direction of the management concept under joint ownership. However, the concept has survived and flourished. It is to the credit of the executive team and board of directors that the team concept has been allowed to develop, given the constraints of the consent decree and mill startup.

A key element in the overall development of team management is visible support from top-level management. Although perceptions of the degree of support from Logan's top managers is somewhat mixed, most individuals acknowledge that top managers are in the position to feel more of the pressure from owners to produce. They must answer directly to questions of bottom-line performance of the organization. A general view voiced among the other levels of the organization was their feeling that top management liked the results but may have little direct understanding of team management, particularly its potential. One individual summarized it with the following comment: "Production has a very distinct bearing. If production is up, I don't think they really care what type of management you have." Another common feeling was that joint ownership and differing philosophy and expectations of the two owners put additional pressures on top management that contribute to the always present conflict between meeting production and developing the team concept.

An exception to the above description of the top management team's involvement in the team concept is the human resources manager. As one business unit manager stated, "Mike Harris is the leader [in developing the team concept]. There's no question about that." Others describe him as the "visionary" on the concept, but also one who has the power to "make things happen." The contribution of Harris to conceptualizing and implementing the team concept at Logan can best be described by looking at his philosophy of the concept and his own management style.

The view that Harris has of the team management concept is based on several underlying principles or assumptions. Two very important assumptions have shaped his thinking. The first is that team management has to be viewed as a different way of looking at work altogether. He believes that preconceived notions of work are normally based on past experiences. Putting away old and often adversarial ways of thinking is not easy. Individuals have to have commitment and an understanding of the "magnitude and potential of the concept." A critical part of developing that commitment and understanding is for management to reinforce and maintain this different view of work, rather than giving it "lip service" until the pressure comes and then reverting to traditional ways of managing.

A second assumption or principle is that team management is a better way to do business than the "traditional, adversarial relationships at many autocratically-run businesses." Harris quotes a statement that he heard to underscore this philosophy: "Get people to do the right thing because they want to, not because it's necessary for them to keep their jobs." He believes this approach creates a different environment that is good for individuals as well as for the company. This area of shared goals should help us "recognize there is potential to improve your competitiveness and also to improve the way people feel about their work at the same time."

Five years of implementing the team concept at Logan has given Harris additional insights into other relevant principles. He notes that you have to look at the total system as a whole and not as pieces. There are a number of major components necessary to support organizational philosophy and one has to put all of those pieces together. It also is important to understand that, if any component of the system is arbitrarily changed, it will affect the entire organization.

Another primary principle is that the team concept has to be managed if it is to be successful. Harris believes that "all the potential in the world is out there," but that there exists varying abilities of management to recognize and take advantage of those opportunities. There are a number of challenging issues that managers must resolve. These include their own ability to "let go" and allow their teams to develop; the tough job of helping define expectations of team members and arriving at some common understandings and goals; and providing an environment where people are contributing, can learn new things, and can grow individually. Harris cites an example of an issue with some team leaders, especially those from union backgrounds. The team leaders were "used to getting nothing from their people and seemed to be satisfied with what was mediocrity in my mind." Developing appropriate expectations and standards is a critical management issue for Logan Aluminum's team concept.

The final principle to be discussed is one that became increasingly apparent as the team concept was developed at Logan—the need for structure. Harris notes there is always a tradeoff in how much structure you put in and in how patient you are allowed to be in nurturing the concept. He believes that a great deal of structure and leadership is particularly important in the early days. Reflecting on the team development process, Harris says that the biggest change he would make would be to put more structure into it initially, because "as pressures or demands for productivity increased, it was more and more difficult to sit down and talk and think about what you wanted to do because you had to do it."

The same theme was echoed among members of the organization at all levels. A business unit manager felt that key managers should have been hired much earlier (at least a year before startup) and been given an opportunity to discuss philosophical issues and reach common understandings but also to determine mechanics for two key issues like pay and progression and general ground rules. Another manager expressed the same insights and added that startup would have been much better because everyone would have been "headed in the same direction." Harris is the first to acknowledge that it has not all been "happy learning, some has been unhappy learning as well." A key point is that those understandings have been developed to great extent even in regard to very similar hindsights!

Conceptualizing and helping create a vision of what the team concept at Logan should be has been a major contribution on the part of Harris. In his own management style, Harris also has demonstrated his belief in the concept. Although some administrative and support staff members view the team concept as "something for the mill," Harris's staff has been encouraged to become involved and contribute. Staff meetings are open and relaxed, with each member expected to participate. The tone for staff interaction is set by Harris's own friendly, easygoing, but business-oriented manner. Staff meetings are usually scheduled around lunch time and it is not unusual for Harris to provide lunch. For example, at one staff meeting barbecued pork (prepared by Harris) sandwiches, coleslaw, baked beans, soft drinks, and desserts were brought in and served buffet-style. This informality helped create an atmosphere conducive to participation and involvement.

Although not everyone agrees that the management team fully understands the actual workings and the potential of the team management concept at Logan, most would agree that overall management support has been instrumental in the development of the team concept. Most team members have little if any direct relationship with top-level managers. Management to them is the team leader and the business unit manager, so the role of these individuals is critical in the development of the team management. A key underlying issue has been that management team continue to reinforce the "we" attitude, which has been successful up to this point in preventing the development of adversarial relationships.

Developing appropriate organizational structures and management team support have undeniably provided the foundation for team management at Logan Aluminum. The success of the concept and its growth and development, however, must be attributed to the men and women who daily meet the many challenges of producing high-quality aluminum in an efficient and effective manner. The employees of Logan Aluminum have made the Logan concept work despite the many changes, particularly in the early stages, that the organization has faced.

THE EMPLOYEES

As noted earlier, the decision to locate ARCO's new rolling mill in Logan County, Kentucky, brought with it the challenge of identifying, recruiting, and training a large (for the area) workforce capable of dealing with both highly sophisticated technology and the concept of team management. The extensive selection process described earlier resulted in Logan's current workforce.

The average Logan employee is a 34-year-old male from in or around Logan County who has completed 13.2 years of formal education. Logan employs approximately 627 regular employees, 300 of whom work in the mill, and about 100 contract employees. The average age is 34 years, with as many in the 18–34 category as from 34–65. The average education is 14 months beyond high school. Approximately 70 percent of nonexempt employees are from Logan and adjacent counties. Females make up 15–18 percent of mill employees, but 35–40 percent of Logan employees when administrative areas are included. The workforce is all salaried but with exempt and nonexempt categories of eligibility for overtime pay. Benefits for all employees are equivalent. The 300 mill employees work on three shifts, most on rotating shifts, so approximately 100 individuals are on the mill floor at any given time.

The in-depth selection process is credited by individuals at all levels for the type of employees Logan has hired. One unit manager states that the selection process has "given us a 95 percent success rate. We don't have the problem of so many marginal performers that other organizations have." By most accounts, the work ethic, an important selection criterion, is very strong among Logan employees. In fact, a team leader with a background in traditional organizations comments, "Some of the worst employees here would stand out in a traditional plant." Overall, Logan employees are viewed as brighter and more motivated than employees in similar traditional plants. The few who aren't "probably shouldn't have made it through the selection process," according to a training team member.

When the Logan facility began screening employees, applicants had only a vague idea about the team management concept prior to the prehire orientation. An important reason that people were initially anxious to work there was that the jobs paid better than those in other area industries. This situation was very positive for Logan, because it allowed them to be selective in the hiring process and to screen for particular characteristics that they felt would help facilitate the development of team management. As one team member noted, "From the very beginning Logan has hired people who need challenge, are well-informed, and have an attitude of wanting to learn and do more." Partly as a result of this selectiveness, Logan employees feel unique and ready to contribute, because they were selected, rather than hired, by Logan Aluminum.

Rather than review particular selection criteria for different attributes, it is very instructive to describe how Logan employees at all levels see themselves and others. A team leader describes Logan employees as self-motivated. He says, "They work as hard when I'm not there as when I'm there. They know what needs to be done and are willing to do it." Another team leader notes that the biggest difference in people in this environment is that they "think like management. There is no us and them." These attitudes are particularly relevant to the self-regulation aspect of team management. An example given by a team member is the use of peer evaluation and peer pressure to deal with the "lazy" worker or problem worker who is not contributing to the team's efforts. Team members, he suggests, are usually in a better position to know who does what than a team leader who may not always be around. Individuals working in a team management environment have more responsibility than those in more traditional settings; but a team member notes that "people seem to enjoy it."

An important element in team management is being sensitive to others. A team member describes it as follows:

> Individuals working in a team environment must enjoy a challenge and be willing to contribute to the team as well as being sensitive to an individual's point of view. This is not a democracy where the majority rules but where one individual may be right and the rest of the team wrong.

It could also be viewed, as a team leader noted, as "caring about people, what's important to them, and realizing that everyone is different."

The characteristics describing the employees of Logan—intelligent, self-motivated, responsible, sensitive to others, and so on—have been very beneficial to the organization in developing the team management concept. These same attributes have created challenges for Logan managers. As one business unit manager commented, "They are intelligent people who have some high expectations." Some have said that the expectations have often been unrealistic. Several individuals felt that the employee orientation had contributed to developing some unrealistic expectations, while others felt that some it came from individuals as well. A team member noted that it was a problem to "get people to understand that participating doesn't mean every day is going to be great . . . you may sometimes have to make sacrifices." He also felt that team members sometimes want the "good parts but not the bad parts of management."

The high caliber of Logan employees has created a need for managers to develop different attitudes and approaches to working with them. Managers at all levels generally note that Logan has the basic talent needed to be successful. One team leader states that Logan is "doing so much more than would be possible elsewhere."

This attitude has an important influence on the various management approaches to nurturing involvement. A key element, according to one team leader, is for the manager to be able to "give up ownership and allow people to make mistakes." By establishing appropriate standards and expectations, managers believe that team members then can make decisions, especially about what happens on the floor, working conditions, and so forth. As one business unit manager explained, "If you give a group of reasonable people the same understanding of a thing, they will reach the same decision; the key is getting everyone the right information and trusting them to do it."

Team members recognize that they must continue to earn additional responsibility and be able to show management that they can make decisions on their own. In some cases, though, one team member noted, management may have to do a certain amount of pushing to get team members to make those decisions.

While recognizing the need for new attitudes and approaches on the part of managers, Logan Aluminum also has acknowledged the difficulty of keeping people challenged. Harris sees a critical future issue as that of Logan's ability to continue to provide meaningful work for employees that will keep them thinking about "the contribution they're making to the organization, the recognition they receive, and their personal growth and development."

Overall, the success to this point of Logan Aluminum and the team management concept includes a number of important elements, not the least of which is its people. The people may in fact be one of the more critical success factors. According to Harris, "If it [the management concept] fails, it will be because we can't manage it, not because there is something inherent in people that you can't accomplish."

Throughout the development of the Logan Team Concept, different factors have played vital roles at different times. The employee orientation manual has identified the keys to successful implementation and operation as employee selection, employee training, team building process and skills, positive mental attitude, maturity, intelligence, commitment, goal-oriented approach, pride, communication skills, and courage. As noted earlier, many of these factors are identified and reviewed in the selection process. Many of the rest, however, are significantly impacted by the training program.

THE TRAINING TEAM

The training effort at Logan Aluminum has been characterized by change and development to respond to the changing needs of the organization. To develop a clear understanding of the current role of training, it is important to establish a context in terms of evolution of training, personnel and facilities, philosophy, current training activities, perceptions of others, and future directions. These aspects of Logan's training program are examined in detail.

The training and development team at Logan Aluminum has evolved as the training needs of the facility have changed. During the late stages of the construction phase in 1983, training activities actually began at Logan. ARCO brought in two experienced trainers, Joe Braun and Pat Shannon, early in 1983 to develop behavioral training and focus primarily on organization development efforts, including working the assessment center and both prehire and posthire orientations.

Concurrent efforts were underway to begin what turned out to be a two-year project to develop approximately 200 competency based, site-specific technical training modules based on task analyses. The two individuals who had responsibility, Stephen Roush and Roger Vincent, were employed by Daniel International, the construction company that built the Logan mill. Daniel Training Services already had an extensive array of training materials, known as Dancraft, for journeyman and on-the-job training for technical programs. Through ARCO's contract with Daniel, Roush and Vincent developed most of Logan's technical training modules.

Late in 1983, Vincent left Daniel to work for ARCO. He worked in technical training at the ARCO Terre Haute, Indiana, facility, which managed as a traditional plant.

Although the first operating technicians were hired in May 1983, there was not a technical training group until 1984. The first operators used Daniel's training materials and later helped write the modules developed for Logan. In April 1984, Del Phillips was transferred from the Terre Haute mill to conduct electrical training and Terry Meadows was promoted from team leader to provide mechanical training. In July 1984, Shannon left the Logan facility and Vincent transferred from Terre Haute to serve as team leader for technical and operator training and to begin some organization development efforts. Braun continued as training coordinator, working out of employee relations (human resources) with a focus on human relations and organization development activities.

After Meadows returned to a team leader position in November 1984, Roush came to Logan in December as a mechanical training specialist. Roush came with the understanding that the role would change as training needs changed. Nine months later, Braun moved from the training position in human resources to join the technical training team while maintaining similar responsibilities.

From later 1985 until February 1988, the training team as part of the human resources business unit functioned with four full-time trainers and an administrative assistant. Vincent, whose training was in industrial psychology, was team leader and had administrative responsibilities for the training area as well as being involved in technical training, statistical process control, team building, and team leader development training. One of Vincent's major projects in 1986 was his involvement in the development of a pay and progression plan, or how to actually implement the philosophy of getting paid for what the employee knows, rather than for what he or she does. This involved the development of measures to quantify what the operating technicians knew about the different tasks within the team. The measures included both written and performance elements.

The responsibilities of the other three trainers were diverse. Braun, with more than 30 years of experience in personnel, employee relations, and training, continued to do pre- and posthire orientations and management development training, including time management, communications, motivation, and the like. He also coordinated some plantwide meetings for the president, including team visits and quarterly communications meetings.

Phillips worked in technical areas with ARCO for approximately 17 years before getting involved in training. He worked with operator and general technician training, statistical process control training, and technical instructor training (train the trainer). Phillips was also the resident equipment troubleshooter and cameraman for onsite film production.

Roush did technical training, including statistical process control, team building sessions, team leader development training, and technical instructor training. Roush's role changed to include more emphasis on organization development, including implementing the Logan Star Concept and conducting the annual employee survey.

Sharon Powell, the administrative assistant for training, worked for Daniel during the construction phase and began working for ARCO when the mill began operation. Powell was responsible for clerical activities, maintaining the training recordkeeping system, coordinating training sessions, and generally keeping everything running smoothly.

When Vincent left to accept another position in February 1988, Roush became team leader for the training area. He kept the organization development responsibilities and absorbed the administrative functions. Many of the administrative responsibilities and teaching of some classes were assumed by Powell. Because of the changing nature of training needs, the vacant position in the training team was not filled.

The training center at Logan Aluminum is located in the building that was used as offices for the construction company during plant construction. It has offices, three learning centers (classrooms), a large shop-type training area with machines for technical training, and resource rooms. In addition, there are three designated learning centers in the administration building, which are used for meetings and various types of training activities, including orientation sessions. Extensive training resources are available, including commercial training packages, films, books, training literature, and state-of-the-art equipment featuring rear screen projection capabilities and an interactive video system.

Although the corporate philosophical commitment to training was evident throughout the company literature and public statements, the commitment had to be translated into a workable training plan. Underlying the development of concrete plans was the determination to prevent training deficiencies, rather than use the conventional "brush fire" approach of merely responding to immediate training needs. According to a 1985 technical training plan summary, an agreement on training philosophy and policies evolved from meetings with business unit managers. The philosophy statement on operator and technical training is as follows:

We believe that training should be:

- Comprehensive in scope.
- Systematic in delivery.
- Job related.
- Fair in its evaluation (written and performance-based).
- Individualized.
- Classroom and performance-based.
- Based on no-fail proposition.

In addition, training policy statements were developed to clearly define the who, what, when, where, why, and how of training sessions. (See Appendix A for complete policy statements.) The training plan was designed to be comprehensive, systematic, and flexible, but also to be responsive to special training requests, such as management development and team leader training.

Initially, employee training needs were assessed through an approach Logan calls DACUM or Developing a Curriculum. This interactive process used a facilitator, a recorder, and five to eight content specialists who met and determined, with consensus, what duties and tasks were required for a particular position and how they were to be performed. The information generated by the meeting became the basis for classes offered to individuals in those positions. This approach individualized training for each particular job. The resulting courses were then prioritized by each business unit, and employees were contacted to select the courses they needed. Although the courses were intended to be offered in a particular order, the actual scheduling of classes for different business units had to remain flexible to respond to changing priorities and needs.

As the above approaches of involving managers, team leaders, and team members illustrate, the philosophy of training at Logan is based on shared responsibility for determining training needs and developing appropriate programs. The training staff does not presume to have all the answers. The staff's approach has been to start with the question of purpose for the training and work with each team from that perspective. As one business unit manager noted, "They talk to people to get an idea of what they want to do and then work toward that end."

Although this approach has been effective in the long term, it has not always been easy to implement. A training staff member described it in relation to team development as follows: "We spent about a month wrestling with the question of teaching at the team's request for making suggestions. We wanted to know what they wanted and they wanted to know what we thought they needed." As a result, the training staff conducted an extensive literature review that included the topics of effective teams, group dynamics, group study, maintenance roles, and so on and resulted in a list of 50 topics. Team leaders narrowed the list to 15 and appropriate programs were developed.

In the implementation of the technical training programs, Logan uses three sources: *(a)* employees, *(b)* vendors, and *(c)* local technical schools. Employees include both the training center staff and subject matter experts who have been trained to teach. Vendors were contacted when specialized training was not available within the organization. Technical schools in the area provided a source of low-cost generalized training. Examples of this type of training used by Logan were welding, pneumatics, and basic electronics.

The issue of cost has been addressed in the technical training plan as well. It is noted that, if students can attend classes on a straight-time basis, the cost is considerably less than when they attend on overtime. The cost of instructors within the organization also varies, depending on individual salaries, the number of times the class is taught, the cost of replacing the instructors while they are teaching, and the time it takes to "catch up" after being away from the job. Varying rates for vendors also affect the cost of training.

As the training emphasis at Logan Aluminum has evolved, the activities of the training staff have changed. The early emphasis was in operator and technical training. In terms of developing curriculum, the training team has accomplished what it set out to do for operator training. The focus of technical training recently has been on developing highly skilled "super-techs" and on cross-training. Greater emphasis has been placed on team development through implementation of the Star Concept and teambuilding as well as on the pay and progression plan, which the organization has been "wrestling with since day one." Team development training includes the basis of conflict resolution, communication, time management, goal setting, peer performance appraisals, giving and receiving feedback, motivation, and positive reinforcement. Most of these training efforts are directed toward teams and team members.

An additional training track has been the team leader development program. Again, this program was developed with the cooperation and assistance of team leaders through a comprehensive needs analysis. Seven or eight broad topic areas were initially identified and developed. The following programs make up the training that has been scheduled over a two-year period: basics of the Logan concept, goals and objectives, performance appraisals, team leader's role, definition of a team leader, salary administration, effective meetings, Logan financial accounting systems, self-regulating teams, conflict resolution, time management, managing teams, communications, decision making, effective presentations, dilemmas of managing participation, and basic metallurgy (see Appendix B).

Obviously, training classes are an ongoing important focus of Logan Aluminum's training staff. In a report of major accomplishments in 1986, the training staff reported teaching and coordinating 85 topics of instruction that were taught on 671 separate occasions.

Beyond training classes, members of the training and development team have been involved in numerous activities that have a significant impact on Logan Aluminum. These activities either fit into the long-range plans of the Logan management concept or had a direct impact on the bottom line according to the same report. The additional dimensions of training staff efforts are outlined below:

1. Designed, implemented, and evaluated the annual employee survey. This includes statistical analysis of data and presentations to executive and managerial levels as well as preparation of format, overheads, and so on for all presentations to teams.

2. Designed and facilitated use of peer appraisal forms for teams. Conducted classes to teach individuals how to do appraisals, avoid pitfalls, and help assure consistency in the appraisal process.

3. Established a "point system" to track and document a pay and progression system for the plant.

4. Facilitated implementation of the Star Concept and served as a clearinghouse for Star Concept information.
5. Monitored and audited team meetings for consistency of process and for any deviations from norms.

6. Conducted team-building sessions for teams throughout the plant. Helped in direction of teams by determining stage of development to facilitate movement to self-management.

7. Audited the assessment center. Developed exercises, served as raters and currently as directors for the center. Conducted prehire and posthire orientations.

8. Developed philosophy and values statements for the human resources group.

9. Participated in community and public relations activities.
   a. Coordinated extended campus course offerings in Logan County through Western Kentucky University.
   b. Conducted plant tours for various types of groups.
   c. Designed and staffed a booth at the Kentucky State Fair for Logan Aluminum.
   d. Coordinated and judged a company forklift competition.
   e. Made presentations to several outside groups.

10. Coordinated all quarterly communication meetings for the president and executive management. Also facilitated and participated in goal-setting meetings.

11. Served as resources for other units in the plant.
   a. Acted as liaison and consultants on statistical research to engineering groups in the plant.
   b. Established a master's level engineering management program with the University of Tennessee, with the training center serving as a satellite point for proctoring and viewing classes.
   c. Served as personal career counselors for Logan Aluminum employees.
   d. Acted as ombudsman to help smooth lines of communication and work with all levels.
   e. Coordinated off-site meetings for managers and teams.
   f. Videotaped machinery in the plant for troubleshooting.
   g. Coordinated with Western Kentucky University to produce a videotape, "Challenge of Opportunity," about Logan Aluminum at no charge to the company.
   h. Assisted in the implementation of statistical process control through teaching, coordinating consultant's visits, and working with managers and team leaders.
   i. Designed a tracking process control chart for the traffic team that increased the on-time delivery from 85 to 90 percent.
   j. Designed a purchasing effectiveness survey for the purchasing department.
   k. Established a crane and forklift truck requalification program for the plant.
   l. Consulted with and wrote articles for the employee newsletter.

12. Served on every steering committee in the plant, including statistical process control, star implementation, and trust committees.

13. Was involved in union-free posture of plant. This included working with consultants to develop a contingency plan for union organizing activities.

14. Provided information on team development to "sister" plant in Canada.
15. Completed a position task analysis (DACUM) for team leader position that included getting management consensus on the duties and tasks. This resulted in the development and implementation of the team leader development team program. Overall, the training and development at Logan Aluminum has been involved in numerous companywide activities and has maintained a very visible profile in the organization.

Developing a clear concept of the role of training at Logan Aluminum must necessarily include a discussion of the perceptions of individuals outside of the training and development team. Interviews with Logan Aluminum employees at different levels of the organization resulted in insights about their views of training. These perceptions are described in the general categories of training needs in a team management organization, views of current activities, perceived need for additional training or other approaches to training, and perceived role of training.

It was generally agreed from all perspectives that training is an essential element in managing with the team concept. A team member described training as "critical in participative management. People have to know what's going on to be a team. The concept absolutely demands that you train people—it won't work without it." Harris, human resources manager, echoes that idea. He said, "People I talk with in these types of organizations say that the biggest way to foul them up is not to do training." A business unit manager feels that training is essential in the behavioral aspects of team management, because it helps facilitate the process of building the concept of the team as a work unit. A team leader states it very succinctly, "Everybody needs training."

Training in traditional organizations often is viewed as expendable overhead. Although the same viewpoint may be expressed in participative organizations, other perspectives also are present. Harris notes, "Training is an easy thing to do away with because it's expensive. It's expensive and it doesn't show an immediate return. You have to be thinking about people's work 10 years down the road." A team member states that it "shouldn't be in an area that, if money got tight and times hard, would be eliminated." He felt that training would be "needed more then; it could help [the organization] get back on track."

Although it was generally agreed that training is essential in team management organizations, the views of current training activities were more diverse and were related to larger organizational concerns. An important issue for team leaders was the difficulty of scheduling training. They felt that additional technical training was needed, yet the demands of production made it difficult to fit training into the regular work schedule. The emphasis on team development through the Star Concept was viewed positively, and training staff members were seen as helpful in facilitating the process with various teams.

The overall view of the training and development team was very positive. A team leader commented, "Everything I've needed, they've provided." According to Harris, "They're there; they can respond to what our needs are; and, they do respond to those needs." This thought was reinforced by a team member who said, "I'm sure they do some great things because I see great things going on in other units." An important element of current training activities is their involvement in the orientation process. Through this process, training is highly visible in the first exposure that people have to Logan Aluminum. Orientation sets the "tone" for an individual's overall work experience.

An important question regarding the training effort is the perceived need for additional training or other approaches to training. Those perceptions are obviously influenced by the individual's exposure to training and his or her overall understanding of organizational needs and capabilities. It generally was felt that technical training and behavioral training were continuing needs.

Both team leaders and team members cited the need for more technical training for operators. They noted that production pressures had made it increasingly difficult to continue technical training, particularly on the third shift. One team member acknowledged that it was the team's responsibility to deal with and felt that the Star Concept would make it easier to handle this issue. Harris echoed the need for additional technical training. He stated, "We have uncharted areas to conquer out there with multiskilled craft individuals; we have years of work to do there to train them."

Individuals at all levels of the organization emphasized the need for a continued focus on behavioral training, especially dealing with the team concept communication. Managers felt that they should have started earlier in the mill's development and concentrated on more extensive training in the team concept. One manager commented that they should have started with questions like: "What is different?" and "What should be different?" It was regarded as particularly important for team leaders to have a greater understanding of their evolutionary role in the team management organization. One manager noted that team leaders needed to be able to discuss problems and issues more. Communication in some form was repeatedly mentioned as an area where additional training was needed. Two aspects in particular, giving feedback and improving communication within the team, were stressed.

Although not a responsibility of training per se, visiting other plants using the team philosophy was seen as a way for both team leaders and team members to enhance their understanding of the concept. Many felt that this type of exposure would help them gain greater insights into the factors that contribute to the success or failure of the philosophy and a better understanding of the organizational "big picture."

The perceived need for additional training as expressed by individuals outside of the training and development team tended to reinforce the training philosophy and overall direction of the team as noted earlier (emphasis on developing highly skilled technical employees through cross-training and on a team development). The only comments regarding what training needed to be doing differently focused on the need for more individualized training and more responsiveness to the training needs of third-shift employees. The statements of one manager summarize it well: "At this point, if I'm not getting what I need from training, I haven't asked for it."

Although the evolution of the role of training, training needs in a team management organization, current training activities, and perceived additional training needs for Logan Aluminum's training and development team have been described in detail, the role of training as perceived by individuals at all levels has not been specifically defined. Many different roles for training were identified by Logan employees. Although different in perspective, these roles have many underlying similarities and may be categorized using Nadler's (1984) HRD roles of learning specialist, administrator, and consultant.

The perceived role of training and development team members as learning specialists was most frequently mentioned by other Logan Aluminum employees. This role included facilitating, designing curriculum, and choosing strategies for learning. The most commonly noted activity was that of facilitation. A manager described the need for an objective outside person who can work with managers, team leaders, and team members. The trainer can "look at a manager or team leader and say 'Here's what they say . . . what's right or wrong?' as an unbiased participant." This facilitation role is "very critical to help build credibility and trust." Additional facilitation skills were identified as needed to help individuals develop critical behavioral aspects, such as communication, conflict resolution, problem solving, giving performance feedback, and giving and receiving criticism. One manager commented, "Training has a critical role in the behavioral aspect—in nurturing those who need it and getting people to a mature level."

Another area where facilitation was described as a training role was in bringing together groups and facilitating philosophical discussions and philosophical understandings. A business unit manager noted, "We need clear philosophical beliefs and standards that we're going to operate from." This same manager felt that training should "probably have been involved in early philosophical discussions aimed at reaching mutual understandings."

Designing curriculum and developing strategies, though those terms were not used, were perceived as a role or responsibility for training at Logan. Aside from developing the technical and behavioral training programs, individuals noted that training should impart the team philosophy in the course of teaching technicians and operators. An important aspect of imparting philosophy is that the trainer have a clear understanding of the manager's philosophy and what that individual looks for in operations. Strategies or methods need to reflect that understanding so as "not to create problems." One such problem mentioned was of raising expectations that a manager or managers do not "buy." One manager commented, "People were told 'You're going to do this and that' and a lot of it didn't happen; that was very frustrating for some people."

Another perceived training role identified by Logan Aluminum employees is what Nadler (1984) would identify as part of the HRD administrator role. According to Harris, "Someone has to identify what should be our involvement at each level and then put together the programs to accommodate that." This role involves the important functions of identifying, proposing, and developing programs to meet training needs.

The role of consultant, again not labeled as such, was frequently mentioned as one perceived to be important for the training and development team at Logan Aluminum. The three aspects of the consultant role as described by Nadler (1984) include acting as advocate, expert, and/or change agent. In the role of advocate, training was viewed as setting the "tone" for new employees particularly through the orientation process. It, therefore, is important for training and development team members to be the advocate for the team concept and its focus on employee growth and development.

Several individuals focused on what they perceived as the training role of providing expert advice and information. A team member described the need for training to stay in touch with how a team is maturing and growing "not so much to influence what we're doing but to let us know how we're doing—providing feedback." This individual felt that it would help the team to know "if a standard somewhere else is better." It also is important to Harris as senior manager that "Training develop the credibility that they are specialized people and they have something to offer that the individual needs." Harris feels that training can be viewed as successful in this respect when team leaders and team members come to them and ask for training.

This final consultant role is that of change agent. This role was identified as an important one for the training and development team. Harris describes the rationale for this role as follows:

> You have to remember that the team leaders and managers are under a lot of different kinds of pressure—none of which are to develop the team concept, normally.
>
> They have more immediate problems so you need someone to sort through the thinking, through the literature, and to introduce concepts to influence their thinking. That's a role for training and employee relations.

Harris goes on to say that training can be a change agent because "they're the people who have the time to think about different types of issues." He believes that having the time to think is one of "the hardest parts of doing something in industry."

Overall, the perception of the role of training closely parallels actual training goals and activities. The evolution of both the team concept and the nature of training at Logan Aluminum continues. The contributions of training to Logan and the team concept up to this point can be summarized in a statement made by Harris: "I don't think we'd be where we are today without training, and they're getting more and more involved in doing the right things, too."

It is difficult to predict, particularly because of the external environment of Logan and most other organizations, what the future role of training at Logan Aluminum will be. Harris says, "I think our training needs will change a lot but our need for training won't change that much." He believes there will always be a need for training at Logan Aluminum, though not always at the same level as today. When asked if he could generalize about the future, Harris offered the following note of optimism:

> I think training's day is still out in the future. Their role is going to become more participative in terms of managing in an organization where they've never been involved. Traditionally, they just put together a program, and the value of those programs was questionable due to their inability to sustain themselves. I think training is going to come into its own.

SUMMARY

This case study of Logan Aluminum was undertaken to view in some depth the roles and responsibilities of training and development professionals in a functioning team management organization. Since training must operate within the context of the larger organization, it also was important to gain an understanding of Logan Aluminum, including the historical development of the mill, the physical facility, the management philosophy, organization structures, the management team, and the employees. These aspects of Logan have been described in detail to provide the context needed to understand the role of training, why it had that role, and its impact on team management policies and practices at Logan Aluminum.

APPENDIX A

LOGAN PHILOSOPHY STATEMENT ON OPERATOR AND TECHNICAL TRAINING

We believe that training should be:

- Comprehensive in scope.
- Systematic in delivery.
- Job related.
- Fair in its evaluation (written and performance-based).
- Individualized.
- Classroom and performance-based.
- Based on a no-fail proposition.

TRAINING POLICY STATEMENTS

1. Through the DACUM (develop a curriculum) process, cross-training has been defined for each technician. Therefore, training classes will be limited to the technician for which the class was intended. However, if a technician wishes to attend a class that has not been identified as the technician's area of responsibility, he or she may do so on his or her own time, space permitting.

2. The company will pay for job-required training for each technician. Attendance should be on company time first; if this is not possible, overtime scheduling is permissible and should be coordinated with the team leader (basic responsibility for scheduling lies first with the individual and then should be coordinated with the team leader).

3. When practical, the same course will be offered at least three times during a given week. This is done to allow maximum scheduling flexibility for all shifts.

4. The company will provide the time required for the technician's designated training program (which is job required). As a guideline, approximately four hours per week has been designated for each technician. This time is not accumulative, is not restrictive. That is, one might attend a 20-hour vendor training session in a one-week period, and, conversely, one might not receive training for an extended time.

5. Technicians who are part-time instructors in the training programs will be allowed adequate preparation time (four to five days per course). All technicians who become part-time instructors will receive a one-day instructor training session.

6. If a trainee receives an unsatisfactory evaluation (written or performance), the instructor will identify the unsatisfactory areas and assist the trainee to overcome the deficiency. If the trainee chooses, he or she may attend the entire course at a later date. All of these activities will be on the trainees's time and the trainee will not be compensated by the company.

TEAM LEADER CURRICULUM

Class No.	*Date*	*Class Identification*	*Instructor(s)*
Kickoff	Sept. 17	Basics of Logan Concept	Mike Harris, Bruce Robson
1	Sept. 24, 30, Oct. 1	Goals/objectives	Roger Vincent
2	Oct. 8, 14, 15	Performance appraisals	Mark Pitchford
3	Nov. 12, 18, 19	Team leader's role	Steve Roush Carol Lee, Mike Zoll
4	Dec. 3, 16, 17	Definition of a team leader	Rich Hammond, Mark Kaminski
5	Jan. 7, 13, 14	Salary administration	Mark Pitchford
6	Feb. 4, 10, 11	Effective meetings	Roger Vincent
7	Mar. 4, 10, 11	Logan financial accounting systems—I	Ev Katz
8	Apr. 8, 14, 15	Logan financial accounting systems—II	Ev Katz
9	To be scheduled	Self-regulating teams	Steve Roush
10	To be scheduled	Conflict resolution	Roger Vincent
11	To be scheduled	Time management	Joe Braun
12	To be scheduled	Managing teams	Steve Roush
13	To be scheduled	Communications—I	Joe Braun
14	To be scheduled	Communications—II	Joe Braun
15	To be scheduled	Decision making	Steve Roush
16	To be scheduled	Effective presentations	Steve Roush
17	To be scheduled	Dilemmas of managing participation	Roger Vincent
18	To be scheduled	Basic metallurgy	Technical Staff
19	To be scheduled	Curriculum evaluation/ future	Steve Roush

APPENDIX B

TEAM LEADER CURRICULUM AND EVALUATION FORM

DATE________________________

Team Leader Class Evaluation Form
(Signature Unnecessary)

CLASS TITLE____________________ INSTRUCTOR____________________

1. Comments on Content

2. Comments on Instructor(s)

3. Comments on Facilities, Materials, Visuals, Methods

4. How relevant was the class to your job? (Circle the number that indicates your perception.)

Not Relevant Very Relevant

1 2 3 4 5 6 7 8 9 10

5. Suggestions for improvement of this class

33 Reforming Russia's Workplace: The Ultimate HRM Challenge*

INTRODUCTION

Maywood International, a successful U.S.-based multinational company (MNC), is holding a closed-door strategic session with its corporate-level planning team and key members of its human resource management (HRM) department. The focus of today's meeting is an ambitious proposal from Maywood's German joint venture partner, Eatenburg, Inc. The American/German joint venture has an opportunity to enter the restaurant market in Russia, which has become more open to Western investors since the fall of communism.

Initial research indicates that Russia may hold the greatest unmet demand for food products and services of any industrialized market in the world. Therefore, this investment ultimately could be the most profitable venture in Maywood's history. However, based on the written report just submitted by Maywood's HRM exploratory team, the Russian culture may represent an insurmountable barrier to success. Maywood's management finally may have met its match in the form of the "Russian mindset."

For those in attendance at today's meeting, a certain amount of personal as well as corporate pride is at stake. Maywood has earned global recognition for successfully integrating its operations into foreign cultures. The decision to go into Russia, therefore, adds a unique emotional component to Maywood's strategic planning decision. No one wants to pass up the chance to be known as the first U.S.-based, full-service restaurant chain in Russia. Even so, the reality of the risks cannot be ignored and the decision makers must do what is best for the long-term success of Maywood and its shareholders.

HISTORY OF THE COMPANY

Based in Dallas, Texas, Maywood International was founded in 1961 as a large-scale, cafeteria-style operation. The company went public in 1968 and now has 342 outlets serving the U.S. market. Expansion into Europe began in 1980, and Maywood now has 36 locations throughout Brussels, Belgium, France, Germany, Great Britain, Spain, and Switzerland. All of Maywood's restaurants are operating in the black and are known to be not only great places to eat but also great places to work.

Maywood recently has gained global attention for its highly successful joint venture with Eatenburg, Inc., of Frankfurt, Germany. In early 1991, the two companies joined

---

*This case was prepared by Professor Donna E. Ledgerwood and doctoral candidate Ruth C. May, University of North Texas.

forces to capitalize on the opportunities emerging from the reunification of East and West Germanys. Eatenburg had watched Maywood's impressive expansion across Western Europe in the 1980s and proposed that the two companies form a joint venture directed at the newly opened markets to the east. Eatenberg, the second largest food manufacturer in Western Europe, has provided food products, supplies, and distribution services to the restaurant facilities set up and operated by Maywood under their joint venture provisions. Of the large-scale restaurants opened in the former East German territory in the past year, each of the three most profitable businesses are owned and operated by the Maywood/Eatenburg joint venture.

MAYWOOD'S UNIQUE APPROACH

Maywood's success in international markets has been attributed to its large investments in research and development (R&D) and its cultural sensitivity. Operations and policies are tailormade to fit the cultural nuances of each location. Maywood's marketing niche has been to offer low-cost, high-quality nutritional entrees prepared in keeping with the traditional culinary style of the region. Each location emphasizes a family atmosphere and is capable of serving 400 patrons.

At Maywood, the underlying philosophy is that "we must become aware of how culturally unaware we are." In other woods, every member Maywood's "employee family" must be proactive in their sensitivity to different cultural environments, and each must respond to the needs of their customers and communities. Each Maywood manager is responsible for blending local talents with corporate policies and practices. Opportunities for selection (i.e., promotions) are based on work performance and not organizational politics or "who you know." Each employee is encouraged and rewarded for contributing his or her knowledge and efforts to the "bottom line" of the organization.

HRM is a line function at Maywood. Each restaurant manager has the responsibility and capability for establishing and maintaining a safe and healthful workplace environment. Each manager's pay and promotion opportunities are tied to job-related performance factors as well as to Maywood's "pay-for-knowledge" incentive pay. Each managerial candidate goes through an intensive six-week training and development course to become a "competent person" after she or he is hired, but before being placed on the job. This course is company paid and is seen as a critical investment in Maywood's organizational development.

Surveys are disseminated to managerial and nonmanagerial employees every six months along with a customer survey. Follow-up training courses then incorporate the findings from these surveys. Potential (behavioral and structural) hazards are identified and Maywood managers are coached in how to anticipate and avoid potentially harmful situations by being proactive. These coaching sessions are participatory in nature and managers leave with techniques they can apply at their restaurants. Maywood also has a free "hot line" to encourage communication and a proactive stance at the local level.

The members of Maywood's internationally diverse HRM department are responsible for generating information on local labor forces to be used by strategic planners in analyzing each prospective location. Seven functions are evaluated in determining the probability of success within a specific culture: training and development (T & D); compensation and benefits; employment, placement, and planning; health, safety, and security; labor relations; validation of the selection practices; and general management practices. If the HRM exploratory research team feels confident that Maywood's HRM strategies can be effectively integrated into a specific cultural setting, then the go-ahead is given to enter that market. Final approval is derived via vote in special planning sessions, involving Maywood's strategic management team and the key officers of the HRM department. Thus, the decision whether to enter a given market is clearly a "strategic HRM decision."

ALL THINGS CONSIDERED

"I'd like to call our planning session to order now," said Mark Leger, head of Maywood's strategic planning group. "We have a very important decision to make today regarding our proposed entry into Russia, and I'd like to begin by turning the floor over to Mr. William Heise, director of strategic planning for our German partner, Eatenburg."

"Thank you, Mark," replied Mr. Heise. "It is a pleasure to be with your group today to discuss this very important opportunity facing our joint venture. I will be brief so we will have plenty of time to hear from your team of HRM experts who have just returned from Russia. As you see in the research data before you, the profit potential for Maywood–Eatenburg restaurant facilities in Russia is phenomenal. We recommend targeting the two largest cities in the country: (1) Moscow with 16 million people and (2) St. Petersburg (formerly Leningrad) with 7 million people. These two metropolitan areas seem to offer the easiest ports of entry into the country; however, two critical barriers have kept most of our competitors out of the market and will be serious challenges for us as well. I am speaking of (1) the poor infrastructure, which limits delivery of goods needed for operations, and (2) the problem of converting Russian currency (the ruble) into hard currency to take our profits out of the country.

"Our transportation analysts have worked diligently over the past few months to negotiate feasible channels of distribution from our production plants in Hamburg and Berlin to the proposed cities in Russia. The close proximity of our German facilities has been a distinct advantage in negotiating with trucking and rail companies in Poland and Czechoslovakia. We believe a reliable system has been worked out for transporting the necessary supplies and equipment to the proposed sites inside Russia.

"The currency problems are not so easily influenced. Though there has been some progress towards convertibility of the ruble, the lack of an efficient financial market and banking system in Russia still hampers the transfer of profits out of the country. Our position at Eatenburg, however, is one of long-term commitment to this area. We feel that it is worth taking initial start-up losses and leaving our profits in Russia to be reinvested in expansion. The returns we are experiencing in our jointly-held East European locations should be more than enough to offset our start up investments in Russia. We must stay out in front of our competitors by positioning ourselves in this market now regardless of short-term losses due to problems with the currency. The long-term potential for profit is phenomenal."

REPORT FROM THE FRONT LINE

"Thank you for addressing those issues for us, William," said Mark Leger. "There certainly are numerous critical points to consider with any opportunity of this magnitude. Now, I'd like to shift our focus to HRM concerns. Vivian Parrott, our director of HRM and Exploratory Team Coordinator at Maywood, will fill us in on what her team discovered about the Russian market firsthand. I must admit, Vivian, that your team's report is absolutely fascinating. In fact, I think 'bizarre' might be a more accurate description. It's hard to believe that your people actually had some of these experiences in a country that I've always associated with high technology and world power."

"You're right, Mark," responded Vivian, "it was certainly an eye-opening experience for all of us who traveled to Russia. Their system of centralized planning has controlled every aspect of Russian life for the past 75 years, and it is still very apparent, even in something as simple as your hot water."

"Your hot water?" asked Mark. "Just what do you mean by that?"

"Well," said Vivian, the evening we arrived in St. Petersburg, we were told to get up the next morning, turn on the hot water and go back to bed for 30 minutes. When we got up again we'd have hot water for our showers. A congenial British woman who was staying on our hall explained that it takes this long to get hot water because there are no hot water heaters in the building. In fact, there are no hot water heaters in Russia, period (except maybe in some of the expensive Western hotels)! Hot water is provided by giant 'hot water heating plants' that literally boil the water for a certain section of the city. When you turn on your faucet, the hot water must travel through miles of pipe in order to reach your sink, and in some cases, it may take as long as 30 minutes to arrive. The British woman also said that if we were to turn on the faucet and only get a stream of air, it was because our area of the city had been cut off from the 'heating plants.' When this happens, Russians just go to a friend's apartment in some other part of the city in order to take a hot shower. Apparently, the hot water is cut off for days and even weeks during the summer to conserve energy and repair plant facilities."

"That sounds like a nightmare for our design people," said Mark. I'm glad that comes under your jurisdiction at Eatenburg, William. We'll leave all decisions relevant to physical design to you and your engineers. I understand from other discussions that these concerns have been addressed and it looks as though the decision to go or not to go into Russia has come down to primarily HRM issues. That's why we're here today . . . So what do you and your people think, Vivian?" asked Mark from across the table. "Can we recruit, train, and retain Russian nationals to abide by our standards of quality and service while not forsaking their own culture?"

"That's the million dollar question," agreed Vivian. "Maybe we ought to review the key points of our report, focusing particularly on the experiences we had inside Russian restaurants . . . You'll remember that in April before we left, we agreed not to travel as official visitors of the Russian Restaurant Association. We didn't want to call a lot of attention to ourselves so we could visit restaurants without any 'window dressing' by the Russians."

"We visited both prospective locations, Moscow and St. Petersburg. In St. Petersburg, there are two very expensive Swedish and German hotels, which have up-scale restaurants on the premises. The average entree is priced at approximately $62 and is only payable in hard currency. Since Russians have few rubles and little access to hard currency, this prevents most people from patronizing the businesses. The only other Western establishments that were evident were a handful of German deli-type bars, which had a limited number of items precooked and flown in from Germany. One of our team members had two slices of a very bad frozen pizza for $6 and then ended up being violently ill later that night."

"Ooh, that's awful," said Mark, "but what about the Russian restaurants? Were they any better?"

"Actually, they were worse," stated Vivian. "One evening, we were sight-seeing with two Russian couples who had agreed to show us the city of St. Petersburg. We ended up near the Hotel Moscow, which is still state-owned and operated. This hotel is supposed to have been the communist party's version of first-class accommodations. Actually, it is very dingy and dark with mostly a black and brown motif throughout. The carpets are buckling and ripped, and there's lots of that fake 1960s plastic "leather furniture."

"So what about the restaurant?" quizzed Mark.

"It took our Russian guides about fifteen minutes find the restaurant since it is secluded in a dark corner on the third floor of the hotel," answered Vivian. "After seating our party, the waiter *told us* we would have to hurry, because he was ready to go home. He also *told us* that we would all have Pepsi to drink and that we would be served the standardized main course of meat and potatoes with ice cream for dessert."

"He *told you* what you would eat?" asked a Maywood strategist. "You've got to be kidding!"

"It gets even better," said Vivian. "We noticed about half-way through the meal that the waiter had given our Russian friends the bad cuts of meat and had given us the tender, better pieces. We were outraged and embarrassed for our hosts until they told us that this is a common practice among Russians. Apparently, Russians tend to treat each other very rudely while foreigners receive somewhat better service."

"Boy, that's quite a reversal from most of the cultures we've worked with in Western Europe," said Mark. "How do you explain that, Vivian?"

"The thing you have to understand about a state-owned Russian restaurant, is that they really don't want you to come in, Mark. Actually, the waiters are 'put out' when you do, and that's because then they have to actually work to serve you food . . . If no customers come in, the employees don't have to work, and they are still paid exactly the same salary as they would be paid with a full house. Again, this is because the restaurants are owned by the state and every worker receives a fixed salary no matter what occurs. There is no such thing as tipping in Russia! The restaurant never has to serve a single meal or turn one ruble's profit to stay in business. Oh, the beauty of centralized planning and socialism!"

"Then how do we compete with restaurants that don't have to consider their bottom line at all?" asked Mark. "They could take tremendous losses just to put us out of business."

"Sure they could, Mark, *if* they had any customers."

"What do you mean, Vivian?"

"I mean that Russians hate to go to Russian restaurants for two reasons: (1) the service and the food is awful and (2) most Russians can't get past the front door. Let me give you an example of what I mean."

"We went to Moscow after two weeks in St. Petersburg and made contact with Mr. Gregory Rachmelivich Raiter, director of the Russian Human Resource Management Association. Mr. Raiter was kind enough to get us into some of the older, established restaurants in Moscow."

"So you had problems getting reservations?" asked Mark.

"No," said Vivian, "The problem wasn't that the restaurants were booked solid; the problem was that the restaurant staff try their best to keep people out."

"Are you telling me they wouldn't have let you in without a call from Mr. Raiter?" Mark asked.

"Mark, they wouldn't even let us in with his call. Mr. Raiter spent three days getting us written permission from the director of HRM for the Russian Restaurant Association."

"I can't believe it," Mark said, shaking his head in disbelief. "So what would have happened if you had just walked up off the street and asked to come in?"

"We would've had to bribe the doorman 200 rubles to let us in," said Vivian. "That's why Russians despise the places so much and why they're empty virtually all the time."

"So who is our competition in Moscow?" queried Mark.

"Well," replied Vivian, aside from a few overpriced Western hotels, which are really targeting a different market than we are, I'd say it's McDonald's and Pizza Hut."

"I'm very curious to hear about their operations," stated another member of Maywood's strategic planning group.

"They are tremendously popular with the Russian public," said Vivian. "They've been in the market for a couple of years now, and it is still common to see lines several blocks long waiting to get in. Their success may have been attributable to "newness" in the beginning, but I think their approach to high quality and customer service has given them real staying power. In fact, one of our interpreters told us that 'We love McDonald's because we do not have to beg anyone to let us in the door. We are treated with dignity and can always be sure that we will get good-tasting food.' "

"Sounds like McDonald's has got a good thing going over there," said Mark.

"Yes," Vivian answered, "But they're not without their problems. As you know, McDonald's has a very strict regimen of training for their new employees regarding how to interact with customers. The McDonald's method is considered "the Gospel" in the restaurant industry, and one of their tactics in "behind the counter etiquette" is to be friendly and to smile at customers. This might seem like a positive gesture to us, but in the Russian culture, smiling is considered to be a sign of weakness. Thus, the workers behind the counter were experiencing a great deal of dissonance between what they were being instructed to do by their employer and what they were being guided instinctively to do by their cultural programming."

"McDonald's also has had a problem with asking employees to interact as a 'family' and to work on a first name basis. The Russian language, like many other languages around the world, has a formal case and an informal case for pronoun usage. Which case you use in a conversation depends on how well you know a person and the status of that individual. Using the informal first name with someone you have just met or a person in authority, can be considered very rude in the Russian culture because this usage is typically reserved for children and subordinates. Also, McDonald's policy of using first names at work does not always seem appropriate to Russian employees. These and other culture-related problems have resulted in a high turnover rate at McDonald's," reported Vivian. "If we decide to go into this market, we absolutely cannot ignore the cultural and behavioral parameters within which we must operate."

"It looks like we've got our work cut out for us ladies and gentlemen," said Mark. "Can we do it?"

Discussion Questions

1. How do you define culture and how is the term used in the context of this case?
2. Discuss some examples of culturally based attitudes in the Russian setting and the impact they will have on the Maywood/Eatenburg joint venture.
3. What factors are most critical to the long-term success of the Maywood/Eatenburg partnership that could be positively or negatively affected by the entry into the Russian market?
4. Are there additional risks that were not identified by the decision makers?
5. Do you think that Maywood's policies and practices will work in Russia? Please explain your reasoning.
6. Do you agree that this is primarily a strategic HRM decision? Are there other HRM questions that should have been considered?
7. What American HRM practices and policies may be particularly difficult to integrate into the Russian culture? Which ones are best suited for effective transfer to Russia?
8. Compare and contrast the temporal (short-term versus long-term) considerations of the risks as well as costs and benefits involved in this venture?
9. Should a decision be made or do you feel that "more research needs to be done"?
10. Are there any additional behavioral or cultural considerations that need to be researched?

Suggested Readings

Brandt, E. "Global HR." *Personnel Journal,* March 1991, pp. 38–44.

Ebrahimi, B.; R. M. and G. Raiter. "Human Resource Management Practices in Russia: Joint American/Russian Perspectives of the Problem." *Southwest Academy of Management Proceedings*, 1993.

Lawrence, P. R. and C. A. Vlachoutsicos. *Behind the Factory Walls*. Boston, MA: Harvard Business School Press, 1990.

Overman, S. "Help Wanted: HR Pros to Help Transform the Soviet Workforce." *HRMagazine*, January 1991, pp. 44–45, 78.

Puffer, S. M. (ed.) *The Russian Management Revolution*. Arkmonk, NY: M.E. Sharpe, 1992.

Puffer, S. M. and O. S. Vikhanski. "Recruiting, Training and Rewarding Employees in the New USSR: The Experience of Moscow McDonald's and Polaroid Corporation." Presentation at Symposium during the Annual Meeting of the Academy of Management, Las Vegas, Nevada, 1992.

Raiter, G. "Inside Intelligence on Soviet Ventures." *HRMagazine*, January 1991, pp. 46–49.

Vlachoutsicos, C. and P. R. Lawrence. "What We Don't Know about Soviet Management." *Harvard Business Review*. November–December 1990, pp. 50–63.

Section F

Management and Development

34 How Do You Evaluate Your Employee Appraisal Program?*

The Hackney Paper Box Company is having trouble deciding what should be done about its employee evaluation program. Hackney operates 46 corrugated box factories from Maine to California and has a highly centralized corporate personnel department in New York City. Each plant employs about 125 persons.

The company policy in the Hackney Company allows a junior employee to be promoted over a senior employee if the junior employee has "noticeably" better qualifications for the job. In the South Bend plant a junior employee was promoted to a combiner operator job over an employee, Bob Peller, with more experience as a combiner, first helper, and two more years of seniority. They went to court. The company correctly contended that the senior employee was not responsible, was lazy, not cooperative, not very bright, and had a horrible attendance record. During the court hearing the attorney for Bob Peller produced copies of all the past employee evaluation forms for his client. These forms were prepared by Bob's immediate supervisors over the past 10 years, the time Peller had been an employee. On a scale of 1 to 5 he was rated (4) above average or (5) excellent in all categories on every evaluation instrument. Bob Peller won the court case, was promoted with back pay, and now the company has to have a qualified operator stay with Peller at all times to get the job done.

The above situation caused Mr. Green, corporate vice president of personnel, to call a meeting of selected plant personnel managers, the corporate compensation manager, and the corporate training and development manager. The purpose of the meeting was to decide what was to be done about the existing employee evaluation program.

---

* This case was prepared by Professor James C. Hodgetts of Memphis State University and is intended to be used as a teaching device rather than to show correct or incorrect methods of operations.

This meeting produced four suggestions that Mr. Green is considering. They are:

1. Junk the employee evaluation program.
2. Substitute management by objectives (MBO) for the present evaluation program.
3. Have the personnel manager at each plant do the evaluation and conduct the evaluation interview that follows evaluation.
4. Leave the program as it is but give every supervisor adequate training in employee evaluation and evaluation interviewing.

The idea to junk the program was advanced by the personnel manager at the South Bend plant. He contended that supervisory personnel were not qualified to evaluate or counsel. He also contended that they would only rate a subordinate "high," as it was much easier to discuss this kind of rating with the subordinate. In addition to this, if an employee was rated "low," the supervisor had to determine and explain to the employee how he could improve. This took effort.

The MBO suggestion was made by a new plant personnel manager who had been transferred to the position from outside the personnel field. He admitted that he didn't know much about MBO but he had heard lots of good things about it.

The suggestion to have the personnel manager do the evaluation and counseling came from a plant personnel manager who had a master's degree in psychology as well as considerable plant experience both as a production supervisor and hourly paid employee. He thought this would work at Hackney as all the plants were small, having approximately 125 employees each.

The suggestion to keep the present evaluation system and train the supervisors in evaluation and evaluation counseling was made by the corporate director of training and development.

Mr. Green is currently trying to decide which suggestion is best or if there is a still better solution.

Discussion Questions

1. What are the personnel problems in this case?
2. What should Mr. Green do? Explain.

---

*35 The Delta Electronics Corporation**

BACKGROUND

The Delta Electronics Corporation is a large national organization with a chain of company owned retail stores specializing in the sale of small electrical home appliances. The company has enjoyed tremendous growth over the last decade, penetrating

---

* This case was prepared by Thomas R. Miller, James M. Todd, and Edward A. Mueller of Memphis State University.

new market areas with store openings at a rapid pace. Corporate sales increases have averaged 17 percent for each of the last six years. Store locations range from large metropolitan areas to small cities in rural settings.

Delta's growth has provided many advancement opportunities for young, aggressive managers who are strongly sales oriented. Promotion is fairly typical of a large retail organization. When an individual is hired as a managerial candidate, he or she enters a training program, which consists of learning store operations, gaining product knowledge, and becoming familiar with company policies and procedures. Most of one's time in the program is spent in personal selling. Promotion to the position of store manager is contingent on mastery of unit operations and achievement of a strong sales record.

Once one has become a store manager, advancement to a larger store is based on effectiveness in increasing sales and profits. After successful performance as a store manager and several years' experience, one may be considered for the position of district manager. Further advancement to the regional or divisional level follows a similar process. Delta's organizational structure is shown in Exhibit 1.

Promotion from within is rigidly observed at Delta Electronics. Upper-level management adheres to the "old school," where employees start at the bottom and work their way up "through the ranks." One's formal education is secondary; performance is what counts.

A NEW EMPLOYEE

As Bob Allan was completing his last semester in the MBA program at Ivy State University, he became seriously interested in taking a job with Delta Electronics. From his research on the firm and his discussions with company officials, Bob learned of the fast growth of the organization and saw an unusual opportunity to rapidly advance his managerial career. Although he was aware of Delta's policy of employees starting at the bottom and working up, he was not discouraged by it. In fact, Bob felt that his educational background would help him progress quickly, since most of his direct competition did not have college degrees. After much deliberation, Bob joined Delta. Within only one month a manager's position became available in a small store in Eagleton, a nearby city, and Bob was selected for the position. Although he had had little experience with the firm, his ability and accomplishments were quickly recognized by Delta's management.

Bob's exceptional performance as a store manager was soon apparent to both his superiors and peers. Often other store managers would call to ask for advice or help. Thus, it surprised no one when Bob was promoted to district manager after only two years with the corporation. Rather than be faced with the customary transfer, Bob persuaded his regional manager, John Frederick, to assign him the open district manager position in the same district where Bob was a store manager.

EXHIBIT 1 Partial Organization Chart for the Delta Electronics Corporation

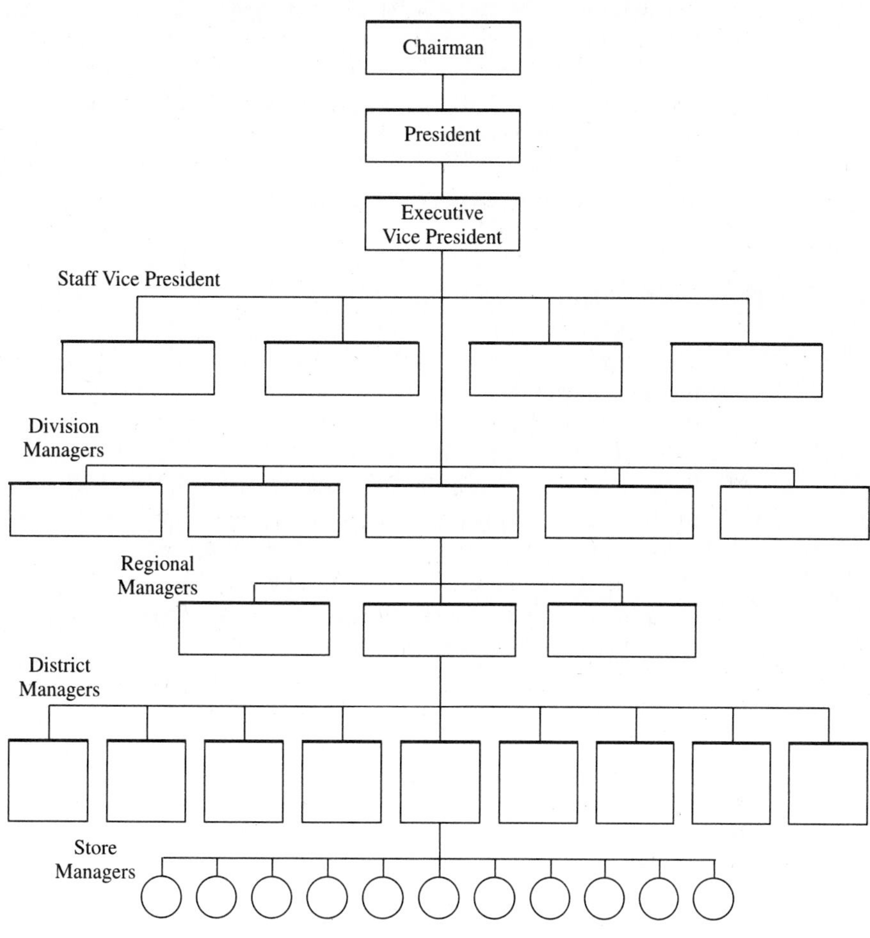

CHANGES IN MANAGEMENT

Soon after Bob's promotion, several major shifts occurred in management personnel. The major change affecting Bob was John Frederick's promotion to division manager from his regional manager position. John had been a friend as well as a boss, and Bob regretted his leaving but was happy that John had moved up. Bob's new regional manager was George Stewart, who had been transferred from the West Coast division and was relatively unknown in his new area.

After a few months working with George, Bob realized that John and George were very different kinds of managers. However, corporate management apparently thought their differences would complement each other. John had been successful as a manager by playing "by the book," adhering closely to corporate policies and procedures. In contrast, George's approach was looser and less straightforward. He was not opposed to bending a rule here and there or even breaking it if he thought it would be to his advantage. Whereas John had always been open and direct in his dealings, George was less vocal with his opinions and appraisals. Initially, Bob felt that the skepticism shown by store managers toward George was normal. After all, isn't any change of management viewed with caution or suspicion? However, even months later he still heard comments from the other managers, such as "George is hard to get to know" or "I just don't know where I stand with him."

DEVELOPING PROBLEMS

During the same period these changes occurred in corporate management, another important development took place. Over the past decade, Delta had grown so rapidly that companywide sales increases of 20 percent per year had become common. Sales growth always had been strong, because general economic conditions never before had been a major limiting factor for Delta. Now, for the first time, sales in existing stores were on the decline, and new markets for outlets were increasingly harder to find. Bob, along with the other district managers in his region, was deeply concerned. The major emphasis at Delta had always been on sales. Now, instead of reporting healthy revenue increases, most of the district managers had sales that were either the same or worse than the previous year. The bad news was no secret, for every week a sales report was sent to each district manager from the home office. The report showed sales for the current week and month compared to the same figures for the previous year. The decline was widespread throughout the company and put considerable pressure on the sales organization.

Although sales were down in his district, Bob felt they would compare favorably with sales in other districts. In fact, when Bob became a district manager, his district was dead last out of nine in percentage of sales increase. One year later, with overall sales declining, Bob's district had risen to third out of nine in sales increase. Nevertheless, it was at this time that Bob was removed as a district manager and, reluctantly, became a store manager in the district again. Bob was surprised when John and George confronted him with the news, but he was even more surprised at the vague reasons he was given. He was told that under his leadership "the district was not working as a team" and that "new managers had not developed quickly enough." George even expressed skepticism that Bob may have been "too smart" for the job. However, no reasons pertaining to measurable performance were given.

The new district manager, Butch Lawson, came from the same area of Delta as had George. Indeed, it was well known that, before his promotion and transfer, George had hired and worked with Butch. George made it clear to the store managers that Butch was "strict and tough and would expect at least 110 percent." Soon after Butch took over the district, the store managers knew he did things differently. He was in favor of working around rules, not by them, and he had stated to the managers that they were "too straight for their own good."

Butch had some ingenious, but indiscreet, methods of improving his district's performance. His favorite piece of advice involved "slightly falsifying" insurance claims. For example, he would advise any store manager who might have a leaky roof to make sure that some merchandise was damaged even if by only one drop of water. Then the store could have a big "water damage sale," sell the merchandise at half price or less to move it quickly, and file an insurance claim for the entire value of the items. Thus, a store manager could increase both sales and profits at the same time. If a store front window should be broken in the middle of the night, that provided an additional opportunity for the "enterprising" manager. Usually, only a few hundred dollars of merchandise was displayed in such a window. However, after one such break-in, the store manager filed an insurance claim for over $8,000 at retail! This incident was known throughout the district. Butch personally assisted in preparation of the insurance claim for the store manager just to make certain it was done "right."

Store employees were uncertain, to say the least, about participating in some of these activities. Butch would try to get them actively involved in the misdeeds to ensure that they would remain "discreet." After a break-in at one store, he asked the employees if they needed a stereo system. He explained that now would be the time to get it and to go ahead and pick one out. No one took up his offer.

With the low level of sales in general over recent months, store managers were discouraged and morale had been suffering. Now, some were even more disturbed to see not only unethical but sometimes criminal actions being tolerated and even encouraged.

After Butch had been district manager for six months, his performance was not better than Bob's in many areas, and in some cases it was worse. Butch was under increasing pressure from above to show an improvement over Bob's performance of the previous year. George, the regional manager, visited the area to talk with Bob, his former district manager, about the situation. During their meeting George stated his belief that one of Butch's main problems was the store managers' continued loyalty to Bob. George felt that these relationships made Butch's job more difficult, and the implication was strong that Bob was turning the store managers against Butch. George suggested that Butch probably could achieve a higher level of performance in the district if Bob were not around. Bob was shocked and indignant at this indictment by George, and he remarked that any problems that Butch experienced were of his own making.

BOB'S DILEMMA

Within a few weeks after Bob's meeting with George, Bob was offered an assignment to manage the largest store in George's region at Lincoln City, which is in another district. George explained that everyone's interests would be served by Bob's taking a new assignment. The store was in a regional shopping mall in a prime location, and the sales and profit potentials were great. Success in this store could mean another district manager's job for Bob. Bob's new boss would be Al

Barnhart, a newly promoted district manager who had worked with George for several years. Al had extended his welcome to Bob to join the district. Several thoughts flashed through Bob's head. The sales commissions and bonus at the Lincoln City store could be fantastic. The prospect of the district manager position was even more attractive. But what would it be like working in another district under George's control? Would Al Barnhart "operate" like Butch? What if he didn't accept this assignment? Could he reasonably stay put under the present conditions? Or should he get out now and give up his comfortable income and three and a half years with the company? What should he do? What can he do? What will his wife, Barbara, think?

George said he must have Bob's answer by the end of the day.

Discussion Questions

1. What problems does the Delta Electronics Corporation face?
2. What course of action should Bob choose?

*36 Time and Change at Evergreen State University**

"I might stick around for another year, but I don't know, Fred, . . . I just don't know. I don't want to leave this place hating it like some of my colleagues who are at retirement age."

Fred reacted with concern. "What do you mean, Oscar, 'hating this place'? I've not been aware that the older faculty have had such bad feelings about the school."

"Well, Fred, some of them do because they feel the university has not really treated them fairly. They've given many years of service to Evergreen State University and don't believe their work has been given its due by the administration. No doubt some of this is just sour grapes, but I can appreciate their feelings since I share some of them," Oscar admitted.

"Oscar, I wish I knew more about this because, if there's something we're doing that's alienating them, I'd like to know what it is. With all of our other problems, the dean's office certainly doesn't need the animosity of our older faculty," Fred replied earnestly.

Oscar smiled and shook his head. "Look, Fred, you've been the dean here for only two years, and there's no way you could understand all that has happened here over the years. There are a lot of reasons the older faculty are unhappy. If you really want to know and are interested in trying to deal with this problem, I'll tell you what I'll do. I know these people pretty well, having worked with them for

*This case was prepared by Professor James C. Hodgetts of Memphis State University and is intended to be used as a teaching device rather than to show correct or incorrect methods of operations.

over 20 years. Let me interview some of them, and I'll give you a report on it. You know I'm an old 'personnel man' from way back, anyway. Maybe I can make a contribution to running this school in my twilight years! But seriously, Fred, the treatment of older faculty here is an important problem. In fact, some of our senior faculty in the college are joining this campus group of older professors that has filed the age discrimination suit against the university."

Fred's interest was sparked by what Oscar had told him. He responded, "Oscar, I'd be pleased to get your analysis of this situation. I certainly won't get much help from the other older faculty in understanding this problem, given what you said about their distaste for the administration. You may be about the only 65-year-old here who'll have much to do with me," he kidded Oscar.

Oscar responded, "Fred, as deans go, I like you about as well as any. But this problem is not really a personal matter, but an institutional policy problem in my judgment. Well, I know you've got other things to do as do I, but I'll do a little field study and report back to you with some recommendations in a few weeks. Then perhaps you can better understand why the old-timers have some of the attitudes they do!"

Fred walked Oscar to the door and replied, "Thanks for your assistance and counsel. I'll look forward to seeing your report, Oscar. Good-by my friend."

"Have a good day, Dean Powers," Oscar answered, assuming a more formal air as he exited the dean's private office.

BACKGROUND

Dr. Oscar Kratz has been a faculty member of the management department at Evergreen State University for nearly 24 years and is approaching retirement. Having had both business and academic experience before he joined the faculty at Evergreen and after rising to the full professor rank 20 years ago, Dr. Kratz is sometimes kidded about having "seen it all" and "having survived" six deans of the business school in his tenure at Evergreen.

Dr. Fred Powers came to Evergreen as dean of the school of business two years ago. Dean Powers met Oscar when Powers was interviewing for the deanship, but the source of their personal relationship was their membership in the same church. Dean Powers and Dr. Kratz visit with each other at school several times a month and have become good friends.

Evergreen State University is a comprehensive institution with about 21,000 students. Evergreen began as a state teacher's college and gained university status about 30 years ago. With the designation as a university, the institution began expansion of both undergraduate and graduate offerings and now offers programs in many diverse fields and grants academic degrees through the doctorate in several areas, including business administration. The school of business has over 100 full-time faculty members in six academic departments.

Although the overall university enrollment has been relatively stable in the last 15 years, the size of the graduate programs has increased somewhat with a corresponding reduction in the size of the undergraduate student body. University resources have shifted markedly over time to provide greater support for master's and doctoral degree programs and for research and scholarly activities.

THE INTERVIEWING PROGRAM

In preparing for his investigation, Dr. Kratz had talked with several older friends on the faculty and with retirees. These general conversations tended to suggest that the problem maybe related to the changing objectives of the university since about 1965. Dr. Kratz decided to survey a cross-section of older faculty who had been in the business school for at least 25 years. To accomplish this, he formulated the following questions to guide his interviews with the participating professors:

1. When did you first join the staff at Evergreen State University?

2. When you were hired, what did you believe were the organizational objectives of the business school at ESU?

3. When you were hired, what did you understand would be necessary for you to do *(a)* advance in academic rank and *(b)* receive increases in salary at ESU? Did you do this? Has your advancement been satisfactory?

4. Since you were hired, have the objectives of the organization changed? If so, when and how?

5. How did you learn about this change of objectives?

6. What were you then told you would have to do (1) to advance in academic rank and (2) to receive increases in salary at ESU?

7. What do you believe are the current organizational objectives of the business school at ESU?

8. Do you believe that you have been treated fairly as a faculty member of the business school at ESU? Why or why not?

Five faculty members who represented a good cross-section of the senior faculty of the business school were selected by Dr. Kratz to be interviewed. Each of the professors had an academic specialty in a different discipline.

Dr. Franks

The first interview was with Dr. Franks, who disclosed the following information. He was hired in September of 1964 as a part-time instructor, and, in the fall of 1965 he accepted a full-time appointment. In 1970, after the completion of his PhD, he was rehired as an associate professor and promoted to a professor in 1975.

When Dr. Franks was employed, he was led to believe that the major objective of ESU was teaching both graduate and undergraduate students and that community service was a strong secondary objective. He also believed that to advance in salary and rank he only had to be a good teacher and serve the business community through speeches, consulting, and building good relationships for ESU. The record showed that he did a good job in both areas. Dr. Franks believes his advancement in rank was satisfactory, but not his advancement in salary.

In 1965, the administration decided that all professional schools should seek accreditation. Dr. Franks was informed that, if he expected to advance in rank and salary, he had to complete his PhD, which he did. By 1975, Dr. Franks had come to believe that community service was now the primary objective of the school and that service had become almost as important as teaching. No one told him this officially, but it just filtered through the organization by word of mouth. Dr. Franks was excellent in community service work and devoted a vast amount of his time to it.

Dr. Franks recalled that in 1970 the vice president of academic affairs addressed the faculty of the business school and advised them that research and publication was to be a third objective and that it was necessary for accreditation by the American Association of Collegiate Schools of Business (AACSB). Dr. Franks understood that publication meant anything that got the name of the school before whomever would evaluate Evergreen State for accreditation. He said that this changed with the passage of time to sponsored research and publication in major learned journals. He believes that the university's change from service to research has robbed him of a successful career at ESU. To back up his case, he points to numerous new members of the business faculty who are paid twice as much as he.

Dr. Franks believes teaching, service, and research are said to be equal, but this has constantly changed and that the administration has not been consistent relative to the value of each promotion and salary increases. Also, he believes that the administration has not been consistent in evaluating the various types of research and publication. Dr. Franks believes that, relative to organization objectives, the organization could have been fairer in faculty evaluations if it had stated objectives as part of the written organization policy. Also, objectives should have been "phased in," thereby allowing older faculty to change as objectives changed.

If Dr. Franks had it all to do over, he would have stopped devoting time to community service activities when they were no longer of value for salary increases. Instead, he would have devoted his time to activities that would have helped him to become an officer in a national academic association where he felt he would have had easier access to journal publication.

Professor Battle

The second interview was with Professor Battle, who was hired in September of 1955 as an assistant professor. In 1960, he was promoted to associate professor and became chairman of his department, a position he held until 1985. In 1965, he was promoted to professor and he served as interim dean from September 1980 until September 1981.

When Professor Battle was employed, there did not appear to be any carefully defined goals at the university or in the business school, other than to teach undergraduate students. When hired he was led to believe that to advance his salary and rank he would have to do an outstanding teaching job. He believes that he did this and that his advancement in rank was satisfactory, but that his increases in salary were not.

According to Professor Battle, the objectives changed in 1960 when a new president was appointed. Teaching remained a major goal, but the main objectives became development of an effective administrative structure to accommodate enrollment growth and the improvement of the academic programs at ESU. This shift in objectives was discussed in administrative meetings and written information was available to all administrators. With this change of objectives, being a good administrator was added to being a good teacher as a requirement for advancement for faculty who held administrative appointments. This expectation was discussed in regular meetings with the president and the dean of the business school.

However, according to Professor Battle, objectives continued to change at ESU. In 1963, the development of a solid master's degree in business administration became an important objective, as did accreditation by the AASCB. By 1970, community service had become a definite objective, and in 1975, research and publication became identified as a major mission. Professor Battle felt he was generally informed of the changing goals in meeting and in memos and letters. He still believed that advancement in rank and salary depended on good teaching and administrative service to the university.

Today, Professor Battle believes that the major objective at ESU is to become a leading educational institution through research and publication. He believes there is less emphasis on teaching at the bachelor and master levels, but more at the PhD level.

Professor Battle believes that he has been treated fairly relative to rank but not relative to salary, as pay increases were not adequate for what he achieved administratively. He believes that his administrative duties were so great that time was not available to do the more financially rewarding activities of research and publication. If he had to do it all over, he would have obtained a doctorate, which would have enabled him to advance further in both administrative rank and salary.

Professor Battle also thinks that the university could have done a better job of adjusting objectives to available funds, and that the school of business has put programs into effect before it had the funds to accomplish them. This has prevented existing faculty from getting deserved wage increases, because available funds had to be spent for new higher paid faculty.

Professor Little

Professor Little was hired as an instructor in September of 1965 on a temporary basis, because he operated his own business (which he has continued throughout his career at ESU.) In 1972, Professor Little was promoted to assistant professor and holds that rank today. He believes that he was hired only to teach students in his area of his expertise. In his first years at ESU, he never thought much about rank or salary since he considered his appointment to be temporary.

Professor Little believes the objectives of the business school started changing in 1975 when a new dean was hired. The reorientation was toward improving the degree of sophistication of the entire college and toward emphasizing research and publication. He found out about these changes in objectives through his annual evaluations by his department chairman. Over time, he believes the importance of research and publication has increased and the importance of teaching has declined. Rank and salary continued to be of minor importance to him since he received substantial income from his business. He believes that the current organizational objective of the business school is to improve its image through scholarly research. Professor Little believes that he has been treated fairly in rank, but that his salary should have increased more than it has. He believes that the attitude of the older faculty toward ESU would have been improved if they had been better paid in comparison with new faculty. If he had it to do over, he would have tried to obtain a PhD in his field.

Dr. Strock

Dr. Strock was hired in July 1965 as a full professor and department chairman. In September 1966, he was promoted to a director-level position in the dean's office, administering management training. He remained in this position until 1975, when he elected to give up his administrative position so he could devote more time to his consulting practice. When he was hired in 1965, he was definitely told by the president and the dean that the objectives of the school of business were changing from just teaching to greater community service and achieving accreditation by the AASCB at both the undergraduate and graduate levels. He was told that to advance in salary he would have to do a good job of teaching and an outstanding job of community service. Dr. Strock believes he did both of these and that his salary increases were adequate until about 1980, when they became almost nonexistent.

Dr. Strock believes the objectives of the business school changed again in 1975, when a new dean was hired. They changed from concern about accreditation and teaching to that of becoming a major research and publication institution with an outstanding PhD program. From this date to the present, the thinks the objectives have continued to deemphasize teaching and stress research and publication. Dr. Strock says he learned of this gradually through general observation of who was hired at what salary and rank, who was promoted, who received tenure, and from memos and letters from various administrative levels within the organization. By about 1986 or 1987, it had become obvious that to receive equitable wage increases, the faculty member would need to publish in an ever-changing group of "acceptable" publications or do research of an "acceptable" nature. What was an acceptable publication or research activity seemed to change with who evaluated it and who did it. And with frequent changes in administration, the expectations and standards were always uncertain.

Dr. Strock believes the current organizational objective of the business school is to gain national recognition as a top research and publication institution with a doctoral program that produces a sizable number of capable graduates. Whether he was treated fairly, the answer is both "yes" and "no." Yes, he knew what was happening but chose to stay and not to devote his time to research and publication. No, the criteria for the type of research and publication needed for pay increases was constantly changing. Many, if not most, of the faculty did not know what was acceptable from year to year. Also, until about 1988, no serious attempt was made to fairly evaluate the faculty. When an evaluation system was installed, the recommendations of the department chairmen who did the evaluation might or might not be accepted.

If Dr. Strock had it to do over, he either would have reduced his consulting activities and devoted more time to research and publication or have sought other employment.

Dr. Morgan

The final ESU interview was with Dr. Morgan, who was hired in September 1957 as an instructor, promoted to assistant professor in 1960, and to associate professor in 1965. While on the faculty, Dr. Morgan completed his PhD in 1970. He served as chairman of his department from January 1980 to September 1984. When he was hired in 1957, Dr. Morgan believed that the major objective of the business school was to provide a practical business administration education for undergraduate students. He also believed that a second objective was community service, such as consulting with local business organizations and participating in various local and statewide business activities. Dr. Morgan stated that the president of ESU in 1965 believed that the business school was to be the "flagship" of the university as it grew and developed in size and strength.

When Dr. Morgan was hired, he was led to believe that, if he did a good job of teaching and was of service to the business community, he would advance in rank and salary. Dr. Morgan thinks that he did both of these and that his salary increased at an acceptable rate until about 1970, when scholarly research and publication began to replace teaching as the major objective of the university. He feels he advanced in rank at an equitable rate until 1965, when he made associate professor.

Dr. Morgan believes the objectives of the business school and the university have changed several times since he was hired in 1957. In the middle 1960s, growth in physical plant and the development of new programs were added as major objectives. Then, starting in the middle 1970s, scholarly research and publication replaced teaching and service as the major objective of the business school. Dr. Morgan says that he found out about these changes through the grapevine and that there was little formal communication.

He does not recall being told anything very specific regarding advancement in rank and salary until 1985, when this was first put in writing. At this time the scholarly research and publication requirement for advancement was first formally explained to the business school faculty.

Dr. Morgan feels that the current organizational objective of the business school is to buy faculty who have done and will do research and publication, and that teaching is of little importance for advancement in salary and rank. He believes that he was treated fairly until 1965, when he became an associate professor, but not since this date.

If Dr. Morgan had it to do over and if he had known about the changing objectives earlier, he would have moved to a school where teaching and service were more important.

THE REPORT TO THE DEAN

At the completion of the five interviews, Dr. Kratz had gained much information about the perceptions, opinions, and attitudes of the older faculty members of the college. Some of what he was told he had anticipated, although several points were new to him. The comments and feelings of the professors he interviewed were, for the most part, consistent. While each of the professors had his own individual concerns over his career progress, they consistently reflected some negative attitudes about their treatment, advancement, and status as faculty members at Evergreen State University.

Certainly Dr. Kratz could understand why the older faculty members were not satisfied with the way they have been dealt with over the years. But his assignment now was to prepare the report for the dean, to help him better appreciate the situation and to provide some recommendations for solving this human resource problem and preventing its recurrence. He poured himself a cup of coffee, sat down at his desk, and began his task.

Section G

Compensation and Benefits

37 *Jergins Department Store (A)*[*]

Jergins is a well-recognized retail department store operating nearly 50 stores in various cities throughout the Southeast. By decentralizing its operations, Jergins focuses its attention on customer service. Management at the store level is responsible for supplying merchandise and services that reflect the tastes and needs of its local community. Each local store's management team consists of a general store manager, several department buyers, and department managers. (Job descriptions for these positions are shown in Exhibit 1.)

Mr. Harvey Hampton is the general store manager of Jergins' Coral Gables store. Harvey has been with the company for 14 years, all spent in the Miami area Jergins' stores. He began as a salesclerk in the shoe department of the downtown Miami store. Later, Harvey became the men's department manager there. He rapidly rose through the ranks. Harvey was promoted to department buyer and then quickly to the general store manager at the Coral Gables store.

Mr. Hampton believes that to best serve the customer you must begin with good salesclerks. He attempts to maintain a "one big happy family" atmosphere. This is attempted despite the fact that there are some 70 employees at the Coral Gables store. As is the case in most retail stores, many of the store's employees are part-timers. This fills the company's needs for flexible schedules and is usually well suited to local students seeking employment. Fortunately, the store never lacks for employees because of the close proximity of the University of Miami. One such student, Bruce Stillwell, was hired four years ago by Mr. Bill Johnson, the men's department buyer. Over the past nine months some things have changed. Both Bruce and Mr. Johnson have noticed a shift in attitudes. The family atmosphere, which Mr. Hampton now is trying to develop storewide, no longer prevails in the men's department.

---

* This case was prepared by Professor George E. Stevens, Kent State University, and Mark E. Nugent, University of Central Florida.

EXHIBIT 1 Selected Job Descriptions

Store Positions

General store manager. Responsible for effective and efficient operation of the local store. Reviews departmental performance and staff support positions. Interfaces with the community and acts as figurehead in representing the company.

Department buyer. Responsible for locating, acquiring, and selling goods desired by the community. Directly responsible for staffing and operations within assigned department. Frequently travels to buying shows and must deal directly with various vendors. Must also coordinate advertising with other local stores and make arrangements with local media. May be responsible for opening and closing store on a rotating basis.

Department manager. Responsible for day-to-day operation of department, including weekly scheduling of salesclerks. Must maintain sufficient salesclerk coverage on the sales floor at all times. May be responsible for opening and closing store on a rotating basis. Must maintain accurate inventory counts. Keep records of all merchandise sold at other prices than at it was originally marked (markdowns). Must effectively display currently advertised merchandise in high traffic areas. May also be required to maintain some level of selling record.

Sales clerk. Responsible for meeting the customer and providing selection assistance where possible. Must effectively use the cash register and be able to correctly handle money.

For Bruce, the part-time job he had had now expanded well beyond the responsibilities of a part-time salesclerk. As a current student at the university, he had hoped to maintain a balance between his schoolwork and a job that was not too demanding. Unfortunately, the store was doing extremely well and there was a need for hard-working, dedicated employees who would not only work during the regular Monday–Friday schedule but would also be available for Saturday assignments. The burden of additional hours and increased responsibility threatened his ability to maintain an acceptable grade point average *and* perform well at work.

In January of 1990, Bruce felt really tired. He sat down and figured out just how many hours he had devoted to the store. Over the period of August 1989 until December 1989, he discovered, he had been working an average of 50 to 55 hours a week. No wonder he had to drop those two finance classes during the fall semester! Bruce knew that the problem was directly attributable to the fact that the men's department had been without a replacement for the manager. During the period cited above, the manager's duties were performed almost entirely by Bruce and another salesclerk. He went to Mr. Hampton asking for either a promotion to department manager or reduction in hours, but Mr. Hampton refused. Mr. Hampton told Bruce that they needed him badly, but a replacement manager would be assigned. Mr. Hampton conceded that he could get all the student help they wanted, but they could not always get *reliable* workers. When Bruce continued to badger him, Mr. Hampton told the department's buyer to make Bruce understand that the store could require Bruce to work as many hours as it wished. When Bruce continued to complain, the buyer gave him a big surprise. He terminated Bruce right in mid-complaint one day. Bruce wanted to file a complaint with someone or some agency—he did not care whom. No one should be required to work excessive hours, even with pay! Bruce believed that overtime should be voluntary.

Discussion Questions

1. Who's correct regarding overtime?
2. What recourse does an employee have if he or she feels that he or she is being required to work too many hours?

---

*38 Karl Ranston's Problem (A)**

Karl Ranston was supervisor of respiratory therapy at Silvertown Municipal Hospital, located in a community of 11,000. Though he worked at the local hospital, Ranston was paid and actually employed by Breathing Care Services, Inc., a contract company providing respiratory therapy personnel and equipment to hospitals nationwide. Breathing Care Services' headquarters was in Boston, Massachusetts.

Ranston reported to Russ Bilderford, area manager. Bilderford was in charge of overseeing Breathing Care's contracts with hospitals in the northern part of the state.

When Ranston began working in Silvertown on December 28, 1988, two full-time certified respiratory therapy technicians reported to him. Karl was a working supervisor. Besides performing administrative duties, he gave patients various types of breathing treatments, obtained blood gas samples, set up respirators as needed, and performed many other tasks that a registered respiratory therapist would do. Karl estimated that he spent 75 to 80 percent of his time on non-supervisory activities.

Ranston had an undergraduate chemistry degree from a state university in Minnesota. Having worked as an orderly and a respiratory therapy aide while going through school, he decided to pursue a career in health care. He was accepted in a two-year respiratory therapy program affiliated with the Mayo Clinic in Rochester, Minnesota. Shortly after finishing this program, he passed an exam to become a registered respiratory therapist.

---

*This case was prepared by Professor Margaret F. Karsten, University of Wisconsin, Platteville.

Karl liked his job at Silvertown Municipal Hospital. Things went well until March 1989 when Gloria Bowman, a respiratory therapy technician, resigned. Russ Bilderford said that he could not authorize Karl to hire a replacement. This meant that Karl probably would have to work more overtime hours, for which he was not compensated. Being an amiable sort and dedicated to his job as well, Karl didn't mind working overtime occasionally. Whenever a patient had to be put on a respirator, which was about once a month, Karl could expect to work around 70 hours a week. He thought that was somewhat excessive, given his salary that averaged slightly more than $9 an hour. At that rate, with no overtime pay, the technician reporting to him could easily take home more money than he did. When Karl talked to his boss about these concerns, Russ just shrugged his shoulders and said, "You're a salaried employee. That means we don't have to pay you for overtime hours. You're expected to work overtime."

In June 1989, Karl Ranston received a promotion of sorts. Silvertown Municipal Hospital recently had affiliated with Leadville Municipal Hospital. Ranston now was in charge of respiratory care in both hospitals. The new organization chart for the combined respiratory care department is shown in Exhibit 1.

Ranston continued to perform nonsupervisory duties 75 to 80 percent of the time. He did not receive a raise and still worked many overtime hours, because his department now had to serve two separate facilities.

Karl again tried to discuss his compensation concerns with Russ. It soon became obvious that Bilderford didn't want to hear about the problem.

EXHIBIT 1 Organization Chart

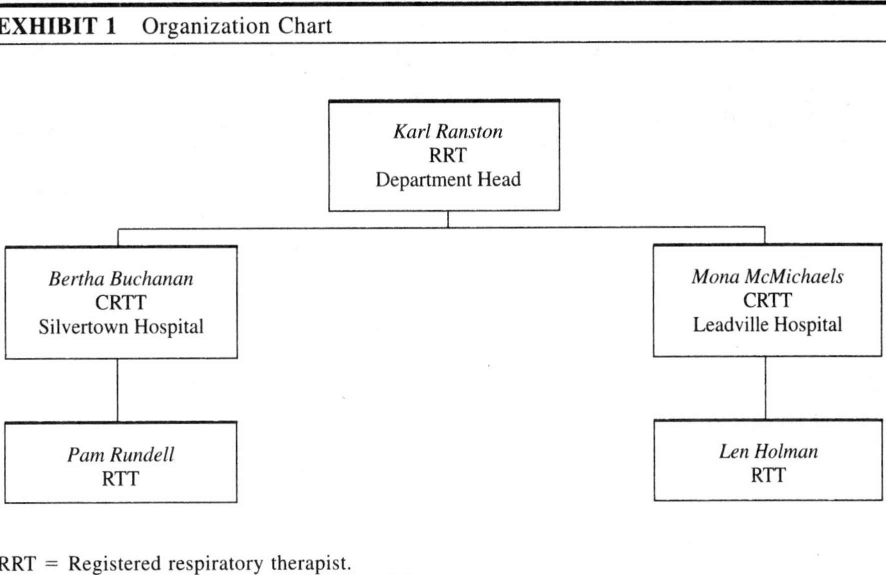

RRT = Registered respiratory therapist.
CRTT = Certified respiratory therapy technician.
RTT = Respiratory therapy technician

Since no help from his boss was forthcoming, Karl decided to call his friend, Fran Magan, who taught personnel courses at Silvertown State University. He thought she might be able to give him some advice. She suggested that he become familiar with a law called the Fair Labor Standards Act and loaned him a book explaining that law.

Discussion Questions

1. What are the issues in this case?
2. Explain, in detail, the parts of the Fair Labor Standards Act with which Karl must become familiar. (What does Karl need to know?)
3. Critique Russ Bilderford's statement, "You're a salaried employee. That means we don't have to pay you overtime."
4. What should Karl do now?

---

*Karl Ranston's Problem (B)**

After studying the Fair Labor Standards Act, Karl still was unsure about whether he was legally entitled to overtime. Some of the examples in the book Fran loaned him just didn't seem to apply in his situation. One helpful item he did find was the address of the nearest office of the Wage and Hour Division of the U.S. Department of Labor. He wrote a letter to that office, and was asked to complete an Employment Information Form (Exhibit 2). As a result of his action, Compliance Officer Dolores A. Bern was sent to investigate Breathing Care Services, Inc.'s operations at Silvertown and Leadville Municipal Hospitals. (See Exhibit 1.) After the investigation, Karl was asked to provide Dolores with a copy of his job description and a list of hours worked from the week of January 2, 1989, through the week of June 30, 1990 (Exhibits 3 and 4, respectively). Dolores told Karl he would be notified of the outcome of the investigation.

Discussion Question

1. Do you think Karl is legally entitled to overtime pay or not? Justify your answer.

EXHIBIT 1

U.S. DEPARTMENT OF LABOR Employment Standards Administration Wage and Hours Division

Date: May 23, 1990

Reply to Attn. of: Dolores A. Bern
(212) 264-5221

Subject: Visit by Wage and Hour Compliance Officer

To: Breathing Care Services, Inc.
c/o Silvertown Municipal Hospital
1000 11th Street
Silvertown, CA 96435

Scheduled visit to begin:
Date: June 14, 1990
Tuesday
Time: 8:30 AM

The Wage and Hour Division is responsible for the administration and enforcement of a number of Federal laws involving labor standards as outlined in the enclosed pamphlet, "The Wage and Hour Representative Is Here."

This is to advise you that I will call at your establishment on the date and at the time shown above to determine compliance with the labor standards laws which may apply to your business. Every effort will be made to conduct this assignment expeditiously and with a minimum of inconvenience to you and your employees. Please note that I will initially need to meet with someone regarding the background of your business (including annual dollar volume of your business and pay practices). Subsequently I will need to review payrolls and time records for all your employees for the previous two years from the date of my visit.

If you or your designated representative or the records mentioned above will not be available on the date and at the time and place indicated above, please let me know as soon as possible so that we can work out some other arrangement. Likewise, since it may be necessary for me to return on subsequent days in that week and/or the next few weeks to finish my check, it is essential that you notify me at 264-5221 should you have potential time conflicts. Please prepare a list of your current employees showing the following information:

Name Address Phone No. Birth Date Starting Date Job Function Pay Rate

Sincerely,

Compliance Officer

EXHIBIT 2 Employment Information Form

U.S. DEPARTMENT OF LABOR EMPLOYMENT STANDARDS ADMINISTRATION WAGE AND HOUR DIVISION	EMPLOYMENT INFORMATION FORM

This report is authorized by Section 11 of the Fair Labor Standards Act. While you are not required to respond, submission of this information is necessary for the Division to schedule any compliance action. Your identity will be kept confidential to the maximum extent possible under existing law.

1. PERSON SUBMITTING INFORMATION

A. Name (Print first name, middle initial, and last name)
Mr. Karl Ranston
Miss
Mrs.

B. Date May 31, 1983

C. Telephone number (Or no. where you can be reached) (214) 843-9435

D. Address (Number, Street, Apt. No.)
338 Pleasant Hill Drive
(City, County, State, ZIP Code)
Silvertown, CA 96435

E. Check one of these boxes
[X] Present employee of establishment   [ ] Former employee of establishment   [ ] Job Applicant   [ ] Other ________ (Specify: relative, union, etc.)

2. ESTABLISHMENT INFORMATION

A. Name of Establishment
Breathing Care Services, Inc.

B. Telephone Number
1-800-256-5031

C. Address of establishment: (Number, Street)
9 Militia Drive
(City, County, State, ZIP Code)
Boston, Massachusetts 02173

D. Estimate number of employees
about 500

E. Does the firm have branches? [X] Yes [ ] No [ ] Don't know
If "Yes," name one or two locations: Central Region, Arlington Heights, IL

F. Nature of establishment's business: (For example; school, farm, hospital, hotel, restaurant, shoe store, wholesale drugs, manufactures stoves, coal mine, construction, trucking, etc.)
contracting service for hospitals

G. If the establishment has a Federal Government or federally assisted contract, check the appropriate box(es).
[ ] Furnishes goods   [ ] Furnishes services   [ ] Performs construction

H. Does establishment ship goods to or receive goods from other States?
[X] Yes [ ] No [ ] Don't know

3. EMPLOYMENT INFORMATION

(Complete A, B, C, D, E, & F if present or former employee of establishment; otherwise complete F only)

A. Period employed (month, year)
From: 12-28-81
To: present
(If still live there, state present)

B. Date of birth if under 19 or if information concerns age discrimination
Month ________ Day ________ Year ________

C. Give your job title and describe briefly the kind of work you do
Department Head of Respiratory Therapy
(See attached sheet)

EXHIBIT 2 Employment Information Form *(concluded)*

D. Method of payment

$ ________ per year
(Rate) (Hour, week, month, etc.)

E. Enter in the boxes below the hours you usually work each day and each week (less time off for meals)

M	T	W	T	F	S	S	TOTAL
2	12	10	12	0	9.5	10	55.5

F. CHECK THE APPROPRIATE BOX(ES) AND EXPLAIN BRIEFLY IN THE SPACE BELOW the employment practices which you believe violate the Wage and Hour laws. (If you need more space use an additional sheet of paper and attach it to this form.)

- [ ] Does not pay the minimum wage
- [X] Does not pay proper overtime
- [ ] Men and women perform equal work but do not get equal pay
- [ ] Discrimination against employee or applicant (40-65 years of age) because of age

Approximate date of alleged discrimination

____

- [ ] Does not pay prevailing wage determination for Federal Government or federally assisted contract
- [ ] Discharged employee because of wage garnishment (explain below)
- [ ] Excessive deduction from wages because of wage garnishment (explain below)
- [ ] Employs minors under minimum age for job
- [ ] Other (explain below)

Though I am a salaried employee and have had professional training, I only devote about 20 - 25% of my work time to supervisory activities. I directly supervise two employees and indirectly supervise two other full time employees

G. Describe briefly the kind of work you do.

I perform the following types of respiratory therapy treatments: chest physiotherapy, hand held nebulizer, incentive spirometry, ultrasonic nebulizer. I perform and analyze arterial blood gas tests, pulmonary function tests, and electroencephalograms. In addition, I set up holter monitors, cold steamers, croup tents, and oxygen. I also set up home oxygen equipment.

My supervisory duties include scheduling employee hours, ordering respiratory therapy equipment, and preparing weekly and monthly reports of numbers of treatments given and types of equipment used. I also attend infection control meetings, department head meetings, and respiratory therapy committee meetings.

(NOTE: If you think it would be difficult for us to locate the establishment or where you live, give directions or attach map.)

COMPLAINT TAKEN BY:

D.A.B.

EXHIBIT 3 Job Description

Title:

Supervisor/respiratory therapist

Definition:

A supervisor/respiratory therapist is defined as an individual providing supervision, direction, and control to the management function of the cardiorespiratory department assigned to and employed at contracted healthcare facilities.

Education requirements:

Individual must be a high school graduate and a registered respiratory therapist (RRT), or be a certified respiratory therapy technician (CRTT), or have advanced training in cardiopulmonary care.

General duties:

In addition to being able to provide all levels of technical skills required of a respiratory therapy technician/therapist (attached) the supervisor/respiratory therapist provides the following:

1. Determines equipment and staffing needs for the shifts or services being supervised. Plans, schedules, and makes determinations of priorities of aspects of therapy and administrative duties.
2. Organizes work load in logical sequences using personal experience and management tools to rate, rank, and modify tasks.
3. Directs the specific tasks by determining the most efficient use of personnel, equipment, and work load.
4. Controls the service by evaluating results of procedures performed. Makes the necessary modifications in the methods used for distribution of services.

Description of Specific Tasks Performed

1. In addition to general supervisory duties, this person specifically performs the following:
   a. Ensures the quality and efficiency of the diagnostic and therapeutic procedures performed by evaluating results of tests in accordance with quality control standards.
   b. Confers with various department directors in need of respiratory therapy services with regard to type, quantity, time, etc.
   c. Participates in the review of care, with the medical director, and shares in studies and data gathering.
   d. Participates in JCAH and medicare audits.
2. Plans and organizes the activities of the respiratory therapy department.
   a. Assists in planning additions to or changes of type of equipment including evaluation of new devices.
   b. Assists in planning the manpower requirements and appropriate wage factors to ensure the maintenance of an efficient and dependable work force.
   c. Plans and implements continuing education programs. Makes presentations on current concepts of cardiopulmonary care to technicians, physicians, nurses, and other paramedical personnel.

EXHIBIT 3 *(continued)*

d. Establishes inventory control of department equipment and supplies.

e. Maintains department files and records. Provides monthly and weekly summaries of department activities. Keeps statistical data for medicare and JCAH audits.

f. Confers regularly with Medical Director concerning the clinical practices and procedures performed by the department. Participates in clinical experimentation and evaluations.

3. Supervises the respiratory therapy department personnel.

a. Is responsible for hiring, orientation, evaluating, training, assigning, and ensuring the efficiency of the technical staff.

b. Provides counseling to subordinates as requested or required. Uses performance appraisal for review.

c. May terminate subordinates as per hospital and department policies.

d. Oversees facilities to ensure that safety precautions are observed.

Title:

Registered respiratory therapist

Definition:

A registered respiratory therapist is defined as an individual providing therapeutic and diagnostic respiratory care for inpatients and outpatients at contracted healthcare facilities and who has been accredited by the National Board for Respiratory Therapy (NBRT) as registered.

Education requirements:

Individual must have successfully completed formal training in respiratory therapy through a program approved by the Joint Review Committee for Respiratory Therapy Education (JRCRTE).

Description of duties:

The registered respiratory therapist possesses sufficient training and experience to perform respiratory care procedures, as prescribed, with supervision in accordance with department policies and approved procedures. The registered respiratory therapist may also be called upon for expert advice in matters of cardiopulmonary care. The respiratory therapist will share in the clinical evaluation of care. The respiratory therapist will share in the clinical evaluation of care, including the establishment of therapeutic objectives and the review of care.

1. Therapeutic Cases

a. Administer therapeutic gases, such as oxygen, as prescribed, in accordance with accepted procedures.

b. Monitor bulk oxygen systems.

2. Treatments

a. Administer positive pressure breathing treatments (IPPB) as prescribed.

b. Administer prescribed medications, including bronchodilators, via inhalation.

c. Administer humidified therapeutic gases, including high-humidity therapy as prescribed.

d. Induce from the patient a sputum specimen for cytological or bacterial examination.

EXHIBIT 3 *(continued)*

e. Perform incentive spirometry treatments as prescribed.

f. Perform bronchial drainage and chest physiotherapy as outlined in department procedures and policies.

3. Critical Care

a. Establishes, maintains, monitors, and evaluates continuous ventilatory support. The respiratory therapist may share in decisions affecting continuous ventilatory support based on clinical findings.

b. Participates in cardiopulmonary resuscitation.

c. Performs airway care, including trachea bronchial aspiration, and other procedures aimed at establishing and/or maintaining natural and artificial airways as outlined in the department procedures and policies.

d. Assists in transport of critical patients as required.

4. Diagnostics

a. Performs sampling and analysis of arterial blood as described in the department procedures and policies.

b. Performs pulmonary function tests in accordance with department procedures and policies.

c. Performs and/or assists in special diagnostic procedures as required by the department.

5. General Duties

a. Performs regular equipment maintenance, preparation, cleaning, and sterilization.

b. Is responsible for documenting procedures in the medical record and department files. Assists in the quality assurance program within the department and the hospital as described by department procedures and policies.

EXHIBIT 4 Hours of Work while Employed by Breathing Care Services, Inc.

Week Starting	*Regular Hours*	*Overtime Hours*	*Call Hours*
01/02/89	40	10.50	24
01/09/89	40	4.25	36
01/16/89	40	3.00	48
01/23/89	40	3.00	36
01/30/89	40	16.50	48
02/06/89	40	3.25	36
02/13/89	40	6.00	48.50
02/20/89	40	9.50	67.50
02/27/89	40	21.75	58.00
03/06/89	40	27.50	60.00
03/13/89	40	9.00	61.00
03/20/89	40	13.50	78.75
03/27/89	40	21.00	75.50
04/03/89	40	26.50	72.50

EXHIBIT 4 *(continued)*

Week Starting	*Regular Hours*	*Overtime Hours*	*Call Hours*
04/10/89	40	10.00	64.00
04/17/89	40	4.25	62.75
04/24/89	40	0.00	60.00
05/01/89	40	8.50	48.00
05/08/89	40	0.25	50.00
05/15/89	40	17.75	37.00
05/22/89	40	28.50	73.25
05/29/89	38.50	0.00	38.00
06/05/89	30.00 + 10.00 (holiday)	0.00	0.00
06/12/89	40	4.50	60.00
06/19/89	40	13.00	51.50
06/26/89	40	7.00	51.00
07/03/89	40	7.00	39.00
07/10/89	37.00 + 10.00 (holiday)	0.00	41.75
07/17/89	40	29.00	38.50
07/24/89	40	25.50	12.00
07/31/89	40	4.50	12.00
08/07/89	40	7.75	23.50
08/14/89	40	3.50	0.00
08/21/89	40	4.25	14.00
08/28/89	40	3.00	14.00
09/04/89	40	4.00	0.00
09/11/89	34.50 + 8.00 (holiday)	0.00	0.00
09/18/89	40	2.00	0.00
09/25/89	40	9.50	28.00
10/02/89	22	0.00	0.00
10/09/89	29	0.00	0.00
10/16/89	40	13.00	65.50
10/23/89	40	8.50	13.50
10/30/89	40	12.00	21.00
11/06/89	40	6.25	13.50
11/13/89	40	19.50	28.00
11/20/89	40	17.50	27.00
11/27/89	40.2 + 8.0 (holiday unpaid)	0.25	73.25
12/04/89	40	6.50	27.50
12/11/89	40	16.50	56.50
12/18/89	40	10.00	43.50
12/25/89	28.5 + 8.0	0.00	0.00
01/01/90	24 + 16 (holiday)	0.00	0.00
01/08/90	40	2.50	0.00
01/15/90	40	4.25	28.00

EXHIBIT 4 *(concluded)*

Week Starting	Regular Hours	Overtime Hours	Call Hours
01/22/90	40	7.50	22.00
01/29/90	40	23.50	70.00
02/05/90	40	19.50	55.00
02/12/90	40	15.00	72.00
02/19/90	40	26.00	83.00
02/26/90	40	17.00	71.50
03/05/90	40	8.00	49.00
03/12/90	40	7.50	58.50
03/19/90	40	17.50	59.00
03/26/90	40	15.50	71.50
04/02/90	40	33.50	14.50
04/09/90	40	1.00	28.50
04/16/90	40	1.50	60.00
04/23/90	40	6.50	73.00
04/30/90	40	23.50	84.50
05/07/90	40	10.50	43.00
05/14/90	37 + 8.0 (holiday)	0.00	42.00
05/21/90	18.5 + 21.5 (vacation)	0.00	45.50
05/28/90	40	2.50	43.00
06/04/90	37.50	0.00	66.50
06/11/90	40	9.50	42.00
06/18/90	40	0.50	0.00
06/25/90	8 + 32.0 (vacation)	0.00	0.00
06/30/90	33.50	0.00	6.50

39 Salary Discrimination at Acme Manufacturing*

Joe Blankenship was trying to figure out what to do about a possible salary discrimination situation he believed he had in his plant.

Mr. Blankenship recently took over as president of Acme Manufacturing from the founder and president for 35 years, Mr. Bill George. The company was family owned and was located in a small eastern Arkansas town. It had approximately 250 employees and was the largest employer in the community. Mr. Blankenship

* This case was prepared by Professor James C. Hodgetts of Memphis State University as a basis for class discussion.

was a member of the family that owned Acme, but he had never worked for the company prior to becoming president. He had an MBA and a law degree, plus 15 years of management experience with a large manufacturing organization where he was senior vice president for human resources when he made his move to Acme.

A short time after joining Acme, Mr. Blankenship started to believe that there was considerable inequity in the pay structure for salaried employees. A discussion with the personnel director led him to believe that salaried employees' pay was very much a matter of individual bargaining with the past president. Hourly paid factory employees were not part of the problem, since they were unionized and their wages were set by collective bargaining. An examination of the salaried payroll showed that there were 25 employees, ranging in pay from that of the president to that of the receptionist. A closer examination showed that 14 of the salaried employees were female. Three of these were frontline factory supervisors and one was the personnel director. The other 10 were nonmanagement.

This examination also showed that the personnel director appeared to be underpaid, and that the three female supervisors were paid somewhat below any of the male supervisors. However, there were no similar supervisory jobs in which there were both male and female job incumbents. When asked, the personnel director said she thought the female supervisors were paid lower mainly because they were women, and Mr. George did not think that women needed as much money because they had working husbands. Also, she said she thought they were paid less because they supervised employees less-skilled than the male supervisors. However, Mr. Blankenship was not sure that this was true.

The company from which Mr. Blankenship had moved had a good job evaluation system. Although he was thoroughly familiar and capable with this compensation tool, Mr. Blankenship did not have time to make much use of this knowledge at Acme. Therefore, he decided to hire a compensation consultant from a nearby university to help him. They decided that all 25 salaried jobs should be in the job evaluation unit, that a modified ranking method of job evaluation should be used, and that the job descriptions recently completed by the personnel director were current, accurate, and usable in the study.

The job evaluation showed that there was no evidence of discrimination in the nonmanagement jobs, but that the personnel director and the three female supervisors were being underpaid relative to comparable male salaried employees.

Mr. Blankenship was not sure what to do. He knew that, if the underpaid women supervisors took the case to the local EEOC office, the company could be found guilty of female discrimination and would have[??] to pay considerable back wages. He was afraid that, if he gave these employees an immediate wage increase large enough to bring them up to where they should be, the male supervisors would be upset and the female supervisors might comprehend the total situation and want back pay. Mr. Blankenship was told that the female supervisors had never complained about the pay differences, and they probably did not know the law to any extent.

The personnel director agreed to take a sizable salary increase with no back pay, so this part of the problem was "solved." Mr. Blankenship believed he had four choices relative to the female supervisors:

1. To do nothing.
2. To gradually increase the female supervisors' salaries.
3. To increase their salaries immediately.
4. To call the three supervisors into his office, discuss the situation with them, and jointly decide what to do.

Discussion Questions

1. Does Mr. Blankenship have only four choices? Discuss.
2. What action should Mr. Blankenship take? Carefully explain.

---

40 The Aria: A Family Restaurant*

The Aria is an 80-seat, elegant Italian restaurant located off Arapaho Drive in a suburb of Boulder, Colorado. The owner, Tony Contos, was originally from southern Italy. As a young man, Tony emigrated to Chicago in the early 1950s, where he tried his hand in the entertainment industry. After an unsuccessful bout in the theater, he began a career in the restaurant business.

Having started at the bottom and worked his way up, Tony became a very well known and financially successful maître d' and restaurant manager. Tony worked in only the finest restaurants in Chicago, made a reputable name for himself, and decided to move on to greater and greener pastures.

In 1979, Tony brought his wife, Gena, and their 20-year-old son, Ricardo, to the Boulder area, where, with the money he had saved, he bought The Aria.

The first order of business was to staff the restaurant with the proper personnel. Tony wanted to bring to Boulder fine, authentic, New York-Italian cuisine and decided to call on some of the many cooks and chefs he had worked with or known in Chicago. After a number of unsuccessful tries at recruiting those he considered the best, Tony finally found a second cook named Paulo, who accepted Tony's offer to relocate and take the position of chef at The Aria. Tony had known Paulo and his wife and two daughters for several years prior to the move they all made to the Boulder area.

Tony then hired three or four other men, already from the Boulder area, to supplement the kitchen staff and to work with Tony in food preparation and cleanup. Although Tony did a great deal of the early morning preparation, including buying fresh food each day, and cooked most of the specialty dishes, Paulo was responsible for the line and the final preparation and presentation of all the food leaving the kitchen and being served to customers.

---

* This case was prepared by Matthew David Popkin, under the supervision of Professor George Stevens. All case names are disguised.

The next group hired was the service staff. Since there was to be quite a bit of tableside cooking done, Tony required that applicants possess a minimum of two years' experience in fine Continental dining room service.

Tony was most fortunate in finding qualified waiters and captains in the immediate area. Most of the men hired were young, in their early 20s to late 30s. All had a reasonable amount of experience in fine dining service and tableside cooking. Of the eight men hired to be captain-and-waiter teams, most held either full-time professional positions or were in the process of completing their educations at local colleges and universities.

As in many restaurants, there exists a fair amount of rivalry or even open hostility between the kitchen crew and service personnel. The back of the "house"—the kitchen—and the front—the dining area—can become battlegrounds for the most heated debates in any fine restaurant. The Aria was no exception and, within a relatively short time, the battle raged nightly.

The kitchen personnel felt that the waiters made much more money than they deserved, for, if it were not for the kitchen, they would be serving frozen dinners. It irritated the cooks working in the hot, stuffy, smelly kitchen to hear the captains and waiters discuss how much money they made in tips each night. It seemed very unfair to them that, although they worked the hardest and longest and with much more expertise, the waiters made considerably more income than they.

The waiters' rebuttal to the kitchen crew's outrage was that anyone could chop an onion and wash a glass. They felt themselves far superior, both personally and professionally.

The fact that all but two of the eight waiters and captains were part-timers in the restaurant business greatly affected the way they perceived their current positions. Many had aspirations of greater things for themselves, considering their jobs as waiters as transitory in nature.

The effects of this blatant rivalry often culminated in sharp words and loud-voiced objections to the most mundane suggestions from either side. Tricks and pranks were played, with the opposing teams going into their neutral corners only long enough to regain momentum and mount a counterattack. Tony, who in his long restaurant career had witnessed this rivalry countless numbers of times, seemed to feel that it was all in a day's work. The business flourished despite the pettiness and childishness, and Tony felt it better to leave well enough alone.

Tony insisted that all dissension and discussion be brought to him as arbitrator so he could have the final word. It seemed to the kitchen crew that all too often, especially on extremely busy nights, Tony sided with the front of the house. It seemed to the service personnel that Tony always sided with the back, and his role as arbitrator was often ignored.

The dissension and discussion carried on into the next day, in the form of employee meals, of which Paulo was in charge. Tony demanded that his waiters arrive at The Aria between one and two hours prior to opening to prepare the tables and side specialties and to share the evening meal with The Aria staff like a family.

These meals were often more raucous than those at a summer camp for hyperactive children. If the kitchen staff was angry with the waiters and captains, the evening meal was often barely edible. If the service personnel wanted to get back at the kitchen crew, they would bring their own dinner and segregate themselves from the rest of the restaurant's staff.

Although the teams that worked together every evening, and sometimes during the lunch hour shift, got along tremendously well and enjoyed a pleasant working relationship, there was sometimes an inordinate amount of strife between the members of the teams themselves. Tony, as maître d', owner, and general manager of all The Aria's operations, was always at the door to greet customers and seat them. As if the problems with the kitchen crew weren't bad enough, Tony would aggravate the situation by seating the larger and better parties with the older waiters and with the family men. He justified his actions with the fact that men with families had greater expenses and, therefore, needed to make as much money as possible.

This was the cause of more agitation and aggravation from the younger men, with no other dependents than themselves, who felt that the job should be done by the man who is most capable. More than once, one or two teams would be extremely busy while the others had little work of their own. On seeing the swamped teams in dire need of assistance, Tony would direct those with little work to help out. This caused a greater amount of ill feelings, because the busy teams never shared their tips with those who assisted them in their hour of need.

Though all of these personnel problems had persisted through the four years The Aria had been open for business, the rate of turnover at the small restaurant was practically nil. Most of the crew that had started with Tony remained. The probable reason for the low turnover rate, in spite of the problems encountered almost daily by the staff, was that many of these situations were considered normal by all parties involved. The crew believed that many restaurants, large and small, suffered from many of the same ailments that plagued The Aria daily.

Another major cause of aggravation for the staff of The Aria was the fact that the restaurant was a family owned and operated business, with Tony's wife, Gena, their son, Ricardo, and his wife, Buffy, all involved in the day-to-day operation of the business.

Ricardo, who before his father opened The Aria had little experience (practically none in the restaurant business), has been the greatest cause of strife for the dining room staff.

Within three years of opening the restaurant for business, Tony placed Ricardo in charge of the waiters and busmen, in the position of restaurant manager. Ricardo was put in charge of all scheduling and the hiring and training of all personnel for the dining room.

Ricardo's wife, Buffy, took care of the daily accounting along with Tony's wife, Gena. Gena was also responsible for assisting Tony in the preparation of specialty dishes and desserts, something they did quite well together. At times, when Tony and Gena were not there, Ricardo and Buffy were in complete authority at The Aria.

The waiters and captains were often offended at the orders given by Ricardo, a person whom they considered to be uneducated in the business, and showed him and his wife the greatest amount of disrespect possible—short of risking their livelihood. The lack of respect was brought on not only by Ricardo's total inexperience but was compounded by his flippant manner in the delegation of his responsibilities. Both Ricardo and Buffy were arrogant toward the dining room staff, probably because they considered themselves totally superior to the patriarch's employees.

Ricardo's parents, especially Tony, worked from daybreak until closing, while Ricardo came to work at the last possible minute and retreated at his earliest possible convenience. While the Contos usually ate a quick sandwich before shutting off The Aria's lights for the night, Ricardo and Buffy would often be seated and served by a team whose evening was over, making the kitchen crew and dining room staff work for them.

Ricardo's parents saw the disgruntled looks and overheard the comments made by many of the staff, but never took their son and daughter-in-law aside to explain the unfairness of other actions. This greatly disturbed the staff.

The staff was also bothered by personal matters in the Contos family. While his father drove a very beat-up old car, Ricardo raced around town in a brand-new foreign sports car. Ricardo was often insolent to his father in front of the staff, and sometimes even in front of The Aria's patrons.

Another problem and the cause of much grief among the staff was the religious beliefs of the Contos family. Tony, Gena, Ricardo, and Buffy were very, very religious—in fact, they called themselves "Born-Again Christians." They were always talking about how they were saved and were always, or so it seemed to the staff, trying to save and convert all "wayward souls" who came their way. It was not unusual for Gena to call members of the staff, either kitchen crew or dining room personnel, into her small office and read them scriptures from the family Bible. It was always very uncomfortable for the persons she called, for, no matter what their own personal beliefs, they could not leave without fear of offending her. An intelligent or rewarding discussion was always out of the question, due to their adamant beliefs.

It always seemed to the waiters and cooks that the Contos family's religious beliefs and business ethics were quite contradictory. Tony would often add extra bottles of wine to large parties to boost the bill. In dishes that called for veal, as described on the menu, the kitchen often substituted less-expensive pork. Ricardo, who often preached the morals of being a Born-Again Christian, carried a pistol in his coat and constantly reminded the staff of its presence. The men found this especially agitating and uncomfortable.

As in many small family owned and operated businesses, the owners always told the staff that they thought of them as family. The Contos would gather the staff and their families for traditional Thanksgiving and Christmas dinners and would often preach gospel during grace. The families of the staff would attend these functions, because they found it obligatory to assist in keeping goodwill with the Contos family. It did not raise morale to hear Buffy comment, "No, that's for the help," as she passed along items she felt were inferior.

The wives and girlfriends of the staff would often gather together in rebuttal to Buffy's feelings of superiority over them. Many times these dinners caused strife in the families of the staff whose livelihoods depended on being two-faced.

Real trouble began at The Aria almost three weeks after the fourth anniversary of the restaurant's opening. It was a very busy Thursday night. The kitchen was extremely backed up; the dining room was buzzing with activity and tempers were flaring. Jim, a very personable and competent waiter (captain) who had worked at The Aria since its inception, had a number of parties whose food was late in coming.

As was customary in situations like this, Jim went back to the kitchen to ask Paulo to speed things up, for the restaurant patrons were getting restless. Paulo, who was often surly with the waiters, especially when the kitchen was backed up, began to curse and carry on, ranting and raving at Jim.

Jim, instead of following Tony's policy of retreating and alerting Tony, returned fire with words as harsh as those of Paulo. The argument went back and forth with voices and tempers rising. Rapidly, the argument escalated from curses to threats of physical violence.

The next thing anyone knew, Jim's black tuxedo jacket was stained red. Jim had been stabbed with a small kitchen knife in his lower left side, under the rib cage. Tony appeared and ordered one of the waiters to take Jim to the hospital and everyone, including Paulo, returned to work.

Jim's wound took 11 stitches and he was told by the attending physician that he was fortunate the knife did not enter an inch higher than it did, for he probably would have left behind a widow. As upset and hurt as he was, Jim decided not to call the police, but instead waited to return to The Aria to speak with Tony.

The next day Jim sat down to speak with Tony about the events that had transpired the night before. At first Tony was very sympathetic toward Jim and told him that he would do everything possible to make it up to him. Jim told Tony that, if Paulo was not fired, he would press charges against him. Jim and Tony, both knowing that Paulo had a family and had been in trouble with the law before, did not want to cause him any grief.

Tony told Jim that he would give Paulo two weeks' notice and place him on the day shift for the remaining time. All of this was agreeable to Jim, as long as he did not have to work with Paulo ever again.

The first week passed quietly without mention of the incident by anyone. At the end of the second week, Tony approached Jim and told him that he needed to keep Paulo another week because he had not found a replacement and the restaurant was booked almost solid. Jim and the rest of the staff were all aware that Alex, the second cook at The Aria, was more than capable and qualified to step into the allegedly vacant position.

Jim began to question the sincerity of Tony's promise to fire Paulo, and he also began to wonder if there were an underlying reason for Tony's not having fired Paulo already. There were rumors to the effect that Tony had loaned Paulo a substantial amount of money, perhaps as much as $5,000.

The following day, Jim confronted Tony and Gena, asking if the real reason Paulo had not been dismissed was an outstanding loan to the Contos. They both confirmed the fact that they had loaned Paulo $5,000 and that they could not afford to lose so great an amount of money. They then asked Jim to understand their predicament and told him that they would keep Paulo on days so they would not have to work together.

Jim, a proud man, realized he had been taken. He asked Tony and Gena what they would have done if Paulo had stabbed their son Ricardo instead of him. He could not believe their reply.

Tony and Gena told Jim that had Paulo stabbed Ricardo they would immediately have called the police, pressed charges, and fired him in one breath. At the end of the week, Paulo was still in the kitchen—and Jim resigned. Jim pressed charges against Paulo, who was released on bail to await trial.

Several months have gone by. Paulo is still the chef of The Aria and Jim remains unemployed. Tony's once almost nonexistent rate of turnover is now quite high, 90 percent. In fact, only one of the original eight dining room staff is still at The Aria.

Patrons of The Aria who once dined there regularly do not feel comfortable with the new staff. They once enjoyed the "family atmosphere" of which the Contos were so proud, and the entire business has suffered from the high rate of turnover.

Those who are no longer employed at The Aria share Jim's feelings of betrayal, for their friend and cohort, and for themselves. They all believe that all the talk of religion and goodness was a front for the true concern of the Contos family—money.

Discussion Questions

1. What could have been done to curtail the dissension between the dining room and kitchen staffs?
2. Is there any validity to the notion of treating employees of any company like members of the family?
3. How do you feel about Tony's pattern of seating larger and better parties to be served by the older waiters?
4. Would the incident between Paulo and Jim have been treated differently in a larger organization?
5. Do you think money was the only factor in Tony's decision to keep Paulo?

*41 Secrid Manufacturing Company, Inc.**

(The case is a technical problem provided for solution, typical of those faced by human resource professionals. The setting is Dayton, Ohio, 199X. The task is to prepare a compensation structure for nonexempt employees of a single-plant local

* Prepared by Professor Theodore T. Herbert, Rollins College, with the assistance of Ann Moss Joyner, MBA, University of North Carolina.

firm, using the technical data provided in the case. The data consist of job titles, salary guidelines, position descriptions, an office salary survey, area wage survey from the Bureau of Labor Statistics, employee information, and the like.)

"This system is no system, Clare, and I want you take it and make some sense of it."

Rosa McMillan, junior partner of Moss and McMillan Associates, Inc., consultants to management, addressed the newest member of the consulting firm. "Here's some information on the current employees and their jobs. Your task is to find relevant market information, evaluate the process Secrid has been using to determine the compensation of its nonexempt employees, and develop a new system. Everything you need is in the library; but with this new librarian in the middle of his work in there, I don't know where things are. You're on your own. Good luck. It shouldn't take more than 10 hours—at least, that's all we can bill Secrid for. Just give me a call if you run into any major snags."

With this, she handed over a stack of papers (see Exhibits 1–5) and left Clare's office. "The first job of any good consultant," Clare thought to herself, "is to come up with an analysis of the problem and a plan for attacking that problem."

EXHIBIT 1 Job Titles

Group I	
PBX operator-receptionist	A. Peler
Order-billing clerk I	L. Parnell
Data entry operator I	P. Pendleton
Group II	
Clerical—sales administrator	J. Carr
Accounts payable clerk II	W. Thorne
Data entry operator II	T. Oehler
Clerk—Accounts payable/inventory control/traffic	S. Joyner
Group III	
Sales department secretary	D. Art, L. Level
	K. White
Payroll clerk III	B. Sellers
Maintenance supply and record clerk	R. Toler
Group IV	
Executive secretary	P. Pulley, M. Tarkington
Personnel generalist	B. Welch
Purchasing department secretary	W. Kale
Traffic and credit administrative assistant	P. Arlington
Group V	
Industrial nurse	J. Jasper

EXHIBIT 2 198X – 198(X + 1) Salary Administration Guide—Nonmanagement Salaried Employees

Secrid Manufacturing Co., Inc.

The following monthly salary guide is to be in effect from February 1, 198X, until superseded to cover nonmanagement salaried office personnel and salaried technicians in the plant and administrative offices in Dayton.

	Group I	*II*	*III*	*IV*	*V*
Start rate	750	810	925	1,055	1,200
Maximum	1,110	1,190	1,370	1,560	1,770
Target	965	1,035	1,190	1,355	1,540

The target salaries will be the expected top rate within the group to be reached by February 1, 198(X + 1). Only employees rated "above average" may exceed the target salary.

Employment should start at the group start rate, or will be commensurate with background experience. The first salary review will be made in no less than four or no more than seven months. Subsequent reviews will be no longer 12 months thereafter.

It is expected that the average new employee with no experience should reach the target salary in about five years. The average new employee with experience could reach the target sooner, based on previous experience.

Performance	*Time in Group to Reach Target*
Above average	3 years
Average	5 years

The salary guidelines for the five groups will be reviewed annually by comparison with the current A.M.S., or other data published for the Dayton area. Necessary adjustments will be made as required to keep Secrid salaries at approximately the average actual salaries in the Dayton area.

EXHIBIT 3 Position Descriptions (Samples)

Secrid Manufacturing Co., Inc.

POSITION DESCRIPTION

Title: Executive Secretary — Location: Dayton
Organization: Secrid Manufacturing — Description No.:
Division/Department: Administration/Sales — Supersedes:

I. Position in organization
   A. Reports to: vice president–finance and vice president–sales.
   B. Directly supervises: None.
   C. Indirectly supervises: None.
II. Major responsibility
   Handle confidential tasks of a broad spectrum for the vice president–finance and the vice president–sales, including payrolls' correspondence and financial records.

EXHIBIT 3 *(continued)*

III. Specific responsibilities (If more space is required, please attach a separate page.)

1. Voucher all expense reports and various other bills for payment.
2. Maintain audit control on cash advances.
3. Maintain audit control on publications and memberships for sales, administration, and manufacturing.
4. Record and pay for all airline tickets and balance airline accounts.
5. Voucher and type special checks.
6. Sign all checks issued by the company.
7. Prepare various monthly reports.
8. Record all absenteeism and vacation for administrative and sales personnel.
9. Make distribution of salaried paychecks to departments.
10. Type management Minutes' extract Management Resolutions; prepare F-800s for salary increases and post to DO 18s.
11. Make bank deposits for factory payroll, civic fund, pension fund, and special account.
12. Take dictation and handle vice president–finance and vice president–sales correspondence.

Personnel Generalist

Job responsibilities:

A. Basic functions

1. Full responsibility for administration of Service Pin Program.
   - *a.* Maintain current employee lists.
   - *b.* Inventory and order pins.
   - *c.* Distribute pins to appropriate managers.
2. Maintain all eligibility records for Secrid hourly employees' pension plan; send annual letters of information to employees.
3. Handle all records for hourly employees' United Way contributions and Flower Fund contributions.
   - *a.* Understand function of Civic Committee; substitute, as necessary, for personnel supervisor at meetings.
   - *b.* Participate in organization of United Way campaign.
4. Control weekly sale of soap to employees.
   - *a.* Order tickets.
   - *b.* Verify number of tickets sold with amount of money received; coordinate with accounting department.
   - *c.* Provide supplies to person who sells soap, tickets/substitute for this person when necessary.
5. Assist with security functions.
   - *a.* Monitor, on a scheduled basis, emergency exit alarm system.
   - *b.* Monitor daily guard logs; take corrective action, as necessary.
   - *c.* Relieve security guard.

EXHIBIT 3 *(continued)*

   d. Participate in organization of review schedule for corporate security department.

6. Maintain current orientation materials; assist with orientation of new employees.
7. Assist in planning and implementation of Christmas gift distribution program.
8. Assume responsibility for special projects.
   a. Compilation of data for negotiations' planning.
   b. Substitute for plant manager's secretary, when needed.
   c. Assist the personnel secretary on as-needed basis.
   d. Plan for retirees' luncheon.
9. Keep records relative to employee payments for medical coverage.
10. Coordinate with department manager/payroll department hourly employees' vacation eligibility.
11. Compile and distribute all hourly employment reports.

Maintenance Supply & Record Clerk

Job responsibilities:

A. Basic functions
   1. Purchasing—locate or select supplier; initiate and/or check purchase requisitions; follow up and expedite orders; receive goods and initial receiving reports for manufacturing expense and AE items. Maintain purchasing files.
   2. Inventory—maintain manufacturing storeroom supplies; issue upon need; reorder when necessary.
   3. Fixed asset accounting—maintain fixed asset books by assigning new equipment numbers, initiating FADO's, maintaining asset file system.
   4. Clerical
      a. Typing and filing; answer phone for maintenance.
      b. Maintain attendance records, time cards, vacation schedules for maintenance and engineering personnel.

B. Behavioral expectations and training requirements
   1. Must be able to organize and plan time in order to complete all tasks.
   2. Must be strong in communication skills to successfully interface with managers, hourly employees, and suppliers.
   3. Must be able to evaluate priorities and self-direct activities based on this evaluation.
   4. Must be able to perform well under critical pressure situations.

POSITION DESCRIPTION

Title: Receptionist	Location: Dayton
Organization: Secrid Manufacturing	Description No.:
Division/Department: Sales/Sales Service	Supersedes:

EXHIBIT 3 *(continued)*

I. Position in Organization
   A. Reports to: Sales service manager.
   B. Directly supervises: None.
   C. Indirectly supervises: None.

II. Major Responsibility
   Handles switchboard.

III. Specific Responsibilities (If more space is required, please attach a separate page.)
   1. Switchboard operator.
   2. Takes messages for Eastern salespeople.
   3. Handles excess typing.

POSITION DESCRIPTION

Title: Accounts Payable Clerk — Location: Dayton
Organization: Secrid Manufacturing — Description No.:
Division/Department: Administration — Supersedes:

I. Position in Organization
   A. Reports to: Manager—traffic/inventory control.
   B. Directly supervises: None.
   C. Indirectly supervises: None.

II. Major responsibility
   Process for payment invoices relating to all items of expense.

III. Specific responsibilities (If more space is required, please attach a separate page.)
   1. Verify receipts of goods and/or services for general expense items.
   2. Audit purchase orders with related invoices and prepare voucher for payment.
   3. Prepare bank deposit for cash receipts.
      a. Mail petty cash, expense reports.
   4. Handle written and phone communications.
   5. Sales—shipment audit.
   6. Bank reconciliation—factory payroll checks.
   7. File maintenance.
   8. Purchase order audit control.

POSITION DESCRIPTION

Title: Clerk—accounts payable/inventory control/traffic — Location: Dayton
Organization: Secrid Manufacturing — Description No.:
Division/Department: Administration — Supersedes:

I. Position in Organization
   A. Reports to: Manager—traffic/inventory control.

EXHIBIT 3 *(continued)*

B. Directly supervises: None.

C. Indirectly supervises: None.

II. Major Responsibility

Maintains financial detail records on inventories of all raw materials and supplies. Maintains inventory control records of most materials and advises purchasing how much of a material to order.

III. Specific Responsibilities (If more space is required, please attach a separate page.)

1. Process all receiving reports.
2. Keypunch all inventory items into computer.
3. Reorder for a bogey system as required.
4. Maintain an essential oils' Hewitt compound, raw materials, additives, and foreign compounds kardex.
5. Distribute daily production report.
6. Request, audit, and post all monthly inventories.
7. Prepare and maintain manufacturing head sheets for production orders.
8. Prepare for sales account managers specific inventories of customer furnished items.
9. Post and file completed production orders.
10. Assist in new manufacturing specification system. All specifications are to be keypunched into the computer.
11. Maintain and update the file retention system.
12. Update and maintain supply master on CRT.
13. Follow up purchasing on all incoming materials and supplies to make sure they were ordered.
14. Follow up all incoming materials and supplies from vendors to ensure timeliness for production and scheduling.
15. Audit and pay invoices covering such items within area of authority and terms of the transaction.
16. Record and establish inventory costs.
17. Record, price, and total all month-end inventories.
18. Typing:
    a. Freight claims.
    b. Steiner and V.T. Bills of Lading.
    c. Miscellaneous correspondence as needed.
19. Keypunch freight bills into computer.
20. Maintain customer master list.
    a. New customers.
    b. Address changes, etc.

EXHIBIT 3 *(continued)*

POSITION DESCRIPTION

Title: Data Entry Operator I — Location: Dayton

Organization: Secrid Manufacturing — Description No.:

Division/Department: Administration — Supersedes:

I. Position in Organization

A. Reports to: Manager—data processing.

B. Directly supervises: None.

C. Indirectly supervises: None.

II. Major Responsibility

Entry of data via terminal into HP3000 computer and serve as backup computer operator.

III. Specific Responsibilities (If more space is required, please attach a separate page.)

1. Ability to enter and verify both production and technical data accurately.
2. Achieve at least 8,000 key strokes per hour.
3. Meet established schedules for production work.
4. Have a thorough knowledge of all data entry jobs in the shop.
5. Be able to use good judgment in detecting errors and determining the appropriate follow-up.
6. Perform occasional clerical duties.

POSITION DESCRIPTION

Title: Payroll Clerk — Location: Dayton

Organization: Secrid Manufacturing — Description No.:

Division/Department: Administration — Supersedes:

I. Position in Organization

A. Reports to: Supervisor payroll/process accounting.

B. Directly supervises: None.

C. Indirectly supervises: None.

II. Major Responsibility

Prepares weekly the payroll for all hourly employees with data processing assistance.

III. Specific Responsibilities (If more space is required, please attach a separate page.)

1. Audit Line Production Sheets for input data to data processing.
2. Record input data relating to all status changes and deductions.
3. Audit input controls and master file update prior to check writing.
4. Prepare payroll distribution summary and weekly check number control count.
5. Promptly advise supervisor or manager of current processing delay affecting completion of weekly payroll.
6. Calculate, prepare distribution of charges, and request payment for monthly hospital care, disability, and life insurance premiums/related reports.

EXHIBIT 3 *(continued)*

7. Make necessary adjustments on payroll for previous weeks.
8. Coding of weekly time cards.
9. Record all special rates affecting current week.
10. Post daily incentive hours to master worksheet.
11. Post time card hours detail to master worksheet.
12. Post status change items to master worksheet.
13. Spot audit of input control and balancing hours.
14. Run balancing tapes.
15. Record details from weekly payroll as needed for future corporate and government reporting/analysis.
16. Process garnishments.
17. Process Employee Savings Bonds.
18. Furnish detailed information as required for corporate, state, and federal reporting.
19. Work with plant accountant auditing production tickets with line production sheets. Also assisting with information for the budget versus actual report.
20. Plan and schedule for short workweek periods.

POSITION DESCRIPTION

Title: Data Entry Operator II	Location: Dayton
Organization: Secrid Manufacturing	Description No.:
Division/Department: Administration	Supersedes:

I. Position in Organization
   A. Reports to: Manager—data processing.
   B. Directly supervises: None.
   C. Indirectly supervises: Data entry operator I—on occasion.

II. Major Responsibility
   Input data via terminal to HP3000 computer.

III. Specific Responsibilities (If more space is required, please attach a separate page.)
   1. Ability to enter and verify both production and technical data accurately.
   2. Achieve at least 8,000 key strokes per hour.
   3. Meet established schedules for production work.
   4. Have a thorough knowledge of all data entry jobs in the shop.
   5. Be able to use good judgment in detecting errors and determining the appropriate follow-up.
   6. Perform occasional clerical duties.
   7. Organize and coordinate the data entry work load.
   8. Collect statistics on production data entry and other related statistics as required.

EXHIBIT 3 *(continued)*

9. Coordinate work schedules of other data entry operators if applicable.
10. Maintain data entry operating instructions.
11. Contribute ideas and evaluate alternatives to improving data entry operations.
12. Train and develop new data entry operators.
13. Learn basic computer operations to be able to back up the computer operator.
14. Aid in designing data entry forms.

POSITION DESCRIPTION

Title: Clerical—Sales Administrator II — Location: Dayton
Organization: Secrid Manufacturing — Description No.:
Division/Department: Administration — Supersedes:

I. Position in Organization
   A. Reports to: Sales service manager.
   B. Directly supervises: None.
   C. Indirectly supervises: None.

II. Major Responsibility
Handles correspondence and reports generated by sales service manager and senior account manager.

III. Specific Responsibilities (If more space is required, please attach a separate page.)
   1. Types dictation to customers.
   2. Takes phone messages.
   3. Handles requests by customers regarding status of contracts, stock, etc.
   4. Handles distribution of mail.
   5. Relief on switchboard.
   6. Does several reports which are sent to customers.

POSITION DESCRIPTION

Title: Order—Billing clerk — Location: Dayton
Organization: Secrid Manufacturing — Description No.:
Division/Department: Administration — Supersedes:

I. Position in Organization
   A. Reports to: Order—billing supervisor.
   B. Directly supervises: None.
   C. Indirectly supervises: None.

II. Major Responsibility
Prepare input for preparation of shipping papers and invoices. Verify machine-prepared ship papers and invoices.

EXHIBIT 3 *(continued)*

III. Specific Responsibilities (If more space is required, please attach a separate page.)

1. Visual checking to verify shipping order data (OSBIC) versus original customer order.
2. Visual checking to verify shipments (yellow copy) versus invoice (OSBIC).
3. Coding, pricing, and furnishing all pertinent data on input form (OSBIC) for each Hewitt-controlled and private brands order entry.
4. Does daily V-T and Steiner orders.
5. Filing orders and shipping copies.
6. Types miscellaneous invoices (other than OSBIC).
7. Mailing invoices and internal distribution of copies.
8. V-T Monthly Inventory report.
9. Auditing—making changes/adjustments on shipments (yellow shipping copy) prior to invoicing (OSBIC).
10. Enters contracts into OSBIC on make and hold orders.
11. Furnish financial analysis department copy of PB orders.
12. Furnish traffic/credit departments copies of shipment when freight charges.

POSITION DESCRIPTION

Title: Purchasing Department Secretary	Location: Dayton
Organization: Secrid Manufacturing	Description No.:
Division/Department: Administration	Supersedes:

I. Position in Organization

A. Reports to: Manager—purchasing department.

B. Directly supervises: None.

C. Indirectly supervises: None.

II. Major Responsibility

Daily work flow in purchasing operation consisting of manager and secretary. Handles all clerical/steno functions while bringing judgment to job.

III. Specific Responsibilities (If more space is required, please attach a separate page.)

1. Reviews purchase requisitions and/or production request material requirements for validity before placing order.
2. Places purchase orders via telephone or mail. Types purchase orders.
3. Chooses suppliers on own or after consulting with purchasing manager.
4. Takes incoming phone calls and handles matters on own or consults purchasing manager.
5. Responsible for record files (purchase orders, Rec. reports, etc.)
6. Arranges for appointments with vendors for purchasing manager.
7. Secures material costs for cost estimating for financial analysis department, when required.

EXHIBIT 3 *(continued)*

8. Expedites materials needed to meet production commitments.
9. Has a large amount of contact with vendors via phone and in person. A good working relationship is a must.
10. Handles manager responsibilities when manager is out of the office. Makes decisions on own or consults with other managers.
11. Annual purchases handled are $8 to $10 million.
12. Handles purchasing manager's correspondence, typing, etc.

POSITION DESCRIPTION

Title: Traffic/Credit Administration Assistant — Location: Dayton
Organization: Secrid Manufacturing — Description No.:
Division/Department: Administration — Supersedes:

I. Position in Organization
   A. Reports to: Manager—Traffic/inventory control.
   B. Directly supervises: None.
   C. Indirectly supervises: None.

II. Major Responsibility
   Perform all traffic-related functions for the company. Provide credit liaison with ASR.

III. Specific Responsibilities (If more space is required, please attach a separate page.)
   1. Handles credit/traffic department mail.
   2. Verify freight rates.
      a. Inbound.
      b. Outbound.
   3. Tracing of freight.
      a. Inbound.
      b. Outbound.
   4. Handles and expedites the following:
      a. Air shipments
         (1) Outbound.
      b. Rail shipments inbound.
         (1) Tallow.
         (2) CNO.
         (3) Miscellaneous.
      c. Glycerine shipments.
      d. Overseas shipments.
   5. Phone communication.
      a. Traffic.
      b. Credit.
         (1) Credit references.

EXHIBIT 3 *(concluded)*

6. Handles freight claims.
7. Handles outside traffic personnel in credit/traffic manager's absence.
8. Vacation relief for credit/traffic manager.
9. Liaison on credit matters between Secrid and ASR.

POSITION DESCRIPTION

Title: Clerical—Sales Administrator III — Location: Dayton

Organization: Secrid Manufacturing — Description No.:

Division/Department: Sales/field sales — Supersedes:

I. Position in Organization
   A. Reports to: District manager.
   B. Directly supervises: None.
   C. Indirectly supervises: None.

II. Major Responsibility
   Handles correspondence and reports generated by district manager.

III. Specific Responsibilities (If more space is required, please attach a separate page.)
   1. Types dictation to customers.
   2. Takes phone messages.
   3. Handles requests by customers regarding status of contracts, stock, etc.
   4. Relief on switchboard.
   5. Does several reports generated by district manager.

EXHIBIT 4 Dayton Area Wage Survey

DAYTON AREA WAGE SURVEY

DECEMBER 198X

U.S. DEPARTMENT OF LABOR

BUREAU OF LABOR STATISTICS

(Bulletin 3000-64)

Secrid Manufacturing Company, Inc.

EXHIBIT 4 *(continued)*

DAYTON AREA WAGE SURVEY
DECEMBER 198X
U.S. DEPARTMENT OF LABOR
BUREAU OF LABOR STATISTICS
(Bulletin 3000-64)
Secrid Manufacturing Company, Inc.

Class A. Work requires the application of experience and judgment in selecting procedures to be followed and in searching for, interpreting, selecting, or coding items to be entered from a variety of source documents. On occasion may also perform routine work as described for class B.

NOTE: Excluded are operators above class A using the key entry controls to access, read, and evaluate the substance of specific records to take substantive actions, or to make entries requiring a similar level of knowledge.

Class B. Work is routine and repetitive. Under close supervision or following specific procedures or detailed instructions, works from various standardized source documents which have been coded and require little or no selecting, coding, or interpreting of data to be entered. Refers to supervisor problems arising from erroneous items, codes or missing information.

* * * * *

COMPUTER OPERATOR

In accordance with operating instructions, monitors and operates the control console of a digital computer to process data. Executes runs by either serial processing (processes one program at a time) or multiprocessing (processes two or more programs simultaneously). The following duties characterized the work of a computer operator.

- Studies operating instructions to determine equipment setup needed.
- Loads equipment with required items (tapes, cards, disks, paper, etc.).
- Switches necessary auxiliary equipment into system.
- Starts and operates computer.
- Responds to operating and computer output instructions.
- Reviews error messages and makes corrections during operation <u>or</u> refers problems.
- Maintains operating record.

May test-run new or modified programs. May assist in modifying systems or programs. The scope of this definition includes trainees working to become fully qualified computer operators, fully qualified computer operator, and lead operators providing technical assistance to lower level operators. It excludes workers who monitor and operate remote terminals.

EXHIBIT 4 *(continued)*

Class A. In addition to work assignments described for a class B operator (see below) the work of a class A operator involves at least one of the following:

• Deviates from standard procedure to avoid the loss of information or to conserve computer time even though the procedures applied materially alter the computer unit's production plans.

• Tests new programs, applications, and procedures.

• Advises programmers and subject-matter experts on setup techniques.

• Assists in (1) maintaining, modifying, and developing operating systems or programs; (2) developing operating instructions and techniques to cover problem situations; and/or (3) switching to emergency backup procedures (such assistance requires a working knowledge of program language, computer features, and software systems).

An operator at this level typically guides lower-level operators.

Class B. In addition to established production runs, work assignments include runs involving new programs, applications, and procedures (i.e., situations which require the operator to adapt to a variety of problems). At this level, the operator has the training and experience to work fairly independently in carrying out most assignments. Assignments may require the operator to select from a variety of standard setup and operating procedures. In responding to computer output instructions or error conditions, applies standard operating or corrective procedures, but may deviate from standard procedures when standard procedures fail if deviation does not materially alter the computer unit's production plans. Refers the problem or aborts the program when procedures applied do not provide a solution. May guide lower-level operators.

Class C. Work assignments are limited to established production runs (i.e., programs which present few operating problems). Assignments may consist primarily of on-the-job training (sometimes augmented by classroom instruction). When learning to run programs, the supervisor or a higher-level operator provides detailed written or oral guidance to the operator before and during the run. After the operator has gained experience with a program, however, the operator works fairly independently in applying standard operating or corrective procedures in responding to computer output instructions or error conditions, but refers problems to a higher-level operator or the supervisor when standard procedures fail.

SWITCHBOARD OPERATOR

Operates a telephone switchboard or console used with a private branch exchange (PBX) system to relay incoming, outgoing, and intrasystem calls. May provide information to callers, record and transmit messages, keep record of calls placed and toll charges. Besides operating a telephone switchboard or console, *may* also type or

EXHIBIT 4 *(continued)*

perform routine clerical work (typing or routine clerical work may occupy the major portion of the worker's time, and is usually performed while at the switchboard or console). Chief or lead operators in establishments employing more than one operator are excluded. For an operator who also acts as a receptionist, see Switchboard Operator-Receptionist.

SWITCHBOARD OPERATOR-RECEPTIONIST

At a single-position telephone switchboard or console, acts both as an operator—see Switchboard Operator—and as a receptionist. Receptionist's work involves such duties as greeting visitors; determining nature of visitor's business and providing appropriate information; referring visitor to appropriate person in the organization or contacting that person by telephone and arranging an appointment; keeping a log of visitors.

ORDER CLERK

Receives written or verbal customers' purchase orders for material or merchandise from customers or sales people. Work typically involves some combination of the following duties: Quoting prices; determining availability of ordered items and suggesting substitutes when necessary; advising expected delivery date and method of delivery; recording order and customer information on order sheets; checking order sheets for accuracy and adequacy of information recorded; ascertaining credit rating of customer; furnishing customer with acknowledgment of receipt of order; following up to see that order is delivered by the specified date or to let customer know of a delay in delivery; maintaining order file; checking shipping invoice against original order. *Exclude workers paid on a commission basis or whose duties include any of the following:* Receiving orders for services rather than for material or merchandise; providing customers with consultative advice using knowledge gained from engineering or extensive technical training; emphasizing selling skills; handling material or merchandise as an integral part of the job.

Positions are classified into levels according to the following definitions:

Class A. Handles orders that involve making judgments such as choosing which specific product or material from the establishment's product lines will satisfy the customer's needs, or determining the price to be quoted when pricing involves more than merely referring to a price list or making some simple mathematical calculations.

Class B. Handles orders involving items which have readily identified uses and applications. May refer to a catalog, manufacturer's manual, or similar document to insure that proper item is supplied or to verify price of ordered item.

EXHIBIT 4 *(continued)*

ACCOUNTING CLERK

Performs one or more accounting clerical tasks such as posting to registers and ledgers; reconciling bank accounts; verifying the internal consistency, completeness, and mathematical accuracy of accounting documents; assigning prescribed accounting distribution codes; examining and verifying the clerical accuracy of various types of reports, lists, calculations, postings, etc.; preparing journal vouchers; or making entries or adjustments to accounts.

Levels C and D require a basic knowledge of routine clerical methods and office practices and procedures as they relate to the clerical processing and recording of transactions and accounting information. Levels A and B *require* a knowledge and understanding of the established and standardized bookkeeping and accounting procedures and techniques used in an accounting system, or a segment of an accounting system, where there are few variations in the types of transactions handled. In addition, some jobs at each level may require a basic knowledge and understanding of the terminology, codes, and processes used in an automated accounting system.

Class A. Maintains journals or subsidiary ledgers of an accounting system and balances and reconciles accounts. Typical duties include one or both of the following: Reviews invoices and statements (verifying information, ensuring sufficient funds have been obligated, and if questionable, resolving with the submitting unit, determining accounts involved, coding transactions, and processing material through data processing for application in the accounting system); *and/or* analyzes and reconciles computer printouts with operating unit reports (contacting units and researching causes of discrepancies, and taking action to ensure that accounts balance). Employee resolves problems in recurring assignments in accordance with previous training and experience. Supervisor provides suggestions for handling unusual or nonrecurring transactions. Conformance with requirements and technical soundness of completed work are reviewed by the supervisor or are controlled by mechanisms built into the accounting system. NOTE: Excluded from class A are positions responsible for maintaining either a general ledger or a general ledger in combination with subsidiary accounts.

Class B. Uses a knowledge of double entry bookkeeping in performing one or more of the following: Posts actions to journals, identifying subsidiary accounts affected and debit and credit entries to be made and assigning proper codes; reviews computer printouts against manually maintained journals, detecting and correcting erroneous postings, and preparing documents to adjust accounting classifications and other data; or reviews lists of transactions rejected by an automated system, determining reasons for rejections, and preparing necessary correcting material. On routine assignments, employee selects and applies established procedures and techniques. Detailed instructions are provided for difficult or unusual assignments. Completed work and methods used are reviewed for technical accuracy.

EXHIBIT 4 *(continued)*

Class C. Performs one or more routine accounting clerical operations, such as: Examining, verifying, and correcting accounting transactions to ensure completeness and accuracy of data and proper identification of accounts, and checking that expenditures will not exceed obligations in specified accounts; totaling; balancing, and reconciling collection vouchers; posting data to transaction sheets where employee identifies proper accounts and items to be posted; and coding documents in accordance with a chart (listing) of accounts. Employee follows specific and detailed accounting procedures. Completed work is reviewed for accuracy and compliance with procedures.

Class D. Performs very simple and routine accounting clerical operations; for example, recognizing and comparing easily identified numbers and codes on similar and repetitive accounting documents, verifying mathematical accuracy, and identifying discrepancies and bringing them to the supervisor's attention. Supervisor gives clear and detailed instructions for specific assignments. Employee refers to supervisor all matters not covered by instructions. Work is closely controlled and reviewed in detail for accuracy, adequacy, and adherence to instructions.

* * * * *

KEY ENTRY OPERATOR

Operates keyboard-controlled data entry device, such as keypunch machine or key-operated magnetic tape or disk encoder to transcribe data into a form suitable for computer processing. Work requires skill in operating an alphanumeric keyboard and an understanding of transcribing procedures and relevant data entry equipment.

Positions are classified into levels on the basis of the following definitions:

LS-2

a. Secretary to an executive or managerial person whose responsibility is not equivalent to one of the specific level situations in the definition for LS-3, but whose organizational unit normally numbers at least several dozen employees and is usually divided into organizational segments which are often, in turn, further subdivided. In some companies, this level includes a wide range of organizational echelons; in others, only one or two; or

b. Secretary to the head of an individual plant, factory, etc., (or other equivalent level of official) that employs, in all, fewer than 5,000 persons.

LS-3

a. Secretary to the chairman of the board or president of a company that employs, in all, fewer than 100 persons; or

b. Secretary to a corporate officer (other than chairman of the board or president) of a company that employs, in all, over 100 but fewer than 5,000 persons; or

EXHIBIT 4 *(continued)*

c. Secretary to the head (immediately below the officer level) over either a major corporatewide functional activity (e.g., marketing, research, operations, industrial relations, etc.) or a major geographic or organizational segment (e.g., a regional headquarters, a major division) of a company that employs, in all, over 5,000 but fewer than 25,000 employees; or

d. Secretary to the head of an individual plant, factory, etc., (or other equivalent level of official) that employs, in all, over 5,000 persons; or

e. Secretary to the head of a large and important organizational segment often involving as many as several hundred persons) of a company that employs, in all, over 25,000 persons.

LS-4

a. Secretary to the chairman of the board or president of a company that employs, in all, over 100 but fewer than 5,000 persons; or

b. Secretary to a corporate officer (other than the chairman of the board or president) of a company that employs, in all, over 5,000 but fewer than 25,000 persons; or

c. Secretary to the head, immediately below the corporate officer level, of a major segment or subsidiary of a company that employs, in all, over 25,000 persons.

NOTE: The term *corporate officer* used in the above LS definition refers to those officials who have a significant corporatewide policymaking role with regard to major company activities. The title 'vice president,' though normally indicative of this role, does not in all cases identify such positions. Vice presidents whose primary responsibility is to act personally on individual cases or transactions (e.g., approve or deny individual loan or credit actions; administer individual trust accounts; directly supervise a clerical staff) are not considered to be 'corporate officers' for purposes of applying the definition.

Level of Secretary's Responsibility (LR)

This factor evaluates the nature of the work relationship between the secretary and the supervisor, and the extent to which secretary is expected to exercise initiative and judgment. Secretaries should be matched at LR-1 or LR-2 described below according to their level of responsibility.

EXHIBIT 4 *(continued)*

LR-1

Performs varied secretarial duties including or comparable to most of the following:

a. Answers telephones, greets personal callers, and opens incoming mail.

b. Answers telephone requests which have standard answers. May reply to requests by sending a form letter.

c. Reviews correspondence, memoranda, and reports prepared by others for the supervisor's signature to ensure procedural and typographical accuracy.

d. Maintains supervisor's calendar and makes appointments as instructed.

e. Types, takes and transcribes dictation, and files.

LR-2

Performs duties under LR-1 and, *in addition,* performs tasks requiring greater judgment, initiative, and knowledge of office functions including or comparable to most of the following:

a. Screens telephone and personal callers, determining which can be handled by the supervisor's subordinates or other offices.

b. Answers requests which require a detailed knowledge of office procedures or collection of information from files or other offices. *May* sign routine correspondence in own or supervisor's name.

c. Compiles or assists in compiling periodic reports on the basis of general instructions.

d. Schedules tentative appointments without prior clearance. Assembles necessary background material for scheduled meetings. Makes arrangements for meetings and conferences.

e. Explains supervisor's requirements to other employees in supervisor's unit. (Also types, takes dictation, and files.)

The following tabulation shows the level of the secretary for each LS and LR combination:

	LR-1	LR-2
LS-1	Class E	Class D
LS-2	Class D	Class C
LS-3	Class C	Class B
LS-4	Class B	Class A

* * * * *

EXHIBIT 4 *(continued)*

APPENDIX B
OCCUPATIONAL DESCRIPTIONS

The primary purpose of preparing job descriptions for the Bureau's wage surveys is to assist its field representatives in classifying into appropriate occupations workers who are employed under a variety of payroll titles and different work arrangements from establishment to establishment and from area to area. This permits grouping occupational wage rates representing comparable job content. Because of this emphasis on interestablishment and interarea comparability of occupational content, the Bureau's job descriptions may differ significantly from those in use in individual establishments or those prepared for other purposes. In applying these job descriptions, the Bureau's field representatives are instructed to exclude working supervisors; apprentices; and part-time, temporary, and probationary workers. Handicapped workers whose earnings are reduced because of their handicap are also excluded.

Listed below are several occupations for which revised descriptions or titles are being introduced in this survey:

Accounting clerk	Drafter
Key entry operator	Stationary engineer
Computer operator	Boiler tender

* * * * *

OFFICE

SECRETARY

Assigned as a personal secretary, normally to one individual. Maintains a close and highly responsive relationship to the day-to-day activities of the supervisor. Works fairly independently receiving a minimum of detailed supervision and guidance. Performs varied clerical and secretarial duties requiring a knowledge of the office routine and understanding of the organization, programs, and procedures related to the work of the supervisor.

Exclusions. Not all positions that are titled 'secretary' possess the above characteristics. Examples of positions which are excluded from the definition are as follows:

a. Positions which do not meet the 'personal' secretary concept described above;

b. Stenographers not fully trained in secretarial-type duties.

c. Stenographers serving as office assistants to a group of professional, technical, or managerial persons;

d. Assistant-type positions which entail more difficult or more responsible technical, administrative, or supervisory duties which are not typical of secretarial work, e.g., Administrative Assistant, or Executive Assistant;

EXHIBIT 4 *(continued)*

e. Positions which do not fit any of the situations listed in the sections below titled "Level of Supervisor," (e.g., secretary to the president of a company that employs, in all, over 5,000 persons);

f. Trainees.

Classification by Level. Secretary jobs which meet the required characteristics are matched at one of five levels accounting to *(a)* the level of the secretary's supervisor within the company's organizational structure and, *(b)* the level of the secretary's responsibility. The tabulation following the explanations of these two factors indicates the level of the secretary for each combination of the factors.

Level of Secretary's Supervisor (LS)

LS-1

a. Secretary to the supervisor or head of a small organizational unit (e.g., fewer than about 25 or 30 persons); or

b. Secretary to a nonsupervisory staff specialist, professional employee, administrative officer, or assistant, skilled technician or expert. (NOTE: Many companies assign stenographers, rather than secretaries as described above, to this level of supervisor or nonsupervisory worker.)

EXHIBIT 4 *(continued)*

Table A-1. Weekly Earnings of Office Workers in Dayton, Ohio, December 198X

Occupation & Industry Division	Number of Workers	Average Weekly Hours[1] (standard)	Weekly Earnings (In dollars)[1] Mean[2]	Median[2]	Middle Range[4]	Number of Workers Receiving Straight-time Weekly Earnings (in dollars) of— 110 and under 120	120 — 130	130 — 140	140 — 150	150 — 160	160 — 170	170 — 180	180 — 200	200 — 220	220 — 240	240 — 260	260 — 280	280 — 300	300 — 320	320 — 340	340 — 380	380 — 420	420 — 460	460 — 500	500 — 540	540 — 580
Secretaries	1,557	39.0	257.00	237.00	202.50-288.50	—	—	16	22	42	60	58	149	237	222	175	112	145	66	46	71	29	38	36	16	17
Manufacturing	1,062	39.5	278.00	255.00	219.00-304.00	—	—	—	—	—	6	33	101	146	155	135	87	120	46	41	57	29	37	36	16	17
Nonmanufacturing	495	38.5	212.00	205.00	167.00-240.00	—	—	16	22	42	54	25	48	91	67	40	25	25	20	5	14	—	1	—	—	—
Public utilities	93	39.0	226.50	191.00	155.00-288.50	—	—	2	—	24	8	7	8	4	3	—	9	6	5	5	11	—	1	—	—	—
Secretaries, class A	138	39.0	339.50	309.50	255.00-361.00	—	—	—	—	—	—	—	—	6	14	24	6	11	21	8	17	4	—	4	6	17
Manufacturing	105	39.5	364.50	320.00	280.50-462.50	—	—	—	—	—	—	—	—	—	6	16	4	11	15	8	14	4	—	4	6	17
Nonmanufacturing	33	37.5	260.50	247.00	224.00-310.00	—	—	—	—	—	—	—	—	6	8	8	2	—	6	—	3	—	—	—	—	—
Secretaries, class B	270	39.5	288.00	280.00	240.00-301.50	—	—	—	—	—	2	2	7	24	27	34	39	64	21	12	13	1	3	11	10	—
Manufacturing	201	39.5	307.00	288.00	264.50-314.50	—	—	—	—	—	—	—	2	10	8	23	31	57	20	12	13	1	3	11	10	—
Nonmanufacturing	69	39.0	232.50	226.00	212.00-259.00	—	—	—	—	—	2	2	5	14	19	11	8	7	1	—	—	—	—	—	—	—
Secretaries, class C	571	39.5	272.50	245.00	210.50-300.50	—	—	—	2	6	2	13	56	87	96	77	30	52	19	21	30	24	35	21	—	—
Manufacturing	425	39.5	291.00	258.00	226.50-351.50	—	—	—	—	—	—	8	29	43	76	58	26	44	11	21	30	24	34	21	—	—
Nonmanufacturing	146	39.0	219.50	209.50	196.00-240.00	—	—	—	2	6	2	5	27	44	20	19	4	8	8	—	—	—	1	—	—	—
Secretaries, class D	452	38.5	212.00	209.50	180.00-232.50	—	—	2	—	30	53	23	76	109	66	31	30	11	5	5	11	—	—	—	—	—
Manufacturing	273	39.0	215.50	215.50	195.00-232.50	—	—	—	—	—	6	15	64	84	52	30	20	2	—	—	—	—	—	—	—	—
Nonmanufacturing	179	38.5	206.50	182.00	162.00-225.00	—	—	2	—	30	47	8	12	25	14	1	10	9	5	5	11	—	—	—	—	—
Public utilities	67	38.5	230.50	170.00	154.00-318.00	—	—	2	—	22	8	4	—	—	—	—	5	5	5	5	11	—	—	—	—	—
Secretaries, class E	114	38.5	190.00	176.00	145.00-229.50	—	—	14	20	6	2	20	10	9	13	8	6	6	—	—	—	—	—	—	—	—
Manufacturing	58	39.0	225.50	229.00	194.50-252.50	—	—	—	—	—	—	10	6	9	13	8	6	6	—	—	—	—	—	—	—	—
						*****																				
Switchboard operators	75	39.5	192.00	176.00	151.00-212.00	—	—	5	1	25	6	1	12	10	6	—	1	1	5	—	—	2	—	—	—	—
Manufacturing	39	39.0	213.50	198.00	161.50-229.50	—	—	—	—	9	3	—	8	6	6	—	1	—	4	—	—	2	—	—	—	—
Nonmanufacturing	36	39.5	169.00	150.00	150.00-182.50	—	—	5	1	16	3	1	4	4	—	—	—	1	1	—	—	—	—	—	—	—
Switchboard operator-receptionists	250	40.0	180.50	176.00	150.00-201.00	—	22	9	23	43	15	22	40	43	15	11	1	—	4	—	—	1	1	—	—	—
Manufacturing	133	40.0	181.00	161.00	150.00-201.00	—	18	—	14	31	6	6	13	21	15	2	1	—	4	—	—	1	1	—	—	—
Nonmanufacturing	117	40.0	180.00	179.50	155.00-208.00	—	4	9	9	12	9	16	27	22	—	9	—	—	—	—	—	—	—	—	—	—
Order clerks	167	40.0	182.00	178.50	150.00-195.00	—	—	2	12	40	10	32	35	20	2	1	12	1	—	—	—	—	—	—	—	—
Manufacturing	72	40.0	196.00	178.50	176.50-212.50	—	—	—	—	12	—	30	11	3	2	1	12	1	—	—	—	—	—	—	—	—
Order clerks, class B	143	40.0	173.00	176.50	150.00-190.00	—	—	2	12	40	6	32	35	13	2	1	—	—	—	—	—	—	—	—	—	—
Manufacturing	7	40.0	179.00	178.50	176.00-195.00	—	—	—	—	12	—	30	11	1	2	1	—	—	—	—	—	—	—	—	—	—
Accounting clerks	1,506	39.5	201.50	190.50	167.00-221.00	—	6	42	108	137	109	191	317	203	144	95	47	22	7	12	43	8	9	6	—	—
Manufacturing	650	40.0	222.50	207.00	186.00-242.00	—	—	—	7	8	28	74	165	120	73	72	42	15	1	6	16	8	9	6	—	—
Nonmanufacturing	856	39.5	186.00	173.00	155.00-200.00	—	6	42	101	129	81	117	152	83	71	23	5	7	6	6	27	—	—	—	—	—
Public utilities	83	39.5	257.50	240.00	152.00-374.00	—	—	2	16	4	4	5	5	5	—	2	—	1	6	6	27	—	—	—	—	—
Accounting clerks, class A	240	40.0	261.50	250.00	215.50-284.00	—	—	—	2	6	8	10	25	25	24	54	21	14	—	—	37	2	6	6	—	—
Manufacturing	125	40.0	273.50	251.00	223.00-282.00	—	—	—	—	—	—	—	9	21	7	38	18	8	—	—	10	2	6	6	—	—
Nonmanufacturing	115	39.5	248.50	234.50	183.00-290.00	—	—	—	2	6	8	10	16	4	17	16	3	6	—	—	27	—	—	—	—	—
Accounting clerks, class B	395	39.5	189.50	186.00	164.50-200.00	—	—	12	34	40	37	56	92	65	26	11	12	—	—	4	1	2	3	—	—	—
Manufacturing	107	40.0	221.50	198.00	176.00-246.00	—	—	—	—	—	11	21	23	12	7	11	12	—	—	4	1	2	3	—	—	—
Nonmanufacturing	288	39.5	178.00	178.00	155.00-199.50	—	—	12	34	40	26	35	69	53	19	—	—	—	—	—	—	—	—	—	—	—

EXHIBIT 4 *(concluded)*

Table A-1. Weekly Earnings of Office Workers in Dayton, Ohio, December 198X

Occupation & Industry Division	Number of Workers	Average Weekly Hours[1] (standard)	Weekly Earnings (In dollars)[1] Mean[2]	Median[2]	Middle Range[4]	110 and under 120	Number of Workers Receiving Straight-time Weekly Earnings (in dollars) of— 120 — 130	130 — 140	140 — 150	150 — 160	160 — 170	170 — 180	180 — 200	200 — 220	220 — 240	240 — 260	260 — 280	280 — 300	300 — 320	320 — 340	340 — 380	380 — 420	420 — 460	460 — 500	500 — 540	540 — 580
Accounting clerks, class C	591	39.5	197.50	193.00	170.00-216.00	—	—	6	35	47	46	76	144	93	85	28	14	2	4	2	5	4	—	—	—	—
Manufacturing	313	40.0	212.00	205.00	186.00-234.00	—	—	—	4	—	—	36	108	69	50	21	12	1	1	2	5	4	—	—	—	—
Nonmanufacturing	278	39.0	180.50	170.00	156.00-202.00	—	—	6	31	47	46	40	36	24	35	7	2	1	3	—	—	—	—	—	—	—
Public utilities	28	38.5	185.00	157.50	147.00-183.00	—	—	—	12	2	3	4	1	—	—	2	—	1	3	—	—	—	—	—	—	—
Accounting clerks, class D	280	39.5	176.50	172.00	150.00-189.00	—	6	24	37	44	18	49	56	20	9	2	—	6	3	6	—	—	—	—	—	—
Manufacturing	105	39.5	193.00	184.00	168.50-206.00	—	—	—	3	8	17	17	25	18	9	2	—	6	—	—	—	—	—	—	—	—
Nonmanufacturing	175	40.0	166.50	155.00	140.00-177.00	—	6	24	34	36	1	32	31	2	—	—	—	—	3	6	—	—	—	—	—	—
Key entry operators	603	39.5	198.50	184.00	161.00-208.50	—	—	35	22	76	49	62	167	87	36	8	3	14	14	2	5	9	14	—	—	—
Manufacturing	268	40.0	220.50	199.00	180.00-223.00	—	—	—	10	17	18	19	71	62	25	5	1	1	9	2	5	9	14	—	—	—
Nonmanufacturing	335	39.0	181.50	178.00	155.50-196.50	—	—	35	12	59	31	43	96	25	11	3	2	13	5	—	—	—	—	—	—	—
Key entry operators, class A	286	39.5	214.50	196.50	184.00-210.00	—	—	—	4	6	11	26	125	62	14	3	2	5	5	1	3	5	14	—	—	—
Manufacturing	159	40.0	226.50	198.00	184.00-218.50	—	—	—	—	2	8	13	59	39	12	1	1	1	—	1	3	5	14	—	—	—
Nonmanufacturing	127	39.0	199.50	196.50	186.00-201.50	—	—	—	4	4	3	13	66	23	2	2	1	4	5	—	—	—	—	—	—	—
Key entry operators, class B	317	39.5	184.00	169.00	154.00-199.00	—	—	35	18	70	38	36	42	25	22	5	1	9	9	1	2	4	—	—	—	—
Manufacturing	109	40.0	211.00	201.50	163.50-224.50	—	—	—	10	15	10	6	12	23	13	4	—	—	9	1	2	4	—	—	—	—
Nonmanufacturing	208	39.0	170.00	160.00	153.00-179.50	—	—	35	8	55	28	30	30	2	9	1	1	9	—	—	—	—	—	—	—	—
Computer operators	470	39.5	264.00	245.00	231.00-297.50	—	4	11	34	43	125	88	23	71	4	21	1	7	13	6	13	5	1	—	—	—
Manufacturing	170	39.5	292.00	260.00	226.00-332.00	—	—	4	10	20	23	27	17	17	3	11	1	7	5	6	13	5	1	—	—	—
Computer operators, class A	144	39.5	310.00	297.50	274.00-326.50	—	—	—	1	9	5	15	12	62	2	10	1	5	10	—	8	3	1	—	—	—
Manufacturing	60	39.0	335.50	301.50	272.00-370.50	—	—	—	1	—	1	10	8	10	2	8	1	5	2	—	8	3	1	—	—	—
Computer operators, class B	168	40.0	260.00	245.00	226.00-258.00	—	—	—	13	17	28	70	10	5	1	11	—	1	1	4	5	2	—	—	—	—
Manufacturing	79	39.5	276.50	253.00	224.50-292.00	—	—	—	4	14	18	14	8	4	1	3	—	1	1	4	5	2	—	—	—	—
Nonmanufacturing	89	40.0	245.50	245.00	245.00-245.00	—	—	—	9	3	10	56	2	1	—	8	—	—	—	—	—	—	—	—	—	—
Computer operators, class C	158	40.0	225.50	233.00	203.50-233.00	—	4	11	20	17	92	3	1	4	1	—	—	1	2	2	—	—	—	—	—	—
Manufacturing	31	40.0	247.00	222.00	187.50-275.50	—	—	4	5	6	4	3	1	3	—	—	—	1	2	2	—	—	—	—	—	—
Registered industrial nurses	59	40.0	390.00	411.00	316.00-452.00	—	—	—	—	—	1	2	2	9	2	1	1	7	6	17	8	3	—	—	—	—
Manufacturing	58	40.0	390.00	414.50	314.50-452.50	—	—	—	—	—	1	2	2	9	2	1	1	6	6	17	8	3	—	—	—	—

EXHIBIT 5 Information Obtained and/or Verified from Secrid

Position	Years with Company	198X Rate	Present Rate	Name	Notes
		Secrid Manufacturing Co., Inc.			
Executive secretary—sales/financial	17	1,290	1,380	Pulley	None
Data entry operations	—	845	—		Vacant as of 5/1/8(X + 1)
Maintenance supply/receiving clerk	8	1,065	1,155	Toler	None
Clerk—sales administration	2	810	925	Carr	Promoted to grade 3
Traffic/credit administration assistant	12	1,240	1,340	Arlington	None
Data processing operations	1	860	925	Oehler	None
Industrial nurse	8	1,470	1,470	Jasper	Last raise 9/8X
Executive secretary—manufacturing	4	1,185	1,300	Tarkington	None
Sales department secretary	10	1,145	1,145	Art	Last raise 7/8X
	14	1,105	1,190	White	None
	2	1,015	1,095	Level	None
Accounts payable clerk	3	880	950	Thorne	None
Order-billing clerk	1	765	820	Parnell	None
Clerk—accounts payable/inventory control/traffic	—	810	—	—	Vacant as of 5/1/8(X + 1)
Purchasing department secretary	18	1,165	1,260	Kale	None
Switchboard operator/receptionist	1	750	805	Peter	None
Personnel generalist	9	1,160	1,275	Welch	None
Payroll clerk	3	930	1,085	Sellers	None

42 Paying for Performance, or What Have You Done for Us Lately?*

(Dr. Phil Roberts, department chair of public administration at Chancellor State University, is puzzled about how he should handle the salary increase recommendations for his departmental faculty. Although he has normally recommended pay increases as a percentage of the professor's current salary, the new dean has clearly stated his preference for the use of absolute dollar salary adjustments. Roberts has recently completed his faculty performance evaluations and has prepared salary adjustment proposals for each of the two methods. The two approaches yield significantly different pay increases for some faculty members, which concerns Dr. Roberts. He must be able to justify whichever plan he recommends in terms of its effectiveness in advancing organizational goals and its fairness to the faculty. At the end of the case, Dr. Roberts is pondering which set or proposals is better, since he must submit his salary increase recommendations tomorrow.)

Dr. Phil Roberts was puzzled. Several hours ago, he had left a meeting with the other department heads and Dr. Rex Anthony, their new dean who had recently come to Chancellor State University. The meeting had been called to discuss how

*Prepared by Professor Thomas R. Miller, Memphis State University.

next year's salary increase program for college faculty was going to be administered. As chair of the department of public administration, Dr. Roberts had attended such meetings each spring for four years, thus the subject was certainly not new to him. Usually, the dean would discuss increase funds that were available, the relationship of the salary increases to faculty performance evaluations, and the procedure and schedule that were to be followed in implementing the salary increase program. Although little new information typically was provided, Dr. Roberts listened patiently to these presentations for any variations from what was done the previous year.

But this year there was something different—quite different—in the new dean's instruction. The dean had encouraged the department heads to use absolute dollar pay increases, rather than percentage increases, in making their recommendations. The dean's final words stuck in his mind: "It is your responsibility to use these salary increase dollars to promote the most effective performance of your departments. You need to have a salary increase plan you can justify to yourself, to your faculty, and to me." Exactly how Dr. Roberts was going to do this was not clear to him. But he had less than two days to think it over and prepare his salary recommendations.

BACKGROUND

Chancellor State University is a large, comprehensive, state-assisted university with an enrollment of about 16,000 students. Located in a medium-sized city in the Midwest, the university offers a wide variety of degree programs at both the undergraduate and graduate levels.

Dr. Phil Roberts has been on the Chancellor State faculty for 12 years and was named department chair over four years ago. The public administration department contains nine faculty members, with specialties in urban planning and management, general public administration, and healthcare administration. The faculty represents a broad mix of disciplinary specialties, industry experience, academic credentials, and orientations to the varied teaching–research–service activities of university professors. Some have chiefly undergraduate teaching responsibilities, others focus on graduate instruction, several are active researchers and publishers, and a few contribute extensively to community and professional service projects. Almost half of the faculty has had 10 or more years experience at Chancellor State, and four have joined the faculty in the last 4 years. The diverse nature of the departmental faculty has contributed to a wide range of salary levels within the department. Indeed, the highest paid professor earns $62,650 and the lowest paid receives $40,953.

In January when Dr. Rex Anthony was named dean of the school of business and public administration, the faculty expressed varying levels of approval and concern about his appointment. On one hand, he presented several years of valuable experience in academic administration and had gained a reputation as an innovator. On the other, he had been characterized as being rather opinionated and controversial at times.

For the past two years, the salary increases at Chancellor State had been quite modest, averaging only about 2 percent annually. The preliminary estimate of a salary increase pool of about 6 percent salary had certainly raised the hopes of the faculty. Indeed, when the announcement of a 7 percent salary increase pool was made early in May, faculty morale seemed to improve with general expectations of sizable pay raises for the next academic year (September through May). Although no one knew what his or her raise might be, given the uncertainty about the raise guidelines, many anticipated a good salary increase after two years of minimal pay improvement.

For several years, Chancellor State had utilized a systematic performance evaluation system for faculty members. Basically, the process involved a modified management-by-objectives approach, in which the department chair and each faculty member established activities and goals at the beginning of the academic year (September) on which the professor would be evaluated at the end of the academic year (May). The process involved evaluation of one's performance in several subcategories of teaching, research, and service by the department chair, giving attention to the plans and goals established earlier for that faculty member. At the completion of the evaluation process, the faculty member's scores in each performance area were combined to produce an overall composite score. Even though this system had limitations and was certainly not perfect, the performance appraisal system had become reasonably well accepted by the faculty as it did recognize individual differences in activities undertaken and accomplished.

University policy specified that the faculty member's evaluation score was to be the major factor in pay increase recommendations. How this was handled varied somewhat among the colleges at Chancellor State, but in the school of business and public affairs the pay raises had to be consistent with performance evaluation scores. Thus, if three professors had composite evaluation scores of 8.1, 8.5, and 9.1, then their respective pay increases had to correlate percentage pay increase with the composite evaluation score. For most of the 12 years Dr. Roberts had been on the faculty, this approach had been used. For the first two or three years he was there, however, the performance evaluations had little impact on pay increases, since salary improvements were largely across-the-board increases, giving scant attention to the faculty evaluation scores. Within recent years, there had been increasing emphasis on "merit" or "performance" in determining salary adjustments.

THE MEETING

Dr. Anthony said that he had reviewed personnel files in the college and had discussed the past practices on salary increases with several administrators. Although he had no doubt that each of the department chairs had tried to administer the pay raise program as well as possible, he had reservations about past practices in handling raises. Of particular concern to him was whether the department heads had utilized the pay increase program as wisely as possible. Were they using the limited funds to optimize the performance of their departmental faculty? Were they providing the right motivational incentives? Dr. Roberts listened intently since he felt he had done a conscientious job of rewarding the faculty in relation to their performance under the university evaluation system. Dr. Anthony continued:

> I think what must be questioned is the way you have handled pay raises here. Now, understand, I'm not at this point concerned with the faculty evaluation system itself. It may need attention, but we'll get to that later. What I'm questioning is why you have percentage pay raises. Percentage pay raises don't enable you to reward the low salaried, outstanding performers enough and they can protect a poor performer who has been paid a big salary.

> What I'd rather see is the use of absolute dollar pay increases which would reflect the existing salary level of the faculty member. If your highest paid person is the weakest performer for this year, he or she would receive the lowest raise, if any, in the department. If your lowest paid person had the best performance, then he or she would get the highest raise. If you handle raises this way, you're not restricted by the person's existing salary.
>
> I realize that what I'm suggesting breaks new ground around here, and I'm not going to insist that you handle the salary increase program this way, at least not this year. But I really want you to seriously consider it.
>
> This year each department will start with a salary increase pool equal to 7 percent of the total faculty salary budget of the department. Note also that the central administration requires that all faculty receive at least a 2 percent raise. I don't particularly like this, but the administration mandated it. So we have no choice in the matter.

Following Dr. Anthony's remarks, there were many comments and questions as well as a lot of side conversation among the department heads. Clearly, Dr. Anthony's idea of using absolute dollars, rather than the traditional percentage pay increases, was controversial. One of the department heads said it was a "bad idea that would create serious morale problems" among the faculty. Also, the remark was made that "absolute dollar raises would wreck the existing salary structure."

In contrast, some comments were favorable or at least neutral. One department head thought the proposed system would "help him keep some good young professors from moving to other schools." Although not endorsing the idea, another department head said he thought the proposal had some merit, but wanted to think more about it.

There also was some disagreement among the group about the required 2 percent raise for all. Some felt it should be more while others opposed any across-the-board raise. But it seemed to be a secondary issue among the department heads.

Near the end of the meeting after an hour of discussion, a consensus on the best method of handling the salary increase program had not emerged. Finally, Dr. Anthony rose and said:

> I've asked you to carefully consider how you're going to make your salary increase recommendations. I will need to have you turn those in to me within 48 hours so we can meet the university deadline for returning these forms.
>
> As in the past, your salary increase recommendations must be consistent with the composite evaluation scores of faculty members' performance. The scores and the recommended pay raises are to be listed on the forms provided. After they are reviewed, I will contact you to discuss any discrepancies or any recommendations which I have questions about or any you want to discuss.
>
> In conclusion, make the salary recommendations you believe are appropriate after you've carefully thought over the system you're going to use. It is your responsibility to use these salary increase dollars to promote the most effective performance of your department. You need to have a salary increase plan that you can justify to yourself, your faculty, and to me.

THE PROPOSALS

When Dr. Roberts returned to his office, he began to review his performance ratings for his department faculty in preparation for making the pay recommendations. In fact, he had earlier calculated preliminary salary recommendations employing the percentage increase system that he had always used before. But given Dr. Anthony's instructions, and his apparent preferences, Dr. Roberts knew he should work up a pay increase scheme based on the absolute dollar system. After over an hour of study and calculation, he had prepared tentative pay increase recommendations for both the percentage increase and the absolute dollar methods. The drafts of the forms completed by Dr. Roberts are shown in Exhibits 1 and 2.

Dr. Roberts then compared the two salary proposals and noted how different the resulting salaries were for some faculty members. The size of the professor's salary base could surely make a difference with the existing pay raise system. But the evaluation score was more strongly reflected in the salary increase using the absolute dollar method. After further reflection, Dr. Roberts was still not sure which pay increase proposal he would submit to Dr. Anthony nor how he would justify his recommendations. He was glad he had another day to evaluate this decision.

Discussion Questions

Was one of these proposals better than the other, given the objectives of the salary increase program? Which method would be more effective? And which system would be fairer? he wondered.

EXHIBIT 1 Proposed Salary Increases Based on Percentages

	Current Salary	*Composite Evaluation*	*Proposed Increase*	*Percent Increase*	*Proposed Salary*
Ken Pett	$ 62,650	9.5	$ 6,887	11.0	$ 69,537
Alex Morgan	40,953	9.0	3,765	9.2	44,718
Joan Martin	57,240	9.0	5,263	9.2	62,503
Allan Ford	43,158	8.6	3,346	7.8	46,504
Catherine Marx	51,780	8.3	3,456	6.7	55,236
Paula Johnson	49,143	8.0	2,751	5.6	51,894
Larry Segner	60,175	7.5	2,284	3.8	62,459
Phil Langston	43,920	7.0	879	2.0	44,799
Total	$409,019		$28,631		$437,650

EXHIBIT 2 Proposed Salary Increases Based on Absolute Dollars

	Current Salary	*Composite Evaluation*	*Proposed Increase*	*Percent Increase*	*Proposed Salary*
Ken Pett	$ 62,650	9.5	$ 5,833	9.3	$ 68,483
Alex Morgan	40,953	9.0	4,842	11.8	45,795
Joan Martin	57,240	9.0	4,842	8.5	62,082
Allan Ford	43,158	8.6	4,049	9.4	47,207
Catherine Marx	51,780	8.3	3,445	6.7	55,235
Paula Johnson	49,143	8.0	2,861	5.8	52,004
Larry Segner	60,175	7.5	1,870	3.1	62,045
Phil Langston	43,920	7.0	879	2.0	44,799
Total	$409,019		$28,631		$437,650

Section H

Occupational Health and Safety

43 Breyer Meat Packing, Inc.

The Breyer Meat Packing, Inc., is one of the largest meat-packing firms in the Midwest. The firm, located in Sioux City, Iowa, employs 580 workers. The administrative staff includes plant management, clerical workers, infirmary staff, and a two-person personnel office. However, most of the employees (540) are considered line employees. Their view of the administrative staff is that that group represents overhead. In private, workers talk about how much more they themselves could make if the plant manager, Melvin Flournoy, would trim some of the "fat." These employees had come to know and like Charmaine, Mel's administrative assistant. There wasn't much that happened around the place that she didn't know about. A number of workers trusted and confided in her. Charmaine never violated anyone's confidence. So, it was no surprise that Brenda and other meat cutters told her about their hopes, dreams, and fears.

"Charmaine, my hands have been bothering me something terrible! I really think it's part arthritis and part having to do the same movements all the time at my workbench. I can't prove it but other veteran meat cutters are having trouble with their wrists and hands, too." These comments were the first indication that Charmaine had that her friend Brenda was having the same kind of trouble other employees in the firm had complained about over the past 10 years. Of course, the workers didn't want to complain too often or too loudly, since there was little support from management to solve or even investigate the problem. In fact, Brenda remembers when Willie Wooten complained to his supervisor about numbness and trouble moving his arms and hands. It wasn't long before Willie had joined the unemployment lines.

Many employees, Charmaine included, had heard the rumors about Willie and other employees who complained about hand, wrist, and arm problems. The grapevine had it that those who complained would be let go, so the company could avoid any workers' compensation claims. Charmaine didn't know what to believe. They had always treated her well. She had worked for BMP, Inc., for 15 years. As a secretary in the plant manager's office, she had seen a number of changes take place, and she also had watched the company grow from a small shop of less than 100 employees to a medium-sized firm of 580 employees.

During the past year, BMP, Inc., had been visited by many compliance agency representatives. Of course, on a continuous basis, U.S. Department of Agriculture meat inspectors remained on the premises, examining the meats to be certain that they were graded properly. In January, the Environmental Protection Agency (EPA) visited and inspected the plant. Their concern was to see that waste and meat by-products were being disposed of properly. The EPA inspectors wanted to verify that there were no air or water pollution violations. The Occupational Safety and Health Administration (OSHA) has jurisdiction over the workplace when it comes to health and safety matters. The OSHA people came during the summer months. Their visit appeared to surprise plant management. The OSHA inspectors spent most of their time checking industrial accident and sickness records. Little time was spent observing the actual meat-packing processes. The last agency to visit was the Immigration and Naturalization Service (INS). It had never been to the plant before. Charmaine had been told by her boss, Mr. Bob Riley, that the INS had taken on the task of enforcing something called the Immigration Reform and Control Act. This fairly new act required that only people who have the right to live and work in the United States be employed by American companies. The companies are responsible for any violations of the law. Charmaine wasn't sure what the INS wanted. She did know that, when their inspectors left, they seemed upset that the company had not modified certain personnel and recordkeeping procedures. One inspector asked Charmaine if she was aware of any changes in personnel background checks or citizenship verification procedures. Mel had gone on a two-day tirade over the federal government and all its recordkeeping demands.

As Charmaine thought about what Brenda and others told her, she wondered if anything should be done about this recurring problem. She wasn't sure what responsibility, if any, the company had to those who complained of arm, wrist, and hand troubles. Finally, she asked herself, what role would any of the government agencies mentioned play in resolving the physical problems?

Discussion Question

How would you respond to Charmaine's questions?

44 The Philadelphia Bulletin (A)

The *Philadelphia Bulletin* is one of three daily newspapers in a thriving market—the metropolitan Philadelphia area. In recent weeks there has been a great deal of talk about news from within the organization, as opposed to the reporting of activities that have occurred outside the firm. All employees were still in a state of shock over the discovery that many of the workers suffered from a debilitating work-related ailment.

The personnel office had to turn its attention from the daily ritual of screening application forms for replacement personnel in a rapidly changing high-turnover environment. Instead of the immediate concern of getting the right person in the right job, the personnel office had to find ways of keeping healthy the employees the *Bulletin* has hired. The problem: RSI. RSI, or repetitive strain injury, affects the wrists, elbows, or arms, and it is caused by spending long hours writing or editing with some kinds of computers.

THE BUSINESS SECTION

Roberta Peters is an author and national financial securities writer for the *Bulletin.* She was told not to pick up a pencil. She has been forced to wear splints and stop writing for weeks at a time. "Of all the injuries I've had in my life, this is the worst. Your hands are so essential to everything you do in this business. I earn my livelihood by using my hands. Writers have no choice in the matter." Other employees in this section are affected. Fortunately, some of them simply report a little tenderness in their elbows or wrists that is relieved by exercises, better posture, or an occasional break from the video terminal.

Roberta describes the progression of the disease. "The pain progressed slowly. It began in the hands and wrists like a twinge of arthritis or numbness. Some of my athletic friends might see similarities between this condition and tennis elbow. I tried to work through it. The result was intense pain; pain so intense that I could not sleep at night. In fact, even the most routine tasks became impossible to do. Picking up a book or folding laundry caused waves of pain to shoot up along my hands, wrists, and arms."

The hard part, Roberta said, was dealing with her feelings. "I alternated between being angry that my work had led to this problem and fearful that I would never be able to return to doing the work I loved."

Requirement

1. What can the employees and the employer do to help overcome the problem of RSI?

The Philadelphia Bulletin (B)

The meeting was a somber one. Crowded into the small room that served as the office of Carter Jones, city editor, were William Hines, associate sports editor; Jonathan Randal, general counsel; Eleanor Randolph, education editor; Sandy Rovner, health editor; Don Colburn, county news; Paul Reisner, science editor; and the managing editor, Daniel Burnside. Last to enter the room was the publisher and editor, Steven Altman. The publisher addressed the group, "As you all know, Frank suffered a mild heart attack two weeks ago. He was taken to University Hospital on the Penn campus. He suffered the attack while relaxing at home. Thank goodness, the hospital is located only a few blocks from his home.

"I've asked William Hines to serve as sports editor during Frank's recovery period. It is a demanding job, but I feel certain that Bill can do what needs to be done during Frank's absence. Bill has worked with Frank over the past nine years and knows the routine and demands of the job.

"One thing I hope you all realize, and I say this for Bill as much as for anyone in this room: Frank's heart attack should help us realize the inherent stress and demanding nature of the jobs we do. The deadlines are 'tight' and the hours are long. Every day we each feel the pressure. Back in journalism school our professors tried to help us understand and appreciate this aspect of the job. Everyone who completed a journalism program was required to do an internship at a newspaper so he or she would have a firsthand acquaintance with the hustle and bustle of our business. We were told that if we wanted a typical 'nine-to-five existence we were in the wrong field of endeavor'.

"You might be wondering why I invited Mr. Randal to this meeting and why I made this previous comment about the demands and nature of the job. These two are connected. I thought that I would ask Jonathan to explain the connection."

Randal explained to the group that there is an increasing amount of litigation occurring in this country. "One area of rapid change involves that dealing with personal legal liability of managers under employment discrimination law. We are discovering that tort claims—for example, assault, battery, defamation, infliction of emotional distress—are being made against employers and their agents. Closer to home—we have been informed by an attorney that Frank and his family have brought a tort action against us in state court. According to the documents we have received, the newspaper and Mr. Altman are judged directly responsible for the stress-related illnesses suffered by Frank. He charges that the nature of the job is such that we knew or should have known that the tasks and demands of the job would directly lead to stress-related outcomes. It is our intent to proceed by hiring independent legal counsel to obtain an evaluation of Mr. Altman's rights and whether there exists any conflict of interest with the corporation."

Discussion Questions

1. Discuss the nature of the job and the lawsuit now filed against the newspaper.
2. What rights and responsibilities do employees and employers have in relation to high-stress jobs?

45 Hargrove Petrochemicals (A)

Hargrove Petrochemicals is composed of 10 autonomous divisions and corporate headquarters, as Exhibit 1 indicates. The case focuses on the Bristol Works. Its organization is given in Exhibit 2.

Bristol Works is housed in a building erected in 1904. The building is five stories high. The top two are not used since the floors are too dangerous. The second and third floors have holes and rotted places in them.

The third floor holds the rock shop lab and the marketing departments. The second floor contains the office, some warehousing, and some buffing compound production lines. The first floor contains the warehousing for heavier materials and the rest of the manufacturing lines. The main operation is chemicals. The work is nonunion.

Jesse Fuller has been with Hargrove for 20 years, all in conjunction with the Bristol Works. He holds a BS in chemistry from City University of New York. He worked his way through college. He's done almost everything at Bristol. He started as a foreman in the manufacturing unit. He's run the rock shop, supervised the warehouse for two years, and sold the compounds. The office and lab are white-collar or technical jobs, so he's not worked there. His employees like him, although they are a bit afraid of him, too. He has a terrible temper, which he loses about once a month. When that happens, everyone tries to get out of the way.

Jesse is now 53 years old. He's happy with the Bristol Works. He likes the town and wouldn't move. Bristol is like his own firm since he's isolated geographically from Hargrove.

Since Bristol makes more money for Hargrove than his budget calls for, they let Jesse alone. He has lower turnover than expected. Absenteeism is also low. His safety and health record is above average. All in all, Hargrove and Jesse are happy with the Bristol Works.

During the past years since the effective date of the Occupational Safety and Health Act, Bristol has been subject to routine but infrequent visits by OSHA inspectors. In February 1984, James Munsey, a new inspector, was assigned to the region. In April, James came to Bristol when Jesse was at a meeting at headquarters. The OSHA inspector determined that the buffing manufacturing was producing unsafe gases. As is his right, he shut down the plant that day. Jesse flew back and modified the

EXHIBIT 1 Hargrove Petrochemicals Organization Chart

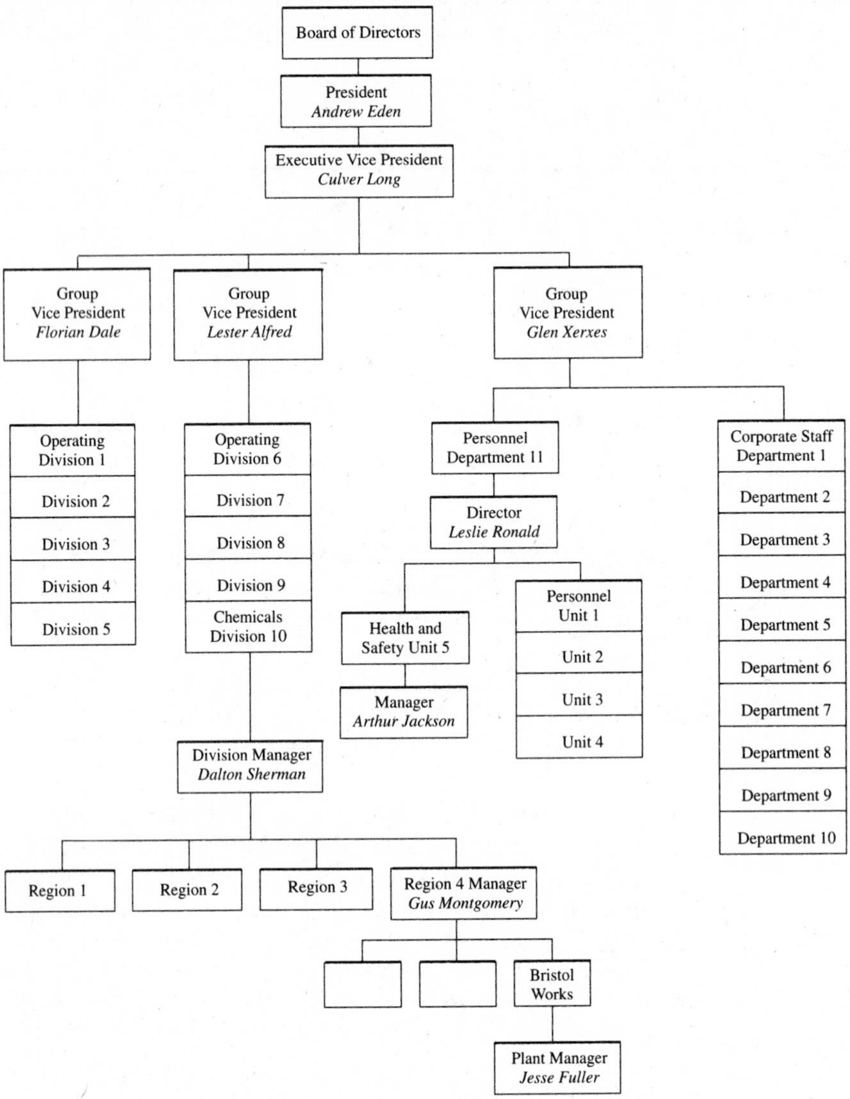

Board of Directors

President
Andrew Eden

Executive Vice President
Culver Long

Group Vice President
Florian Dale

Group Vice President
Lester Alfred

Group Vice President
Glen Xerxes

Operating Division 1
Division 2
Division 3
Division 4
Division 5

Operating Division 6
Division 7
Division 8
Division 9
Chemicals Division 10

Division Manager
Dalton Sherman

Region 1
Region 2
Region 3

Region 4 Manager
Gus Montgomery

Bristol Works

Plant Manager
Jesse Fuller

Personnel Department 11

Director
Leslie Ronald

Health and Safety Unit 5

Manager
Arthur Jackson

Personnel Unit 1
Unit 2
Unit 3
Unit 4

Corporate Staff Department 1
Department 2
Department 3
Department 4
Department 5
Department 6
Department 7
Department 8
Department 9
Department 10

gas filters. James passed the filters, and Bristol started production again. Before leaving the plant, James informed Jesse that, because various toxic substances, such as benzene, were utilized at Bristol, he thought it best to inspect the plant more frequently.

EXHIBIT 2 Organization Chart: Bristol Works

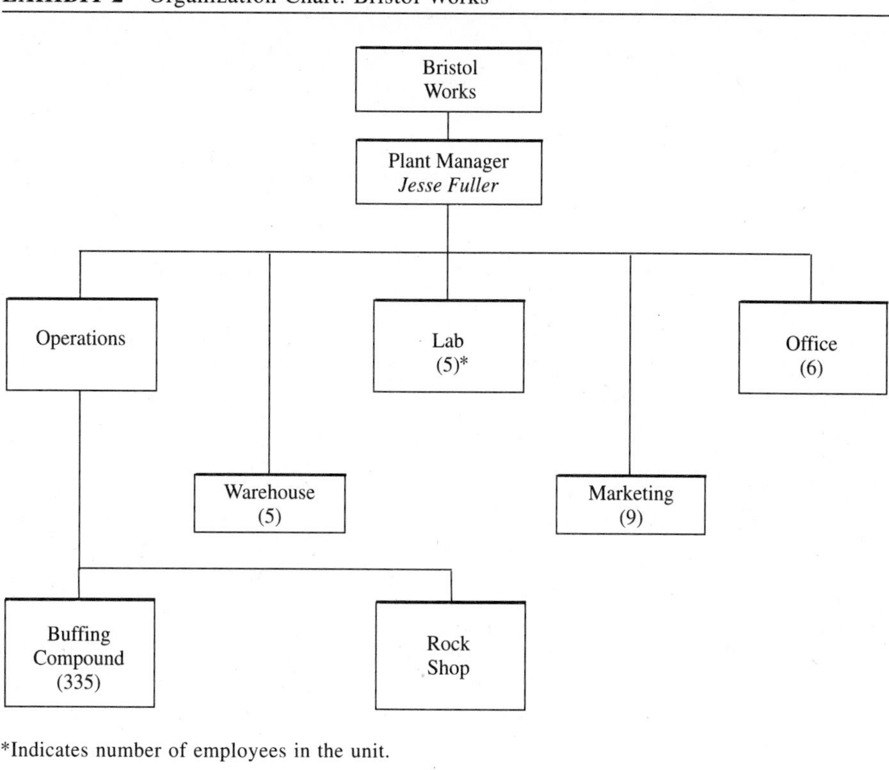

*Indicates number of employees in the unit.

In May, James came back and shut the plant again when Jesse was at a Rotary meeting. Again, the filters were cleaned and modified. This time Jesse was really angry. After the plant was reopened and James was gone, Jesse held a meeting of all employees. At the meeting he said:

> Look, this OSHA guy is killing us. This is an old works. We can't afford to be shut down. At my recent meeting at corporate headquarters, I tried to make the case that we needed a new building here. The sharp-pencil boys pointed out that we are profitable now, but not if we have to build a new plant. The industry is overcrowded, and Hargrove will close this plant, rather than spend money on it. If we get shut down or have to buy a lot of antipollution crap, they could shut us down. That OSHA guy is the enemy—just like a traffic cop. We've got to pull together, or we could all sink together.

The employees had never seen Jesse so angry before, and they feared for their jobs now more than ever. There was a lot of unemployment in the area. Before adjourning the meeting, Jesse asked his people for ideas on how to deal with the OSHA inspector. Responses ranged from beating up James to barring him from the plant.

In July, James Munsey appeared at the Bristol Works gate. In accordance with their instructions, the guards stopped James until he could be signed in and given a badge. Once the guards received authorization, then he could be allowed on the premises. Security guard Clarence Smith phoned Jesse.

Smith [to Fuller]

The OSHA inspector is here to see you.

Fuller

Oh, my God! [pause] You go out there and tell him I'm too busy to see him today.

Munsey

Ask your boss if he's too busy tomorrow.

Smith [on the intercom]

Mr. Fuller, are you too busy tomorrow to see the inspector?

Fuller [on the intercom]

What do you want this time, Munsey?

Munsey

Because of previous violations, you're due for another inspection.

Fuller

Look, I'm busy. I am not sure when I will be able to see you. In fact, I don't feel obligated to let you in unless you can produce a search warrant. That, and only that, will convince me that you have a legitimate purpose.

After Munsey left, the place was bedlam. Everyone was put on red alert. No work was done. The whole plant was cleaned up. The lab was put in order. Bottles that leaked were secured. Shelves were straightened. The rock shop was cleaned up. Machines without safety guards were moved and covered up, as if they were no longer used. Machines too heavy for the third floor were moved. The filters were cleaned. The water bath was cleaned. The slippery floor made of metal, which was supposed to be neutralized and scrubbed daily (though it usually got it monthly), was neutralized and scrubbed. Everyone helped. Even the secretaries and lab technicians helped with the cleaning. The lab was put in order.

The next day the inspector returned. He did not have a warrant. The guard waved him on and sent him to Fuller's office. James and Jesse toured the plant and the inspector passed the Bristol Works. But the employees wondered if the inspector didn't have to realize what had happened.

Discussion Questions

1. Under what conditions does a company have the right to refuse OSHA inspectors admission to the facilities?
2. What are the real problems and issues in this case? Explain.

Hargrove Petrochemicals (B)

On August 15, a group of federal inspectors pulled up to the Bristol Works gate. They stopped there and asked to see Jesse Fuller, the plant manager. Security guard Wesley Walker called Fuller.

Walker [to Fuller]

Federal inspectors are here to see you.

Fuller

Inspectors! Don't tell me James Munsey thinks he needs help?

Walker

No, sir. I met Mr. Munsey. He is not here. These gentlemen are from an agency called the EPA.

Fuller

EPA! Keep them there. I will come down to the gatehouse to meet them.

Walker

Issue badges and sign them in, sir?

Fuller

No. Just wait until I get there.

Fuller went over to the gatehouse. When he arrived, he introduced himself. He met the five representatives of the Environmental Protection Agency. The agents were armed with a search warrant from a U.S. magistrate. The team had been sent to check compliance with the Toxic Substances Control Act. The team's makeup was interesting. Of the five people, two were agency officials, one was a state environmental worker, and two were employees of a private company, Bildisco Environmental, Inc., which was one of a number of consulting corporations hired by the EPA to conduct inspections.

Jesse looked thoughtful for awhile, then turned to the security guard. He told Walker not to issue badges or to sign in anyone. Jesse told the EPA inspectors that they would not be admitted to the plant. After a very lengthy argument, the five men left the premises waving the search warrant and vowing to return.

In a formal letter to the Environmental Protection Agency, the company explained that it did not object to an inspection but it was dissatisfied with the makeup of the EPA inspection group. Hargrove management claimed to be particularly concerned about protecting its trade secrets. If the EPA sends a team consisting of its own agents, the company said, they will have free access to the plant and be made privy to the specifics of any chemical process. Hargrove felt that it was protected by federal law because EPA employees were restricted in terms of the information they learned. Few private consultants are subject to the same sanctions imposed by the Trade Secrets Act or other federal law. Also, the company believed that private consultants abuse their power. These outsiders like to throw their weight around.

The federal agency's response wasn't long in coming. The EPA did not accept the company's position. The EPA believed it was a smoke screen used to prevent the government from detecting noncompliance with the Toxic Substances Control Act. Further, the worry about consultants being untrustworthy was seen as unwarranted. Since the EPA began using large numbers of consultants, it has encountered no increase in complaints regarding trade secrets. The EPA also informed Hargrove that a lawsuit would be forthcoming. When Jesse Fuller received his copy of the letter, he wondered if he had gotten the company into big trouble.

Discussion Questions

1. Does a company have a right to bar EPA inspectors from the company's facilities?
2. Evaluate the company's stated reasons for barring the EPA inspection team. Are the reasons legitimate? Tell why or why not.

Hargrove Petrochemicals (C)

Arthur Jackson is manager of the health and safety division of Hargrove's personnel department. Arthur is a graduate of Case Western Reserve University, with a BS in industrial engineering. He has taken additional short courses in safety management offered by various professional associations. He had five years' experience in the safety department of Allied Chemical before coming to Hargrove a year ago. He was safety manager for several operating divisions (including this division) prior to coming to the home office staff last year. He has tried to visit each division and plant since then, although he has never been to the Bristol Works. Hargrove has many plants, and he has personally visited about one-third of them since he went to the home office.

The role of corporate-level health and safety is to set policy for the corporation. The office keeps the divisions and plants informed on the latest information, trains divisional and (where appropriate) plant-level people, and is responsible to the president for safety for the whole company. It also is responsible for seeing that all operations meet all health and safety standards of the company and OSHA. Jackson has three professionals on his staff.

Arthur has received word about Bristol's recent experiences with OSHA and has decided to go down to Bristol and see what's going on. He arrives the week after the EPA visit. Jesse is sick that day. Arthur inspects the works and finds numerous OSHA violations. The Works also violates a number of Hargrove's own safety and health regulations.

When Arthur returns to his office, he decides to call a meeting of his subordinates to discuss how the company might approach the problem of making Bristol Works safe and hazard-free for employees there. He decides to generate his own list of alternative actions, just in case his subordinates come up empty. In rummaging through his files he discovers a report on genetic screening for employment purposes.[1] The more he reads, the more he likes the idea. A professor at the University of Maryland, Judy D. Olian, had done an extensive study on the current level of corporate involvement in genetic screening, and she identified a series of public policy issues related to the use of genetic screening devices. Arthur silently thanked her for her thoroughness. He believed that the home office would be unwilling to make major improvements at Bristol, but that minor improvements, emphasis on the use of protective clothing, including respirators, and genetic screening might do the trick. So, he would propose this short-term solution. He had his secretary reproduce Professor Olian's study as well as a report by the Office of Technology and Assessment, "The Role of Genetic Testing in the Prevention of Occupational Disease." These materials, along with a couple of recent newspaper articles on the subject, were distributed to his subordinates.

Discussion Questions

1. Assume you are one of Arthur's subordinates. How effective do you believe genetic testing would be in making Bristol Works a safer and healthier workplace?
2. What kinds of issues and legal implications are raised in using genetic screening for employment purposes?

---

*46 A-1 Electronics**

A-1 Electronics, located in Cincinnati, Ohio, is a wholesale distributor of electrical equipment and parts. During the past few years, A-1 has enjoyed a steady sales growth, which has allowed for an expansion in the geographical territory A-1

1 Genetic screening in the employment context involves the identification of applicants hyper susceptible to occupational disease, thus facilitating selective placement or exclusion of candidates on the basis of the genetic information.

* This case was prepared by Professor William P. Smith, Hofstra University.

covers and a broader product line. Six years ago A-1's sales were limited to the greater Cincinnati area. Currently there are customers in a five-state region. Over the same period, the number of inventory items has increased from 14,000 to approximately 20,000 items. Business growth and the need for greater efficiencies, particularly in A-1's recordhandling, are responsible for a modernization plan in the main office. This modernization plan includes purchasing more automated office equipment and recruiting qualified persons to operate such equipment.

The company's main office is the workplace for three managers and 16 clerical staff. Robert Riley, the general manager, has his own secretary, as do the purchasing manager, Steven Phillips, and the accounting manager, Elizabeth Seale. All of the managers' offices are adjacent to a large work area, where all of the office employees are located. Of the remaining 13 office staff, 5 are responsible for purchasing and accounts payable functions, another 5 oversee inventory control, outgoing shipments, and accounts receivable records, and 3 employees perform typing and filing tasks. See Exhibit 1 for a basic floor plan of the office.

The area where all office employees work is basically a large room, 1,000 square feet in area, with no subdivisions, partitions, or walls to separate the workers. There is one door at the front of the office that is used as a main entrance. A corridor at the rear of the office leads to the main warehouse. There are no windows in the main office area and the building is centrally heated and air-conditioned.

All of the 16 office employees are women. Nine have been with the company 10 years or more, 11 are 45 years or older, and 12 are married. Their pay is average for those persons with comparable skills in the local labor market. A basic benefit package includes life and health insurance, a pension plan, and paid vacations. These benefits are modest, but typical for the labor market, and accrue slowly as a function of seniority.

As part of the modernization plan for A-1's office, a word processing system was leased. None of the current employees is sufficiently skilled or particularly interested in learning to operate this new piece of equipment. Thus, the decision was made to hire someone who already possessed word processing experience. To assist with recruitment, the services of a local employment agency were retained. A-1 had had good success in the past with this agency.

By the end of the second week of recruitment, two qualified persons had been referred by the employment agency. After interviews with both applicants, Robert Riley and the office manager offered the job to Kathryn Palmer. Riley was quite satisfied with the selection and was anxious to have her begin work, because the expense of leasing word processing equipment and of the recruiting process was making this transaction a costly one.

Kathryn's first few days in the job appeared to go very well. Her past experience on an identical word processing system was a definite asset. She also seemed to get along quite well with the other people in the office. However, the afternoon of her fourth day on the job Kathryn complained of headaches and nausea and asked to go home. The following morning she reported to work in apparently fine health. After working a couple of hours, she began suffering from the same complaints and again asked to go home. Later that day, Kathryn called Riley from her home and apologetically submitted her resignation. She said the cigarette smoke in the office created by other employees was responsible for her illness. Kathryn's resignation and her reason caught Riley totally by surprise. He sensed Kathryn must have really had another reason for wanting to quit and was looking for an excuse in the cigarette smoke. Riley knew a majority of the office employees smoked at their desks. Occasionally, jokes were made about "air pollution" in the office, but the jokes never seemed too serious or critical. No one had ever formally complained about the smoking. Riley was tempted to dismiss Kathryn as some sort of fanatic, yet he realized he now faced a rather serious problem. A-1 was back at "square one" and would have to reinitiate a search for another word processing operator.

Riley informed the employment agency of Kathryn's resignation on what he felt to be spurious grounds. The agency assured him they would not charge a fee for placing Kathryn and would commence a new search immediately. Unfortunately, they told him, the other qualified applicant was no longer available and that, at this time, the supply of experienced word processing operators was not keeping pace with demand. In the meantime, another division of the employment agency specializing in temporary employment could refer experienced persons who were available strictly for short-term assignments. Riley contracted to have a temporary employee come to work at A-1 while a search for a full-time replacement was conducted. Riley was anxious to settle on someone and get the word processing operation going, because by now there were other, what he considered more pressing, matters for his attention. It was Friday afternoon and the temporary employee was contracted to begin work on the following Monday for two full weeks.

On Monday, the temporary employee reported to work and remained all day. She also had experience on this same system and caught on quickly for her first day. Later that evening, Riley received a call at his home from a representative of the agency, saying the temporary worker had asked to be removed from the assignment and that another temporary worker would have to be assigned. The reason for the reassignment: the temporary employee could not tolerate the smoke in the office.

On Tuesday morning the second temporary employee (or third, as Riley had come to think of it) reported to A-1. Both the temporary service and Riley spoke to the new worker about smoke in the office, and the employee, although a nonsmoker, indicated smoking did not bother her. Over the course of the next several days this employee would remain with the assignment. Riley considered her performance to be adequate.

The sudden resignation of two promising workers for the same reason gave Riley cause to consider their complaint. As the search for a permanent replacement continued into its second week without success, Riley began to contemplate the "fish that got away" and if there might have been a way both resignations could have been avoided. He began to examine the situation more fully.

Of the 16 people in the office, 10 were smokers. Most of the smoking employees were among those who had been with A-1 for several years and had a demonstrated loyalty to the firm. It was true that, despite the centrally controlled cooling system, by late afternoon a hazy fog would accumulate and the temperature might increase to 80 degrees. These factors had never seemed important before, but they began to take on a new significance as Riley reflected on a recent article he had read in the newspaper citing nonsmokers' complaints about public smoking. The article referred to recent legislation in San Francisco, California, and in Suffolk County, New York, which required employers to accommodate a smoke-free work environment for nonsmoking employees who request one. Riley felt sure nothing like that would happen in Cincinnati, but it did cause him to speculate on the challenge his own firm might begin to face in the near future. Several of the younger, more promising office employees were nonsmokers and with time might become more assertive about their right to work in a smoke-free environment. At the same time, Riley sensed nothing but problems should he try to restrict what had become a well-entrenched social norm among a group of dedicated and loyal employees. He did not want a potential conflict on this issue to escalate into a situation where one group or the other would feel as if their rights were being unfairly sacrificed. At this time A-1 did not have a smoking policy, but Riley considered it a matter of time before one would have to be implemented. He wondered if he should wait until more complaints were raised or try and initiate a fair-minded policy now.

Discussion Questions

1. Should Riley institute some sort of no-smoking policy at A-1 at this time?
2. Should the failure to attract a qualified word processing employee be a significant factor in deciding how to handle this situation?
3. Since some localities (e.g., San Francisco and Suffolk County) have adopted "indoor air" laws, what guidelines would you suggest to an organization forced to implement a no-smoking policy?

---

*47 Andromeda Chemical, Inc. (A)**

Andromeda Chemical, Inc., had its start at the beginning of the 20th century. Today, the company operates 110 plants throughout the world. Andromeda also has 17 research laboratories across the country. It is a chemical company engaged primarily in the manufacture and sale of a diversified line of specialty chemicals. The firm's products include:

---

* This case was written by Professor George E. Stevens, Kent State University, and by Kendra Clausen and Cliff Hodge, Arizona State University. All names in the case are disguised.

1. *Consumer products*—Personal care and grooming products, women's fragrances, and household maintenance and cleaning aids.
2. *Specialty chemicals*—Specialty chemicals for industrial water treating; mining and paper chemicals; enhanced oil-recovery products; aerospace products, process chemicals, and catalysts; dyes, plastics additives; fine, rubber, and textile chemicals; inorganic and organic pigments; industrial safety equipment; and acrylic fibers for apparel, home furnishings, and industrial applications.
3. *Medical*—Antibiotics, steroids, vitamins, and other pharmaceuticals; vaccines; fine chemicals and bulk pharmaceuticals.
4. *Formica*—Formica brand decorative laminates for residential construction, commercial construction, furniture, and adhesives.
5. *Agricultural*—Animal feed, health and veterinary products, insecticides, herbicides, fungicides, and phosphate and nitrogen fertilizer products.

In 1978, Paul Green was promoted to the position of personnel director of the Denver plant of Andromeda Chemical, Inc. When interviewed for the position, Paul was led to believe that the problem areas of the job related to recruitment of technical people, turnover, and union demands for a stronger role in decision making. Once he landed the job, however, he was to learn about a more pressing problem.

Paul was really pleased that he was chosen for the personnel director's job. In his seven years with Andromeda Chemical, he had worked in a variety of positions. After graduation from Colorado State University, he accepted a personnel assistant's job with the company. He was lucky that his first assignments were all at the corporate headquarters. He received his MBA from Rutgers University exactly two months prior to leaving to take his first plant personnel assignment. Paul believed his two-year stints as assistant personnel director in plants at Omaha, Nebraska, and Cedar Rapids, Iowa, would prove invaluable to him in his new job. The Denver plant assignment seemed to be an excellent indication of the company's confidence in his abilities. Paul considered the promotion as a reward for top performance and completion of degree requirements. The plant was one of the company's largest unionized operations. The position of personnel director is critical to the successful operation of the facility.

One day, Paul looked up to see Dr. Rick Morrison, the plant's physician, striding purposefully toward his office. Seldom did he see or hear from Rick, so Paul was surprised and puzzled by this unexpected visit. Rick must have noticed Paul's bewilderment because the following conversation ensued as they met at the door:

Rick

Paul, I hate to burden you with another problem since you've only been on the job a matter of months, but I have little choice in this instance.

Paul

What's up? Is it anything serious?

Rick

I am afraid so. For some time, corporate has been studying the problem of worker exposure to toxic substances. As plant physician, my charge was to determine the existence of any work-related health or safety problem here. A plant area which has come under close scrutiny is Building 21. This building contains our lead pigment division.

Paul

Yes it does. We have a number of lead smelter workers in there who have responsibility for manufacturing and assembling certain key products.

Rick

Our studies and those of other researchers indicate a link between lead exposure and anemia, central nervous system damage, kidney disease, and "female problems."

Paul

What does that mean? We have eight women, ages 26 to 43, working in the lead pigment division. They have done an excellent job there. Women don't leave as quickly as men, and the quality of their work is higher. Is there anything wrong about women working in Building 21?

Rick

We now know that lead exposure may lead to sterility, miscarriages, and birth defects in the employees' unborn children. These problems are particularly tragic. I focus on women because their health problems are more visible and affect their babies as well.

After the conversation, Paul sat there thumbing through the report that Rick had left with him. Clearly, there was a problem. A breakdown by production process and by building location indicated that the incidence of certain medical problems was significantly higher in Building 21. That building was the only one that involved a lead chromate pigments process. The kinds of problems found were consistent with the National Institute for Occupational Safety and Health (NIOSH) research studies concerning the potential dangers of lead. If there is a link between these workers' health problems and the production process (and there seems to be), then Paul must develop alternative courses of action.

Three days after his meeting with Rick, Paul wrote a memo to Patrick Livers, the plant manager. He reviewed the events leading up to his meeting with the plant physician and the implications of the medical data. In concluding his memo, he identified a few alternative courses of action that might be taken: (1) take no action, (2) forbid women of child-bearing age from working in Building 21, and (3) discontinue the production process. Although Paul recognized that his list was not exhaustive, he felt these alternatives were the most obvious.

Discussion Question

You are Patrick. The company has given you a great deal of responsibility and autonomy. What can you do about the health problem? What other alternatives might you consider? On what basis (criteria) will you choose the best alternative?

Andromeda Chemical, Inc. (B)

In 1979, less than 12 months after Paul had been promoted to personnel director of Andromeda Chemical's Denver plant, five women filed a complaint against the company. They claimed that Andromeda had forced them to be surgically sterilized to keep their jobs. All females who worked in the plant were made an offer. The women could accept other positions in the plant. They would be transferred from their present jobs (which paid $225 a week plus overtime) to "utility" jobs that paid $175 a week without extras or to jobs in other departments. For a 90-day period,each transferee would be kept at her old pay rate. The offer to female workers in Building 21, however, went one step further. The company believed that female workers in certain jobs in Building 21 were exposed to concentrations of lead that might cause miscarriages and serious disorders. The executives felt that it was impossible to reduce the lead concentrations to even safer levels without committing large amounts of capital to that purpose. In the interest of "fetus protection," the company excluded women from such areas unless they had proof that they were sterile. A staff report by the Occupational Safety and Health Administration (OSHA) revealed that those female workers who actually were sterilized all retained their jobs.

OSHA cited Andromeda for violations it detected during its October 1979 inspection of the Denver plant. The agency alleged that the company's sterilization policy violated OSHA's 1970 charter. By the end of the month, Andromeda received notification from OSHA that the agency had proposed total penalties of more than $40,000. These penalties were the result of a number of citations issued following the recent comprehensive safety and health inspection of the plant. OSHA issued a citation in which the agency alleged that Andromeda Chemical "adopted and implemented a policy which, as a condition of employment in certain specified areas, necessitated sterilization of female employees." This policy, in OSHA's words, "did not fulfill the general duty requirements"[1] of the Occupational Safety and Health Act of 1970. Furthermore, one OSHA medical officer condemned the company when she stated her belief that no worker must be forced to sacrifice his or her right to conceive children to hold a job. As the company was preparing to defend its position on the alleged policy before two federal administrative law judges, word arrived that a class action suit had been filed on behalf of five of the women who worked in Building 21. The Colorado Civil Rights Commission had notified the company of the suit and the allegations made by the plaintiffs.

A lump formed in Paul's throat as he thought about the events of the past year. The company had acted quickly once it discovered a lead-exposure problem, and

[1] The general duty clause of the act requires employers to provide employment free from recognized hazards likely to cause death or serious physical harm.

the decision to offer women of child-bearing capacity other jobs was an indication of its concern and benevolence. The class action suit was a shock to management. The women had given not the slightest hint that they would sue the company. Thirteen women were party to the sex discrimination suit. The OSHA citations were another matter. The company, in general, and the Denver plant, in particular, seemed to be a favorite target of OSHA. Now the newspaper and other media coverage of the situation was making the company look like an insensitive, money-grubbing monster. The public relations department was working hard to counteract the negative publicity and to salvage the company's image.

The situation was viewed quite differently by Andromeda. Back in 1977, the company had made a statement regarding a medical policy excluding women from the lead pigment division at the plant. The women were told that no one would lose her job or sustain a loss of wages as a result of the policy. According to company officials, at no time were female workers pressured. In fact, Rick Morrison said they were discouraged from seeking sterilization procedures.

In two days, Paul must attend a big meeting at the headquarters office in New Jersey. As plant personnel director, he has responsibility for all personnel matters so he has no choice but to go. Key executives, including representatives from the legal department, will have lots of questions to ask him. His answers and those of the plant manager are to be used to help the company develop a legal strategy for the upcoming hearings and determine the likelihood of a successful defense.

Discussion Questions

1. Can a company exclude female employees from hazardous work areas unless they're sterile?
2. Does a company sterilization policy as described here fulfill the general duty requirements of the Occupation Safety and Health Act of 1970?
3. Evaluate the positions of OSHA and that of Andromeda Chemical on the sterilization policy issue. As the federal administrative law judge, how would you rule? Why?

---

48 Missouri Mining & Metal Works, Inc.

If you are in conformity with OSHA regulations and any of its state counterparts, if you are actively promoting a safe workplace, and if you respond when unsafe conditions are called to your attention, then you are unlikely to open yourself up—as a corporation or as an individual—to criminal liability. But if you believe that ignorance is bliss, then criminal culpability is one more reason to change your ways. (James O. Castagnera, *Personnel,* September 1985, p. 12)

Missouri Mining & Metal Works, Inc. (MMM), is a small company that prepares electrical wire for manufacturers' use. The electrical wire is fed through a production process that coats wires with liquid enamels and polyvinyl chlorides. The company has been in business in the same neighborhood for 48 years. Workers at the plant often are related to each other and learned about their jobs from friends, neighbors, and relatives who served as co-workers, subordinates, and supervisors. The company seldom employed more than 75 employees. Despite its size, however, MMM was well known among regional building trades and industrial firms. The company supplied many firms in the St. Louis area with the quantity and quality of wire each desired for the job that had to be done.

Sales of the small wiring company had continued on an upward trend since 1941, when this country was at war. The president, two vice presidents, and the plant manager had all been with the company for more than 30 years. These company officers and all other company employees knew that the company's success meant a great deal to them because of MMM's profit-sharing plan.

The economic aspect of working for MMM had become a most important issue and the major factor in understanding why so many people had long years of service with the company. One area of improvement had been largely ignored—the cleanliness of the plant floor and limited attempts to remove certain fumes from the air system. Many employees had complained over the years that the ventilation system could not handle the fumes from the polyvinyl chloride and liquid enamel coatings.

Employee complaints don't tell the whole story. Over a period of approximately one year beginning in November 1988 and ending in December 1989, 40 employees became ill. It was discovered that some of them suffered from lung and nerve disorders. According to the employees' doctors, the cause of the illnesses was overexposure to a dozen hazardous chemicals at the plant. Company officials considered taking action to overcome the ventilation problem and exposure to hazardous chemicals, but they realized that the old plant and equipment would be hard to replace economically. If protective measures were taken, it was likely that the plant would no longer be profitable. The officials weighed their options.

A letter from an attorney spurred them into action. An employee talked to the attorney general's office about filing *criminal* charges against the company. He believed, according to his attorney, that the company "willfully and knowingly, exposed its employees to great harm. . . ." The attorney also mentioned that the state environmental agency and the Occupational Health and Safety Administration were being made aware of conditions at the plant.

Given the threat of litigation, the company retained an attorney. After weeks of review, the attorney for the company reported the following:

1. That something called *preemption* implies that federal health and safety laws preempt the enforcement of state criminal laws by local and state prosecutors when an unsafe workplace causes death or injury to a worker.
2. Other defenses protect the employer as well.
3. He identifies three "tried-and-true" legal theories that allegedly protect employers from tort liability:

a. Assumption of risk.
b. Contributory negligence.
c. The fellow-servant doctrine.

After hearing the company appointed attorney's presentation, the president had a queasy feeling down in the pit of his stomach. It was all too neatly packaged, too smooth, too certain. There was a great deal at stake, yet the attorney seemed all too smug. Vaguely he recalled a case about the experience of Film Recovery Systems. Now he remembered. The television show "60 Minutes" did a program on a suburban Illinois plant where a worker allegedly died from overexposure to cyanide. That case was tied up in the courts, but the state attorney brought criminal charges against the top management. As he gathered up his briefcase to go home that night he wondered how greatly exposed the company was to legal liability.

Discussion Questions

1. Are companies preempted from state criminal prosecutors when federal health and safety rules apply?
2. What action(s) should the Occupational Safety and Health Administration and other similar agencies play in preventing such problems as are described in this case?

Section I

Negotiation with Employees

49 Employee Relations at the Washburn Division*

The Washburn Division of the Cohack Manufacturing Corporation came into existence in August 1980 when Cohack completed building a new production plant at Crooked Tree, Montana. Crooked Tree is a small town in a rural resort area approximately 125 miles from Butte, Montana, the home office of Cohack Manufacturing.

The workforce had grown to approximately 900 employees by July 1, 1986. They were recruited from Crooked Tree and the surrounding 10 counties. Almost all new employees were completely without past industrial experience. However, employment standards were high, and all persons hired appeared to have considerable potential. With only five exceptions, on July 1, 1986, all production supervisors in the lower three echelons of management had been promoted from within. Washburn Division had the usual problems of all new plants plus the technological problem of a manufacturing process completely new to industry.

In January 1983, the plant was organized by the Amalgamated Workers of America after a long and costly strike. Good employee–management relations never returned. There were numerous changes in top management and union leadership. The union refused to follow the grievance procedure and demanded instant affirmative answers to all problems. The wildcat strike was frequent. Lower echelons of management suffered repeated abuses and threats from a limited number of employees. Sleeping, loafing, gambling, and even sabotage of production were not unusual. Higher management had, at times, failed to back lower management when it attempted to take disciplinary action.

---

* This case was made possible by the cooperation of a business firm that remains anonymous. It was prepared by Dr. James C. Hodgetts of Memphis State University as a basis for class discussion, rather than to illustrate either effective or ineffective administrative practices. The letter from the president appears as it did in the original, except for changes in names and places that would reveal the company's true identity.

EXHIBIT 1

Cohack Manufacturing Corporation
Butte, Montana
July 29, 1986

To all Washburn Division employees:

As you know we have recently made many changes in the top-management group at Butte. There were also some changes made at Washburn. These were made because mistakes in the past had taken us to the point of bankruptcy. It was recognized that there were two (2) basic problems. One was the deterioration and lack of proper operating facilities, and the other was the small percentage of our employees who were seriously affecting our operating efficiency.

With regard to the first problem, this new management team immediately appropriated approximately four million dollars ($4,000,000) to improve facilities over the next three (3) years. Some improvements can already be seen; others will take time because of engineering and delivery delays.

Concerning the second problem, there are some employees who loaf, sleep, play cards, abuse and threaten our management, or just plain don't do the job they are being paid to do. We know, as you do, that no business can operate for long under these conditions. Their actions have caused us to reach the point where our operations are being seriously affected. When this happens, the security of everyone is threatened—we will not allow this to continue. Some feel that we were afraid to correct these problems. Nothing could be further from the truth. We honestly believe that since the future of so many employees and their families were at stake we, as management, had to first try persuasion and cooperation before resorting to disciplinary action. This approach has not been successful; in fact, matters have gotten worse.

In the interest of the job security of everyone concerned, we are hereby serving notice that we will no longer tolerate such things as sleeping, loafing, gambling, or game playing on company property, threats or abuse to management, or other interferences which affect production. Our management has the authority to take the necessary corrective measures to stop these practices.

We feel confident that most of our employees will do the job that has to be done. They performed magnificently in our recent production crisis. The only thing which good employees have to worry about is what the few bad ones can do to their job security. We ask for your cooperation in helping us make this a better, safer, more secure place to work. We are doing everything humanly possible and within reason to reach this goal.

C. J. Cohack, President

By the end of 1985, the Washburn Division had forced the Cohack Manufacturing Corporation to the verge of bankruptcy. Early in 1986, the company was able to borrow $4 million on the physical facilities at Washburn, and local top management was again changed. By July 1986, the technical problems were decreasing, but the human problems remained unchanged.

On July 29, 1986, the president of the company wrote the letter shown in Exhibit 1 to all Washburn employees with the hope that it might help to correct the situation.

Joe Grisson, human resources manager at Washburn, does not believe that Mr. Cohack's letter will do much good. To him this is just another threat that will not be backed up. He believes there are only about 10 employees, all union officers or stewards, who are the ring leaders relative to the employee relations problem. Joe wants to start collecting concrete evidence that will enable the company to proceed with disciplinary action as permitted in the union–management agreement. Since all 10 employees have been given written reprimands, he wants to give all 10 employees disciplinary layoffs as soon as the company is sure they can defend their position, if the union decides to use the grievance and arbitration procedures. This was tried once before but, when the union closed down the plant with a wildcat strike, the company let the employees return to work with back pay. Joe is certain the union will do the same, again and when they do the company should take legal action against the union and fire the 10 ringleaders.

Requirement

Given the information presented, what specific personnel actions must Joe take? Identify the specific personnel problems to be addressed.

50 Smith Radiators, Inc.

On April 14, 1991, Mr. Daniel Smith II, the president of Smith Radiators, Inc., received a letter from Automobiles of America, Inc. (AAI), a major customer of Smith Radiators. Mr. Smith is concerned about the contents of the letter. In the letter, Mr. Brown, the director of purchasing for AAI, made it clear that AAI expects just-in-time (JIT) delivery of radiators in the next three months and requires Smith Radiators to be a fully certified AAI supplier by the end of 1992. Certification will result in increased business from AAI. On the other hand, loss of the AAI's account is inevitable if the stated conditions are not met (see Exhibit 1).

Mr. Smith, concerned about the proposed reduction in the number of AAI's radiator suppliers, called Mr. Brown for further clarification. During their conversation, Mr. Brown made it clear that AAI's goal is to certify only 3 of the 10 radiator suppliers (see Figure 1). Certified suppliers will be exclusive suppliers of radiators for AAI. AAI will not give special preference to U.S.-owned companies during the certification process. Mr. Brown also said that, even though AAI and Smith Radiators, Inc., have had a long and fruitful relationship, this relationship will come to an end if Smith Radiators is not certified by 1992.

EXHIBIT 1

April 10, 1991

Mr. Daniel Smith
President
Smith Radiators, Inc.,
Detroit

Dear Mr. Smith:

Smith Radiators has been a valued supplier to AAI for the last 30 years. You will agree that this relationship has brought prosperity to both Smith Radiators and AAI. However, foreign competition in the automotive industry and the current recession have forced us to reduce cost, improve quality and respond effectively to customer needs. As one of the major supplies of radiators, I am counting on you to help us become more competitive.

Specifically, our new purchasing program requires that suppliers deliver parts on a just-in-time basis. Such a purchasing strategy results in receiving frequent and reliable shipments of high-quality parts in exact quantity and at a fair price. Although other suppliers can supply radiators for a lower price than Smith Radiators, because of our long-term relationship, we are not seeking price concessions at this time. However, we expect significant improvement in the quality of supplied radiators. Also, radiators will be picked up by our carriers twice a day in containers that hold 10 units each. We are expecting our suppliers to be in full compliance with JIT delivery policy by July 15, 1991.

As you know, successful JIT implementation requires mutual, long-term relationships with a few certified suppliers. AAI management is convinced that there are too many suppliers for each part. In order to streamline purchasing operations, a reduction in the number of suppliers is inevitable. AAI's purchasing division has been instructed to evaluate the 10 suppliers for radiators by the end of 1992. Only those suppliers that successfully meet the certification criteria will be retained. Obviously, these certified suppliers will receive a bigger share of AAI's radiator business. AAI is fully aware of the fundamental changes needed in suppliers operations to successfully meet the criteria. However, 18 months should prove to be enough time for the changes to take place and for us to evaluate Smith Radiator's performance on the following criteria:

1. The JIT delivery.
   a. Quality of supplied parts.
   b. Delivery frequently.
   c. Reliability of delivery.
   d. Number of shipments received in exact quantities.
2. The price of delivered parts.
3. Supplier's ability to seek continuous improvements.

EXHIBIT 1 (concluded)

a. Technical expertise.
b. Implementation of statistical process control.
c. Willingness and ability to share information with AAI.
d. Willingness to get involved in AAI's product design.

As I noted earlier, we value AAI's relationship with Smith Radiators. I firmly believe that your firm will make the necessary changes for certification.

Sincerely yours,

Jeff Brown

FIGURE 1 Current Radiator Suppliers to AAI

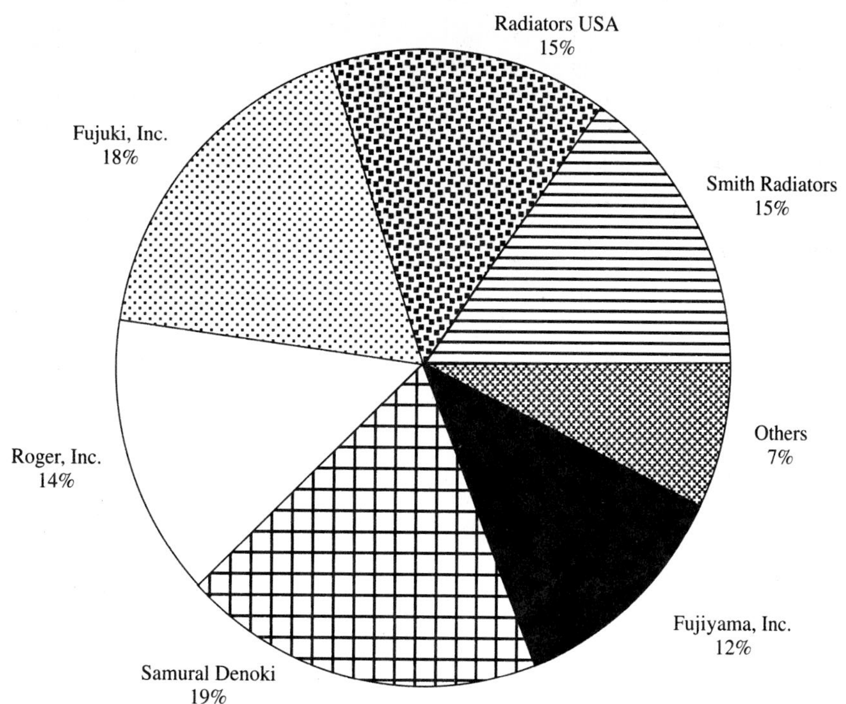

Percent market share.

BACKGROUND OF SMITH RADIATORS INC.

Smith Radiators is a privately held company. It was founded by Mr. Smith I, grandfather of Daniel Smith, in 1950. From a garage shop, the company has grown steadily over the last 40 years (see Exhibit 2). Last year, it netted $50 million in sales. The firm currently employs 475 workers. Although the firm is small, it has acquired a reputation for manufacturing reliable radiators and has supplied radiators to major U.S. automobile producers (see Figure 2). Radiators are technically sophisticated and require specialized equipment and a skilled workforce. The production plant is a typical job shop operation. Machines that perform similar operations are grouped together. Manufacturing operations for radiators include casting, drilling, welding, machining, and painting. Of the 475 employees, 400 are production workers (see Exhibit 3). The production workers are unionized. Current job descriptions allow little flexibility for management to assign these workers to different tasks.

The company is located in Detroit, where a skilled workforce is readily available. Because of the concentration of automobile manufacturing facilities, many automobile parts suppliers are located in and around Detroit. An abundance of suppliers has resulted in intense competition for Smith Radiators. To maintain its market share, Smith Radiators has used low wages (see Exhibit 4) and layoffs as cost reduction strategies. Not surprisingly, union leaders have been demanding competitive wages and job security for their members. Unfortunately, the current recession has caused a lot of unemployment locally. This has shifted union focus

EXHIBIT 2 A Chronology of the Evolution of Smith Radiotors, Inc.

1937	First garage shop opened by Daniel Simth I and two partners in South Detroit.
1942	Daniel Smith I buys out his two partners and opens a second garage shop specializing in radiator repairs.
1945	Smith starts a small firm making replacement radiators for popular models.
1949	Smith sells his two garages to concentrate on making radiators.
1950	With $1.5 million in annual sales, Smith Radiators is incorporated.
1962	Smith Radiators, Inc., net sales cross $10 million.
1971	Smith Radiators, Inc., wins a major contract with Automobiles of America, Inc., to supply radiators to its Lamda division. The company expands its factory and workforce.
1975	Daniel Smith I dies at the age of 79. His son Tom takes over the company.
1980	Smith Radiators' net sales top $30 million.
1988	Tom Smith dies at the age of 49. Daniel Smith II, 29, becomes the CEO of Smith Radiators.
1990	Smith Radiators' net sales top $50 million.

FIGURE 2 Major Customers of Smith Radiators

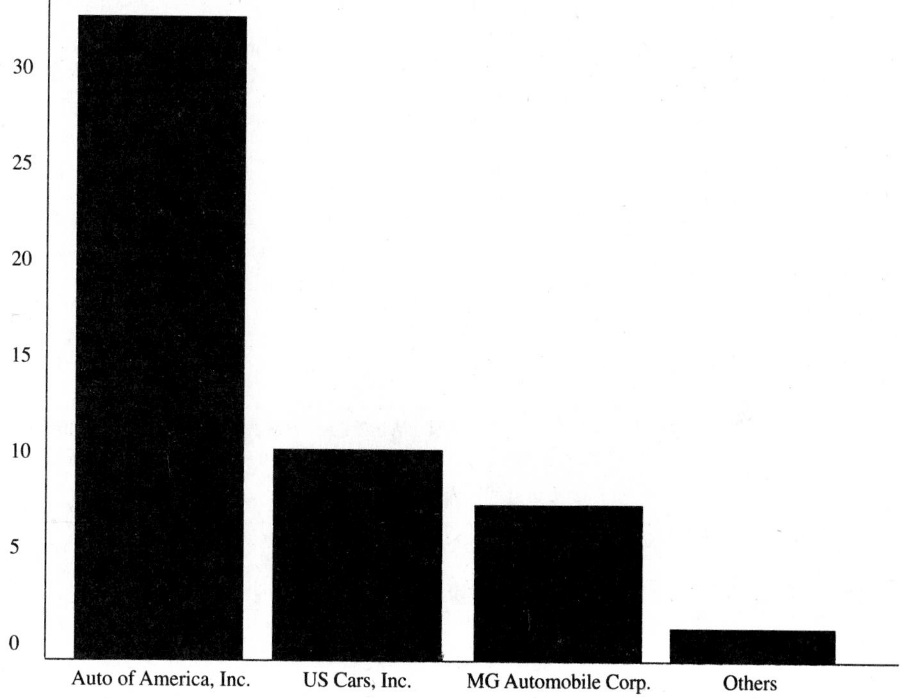

Sales in millions of dollars.

from wage increases to job security. As a matter of fact, the union fought hard to win a "no layoff" concession from management in the current contract. In exchange, they gave up demands for higher wages and the right to strike.

STATUS OF SMITH RADIATORS

Union

Historically, there has been an adversarial relationship between the union and Smith Radiators' management. The primary areas of disagreement are job security and low wages. Lack of open communication and previous layoffs has convinced union

EXHIBIT 3 Number of Smith Radiators, Inc., Employees by Seniority

Years	*Total Workforce*	*Production Employees*
0–5	195	180
5–10	110	100
10–15	75	64
15–20	48	26
20–25	22	17
25–30	13	10
30 or more	12	3
Total	475	400

EXHIBIT 4 Average Hourly Wages for Production Workers in the Radiator Companies around Detroit

Company	*Wages (in $)*
Fujiyama, Inc.	$11.0
Fujuki, Inc.	10.2
Radiators USA	10.9
Roger, Inc.	11.1
Smith Radiators, Inc.	9.5

officials that any improvements or changes in the workplace will result in layoffs. Narrowly defined job descriptions are used as a protective measure by the union to save jobs. Management's refusal to assign female workers to higher-paying jobs in soldering and painting is another thorny issue.

Workforce

Most of the workers at Smith Radiators are high school dropouts. They are skilled in their trade but earn low wages. A constant fear of layoff coupled with low wages has resulted in a dissatisfied workforce with high turnover. Typically, workers use Smith Radiators as a training ground and move to better jobs when they have acquired proficiency in their trade. High turnover and absenteeism has forced management to keep more workers on the payroll than needed. Currently, the company has 20 percent surplus of production workers.

Management

Mr. Smith is highly committed to retaining the firm's competitive edge. Through AAI, Mr. Smith sees an opportunity for his business to grow. Smith Radiators is financially sound and has enough capital to make necessary changes. The company also has a network of reliable and long-term suppliers. With some persuasion from management, these suppliers can easily deliver parts on a JIT basis.

SMITH RADIATORS' COMPETITION

Global competition has increased tremendously in the last decade. The U.S. government's commitment to promote free trade with its neighboring countries suggests that competition will continue to intensify. The U.S. automotive industry has been particularly hit hard by global competition. In addition to domestic suppliers of radiators, Smith Radiators competes with two types of international suppliers: firms whose manufacturing facilities are located offshore (importers), and subsidiaries of foreign companies operating within the United States. Importers benefit from lower labor costs, less-stringent environmental laws, and weak unions in their home countries. Savings, thus achieved, usually outweigh the increased costs associated with importing goods, such as transportation and tariffs. Hence, importers can often sell their goods in the U.S. market for a low price. Also, the foreign subsidiaries (particularly the Japanese companies), with production facilities located around Detroit, have a clear advantage over Smith Radiators. Managers of these firms are committed to the JIT philosophy implementation. Hence, the new production facilities are designed for the JIT production. Typically, these firms are not unionized. As new startups, their selection and recruitment strategies are thorough and directed toward identifying potential JIT workers. These competitors also are providing performance-based pay and incentive schemes that tie a worker's wage to overall company performance. A satisfied and dedicated workforce takes pride in its workmanship and shares the firm's goal of producing quality parts at reduced cost. As a result, these firms can supply better-quality radiators at a very competitive price.

SMITH RADIATOR'S INITIAL RESPONSE

A couple of days after receiving AAI's letter, Mr. Smith called an emergency meeting of all department heads. In the meeting he read the letter from AAI and discussed the serious ramification of losing the AAI account. Mr. Smith stated that in order to remain competitive and profitable, Smith Radiators must meet AAI's demands. He charged each vice president with the identifying of problems and with describing the JIT environment for their functional area. To get them started, he handed out a description of the JIT philosophy. In addition, Mr. Gary Jones, the vice president of human resources, received a brief writeup on human resource management's role in the JIT environment (see Exhibit 5). Within two weeks, Mr. Gary Jones was charged with identifying short-term and long-term HRM strategies to facilitate compliance with AAI's request. In his recommendations to Mr. Smith, he also was required to propose solutions to the HRM problems identified. To accomplish this, Mr. Jones intends to review current HRM practices at Smith Radiators, discuss JIT implementation with the employees, and talk to other firms about their experiences with JIT implementation.

CURRENT HRM PRACTICES AT SMITH RADIATORS

Smith Radiators almost always uses internal sources to recruit new employees. Current employees are asked to recommend prospective candidates and receive $500 if their candidate remains with the company for more than two years. Because the employees earn extra money, the union supports this policy. The selection process is simple, based on job tryouts and interviews conducted by the appropriate operating manager and Mr. Jones. New employees are trained on the job by fellow co-workers under the supervision of a foreman. Smith Radiators does not have a formal training department or a training manual.

Smith Radiators has a centralized decision-making process. In fact, most of the final decisions are made by Mr. Smith. The vice presidents are expected to assist him in the decision-making process and implement the decisions taken. The firm is highly structured with a traditional line of command. Employees are expected to perform assigned tasks. Employee feedback is not common. Not surprisingly, the Smith Radiators' workforce is dissatisfied with current work environment. As a matter of fact, Mr. Jones spends most of his time dealing with employee grievances and the union.

There are several areas of conflict between the management and union. In return for a "no layoff, no strike" policy, the union agreed to lower wages in the last negotiations. The company is overstaffed by 20 percent. In addition to lower wages, the union is concerned about layoff when the current contract expires on December 31, 1991. Blacks are under-represented in the company; only 10 percent of the workers are blacks and most of them have been hired in the last 10 years. Another area of conflict between the union and the management is the company's policy that bans women from working in such departments as soldering and painting. Jobs in these departments traditionally pay a higher wage. However, lead or lead-based products are used in these departments. These products are known to be harmful to employees' health. In particular, the medical community suspects that pregnant women who are exposed to lead may give birth to deformed babies. Smith Radiators management believes its policy protects female workers and the company.

EXHIBIT 5 Mr. Smith's Report

The Just-in-Time Philosophy

The JIT philosophy is broad in scope and requires fundamental changes in every aspect of the business. Success of the JIT philosophy depends on the implementation of four tenets: elimination of waste, total quality control, supplier participation, and employee involvement in decision making. Benefits of JIT implementation include reduced inventory, higher quality of produced and supplied goods, flexible manufacturing, shorter production lead times, and increased productivity. Since JIT requires fundamental changes in doing business, practitioners report difficulties with its implementation. For small firms, lack of capital to undertake the required changes, lack of in-house JIT expertise, and lack of clout with suppliers and customers are identified as problem areas. Unionized labor, employee resistance to change, lack of top-management commitment, and adversarial relationship between union and management also are problematic for both large and small firms. However, the benefits of JIT implementation outweigh the problems. As a result, an increasing number of manufacturing firms in the United States are successfully implementing the JIT philosophy.

Human Resource Management in the JIT Environment

A JIT worker performs multiple tasks. The multiskilled workforce gives management flexibility in assigning these workers to different tasks. This flexibility is essential to quickly respond to production schedule changes. Because each worker performs multiple tasks, job descriptions are loosely defined. A JIT worker also participates in a companywide problem-solving network. Employee participation in quality circles is equally important.

Quality circles are established to identify problems with current operations and suggest improvements. The success of quality circles depends on open communication between management and workers. Further, to evaluate, recommend and eventually implement the proposed changes, workers must articulate their opinions effectively. Thus, a group-oriented workforce with good communication skills is critical to seeking continuous improvements.

JIT workers also inspect their own work. If the production process is not operating satisfactorily, workers have a responsibility to stop the line and rectify the problem. This requires a self-disciplined workforce with a good work ethic. Problems are usually identified via statistical process control. Workers monitor the process and chart its performance regularly to check for conformity. Thus, only a worker with good quantitative and diagnostic skills can perform these task, successfully.

A JIT workforce is self-disciplined, multiskilled, group-oriented, and has good quantitative and diagnostic skills. JIT workers are amply rewarded for their dedication to work. Management is expected to provide job security to workers, pay fair wages, implement group incentive schemes, and respect workers.

EMPLOYEE REACTION TO JIT IMPLEMENTATION

Mr. Jones talked to several employees in the plant to find out if they knew about the JIT philosophy. To his surprise, many of them had heard about the new manufacturing approach through their friends and relatives working with JIT firms. It was the perception of the employees that JIT implementation would require a lot of changes in the workplace. Such changes could result in layoffs after the current contract expired.

The union also was concerned. When informed that Mr. Smith was exploring the feasibility of JIT implementation, a union official stopped by Mr. Jones's office to share his reservations. His concerns were: loss of seniority, weaker union power, and the loss of job security provided by the current contract. The production supervisors also had serious reservations concerning JIT implementation. At a luncheon with the supervisors, Mr. Jones asked if production workers could be given more responsibility for planning and controling their work. He also explored the potential of more employee involvement in decision making. The supervisors felt that worker involvement was impossible at Smith Radiators. Because workers did not feel responsible for their work and were generally noncooperative, communicating with them was problematic.

On hearing the employees' negative response to JIT, Mr. Jones decided to approach his friend Guy Niles, a human resource manager at Tippon, a muffler manufacturing firm. Mr. Niles played a major role in devising new HRM strategies when Tippon implemented the JIT philosophy in 1989. Guy was very enthusiastic about the results of JIT implementation. According to him, Tippon earned record profit last year, which was 20 percent higher than any previous year. Increased productivity had resulted in increased market share for the company and higher wages for workers. Labor turnover was at an all-time low. Mr. Jones was encouraged by Tippon's success with JIT implementation. This was particularly heartening to him, since Tippon's HRM practices two years ago were comparable to Smith Radiators' in every respect.

After gathering the information, Mr. Jones realizes that, for JIT implementation at Smith Radiators, fundamental changes in current HRM practices are required. Mr. Jones' task is to identify the issues and propose solutions to the problems currently facing Smith Radiators. For the successful JIT implementation, recommendations are required for both short-term and long-term HRM strategies. He also knows that, in the JIT environment, union cooperation will be critical.

APPENDIX 1

Smith Radiators, Inc.,
Balance Sheet 1990

Assets

Current assets:	
Cash	$ 724,030
Accounts receivable	22,112,222
Inventories	21,123,315
Prepaid expenses	656,321
Total current assets	43,316,102
Fixed assets:	
Land	8,501,120
Buildings	22,222,234
Machinery and equipment	15,636,232
Total fixed assets	46,339,586
Total assets	89,655,688

Liabilities and Stockholders' Investment

Current liabilities:	
Accounts payable	13,286,123
Accrued payroll	850,254
Taxes (local, state, federal)	24,896,190
Total current liabilities	39,032,567
Stockholders' investment: stock (@$1,000 per share)	22,000,000
Earned surplus	28,623,121
Total stockholders' investment and earned surplus	50,623,121
Total liabilities and stockholders' investment	89,655,688

APPENDIX 2

Smith Radiators, Inc.,
Income Statement 1990

Net sales	$50,123,452
Cost of goods sold:	
Production (labor, materials, overhead, etc.)	33,000,123
Administrative	4,324,675
Sales	3,675,245
Other	976,783
Total cost of goods sold	41,976,826
Income before taxes	8,146,626
Taxes (local, state, federal)	2,145,426
Net Income	6,001,200

APPENDIX 3

Smith Radiators, Inc.,
Net Sales and Income

	Net Sales	*Net Income*
1986	$36,456,325	$5,124,843
1987	40,234,678	5,121,456
1988	42,234,789	5,412,565
1989	46,123,562	5,932,987
1990	50,123,452	6,001,200

51 Southwestern Bell Telephone Company

The chill of the late fall was starkly apparent the morning of December 10. The breath of the picketers rose like wispy smoke as they walked around the central telephone exchange in Kirksville, Missouri. The placards they carried were inscribed "Wilson Construction and Southwestern Bell violate area standards, Local 307 United Iron and Steelworkers of America." The word strike was not present on any of the posters. The steelworkers had been displaying their signs since 7:30 AM, and it was increasingly obvious that they had no intention of removing themselves before 8:00 AM, at which time the Southwestern Bell employees would normally report for work.

THE "INFORMATIONAL PICKET" ACTION

As noted by the placards, the picketers were representatives of Local 307 of the United Iron and Steelworkers of America (UISA), headquartered in Ottumwa, Iowa. During a meeting held the evening of December 9, it was agreed by the rank and file that they would erect an "informational picket" at the telephone office in Kirksville. Presiding at that meeting was William Johnson, president of the UISA local, and Ron Mikel, vice president and steward, representing the Kirksville membership. The informational picket action was being taken due to the presence of Wilson Constructors, Inc., of Lenexa, Kansas, at Southwestern Bell's telephone office on Washington Street in Kirksville. Wilson Constructors is a nonunion general contractor that presented the low bid for the construction of a new microwave tower on top of the existing telephone building. Southwestern Bell Telephone Company must, by law, consider all bids submitted to it for new construction. The company cannot discriminate against bidders because they are either union or nonunion. The local steelworkers had been carefully monitoring the progress that Wilson was making on the tower project for several weeks. To this point all of the work performed had been in preparation for the actual handling and erecting of the steel tower.

On December 9, however, preparation work was not the steelworkers' concern. The first truckload of steel had arrived at the job site, along with a 15-ton crane on December 4. All attempts by Mikel to get Wilson Constructors to hire some of his people had failed. As a result, the union felt that its next course of action was to set up a picket line. A problem of common situs picketing was on its way: the operations of a secondary employer were being disrupted. The secondary employer was being picketed.

FROM THE WINDOW PANE

Jim Thompson, network service supervisor, switching (local service), and Jim Ball, network service supervisor, toll (long distance), watched the patroling picketers through the windows of a large office inside the telephone building.

"Why did the company [Southwestern Bell] wait until it was too late to talk to these people?" Ball asked. Thompson answered with only a shake of the head.

Ball recalled many of the events of the last few weeks that had led up to the current situation. During a preconstruction meeting held in Kansas City on November 10, he and Thompson had stated that, once construction on the tower started, some kind of work action from the steelworkers local was almost 100 percent certain if Wilson did not use some union labor. They also informed the legal department representative that this particular union had a reputation for "busting heads" if anyone tried to cross its picket lines.

"Yes," Ball thought, "we've told them several times." But, given the present situation, that thought alone provided very little consolation.

As 8:00 AM approached, both supervisors felt crippled. "Is there anything that we can do to get these guys away from our employees' entrance?" Thompson asked.

"No," replied Ball, "the boss [Wes Storm—manager] said for us to hang loose until we see what legal has to say."

"Gee, that will take all day," responded Thompson. "You and I know that our craft people will not cross that picket line!"

About that time the phone rang. Ball put the call on the speaker so he and Thompson could both hear what Wes had found out from the legal department.

"OK," Wes began. "Legal is trying to contact the steelworkers' local office right now. The lawyers will attempt to get the picketers to clear the telephone employees' entrance so our people can come to work. Heck, their 'grievance' isn't with us anyway. It's with Wilson for refusing to hire some of the union steelworkers."

"Darnit, Wes," Ball countered. "Why didn't legal take Thompson and me seriously three weeks ago in Kansas City—when we told them that there would be trouble if Wilson uses strictly nonunion labor in our building?"

After a slight pause, Wes replied, "Nobody actually thought there would be any problems. We are building towers in Moberly, Sedalia, Chillicothe, and downtown Kansas City, and to this date we have not had any problems with any of the other local unions."

Just about that time, 7:55 AM, another one of the office phones began to ring. Jim Thompson answered and talked for several minutes. He then hung up and returned to the speaker phone.

"That was one of our repeatermen [telephone craft title]," Thompson stated. "I'm sure it was Eldon Coy. He says that everyone is waiting over at Doughboy's Donut Shop to see what happens." They had contacted Scat Davis, president of their own union, the Communications Workers of America (CWA), local chapter, to see what the union wants them to do. But at that time they still had not heard from St. Louis headquarters about the next course of action.

"Eldon maintains," continued Thompson, "that regardless of what the union says, none of the Kirksville craft people have any intention of crossing that picket line. They think that someone will get hurt if they try to cross. They're a little scared."

"I understand that," Wes replied. "But they have to come to work, nonetheless. Legal says that this is only an informational picket set up against Wilson, and that it does not bind our people not to cross."

The legal staff had, indeed, added quick references to a certain National Labor Relation Board's (NLRB's) "Reserved Gate" doctrine, as well as to a Denver case, and to another International Union of Electrical Workers (IUEW) case. But they did not elaborate. They had some more "checking into" to do before jumping to the conclusion that any of these applied to Bell's situation.

IN VIEW OF RESPONSIBILITIES

Eight o'clock came and went and still no telephone employees had come to work. Shortly after 8:00, another of the repeatermen called the office and asked if he and the other outside repairmen could report to their company vehicles and drive to their work sites. All company vehicles had been removed from the telephone exchange parking lot several weeks earlier because Wilson was using the company parking lot to store materials for the new tower. Therefore, the telephone vehicles were not on Southwestern Bell's property but, instead, were parked in the municipal parking lot a few blocks away. This would allow some of the employees to report for work without having to cross the picket line.

John's request was, however, refused by Ball, his immediate supervisor. Wes supported Ball's refusal to grant the request. "The first floor of the telephone building is the reporting location, and not the front seat of a company vehicle," Wes stated flatly.

"Besides," added Ball, "it is the company's view that we, and not the union, should decide where the craft people report for work. We do not alter policy in order to allow union members to circumvent their contract responsibilities. In this case, the union is asking us to make an exception for them, which could constitute a dangerous precedent should a situation like this occur again."

According to one member of the management staff, the union's responsibility in matters of this nature had been made clear under the "service interruption" provisions of the contract. (See Exhibit 1.) Once it was determined that the picket was informational in nature, it was the union's responsibility to ensure that its members reported to work, whether or not picketers were present.

The picketers remained in place at all entrances until approximately 10:30 AM. At that time, the picketing steelworkers were asked by their union to reposition themselves only at the entrances that had been clearly designated as those to be used by the "contractors only." An agreement had been reached between the steelworkers and the company's attorneys.

EXHIBIT 1

Article II

Service Interruption

The Company and the Union recognize their responsibility in the interests of the public and the employees to avoid interruptions in telephone service. Accordingly, they will process promptly employee complaints and grievances which are subject to handling under the grievance procedures for the purpose of avoiding interruption of telephone service to the public and economic loss to employees from work stoppages.

Any employee complaint or grievance which is subject to handling under the grievance procedures shall be presented and heard promptly in accordance with the provisions of those procedures and the arbitration procedures, where applicable.

As to those employee grievances which are subject to arbitration, the Union, its officers, or representatives will not order or sanction a work stoppage or slowdown at any time.

THE 10 O'CLOCK SETTLEMENT

The agreement was reached between 10:00 AM and 10:20 AM By this time, all of the damage had already been done. The telephone employees (represented by CWA) who had refused to cross the picket line were docked for two and one-half hours of pay, and the lost time was charged to their payroll records as unexcused absence. Unexcused absence is one of the criteria that help to determine whether employees receive a satisfactory or an unsatisfactory appraisal for their yearly performance. Their appraisal, in turn, will affect their hopes for transfer or promotion. It was not very surprising, therefore, that the employees involved had no intentions of accepting the unexcused absence charged to their records without a fight.

The first step was taken by Roger Elmore, union steward for the Kirksville telephone employees. Roger promptly informed the local CWA president, Scat Davis, of the situation, and that all of the telephone craftpeople at the Kirksville office wanted the unexcused absence removed from their payroll records. They also wanted to be reimbursed for the two and one-half hours of pay that they had lost.

EXHIBIT 2

Article III

Unusual Grievances

Whenever the Vice President of the Union (or in his or her absence, the Assistant to Vice President) informs the Vice President–Personnel of the Company (or in his or her absence, the Assistant Vice President–Labor Relations) that a complaint or a grievance exists which in the opinion of the Vice President of the Union involves a condition which constitutes a serious and immediate threat to the health or safety of an employee or group of employees and which in his or her opinion requires prompt handling, and it is mutually agreed that such a question of health or safety is in fact involved, then such complaint or grievance may be presented and heard at such level of the Grievance Procedure as the Vice President of the Union may select. The first meeting with respect to such complaint or grievance shall be held at a time and place to be agreed upon and as promptly as conditions permit; the two-week time limitation set forth in the Grievance Procedure shall be applicable. There shall be no obligation on the part of the Union to appeal such complaint or grievance to any higher level, and the grievance if arbitrable shall then be subject to the provisions of the arbitration procedures of this Agreement.

While Roger hoped that Scat would decide on an appropriate line of action, it was Roger's contention that this vexing and dangerous situation should have been averted by the company (Southwestern Bell) and the union (CWA). Failure to react according to the evidence of an imminent strike action, by both the company and the union, was clearly a case of negligence on both sides. Roger also contended that the failure of both sides to act in the face of this situation was a violation of Article III of the General Application section of the 1980 Collective Bargaining Agreement (see Exhibit 2). Moreover, he saw the refusal of the Kirksville CWA members to cross the steelworkers' picket line as the culmination of a month-long "ignore it and it'll go away" course of action.

At any rate, tempers were reaching the boiling point, and the Kirksville employees were demanding that some action be taken. Subsequently, Scat Davis scheduled an emergency union meeting for the evening of December 15. The major item up for discussion by the membership was whether CWA should reimburse the Kirksville employees for their lost time out of the union's general fund, or whether the union would formally grieve the work stoppage and the subsequent withholding of pay.

Discussion Questions

1. How would you evaluate the activities of the Steelworkers, Local 307?
2. What options are available to the Communication Workers of America?
3. Evaluate the activities of Southwestern Bell.

52 The Discharge of Stanley Thompson: An Arbitrator's Dilemma

South Bay Corporation is a multimillion-dollar northeastern company engaged in manufacturing structural beams, engines, valves, and other support equipment for the petroleum industry. With recent interest in U.S. oil exploration, the corporation has experienced substantial growth through customer demand. This growth has caused the company to increase its workforce in addition to working significant amounts of overtime to meet customer needs. Overtime requirements have been particularly heavy in the engine department, where mechanics and machine operators work long hours producing and assembling both standard and specially built engines for oil drilling equipment.

Employees of South Bay have been represented by an independent union—South Bay Employees Association—since 1968. Labor–management relations are described as friendly, although during the past six months relations have become strained due to impending contract negotiations. Grievance activity has increased 40 percent, and more cases are being finalized through the arbitration process. On December 10, 1979, the union requested the arbitration of a discharge case after repeated attempts to resolve the issue through the grievance procedure produced no results. The following facts and issues were presented to the arbitrator during the arbitration hearing.

FACTS OF THE CASE

The grievant, Stanley Thompson, had been employed by South Bay for six years. Thompson is an experienced and qualified engine mechanic, having worked 12 years in related jobs before joining the company in January 1974. At the time of his discharge, he was classified as a senior engine mechanic in the engine department. Thompson has received company recognition for his ability as an engine mechanic. His annual performance reviews are very good, and they acknowledge superior quantity and quality of work performance. He received a commendation letter on March 26, 1979, from his department manager for early completion of a job assignment involving a specially built engine.

During the first five years of Thompson's employment, his attendance record was excellent. He missed only one workday during this entire period.

However, the company maintains that, during the past year, Thompson has developed an excessive record of tardiness and absenteeism. Evidence submitted during the hearing shows that over a 10-month period—September 1978 through June 1979—the grievant was absent 9 full days, and he had 11 partial days of absence. On February 16, 1979, and again on April 10, 1979, Thompson received verbal warnings about his attendance problem. On May 25, 1979, he received a written warning notice about his excessive absenteeism. The written reprimand advised the grievant that continued absenteeism or "other evidence of lack of interest in job performance would not be tolerated and will result in termination of employment." Company procedures allow employees to respond to disciplinary action taken against them. When responding to the written warning, Thompson wrote on the note that he did not remember receiving prior verbal warnings. During the hearing, however, Thompson did testify that he had received one verbal warning prior to receipt of the written notice. Thompson claimed that his attendance problem was caused by the fact that his wife and young daughter had been critically ill.

After receiving the written reprimand on May 24, and up to his discharge on September 24, 1979, Thompson's attendance record shows an additional seven full days of absence, six partial days, and four incidents where he agreed to work overtime but did not report to work. His attendance record again was verbally reviewed with him on August 16, 1979, but no further disciplinary action was taken.

Thompson's discharge took place after an incident that occurred one Saturday morning. On Saturday, September 22, Thompson was working overtime due to the heavy workload in the engine department. At approximately 10:40 AM, Thompson's supervisor, Tom Avey, while passing a window in the work area, observed Thompson sitting at his workbench with his feet up, reading a magazine. Avey did not approach or discuss the incident with Thompson at that time. At the time of the incident, the grievant was working on company time, and his lunch period did not begin until 11:00 AM Except for a slight disagreement over the exact time the incident occurred, Thompson admitted under oath to the conduct observed by his supervisor. Thompson does not, however, admit to loafing. Rather, his explanation for sitting at his workstation was due to the need to receive parts for completion of a special engine. Without these parts, work could not proceed and no other jobs had been assigned to him. The parts were to be delivered from supply services at 1:00 PM that day.

Early Monday morning, September 24, 1979, Thompson's supervisor met with the manager of employee relations, Mrs. Gail Gorton, to discuss the incident observed on Saturday. After a brief discussion of Thompson's work record, it was decided to immediately terminate his employment. Thompson was given his discharge notice at 10:00 AM, along with his final paycheck.

POSITIONS OF THE PARTIES

Company

The company maintains that Thompson was properly terminated according to the employment policies of South Bay. These policies were verbally covered with the grievant during his employment orientation, and they were listed in a handbook given to all new employees. The company argues that there are 19 different work infractions for which employees may be disciplined or terminated. Specifically, the company believes that Thompson violated rule number 9, "loafing or sleeping on the job," and number 17, "careless or inefficient performance or productivity." The company maintains that Thompson's admission of guilt, regardless of the reason, is sufficient to uphold the discharge. The company also believes Thompson's loafing is most serious since he was being paid time and a half for the Saturday assignment.

Given the gravity of the offense on September 22, Thompson's poor attendance record, and the proper application of the progressive disciplinary system over the past year, the disciplinary action the company applied was reasonable and was properly within managerial discretion.

Grievant

Thompson maintains the 19 causes for discipline spelled out in the employee handbook may result in termination, but that an infraction of any one cause does not mandate discharge. Due to the extenuating circumstances surrounding the incident on Saturday (i.e., unavailable parts), the actions of the company are too severe to warrant termination. Further, Thompson contends that the company neglected to properly investigate the Saturday incident prior to his termination on Monday. The grievant maintains that, when discharge is involved, the company bears the responsibility to consider any and all facts that could influence the extent of discipline. This should include a meeting with the employee to review his or her side of the story. Thompson believes this omission is a general violation of industrial due process and a right of employees before discipline is administered.

Finally, the grievant argues that certain procedural errors were made during progressive discipline for his excessive absenteeism. Company policies state that, when employees receive written reprimands, at 45-day intervals or less, the company will investigate and counsel the employee until the problem appears to be corrected. This procedure was established to continually advise employees of how they stand in regard to achieving company standards. Therefore, based on Thompson's fine performance record, the procedural irregularities in applying progressive discipline, and the extenuating circumstances surrounding the Saturday incident—combined with the lack of due process—Thompson's discharge was not warranted and he should be reinstated.

CONCLUSION

The arbitration described above was conducted under the rules of the American Arbitration Association (AAA). All parties were given a full and fair opportunity to present witnesses and evidence. All witnesses testified under oath. According to AAA procedures, the arbitrator has 30 days from the close of the hearing to render his or her final and binding award.

Discussion Questions

You are the arbitrator and have heard the above case. Based on the facts presented and the arguments of each side, how would you rule?

Would you uphold or reverse the discharge of Mr. Thompson? You may wish to consider the following points before reaching your decision:

1. Thompson's attendance record.
2. Thompson's quantity and quality of work.
3. The progressive discipline given to Thompson and the manner in which it was administered by the company.
4. The discharge of September 24 and the facts surrounding the incident.
5. Management's right to discipline and discharge an employee for just cause.

---

53 Inspiration Consolidated Copper Company

BACKGROUND

Inspiration Consolidated Copper Company is an integrated natural resources company. Its principal business is the production and sale of copper from its Arizona operations, which include mines, smelter, refinery, solvent extraction, rod fabricating, and sulfuric acid plants. Inspiration also smelts copper-bearing materials for other producers and owns and operates a silver-bearing silica flux mine in Montana. Its exploration activities, which cover most of the western states and Alaska, are aimed at diversification, both geographically and among natural resources.

The company's Arizona facility, located in Miami, Arizona, is the only facility involved herein. At the Arizona facility, the company is party to several collective bargaining agreements, including one with the United Steelworkers of America, Miami Miners Union Local 586. Failure to resolve the following grievance has required that it be submitted to an arbitrator. Your name was on the panel the American Association of Arbitrators sent to the parties, and they selected you to hear the grievance. You agreed and have just heard each party's position. Now you have to prepare your award. The issue emerging in the instant case is: Did the company violate the collective bargaining agreement when it terminated the grievant, Douglas Peterson, on February 14, 1982? If so, what is the appropriate remedy?

CIRCUMSTANCES

Douglas Peterson, the grievant, had been employed by the company for approximately six years, prior to his termination in February 1982. At the time of his discharge, Peterson was classified as a steam plant operator in the smelter department.

The grievant's last day of work for the company was February 7, 1982. He was scheduled off on February 8 and was scheduled to work the B shift on February 9, 10, 11, 12, and 13. Following his regular work shift on February 7, Peterson was arrested and incarcerated and, subsequent to that date, was unable to report to work because he was in jail.

On February 11, 1982, Steven Slepian, the grievant's attorney in the criminal matters, telephoned Peterson's general foreman, who referred the attorney to Jim Yingst, the smelter production superintendent. Slepian told Yingst that Peterson had been incarcerated and that he was trying to obtain Peterson's release. Slepian asked Yingst what impact Peterson's failure to report for work would have on his employment status. Yingst replied that the company's policy dictated that a failure to report for work due to incarceration would be treated as an unexcused absence. Yingst informed Slepian that Peterson faced termination if he accumulated more than four successive days of absence. Although Slepian did not specifically request that Peterson be granted a leave of absence, the company treated the attorney's inquiry as a verbal request for a leave of absence.

On February 13, 1982, Peterson accumulated his fifth successive day of unexcused absence. In accordance with normal procedures, the company then processed his termination. Manny Casillas, a company labor relations representative, while processing the termination paperwork of February 14, 1982, showed Richard Guerra, one of the union's stewards, Peterson's termination papers. According to the company, when Casillas told Guerra that Peterson was being terminated, Guerra replied that Peterson was in jail. No written request for a leave of absence was ever filed by Peterson or on his behalf.

The following week, Peterson's name was absent from the work schedules posted throughout the company's facility. On February 27, 1982, after the criminal charges against him were in the process of being dismissed, Peterson was released from jail. On that same day, Peterson called the company to check on his employment status. Peterson contends that he was told by the company that it would be necessary for the personnel representative to talk with labor relations and that he should call back. After additional unsuccessful attempts to determine his status on February 28 and 29, on March 3, Peterson filed a formal grievance protesting his termination. On March 4, he received official notice from the company that he had been terminated.

RELEVANT CONTRACT PROVISIONS

Paragraph 4.16 Discharge and Discipline

In the event an employee shall be discharged, suspended, or disciplined by the Company after the date of this Agreement, such employee shall be given full reasons for such discharge, suspension, or disciplining, in writing.

Paragraph 9.3 Granting of Leaves of Absence

Leaves of absence, without pay, may be granted for reasons such as jury duty and other good and sufficient reasons. Leaves of absence, without pay, for other good and sufficient reasons shall be granted to employees for a period up to thirty (30) days, which period may be extended by mutual consent.

Paragraph 9.4 Request for Leave in Writing, Separation of Employees, for Unauthorized Leave

Request for leaves of absence must be made in writing to the immediate supervisor, and each case must be considered on its merits. One copy of the leave of absence shall be given to the employee at the time the leave is granted and one copy to the Union. Upon return from leave of absence, the employee shall be reinstated without loss of his seniority rights. Leaves of absence shall in no way jeopardize the standing of rights of employees. Upon the employee's return, he shall be reinstated with seniority accumulated throughout his leave of absence. Employees absent for more than four (4) days, without having obtained a properly authorized leave of absence, shall be separated from the payroll.

The company's absentee program is described in Exhibit 1.

COMPANY POSITION

The company contends that Peterson's failure to report to work for the five consecutive days without having obtained a prior leave of absence, coupled with Peterson's failure to provide a written request for leave of absence, formed the basis for its decision to terminate him. To justify its action, the company relies on paragraph 9.4 of the agreement and a prior arbitration award involving this same company and union and issues as contained herein. Paragraph 9.4 of the agreement clearly and unequivocally provides that a request for leave of absence must be in writing. It also provides that an employee who is absent for more than four days without having obtained a leave of absence shall be "separated from the payroll." As it has consistently done in the past, the company enforced the policy manifested in paragraph 9.4 and properly terminated Peterson.

At the hearing, the union argued that Peterson's termination was improper under the terms of paragraph 4.16 of the agreement (which relates to typical discharges) and points to the company's forms, used internally, to claim that Peterson was

EXHIBIT 1 Absentee Program (adopted July 22, 1974)

TO ALL EMPLOYEES:

Please review the following procedure so that you are completely familiar with its provisions:

1. Excused absences will be granted only for:
   a. Prearranged absences for good and sufficient reason.
   b. Leave of Absence.
   c. Injury—immediate family or per contract.
   d. Sickness—immediate family or per contract.

A LEAVE OF ABSENCE may be granted for good and sufficient reasons by requesting a leave from this foreman in accordance with the applicable union contract. Employees who because of emergency situations are unable to arrange for a leave prior to the days needed may have a representative arrange the leave in accordance with the applicable union contract in their behalf by transmitting the required information to the department head.

2. Unexcused absences are those absences not covered in the above paragraph. The following steps will apply for unexcused absences:
   a. Each employee will be allowed two unexcused absences in any consecutive 12-week period.
   b. For the third absence, a written warning will be issued by the shift foreman.
   c. For the fourth absence, the employee will be interviewed by the department head or representative, and, after investigation of the circumstances and absentee record, he will receive a second written warning if warranted.
   d. For the fifth absence, the employee will be interviewed by the department head or representative, and, after investigation of the circumstances and absentee record, he may be subject to a five-day layoff.
   e. After receiving five days off, the employee may be discharged following the next unexcused absence.

3. Any employee can clear his record with 12 weeks without an excused absence. If the record is not cleared, the above sequence of steps will follow.

4. Consecutive days of 1, 2, 3, or 4 are to be counted as one absence.

5. The program will be administered as follows by all departments:
   a. Consecutive days of 1, 2, 3, or 4 are to be counted as one absence. On the fifth day, in accordance with the contract, employees are automatically terminated if they have not reported off.

6. The Company agrees to clear all absentee records as of the Date of Settlement (8/23/74).

really "discharged" and that, therefore, paragraph 4.6 applies. In this regard, the company refers to a prior arbitration, involving a Mr. Salvador Reco. Essentially, the issues raised in both the prior arbitration and the instant case are the same. However, Reco had filed a written request for leave of absence, which serves as further evidence of the propriety of the company's action in the instant case. In his decision, arbitrator Donald Daughten held that section 9.3 of the agreement gives the company total discretion in its determination of leaves of absence. In addition, arbitrator Daughten noted that the company has maintained its long-standing history of denying leaves of absence to incarcerated employees. As in the instant case, the union cited the company's internal documents in support of paragraph 4.16 as its defense to the grievant's termination. Arbitrator Daughten dismissed this argument and noted that the company views an employee that is separated from the payroll in accordance with section 9.4 as having quit.

Finally, arbitrator Daughten made it perfectly clear that paragraph 9.4 is controling and gives the company the unequivocal right to terminate an incarcerated employee for more than four absences without having obtained a prior leave of absence. Due to the fact that arbitrator Daughten's decision makes no mention of the criminal guilt or innocence of the grievant, it is clear that criminal culpability is not a relevant factor in adjudging the propriety of a termination under paragraph 9.4.

It is standard "arbitration law" that a prior arbitration between the parties becomes part of the current agreement. Having lost the prior arbitration, the union cannot raise the identical issues before a new arbitrator (Reynolds & Reynolds Co., 67LA157, 1974.)

However, even if there has not been a prior arbitration, the company clearly acted in accordance with the agreement in separating Peterson from the payroll due to his failure to secure approval of a written request for leave of absence prior to being absent for more than four days.

UNION POSITION

The union alleges that the company acted in an arbitrary and capricious manner in terminating Peterson. The rationale forming its position is twofold. The union contends that the company's decision to terminate Peterson was premature in that Peterson's attorney, Steven Slepian, reported him absent on February 11, 1982, and thereby complied with the current absentee policy. In addition, on this same date Slepian requested a leave of absence to secure Peterson's job. The company denied this request and subsequently discharged the grievant on February 14, despite the fact that paragraph 9.3 plainly states that leave may be granted for good and sufficient reasons, and that, in the past, other phone-requested leaves of absence have been granted. The fact that the company has, in the past, approved phone requested leaves serves to indicate its arbitrary treatment of the grievant.

In addition, the company's discharge of Peterson and subsequent failure to provide the benefits stipulated in paragraph 4.16 of the agreement constitute another violation of the collective bargaining agreement. Management's failure to notify Peterson of his termination, coupled with its failure to reinstate the grievant after he filed a grievance and provided documentary proof that the criminal charges against him had been dismissed, serves as proof of company capriciousness.

If the company were to have the sole right to deny a leave of absence, this would take away the right of an employee to grieve the company's decision. The very fact that paragraph 9.3 appears in the agreement gives credence to the union's contention that company decisions regarding leaves of absence are subject to both review and reversal.

The union requests that the grievant, Douglas Peterson, be reinstated to his former position with full back pay and restoration of all seniority and other job rights.

Discussion Questions

In this case, your award should contain:

1. Your rationale in finding on the merits of this case.
2. The degree to which you would grant the relief Peterson is asking or uphold management.

---

54 Management Campaigns and Union Organizing at KCOM-KOHC Medical, Inc.

BACKGROUND

It was February four years ago. A group of employees at the Kirksville College of Osteopathic Medicine, Inc., and Kirksville Osteopathic Health Center (KCOM-KOHC) approached some of the management personnel at the institution and informed them of a union organizing campaign being conducted by Service Employees International Union (SEIU), Local 50. The effort had been initiated during the summer of the previous year. SEIU's intent was to organize service, maintenance, and professional employees within a 12-month period, in the complex employing over 900 people. A representation election was eventually scheduled; but five years had elapsed after the initial campaign effort began.

THE TRAINING FACILITY AND THE HEALTH CENTER

Kirksville College of Osteopathic Medicine and Kirksville Osteopathic Health Center (KCOM-KOHC) were founded by Dr. Andrew Taylor Still in Kirksville, Missouri, in 1892. KCOM, the first school of osteopathic medicine in the world and the Harvard of osteopathic colleges, offers a four-year post-baccalaureate training program that leads to a doctor of osteopathy (DO) degree. It also offers a bachelor of science (BS) degree program in medical technology. The facility sponsors and houses numerous medical research projects in addition to its degree program.

The Kirksville Osteopathic Health Center began operating a few years after KCOM as the first hospital of osteopathic medicine. A part of the KCOM-KOHC complex, KOHC is a 254-bed hospital comprised of Kirksville Osteopathic Hospital, Laughlin Osteopathic Hospital, and several clinics. KOHC is a nonprofit organization that serves as the hands-on training unit for KCOM students.

WHEN WORKERS CALL: THE UNION AND ITS INVITATION

The Service Employees International Union (SEIU), an AFL-CIO affiliate, was headquartered in St. Louis, Missouri. The union was 230,000 employees strong and had been attempting to organize hospitals throughout the states of Missouri and Illinois. Its campaign efforts had been fairly successful, especially in the St. Louis area, where it had won a number of elections. Nationwide, SEIU had been more successful on the East and West Coasts than in the central section of the country. The union's activities were oriented toward people in the healthcare industry. Particular targets were service-type employees (e.g., dietary, housekeeping, and maintenance workers) as the union's name implied. In addition, however, SEIU was beginning to seek membership among professional employees, such as nurses and lab personnel.

The emergency room personnel at KCOM-KOHC were the original group that contacted SEIU for assistance, although there were strong sentiments in favor of union presence in the nursing, dietary, housekeeping, and medical lab departments as well. Nurses in the emergency room felt that they received little recognition and were underpaid. All of the emergency room employees, like others in the KCOM-KOHC complex, were worried about rumored staff reductions and the status of their jobs. Grapevine discussions of impending layoffs at KCOM-KOHC had become something of a historical phenomenon. The hearsay often had turned out to be true. Also, major changes were being implemented within the complex that were ineffectively communicated to workers; these fueled concern with confusion.

Sensing that the workers were becoming increasingly dissatisfied with the existing employee program and work-related policies, management decided it was time to introduce some necessary changes. One example involved a concerted effort to improve the communication between employees and their managers, as well as between middle managers and top management. A number of communication-related seminars were sponsored to achieve this. Another example was the initiation of a wage survey, with the intent of overhauling the organization's compensation system.

These changes had been initiated by KCOM-KOHC, partly to forestall any of its workers' inclinations toward inviting a union. Indeed, the administration had always clearly voiced its opposition to the unionization of its employees even though, according to one employee, "no one could remember the last time KCOM-KOHC offered much to its workers in terms of good pay, benefits, and working conditions." Nevertheless, management's systematic, straightforward approach seemed to have kept the organization from alienating its employees. As one medical lab attendant noted, for example, "There's no one here in the organization or in the entire county who does not know that things have been pretty tight, financially, for KCOM-KOHC in the last several years." This time, however, the camel's back had been broken—not by a specific last straw, but by perennial cycles of underpayment and insufficient recognition for a job well done. As a result, some emergency room nurses secretly invited SEIU. Union officials at the St. Louis headquarters surveyed the workers' request and approved an organizing effort at KCOM-KOHC. In their assessment, the workers' concerns were with the types of issues with which "winning union campaigns" were made, and included serious problems of wages, communication, job security, staffing levels, and worker "floating" policies. Later, the employee grievance procedure would be another area raised by SEIU.

CAMPAIGNING FOR WORKERS' SUPPORT: THE FIRST YEAR

The campaign actually began in June, five years ago. The union initially acted by holding secret organizational meetings to acquaint union organizers with employees and to try to identify key people within the KCOM-KOHC complex. These people would be used to help promote SEIU by passing out pamphlets and starting word-of-mouth communications in general support of the union. If the organizing attempt proved successful, some of them would eventually become officers of the local union. SEIU representatives had somehow been able to obtain a variety of pro-union mailings. The union's effort at this point was to contact as many employees as possible, as a way of raising their awareness with regard to union presence.

Soon after the first contacts, the union began to ask KCOM-KOHC employees to sign authorization cards. The number of cards signed would indicate the magnitude of workers' interest in having SEIU, Local 50, represent them in collective negotiations with the employer. Union authorization cards were left on the tables in the cafeterias, lobbies, and near time clocks. A SEIU bulletin (Exhibit 1) stating wages, vacations, sick leave provisions, and other benefits that some SEIU members were receiving at other SEIU institutions were also placed at locations throughout the complex. It was at this point that some employees informed management of the increasing union activity at KCOM-KOHC.

THE SECOND YEAR

Management was not aware of the union's presence at the complex until February, the following year. However, the administration wasted little time in preparing itself to defend against the union's campaign, when the organizing attempt by SEIU was brought to its attention.

EXHIBIT 1

SEIU Bulletin
Service Employees International Union AFL-CIO, CLU
Local No. 50

TO: All Hospital Employees

Service Employees International Union, AFL-CIO, CLU, is attempting to unionize all hospital workers in the states of Missouri and Illinois. Hospital workers' wages and benefits are far below those of other workers in the workforce, and, because of this, Local No. 50 will assist hospital workers in upgrading their wages and benefits. The following are a list of wages and benefits that are enjoyed by Service Employees International Union Members.

Wages	*Per Hour*
RNs	$8.09
Nurses aides	6.35
Dietary and kitchen employees	6.73
Housekeepers	6.52
Central supply	5.90
Laundry workers	6.04
Maintenance workers	6.74

Employees working the afternoon and midnight shifts shall receive more per hour for working these shifts. All employees shall receive 50 cents more per hour when the hospital is short of help. Employees working the weekend will receive one and one-half (1-1/2) time per hour.

Holidays

All employees shall receive 12 paid holidays per year: New Year's Day, Good Friday, Easter Sunday, Memorial Day, Independence Day, Mother's Day, Labor Day, Thanksgiving, Christmas, Employee Birthday, Personal Day, Father's Day.

a. Double time and one-half (2-1/2) shall be paid for all hours worked on a holiday.

b. If employee is off on holidays, he or she shall receive pay for that day.

Vacation

All employees shall receive vacation as follows:

2 weeks after 1 year of service
3 weeks after 2 years of service
4 weeks after 4 years of service
5 weeks after 6 years of service

EXHIBIT 1 *(concluded)*

Paid Sick Days
All employees shall receive eighteen (18) paid sick days per year and three (3) paid personal days. Any unused sick days may be paid at the end of the year.

Funeral Leave
All employees shall receive five (5) paid funeral days per each family member.

Uniforms
Paid for or furnished.

Hospitalization
Paid hospitalization for employees and family.

Disability Paid
Employees will receive seventy-five percent (75%) of wages if off from work ill.

One of the first decisions made by administration was the hiring of a management consulting law firm that had previous experience in antiunion tactics. This firm, Elliott, Kaiser and Freeman, whose main office is in Kansas City, Missouri, arrived within a matter of days and began to interview members of the KCOM-KOHC supervisory and management staff. The main purpose of these interviews was to determine how the supervisors and managers felt about the union campaign, identify what they felt were the key issues, and use the information to develop the type of training and support the supervisors and managers would need to prepare them to carry out the strategy that would be used by KCOM-KOHC.

At the first group meeting between the management consultants and the supervisory and management staff, supervisors and managers were given handouts on the "Dos and Don'ts of a union campaign," emphasizing what members of management could do and say, as well as what they could not do or say to employees during an antiunion campaign. Included in the handouts and discussed at the meeting were such items as those listed in Exhibit 2. Films of a firm dealing with a union campaign and of a strike at an inner-city hospital in New York also were shown. The importance of promptness in forwarding all the information and rumors heard to the attention of the administration also was discussed.

In April 1981, the union began to educate employees about their rights under the National Labor Relations Act by distributing letters explaining them. The first of these letters pointed out to workers that punitive actions by corporate management, such as terminating and transferring employees for union activity, were illegal. At this time, the union started to file unfair labor practice charges on behalf of KCOM-KOHC employees for all conceivable disciplinary warnings, regardless of how trivial. This was done in an effort to show KCOM-KOHC employees that the union was willing to fight management for them. The union also hoped to use up the management consultant's time by giving the consulting firm too many unfair labor practice charges to defend. To further persuade employees of the union's

EXHIBIT 2 Some Things the Employer Can or Cannot Do during a Campaign

The "Cans"

1. Tell the hospital employees that, if a majority of them select the union (an outside organization), the hospital will have to deal with it on all their daily problems involving wages, hours, and other conditions of employment. Advise them that the hospital would prefer to continue dealing with them directly on such matters.
2. Tell hospital employees that you and other members of management are always willing to discuss with them any subject of interest to them.
3. Tell the hospital employees about the benefits they presently enjoy, all of which may have been obtained without union representation. Avoid promises or threats, either direct or veiled.
4. Tell the hospital employees how their wages, benefits, and working conditions compare favorably with other hospitals in the area, whether unionized or not. Information should be factual.
5. Tell the hospital employees some of the disadvantages of belonging to a union—such as the expense of initiation fees, monthly dues, fines, strike assessments, and membership rules restricting their personal freedom. Quote from the specific union's constitution and by-laws granting the union power to impose punishment and discipline against its members.
6. Tell the hospital employees there is a possibility that a union will call a strike or work stoppage even though many employees may not want to strike and even though the employer is willing to bargain or has been bargaining with the union. Inform employees that any strike can cost them money in lost wages.

The Cannots"

1. Promise hospital employees a pay increase, promotion, betterment, benefit, or special favor if they stay out of the union or vote against it.
2. Threaten loss of jobs, reduction of income, discontinuance of privileges or benefits presently enjoyed, or use intimidating language which may be designed to influence a hospital employee in the exercise of his or her right to belong, or refrain from belonging to a union.
3. Threaten or actually discharge, discipline, or lay off a hospital employee because of his or her activities in behalf of the union.
4. Threaten, through a third party, any of the foregoing acts of interference.
5. Threaten to close or move the hospital, or to drastically reduce operations if a union is selected as a representative.
6. Spy on union meetings (parking across the street from a union hall would be suspect.)
7. Conduct yourself in a way which would indicate to the hospital employees that you are watching them to determine whether or not they are participating in union activities.
8. Discriminate against hospital employees actively supporting the union by intentionally assigning undesirable work to the union employee.
9. Transfer hospital employees prejudicially because of union affiliation.
10. Engage in any activity favoring nonunion hospital employees over employees active in behalf of the union.

good intentions, a letter from the president of SEIU, William Stodghill, was posted that stressed the intent of the union to be that of improving patient quality care through increasing staff.

Early in May, a class on union authorization cards was given to management personnel. Its purpose was to enable managers to answer questions often raised by some employees about authorization cards. Discussed also were different approaches the union could use to ask workers to sign cards and whether each could stand up under the law. The class culminated in a test on when an authorization card could be viewed as valid or invalid by the National Labor Relations Board. Examples of the reviewed items were as follows:

Union Organizer: "Don't be a renegade. Sign the card just like everyone else. If you do, you won't have to pay either regular dues or initiation fee."

Employee: "That sounds pretty good to me. I'm always looking for a bargain."

Valid [Invalid]

Union Organizer: "Well, it looks like you could be the lucky person. We need one more person to get an election at this facility. If you sign this card, we can go down to the Labor Board and ask for an election."

Employee: "Well, I'm not saying I'll vote for the union, but I'll sign to get an election."

[Valid] Invalid

The union responded by preparing and mailing a one-page leaflet to employees entitled, "Have you heard this message yet?" This leaflet posted and addressed seven questions that the union felt would be raised by management. It consisted of counterarguments to standard management objections during an organizing campaign and included such statements as "All the Union wants is your dues money" and "The Union will be run by outsiders." The leaflet was poorly timed to the extent that the issues it raised had not been originated by management, and thus, prematurely opened a can of worms; it began to raise and address questions that had not yet been raised by management. Therefore, it provided management a perfect opportunity to bring out the administration's views and responses to the raised questions. On May 8, Dr. H. Charles Moore, president of KCOM, sent a memorandum to all employees, appealing to them not to sign the union authorization cards. In addition, Dr. Moore's memo stated, in part: "We do indeed have problems and are working as quickly and as positively as we can to work out those problems. We ask that you bear with us during this time of change, and we believe that our future together will be positive and rewarding to all." He went on to explain that, if employees were patient with KCOM-KOHC during the turbulent times, both worker and employer would benefit more if unencumbered by a union. On May 19, the vice president and administrator of KOHC, Mr. William Greene, sent another memo on union authorization cards to the employees. Mr. Greene's memo used a question and answer format to discuss such items as what a union authorization card is: whether it obligates employees (it does); what the union does with the signed cards (to seek an NLRB certification election and/or to try to force the employer to recognize it without an election); the types of pressure workers are subjected to so as to get them to sign union cards (while sweeping under the rug the equally important right not to join a union); the difficulties of getting rid of a union; and how to revoke a signed card (simply, by writing the union and asking it to withdraw the signed authorization card). One of the interesting revelations underscored by Mr. Greene's memo was that SEIU had won an election a few years earlier at Jefferson Memorial Hospital in nearby Festus, Missouri. Some years later, the employees at Jefferson Memorial were very disenchanted with the union and voted to get rid of it. However, this was done after the union had already dragged its suffering members through an unpopular strike of over one year in duration.

KCOM-KOHC administration, feeling that communication between the employees and the frontline supervisors and managers was a key point, continued to have seminars on better communication skills for supervisory and middle-management personnel. They were encouraged to discuss with the employees any issue that would arise in their everyday dealings on the worksite.

By the end of May, management also had put into effect the "Hotline," an anonymous call-in service for workers. The purpose of the hotline was to improve communication between the employees and administration. An employee could call the hotline and ask a question without having to leave his or her name. Once a week a printed edition of the hotline was given to all of the employees and the questions asked the previous weeks and the answers were given. This was the beginning of a management-supported, employee-oriented weekly newsletter called the *Health Center Hotline.*

Early in August, the union sent a letter to the employees that was cosigned by Mr. William Stodghill, president, and Mr. Kevin Gallagher, business representative, of SEIU, Local 50. In this letter it was stressed that the intent of the union was to improve the quality of patient care by increasing staff, and to improve wages, benefits, and working conditions and to create a functional grievance procedure. This letter also contained a cartoon to demonstrate the strength of the union. The union was hopeful that the cartoon, which made a caricature of management's powerlessness in the union's presence, would show KCOM-KOHC employees that they had nothing to fear from management as long as they had the union behind them.

CONTRACT SAMPLER

On August 17, KCOM-KOHC management responded (to SEIU's letter of early August) with a letter to the workers from Mr. William Greene. This letter began by indicating that the union was an outsider to the local community, the medical complex, the ways of life of the people who worked in the complex, and to the effective running of a healthcare business. Mr. Greene lamented that it would be a tragedy to be represented by "someone" who did not "know anything about 'our Health Center,' and [hadn't] ever taken the time to find out." He characterized the union's statement of intent to "improve patient care by increasing staff" and to achieve "optimal patient care" by decreasing patient load per employee as "empty promises." He illustrated by pointing out that the organization's nurse staffing problems were due to a nationwide shortage of licensed nursing personnel, which KCOM-KOHC had attempted to ease through a widely publicized nurse recruitment and retention program. Further, he underscored that no union could possibly guarantee the hiring of additional licensed nursing personnel anywhere that he was familiar with. But this was not all.

Mr. Greene admitted that, in terms of wages, benefits, and working conditions, KCOM-KOHC needed a great deal of improvement and explained why a wage and salary study was already being conducted by the organization. However, he revealed that even the complex "looked good," compared to contracts negotiated by the union at other medical facilities and hospitals. Reference was made to the terms of a contract that had been negotiated and signed between SEIU (representing the housekeeping employees at St. Louis University Hospital in St. Louis, Missouri) and Service Master Industries (a contractor that was the primary employer of those employees at the hospital). Mr. Greene did not excerpt and attach any specific parts of the contract to his letter. Instead, copies of the entire contract were given to supervisors and managers who, in turn, passed them along to workers. In addition, copies were kept in the employee relations office by Mrs. Sueanna Hannah, director of employee relations. Employees also were encouraged by their supervisors to go to the employee relations office to look at the contract.

All workers who inspected the contract found comparisons similar to those in Table 1. The wages earned by housekeepers at St. Louis University Hospital were generally lower than those that already existed at KCOM-KOHC. In addition, the SEIU contract with Service Master Industries revealed wages that were by far lower than those publicized by the union, in Exhibit 1, as typical results of its negotiations. Furthermore, all benefits announced in Exhibit 1 as representative of SEIU agreements were considerably higher than those on the signed contract. One of the most talked about benefits in the contract concerned sick pay. Under the SEIU/Service Master Industries contract, an employee would not receive sick pay for the first day he or she called in sick, unless the individual was hospitalized. Thus, if a full-time employee was ill on Monday and Tuesday without being hospitalized, he or she would only be paid for Tuesday. On the other hand, the individual would receive pay for both days under the prevailing terms at KCOM-KOHC.

Management personnel kept referring back to this contract throughout the campaign. For example, it was often underscored that the cost of living was very high in St. Louis, a large city of a few million people, compared to small Kirksville, a city of only 17,000. Yet KCOM-KOHC workers had relatively better wages, benefits, and work conditions, even if marginally so.

HOPE NEWS OR NEWSLETTER WARS?

The union began its own newsletter in late August. The publication was called *Hope News* and did not appear regularly. "Hope" originally stood for "Help Our Patients and Employees." Later, it would also stand for "Help Our POOR Employees."

TABLE 1 Comparisons Based in a Contract Sampler

Minimum Wage Rates Effective June 1		
Length of Service	*SEIU/SMI* Contract per Hour*	*KCOM-KOHC† per Hour*
Start	$3.65	$3.85
After 60 days	3.75	4.00
After 1 year	3.90	4.15
After 3 years	4.00	4.25
After 5 years	4.10	4.45
After 10 years	4.20	4.60

* The SEIU/Service Master Industries contract stipulated that employees with ten (10) years or more of service on June 1 would receive the indicated rate or forty cents (40) per hour over the current rate, whichever was higher.

† Reported here are approximations of prevailing wage rates at KCOM-KOHC, for the same category of workers (housekeepers), at the time. They are based on estimations by KCOM-KOHC managers.

Because SEIU had its local headquarters in St. Louis, it found itself having to fight the "outsider" image. For example, management often referred to the union as an outsider that did not understand the local problems of the Kirksville area. *Hope* was an attempt to improve the union's outsider image by associating familiar names with SEIU. Although the union had about half of the workers interested in organizing, many of the rest were still uncertain about what the union would do to their local work life. The others seemed to have been afraid of change in general, and particularly those underscored by the presence of the union. To show those with doubts that the union had become part of the local community, the newsletter contained comments from employees of KCOM-KOHC concerning working conditions, recipes for cookies and salads, and other such items from the local people. Comments in the *Hope News* also would be used to raise such issues as grievance procedures, floating, and acuity levels. Acuity level was a factor used to decide the number of nursing personnel that would work a particular shift on a particular floor. It was based on the type and seriousness of the patient's illness. For example, the number of nurses assigned per cancer patient may be higher than for a routine tonsillectomy.

FLOATING THE PERSONNEL

The floating issue grew in importance, and it became obvious to management that the strength of the union was in the nursing department. Nurses were the employees most often asked to float between buildings. In fact, floating was not even a policy in some departments, such as dietary and housekeeping. The purpose of floating employees, from management's point of view, was to spread the workload evenly throughout the medical complex. For example, if the 5-South wing had four nurses, three aides, and three patients, and 2-South had two nurses, one aide, and six patients, then one nurse and one aide from 5-South would be floated to work on 2-South. The union, on the other hand, maintained that it was harassment to make employees work at areas that they were not permanently or originally assigned to. The union stated that more employees were needed to overcome the practice of employee floating. The nurses themselves felt it unfair that they were moved around when other employees were not. Furthermore, they were bitter about being originally hired to work on particular floors by virtue of their specialties and then "forced" to work outside their primary skill areas.

THE TALK, LISTEN, AND COMMUNICATE COMMITTEE (TLC)

Not all classifications of KCOM-KOHC workers felt as strongly for their own self-interest motivations to unionize as the nurses at this point in time. As a result, a splinter group emerged around the months of August through November. Several employees had started being upset with the union and decided to form a committee of their own. Indeed the committee was neither originated by nor connected in any way as a stooge to either SEIU or the KCOM-KOHC management. Rather, the group was an independent movement started by a certain Tom Auxter and a handful of his friends. Its purpose was to solve problems of the organization within the organization and without the benefit of a union. This committee sent two letters to the employees, in a membership drive, during this period. The letters read in part:

> WE ARE THE EMPLOYEE COMMITTEE THAT CARES! WE KNOW that we can work with the staff, physicians, administration, community, with each other and with you to make KOHC the best possible health center. WE THINK it's time for the union to leave us alone so that we can all work together to improve the things that we all care about . . . JOIN US, and let's work together to get things done for KOHC and each other!

Out of this employee committee grew the Talk, Listen, and Communicate (TLC) Committee. This committee, which is still functioning (as of data collection date), meets with administration to communicate suggestions and concerns that have been given to them by their fellow employees. The union contended that the employee committee was actually initiated by the administration of KCOM-KOHC, but lacked concrete evidence to prove that effect.

ECONOMIC AND FINANCIAL HARDSHIPS

During this entire year, KCOM-KOHC experienced severe financial troubles. Like many other healthcare organizations in the country, the patient census had dropped well below the normal average. The cost of new equipment, supplies, and other expenses had skyrocketed. When this was combined with the fact that Medicare and Medicaid reimbursements to the institution no longer covered the costs laid out by the institution, KCOM-KOHC had to absorb over $2 million in bad debts that it could not pay. Some managers estimated that the organization was already about $1.5 million in the red. Because the financial picture of KCOM-KOHC was anything but rosy, management announced in late November that no merit increases would be given to employees of KCOM-KOHC for one year, beginning on December 1. On December 2, the union sent a letter asking the employees to consider the fact that they would be receiving no pay increases and that the practice of floating was still taking place. The union stated that it could negotiate regular wage and benefit increases if given the chance. Sections of the letter read as follows:

> NO pay increases for (the entire next year)?
> NO overtime pay for working a holiday?
> NO reimbursement . . . for completing the LPN training program?
> A floating policy still in effect, whereby employees are moved back and forth between the two hospitals without advance notice and NO reimbursement for gas?
> NO disability insurance?
> NO hospitalization coverage while you are not working?
> And after all of this the (administration) hires a management consultant to conduct a "compensation study" for . . . computing new wage rates that (management) claims it can't afford to pay anyway???

The union did not know how bad the financial situation of KCOM-KOHC had become. After several weeks of discussion and planning between management and the institution's board of directors, a plan to reduce KCOM-KOHC's expenses was developed. A main component of the plan called for the reduction of 140 full-time equivalents from the KCOM-KOHC personnel. The decision on which employees would be terminated was based on employee seniority within the individual's current department at the time. In addition, all part-time positions were eliminated in each department before any full-time employee was terminated. On December 10, those people that represented the 140 full-time equivalents were told that they were in positions that had been declared excessive by the institution, and, therefore, their services were no longer needed. Each of these employees was given two weeks' severance pay and also was paid for any unused vacation and holiday time. Unemployment compensation would not be contested by the institution for any of the excessive personnel that had been terminated. SEIU had something of a field day with the mass terminations that were taking place. During the three months prior to the December 10 dismissals, the union had been losing much of its support among the employees. The mass discharge was just what the union needed to bolster its waning campaign. Employees began to question their job security. Rumors of more mass terminations began to spread like wildfire.

A QUESTION OF IMAGE

In late December, Mr. William Greene sent to all employees a "facts versus rumors" handout. His foremost intent was to put an end to some of the rumors concerning additional terminations; but the handout also attacked the union as being an outsider. Mr. Greene pointed out that the union's closest office to KCOM-KOHC's location was in St. Louis—about 260 miles away from Kirksville. Further, he indicated that "SEIU (was NOT really SEIU), but SEIU-RWDSU." [RWDSU stood for Retail, Wholesale, Department Store Employees Union (New York City).] In addition, his letter uncovered that SEIU, Local 50, had 19 members on its executive board out of which only 1 was a hospital employee. Based on this and similar revelations, the letter left the workers with a question: How could SEIU, Local 50, be "your union?" Mr. Greene encouraged the employees to call the hotline to get factual answers to any other uncertainties they may have. During the last few weeks of December, SEIU's representatives were being quoted on an almost daily basis in the Kirksville *Daily Express,* the local newspaper, and on the local television and radio stations. The mass terminations and the need for union protection of KCOM-KOHC employees were the main topic. This left the union with the feeling of having the local press behind its cause. However, that was not and did not translate to the strong endorsement the union had hoped for. Public opinion did not take a swing for the worse against KCOM-KOHC, as the union had hoped for. The fact, however, was that, due to perennial hardships, KCOM-KOHC had been receiving a great deal of local bad press for several years. This consistently had produced a curious mixture of low public image and immense public sympathy for the organization. In a sense, therefore, hearing negative remarks concerning KCOM-KOHC had become "old hat" in the Kirksville community. Thus, a dismayed SEIU official lamented that the union's strategy of getting the local press on its side was not as helpful a tool as in other SEIU campaigns he had been associated with.

THE THIRD YEAR

The union petitioned for an election and, on January 18, a representation hearing commenced in Kirksville before the National Labor Relations Board (NLRB). The purpose of the hearing was to determine the right of the KCOM-KOHC employees to be represented by SEIU, Local 50, for purposes of collective bargaining. An issue of *Hope News* came out at this time encouraging the employees to keep faith and to stand up for their rights. This edition of the newsletter also questioned management's tactics and implied that the institution could not be trusted to tell the truth. For example, it stated that "Mr. Greene is lying when he claims that SEIU is not really SEIU." It explained that a merger between SEIU and RWDSU had been proposed, but final action could not be taken on it until a convention in May or June. It further argued that perhaps the merger, nevertheless, would be an advantage to workers in the medical and healthcare industry.

THE BARGAINING UNIT CONTROVERSY

The representation hearing took much longer than anyone had anticipated. Due to a scheduling problem, the hearing was on recess for several days and then reconvened on February 16. SEIU took the position that there should be two bargaining units—one for professional and the other for nonprofessional workers. The professional unit would include the registered nurses and the medical and X-ray technicians. Everyone else would be in the nonprofessional unit. The union argued vigorously for including only KOHC employees and no KCOM workers in the bargaining units. KCOM-KOHC management took the position that three bargaining units were needed to represent each of the professional, service and maintenance, and nonprofessional groups of employees. The professional unit would be made up of the same group of workers proposed by SEIU (i.e., RNs, medical, and X-ray techs). The service and maintenance unit would include nurses' aides, maintenance, housekeeping, and dietary employees. The nonprofessional bargaining unit would include all other employees. In addition, the administration argued that clerical personnel should be included in one of the three bargaining units and that all employees (KCOM and KOHC) were to be included in the bargaining units. The biggest battle during the hearings centered around the inclusion of KCOM employees. The union contended that KCOM was a separate organization by itself and had no connection with KOHC in any shape or form. To support this premise, the union called numerous witnesses in an attempt to establish that KCOM and KOHC could each function on its own, without any support or help from the other. Management's lawyers also called numerous witnesses to provide evidence that KCOM and KOHC were two arms of the same private organization. The KCOM-KOHC lawyers began by establishing that traditionally, the dietary, housekeeping, and maintenance departments all functioned between both KCOM and KOHC. Further, Mr. Don Hunter, director of budgets, presented data showing that the budget was based on the operation of KCOM-KOHC as a whole and that separate budgets were not prepared for each arm of the organization. Testimony was given on the fact that some departments, such as audiovisual, did work for both units. Moreover, a number of departments, such as X-ray and medial lab, testified that some pieces of equipment were shared between their departments at KOHC and the research labs at KCOM. It was noted that all employees' checks were issued by the same organization, and that the institution's major regular newsletter, the *Intercom,* was distributed to all employees and also stated on its cover that it was the biweekly "KCOM-KOHC" newsletter. Finally an examination of the corporate organizational structure during the hearings underscored that KCOM-KOHC had the same board of directors, and that Mr. William Greene, vice president of KOHC, reported to Dr. H. Charles Moore, president of KCOM. A manager at KCOM-KOHC later explained why the administration wanted all KCOM-KOHC employees included in the bargaining units. Union support was much stronger among KOHC employees than in the ranks of KCOM employees. Besides, the management's lawyers felt that if all employees were in the unit the chance for a union victory would be greatly reduced. A labor relations expert added that it was quite possible that the union did not have enough authorization cards signed to warrant an election by all KCOM-KOHC employees; hence, the union's unequivocal contention for the exclusion of KCOM employees. Management also felt that three bargaining units would decrease the chance for a union victory. In a three-unit bargaining structure, nursing aides would fall into the service and maintenance employees unit. Nursing aides had become a union strength, while union support among service and maintenance employees had begun to slide downhill. This meant that in an election, the pro-management support of the service and maintenance employees could cancel out the strength of the nursing aides. The clerical personnel also hoped to dilute the union vote in the nonprofessional unit. Tactical or fortuitous? The waiting begins! The representation hearing ended in late February. The union sent out a *Hope News* in late March. This issue of the newsletter contained several comments from KOHC employees about the right to organize and the benefits of a union. It also contained a section entitled "The Pope's on Our Side," which discussed the pope's view of working conditions in Italy and the pope's belief that workers have the right to organize. An appeal to vote yes on election day was included. The union and its supporters were confident that an election would take place around the middle of April. Little did they know that the long wait had just begun. April came and no election date had been set. Meanwhile, the management lawyers had been hatching their own "grand design." They had filed a brief with the regional office of the National Labor Relations Board in Kansas City, Missouri, requesting that the SEIU, Local 50, KCOM-KOHC case be heard and decided on by the nation's National Labor Relations Board (i.e., the national board) in Washington, D.C. Management's lawyers stated in their brief that due to the difference in opinion on the number of bargaining units and on whether all employees should be in the bargaining units, as well as the fact that few decisions on bargaining units at colleges of medicine had ever been made, it was in the best interest of the union and the institution to have the national board make the ruling. Shortly after this brief was filed, both the union and the institution were advised that the regional National Labor Relations Board had passed on their case to the national board. The union's campaign officers were upset by this new development. SEIU had been telling the employees to "hang tough," because an election was near. Now, however, the election date would be delayed by, well, a few months more; or so it was thought.

THE SECOND CONTRACT SAMPLER

During the first week of May, the administration began to distribute to the management staff copies of an agreement between SEIU, Local 513, and Mount Carmel Medical Center in Pittsburgh, Kansas. This was soon after the union had mentioned the contract as one of those it had negotiated for a unit of registered nurses in an issue of the *Hope News.* Management had observed that the SEIU/Mount Carmel contract compared with the SEIU/Service Master Industries contract, and, therefore, contained wages, terms, and conditions that were not as good as those prevailing at KCOM-KOHC at the time—even though, as the union would later clarify, the Mount Carmel contract reflected a twelve percent (12%) wage increase. On May 13, the union sent to the employees a letter signed by William Stodghill, president of SEIU, Local 50 (and addressed to "Dear KCOM, Inc., employees"), concerning the Mount Carmel Medical Center contract. The union called attention to the fact that the contract established an Educational Reimbursement Program for registered nurses (RNs); a shift differential of thirty-five cents (35¢) per hour in the afternoon and forty-five cents (45¢) per hour for the night shift; pay for being on-call or on standby time and one-half if actually called back to work; and a general 12 percent raise in wages. The letter expressed that "The Mt. Carmel contract, which covers 77 Registered Nurses, is far from the 'best' the union had negotiated for its 230,000 members in the United States and Canada." Furthermore, it stated that "It is ridiculous to waste time and energy worrying about someone else's contract. Each facility negotiates its own contract. Language which KCOM, Inc., employees find unacceptable in other Union contracts does not have to end up in your contract." Thus, the letter also attempted to underscore that the workers could refuse to ratify any contract negotiated by the union, if they did not like its terms. This was the first time that SEIU specifically addressed any piece of correspondence to "KCOM, Inc., Employees." All future union letters and memos would follow the same example, in an effort to establish a better relationship with KCOM employees that the union had previously snubbed.

THE UNFAIR LABOR PRACTICE CHARGE: A DOUBLE-EDGED SWORD?

When the union started filing unfair labor practice charges against KCOM-KOHC about one and a half years ago, its intent was at least threefold. First was to provide the workers some quick evidence of the fine job SEIU could do in their defense; second was to overwhelm and distract management's "antiunion" consultants by confronting them with a barrage of cases to deal with; and third, to provide some martyrs for the union's cause by seizing on some unjust, ill-conceived, recklessly reactive, or vindictive disciplinary actions by the organization. As a result, the union eagerly filed more than 25 unfair labor practice charges by the end of June during the second year. The number of the charges exceeded 60 by May of the third year and dealt with a variety of KCOM-KOHC disciplinary actions, ranging from warnings and suspensions to terminations. The first major wave of decisions was received by July of the second year, from NLRB's regional office in Kansas City. Not even one disciplinary action by KCOM-KOHC was reversed. (This was one of the events that preceded the formation of the TLC committee.) The union followed with two actions. First, SEIU appealed the findings of the regional NLRB office to the National Labor Relations Board's national office in Washington, D.C. Second, the union distributed a leaflet toward the end of July, attacking the campaign strategies of management's "antiunion consultants" and suggesting to the workers that they were not receiving better wages because all of the money was being spent on the consultants. The leaflet read in part:

> Big business's attack on the labor movement is occurring on many fronts. The prime movers in this attack are an army of lawyers and consultants whose major purpose is to help business maintain outlandish profits by preventing workers from organizing. But the consultants constitute a Big Business of their own—bringing in up to $1,000 a day for their services.

The second major wave of decisions was received in early May, during the third year, from NLRB's Kansas City regional office. The regional NLRB ruled against five of the organization's disciplinary actions and ordered it to reverse or correct them. However, the union could not enjoy the victory. Winning only five reversals in almost one and a half years and after filing more than 60 unfair labor practice charges was not something to brag about. Besides, management was immediately appealing the decisions to the NLRB, which meant that SEIU could not take credit for the victory, yet. Management's legal consultants decided in June to discontinue the fight against the five reversals of management disciplinary actions. The lawyers felt that, even though they could probably win four of the charges, it was not worth the time and money it would take to contest the decisions. Therefore, in July, KCOM-KOHC was required by the NLRB to post the findings of unfair labor practices for a period of 30 days. The posting of the NLRB findings created little discussion among the employees. Most employees would begin to read the announcement and then would say "big deal" and walk away. Union supporters did little to spread the word of their small victory. They were apprehensive that some employees might ask about the other charges that the union was unable to reverse. Besides, by initiating an appeal in May and then dropping it by early July, KCOM-KOHC management allowed the findings to slip out through the grapevine and, thus, diffused the punch which the release of the news would have had otherwise. It was during the month of July that KCOM-KOHC received word that the National Labor Relations Board in Washington, D.C., had upheld the findings of the regional board in Kansas City, concerning the termination of a housekeeping employee in January that year. The Kansas City board ruled that KCOM-KOHC had just cause to terminate the employee. Both union and management officials conceded that this was the most important of all the unfair labor practice charges. Indeed, management and its legal consultants viewed the case as the only important one of the charges. First, it was the only termination case that was directly related to the presence of the union. Second, the worker was discharged soon after he was found sharing and distributing union cards and discussing union organizing activities during work time. Management based its arguments on the grounds that he was negligent in his own duties, while at the same time disrupting the performance of other workers. Third, he was one of the most outspoken supporters of the union. On the night that the employee was terminated, he made several statements that the union would protect him and he would be back on the job in a few days. At a union meeting the next day, he was used as an example of a poor employee who was abused by management and was terminated for supporting the union. When KCOM-KOHC publicized its victory in this case, the union once again began to lose employee support. Several employees began to question just how much protection the union could really give them. Shortly after, several of the stronger and more vocal union supporters began to quit their jobs at KCOM-KOHC and to work or look for jobs in other organizations. Late July saw another issue of *Hope News,* asking the employees to remain united and faithful to the union's cause. It contained an open letter from William Stodghill and described the "long and hard" union fight by the SEIU-supported employees of Baptist Hospital in Beaumont, Texas. The union-organizing effort in Beaumont had lasted for almost 16 months.

STRATEGIC REPOSITIONING

As August approached, management and its consultants decided to slightly change their strategy. Seminars and classes on communications and management techniques would continue on a regular basis. The administration believed that the seminars had been improving the quality of the institution's supervisors and managers and that continuing them would be in the best interest of all. Management also decided to hire a training manager for KCOM-KOHC. This person would not only develop and give seminars for the supervisors and managers but would also develop a new employee handbook, an employee orientation program, and other training programs for the employees. Any new unfair labor charges would be fought, as in the past. However, the union had not filed any charges for several months. Management would no longer answer any union letters, memos, or announcements that would appear in the future. For example, from August (of the third year) to April (of the fourth year), the union sent out two issues of the *Hope News.* In neither case was there any response from management. Management personnel also ceased to discuss the union and its activities with the employees, unless it was absolutely necessary. Supervisors would no longer encourage discussions about the union. Any changes taking place at KCOM-KOHC continued to be communicated to the employees by letter and through the TLC committee. For example, if a change were to be made in the insurer for KCOM-KOHC employee health insurance, a letter would communicate the information to the employee. In addition, management planned to write more letters to the employees to enable them to become more comfortable with receiving letters from the administration. As one KCOM-KOHC manager explained, the purpose was to preempt the time when a letter-writing campaign against the union would become necessary.

A PERIOD OF QUIET WAITING: THE FOURTH AND FIFTH YEARS

The campaign remained extremely quiet through the early part of the fifth year. Management was very faithful to the strategic repositioning which it adopted in August, during the third year, and never mentioned SEIU. The union filed no additional unfair labor practice charges. An issue of *Hope News* appeared in April; only one or two more appeared in the fourth year.

The lack of an election date added to the lack of campaign activity. Some observers speculated back in April during the fourth year that an election would be held by November. However, December came and went, but there was no election. Meanwhile, more and more union supporters were leaving the employ of KCOM-KOHC. The organization, itself, was hiring new employees who were not familiar with the union or what it stood for. The compensation study had been completed and management approved and established the new salary and wage structure. Workers also began to use the employees' grievance procedure that had existed but was rarely used in the past and found that, in some cases, management was willing to reverse a disciplinary action. Word was finally received by April, during the fifth year, that the selection date had been set for June 28. The management and union teams pondered their respective plans of action for the next few weeks.

Discussion Questions

1. How would you describe, from a collective bargaining perspective, the internal environment at KCOM?
2. Is it likely that an organizing campaign will be successful? Explain.

Section J

Managing a Difficult Employee

55 Speedy Cable Company

After getting a theft problem off his back, now Angelo Kinicki finds himself dealing with a mutiny over the use of temporary and other contingency employees and a privacy issue. How can he meet his budget target, be productive, *and* keep these ungratefuls happy? Angelo, the person responsible for all personnel matters at the center, leaned back in his comfortable chair and gazed out the window. His thoughts turned to his stormy meeting with Mrs. Cecilia Gambiccini, the Speedy Cable Company's equipment records associate. What could he do?

Until today, his job seemed simple enough. All he had to do was keep Speedy Cable running smoothly, make his numbers with regard to cable company sign-ups and expenditures for things like personnel, equipment, vehicle repair, overtime, and the like, plus make sure sufficient crews were out to install, repair, and remove cable TV as needed. He thought this piracy business was enough headache for him. Angelo consoled himself with the thought that every manager seemed to have a cross to bear! He remembered the cable company manager he met at the convention in Florida who told him, "Hey, if there weren't alligators in the swamp, they wouldn't pay us the big bucks!" Right now, that thought was no consolation to him.

As manager of the Webster Groves office of Speedy Cable Company, he had responsibility for all administrative matters. After 15 years as a civil servant in Saint Louis area city government, including 10 years working for the Clayton city manager, he had grown accustomed to handling any kind of problem. He liked the staff here, and he wanted them to like him. Angelo had a special knack for getting the customers, staff associates, installation crews, and others he encountered on a daily basis to cooperate most of the time. He emphasized the need for all of the company's employees to work as one big family. Angelo knew the ideal would never be reached but it was something to strive for. Critical to his operation were the staff associates and installation crews. The associates provided a front-line defense and had developed the knack to handle the most irate customer call. God knows, on the days when the weather was lousy or there was a major electrical problem, each of these folks was worth his or her weight in gold. The associates also were crucial in their ability to sell cable TV services. A good associate could get nearly everyone who called to upgrade their request by adding premium channels or additional converter boxes in the home or other features.

Angelo's job, in general, became especially easy when Barb Fisher, his secretary, arrived two years ago. Barb was a super organizer and planner. Performance evaluations were properly scheduled, files were up to date, people were paid on time. There hadn't been a single snafu of this type since she came. Kinicki had thought that the toughest part of his job was the friction caused by just these kinds of snafus. Given this current problem with Cecilia, he wasn't so sure.

THE WEBSTER GROVES LOCATION

The Speedy Cable Company location in Webster Groves is one of seven such cable TV operations in metropolitan Saint Louis. The locations were built for the express purpose of serving the cable TV needs of Saint Louisians within key geographical boundaries, given that the metropolitan area includes nearly 100 municipalities. It was not a simple task to determine who would receive service from which cable TV company. A wide range of services, from basic services to multiple premium channels, special equipment, customized installations, and attractive discount programs for heavy cable users, was offered by Speedy Cable and its counterparts. The cable TV business, however, is closely regulated but within its immediate area maintains a monopoly. The company is quite typical of the other cable TV companies located in a metropolitan area. This one is located in a densely populated area of the city. The company boasts of nearly 300,000 subscribers and is growing steadily. It serves a large geographical area. People in the area are a mix of professionals, managers, and executives who have discretionary income with which to purchase multiple cable TV services. Most subscribers have at least two converter boxes in their homes.

Angelo Kinicki, directs the activities of a 45-member staff. The staff consists of 15 associates, 4 secretaries, 5 salespersons, and 10 cable TV crews (each one-man crew member has his or her own minivan). Despite this very broad chain of command and diversity of the employee background or training, the company is noted for its warm and friendly environment. Over the years, staff members have worked well together and many employees participate in various activities together after work. Unlike many employment settings, employees have avoided forming cliques on the basis of professional or status differences. One reason for this is the lengthy associations that exist among employees. Most have been at Webster Groves for at least five years. Employees know their jobs and go about their duties with little or no direct supervision. Unfortunately, Angelo notes that turnover has been occurring in recent months that has negatively affected the morale of some employees.

THE CLERICAL STAFF

It takes a lot of people, people of various skills and abilities, to make an operations such as a cable TV company function smoothly. One such group of people is the small group of secretaries Speedy Cable employs at Webster Groves. Although their task seems rather simple—have the customer records where they are needed when they are needed—accomplishing this objective is often made difficult by folks who misplace or misfile cases, absentminded installation crew members, and the boss, Angelo, who is known for his unsuccessful attempts to do too many things at once.

As recently as six months ago, everything ran quite smoothly. Few people had anything negative to say about the clerical unit. Over the years, this group had become the closest, most efficient team of any at the center. Everyone worked to get the job done. There was some play, however. The workers arrived at 8:00 AM each morning, but it was not uncommon to see them on long coffee breaks that concluded at 8:30 AM Such long breaks tended to occur on the average of twice a day. People could set their watches by the afternoon coffee break. At exactly 3:00 PM, people seemed to gravitate toward the vending machine and employees' lounge area. Around 3:20 PM, people would begin to quietly excuse themselves. Although an outsider would deem the 50 minutes of time spent on such breaks a total waste, such was not the case. Break time was used to unwind. Except for these two long breaks, people worked hard right through the day. Often workers would pass up lunch to get paperwork finished so the installation crews had the daily work assignments, directions to unfamiliar locations, and appropriate work orders. Things started to fall apart in the office when customers who came in to complain or wanted service noticed that folks were there but not serving them. Occasionally, vendors informed Angelo that there was a problem or a crew member wondered why secretaries weren't picking up or responding to call-ins as quickly. The biggest change to occur was the departure of two of the secretaries. One decided to go back to school to pursue a degree in physical therapy and the other moved to Milwaukee because of her husband's relocation to the General Motors plant there.

Cecilia was liked for a lot of reasons. One of the reasons was the manner in which she related to other people. She had the respect of all because of her knowledge of the company's operations, skill in relating to others, and a special skill for getting things done through others. She seemed to know just the right technique to use on each person. The clerks loved her. She demanded a lot from them, but she never asked anything that she would not demand of herself. During the past few years, she directed the activities of the secretarial staff with a light touch. The staff knew the work and the routine. And, having been well trained by Cecilia, the workers needed little direct supervision. Until recently, Cecilia could not remember the last time she had had a complaint about anybody. She knew the two daily breaks were long, but the secretaries really made up for it during the other eight hours of the day. Liz also knew that her own superior performance ratings had been a true reflection of the kind of quality staff Webster Groves had had. Now, she strongly considered leaving.

On July 6, Louise Nichols, the newest secretary, reported to Angelo Kinicki for her first day of duty. Angelo welcomed Louise warmly and, with little in the way of orientation, proceeded to take her to the clerical staff's work area. Afterward, he returned to his office, where he decided to look over her personnel file. In reading through the file, he discovered that she had worked six years in city government. Louise had quickly risen through the ranks in a minimum amount of time. Her test score on the supervisor's examination was a 99, the highest score he had ever seen. Her work as a clerk and clerk-typist was consistently superior. According to her supervisors, Louise was viewed as meticulous, dedicated, hardworking, and intelligent but a perfectionist to an extreme.

THE MEETING

Five months had passed since Louise first arrived at Webster Groves. Although Angelo had not formally met with her to conduct her probationary performance review, he assumed that all was well. He had planned to talk with other staff members before conducting the formal performance review. This review, he realized, would be extremely important because passing grades would mean she now had permanent status as a clerical supervisor. As Angelo contemplated this decision, he heard a commotion outside his office door. The intercom crackled.

"Angelo, Angelo!" It was Cecilia. There was the sound of urgency in her voice.

"Yes, Cecilia, what's the matter?"

A very upset and angry Cecilia came into his office. What he learned was that both Liz and Cindi, both of whom had been hired by Angelo through a local temporary agency, simply were not working out. In fact, he learned that they were hardly working at all. Cecilia described both as having an "attitude problem." However, Cecilia noted that Liz *could* do the work. Despite all coaching, training, and guidance, Cindi could not. Unfortunately, that meant that Cecilia and the one holdover secretary, Gloria Boddy, were left to do the lion's share of the work. In fact, neither Glorida nor Cecilia were taking those luxuriously long breaks anymore because they didn't have time! Cecilia went on to say that both of the new secretaries refused to work very hard because they viewed themselves as second-class citizens because of the temporary help status! Cecilia said something had to be done. It was either her or them!

After Cecilia left, Angelo began to check out her allegations. He talked to both Liz and Cindi and learned that both resented having to take the company's written honesty test and drug test. Angelo had tried to explain that the honesty test provided a psychological profile and, in his view, results which are useful in predicting on-the-job behavior. The drug test, he said, is required of all potential hires because the company could not afford to hire "unreliable people." However, the biggest complaint the two women had was that they felt it was an invasion of privacy to have Cecilia monitoring employee performance and having calls as well as electronic mail monitored. One by one, each of Cecilia's concerns was proven to be true. He could not believe it! The more he asked, the less he liked what he heard. Why hadn't anyone talked to him? He had not conducted employee surveys before, but maybe now he should. Is the behavior a problem consistent with nonpermanent employees? He wished he knew the answer to that one. He needed to know when people had a problem up front, not several weeks or months later. As he sat back, he tried to determine what he should do.

Discussion Questions

1. How would you describe this Speedy Cable Company office?
2. Could anything have been done to prevent the friction that seems to have occurred?
3. If you were Angelo Kinicki, what would you do? Why?

56 The Right Nurse for the Job

Frances Matthews, the director of clinical services at Appalachian Home Health Services, Inc. (AHHS), was concerned. AHHS needed to hire a nurse quickly. One of the staff nurses had just handed in her resignation because her husband was being transferred out of state. The nurse who was leaving gave AHHS two weeks' notice, which complied with the agency policy; however, it still left the agency in a bind. Frances knew that recruiting and interviewing of home health nurses was a time-consuming process, and, even after a nurse was hired, several weeks of orientation usually were required before the nurse could perform independently. She knew that all of the regular staff were working to capacity, and that the loss of even one nurse at this time would have major implications. She walked over to Kate Hennessey's office to discuss the situation. Kate was the director of administration services. Frances and Kate had started AHHS four years ago as a partnership. Together, they made all final hiring decisions.

Frances knocked on the door, saw that Kate was sitting at her desk, and walked in. "Sue is leaving. She sure picked a bad time to move!" She laughed halfheartedly and said, "We need to replace her quickly. Do you have any brilliant ideas?" Kate sighed, and responded, more in the form of a statement than a question, "We don't have any decent applications on file, do we?"

"Nope."

"Great. Well, let's get our ad into the paper today, maybe something will turn up."

Appalachian Home Health Services, Inc., is a private, not-for-profit home health agency, located in a rural area of a midwestern state. The stated purpose of AHHS is to provide healthcare services at home, to elderly and disabled individuals, and to persons with a short-term, specific healthcare need that could be handled at home.

AHHS, as a "fee-for-service" healthcare organization, provides in-home services, then bills for the services, either to a public or private insurance carrier (e.g., Medicare, Medicaid, Blue Cross/Blue Shield), or the patient directly. AHHS receives all (100 percent) of its revenue from billed services. As a private organization, it does not receive government subsidies or tax support.

Competition in the home health field is intense, particularly in rural areas where the need for service fluctuates. Because services are expensive to provide, it is critical for agencies to generate a volume of visits sufficient to cover fixed expenses plus make a small profit. Competition for the AHHS comes primarily from Care One, Inc., a multicounty operation that has been established in the area for well over 10 years. AHHS surpassed Care One in total number of visits after its second year of operation and has been steadily growing. Many of the physicians in the area, however, continue to use Care One, and they receive more referrals from nonlocal hospitals than does AHHS.

AHHS currently has 32 employees: 15 registered nurses (full-time and part-time), 8 nursing aides, 1 physical therapist, 1 speech therapist, and 7 administrative staff. All but two employees at AHHS are female.

REFERRALS FOR SERVICE

Most of the business generated for AHHS is in the form of referrals. Hospitals (social workers, discharge planners), account for over 70 percent of patient referrals; of this total, approximately 85 percent are from the two local hospitals, and 15 percent are from out-of-town hospitals. The second most frequent source of referrals is the general public; former patients, potential patients, family members, clergy, and so on may request services directly. Approximately 20 percent of referrals come from this source. A small number of referrals come directly from physicians. Although this source is less than 10 percent of the total, it is important to the AHHS, because of the power and status that physicians have in the community.

PATIENTS WHO RECEIVE HOME HEALTH SERVICES

Most of the individuals who receive in-home care are elderly. They usually have a chronic illness that requires monitoring, or they have a need for rehabilitation therapy following an acute episode, such as a stroke or hip fracture. Some patients are disabled and require ongoing therapy at home. Some are convalescing from a hospital stay and need short-term care (e.g., dressing changes). Others have a special type of medical care need that does not require hospitalization, such as intravenous antibiotics or chemotherapy.

Most of the patients cared for by AHHS are indigenous to the area, live in the country (some without running water or bathrooms), and are religious. Although not all patients fit this description, it is fairly safe to say that the patient population is elderly, traditional, and conservative.

THE ROLE OF THE HOME HEALTH NURSE

The registered nurse is the central caregiver in the home health field. The nurse must be able to function independently and comfortably in the patient's home and must be capable of performing a wide variety of clinical procedures (e.g., injections, inserting catheters, obtaining specimens). Furthermore, the RN is considered both a "case manager," and a "gatekeeper," in the coordinating medical, health, and social services. This position requires high-level skills in nursing and communications. Nurses with a BSN (bachelor of science in nursing), plus experience in home health or community nursing are usually sought for these positions.

After Frances left, Kate asked the office manager to run off a copy of their standard classified ad for a home health nurse and take it out to the local newspaper's office. The next day, the newspaper carried the ad in the classified section. The advertisement ran for three consecutive days. Applicants were requested to call the office, or to send a résumé to the director of clinical services.

AHHS received two responses to the advertisement. One was a résumé from a student at a nearby technical college. The college had a two-year (associate degree) registered nurse program, and the applicant was in the last quarter of her second year. Frances read over the résumé. She knew, from past experience, that RNs from two-year programs lacked many of the skills needed for this type of work. She decided not to interview this applicant.

The other applicant, Margaret Jenkins, called to express interest in this position. The conversation was pleasant and informal, since the women knew each other. Margaret had lived in the area all of her life, had family there, and was well known for her community activities.

Margaret Jenkins was a registered nurse with a BSN from a local university. She had been working for the past eight years for Dr. Edward Smith, a general practitioner in town. Prior to that time, she had worked at the state mental health center. References from both employers indicated that she was hardworking, responsible, professional, and got along well with patients, staff, and physicians.

Eighteen months ago, Margaret was involved in a domestic violence situation in her home. During an argument with her husband, according to the press, Margaret was physically attacked and the argument ended in the death of her husband. Margaret was charged with murder. During the course of the trial, most of the details were made public. Episodes of violence had occurred previously, resulting in a separation of Margaret and her husband, with a restraining order against the husband. Margaret testified that, on the night of the fatal argument, she was home with her two children when he appeared and threatened all three of them. While he was beating her, she managed to pick up a kitchen knife and killed him. The court convicted her of involuntary manslaughter and sentenced her to 10 years in prison. While she was in prison, her attorney petitioned for early release, based on her standing in the community and the fact that she was the sole support of two young children. Also during this time, several concerned friends led a successful campaign to have her nursing license reinstated. The state board of nursing had revoked her license to practice nursing (standard practice for convicted felons).

Margaret's immediate concern was finding employment. Dr. Smith, her former employer, was semiretired and not able to rehire her. When she saw the AHHS ad in the paper, she thought it was her answer. Now that she had her license back, she could begin working immediately.

THE INTERVIEWS

Because of Margaret's good work record, and because no other suitable applicants were available, Frances asked Margaret to come in for an interview and set up an appointment for that afternoon. The procedure at AHHS was for all RN applicants to be interviewed first by the nursing supervisor and then by the two directors, Frances and Kate.

Margaret Jenkins walked into the AHHS offices and greeted everyone warmly. A Caucasian woman of average height and weight, she appeared to be in her mid-30s. She was on time, was dressed appropriately, and looked a little nervous. Barbara, the nursing supervisor, introduced herself and led her into the conference room. A half hour later, Barbara brought Margaret to Kate's office, where the second interview would take place. Barbara went in first and briefly summarized her interview. Although she had a positive overall impression, she was concerned about Margaret's lack of experience with home health procedures, particularly interviewing and assessment skills. (Since this part of the job was so important to the overall plan of care, it was essential that RNs have experience in this area.) She then left the office and Margaret went in.

Margaret sat down with Kate and Frances. The three women discussed AHHS policies and general personnel issues, including benefits. It was clear that Margaret had the abilities and skills needed, she knew the geographical area well, and could communicate effectively with area physicians. Her only weakness was that she did not have home health experience. Her personal life was not discussed, but she did remark at one point, "You know I really need this job." At the end of the interview, Frances thanked her for coming, and said, "You do meet many of the qualifications, but I'm not sure if you're the right person for this job." Margaret smiled grimly and said, "I wouldn't blame you if you don't want to hire me." With that, she picked up her things and walked quietly from the office.

Frances and Kate looked at each other. "I don't know," Kate said. "I don't know either!" responded Frances. They usually based their hiring decisions on qualifications, plus "intuition" and usually agreed on an applicant's suitability. This case was different, however, and neither was sure whether they should hire Margaret Jenkins.

Discussion Questions

1. What specific factors must the directors consider in deciding whether to hire Margaret Jenkins?
2. If AHHS does not hire Ms. Jenkins, does she have grounds for legal action?
3. What could AHHS have done to increase the number of applicants?
4. What selection devices did AHHS use? How valid are they? What other methods could they use?

Suggested Readings

Arvey, R. D., and R. H. Faley. *Fairness in Selecting Employees.* Reading, Mass: Addison-Wesley Publishing, 1988.

Caldwell, D. F., and W. A. Spivey. "The Relationship between Recruiting Source and Employee Success: An Analysis by Race." *Personnel Psychology* 36 (1983), pp. 67–72.

Klimoski, R., and M. Brickner. "Why Do Assessment Centers Work? The Puzzle of Assessment Center Validity." *Personnel Psychology* 40 (1987), pp. 243–60.

Latham G. P.; L. M. Sarri; E. D. Pursell; and M. A. Campion. "The Situational Interview." *Journal of Applied Psychology* 65 (1980), pp. 422–27.

Taylor, M. S., and D. W. Schmidt. "A Process Oriented Investigation of Recruitment Source Effectiveness." *Personnel Psychology* 36 (1983), pp. 343–54.

57 The Courtland Hotel (A)

BACKGROUND

The Courtland Hotel has been in operation nearly 15 years. It operates in the central Florida area near the numerous and popular theme parks. The Courtland Hotel is considered one of several luxury resorts. It is owned by a very prestigious European hotel corporation, and it is managed by officers who are located in Houston, Texas. The Courtland has 400 rooms, two restaurants, a lobby bar called The

Lamplighter, and a nightclub/lounge called After Hours. Many parts of The Courtland have been renovated over the past few years. The renovation was done so the hotel would remain competitive with new hotels in the area.

The Courtland's market consists mostly of middle-class families who take annual vacations together. The hotel is price-competitive for this target group and the management believes in the philosophy of "the best value for the dollar spent." Also, The Courtland offers many "extra" services to its guests, including free coffee and newspaper each morning, health club privileges, room service, in-room safes, and in-room stocked mini-refrigerator.

Many of these services are the brainchild of the present general manager, Peter Starke. Starke has been the general manager for approximately three years. This is considered to be a record at The Courtland. One hotel veteran believes there have been about 20 general managers over the past 15 years. This is a very high number, but not so high in the hotel business. Employees at all levels of a hotel—from maids to managers—tend to "drift" from one property to another during their respective careers. Hourly employees often will change jobs for one that pays just 10 cents more per hour, even if the overall benefits are not as good. Wages are often an incentive for managers as well, but more often prestige, power, and the freedom to manage are more important factors. Peter Starke had learned to play the corporate game; that is, he knew the balance of following corporate directives and subsequent red tape, and managing his property like he wanted. He believed in a "personal style of management" and an "open-door policy" with all members of his staff. He made an effort to learn the names of all 200 employees at The Courtland.

Peter Starke reflected on the lessons learned at a recent meeting of the Florida Hotel & Motel Association. The association estimated that, of the state's 50,000 hospitality jobs, as many as a fifth, or 10,000, are going begging. Most of those positions are entry level. One speaker at the meeting estimates the industry will need 500,000 new workers by the year 2000, yet hoteliers have failed to tap adequately two large pools of talent: older people and disabled individuals. Peter was wondering what he might do to tap into the pool of 60 million Americans older than 50. All studies indicate that these people have fewer absences and accidents than younger workers and are highly motivated. Peter also noted that there might be something he could do to consider for hiring from the local pool of the nation's 35 million disabled adults. He thought about these workers as he concerned himself with the lack of motivation and commitment, turnover, and absenteeism he noticed in some of his employees. Although The Courtland had experienced a high employee turnover rate, there were still many employees who had been with the company for 10 years or more. Some of these employees truly enjoyed their work; some stayed for the better-than-average benefit package; others stayed because they have attained a certain level of seniority in their own departments. While it is true that many of these employees are considered valued members of the "team," there are several who cause problems among their co-workers. These problems often are initiated by these senior employees who display the attitude that they are "permanent" employees of The Courtland. This often causes disciplinary problems, because these employees feel they are "above" directives from their immediate supervisor or department manager. Co-workers often feel they, too, are above any new rules or procedures that are instituted by their superiors.

THE MISSING JUICE

As he was leaving the banquet area of the restaurant, Wally Reiff was approached by his supervisor, who had observed him hiding a six-ounce can of orange juice under his coat. After he was stopped, Wally dropped the juice on the floor and left the premises. The next day, when approached by management regarding the incident, the employee denied that he had attempted to steal the juice. Wally was fired, and he filed a grievance.

The union maintained that the company failed to establish "beyond a reasonable doubt" that the grievant had stolen the juice or even seen the container on the floor. Firing, the union said, should not be considered because of the nominal value of the stolen juice. The punishment was not, in the union's judgment, commensurate with the crime. The union also argued that, while the grievant was a low-seniority employee with a poor disciplinary record, it was improper to discharge him due to theft.

Requirement

You are the arbitrator. Would you uphold the company's decision to dismiss or would you reverse it? Explain your ruling.

The Courtland Hotel (B)

THE FUNERAL

Many of the hotel employees attended the memorial service for their former comrades at the hotel. It was an unfortunate and tragic situation. On payday Fridays a bunch of employees would walk down to the local branch bank to cash their checks. Last Friday was no different at first. Unfortunately, tragedy struck. While waiting in line to cash their checks, two employees found themselves in the line of fire when a bank security guard went berserk. The bank's lobby was full of people, most in a somewhat festive mood as they waited to have their checks cashed. When the shooting had subsided, eight people were wounded and three were dead. Of the three who died, two were from the hotel and the other person was a bank employee.

After the memorial service was held it was learned that the survivors of both hotel employees who had died made clear their intention to sue the bank. They now want to talk to an attorney. It was their intention to sue the bank because they shouldn't hire "dangerous people." Someone found out that the bank guard had a lengthy arrest record. Other employees were surprised to hear that a lawsuit was being considered. Their friends at the bank said that the bank routinely does background checks on their employees. Judy Ryder, who works at the hotel's front desk, knew people in the bank's personnel office. According to Judy, the personnel director was always complaining that the privacy laws really made it difficult to investigate the background of prospective employees, and the new polygraph law took away an important tool that the bank had relied on. She said that the bank had just started using paper-and-pencil-type honesty tests.

Discussion Questions

1. In general, can a company be held responsible for the actions of an employee? If so, under what conditions?
2. Can the bank be held responsible for the behavior of this bank guard? Explain your answer.

The Courtland Hotel (C)

TENDING THE BAR

In February of 1989, a new food and beverage director was hired at The Courtland. Brett Simpson had worked previously as an assistant food and beverage director and dining room supervisor with other large hotels in the area. Simpson quickly met all his staff members, including Barbie Danforth, the head bartender at the hotel's bar, After Hours. Barbie had, as was the case with other bartenders, worked initially in the hotel's Lamplighter Restaurant. So, she was proud to become the head bartender after five years of experience at The Courtland. Simpson knew that there was a need to make some changes in the beverage department but did not feel rushed since he believed that Barbie was "holding down the fort."

Penny Martin had been a bartender at The Courtland for three years, second only in number of years to Barbie. Penny was a rather plain looking girl who tended to bring her problems to work, in that she was often rude or curt to patrons. For this reason, unlike many of the other bartenders, she did not have any "regulars." However, Penny enjoyed certain special privileges from Barbie because they had outlasted so many other employees. These privileges included schedules tailored to fit her other appointments, and all of her shifts at After Hours, behind the bar. This did cause some resentment among newer employees, but Barbie had the attitude that the others could "take it or leave it." Despite these problems, After Hours enjoyed high revenues and the bartenders usually tipped out at $50–$100 for each girl per night. Of course, the norm for these tipped employees was that they only declared about $10.

Later in the year, Penny learned that she was pregnant and was due to deliver in early December. She was happy about this but was also somewhat distressed since she had recently separated from her husband. She knew that she would have to support herself for an indeterminate length of time but felt she could manage given her tip income. Penny said nothing to anyone about her pregnancy until she began to show. Penny and Barbie had no discussion about the possible problems her pregnancy might cause if Penny continued as a bartender. Barbie knew, however, that it was not doing anything for business. Simpson and Starke made no attempt to transfer her. They were aware of the recent court cases and the need to treat expectant mothers fairly.

In early September, Penny asked Joyce McDonald, front office manager, about possible openings in the front office or in the reservations office. Penny accepted the only available position for someone who was untrained and did not want to stand for long periods—PBX switchboard operator. The job was at the same hourly rate as her previous position but there was no opportunity to earn tips. The actual rate for the job was $1 an hour less but Penny's pay rate was not changed because the job in question was about the only practical one for someone pregnant.

After a couple months on the job, it was obvious that Penny was a very poor operator. Despite intensive training and the emphasis Joyce placed on being pleasant and congenial, Penny refused to comply. The desk clerks and others complained about Penny's demeanor and her failure to be cooperative, even when they asked her to do simple tasks. Soon Peter Starke, the general manager, heard of these problems. He personally received complaints from hotel guests, too. Joyce repeatedly warned Penny about her behavior. In fact, she counseled her, verbally warned her, and prepared a written warning which was placed in Penny's file. It seemed to do no good.

In November, Penny informed Joyce that she would take maternity leave from November 20 until six weeks from her expected date of delivery of December 5. At the same time, another employee, Ann Lyle, planned her maternity leave for an expected delivery date of December 1.

After giving birth to her baby on December 10, Penny contacts the new food and beverage director, Barry Cotton. Barry has had only limited contact with her, and that when she was on the switchboard. He is surprised when she asks if there are openings in the beverage department. He, not knowing her background, honestly replies that there are no openings. Penny does not accept Barry's word. She contacts Barbie (who does not return Penny's calls). Peter Starke, when he learns of the situation, fills Barry in on Penny's past history with The Courtland. Penny next calls Joyce McDonald about work. Against her better judgment, Joyce gives in after Penny begs her for work.

Penny returns to work on December 24, 1989. Her attitude has not changed. It is obvious that she was dissatisfied with having to return to the switchboard. She made sure that everyone in the hotel knew of her displeasure. The verbal and written warnings began all over again.

In January, Cotton received a notice from the state that Penny had filed a sexual discrimination suit against the hotel and named Cotton as the chief defendant. Penny claimed that she had been discriminated against on the basis of her sex, because she was not able to reclaim her former position as a bartender when returning from her maternity leave. She also claimed that McDonald had forced her to return early from her leave, but that she had let Ann Lyle stay home for her total six weeks after childbirth. Cotton and McDonald were outraged by these fabrications. Starke was particularly upset, because he felt that The Courtland had acted as a fair and responsible employer in Penny's case. Starke immediately contacted his superiors as well as the corporate legal staff. Although they had dealt with many cases of disgruntled employees, they were not entirely familiar with how to handle a sexual discrimination case.

Penny continued to work at The Courtland until one particularly nasty and vexing confrontation with another employee. The verbal altercation with the executive housekeeper was witnessed by several people. Penny was suspended for three days. She demanded a meeting with Joyce McDonald and later with Peter Starke to protest her treatment. At a meeting with both Joyce and Peter, she was insubordinate to both. She directly confronted each person, screaming and cursing at both. Finally, her actions had gone too far. Peter terminated her on the spot.

Discussion Questions

1. Did Penny have a strong case against The Courtland?
2. Was it a coincidence that Joyce submitted more warnings on Penny after she had filed the case against the hotel?
3. Was Starke justified in his dismissal of Penny?

---

58 Harding Space, Inc.

KEEPING 'EM HONEST

Harding Space, Inc. (HSI), is a medium-sized firm located in Melbourne, Florida. The firm essentially has been a subcontractor on many large aerospace contracts, which have been acquired by such firms as Rockwell International, Martin-Marietta, and Harris Corporation. In 1989, the newly elected Bush administration sought ways to bring the federal budget in compliance with the Gramm-Rudman Act. Although it was unlikely that full compliance would occur, it was certain that certain cutbacks in spending would be necessary. Military, social, and space programs would be affected. With the cutback in many of the National Aeronautics and Space Administration programs, Harding anticipates declining revenues. In anticipation of these cutbacks the firm is looking very closely at ways to cut labor and other significant costs. Sick leave, medical, and hospitalization, as well as long-term disability policies and other payments for time not worked, are all being carefully examined by the financial officers.

"Have you seen our most recent telephone bills?" the company's controller asked supervisors at the department heads meeting. In reviewing telephone bills over the most recent three-year period, he had noticed a 150 percent increase in the size of the monthly bill and a substantial increase in the number of long-distance calls. The controller informed the group that the supervisors' gentle prodding, posted rules, and memoranda circulated to employees asking them to curb long-distance phone calls and to eliminate personal calls just seemed to have no effect. At present he had no way to identify the culprits, but he had an idea for them to consider. "If someone is speaking five times a day with a friend who works across town or making long-distance calls to relatives, the company cannot find out." He wanted their feedback before he moved to implement the plan. "Every time I look at a telephone on someone's desk, it looks like a blank check."

After the announcement of the company's new telephone monitoring system was made, a great debate raged among employees about whether the company had a right to track calls made by employees. The new system consists of software for personal computers and a cable connecting the PC to the telephone system. The system tells the employer who was called how long the worker spoke and how much the call cost. Some employees, especially managers, approved of the company's actions. These employees believed that keeping tabs on personal calls made from the office should not be a problem, as long as it is the company that's doing the paying for the calls.

Many employees, however, felt that the company had overstepped its boundaries. They felt that it is bad enough that they work under surveillance by way of TV cameras, but now some management type wants to listen in on their calls. These employees believed that the worker is entitled to personal privacy in the workplace and at home. A company spokesman acknowledged that the potential for going overboard does exist, but he did not believe that the company would use the system to check up on employees. He felt that the company would probably track only those calls that exceed $10 or some other limit.

What the spokesman didn't say was that the company was planning to use other electronic monitoring techniques to observe worker performance, to guard against materials thefts, and to provide security. Hindsight is 20-20, he thinks, but he wishes the company had carefully thought about the ramifications of the planned and recently implemented surveillance techniques. He almost said out loud, "Thank goodness we don't have a union!"

Discussion Questions

1. What rights of privacy do employees have while on the job?
2. Should employers be restricted in their ability to monitor calls made by employees while at work? Why or why not?

59 Ben Franklin Hospital (A)

The patient, a 42-year-old Philadelphia woman, ended up on the doorsteps of Ben Franklin Hospital, so to speak. She was brought into the emergency room by paramedics. The paramedics said the woman informed them that she was infected with the virus that causes acquired immune deficiency syndrome. It is not clear whether AIDS was a factor in the treatment the woman received. What is clear is that her blood pressure was dangerously high—230/120, compared to a normal level of 140/90 or lower—and that her heart rate was elevated. She was taken to Ben Franklin Hospital by paramedics shortly after midnight on November 14, 1989, after she dialed the 911 emergency number for help. According to state officials who later investigated the case, no treatment whatsoever was provided. The state licensing agency claims that the hospital refused to treat the indigent emergency room patient and then paid a taxi to take her to Philadelphia General Hospital (PGH). A Ben Franklin Hospital administrator claimed the hospital *did* examine the woman but failed to document her care. He claimed that the hospital provided the taxi because the woman wanted to go to PGH where she had been treated in the past.

Philadelphia General Hospital is a large, city owned and operated hospital in the City of Brotherly Love. It has 650 beds and has all of the departments one would find in a general public hospital of its type that's located in a metropolitan area. Unfortunately, PGH has some of the same problems that have beset other metropolitan hospitals. The patient load continues to increase at a rate that is much faster than the hospital's ability to acquire resources (human, equipment, money). When the for-profit hospitals in the area decide that ability to pay is a "test" prospective patients cannot meet, these patients often become the victims because the for-profit hospitals turn them away.

Unlike the many half-empty hospitals around the country, PGH is bustling. At least 25 percent of its patients occupy "public beds"—admitted under Medicaid or with no resources at all. For those without resources, their care may be paid for by the city government or simply written off by the hospital. The length of stay at PGH averages 12 days, much longer than the national average, because poor people who come in are usually sicker than the middle-class. The poor may not eat properly, their living conditions may be unhealthy, they don't have access or can't afford preventive care, and there are those individuals who are irresponsible about caring for themselves. With the hospital's location being in easy walking distance of the University of Pennsylvania and Drexel University, those among the poor who live in nearby Powelton Village and the surrounding area are well served. In the immediate area the poor and the rich are compressed together.

Discussion Question

What rights to admission do indigent patients have? Discuss in terms of the various types of hospitals.

Ben Franklin Hospital (B)

Ben Franklin Hospital, unlike Philadelphia General Hospital, is an investor-owned (for-profit) hospital. It has 358 beds. Nearly every form of surgery and treatment is offered at its facility. There is a psychiatric center, cancer and physical rehabilitation facilities, a gynecology building, a day-care center, and some apartments for medical residents. The 374 doctors are certified to admit patients. Technological expense in medicine is significant. However, labor is the hospital's greatest cost. More than 55 percent of the typical hospital bill is for staff—and that *excludes* doctors! Hospitals such as Ben Franklin require doctors, nurses, pharmacists, technicians, orderlies, accountants, lab technicians, cooks, maintenance crews, and so forth, all day every day. During the 1970s the number of hospital beds grew quite rapidly. Then came the 1980s; between diagnosis-related groups (DRGs) and the advent of less-debilitating forms of surgery, the call for beds declined. In recent years, however, the hospital's census has fallen drastically. The hospital finds itself bigger than it needs to be and it is forced to manage its costs better. Charlotte Wilson, unit coordinator, really had her hands full. Never could she recall having such problems scheduling registered nurses, technicians, and others needed for various operating rooms. The problem seemed not to be associated with the nature of the operations, the days of the week, or the time of day when scheduled. Everyone worked long, hard days at the hospital, but the work schedule was in no way different than it had been in recent months. Of course, turnover is *always* a problem, but what else is new! Recent efforts to attract and retain nurses with the offering of "bounties" had proved successful. These bounties allowed current employees to get a special bonus if they identified people in scarce job categories (e.g., registered nurses) and these folks were actually hired. In addition, payment for training and education both on and off the premises as well as the on-site child-care facilities had really reduced absenteeism and turnover. After weeks of struggling with the problem, she decided to let Cheryl Ransburg, director of the operating rooms, know about the extent of the problem.

Cheryl and Charlotte talked about the coverage problem at length. They decided that Cheryl should take a more direct approach in seeking a solution to the problem. Informal discussions with circulating technicians and circulating nurses did reveal a pattern. In general, many of them were reluctant to work with Dr. Benjamin Cooper. Dr. Cooper has had admitting privileges for at least nine years. In fact, he is responsible for about 20 percent of the elective pulmonary admissions.

After three weeks of quietly investigating the matter, the pieces began to fit together. Selected hospital staff came to see Cheryl and offered to provide information if they could be assured of confidentiality and anonymity. Several people knew that Dr. Cooper was in trouble. Rumors were persistent. He loved to snort. He was hooked on "snow." At first he tried to hide his habit but after awhile he seemed not to care. People knew that he had a razor blade, pocket mirror, hypodermic needle, and other possible drug paraphernalia in his office desk. Some co-workers mentioned that his marriage had fallen apart over his dependence on drugs but he clung tightly to his job. Not much could be ascertained from his physical appearance. He was tireless, seldom ate, and his pupils did not seem quite normal in size. Without his medical practice, there was no possible way that Ben could support his habit. Dr. Cooper and Ms. Ransburg had maintained a good working relationship, but the information she received was corroborated by too many people. Something had to be done. A medical doctor who does drugs could put himself, his patient(s), and the hospital at great risk.

Discussion Questions

1. What should Ms. Ransburg do?
2. What's the likelihood that disciplinary action will be taken against Dr. Cooper?
3. Are personnel or other laws relevant?

Ben Franklin Hospital (C)

Judy Ryder had been in nursing for 15 years. She knew that one of the occupational hazards people in the profession face is that of drug dependency. From her perspective this society looks the other way when it comes to so-called legal drugs. Folks don't go to jail for possession or abuse of alcohol unless they harm someone, as in automobile accidents. Even then the sentence may be lighter. Judy has seen legal drugs as an issue from a different perspective. She has always worried about the overprescribing of drugs and a failure on the part of some doctors and patients to be knowledgeable about the effects of certain drugs' interaction. Fortunately, pharmacists are playing a greater role and taking the initiative in explaining to patients what effect certain drugs have and whether they should be taken with other drugs.

Judy also knows that some patients abuse stimulants, depressants, and other common drugs. Patients have been known to complain to different doctors about their (rehearsed) symptoms, then collect prescriptions to take to the pharmacist of their choosing.

Judy's greatest fears have less to do with the situations described above and more to do with other professionals in her own field. She knows that nurses and doctors have access to various medical cabinets. If one wants something to keep him or her going, that person knows just which medication will do the trick. What starts out as something innocent—just a pill to keep the energy flowing—becomes a habit that gets out of control. The people who get "hooked" tend to deny their dependence and many can mask the fact that they have an abuse problem. Unfortunately, the habit does not disappear. Sooner or later, behavior changes or the ability to function on or off the job suffers. However, the changes may be difficult to detect.

Judy hated to be the one to break the news to the director of nursing, but she knew that she would have to report her friend and co-worker, Pat Clement. They had worked together at the hospital for 11 years. Pat had marital problems. She has been a single parent with the responsibility of raising three children. Handling the demands of family and a nursing career was difficult for her. When she realized that Judy knew about her thefts from patients, she just told Judy that the patient would not miss the reduction in dosage and Pat wanted to get something to "calm her nerves."

Discussion Questions

1. What action should be taken (from a personnel perspective)?
2. What's the likelihood that Pat will be disciplined?
3. Are any personnel laws relevant here?

Section K

Employee Discharge/ Turnover

60 *Taking a Bite Out of Former Diet Firm Partner**

Call it the war between weight loss women—with the winner to be decided in court.

This battle pits Jo Hairston, president of World Weight Off Group, the Cuyahoga Falls-based diet company, against Susan Gerrits, a five-year former employee of Hairston's who now runs Worldwide Weight Off Systems in Portage County. Hairston has run her World Weight Off Group franchise in Ohio and nine other states since 1969 and now has 475 regular meeting locations. Gerrits opened her weight-loss center inside a gym in mid-September—and was sued by Hairston's company the day after she opened.

As charges and countercharges fly, each says she was wronged and treated unfairly.

Tough competition is common in the diet business, but Hairston has prided herself on her upbeat, caring image. She frequently talks about her family—many of whom work for her. As for most of her staff of 2,200, she hires only people who have lost weight—and kept it off—through World Weight Off Group. But Gerrits claims there's another side to World Weight Off Group and Hairston. Employees are poorly paid and morale is low, so some workers are leaving the firm, Gerrits and other former employees claim.

Gerrits was eager to work for Hairston when she started at World Weight Off Group in October 1989 in its On the Job department, which markets its weight-loss programs to area employers. At that time, she signed a two-page employment contract that stated among other things that she would not "entice any customer or employee away from WWOG" for a year after she left the company.

---

* Adapted from news story that appeared in the *Detroit Free Press,* October 21, 1994.

WWOG attorney Shirley Hairston, one of Jo Hairston's daughters, says all employees sign the contract, which also contains an agreement not to compete with Worldwide Weight Off for a year after an employee leaves, to protect WWOG's confidential information and client information.

Employment contracts with non-compete agreements are common in many industries and they're often upheld in court if their terms aren't too broad. But Gerrits' attorney says the working of WWOG's contract is ambiguous. Because the agreement says it's effective for a year after "termination of my employment by WWOG," it does not apply to Gerrits, who quit voluntarily, says her attorney Frank Cardimen.

Shirley Hairston says it's only the second time the company has sued former employees under terms of their employment contracts.

After Gerrits quit, she opened Worldwide Weight Off Systems inside World Gym in Cuyhoga Falls, and she hired three other former World Weight Off Group employees. Two of them left to join Gerrits' business, but one had left earlier.

WW Off Group sued Gerrits and the three former employees in Portage County Circuit Court the next day. The suit charges that Gerrits and others used World Weight Off Group's confidential information and sought out its customers and employees for her company. It also alleges that, before she left, Gerrits copied documents, program materials, and client lists to use in her new company.

Gerrits denies all allegations. She says she's using not World Weight Off Group techniques but rather materials from the American Heart Association. She says her program focuses on "wellness" and not just weight loss. "I guess I should feel flattered that they feel so threatened," she says.

The Hairston-Gerrits dispute is similar to one in 1989 in which Cheryl Ransburg left Hairston's employ after 15 years to start Ellie's Weigh Loss Clinic in Aurora. WW Off Group sued Ransburg, saying she was using confidential information to attract WWOG's customers and employees. Ransburg eventually prevailed and the case was dismissed. Ransburg now teaches her weight loss classes throughout the Akron, Kent, Stow area and employs about 26 people. But she still gets angry at World Weight Off Group and Hairston for the way they treated her.

For her part, Jo Hairston says the multibillion dollar diet business has "lots of room for competitors," and she wishes Gerrits well. However, she is clearly annoyed at her tactics. "When she started taking our employees and badmouthing us and taking our clients we'd had, the company decided to sue," Hairston said. "She had been a trusted, loyal employee."

This week, the suit is moving forward with attorneys asking questions in depositions from key people.

World Weight Off Group has asked a judge for an injunction to stop Gerrits from contacting WWOG employees or clients or members or using its confidential information. The judge has already issued a temporary restraining order that prohibits those actions for a period of 45 days. A hearing on the injunction is scheduled for next month.

61 Making Partner in an Accounting Firm

Public accounting firms and law firms provide an ideal setting to study and attempt to model promotion opportunities. Such firms hire highly motivated, task-oriented achievers who put many, many hours into getting the job done. During the past decade there has been a dramatic rise in the number of women who have entered the professions that these firms represent. Specifically, large gains in the number of employed female professionals have occurred in law schools, business schools, medical schools, schools of architecture, and schools of accountancy, among others. However, the fact that women gain entrance into the organization or a profession does not ensure that upward mobility will follow. Significant inroads are being made in many industries. However, the female workers in many occupations continue to encounter the glass ceiling writers now talk about.

THE ANN HOPKINS CASE

In 1978, Ann Hopkins was hired as a senior manager in the Washington office of Price Waterhouse. Price Waterhouse is one of the giant nationwide firms that dominate the public accounting field. Prior to the merger of certain large accounting firms (e.g., Arthur Anderson and Arthur Young), Price Waterhouse was one of the so-called Big Eight, a major player on a nationwide basis. The senior manager position is a position of high responsibility and visibility, and one that makes tremendous demands on one's time. Coming in at such a high level would seem to indicate that the firm both acknowledged Ann Hopkins' competence and had high expectations of her. A senior manager is one step below the highest rank—that of partner. Typical levels of progression in an accounting firm range from the lowest (staff accountant or junior accountant, senior accountant, manager, partner, and managing partner) to the highest rank. The partners share in the revenues derived by the firm. Both they and senior managers have the responsibility of attracting new and repeat business for the firm.

In 1982, Ann Hopkins was nominated for promotion to partnership. She was the only woman among 88 candidates that year. Her record was outstanding. Despite the demands that go with raising three children, she had helped bring in between $34 million and $44 million in business to the firm. In addition, she had billed more hours in the preceding year than any of the other 87 partnership candidates.

The road to partnership, however, is fraught with peril. The results *were* excellent. Written evaluations uncovered perceived problems. Specifically, brought into question was the femininity, personality, and attire of Ann Hopkins. Questions were raised both verbally and in writing by certain (male) partners. She received written evaluations that described her as "macho," harsh, and foulmouthed to co-workers.

According to a report in *Time*, a partner said she needed to take a "course at charm school." After her candidacy for partner, the decision was delayed for a year. A partner who supported her candidacy advised her that she might improve her chances if she "learned to walk, talk, and dress more femininely . . . wear makeup, have her hair styled, and wear jewelry."

Hopkins remained with the firm for another year or two. Later, she left the firm and brought suit, contending that the promotion process had violated Title II of the 1964 Civil Rights Act. This act prohibits job discrimination.

One aspect of the *Hopkins* case dramatizes a dilemma women in professional positions face. Firms ask women to walk a narrow line between appearing serious and seeming overly severe. Those who have worked in male-dominated occupations expect women to act both feminine and businesslike. Males may not realize that they are sending out a conflicting message. Brenda Taylor, a former assistant state attorney in Florida, learned that dress codes and one's taste in clothes can cause problems. Taylor had a penchant for short skirts, designer blouses, ornate jewelry, and spike heels and colored hosiery. In general, the law permits officers to establish dress codes, as long as they impose equivalent restrictions on both sexes. Taylor's office has such a dress code, which mandates conservative dress for all. An issue not addressed is captured in a statement by Professor Mary Coombs of the University of Miami, "Almost anything you wear runs the risk of looking like you're trying to appear just like a man, or too feminine."

Discussion Questions

1. Do partnership organizations (e.g., law, business, architecture) differ in personnel decision making from the other business organizations?
2. Are partnerships to be exempt from provisions of nondiscrimination or equal employment opportunity laws?
3. What actions can companies or individuals take to avoid the conflicting messages mentioned in this case?

---

62 Food King Super Markets, Inc. (A)

"Charlie, I am getting too old for this job. Supervising today's young people is putting lots of gray hair on my head!"

"Joe, when you're bald like me, you might prefer *any* color hair to having no hair at all. I'm just kidding. I wonder myself sometimes why I waste my time and energies trying to supervise these employees."

"Tell me what happened . . ."

THE STORY

The city of Sanford's Food King Super Market had developed a grooming policy 15 years ago. The policy included a dress code, which made explicit how employees, whether full-time or part-time, should dress. Over the years, applicants were told about the dress code and made aware of the company's expectations. Those who were hired were reminded of the dress code. Attire was not a major problem. Oh, occasionally someone would forget his or her "uniform"; the supervisors and managers expected that out of their predominantly teenage work force. In recent years, the "punk" hairdos and scuffed jeans look was out so the dress code/attire problem was a nonissue.

The year 1989, however, became the year of notoriety for Food King. The firm didn't want the publicity but they got it anyway. The first complaint involved Sylvia Foreman, a black cashier who had been with the supermarket chain since 1987. She was an extremely competent, reliable, and friendly employee. Sylvia managed the high stress and the grumpiest of customers with ease. For all of 1987 and 1988, she was a model employee. The problem was her hairstyle. Charlie constantly reminded his cashiers that they were very critical to the success of the store. They were, in Charlie's words, "the last line of defense" between the customer and the store when there was the potential for a complaint. Apparently, at least one regular customer violently objected to Sylvia's new hairstyle. During the latter part of 1988, Sylvia had taken to having her hair tightly braided in a cornrow hairstyle. Her co-workers were noncommittal about it at first, but over time they grew to like it. Sylvia was an attractive person who got along with her fellow employees. Her behavior toward others did not change. However, the complaint letters stating an objection to the hairstyle came in on a regular basis. Finally, Charlie felt compelled to act. He did not find her appearance objectionable, but, if a customer or customers objected . . .

Following a progressive discipline approach starting with a verbal warning, he proceeded to discipline Sylvia. In the end, he gave her an ultimatum—"get rid of the cornrows or face dismissal." Sylvia refused. She was terminated on March 19, 1989.

It did not take long for the summons to arrive. Sylvia felt that the cornrow hairstyle had no effect on her ability to do her job as cashier. Her attorney claimed the company was overreacting to the complaints of one or a very few customers. The dress code was too vague and she was not informed previous to formal discipline interviews that any rule was violated. The real troublesome issue, though, was her claim that the requirement banning the hairstyle had a racial connotation, because the requirement was more likely to affect blacks or other minorities, since few whites wore their hair in the cornrow style. Charlie wondered what the company would do. He was interviewed by the company's counsel, but they didn't volunteer any information about the strategy they would take.

Discussion Questions

1. What should Charlie have done?
2. How would you have handled this situation?
3. Was the dismissal appropriate? Explain.

Food King Super Markets, Inc. (B)

The Sylvia Foreman case was not the only dress code/grooming issue the food market chain faced in 1988. The Chris Carter "problem" occurred in Casselberry, Florida. One little round object was the focus of attention in the local newspapers. When the object in question is an earring in a young man's ear, people sit up and take notice!

Joe Newsome was one of Food King's most experienced managers. This was his fourth managerial stint. He had been manager of the Casselberry Food King store for five years. He had devoted most of his time and energy to the problem of handling the administrative duties related to the store. He left the day-to-day operation of the store to his subordinates. He had been pleased with the development of his assistant store managers. His ability to develop people was evidenced in the upward mobility of so many of his people over the years. The stickiest problem he faced in 1988 was a *people* problem. Often, he lectured his assistants that the people problems were the problems that really tested the mettle of those who manage. "Working with data and with things was simple by comparison," Joe claimed.

In July of 1988, Chris Carter applied for a position at Food King. Chris was only 16 years old. Chris was hired as a bag boy. He was a good student and appeared to take orders well. He got the nickname Odd Job because he willingly did a little bit of everything from assisting customers with their packages and taking loaded shopping carts to the customer's car to bagging groceries and helping with stock. He appeared to be a fast learner. Everyone liked him, but when he started wearing his earring during working hours, he lost a few friends. His peers had no problem with the ornamentation, but not so for his supervisors. Chris argued that he had a right to wear the earring. He wanted to know why he was being persecuted. As he stated, "No one bothered women when they wore earrings."

After discussing the earring situation with his assistant managers, managers at other stores, and the food chain's personnel director, Joe decided to send Chris home. He told Chris he would have to remove the earring before he could return to work. Chris refused and hired an attorney. Chris's attorney was a member of a law firm that was well known for its handling of Title VII (Civil Rights Act of 1964) cases. A sex discrimination complaint was filed with the Equal Employment Opportunity Commission and the Florida Commission on Human Relations. The case is currently being investigated by these agencies.

Requirement

Considering the facts of this case, is the company's position legally defensible? How would you have handled this situation? Explain.

Food King Super Markets, Inc. (C)

"Why do these things always have to happen to us?" That was the commonly heard lament that echoed across the boardroom where the store management team of the food King Super Markets was holding its monthly meeting.

No one would have believed, when the Maxine Garnett situation developed, that the issue would still be in the news 12 months later! The media were like bloodhounds once they got the scent of a good, juicy, gossipy story that would make *somebody* look bad. It was hard to blame them, because the company's policy made the supermarket look like bad guys. The issue was very simple and began simply enough.

Maxine had worked with the company for all of three years. During that time her store manager had gently chided her for wearing pants on the job. There were jobs in the back room where that was not a problem; but in the store front area where supervisors and managers interacted with customers was another matter. Maxine had served as assistant manager of the records and electronics ware area. The area is one of those that the powers that be had seen fit to enhance, because they believed that a significant share of their profit could be derived from the area where CDs, portable radios, boom boxes, and similar items could be sold. The store, therefore, had invested considerable resources in assuring that Maxine's area was well staffed and the inventory was maintained at a sufficiently high level that customers could find exactly the merchandise that they needed. As Maxine had watched this development, she came to feel that "food store" or even "supermarket" had become misnomers when it came to describing the products today's shopper might purchase at Food King's. Maxine didn't mind a bit, because this development enabled her to increase her income as well gain additional responsibility as well as recognition for her contributions. However, Maxine had one little "problem." She just *loved* the comfort that pants provided. No, she did not walk around in jeans. She always wore attractive clothes and her pants selection was no exception.

SIX WEEKS AGO

After repeated gentle warnings about her attire, the store manager took a formal approach. He pointed out that the store had a "no pants" rule for female employees who acted in supervisory or managerial capacities. He told Maxine that he would have to enforce the rule and did so. Maxine, in a very professional way, said that she would not change her attire to suit the "male establishment" since the store's rule had no legitimacy. Unfortunately, the store manager refused to budge on the issue. Equally unfortunate was the fact that Maxine became an overnight sensation and darling of the media when they learned of her situation. Every local newspaper and some national ones picked up the story of the news service wire.

Now the store manager is wondering if he made the right decision. Given what he knows now, he wonders—if he had another chance—whether he would make the same decision.

Discussion Questions

1. What went wrong in this situation?
2. If you were the human resource consultant and had an opportunity to advise the store manager, what would you tell him?
3. What, if anything, should he do now?

---

*63 The Dallas Computer Caper—A Newspaper Account**

Richardson, Texas—at about 3:00 AM on a Saturday morning, Joe DiMaggio Sykes broke into the offices of WWPA, Inc., and UGP, Inc., and sat down at his old terminal. He signed on and signed off. He immediately signed back on with a three-day-old security password that let him perform his job—computer security officer. He then erased 168,000 payroll records on the company's Zenith System 326/38 and invoked a time bomb intended to erase records on a monthly basis. Sykes had been fired three days before, on September 18, 1989.

In a case that was initially considered too technical to pursue, a jury, including three computer professionals, convicted Sykes on a felony charge of harmful access to a computer last week. He faces up to 10 years in prison.

Computer security experts agree that the case will likely not deter this criminal activity, but the precedent may persuade more law enforcement officials to pursue computer criminals.

NOT CLEVER ENOUGH

While Sykes may have been clever about covering his audit trail, the break-in and a coincidental weekend work session of a fellow programmer led to his discovery.

---

* The names and places used in this case are, for obvious reasons, fictitious but the events described are real.

"He was having continual conflict with the company and anticipated being fired," said David Bob Johnson, Dallas county assistant district attorney. Johnson said that the time bomb was created in a new account, which Sykes gave a name beginning with the letter Q—the same letter that begins account names provided in IBM software—so it would remain undetected. Sykes apparently used it to create a program that gave it security clearance. According to Johnson, he tied this program, which was intended to erase files, to legitimate files and put it on a time switch.

The company, an insurance and brokerage firm, made a cursory check of the accounts after Sykes was fired but did not find the hidden account, according to Johnson. Computer system officials at the company would not comment.

Saturday morning, after Sykes's break-in, a programmer came into the office to figure out how a new bonus system would affect the company's payroll. Johnson said that every time the programmer ran the simulations, the payroll came up with zeros, signaling that the initial payroll deletion had occurred. This led the company to shut down the computer for two days to cleanse the system, a move that allowed the time bomb to be discovered.

Johnson, who had little past experience with computers, said he wanted to pursue the case even though the district attorney thought it was too technical to try and was willing to negotiate out of court. The jury was more technical than most, Johnson said; it included one systems analyst and two computer designers.

Also, the case was not attractive to the prosecution because the actual damages were rather small; the county only proved $12,000 in damages for downtime and the cost to fix the payroll accounts.

"In the scheme of things, it was not a large loss. But 550 people didn't get their checks for a week or two; and if the program had gone off as planned, it would have created havoc," McCown said.

SHOW SOME SPINE

The conviction most likely will help other prosecutors overcome an apparent fear of prosecuting high-tech crime cases, Johnson said.

"One of the most pressing needs in the criminal area of viruses is the education of attorneys," said John McAfee, chairman of the Santa Clara, California-based Computer Virus Industry Association. McAfee noted that there has been a rapid increase lately in requests for virus-related information from police organizations.

The *Sykes* case is thought to be the first to win a felony conviction. A 1985 case involving a similar time bomb planted by a disgruntled employee in Minneapolis only involved a misdemeanor, although the original charge was extortion. Sykes was sentenced on October 21, 1989.

Requirement

Identify and discuss the personnel issues raised by the situations described in this case.

64 Western Lighting and Electric Co.

The Western Lighting and Electric Co. is a company of 210 employees. It had made its mark in the southeast corner of Pennsylvania. In addition to supplying power to a limited number of customers in counties surrounding Philadelphia, it sold some electrical appliances to consumers and dabbled in the sale and manufacture of some consumer goods. Unfortunately, in recent years it has had to rely on the power supply aspect of its business to generate revenues to offset losses in the consumer goods division. The principal reasons for these losses were the overwhelming consumer acceptance of foreign products, especially those from Japan and Korea, and the incredible price competition that high-import tariffs seemed not to affect. The result: continued loss of market share, movement back to its basic business, and belt-tightening that has led to a reduction in the workforce. However, heavy losses continue.

"Mark, I am telling you, we *have* to cut back! We have attempted to rely on attrition but it is just not working. After three years of being benevolent, it's time for folks here to face the harsh reality of the bottom line. You and Paul Silas came up with a fantastic early retirement program for these old guys nine months ago, yet few of them wanted to take advantage of it. I just don't understand it. Many of them might as well be at home tending their gardens for all the good the slow-moving old farts do us!"

"Jim, I really think that you are losing your objectivity on this one. These folks have given us 20 or more good years of service. I don't think that it's right to just cast them out. Where would we be without the technological breakthroughs of Pete Johnson, Robert Wells, and John Corrigan, for example? All of those guys started here when they were in their 20s. The oldest is John at 59."

"Jim, you're my boss and you're my friend. In fact, I am glad that you will make the decisions. You certainly seem more objective and positive about these guys than I am. It is too bad that I am not convinced. These old clowns might have made contributions years ago, but when is the last time one of them had something patented? Age is a problem. I'd get rid of the lot of them. You can sit around and wait for them to croak if you want. By then our business will be in bankruptcy. One word of advice: Fire the bunch of them. They are slow, obsolete, and our most expensive employees, from a compensation standpoint."

Just one year after the discussion between Mark and Jim, a downsizing plan was implemented. This plan was based on employee performance evaluation data, projected labor cost data for all job categories, seniority, and anticipated profitability of various units. Jim knew that regardless of the workforce reduction strategy taken, there would be opposition. Someone would be hurt. He tried to make the selection scheme as objective, consistent, and impersonal as possible. The end result would be that approximately 45 people would be terminated. The *headache* came a great deal sooner than he expected.

Several older employees were terminated. At a recent EEOC hearing, these discharged employees testified that their supervisors made derogatory comments, like "old farts" and "old clowns," and argued that these statements were evidence causally linking their termination to prohibited age discrimination. Jim was really worried because he knew that a number of supervisors, not just Mark, felt this way. Although he developed his reduction in the work force scheme without using age or seniority as a negative factor, he knew that the termination decisions were based on his model.

Discussion Questions

1. Should Jim be worried? Why or why not?
2. Do these remarks provide sufficient evidence that the decisions were discriminatory?

*65 Arizona Highway Patrol**

The Arizona Highway Patrol (AHP) has a long, proud, illustrious history and a reputation for having a professional, well-trained group of officers. Most of the officers turn down opportunities to make more as city police officers or county sheriffs so they can be an integral part of the most highly respected police officers in the southwestern United States. The job of patrolling the many hundreds of miles of state highway is a difficult one. Officers, traveling alone, cover many miles a day checking motor vehicles for near compliance with posted speed limits. When it comes to speed, the judgment is made on the basis of the weather and road conditions as well as the speed of other traffic. Informally, officers allow drivers to exceed the speed limit to some degree, especially in the wide open spaces that is much of Arizona. Arizona does have its contrasts, though—from the desert landscape of Tucson to the mountainous terrain of Sedona or Flagstaff. Other major duties of these officers are to identify unsafe trucks hauling goods through the region, assist motorists who need help, and determine if individuals are bringing plants or other contraband into the state.

Over the past 10 to 15 years the composition of the AHP has undergone significant change. More women, Hispanics, native Americans, and blacks have been added to the force. Increased development and growth in the Phoenix and Tucson areas has led to a need to increase the size of the Arizona Highway Patrol and to provide more of a concentration of officers in the troops around these two metropolitan areas.

"I know he's a hard worker and a good officer, but I want him dismissed anyway . . ." So ordered Major Ted Herbert to Captain Mark Peters.

---

*The names, places, and organizations used in this actual care are disguised for obvious reasons.

BACKGROUND

Tom Woodson joined the Arizona Highway Patrol about three and a half years ago. Tom had a spotless record. In fact, his personnel file at the headquarters shows his work was above average and that supervisors considered him "a hard worker," "professional, eager to learn, dedicated, and very personable." Such a record is not surprising since Tom's parents are officers elsewhere in Arizona and he has been a police "brat" for as long as he can remember. Law enforcement is his life and he would love to continue his career.

Tom didn't want notoriety or publicity but what he got was a scandal. Tom never thought that he would see his name in headlines but there it was, part of the lead story in *The Phoenix Gazette:* "Bisexual deputy forced to resign." He was a good officer who worked well with others and had no difficulty in doing his job. He had the respect of his fellow officers and that of his neighbors, associates, and friends. Now, this story might change all that.

In April of 1989, during an investigation conducted by Mesa Deputy Sheriff Paul Butler, Jr., Woodson admitted he had had a homosexual affair with a man about one and a half years before. Woodson also told investigators he has had numerous relationships with women. The report concluded that "Woodson's chosen sexual preference could compromise his position as a highway patrol officer and public servant. His decision . . . could bring dishonor or disrepute to the AHP Commander, who holds that homosexuality is unnatural, immoral, and inexcusable."

An internal investigation, which led to Woodson's dismissal, was begun when Mesa police Captain Fred Ware told internal investigators that Woodson had a sexual encounter with another man. AHP spokesman George Solomon said the officer's sexual preference is not congruent with the standard of behavior we'd like to see in a member of our state highway patrol. We informed Tom that termination was a definite possibility but he would have the option to resign. The department also told him that the case could become public if he refused to resign, was fired, then chose to fight the decision. "If you have a drinking problem, a drug problem, you beat your wife, write bad checks, or you're a homosexual, you'll have problems in this agency," Solomon said.

When interviewed by the press, Woodson took issue with the views of his former employer. He said that his sexual affairs were with consenting adults while off duty. He did not believe that the Arizona Highway Patrol had a right to investigate his private life.

"If they want to investigate me because they heard little kids were involved or I was doing something on duty, I'll take my medicine. But I didn't do anything wrong," he said. According to Solomon, the major concerns of AHP were along those lines—whether the activity was conducted while on duty and whether it involved minors. The internal report, however, states there were never any allegations that Woodson was engaging in sex while at work or with children. Solomon also claimed that the AHP does not screen out homosexuals or bisexuals in hiring. He said there is no written policy preventing their employment.

After consulting with an attorney, Bill Peterson, Woodson has decided to withdraw the resignation he submitted on April 27 (less than a week ago). He wants to be reinstated. On advice of his attorney, if the AHP refuses, Woodson will sue to get his job back. According to Peterson, AHP "doesn't have a leg to stand on. . . . This threat of termination is not legally defensible. They should be ashamed to discharge an otherwise competent highway patrol officer because of his sexual predilections. The AHP has violated some of his basic civil liberties."

When the attorney completed his interview with the media, he spoke off the record to a couple of associates. He noted that court rulings on the rights of homosexuals have been mixed. Certain recent cases (since about 1986) have wound their way through the federal courts. Peterson stated his belief that the Arizona constitution specifically protects privacy.

EPILOGUE

Members of the state's two largest metropolitan (Phoenix and Tucson) areas' Fraternal Order of Police (FOP) voted by a 2-1 margin to support Woodson in his bid to gain reinstatement to his job as a highway patrol officer. Two of the Arizona Highway Patrol's top administrators abstained from voting but more than 800 of the state's troopers are members of these two FOP groups. According to veteran officers, this is the first time in anyone's memory that FOP lodges had taken a stand opposing a commandant's action.

Several troopers, in fear of losing their jobs, spoke off the record to reporters. They said they personally oppose homosexuality. But they said they support Woodson's right to do as he pleases with his private life as long as his off-duty activities are legal and do not interfere with work. These officers believe that the commandant has overstepped his duty to enforce state laws and was regulating the morality of his state troopers. This action against Woodson, they said, set a bad precedent that could affect other deputies—homosexual and heterosexual—in the future.

Not everyone disapproved of the commandant's decision. The following excerpt is typical of some of the recent mail received by the commandant: "The gay situation is a travesty—a holy sin, the same today as when the Bible was written. When sin walks in, we have pestilence (AIDS), much degradation. All morals are cast out. We used to arrest on sodomy cases."

Another person wrote: "I stand in prayerful support of your recent action. . . . How can a state trooper live an openly immoral or even amoral lifestyle and then protect my family from the activities associated with prostitution and pornography?"

Requirement

Research this issue, the relevance of sexual preference as grounds for dismissal. How would you rule if you sat as a judge to hear this case? What factors would you consider in making your decision?

66 Jergins Department Store (B)

"Working in the back room has never been a problem for me. Once in awhile we have an irate customer but usually I can shake that off as part of the job. This, however, is the first time that I've ever been injured on the job."

WHAT HAPPENED

John Haviland joined Jergins in January 1987. He took his job seriously. He worked in the customer package pickup area. He was a quick learner. In no time at all he had mastered the filing and inventory system for merchandise ordered and later delivered to the Coral Gables store. As a package/materials handler for Jergins, he had earned good performance evaluations. The evaluations were a tribute to his competence and good-natured manner of getting the job done. His supervisor, Charlie Winner, was convinced that John worked hard when you watched him but took things easy when the boss was out of sight. Charlie just thought that John was a guy who spent most of his time thinking up ways to get out of work, so for Charlie to give John a good rating suggests others' feedback about John is quite positive.

A recurrent problem in the loading dock area had never been addressed. Over the years, the Miami heat and humidity took its toll on the rubber seal surrounding the loading dock door. During the summer, heavy thunderstorms would lead to a great deal of rain in a very short time. The result of these torrential rains was that puddles of water formed inside the bay area. Peter Smith, one of three package handlers, informed Charlie of his concern about possible injury to anyone working in the area when the floor near the loading dock was wet. Charlie told Peter to mind his own business and get back to work.

In January, one month into the start of his third year on the job, John made Peter's nightmare become a reality. While moving a customer's television and video recorder off a cart and into position for loading, John slipped on a wet spot. His feet flew from under him and he landed hard on his back. At first, he thought that he was fine but, when he tried to get to his feet, he knew that he had a serious problem. He felt sharp pains in the lower back area. John was off duty for nearly seven work days. When he returned he brought a doctor's note, which stated there was damage to discs in his lower back and that his lifting should be restricted to no more than 50 pounds. John asked the personnel manager to transfer him. The personnel manager called Charlie Winner. Charlie informed him that the job could not be done by someone with the stated lifting restriction. John had made a case for his transfer or retention in the same job. He said that heavy lifting was only required a small percentage of the time and there were other workers in the department who could lift for him; therefore, the employer could accommodate without undue hardship.

From John's perspective, he saw himself as handicapped and believed that the company was required to accommodate him. Unfortunately, the company's decision was to terminate John. They felt no need to accommodate the employee.

Discussion Questions

1. Should John be treated as handicapped?
2. What obligation does the company have to accommodate him?

---

*67 Drinking His Job Away**

"Do you know how many days of work you've missed over the last two or three years?" Harry Harvey, supervisor of the purchasing department, could contain himself no longer. "I'm tired of covering for you, Clarence. You have been slipping, slipping, slipping for a long time. I have talked to you until I've become blue in the face. Despite all the verbal and written warnings you refuse to stop your drinking. This is official: Your dismissal is imminent. Anyone who can miss 389 days in three years deserves the opportunity to find a job elsewhere." Three months later, after repeated verbal warnings, Clarence, an 11-year veteran of the National Marine Fisheries Service, was fired.

WHAT HAPPENED

Clarence Peterson, 47, served as a purchasing agent for the National Marine Fisheries Service, a federal agency in Madison, Wisconsin. Family and financial problems had really been difficult for him to handle over the past few years. He had one thing after another go wrong. The worst of the financial setbacks was the Black Thursday on Wall Street when he took a $38,000 loss. He had recently bought some stock short and it had started to rise in value when the bottom fell out. Repeated calls that day to his stockbroker went unanswered. By afternoon, additional attempts to reach the stockbroker were met with a constant busy signal.

His marriage of 25 years abruptly ended three years ago. No one could describe the shock and utter despair he felt when his wife calmly informed him that her lawyer would be getting in touch with him about the divorce decree. Clarence didn't realize that his marriage was in trouble! He asked himself why he had been so blind to what was going on. His three kids were going to go with their mother. He wasn't exactly thrilled that he would only have occasional visitation privileges.

---

* The names of the individuals and organization are fictitious, but the situation described is based on an actual incident.

The divorce and loss of his children seemed to devastate him and cause him to lose interest in his job. Nothing seemed to matter anymore. He began to drown his sorrows in a bottle. He drank alone; he drank with others. Co-workers and friends began to notice that he had become more than a "social" drinker. Some even asked if he could "handle it." Clarence's drinking got out hand. Everywhere he went he took a bottle. Finally, he started bringing a bottle to work each day. At the dismissal hearing, Clarence admitted to drinking a pint of gin a day while at work. He claimed that he could control his drinking and, whether he drank or not, he could maintain good performance. What he did not acknowledge is that concerned co-workers and subordinates served as "enablers" who helped him to get his job done, took telephone messages when he was too inebriated to do so, gave excuses when he was indisposed, or otherwise helped him get through his workday.

As the years went by it became increasingly obvious that he could not do the job. Friends grew tired of pinch-hitting for him. In fact, some co-workers became downright resentful of having to cover for him. His $48,000 mistake on a purchase order served as the impetus for his dismissal. The 389 days missed from work over the last three years didn't help his case at all. The dismissal hearing was held shortly after the auditors uncovered the $48,000. At the hearing, the employee's attorney claimed that his client was sick. His alcoholism was an illness requiring treatment—not dismissal. The attorney also argued that although many people told Clarence that he should stop drinking, no formal counseling took place. "Rehabilitation, not retribution, should have been the order of the day," the attorney claimed. "My client had a crippling disability and the agency failed to make reasonable accommodation. Federal agencies, more so than do local or state agencies, have a special duty to assist handicapped workers."

Discussion Questions

1. What issues does the case raise?
2. Should an employee miss 389 days over a three-year period yet still retain his job?
3. Should alcoholism be treated as a disease? How would you rule in this case?

*68 Consultants' Advice at WTAM—Channel 4**

WTAM encountered great difficulty in its attempts to compete with the current news leader, WCAU-TV. WCAU is the pride of CBS's southeastern U.S. market. The Tampa-based affiliate consistently places first in all the "sweeps." The station's

*The names, places, and organizations identified have been disguised. The personnel situation is real.

stranglehold on first has been very frustrating to other local TV competitors. WCAU's dominance has been most pronounced in the news department. No one has been able to unseat the evening and late night news teams from the number 1 perch over the last four years. These competitors have *not* stood idly by. The turnover rate among the anchors and others on the evening and nightly news teams has been astronomical.

For many, many years WCAU was the doormat of the sweeps process. The competing television stations, WPIX and WTAM, had taken turns as leader in the region. In fact, until 1982, WCAU trailed both stations in the viewer ratings process. Bill Baxter, the original owner of WCAU, encountered financial difficulties. He then decided to sell out to a new owner. The highest bidder for the station was the flamboyant, hard-driving Charlie Stevens. Dr. Stevens had spent much of his life as a professor at the University of South Florida. He later became dean of the college of business administration. His financial moxie, personal contacts he had developed and nurtured over the years, and his wife's inheritance enabled him to purchase the station. Charlie had become accustomed to success. He was one of those city fathers who got in on the ground floor of Tampa's incredible growth spurt of the 1970s and 1980s. He had purchased a great deal of real estate, and his financial holdings had multiplied dramatically as well. He was, as he liked to say, fond of "winning." The station was *not* a toy. He wanted it to be the best. He told all the employees at their very first meeting under his ownership that he "took no pride in being the Avis of the television industry."

Charlie was willing to recruit the best, even if it meant raiding neighboring stations. He spent thousands on promotions and marketing of the station, its programs, and its television personalities. During the early years of his ownership there was rapid turnover. He established a new top-management team, beginning with the station's general manager. His "real baby" was the evening news. During 1982–84, he tinkered constantly with that program, and program format changes were made. He experimented with anchors and co-anchors, and he changed the key people who delivered the news, weather, and sports. Most of his efforts were designed to change the image of the television station. He was determined to see the station become number 1 in viewer audience. The 1984 ratings results placed WCAU in first place for the first time in over a decade. Dr. Stevens did anything and everything needed to remain at the top of the local television market. Not unlike other station management, Charlie relied on consultants to provide marketing suggestions and to gather marketing research. However, Charlie was a maverick. He was as likely to implement their recommendations as he was to discard them. He liked the motto "if it ain't broke, don't fix it."

WCAU's efforts left the other Tampa television stations in a panic. They did not know what to do. Their corporate owners weren't happy being also-rans in the television sweeps. These stations tried rather drastic moves in an effort to entice viewers away from WCAU. In some instances, the move of lineups, use of syndicated programs, and evening schedule changes were made. Each of the stations has modified its news format as well. Nothing has worked. WTAM is just a station. If anything, its most recent move may have helped WCAU strengthen the hold on first place.

The consultants have spoken. The surveys have been done. The ratings over the past two years have been carefully examined. *Somebody* from the evening news team must go. The news team consists of two co-anchors, Gerald Rising and Michelle Murray, weather forecaster Al Donnelly, and sportscaster Ray C. Jurgensen. They all knew that the ratings weren't what they should be. None of them knew why they were so low. The team itself had changed in recent years. People who worked for WTAM viewed the team as being a pretty good one—with one notable exception.

The exception was Al Donnelly. Not only was he popular with the station's television audience but everybody at the station liked him. His personal mark of distinction and touch of individuality was his neatly trimmed beard. (Few in the industry dared to break the unwritten rule of "no facial hair.") Al was really good at what he did. He brought to the team an air of professionalism, a touch of humor, and the knack of interjecting a remark or two that made people feel that he was talking to them.

A LOOK AT AL DONNELLY

Al Donnelly is a native of Fort Wayne, Indiana. He has had two loves—sports and meteorology. For many years he wrestled with the need to balance his dual loves. He wasn't a great athlete, but he certainly had accumulated his share of trophies and medals as a high school star at a Class A (small) school. He learned very quickly, however, that sports offers a very short-lived career with risk of injury hanging over one's head. A rather mediocre college athletic career helped reinforce his decision to become a weatherman. He did earn four letters, two each in baseball and basketball, but competing for a varsity position at an NCAA Division III was not all that difficult.

Since earning his bachelor of science degree in physical sciences in 1979, Al has worked for three different TV stations during the past nine and one-half years. His first job, which took place at a television station in Indianapolis, left much to be desired. He was more of a gofer than a weather person. The station was small and ranked number 3 out of the three local stations. One value of the station was that he was more of a generalist. He had the opportunity to learn how everything works. It provided a nice overview of television—from management to the lowliest (but essential) technician. He learned quite a bit.

The experience helped him land a full-time position doing the weather for a top-rated station in Toledo, Ohio. He thoroughly enjoyed his work at WTOL-TV. Despite the severe winter weather and the depressed state of the economy during his first two years there, he turned down two employment opportunities. As he gained in stature at the station, he watched Toledo begin its slow but steady recovery. Business opportunities, such as the retention of the Jeep plant, revitalization of the downtown and the water front areas, and the attraction of new industry, including the city's first mini-mill for steel production, helped keep Al in Toledo. When the offer to join WTAM came along, however, Al decided that for professional reasons it was the best thing to do. He also decided that the Florida weather would not be too hard to tolerate. So, in 1986, he joined Tampa's WTAM-TV. He'd been in the business for seven years and had become a very competent, seasoned veteran.

WORDS TO A COLLEAGUE

"There's nothing wrong with my beard. I don't even want to hear that malarkey! In fact, many of the viewers who write to me take time to compliment me on having such an attractive beard. Some say that they don't care what the consultants and so-called experts say, the beard should stay; the consultants should go! From my perspective, the smart boys raise the beard issue, but it is really a straw man. They just want to justify the big bucks they get. They haven't got a clue what is wrong. There is no concrete evidence that I'm the cause of the news program's persistent low ratings.

"I know that I am not the problem. No one person, especially not the meteorologist [who is responsible for weather reports], makes or breaks the evening news program. The program format, the personalities, and the competence of the anchor, co-anchors or production crew, or strength of the news-gathering function, have a much more dramatic impact on ratings. I have watched news anchors come and go so often during my years here that it looks like a trapdoor instead of a softly contoured chair that should be their homes when they are on the air. These previous changes and my gut lead me to believe that the real problem may be management malfeasance. However, I have learned that being forthright around here is a sure ticket to somewhere else. Clearly, there's little security in this business. Clive Thomasson, my counterpart at WCAU, warned me not to sign an employment contract that included a noncompete clause. [See Exhibit 1.] I wish that I had listened. Today I received my 'pink slip.' The owner terminated me. He believes the consultants know what is best. I asked what it was that I did wrong. He said that he had no complaints with me regarding my performance, just that it was time for a change. Obviously, the accumulation of wealth doesn't mean that you are smart. I'm not happy about the situation. I don't think I should just be gotten rid of. I'm going to talk to my attorney about my discharge to see what recourse I have."

EXHIBIT 1 Employment Agreement

Employment Agreement

EMPLOYMENT AGREEMENT (this "Agreement"), dated August 17, 1989, is between Television Station WTAM, a Delaware corporation (the "Company"), and Al Donnelly (the "Employee").

WHEREAS, the nature of the Company's business is broadcast media in a highly elastic market and the Company has provided significant compensation to the Employee, the parties enter into this Agreement.

EXHIBIT 1 Employment Agreement (continued)

I, Al Donnelly, of Plant City, Florida, in consideration of my employment by Television Station WTAM-Channel 4, and the consideration of the premises and the mutual covenants contained herein, the parties agree as follows:

1. *Employment and Acceptance*

The Company has hired the Employee to work in the position of meteorologist or weather forecaster on the station's nightly and early afternoon news programs. This employment is not guaranteed to last a specific, determinant length of time. The employment may be terminated with or without cause at any time.

2. *Duties and Authority*

During this unspecified term of employment the Employee shall devote his full time and energies to the business and affairs of the Company. The Employee agrees to use his best efforts, skills, and abilities to promote the Company's interests and to serve as meteorologist or weather forecaster and to perform such duties as may be assigned to him by the Company's management. The Employee shall, as part of the employment agreement, perform his job in an exemplary manner, obeying all rules, regulations, procedures, and policies established by management.

3. *Compensation*

3.1 As base compensation for all services to be rendered by the Employee of the Company pursuant to this Agreement, the Company agrees to pay the Employee, during the term of his employment, a salary ("Salary") at the rate of $90,000 per annum, payable in equal biweekly installments, subject to increase during the term in accordance with the Company's salary review policies as in effect at the time of employment.

3.2 In addition to the base compensation specified above, the Employee shall be entitled to receive a bonus (the "1989 Bonus") determined in accordance with the Fall 1989 TV news program "sweeps" results.

3.3 The Company shall pay or reimburse the Employee for all reasonable expenses actually incurred or paid by him during the term of employment in the performance of services to the Company under this Agreement, on presentation of expense statements or vouchers or such other supporting information as the Company may require.

3.4 The Employee shall be entitled to all rights and benefits for which he shall be eligible under any pension, group insurance, and other forms of insurance, as well as other "fringe benefits" which the Company provides for its professional and managerial employees. Without limiting the generality of the foregoing, the Employee shall be provided, at the Company's expense (including fuel, lubricants, maintenance, and insurance), an automobile of the same make and model (or comparable) as is now provided to him by the Company.

4. *Termination*

4.1 In the event of (i) the Employee's willful, material and bad faith failure to perform his duties hereunder, (ii) the conviction of the Employee of (x) any felony, or (y) of any lesser crime or offense involving the property of the Company or any of its subsidiaries or affiliates, (iii) the gross misconduct by the Employee in connection with the performance of his duties hereunder. These items constitute, among others not stated, "for cause" reasons for dismissal. The employee so terminated forfeits any rights to unaccrued benefits. The company shall have no further obligation to make any payments to, or bestow any benefits on, the Employee from and after the date of said termination, other than payments or benefits accrued prior to the Date of Termination.

EXHIBIT 1 Employment Agreement (continued)

4.2 If the Employee shall die during the Term, the Employee's employment under this Agreement shall terminate, except that the Employee's legal representatives shall be entitled to receive the compensation provided for hereunder to the last day of the month in which the Employee's death occurs.

4.3 If the Employee becomes so disabled during the term that he is unable substantially to perform his services hereunder for an aggregate of 6 months within any period of 12 consecutive months, this Agreement may be terminated by the Company. Such termination shall be determined by resolution of the Company's board of directors after the expiration of said six months, and shall be effective upon written notice to the Employee of the adoption of such resolution. The compensation due the employee hereunder shall be paid through the last day of the calendar month in which such termination shall have become effective.

4.4 In the event the site of the Employee's employment is relocated outside of Hillsborough, Osceola, Seminole, or Orange Counties, the Employee shall have the right to terminate this Agreement, and following such termination shall be entitled to receive six month's salary.

5. *Protection of Confidential Information: Non-Competition*

5.1 The employee shall not divulge to anyone, either during or at any time after the termination of his employment, any confidential information concerning the Company and its subsidiaries and affiliates or its or their customers. The Employee acknowledges that any such confidential information is of great value to the Company and its subsidiaries and affiliates, and on the termination of his employment the Employee shall forthwith deliver up to the Company all documents, memoranda, and other data in his possession relating thereto. The Employee shall not, either during, or at any time after the termination of his employment, make any public or private statement reflecting adversely on the Company and its business prospects or otherwise disparage the Company. The employee shall not, either during his employment or during the first 18 months after the termination of his employment, solicit or encourage any employees of the Company to leave the employ of the Company, consult with any such employee with respect to other employment opportunities, or on behalf of any future employer, hire or offer to hire any person while he or she is an employee of the Company.

5.2 The Employee shall not directly or indirectly appear in the position of meteorologist, weather forecaster, or other on-the-air capacity on any television station program within a restricted area of 90 miles radius of Tampa. This geographical restriction applies to major television markets (e.g., Orlando) as well as smaller markets (e.g., Lakeland) and covers a period of 18 months after the date of termination of the employee's employment, whether this termination is with or without cause. This covenant on the Employee's part shall be construed as an agreement independent of any other provision in this Agreement; and the existence of any claim or cause of action on the Employee's part against the Company, of any kind whatsoever, shall not constitute a defense to the enforcement by the Company of this covenant. The Employee shall be entitled to seek or arrange for any such position, ownership interest, or association, so long as it does not go into effect until the expiration of this Agreement's stipulations. In addition to any other right and remedy it may have, at law or in equity, the company shall be entitled, on a proper showing, to an injunction enjoining or restraining the Employee from any violation or threatened violation of this Section, provided, however, that the foregoing shall not prevent the Employee from contesting the issuance of any such injunction on the grounds that no violation or threatened violation of

EXHIBIT 1 Employment Agreement (concluded)

this Section had occurred. If any of the restrictions contained herein shall be deemed to be unenforceable by reason of the extent, duration, geographical scope, or other provisions hereof, and in its reduced form, this Section shall then be enforceable in the manner contemplated hereby.

6. *Intellectual Property*

The Company shall be the sole owner of all the products and proceeds of the Employee's services, including, but not limited to, all materials, ideas, concepts, formats, suggestions, developments, arrangements, packages, programs, and other intellectual properties that the Employee may acquire, obtain, develop, or create in connection with and during the Employee's employment, free and clear of any claims by the Employee (or anyone claiming under the Employee) of any kind of character whatsoever (other than the Employee's right to receive compensation hereunder).

7. *General*

7.1 This Agreement shall be governed by and construed and enforced in accordance with the laws of the State of Florida without regard to the principles of conflicts of laws thereof.

7.2 This Agreement sets forth the entire agreement and understanding of the parties relating to the subject matter hereof, and supersedes all prior agreements, arrangements and understandings, written or oral, relating to the subject matter hereof.

7.3 The invalidity or unenforceability of any provision or provisions of this Agreement shall not affect the validity or enforceability of any provision of this Agreement, which shall remain in full force and effect.

IN WITNESS WHEREOF, the parties have executed this Agreement as of the date first above written.

TELEVISION STATION WTAM CHANNEL 4

By:______________________________

____

Al Donnelly

Clive Thomasson had talked to Al about employee noncompetition clauses. Although the concept wasn't new to Al, he had never been asked to sign a contract with such a clause. Since his arrival at WTAM, Al has signed a contract that has an employment-at-will clause and a noncompetition clause. The employment-at-will clause makes clear that the employee serves for an indeterminant period and that he or she may be terminated "for good cause, no cause, or a cause morally wrong provided that cause does not violate a statute. . . ." The noncompetition clause bars the former employee from working in the same career field for a competing television station in the same geographical region.

Discussion Questions

1. Discuss the employment relationship between Al Donnelly and WTAM-Channel 4. In particular, examine the employment agreement. Pay special attention to noncompetition and employment-at-will clauses. What personnel issues does this agreement raise?
2. What factors should a television station consider in determining whether to dismiss or retain a television personality?

Part 2

Incident Cases and Role-Playing Exercises in Human Resource Management

Active learning is a critical aspect of maximizing the time and effort a student commits to the classroom. This text includes many different types of material that are designed to enhance learning while blending theory and practice. Here we shift from cases to incident cases and role-playing exercises.

As noted in the preface, **Incident Cases** are "minicases." These incidents are typically a page or so in length, focus on an especially timely and relevant aspect of human resource management, and contain information that requires students to ask themselves the right questions. The role-plays require a small group of individuals to take on assigned roles in acting out a situation involving people and a key human resource issue that impacts the role players.

Section A

Incident Cases and Role-Playing Exercises: A Discussion

Paul and Faith Pigors observed that sometimes cases do not simulate reality as well as they might.[1] They believed that this was so because cases can give the impression that all the material necessary to deal with a situation is given at one time. In fact, they argue, usually problems unfold over time and require the problem solver to act to gather more information than is first given.

Thus, the Pigors advocated the use of the *incident* case method. The method works like this [2]:

Step 1. A short statement or incident (usually 100 words or so) is presented to the participants.

Step 2. Each participant examines the incident and asks, "What's going on here?" The participant tries to decide the main issues at stake.

Step 3. The participant formulates a series of questions that are essential or useful in solving or coming to grips with the case. Usually, these questions focus on the who, what, when, where, and how of the incident.

Step 4. The focus becomes: What is the most important issue here, and what needs to be decided and done right now?

Step 5. The case as a whole is examined, and all major issues are dealt with.

Thus, the incident method is similar to cases, but in some ways different. Typically, this is how an incident case is handled:

---

[1] Paul Pigors and Faith Pigors, *Case Method in Human Relations: The Incident Process* (New York: McGraw-Hill, 1961).

[2] Ibid., pp.142–45

In step 1, each participant reads the incident alone and makes notes about his or her reaction to it. He or she also answers the questions in step 2. Then, the participant discusses the conclusions of steps 1 and 2 with a small group in the class or seminar. Typically, this is a group of three to five persons. Together they come to agree on steps 1 and 2, at least initially, and formulate the questions in step 3.

When step 3 is completed, the discussion leader for the group is chosen by the group. It is suggested that this role rotate among the members from time to time. This leader calls over the person conducting the session. The discussion leader asks the questions the group formulated of the person conducting the session. He or she has additional information available about the incident, and, thus, this simulates the search for information in the real problem-solving experience.

At this point, the groups formulate the responses to steps 4 and 5. Finally, there is a group discussion of all the groups in which all the ideas developed are examined. This process involves more active participation by all present and is a useful learning experience in most cases. The incidents given in this text involve a variety of problems and settings, as was true with the case situations.

Section B

Incidents

69 The New Guy*†

Steven, prepared for a new venture, had just moved to Denver. At 21, he had just graduated from college and was eager to get started in the "real world." One of his first activities on his arrival to the city in August of 1992 was to sign up with an employment agency. Since he was in a new environment with no professional contacts, he thought the agency was his most reasonable option.

The first job he was referred to was route salesperson for the All-Star Company, an industrial linen supply company. All-Star employs approximately 50 people at this site. The company is unionized. The job opening was for a driver; but other job duties included delivering clean supplies of linens, picking up bundles of soiled materials from route sites, and unloading these at All-Star.

Steven was hired for this position. Upon his hire, Steven notified his supervisors that he had diabetes. His supervisor had no reservations about the disease. In fact, he was familiar with it because his friend also had diabetes. Steve did not, however, mention this to his partner with whom he rode in the truck.

Because of the strenuous nature of the job. Steven had some problems maintaining his blood sugar levels.[1] On one occasion, Steve had a "reaction" and his partner suspected him of using drugs. At that point, the supervisor informed the partner of Steven's medical condition.

On a second occasion, Steve experienced a more severe reaction, which resulted in unconsciousness. His employer sent for an ambulance to ensure proper medical

* Fictional names have been used in this case.

† This case incident was prepared by Professors Wendy Eager and Dianne H. B. Welsh, Eastern Washington University.

[1] Exercise can cause blood sugar levels to drop, resulting in dizziness, sweating, and mental confusion. This can be prevented by eating a snack or by adjusting medication.

treatment. On Steven's return to work, his supervisor called him and told him that he'd have to let him go. The supervisor was very upset during this meeting.

Steve did file a grievance with union officials. He was still in his probationary employment period and was not yet a union member.

---

70 Franklin's Department Store

The Franklin's Department Store branch at Scottsdale Avenue and Broadway had been in business for 16 years. It was a very good volume store that more than held its own when it came to sales. The store's close proximity to Arizona State University in the city of Tempe certainly didn't hurt. The store got its fair share of sales from a portion of the 40,000 students in the neighborhood. In addition, the location was a good one. Scottsdale Avenue was one of the busiest streets in the Tempe, Phoenix, and Scottsdale areas. The store is one of eight in the Phoenix metropolitan area. Although its sales have increased somewhat, store size in terms of square footage and workforce has remained constant since 1988.

The store's previous manager, Roxana Bacon, had done an outstanding job of cutting costs by managing employee turnover well, using appropriate recruitment sources and methods, and keeping pilferage and spoilage to a minimum. Her reward for her excellent performance was a promotion to a regional management position. All the employees at the Scottsdale store were happy for her until they met the new department store manager.

Rick Cohen, the new store manager, is a native of Los Angeles. Coming to Arizona from a California store was just one more stop in his climb to the top of Franklin's. He was an ambitious sort who let nothing stand in his way. From top management's perspective, they liked the fact that he was a highly motivated, intelligent, and determined workaholic who kept himself in top physical condition. Tennis and jogging were two of his greatest loves. His motto was "work hard and play hard." After two weeks on the job, Rick issued a memorandum to all employees appealing to them to get in shape. Specifically, he mentioned that lower medical costs and higher productivity could be obtained if employees exercised and ate nutritious meals. Within one month Rick had issued individual memoranda identifying each employee's proposed weight given that person's height.

Bob Johnson, a 6-foot, 3-inch, 300-pound department store salesman, knew he was in big trouble. He broke into a cold sweat every time he saw Rick approach. Bob had been given orders to lose 90 pounds in six months. Bob had been able to shed only 49 pounds, and he feared for his job. The six-month grace period ends next Friday. Bob was not the only fearful employee. The new boss, whom all described as a "health nut," had all the store's overweight workers in a tizzy. Several had been informed of their pending terminations. The reason: It was unlikely that they could meet his weight mandates.

Sure enough, Bob lasted another two weeks, then received his pink slip. Off the record, Rick believed that not only were there savings in terms of medical care expenditures and lost time, but those who are obese, in his mind, possess undesirable characteristics. In Rick's view, the overweight are lazy, slothful, and dishonest. He told employment agencies not to send overweight candidates to him because "fat people steal."

Quite a few employees, among them some who are not overweight, believe that the store manager is overstepping his bounds. They feel that Rick is discriminating against those who are heavy. "The focus should be on whether the person does a good job, not whether he is good looking," was the view of many workers. The "fatty" dismissals seemed hard to prevent. No one could think of any laws or regulations that protected someone who was discriminated against on the basis of his or her weight. One person recalled a man being denied a job at a health club because he didn't have a muscular build and another health club applicant was rejected because he was overweight. In each case, the employer argued that the people did not project the image a health club needed its employees to project. Neither looked like the "after" in a health club commercial, so the employer turned them down because they would destroy the club's credibility and make it difficult to recruit clients.

Employees later learned that one fired employee had gone to an attorney who admitted that there were gaps in the law that could make obese workers vulnerable to discrimination in the workplace. The attorney also mentioned that employers were not required to give a reason for dismissal so those cases are even more difficult to win.

Discussion Questions

1. Under what conditions does an employer have a right to dismiss a person because of an employee's overweight condition?
2. Are there are federal laws that prohibit discrimination on the basis of obesity?

---

*71 The Contract Settlement**

You are the plant manager of a large chemical plant of a multiplant, multiproduct company. Some of the company's plants are union, some are not. Your company has the typical wage–salary structure, with wages and salary structures determined by such factors as area rates, economic conditions, law of supply and demand, starting wage and salary rates, and the like.

---

* Prepared by Professor Henry F. Houser, Auburn University at Montgomery.

Your union plant has recently negotiated a three-year contract for hourly employees. The contract calls for total increases, including fringe benefits, or a total of 25 percent over the three-year period. You and other members of your management team feel the contract is a generous one, and the workers voted overwhelmingly to accept it. You felt, with a sigh of relief, that now you could devote more of your time to long-range planning, particularly on cost-reduction methods to permit your plant to continue to remain competitive in spite of the increased labor costs.

Today you received a shock in the form of a committee of salaried employees, consisting of technical supervisory personnel. The committee had asked for a meeting with you, and in the course of the meeting had outlined a number of grievances. First, very few of them had received, in recent years, pay raises of an equivalent percentage to the contract increases. Also, the hourly workers consistently received overtime and other premium pay equal to approximately 15 percent of their regular income, so many of the skilled workers made more annually than the engineers and supervisors. Many of the committee members were very belligerent and resentful, and you could tell that they had discussed this problem among themselves before asking for the meeting.

Without making any specific concessions, you agreed to look into their grievances and to meet with them again in two weeks. Meanwhile, at your suggestion, they selected a committee of their members to study the problem and to present some specific suggestions at the next meeting.

Required

Outline the analytical and action steps you will take between now and the next meeting.

---

72 Fat Is Fabulous

Sarah Burns told herself that she was not going to quietly walk off and simply accept the college's decision. She had been passive long enough. All of her life people have been discriminating against her because of her size. Enough is enough. She knew what she weighed—280 pounds—down from the 328 pounds she weighed when her former nursing college forced her to resign. Sarah had been in a state of shock and inertia for six months. She was devastated that her college saw fit to pressure her to leave. Overweight since childhood, Sarah notes that she has endured a lifetime of discrimination, beginning in kindergarten where she bore the brunt of classmates' jokes. Some students called her Tubby or Fatso. According to Burns, "Fat is an OK word. I think this is an important issue. I don't think people really accept the fact that society can be very cruel."

Sarah believed that the college's explanation for forcing her to resign from the school's nursing program was bogus. They claimed that they had made an agreement with her. The agreement: Maintain her good academic standing, lose two pounds a week, and keep in contact with faculty who had the responsibility of monitoring her diet. A school spokesman claimed, "We were trying to get her to do two things: one was helping her to address her condition of morbid obesity. Two was in terms of the academic requirements. She flunked a course because she could not successfully integrate information related to diet and nutrition."

Later, she enrolled at another nursing school. There she completed all requirements of the program, and she now serves as a pediatric nurse. After consultation with an employment law attorney, she filed a lawsuit. No verdict has been rendered but arguments for both sides have been heard. Before the verdict was reached a friend brought news of a former Xerox Corporation employee who had filed discrimination charges. The woman, who weighed 249 pounds, claimed that her weight in no way detracted from her performance as a marketer for the copier-duplicator giant. The woman lost her case in trial court but has appealed the decision.

Discussion Questions

1. Does a school have a right to dismiss a student because of his or her physical condition, in this instance, obesity?
2. If so, what basis does the school have for such a decision?

---

*73 St. Luke's Children's Hospital**

You are the director of facility services for a 600-bed urban hospital located in a large southwestern city. Your unit is responsible for cleaning all patient rooms, maintaining all public areas, removing ordinary trash from offices and laboratories (hazardous materials are handled separately), and making various physical repairs. There are about 150 people in the facility services unit. This includes yourself, 2 assistant directors, 11 supervisors, 7 clerical workers, 35 skilled craftspeople (electricians, plumbers, painters, and so on), and about 90–100 unskilled cleaners and janitors.

The skilled craftspeople are represented by five different trade unions (all AFL-CIO affiliates). Most of the craftspeople are male (70 percent). Their ages range from mid-30s to early-60s (St. Luke's doesn't hire apprentices). About half are white, 35 percent Hispanic, and 15 percent black. They come from all over the city and suburbs. Their wage and benefits package is comparable to local industry packages and much better than other local hospital packages.

---

* This case was prepared by Professor Donald P. Rogers, GMI Engineering and Management Institute.

The unskilled cleaners are represented by a rather militant local of an AFL-CIO affiliated industrial union. Almost all of the cleaners are women (88 percent). They range in age from teens to late-60s, although most are between 25 and 45. More than half are single parents. About 60 percent are black, 35 percent Hispanic, and 5 percent white. Most live in the city, within two miles of the hospital. Their wage and benefits package is one of the best in the city—better than most local industry packages.

Absenteeism for both groups is getting out of hand. People don't show up when they are scheduled to work. During the last three months, daily absenteeism for the craftspeople averaged 15 to 20 percent. For the cleaners, daily absenteeism is running at 20 to 24 percent; these rates are three to four times higher than the national averages. To ensure that you can cover any given shift you have been overscheduling by about 20 percent. In other words, you have to schedule 50 people a day on a day shift to make sure that 40 will show up, or 25 people on an evening shift to get 20, or 12 on a night shift to get 10.

Maintaining buffer staff is expensive. Most employees receive full pay for the days they miss, because of vacation day, sick day, and personal leave provisions of the various union contracts. Employee benefit costs accrue even when the person is absent. The hospital's chief financial officer has been tracking your payroll costs and considers them excessive. You need to do something to reduce labor costs without reducing levels of service.

Discussion Questions

1. What reasons do workers have for not showing up for work?
2. What can you do to motivate them to show up?
3. Is absenteeism really the problem in this case?

---

*74 The New Mexico Railroad "Red Light" Case**

The history of the New Mexico R.R. system dates back to 1871 when the idea was first envisioned by D. B. (Gizmo) Jackson. During this period there was an increasing need to "link" widespread regions for trade and transportation. Formal organization was completed on September 6, 1872, and the name of the company was changed from the Albuquerque & Santa Fe System on November 24, 1875.

---

* This case was prepared by Professor George E. Stevens, Kent State University with assistance from Paul Stephenson, Paulius Birutis, John Dottore, Steve Droze, Brad Glass, Laurie Shapek, and Diane Wharton, all of whom are students at the University of Central Florida.

Paul Hearn comes into the personnel office one day. He has always loved trains and his lifelong dream is to become a train engineer. Hearn completes the employment application, passes a screening interview, and he gets the highest score that anyone has earned on the railroad's fireman test. (The position of fireman leads, with experience, to the job of engineer. An engineer is required to be able to distinguish red, green, amber, blue, and white traffic signals.) In addition, he takes and successfully passes the company's comprehensive physical examination. The two of you talk salary and benefits. You have done everything just short of hiring him when you notice that he did not pass all parts of the physical examination. He has failed Ishihara's test, a pattern of different color dots forming figures, but he passed a "bright color" test. Even though he failed Ishihara's test, the examining physician recommended that he be accepted for the fireman training program. This recommendation has been passed on to the railroad's chief medical officer, who informs you that he would like to overrule the examining physician and declare the applicant unfit for service on engines. The chief medical officer reminds you that ". . . as a carrier, it has an extraordinarily high duty to ensure the safety of its passengers and that the rejection of Hearn would be based on company standards that are justifiable and reasonable."

Discussion Questions

1. Do you let the examining physician's recommendation stand or do you reverse the decision? Explain.
2. What factors should you consider in making your decision?

75 The Cleaning Woman

When Cheryl Green of Rockville, Maryland, realized that she was just too hurried and too harried to keep her house clean, she came up with the perfect solution—hire someone. She didn't need to have someone perform those duties every week, so she hired a woman to clean her house on a biweekly basis. Cheryl paid Carole Washington, the housekeeper, $50 once every two weeks to do the cleaning for her.

Carole was especially pleased to have Mrs. Green for an employer. Mrs. Green faithfully paid her employee's Social Security. Carole had previously been "burned" by an employer who failed to do so, despite the fact that the employer deducted the employee's contribution from her paycheck. Mrs. Green also kept track of sick leave and holidays. These efforts were even more remarkable given that Mrs. Green lived on a very limited budget. Paying Carole $1,300 a year really strained her financial resources. The working relationship between the two women was excellent. Carole believed that her working relationship was more than satisfactory. Cheryl was convinced that she was doing everything the law required.

She was not. To her amazement, the Rockville woman received a letter informing her that she was a lawbreaker. Mrs. Green was told that she was violating Maryland's worker's compensation law. The Maryland law covers any employee who is paid at least $250 a quarter in wages. The employer must buy a worker's compensation policy that costs $350 a year. (Carole is paid $1,300 a year.) Mrs. Green finds herself in an unenviable position. She can hardly scrape up the $1,300 in wages needed, but now she must pay additional money if she is to comply with the law. She must decide whether to continue to employ Carole illegally without paying the policy premium or risk going into debt if she wants to keep her cleaning lady legally. The former option means risk for the employer should the employee become injured. In this case, the employer did act in good faith. There was a communication breakdown between the Maryland Workmen's Compensation Commission and the insurance companies. Each thought that the other would notify the employer-client about his or her obligations.

Requirement

Research your own state's workers compensation law. When you do see these laws, tell how those laws differ from the ones described here. Do such laws actually protect the worker?

*76 The "Great" Professor**

Dr. Harvey Davis, a professor of management, has taught at the University of Southwest Florida since 1980. During this time he has gained tremendous recognition from students for being a dedicated, caring, and knowledgeable instructor. He spends hours with students. He helps them with their student organizations and assists students who need encouragement in the classroom. In fact, for the last two years, Dr. Davis has been chosen recipient of the teacher of the year award. To Dr. Davis's credit, the recognition has not been based on a popularity contest. Student evaluations are examined, a special midterm evaluation and a student evaluation are done, student interviews are conducted, and the professor's teaching is observed by a team consisting of students, faculty, and administrators.

Today, you receive the results of an investigation initiated by the Federal Bureau of Investigation. While investigating charges of misrepresentation and mail fraud concerning administrators of an Arizona university, it was determined that 73 individuals bought their degrees from a diploma mill. "Dr." Davis is among those individuals

* The names of the university and people listed are fictitious. The personnel issues described are real.

identified in the FBI report. The report reveals that Davis bought two degrees from the same institution. He did no academic work for either. Basically, he paid a fee and, in return, was given fabricated transcripts, diplomas, and even parking decals. Your first inclination is to fire him and then have the university sue him for fraud.

Requirement

Research this type of case. Determine what action(s) you should take to handle this specific situation and to possibly avoid recurrences of this type in the future.

---

77 Tastee Donuts, Inc. (A)

Michael Creighton, owner of two Tastee Donuts shops in Tampa, Florida, felt great about the revenues generated by his businesses. When he opened his first shop five years ago, he was afraid that donut lovers might be loyal to Mr. Donut and other established franchises. Fortunately, his fears were never realized. He had done a great job of identifying and studying factors most crucial to the success of his business. He had identified capital, location, promotions, advertising, overhead costs (e.g., rental fees), equipment, and staffing as the most critical factors. Now he is the proud owner of two money-making shops that employ a total of 12 employees, 6 in each shop. His turnover has been high, but he has been able to hold onto his doughnut makers and he has been able to easily replace those who work the counter, drive-in window, and operate the register. Most of his employees are women. About half of the women are married. The single ones tend to be in their 20s and attractive. Mr. Creighton wants women who meet all his criteria—job related and nonjob related.

Creighton had believed that 1989 would be a great year. According to his timetable, this would be the year that he doubled his shops and eventually doubled his profit. Now, he's afraid that 1989 could be the year that he loses it all. His greatest fear could be realized. He knows better than anyone else that he sees the culprit each time he looks in a mirror. He just couldn't keep his hands off his workers. He was always saying things of a sexual nature to his employees. Until Arlene complained, no one had had the guts to file a complaint. Her repeated attempts to get him to stop the jokes, touching, and other objectionable behavior failed. She told him that she was going to the local office of the Equal Employment Opportunity Commission. There she would file a sexual harassment complaint. Arlene said that she had met with a couple of his former employees who would provide depositions supporting her case. According to Arlene, she had learned from a personnel class that she could file a complaint under provisions of Title VII of the Civil Rights Act of 1964 and EEOC guidelines. Over the years, Creighton had come to believe that a sort of contract existed between himself and his "girls." If they wanted to work for him or wanted a raise then they had to go out with him when he wanted. Much of the turnover was caused by voluntary resignations or his firing of those who did not want to "cooperate."

Discussion Questions

1. Which laws cover unlawful sexual harassment?
2. Is Michael Creighton violating the Civil Rights Act (1964), the EEOC's guidelines, or any other statute that might cover sexual harassment?
3. What legal recourse, if any, does Arlene have?

Tastee Donuts, Inc. (B)

"Look, Phil, I could fire you! We run a very small operation here so every worker is doubly important. I can't have people taking time off for weeks at a time even if it is for jury duty. Now, it looks like you're going to be involved with a grand jury case that will keep you occupied for weeks. You can demand your full salary and declare your right to serve jury duty but I want you to know two things: (1) Your salary will be reduced by the amount of money you're paid for being a juror; and (2) if this thing goes more than three weeks you can consider yourself fired."

When Creighton hung up the telephone, Phil's angry retort still echoed in his ear. Phil Richards threatened to get an attorney immediately if Creighton took any type of adversive action. Richards said Creighton put him in a classic Catch-22 position. To do so to an employee is grossly unfair. He claimed that he was just doing his patriotic duty. Creighton felt that he had a business necessity reason for terminating Phil should the trial go on because accommodation should only go so far. If Phil was in prison, Creighton reasoned, he could replace him, so why should this situation be different? After all, a small operation has practically no slack. Everyone had to be present to get the job done. Just to be on the safe side, though, the store owner decided to talk to a labor attorney friend about the situation he now faced.

Discussion Questions

1. Did Creighton make a good personnel decision?
2. Does an employer have a right to pay an employee's salary less the amount paid by the court for jury duty?
3. Can an employee be fired because of jury duty commitment?

78 Fort Pierce Truck Personnel Company

The Fort Pierce (Florida) Truck Personnel Company is a subsidiary of Worldwide Corporation of Pennsylvania. The Florida company's principal business is long-distance hauling up and down the eastern seaboard. In 1988, the trucking company hired its first woman driver, Gina Hall.

Mrs. Gina Hall, a former corporate accountant, gave up her white-collar job in Elizabethtown, Pennsylvania, in 1986 to enroll in tractor-trailer school. There she met her husband, Harry, who was a 20-year veteran of the road. Harry was certified to teach truck driving in Pennsylvania and Florida. When Gina and Harry met, he was an instructor and she was a student at the MTA Truck Driving School in Elizabethtown. During the summer of 1988, the Halls decided to apply for driving jobs with Fort Pierce Truck Personnel Company. They did so on the advice of a friend who was a company employee. During the period 1986–88 she gained experience with three different trucking companies.

As a strategy, the couple decided to have Harry apply for a job there first. However, when Gina returned her husband's completed application to the company, the office dispatcher asked her where her application was. She told the dispatcher that she had not completed one. After learning of her driving experience, the dispatcher encouraged her to do so. Harry was hired in one day and put on the road the next. She waited 40 days to be hired. The company representatives stipulated that she would work primarily with her husband. There were a series of delays until finally she called the operations manager in Pennsylvania to ask if her being a woman was a problem. The manager said no. She next had to pass an extremely difficult road test. (Her husband was not subjected to any road test.) Before she could be hired, though, she faced an interview by a headquarters manager who flew down from Pittsburgh. Finally, in October 1988, she was hired officially as the company's first woman driver. On her first day the dispatcher told her that they needed a driver to substitute for a sick team member and asked her if she was ready to go, right then. She would have been riding with another man, and the manager said right in front of her that he did not want to face that issue yet. So, someone else was assigned. According to Gina, "Trucking is a tough business. Being a woman driver clearly puts me at a distinct disadvantage." Despite the perceived disadvantage, she was earning $500 a week with the company. In late November an event occurred, she says, that led to the dismissal of both her and her husband Harry. On a trip to Paoli, Pennsylvania, the Halls met a southbound company team that shouldn't have been where it was. "We knew when that team left the Fort Pierce terminal—we were there—and there was no way they could be where they were on the road without grossly exceeding the speed limit," Gina said. "Not only that, they were off route, on the wrong interstate." During their visit to Worldwide headquarters in Pennsylvania, the Halls reported the incident to a company official. After they returned to Fort Pierce the next day, they were fired.

When the couple asked why there were being fired, they were told that they did not have "a Worldwide attitude" and that their performance was poor. The company spokesman refused to define the poor performance. Later, the dismissal decision was referred to a Worldwide grievance committee. That committee refused to hear her complaint. Afterwards, she decided to seek legal recourse. She retained an attorney to represent her when she presented her case before the state's deferral agency, the Florida Commission on Human Relations. In the 1989 hearing concerning her dismissal, the company stated that they terminated her at the end of her 30-day probation period "as a result of her poor performance." The briefs submitted by the company stated that "Gina Hall's team was taking too much time to complete a trip."

Gina counters Worldwide's claims by saying the company's subsidiary discriminated against her by:

- Hiring her as someone who occasionally would ride and drive with other drivers than her husband, then refusing to allow her to work with anyone but her husband because other drivers' wives complained.
- Subjecting her to sexual harassment by telling her that "all she had to do was show appreciation and play along."
- Firing her at the same time they fired her husband, who they considered to be a whistle-blower, because she became a personnel problem without him.
- Only once did a dispatcher inform her team that they took too long to make a trip. Their destination dispatcher, however, said that was not a problem. This delay was caused by a truck that was not roadworthy. Gina wrote up 10 safety violations on the vehicle when she returned from the trip.
- At no time were the Halls given a written time schedule to follow.

Discussion Questions

1. If you were the hearing officer in this case, how would you rule and why?
2. Are there federal or, in the case of Florida, state laws that would prohibit the company from discharging either Gina or Harry or both?
3. Under what conditions may a company legitimately fire a whistle-blower? Do any of those conditions exist here? Explain.

---

*79 Recruiting at RUF Corporation**

RUF Corporation is a medium-sized manufacturer located in a large midwestern city. The corporation is a subsidiary of a multinational corporation specializing in consumer home products. Each subsidiary has its own staff departments. Job openings are

---

* Prepared by Professor Floyd G. Willoughby, Oakland University, and James Klonica. Copyright © 1995, Professor Willoughby.

initially posted within the RUF Corporation, which includes all sister subsidiaries and parent corporation. Only then are unfilled openings advertised to external applicants. Regardless of whether the job applicants are internal or external, they all must go through the same recruitment procedures.

Job applicants are interviewed by three individuals. The three interviewers are a member (a potential co-worker) from the hiring department, the director or staff head of the department, and a member of the human resources department. Management feels that these interviews are thorough and meet the needs of the organization and applicants.

The first interview is held with an area supervisor who assesses the technical abilities of the applicant. The supervisor evaluates the applicant's capabilities and potential by comparing the applicant's résumé with the job description. The supervisor uses the interview to clarify any discrepancies in the résumé, ask any questions about the applicant's technical work-related experience, and tries to judge the applicant's ability to learn. The supervisor tries to gain information about the applicant's work history, chronological data, and experience. The educational background of the applicant is assumed to indicate how well the applicant learns new skills.

The second interview is with the department's staff manager. The purpose of this interview is to assess the applicant's conceptual skills. This is accomplished by evaluating the applicant's responses to a series of "true to life" scenarios. This allows the manager to assess the applicant's cognitive skills and the degree to which she or he may possess managerial skills. The manager also evaluates the applicant's résumé, goes over the job application, and, if the applicant is an organization member, calls around to get "word-of-mouth" recommendations. This enables the interviewer to determine if there is a fit between the applicant and the organization.

The third and last phase of the interviewing process involves a member of the human resources department. This staff specialist evaluates the job application and résumé; makes the necessary employer checks and references. (If an applicant is a current organization member, the specialist calls the applicant's immediate superior for a reference.) Also, the staff specialist administers conventional, standardized testing. The applicant's interaction skills also are checked at this point, because it is felt that having good interpersonal skills ensures a productive atmosphere in the workplace.

The organizational level of the job opening and the nature of the job determine which standardized tests are given to the applicant. Tests such as the Myers-Briggs, aptitude and ability, and personality tests are administered to the applicant. The staff specialist has complete discretion over which tests are administered. After the third interview is completed, the three interviewers meet to decide whether an offer should be extended to the applicant.

Section C

Role-Playing Exercises

This section also contains a series of descriptive settings that can be used as a basis for role-playing. Role-playing has some similarity to case studies and incident cases; that is, the individual or group assesses the data presented in the exercise. The problem is isolated, possible causes are considered, and attempts are made to solve the problem.

At this point, however, individuals are chosen to represent each of the key persons in the exercise. Each role-player absorbs all he or she knows about the role to be played. The person attempts to determine how the role-occupant would respond to problem solutions.

Then the role-players come together. They react to each other as the persons in the exercise would likely react to the approaches made by the focal persons. Role-playing allows the participants and observers to simulate how various solutions to problems might be concluded. The involvement of the role-players provides a new dimension to learning experiences in personnel administration.

*80 Selection Interview: A Practice Session**

OBSERVER'S ROLE SHEET

In this round, you will play the role of observer while a manager interviews an applicant for the position of manager trainee, an entry-level management position in a large bank. The position requires a person who is intelligent, educated, and motivated; and who can make decisions, communicate with people at all levels (managers, employees, and customers), and protect and use the bank's assets efficiently.

* This exercise was prepared by Professor John E. Oliver, Valdosta State University.

As an observer, you should take notes on three things:

1. What worked well for the interviewer? This includes questions that elicited good information and actions like smiling, eye-contact, or silence that led applicant to share more information.
2. What worked well for the applicant? This includes questions, answers, or behavioral responses that resulted in positive responses by the interviewer.
3. What questions or behaviors did *not* work well for either party? How could these less effective efforts be redesigned to make them more effective?

The interviewer is trying to learn as much as possible about whether the applicant is qualified for the job based on what he or she knows about job requirements. The following is a list of some types of information that can be gained from the interviewer:

1. Appearance.
2. Self-expression.
3. Responsiveness.
4. Relevance of work experience.
5. Sufficiency of work experience.
6. Skill and competence.
7. Adaptability.
8. Motivation.
9. Interpersonal relations.
10. Leadership.
11. Relevance of schooling.
12. Sufficiency of schooling.
13. Intellectual abilities.
14. Versatility.
15. Breadth and depth of knowledge.
16. Level of accomplishment.
17. Reaction to authority.
18. Ability to work in a group.
19. Attitudes toward achievement.
20. Emotional and social adjustment.
21. Basic values and goals.
22. Self-image.
23. Vitality and energy.
24. Management of time, energy, and money.
25. Maturity and judgment.
26. Cultural breadth.
27. Diversity of interests.
28. Social interests.

The interview should last 10 minutes. After the interview is over, you are to recommend that all three participants (you the observer, the interviewer, and the applicant) take three minutes to reflect silently and in writing, any feelings, ideas, or comments you may wish to share later during the discussion of the interview.

Only after the three minutes of silent note-taking will you begin giving feedback to both the interviewer and applicant on the things that worked well or that could be improved. Be sure to let them talk over your comments and suggestions, their own notes, and anything else they want to discuss.

Remember, your goal as observer is to give positive feedback to both the interviewer and applicant and to make sure they have shared their feelings and knowledge to insure that maximum learning occurs during the experience. Your feedback should take only about five minutes.

APPLICANT'S ROLE SHEET

In this round, you will play the role of a recent college graduate, interviewing for the position of manager trainee, an entry-level management position in a large bank. The position requires a person who is intelligent, educated, and motivated; and who can make decisions, communicate with people at all levels (managers, employees, and customers), and protect and use the bank's assets efficiently.

As an applicant, you can prepare for the interview in three ways:

1. Learn all you can about the job and the organization before the interview.

2. Prepare a list of questions you would like to ask about the job, the organization, promotional opportunities, pay, and benefits.

3. Prepare yourself mentally by relaxing. Remember that the interview is *not* a competition. It is an activity that allows you to see whether there is a match between the job requirements and your qualifications. If the match does not exist, you don't want the job. If the match does exist, the more relaxed you are, the more qualified you will appear. If you do not get the job you are still a "good person." There is nothing you can do in the short-run to better qualify yourself for a job; and you do not want to get a job for which you are unqualified. This leads to dishonesty, failure, or both. Therefore, relax, be confident, and approach the interview as a fact-finding mission. Find out if you can *do* the job, and if you *want* the job.

You may want to ask the questions like the following:

1. What would my duties and responsibilities be?
2. Who would I be working with?
3. If I do a good job, how will I be rewarded?
4. What jobs could I expect to do in the future?
5. What do you like about being a manager in this organization? Dislike?
6. What is the pay range for people in this job?
7. What fringe benefits does the company offer?

As the interview progresses, you may be asked questions to determine your qualifications. Opening questions like, "What college did you attend?" may be followed by probes like, "In what subjects did you do well?" and "Why?" Try to be relaxed and honest.

As the interview comes to a close, try to find out when, where, and how you will be contacted again.

Remember, your goal is to determine whether this job is one for which you are qualified, and one in which you will be satisfied and successful. The interview should last 10 minutes.

INTERVIEWER'S ROLE SHEET

In this round, you will play the role of a manager, interviewing an applicant for the position of manager trainee, an entry-level management position in a large bank. You are seeking to fill the position with a person who is intelligent, educated, and motivated; and who can make decisions, communicate with people at all levels (managers, employees, and customers), and protect and use the bank's assets effectively.

A good interviewer uses three tools effectively:

1. Use *questions* to probe for information (what, how, why).
2. Use *silence* to be receptive to information and to prompt further comment by the interviewee.
3. Use *observation* to see things that are not verbally transmitted.

In addition, a good interviewer recognizes that an effective interview process has three stages *before* the interview, *during* the interview, and *after* the interview. Several important activities are accomplished in each stage.

Before the interview, review key job requirements, review the applicant's résumé or application if available, plan questions to ask based on the applicant's apparent strengths and weaknesses compared to job requirements, and insurance compliance with equal employment opportunity guidelines.

During the interview, use an *opener* (statement or question) to relax the applicant. For example, "Let me tell you a little about the company . . . " or "I see you're from Albany. I used to live there, too." When the applicant is relaxed, use *lead-in statements* to begin the interview. Something like, "What college did you attend?" works well. Make statements and ask planned questions about *relevant* issues, using lead-in questions followed by more in-depth probes like, "Tell me more about that," "When did that happen," "Why?," "Who else was involved?," and "What did you learn from that?"

Relevant issues might include the following:

- Education and training.
- Work experience and skills.
- Job performance evaluations.
- Career interests and work goals.
- Interest in job and company.
- Salary and benefits.
- Self-assessment (*if job related*):
  a. What has led to your success to date?
  b. What motivates you?
  c. What are the important traits of a manager?
  d. What would be a good reason to fire an employee?
  e. What strengths do you have that would help you be successful in this job? Weaknesses?

As the interview progresses, give the applicant a chance to ask questions. Close the interview with a "thank you" and a definite date, time, place, and method of next contact—i.e., "We'll call you at this number next Friday to let you know what comes next. We still have three people to interview".

Ordinarily, a good interviewer waits until after all candidates are interviewed, then reviews all applicants before making decisions. The decision then is communicated as promised.

Remember, your goal is to determine whether the applicant has the necessary skills, knowledge, abilities, and motivation to perform the job well. The interview should last 10 minutes.

81 Follow-Up Recruiting Effort*

A. Preparation for role-playing.
   1. This case features a follow-up recruiting effort on a good prospect. Two years earlier, the applicant had rejected your offer in favor of another firm's offer of employment.
   2. Background information is read aloud to all.
   3. The class is divided into groups of three, and three roles (Pat, recruiter; Terry, applicant; and observer) are assigned by mutual agreement of the group members.
   4. The roles should be played spontaneously, after reading the role instructions. Players should not read each other's roles.

B. The role-playing process.
   1. Each group starts on signal and plays each case segment as directed. Total time will be 15 minutes.
   2. Observers watch and prepare to report.

BACKGROUND INFORMATION

This case involves three follow-up telephone calls from Pat to Terry, a young person who two years ago rejected the firm's offer in favor of other employment. The telephone calls are independent. Each contact has a different outcome. After these segments are completed, a final scene takes place in Pat's office. We listen first, however, to a telephone call.

ROLE FOR TERRY

About two years ago you graduated from a local college and took a job with a small company that manufactures various kinds of electronic equipment. You took this job after a great deal of soul searching because it looked like a great opportunity.

The first part of this exercise is divided into three segments, each one representing a telephone call to you from Pat, a recruiter you got to know and like when you were trying to decide which job offer to accept. Pat will be "calling" to see how you're getting along in your job; and each of the three times you will have a different answer.

1. On the first call, say you're happy with your work, but the training wasn't very good and your boss is a problem.

---

* Prepared by Professor Allen J. Schuh, California State University, Hayward, California.

2. On the second call say you are completely happy with the job, your supervisor, your co-workers, and you know you made the right decision. But offer to get together for lunch sometime.
3. On the third call say you're not sure about your decision anymore because the job isn't very challenging. The people are fine, but you don't seem to be getting anywhere.

The second part of this exercise is set in Pat's office where you've come in to talk about your career. Let Pat try to sell you again, but don't be an eager buyer. Remember, another company could be worse than your current employer.

ROLE FOR PAT

You are a recruiter in a personnel department in a smaller city. Several years ago you became acquainted with Terry, a sharp young person who was graduating from a local college. You had high hopes for a recruitment, but at the last minute the applicant accepted other employment after a great deal of wavering. Today is a slow day in your office and on these occasions you go through your follow-up file. You've decided to call Terry to see how the current job is going.

The first part of this case is divided into three segments, each one representing a telephone call to Terry. Your purpose in calling is the same each time, to consider a new employment offer from you. Assume that each call you make to him is the first one in six months. Terry will have a different answer each time. Each "phone call" should last two to four minutes.

Following the telephone calls, the second part of the exercise is set in your office when Terry comes in to talk once again about your company. Good luck in your recruiting.

INSTRUCTIONS FOR OBSERVERS

This exercise allows you to pretend you are wiretapping three telephone conversations between Pat (recruiter) and Terry (applicant), and then you will eavesdrop on a meeting in Pat's office. The first three segments of the exercise involve telephone conversations in which Pat calls Terry to find out how the job has gone; and to see whether Terry might now be ready to switch companies, after finding out that the present employment has some drawbacks.

Focus your attention on Pat's approach. For each of the "calls," what could be done differently? Summarize your reactions to the telephone calls after all three have been completed.

Segment Four is set in Pat's office. Note these things:

a. Pat's opening and the development of appeals.
b. How you would react if you were Terry.
c. Whether Pat pushes too hard, given that Terry has already come into the office.

82 Turning Down an Eager Applicant*

A. Preparation for role-playing.
   1. In this exercise, participants will be asked to role-play a case involving an eager but unacceptable applicant.
   2. Participants are divided into groups of three (one or two groups may contain two persons to handle groups not divisible by three).
   3. In each group, one participant takes the role of the recruiter, another takes the role of the applicant, and the third acts as observer (in two-person groups, the observer is omitted).
   4. When all have completed reading the instructions and background material, the role-players will set aside their instructions and prepare to act their parts in a natural way.
   5. Observers should be ignored by the role-players and should make themselves as unobtrusive as possible.

B. The role-playing process.
   1. The applicants are asked to turn away from their groups. At a signal they will return, indicating their arrival at the personnel department. From this point in, participants will act in their roles.
   2. Role-playing ensues for about 10 minutes of interaction.
   3. Observers watch and prepare to report.

C. Reports from observers and participants.
   1. The observer reports with references to the instructions to the observer.
   2. The applicant (Bobby) reports on how they felt as they talked with recruiter Kim, especially when they learned of rejection.
   3. The Kim's report, on what they would do differently next time in similar circumstances.

BACKGROUND INFORMATION

The case involves recruiter Kim and an applicant named Bobby. Bobby will soon graduate from college. Bobby is a conscientious student who gets slightly better than average grades, is a persistent worker, and does a good job of career planning. Two-and-a-half-months ago, Bobby met Kim on campus and began to talk seriously about joining the company. After two interviews, Bobby took the screening tests and completed the application, which has been pending for several weeks now. At this point, Bobby has just decided to drop in on Kim in the personnel department to see if any word has been received on the application.

---

* Prepared by Professor Allen J. Schuh, California State University, Hayward, California.

ROLE FOR KIM

For the past two-and-a-half weeks, you have been recruiting Bobby for the company. In today's in-basket you found a memo indicating that Bobby's application had been rejected by the prospective department manager. Your task now is to contact Bobby and give the bad news, a task which is especially difficult because Bobby is quite eager to join the company.

ROLE FOR BOBBY

On the spur of the moment, you've decided to drop in at the personnel department to talk with Kim about your pending application. It's over two weeks since the application was filed, and you are especially eager to get official word of your acceptance since you've told all your friends about the company. Also, you know how pleased your parents will be, because one of them is now employed with the company in another division.

You are about to be told by recruiter Kim that your application has been rejected, an outcome you didn't expect and cannot accept. Your task is to give Kim as hard a time as you can. Make Kim uncomfortable. As far as you know, you meet all the qualifications. Kim had led you to expect acceptance. Maybe an error has been made somewhere. Maybe Kim was just stringing you along. You don't know the reason for taking so long to find out, and you don't care about it, you just want to know what went wrong.

INFORMATION FOR OBSERVER

You are overhearing a conversation between Kim, a recruiter, and an applicant Bobby. Make special note of the following:

a. The manner in which recruiter Kim leads to and breaks the bad news to Bobby.
b. The way you would have felt if you were Bobby.
c. What Bobby did that made Kim seem to feel uneasy.
d. The ways Kim tries to accommodate Bobby's disappointment. Do not enter into the discussion in any way. Learn what you can by "listening in."

---

*83 The New General Supervisor**

You have just been promoted to the position of general supervisor, department two, of Colby Manufacturing, Inc. Your department is one of three manufacturing departments reporting to a manufacturing superintendent.

---

* This exercise was prepared by Professor Ronald W. Clement, Murray State University.

Colby employs 250 people, as revealed by the organization structure, and most of them work in manufacturing. Table 1 presents a demographic breakdown of the company; Exhibit 1 shows the organization structure of the company.

You joined Colby as a manufacturing supervisor in department one in June 1978, after graduating with a bachelor's degree in business from a southwestern U.S. university. After one year, you were transferred to a similar position in department three. Your recent promotion (January 1982) was a result of your excellent performance as a supervisor. You seem to be well known and well liked in most parts of the organization, although there appeared to be some resentment (especially among the nonsupervisory employees) when you first joined the organization. Apparently some of the veteran employees disliked having to work for a newly hired white woman, age 22.

Now that you have been promoted to the position of general supervisor of department two, you have heard new rumors of discontent about working for a woman. These rumors regard the attitudes of your two new peers in departments one and three, and two of your subordinate supervisors in department two.

TABLE 1 Company Breakdown

	Supervisory			*Nonsupervisory*		
	Total	*Women*	*Black*	*Total*	*Women*	*Black*
Accounting	1	—	—	3	—	—
Personnel	1	—	—	2	—	—
Sales	1	—	—	10	—	1
Purchasing	11	—	—	1	—	—
Manufacturing	19	1	2	210	105	110

Note: There are 50 black women.

EXHIBIT 1 Organization Chart for Colby Manufacturing, Inc.

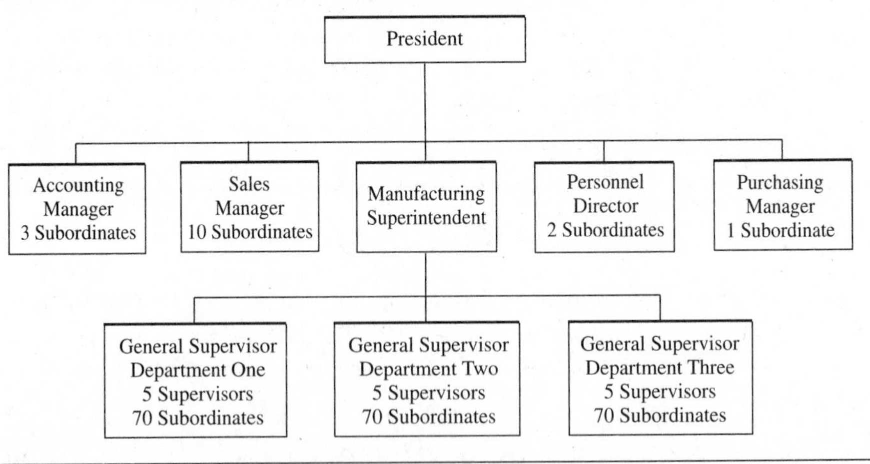

Although you do not consider yourself to be a militant feminist, you are concerned that there are so few blacks and women in supervisory positions in your firm. Although no charges of discrimination have been filed against Colby Manufacturing, you believe this is a likely possibility, especially in manufacturing. Even your department could be the focus of such a charge.

You would like to investigate to determine whether the firm is in violation of equal employment legislation. If you find that a real problem exists (and it probably does), you would like to propose a way to correct the situation.

Discussion Questions

1. How would you go about investigating the extent of the problem (e.g., to whom would you speak? What records or procedures would you check?).
2. Assuming you conclude that the changes for discriminatory charges are great, what action would you propose? To whom? How?

---

*84 Termination Interview: The Pink Slip Exercise**

BACKGROUND INFORMATION

The pink slip has long been a signal of employment termination. It can be quite a psychological blow to a person to hear this phrase: "Your services are no longer required." Naturally, the termination may cause desperate financial problems, too.

On the organization's side of the ledger, there are any number of situations in which termination—the pink slip—is necessary. From the perspective of an individual manager, there may be no choice in the matter. It may simply be the manager's job to pass along the bad news to the other person. The experience may be associated with anxiety, regret, and guilt.

Because many people have not had experience terminating an employee, some guidelines are offered:

1. The manager's major task is to be clear in letting the person know that he or she has really been terminated.
2. The other person may try to reverse the decision, but this is not possible. The manager can save unnecessary argument if the finality of the decision is made very clear.
3. The manager wishes to communicate the terms of the termination clearly, including the effective date, information about severance pay (if any), information about other benefits and rights, and other information.

---

* This exercise was prepared by Professor Jack L. Mendleson, Radford University.

4. While the manager may wish to help the person find a new job, that help could be postponed for now. The other person probably needs to absorb the fact of the termination for a while.

In short, the termination interview is primarily a one-way communication from the manager, in which he or she presents the facts and checks to see if the other person understands those facts. The termination interview need not be lengthy. Ten minutes is probably enough time.

THE EXERCISE

Two or three rounds of multiple role-playing are best. The group should be divided into small groups of three. The instructor will tell you how the three roles will be allocated:

Note: The regional manager should read *only* the "role for regional manager." The store manager should read *only* the "role for store manager." The observer should read *both* roles and "observer instructions." NOW STOP READING! Do not read on until assignments have been made.

Instructions

1. Be sure you know which role you are to play.
2. Read your assigned roles carefully and decide what you plan to say to the other person in playing your part.
3. Set aside the papers. The observer should sit to the side and should not intrude.
4. Conduct the interview for 10 minutes.
5. The observer should report his or her findings to both people, and all three should discuss how the interview went and how you felt about it.
6. The instructor may have further instructions for you.

ROLE FOR THE REGIONAL MANAGER—(Not to be read by the store manager)

Today you have an unpleasant job. You must terminate X, a store manager with 15 years of service.

This store manager has been warned many times about his or her customer relations. He or she promises to work on it but never seems to improve. He or she was sent to a Dale Carnegie course and to an executive program in human relations at the local university. Some of it may have helped, but only temporarily.

You don't want to get into all the old disagreements again. You want to terminate the manager. Here is what you want to do:

1. Let X know that this is the end of the line. There is no appeal. X is terminated. This is his or her last day on the job.

2. Follow the guideline of procedures in the attached memo from the director of personnel.
3. Let X know that you personally are willing to help him or her find a new job with another company.
4. Prepare yourself as best you can to deal with whatever X may say. He or she may be mad at you, the company, or the world—and may yell or cry.
5. Review the performance summary for X.

One thing in your favor is this: The termination should not come as a big surprise for X. He or she has been warned many times. He or she will not be the first store manager to be terminated.

A performance summary for X is attached.

When you have studied the materials and have an idea of what you need to say, call the store manager into your (imaginary) office and discuss the termination with X. Limit the meeting to about 10 minutes. Address X by his or her real first name.

MEMORANDUM—(Not to be read by the store manager)

To: (You), Regional manager

From: Marion Karline, Corporate Director of Personnel

Subject: Termination of X, Store Manager

It is always a difficult task to terminate someone with long service. I hope I can help you a little in this assignment. Let me review the corporate policies and procedures with you. It is essential these be followed to the letter.

1. Today is X's last day at the store. This is company policy for terminated people so they don't damage other people's morale. He or she should be instructed to turn in all keys to the regional office at the end of his or her shift today.
2. In lieu of notice, he or she will be given two weeks' of full pay.
3. Then he or she will receive the regular severance. It is two weeks' pay for every year of service. In this manager's case, that means 30 weeks of full pay. The checks will continue to be deposited in the person's checking account.
4. The company's portion of insurance premiums will be paid until X accepts a new full-time position or until the end of the 30 weeks, whichever comes first.
5. If X has any questions about these severance arrangements, he or she may phone me at 555-0007 or visit me in my office.
6. I am knowledgeable about jobs in this industry and will help X find a new job if he or she wishes. I also have some ideas on résumés, interviewing, and the whole job search process. I have known X for a long time, and we have a friendly relationship. I really want to help.

FOR THE REGIONAL MANAGER—(Not to be read by the store manager)

Performance Summary for X, Store Manager

Hired in January, 15 years ago, as a stock person.

Worked up through numerous positions, becoming store manager 10 years ago.

Performance as Store Manager

Rated as an adequate manager through last year. Continuously rated "not immediately promotable."

Last year, with the new corporate policies regarding customer relations, X was rated low on customer relations; while ratings for performance against quota and cost savings continued as before, adequate but not outstanding.

X was informed three times during the year that his overall performance was rated unsatisfactory, mainly because of his inadequate customer relations. X was shown the complaints received by several customers about his rude behavior in dealing with refunds and exchanges.

X has met with the regional manager on three occasions about customer relations and once with the corporate director of personnel. X was coached carefully and specifically over a period of one year.

ROLE FOR THE STORE MANAGER—(Not to be read by the store manager)

You have been with the ABC Stores for 15 years and have been a manager for the last 10 of those years.

You are about to meet with your boss, the regional manager. This may be the day you get fired. You've been warned about customer relations a lot, but you just don't agree with the company's liberal policy.

You would hate to be fired. Your spouse is out of work, and you are sole support for your three kids. You have always worked here at the store. You don't know any other kind of work. You have no idea what you might do for a job if you lose this one.

If the regional manager does talk about firing you, talk him or her out of it. After all, the company owes you something for your 15 years of loyal service.

If the manager finally does fire you, you're not going to take it without telling him or her off.

Call the regional manager by his or her real first name.

OBSERVER INSTRUCTIONS

1. Study the regional manager's role with him or her. Do not give advice.
2. Keep notes on how well the interview progresses:
   a. How clear is the communication of termination?
   b. What is the regional manager doing or saying which detracts from the message?

- How would you characterize the regional manager's behavior?
- Rough (too harsh, etc.).
- Too soft, wishy-washy.
- Professional.
- Friendly.
- Helpful.
- Others.

   c. How would you assess the regional manager's overall success in the meeting?

- Very effective.
- Effective.
- So-so.
- Not every effective.
- What feelings do you have for the store manager?
- No sympathy, he got what he or she deserved.
- Strong sympathy for him or her.
- Other.

Part 3

Other Exercises and Experiences in Human Resource Management

The following is a series of exercises to be completed by the user of this book. Some of them are cost-benefit exercises. They require the participant to calculate specific costs of a personnel function, to calculate or infer its benefits, and to recommend whether to continue the activity. If it is to be continued, the participant must specify the future form or approach.

The other exercises require the participant to take part in data-gathering before analysis takes place. In some of the exercises, the participant enters the field, observes, and gathers and analyzes the data. In others, the participant interacts with other participants in the classroom or other settings. The exercise takes place and analysis and recommendations follow. Both of these approaches have in common participant input to the exercise before analysis can take place.

The purpose of these exercises is to provide the participant the opportunity to put his or her knowledge of personnel activities to work. Not only are participants building their decision-making skills in these exercises but they are also developing some more specific skills in designing and evaluating such activities as human resource planning, recruitment and selection programs, performance evaluation systems, work scheduling, and compensation and benefit plans. The participant will realize there is still much work to be done after the decisions are made and also will realize some of the problems involved in implementing the decisions. Participants find these specific skills useful, because most managerial positions are involved in implementing and evaluating personnel policies and programs.

Section A

Cost-Benefit and Field Exercises

*85 Total Quality Management in Human Resource Management**

CASE OVERVIEW

TQM announced by top management as a new program. Management has a desire to jump on the bandwagon of "quality" but has not a real understanding of TQM. What should HR do to maximize the success of the company's TQM efforts?

CASE BACKGROUND

StarShade, a publicly traded company, has experienced steady growth in market share since its founding in 1984. StarShade is a manufacturing company specializing in the design, manufacture, and sale of fashion sunglasses in the United States. The domestic market for up-scale, fashion-oriented sunglasses has been increasing on average by 20 percent since 1986. However, during the past year, high-quality and low-cost foreign imports have been flooding the domestic market and threaten to seriously erode both StarShade's present market share and its profits. Forecasts by the U.S. Department of Commerce suggest foreign imports to the U.S. sunglass market will continue to increase. StarShade is at a critical stage in its existence and needs to develop a strategy that will allow it to successfully meet the challenge posed by foreign competition. StarShade's president is committed to developing a

* This exercise was prepared by Professor James H. Browne, University of Southern Colorado.

strategy for StarShade that will protect existing market share while maintaining historic levels of profitability. Toward this end the president met with StarShade's management team in a weekend "strategic planning meeting" to develop the required strategy. The strategic planning meeting resulted in the identification of three specific strategies. The basics of these strategies are:

1. To achieve an annual 10 percent cost reduction in both the design and production departments in each of the next three years.
2. To increase annual sales by 10 percent in each of the next three years.
3. To achieve a "world-class quality" reputation in the sunglass industry within three years.

During the month following the strategic planning meeting, the management team held numerous meetings to identify the means by which these new strategies can be implemented. During these meetings StarShade's management agreed that, by emphasizing the"world-class quality" strategy, the other two strategies would likely be implemented by default. After much discussion StarShade's management team has agreed to launch a total quality management (TQM) initiative as soon as possible. The primary obstacle StarShade's management faces in implementing TQM is that only a few of the management team members really understands all that is involved in TQM. Although there was consensus that TQM is desirable there was no agreement on how to begin. StarShade's HR director was better acquainted with the TQM concept than most of StarShade's other managers, because she recently had attended a series of teleconferences on TQM offered through the local Chamber of Commerce. While the HR director admits she is no "TQM expert" she has persuaded StarShade's management to engage in a brainstorming session to identify some good ideas for implementing TQM.

On the day of the brainstorming meeting the HR director solicited any ideas that StarShade's management believed were relevant to consider regarding TQM. Some of the ideas suggested by StarShade's management during this meeting are presented in Exhibit 1.

EXHIBIT 1 Some Ideas from StarShade's Brainstorming on TQM

1. Invite voluntary participation from all StarShade personnel in TQM (e.g., training, planning sessions, etc.).
2. Require mandatory participation of all StarShade personnel in TQM (e.g., training, planning sessions, etc.).
3. Involve only representatives of various employee groups in TQM first by asking for volunteers and secondarily by mandatory assignments.
4. Hire an outside TQM expert to manage StarShade's TQM efforts.
5. Provide TQM training only to StarShade's management so present management personnel can develop and implement TQM.

EXHIBIT 1 Some Ideas from StarShade's Brainstorming on TQM *(concluded)*

6. Provide TQM training to all StarShade's personnel (i.e., management and nonmanagement) so all organizational members will be active participants in TQM.
7. Provide individual incentives for TQM involvement.
8. Provide group incentives for TQM involvement.
9. Once basic TQM responsibilities are identified for StarShade employees, write that responsibility into each employee's job description.
10. Obtain an "off-the-shelf" TQM program for immediate implementation by StarShade.
11. Focus primarily on improving StarShade's ability to meet *external* customer requirements as the number 1 priority.
12. Focus primarily on improving StarShade's ability to meet *internal* customer requirements as the number 1 priority.
13. Immediately require that every department begin collecting data that will serve as a benchmark for any improvements in performance (e.g., percentage of defective products, average number of days to move from new product design to actual production and marketing, etc.)
14. Establish the human resource department as the responsible organizational unit for StarShade's TQM efforts.
15. Identify both the production and design departments as having the highest priority in TQM implementation.
16. Target all departments as having high priority in TQM implementation.
17. Establish a new department that will have responsibility for TQM organizationwide.
18. Commit to one or two major problems regarding present quality and develop a timeline for their resolution.
19. Commit to adopting incremental change as preferable to attempting quick successes in resolving major quality problems.

ASSIGNMENT

Using the form below individually assign merit ratings of 1 through 5 to each TQM idea, using these ratings:

1 = idea greatly inhibits TQM.

2 = idea somewhat inhibits TQM.

3 = idea neither inhibits nor facilitates TQM.

4 = idea somewhat facilitates TQM.

5 = idea greatly facilitates TQM.

Then, provide a brief rationale to support each merit rating. Lastly, break into groups of 4-5 students and discuss the relative merits of each of the 19 ideas and share your rationale with others in your small group.

Idea No.	*Merit Rating*	*Rationale for Rating of Ideas Merit*
1	______	______
2	______	______
3	______	______
4	______	______
5	______	______
6	______	______
7	______	______
8	______	______
9	______	______
10	______	______
11	______	______
12	______	______
13	______	______
14	______	______
15	______	______
16	______	______
17	______	______
18	______	______
19	______	______

86 Job Description Exercise*

Job analysis is a term that is applied to the systematic study of work in industries. It is the process of identifying by observation, interview, and study all of the significant worker activities and:

1. To establish job specifications.
2. To determine wage structures.

---

* Prepared by Vandra L. Huber. Copyright © 1984 by Vandra L. Huber. This exercise is an adaptation of class materials originally prepared by E. J. McCormick and William E. Scott, Jr.

3. To resolve issues of comparable worth and equal pay.
4. To determine qualifications to be use in employee selection.
5. To derive training programs.
6. To identify job parameters so that performance appraisal can be based on job duties and tasks.
7. To design or restructure jobs.

While job analysis can be conducted in many different ways (i.e., interviews, structured questionnaires, behavioral sampling, participant-observation), the culmination of the analysis is a written description of the job. Sometimes called the *job specification*, the job description is a written statement of purpose, duties, equipment, working conditions, and relation of a particular job to other jobs. While job descriptions may detail many different aspects of a job, nine functional areas are primary. They include:

1. Identification.
2. Job summary.
3. Supervision.
4. Work performed.
5. Training and experience.
6. Working conditions.
7. Job hazards.
8. Physical demands.
9. Relationship to other jobs.

EXHIBIT 1 Position Description

1. **Identification**

Job title ______________ Code ______________
Alternative title ______________ Date ______________
Department ______________ Analyst ______________
Name of incumbent ______________

2. **Job Summary**

____

3. **Supervision**

A. *Supervision Received*

Immediate supervision ______________ Overall supervision ______________
Direction only ______________ Understudy ______________

____

B. *Supervision Given*

Coordinates systems ______________ Supervises assistants ______________
Supervises work group ______________ Supervises fellow workers ______________
Number of departments or units supervised ______________
List: ______________

____

____

____

EXHIBIT 1 Position Description *(concluded)*

Number supervised:
Full-time employees ________ Part-time employees ________

4. **Work Performed**
   Descriptions:

5. **Training and Experience**
   A. *Previous Job Experience* (desired or necessary, or both)
   B. *Schooling and Training*
      1. General schooling
      2. Special training
   C. On-the-job training

6. **Working Conditions** (specify percent of time exposed to conditions)

___ Inside	___ High Temp	___ Toxic Conditions	___ Odors
___ Outside	___ Low Temp	___ Vibration	___ Dust
___ Noise	___ Fumes	___ Poor Ventilation	___ Other
___ Slippery Floors	___ Moving Objects	___ Electrical Shocks	

   Remarks:

7. **Physical Demands** (specify percentage of time)

___ Lifting	___ Pushing	___ Standing	___ Other
___ Carrying	___ Pulling	___ Sitting	

   Remarks:

8. **Relation to Other Jobs**
   A. Promotion
      from ________________________________
   B. Promotion
      to ________________________________
   C. Transfer to and from ________________________________

IDENTIFICATION

Job title. Record in this space the name by which the job is usually known. When jobs are known by various titles, the most commonly known title should be used. A list of common job titles is contained in the *Dictionary of Occupational Titles*, which is published by the U.S. Department of Labor.

Code. In this space write the job code that is listed by the Department of Labor.

Alternative title. Some jobs in an organization have more than one job title. If this is so, for the position you are examining, write in the alternative title in this space.

Department. Because organizations may have individuals performing similar identical work in different departments, it may be important to identify for which department the job is performed. This may be critical in determining wages, since job incumbents performing jobs of the same title may in actuality be performing different work (i.e., a secretary in the legal department may prepare briefs, while a secretary in another department may prepare accounts receivable records).

JOB SUMMARY

(Complete this section after all other sections.)

The purpose of this section is to define the job, pointing out the basic factors that differentiate this job from other jobs. The writing should be concise, complete, and accurate. In this section, action verbs should be used to summarize:

1. What the worker does.
2. How the worker does it.
3. Why the worker does it.

In describing "what" the worker does, include physical and mental actions. In describing "what," avoid general such terms as *prepares* or *operates* because they cannot give a precise picture of the job. Record "how" the work is done, including the machinery and tools used, job knowledge applications, and decisions. Finally, record "why" the worker does the job—in other words, the purpose or expected result or product.

SUPERVISION

In this section, the supervisory relationship is specified. Place an X next to the appropriate descriptor specifying the *amount* of supervision received.

Immediate supervision. Applies to jobs with detailed instructions given to worker and frequent monitoring of work outputs. Applies to well-structured situations with little deviation from established work procedures.

Overall supervision. Worker receives overall supervision but is responsible for determining work procedures within a broad area of operations.

Concerning the supervision given, record:

1. Number of departments supervised.
2. Number of workers supervised.
3. Job titles held by employees who are supervised.

Then put an X next to the *nature* of the supervision given.

Directions only. Worker is permitted to do work without any type of direction or instruction and with little work inspection.

Understudying. This is a special supervisory relationship. Usually associated with job coaching or apprenticeships. The objective is for the subordinate to learn the duties of a higher-level job.

Coordinates operations. Coordinates an organization or phase of operations within an organization. Gives general directions.

Supervises work group. Supervises individuals in a work group. Individuals who fall in this category usually have supervision as a primary job task or duty.

Supervisor's assistants. Supervision is an incidental part of other primary duties. A professor who supervises a secretary is an example of someone in this category.

Working supervisor. This person operates as a worker-supervisor. The individual performs work that is comparable to that performed by the workers he or she supervises. An example is an office manager who coordinates and distributes work to other secretaries.

WORK PERFORMED

In this section, the duties and tasks that the worker (sometimes called a "job incumbent") performs are recorded. Complete statements beginning with action verbs should be utilized. Each descriptive statement should describe *what* the worker does, *how* the worker does it, *why* the work operation is performed, and *what tools and equipment* are used. The writing style should be uniform. Begin each sentence with a verb in third-person singular. Avoid unnecessary words or words that have more than one meaning. Avoid vague terms, such as *performs* and *coordinates*. Be specific.

Break each job apart into its relevant duties. You may wish to summarize, under each duty, the specific tasks which comprise that duty.

Time. Because it is important to determine which job tasks are the most important, you also need to identify the amount of time devoted to each task. Use multiples of 5 for the percentage. Use "N" for those operations requiring less than 5 percent of the time. Some job cycles involve hours or days; some, weeks; and some, months. Record the percentages of time for each operation in the same manner, regardless of the length of the cycle. List first the job tasks that take the most time and follow with those of decreasing time importance. If time figures cannot be calculated, explain why not. Be sure to specify what time dimension you are using when you figure the percentages.

TRAINING AND EXPERIENCE

In this section, it is important to carefully describe previous job experience and the schooling and training necessary to perform well on the job. You should describe the training and experience necessary to do the tasks that comprise the job, rather than the specific training that the job incumbent possesses. Your description should include:

A. *Previous job experience*. Describe the type, amount, and level of previous experience that is considered necessary and desirable. Differentiate between *desired* and *required* experience.

B. *Schooling and training*. Schooling and training refers to job-related knowledge that is not acquired on the job. Required job training is the minimum amount of training necessary to perform the job acceptably.

General schooling refers to education of a general academic nature that contributes to the worker's ability to follow instruction and to acquisition of knowledge, such as computer languages or shorthand. This education refers to what is acquired in liberal arts programs of a high school.

Special training refers to job-oriented training, which may be obtained through apprenticeship, business colleges, and correspondence courses. You should list the specific courses, such as bookkeeping, machinist apprenticeship, and so on.

On-the-job-training refers to skills acquired on the job. It is training beyond that obtained from experience in other jobs or from special training programs. For example, an accountant may have to learn the specific account receivable processes used by the firm. Specific skills that must be learned on the job should be *listed* (e.g., two weeks required to learn computer-monitoring procedures).

WORKING CONDITIONS

In this section describe the environment in which the work is to be performed. List the approximate percentages of time the worker is exposed to each condition. Be specific when describing the environment in which the work will be performed in. Add clarifying statements, such as "works in temperatures ranging from 40 to 65 degrees." If time percentages cannot be accurately estimated, use "O" for "occasionally" and "F" for "frequently."

JOB HAZARDS

Each work environment contains special dangers (e.g., molten steel or a line drive) both inside and outside (e.g., a windowless swinging door to a fast-food kitchen). Conditions to be observed and noted may include high temperatures, fumes, rickety shelving, waxed floors, and . . . the list can be endless.

PHYSICAL DEMANDS

Record the percentage of time the workers performing the job spend lifting, carrying, pushing, and pulling. For lifting, indicate the amount in *pounds*. Be sure to indicate the percentage of time spent standing and sitting, and list other physical demands as necessary for the successful performance of the job.

RELATIONSHIP TO OTHER JOBS

If the job is an established career path or promotional sequence, then it is important to indicate the relationship between the job being analyzed and other jobs. *Item A* indicates the position from which workers are promoted. If the job traditionally is associated with promotion to a particular position, this should be noted in *Item B*. If there are no advancement possibilities, such a fact should also be noted. *Item C* should include the titles of jobs to which the worker may normally be laterally assigned within the department on a permanent basis. *Item D* should be used to list the titles or job specifics to which the worker may be temporarily assigned or transferred (i.e., proofreader to paste-up artist).

*87 A Field Study of Business Recruiting Practices**

Different companies in different areas of the country use varying sources to obtain their employees. Most texts provide a model which describes these practices and one is duplicated in Table 1. You will notice that each category has one additional column, which is the point of this exercise.

First form a group of three to four persons, then elect one of your group to be the spokesperson. Call a business in your area (preferably a larger business with several hundred employees) and speak to the personnel manager or a knowledgeable person in the personnel area. Ask this person the following question: What (internal, external) sources of recruits do you use for your (blue) (gray) (white) (managerial, technical, professional) employees? You will probably find that you may have to mention a few of the sources to aid them in understanding what you are referring to, and you will probably find it most advantageous to divide the questions into internal versus external by level of job.

The professor will make sure that each group in the class obtains information from a different business and thus maximizes information obtained and minimizes time lost for the business. Check the chart each time the business mentions a source and be careful not to imply that they are right, wrong, or different from others in the responses they give.

When the personnel representative has finished all of the questions, quickly compare your findings with those listed as "usual." Notice any differences and ask the personnel representative why he or she does not use that source. Write down any comments the representative makes in the space provided on the next pages.

---

* Prepared by Jerry L. Wall. Copyright © 1982 by Business Publications, Inc. Reprinted by permission of Business Publications, Inc.

TABLE 1 Sources of Recruiting Various Types of Employees

Sources	*Blue-Collar*	*Gray-Collar*	*White-Collar*	*Managerial, Technical Professional*
Internal:				
Job posting and bidding	X	X	X	
Friends of present employees	X	X	X	
Skills inventories	X	X	X	X
External:				
Walk-ins, including previous employees	X	X	X	
Agencies				
Temporary help				
Private employment agencies			X	
Public employment agencies*	X	X	X	
Executive search firms				X
Educational institutions:				
High school	X	X	X	
Vocational/technical	X	X	X	X
Colleges and universities				X
Other:				
Union	X			
Professional associations				X
Military services	X			X
Former employees	X	X	X	X

*Normally called U.S. Employment Services.

COMMENTS

Discuss the comments obtained within your group. Does your group agree or disagree with the commentary about that source? Jot down your feelings:

Are there any characteristics of your labor market the businesses have mentioned that would cause it to vary from the average? If so, note these below:

Each group of the class now should be given an opportunity to present and discuss their findings. Do you find substantial differences between groups? If so, note these below as the groups make their presentations:

Discuss in the class how any common differences from the model in the text reflect characteristics of the local labor market. Examples:

____

____

____

____

Discuss how any individual company differs from the local average (or the text model). Could such differences reflect company idiosyncrasies? Discuss how these can emerge and indicate your responses below:

____

____

____

____

88 Standard Interview Form*

(You may look back and forth between the application and this interview form during the interview. Make all of your notes only on this form. With young applicants, start the interview with education. With older applicants, you should start the interview with work history.)

Applicant's Name ______________ Date of Interview ______________

Interviewer ______________________________

Education and Activities

a1 Tell me about the grades you made in high school (and college).

a2 Compare grades in your major versus overall/first-year versus last-year attendance.

a3 Why did you go to college?

a4 Why did you go to this particular college?

b1 How were your college expenses paid?

b2 Are all of your full-time and part-time jobs reported on the application form?

b3 What were your housing arrangements? What were your responsibilities?

c1 Were you in any student activities? Which ones? (List them if they are not reported on the application form.)

c2 How did you get into these?

c3 Did these organizations have any special purposes? How effective were they at those purposes?

* Prepared by Allen J. Schuh, California State University, Hayward.

c4 How much time did they take?

c5 What responsibilities did you have?

c6 How effective were you? Give some examples.

c7 Any connection with any of these now?

c8 How well did you get along with the other people in these activities?

d1 Were there any courses in college you did not complete?

d2 Did you change your major while in college?

d3 When did you study?

d4 How much did you study?

d5 What did you think of your teachers?

d6 How would you evaluate your overall effectiveness as a student?

e1 Did you participate in any sports?

e2 What did you think of your coaches and teammates?

f1 How did you spend your weekends during the academic year?

f2 How did you spend your summers while going to college?

f3 Was there anything you particularly liked/disliked about your school years?

f4 Were there any experiences in school that have been particularly helpful since leaving school?

Military Experience

g1 What is your present situation with regard to military service?

g2 If you have been in military service, start at the time you entered service and describe your different jobs.

g3 What were your responsibilities? How effective were you at these jobs?

g4 Was there anything you particularly liked/disliked about your military experience?

g5 Were there any experiences in the service that have been particularly helpful since leaving the military?

Work History and Experience
(start with first full-time employment)

h1 What was the first full-time job you had?

h2 When was that exactly?

h3 What other jobs did you consider at that time?

h4 Why did you take the one you did?

h5 How do you feel now about your experiences with them?

h6 Why did you leave?

h7 When was that exactly?

h8 What did you do between jobs?

h9 How did you decide to go with the next company?

Note: cycle h2 to h9 for each job.

h10 What are you looking for in your next job?

Specific Job Activities
(start with the most recent employment)

i1 What did you do on this last job?

i2 How effective were you at that job? Give me some examples of your effectiveness.

i3 Describe any record-keeping.

i4 What kind of hours did you have?

i5 How much and how often were you paid?

i6 How much and what kind of travel was involved?

j1 What other people did you work with?

j2 Were there any people you worked with who disliked you?

j3 How well did you report?

j4 To whom did you report?

j5 How often and what did you report?

j6 How did your supervisor know what you were doing?

j7 How well did you and your supervisor get along?

j8 Did you get things done correctly and on time? In general. Specifically.

j9 Did you need to work much overtime?

Your Next Job

k1 Have you discussed this possible job change with (family)? What was the reaction?

k2 How do you and your family feel about your working nights?

k3 How do you and your family feel about your working weekends?

k4 What would be your reaction to being confronted with a mistake that others thought you committed? Has this ever happened? How did you handle it?

Note to interviewer:

Consider the following for Sales, Management, Scientist, and Engineer positions.

Family Responsibilities

l1 Describe for me the neighborhood where you are presently living.

l2 How long have you lived there?

l3 Why did you decide to live there?

l4 How well do you get along with your neighbors?

l5 How do you feel about education?

l6 What do you do around the home? Lawn/house/car?

l7 Do you have any hobbies? What/where/how often/with whom?

l9 What kind of vacations do you take (what do you do)? Describe the last one.

l10 How much time do you spend each week reading: books/magazines/newspapers?

l11 How much time do you spend watching television: favorite programs/those you like less well?

l12 How do you feel about the doctors and hospitals available to you?

Social Life

m1 How often do you entertain?

m2 How often do you go out?

m3 How do you usually spend your lunch time?

m4 How do you spend weekends and holidays?

Social Mobility

n1 To what organizations do you belong?

n2 How long have you been a member?

n3 Why did you join these organizations?

n4 Have you held any offices or been on any committees? What were your responsibilities? How effective were you?

Insurance

o1 What life insurance policies do you have?

o2 How about other forms of insurance?

o3 When did you have your last physical examination?

o4 Any illnesses during the last year?

o5 Any minor chronic conditions? (allergies, lower back)

Financial Picture

p1 What do you think about the income from your present job? How about income from other sources? (How permanent is the source?)

p2 Do you have a checking account? Who handles it? What is its balance?

p3 How do you feel about charge accounts and credit cards?

p4 What kinds of automobiles do you have (make/model year)? How were these cars purchased?

p5 How do you usually pay for major items?

p6 Are your parents/in-laws living? What is their health? Do they get any financial help from you? How much? How often?

p7 Is there any chance that any of them would need to live with you during the next year? How would you handle that?

p8 Do you have any financial obligations of any kind that have not been discussed?

The Future

q1 What would you like to be doing five years from now?

q2 How much money would you like to be making five years from now? Why this amount?

q3 What kinds of people would you like to be working with five years from now?

q4 What kinds of people would you like to associate with socially five years from now?

q5 What do you believe is an ideal job for you?

q6 What do you plan to do after you retire?

Note: Deficiencies in interpersonal relations, motivation, trustworthiness, responsibilities, and effectiveness.

89 Friends Can Get You in Trouble!*

Arthur Nelson smiled expansively at his guest and remarked, "Yes, I do run a tight ship here. I'm very proud of the way I took over this personnel department and made it one of the best around. You can't fault the way I moved Rondo Manufacturing from a 15 percent a year turnover to about 1 percent. That speaks well of my efforts in the company as a whole, too."

Ron Clark looked at his friend and said, "I wish I was in as good shape as you, but this EEO thing really has me bothered." Ron was referring to the fact that he had just received a notice from the State Fair Employment Practices Commission that his company had been charged with discrimination by a minority male. He was expecting a visit from the state EEO investigator in two weeks. "I remember the guy. I talked to him but I could see he really didn't fit in. He'd just moved to town and didn't know anyone in the plant or in town. And you know how close-knit my work groups are."

"You know that reminds me of the way I combated the attitude and motivation problems in my company, too," Arthur remarked. "You remember that we discussed how letting the workers pick who they wanted to work with and recommend their friends for employment would work wonders for morale. And sure enough, it did. Why, that's all we use now!"

"You're right, those recommendations from friends and promotions from within have totally satisfied our employment needs for several years now, too," Ron sighed. "I really can't understand what's wrong with letting your employees pick who they want to work with. It seems to be a great motivational tool, but I have a feeling that's what the state EEO people want to talk to me about. And, Arthur, I have a hunch you may be next in line!"

Do you think there's some truth to Ron's observation on the appropriateness of recruiting from within? Why?

Discussion Questions

1. What are the characteristics, advantages, and disadvantages of the following:
   a. Promotion from within:
   b. Using recommendations from friends:
2. Under what circumstances would these be acceptable sources? Unacceptable?
   a. Acceptable:
   b. Unacceptable:
3. What sources would be more acceptable in terms of providing equal employment opportunity and demonstrate positive recruiting efforts?

---

90 Looking at Résumés*

Your organization has an opening for manager of accounting, a department head position with mid-level management responsibility. The job is a high-stress one, since the incumbent must supervise some 25 professional and clerical employees handling diverse duties. The manager of accounting reports directly to the president, who is a hard-nosed stickler for detail. The president manages with a tight rein and expects not only perfection but immediate solutions to problems.

A newspaper advertisement of the position has yielded, unfortunately, only one response. The following résumé was received in this morning's mail. Because the organization has had a great deal of difficulty filling this job in the past, and turnover in the job has been frequent, you want to give this résumé your immediate attention to see whether the applicant should be hired before he gets away.

Discussion Questions

1. Do you think the applicant is qualified for the job?
2. What additional information would you like to know before answering question 1?

Résumé

NAME:	GEORGE JONES
ADDRESS:	715 Judy Drive Nashville, TN Telephone: (123) 456-7890
PERSONAL:	Born 11-6-32 (Nashville, Tennessee) 5′11″, 185 lbs. Married to Ola Mae Jones 4 children, born 4-20-52, 10-5-58, 2-15-60, 8-2-71
EDUCATION:	H.S. Diploma, Jackson High School Jackson, Mississippi, 1951 BS Degree, University of Southern Tennessee, 1962. Double Major: Accounting and Business Administration MS Degree, Business, California State University, 1978 PhD Degree, Business Administration, University of Mississippi, 1981. Certified Public Accountant—Mississippi and Tennessee Special Courses: "Growth Through Acquisition and Merger Seminar," National Association Wholesalers, 1972. "Sales Management Seminar," National Association Wholesalers, 1968

* Prepared by Professor John E. Oliver, Valdosta State University.

Résumé *(continued)*

PUBLICATIONS AND RESEARCH:	"Transportation Rates," co-authored with Joe Smith. Paper to be presented to Southwest Marketing Association, Atlanta, Georgia, March 1985 Currently doing research in the area of cash budgeting practices in small organizations.
TEACHING EXPERIENCE:	Undergraduate: Principles of Accounting, Intermediate Accounting, Advanced Accounting, Accounting Standards, Cost Accounting. Graduate: Specialized Accounting Problems, Theory Seminars and Special Courses: Program Budgeting Seminar, Florida Department of Health and Rehabilitation, CPA Review Course (Practice), Certified Professional Secretary Review (Accounting).
PROFESSIONAL ORGANIZATIONS:	American Institute Certified Public Accountants American Accounting Association American Society Traffic and Transportation Tennessee Society Certified Public Accountants (member, scholarship committee)
COMMUNITY ACTIVITIES:	Former member of Jackson Junior Chamber of Commerce Former President of Jackson Exchange Club, 1971 (Club won National Big E Award for Excellence during my term of office) Jackson Chamber of Commerce activities: Director 1971–1972 Member of Wholesale-Retail Promotion Committee Chairman—Community Minimum Wage Clinic, January 1970 Salvation Army Building Fund Committee, 1980 Dawn of Hope, Nashville, Tennessee Member—Sheltered Workshop Committee, 1983–1984
WORK EXPERIENCE:	
August 1951 to December 1951	SEARS, ROEBUCK & CO., Jackson, Mississippi Salesclerk
January 1952 to January 1955	EQUITABLE LIFE ASSURANCE SOCIETY, Nashville, Tennessee Assistant Teller Cashier's Office
1955 1956	USAF, Korea & Japan Personnel Specialist. Worked at Wing Headquarters level.

***Résumé** (continued)*

October 1965	SOUTHERN DRUG COMPANY, Jackson, Mississippi Accountant—Operation Manger, Sales Manager Secretary & Treasurer and share in General Management. I am familiar with all phases of Wholesale Drug House operation and have supervised a warehouse employing 33 people. Directed the installation of data processing Unit Record Equipment in 1974. I was responsible forthe activities of 10 salesmen, two buyers, and shared in top management decisions. I have visited several wholesale drug firms and have been active in trade associations.
June 1978 to March 1981	Graduate Student, University of Mississippi
March 1981 to July 1983	Assistant Professor, Accountancy, Tennessee College, Nashville, Tennessee
September 1983 to Present	Associate Professor, Accountancy, Tennessee College, Nashville, Tennessee
TRADE ASSOCIATIONS ACTIVITIES:	Past President, Southern Drug Club, 1973–74 Served four years as Secretary, Drug Travelers of Mississippi.

*91 A Problem of Orientation**

You are Phil Myrich, personnel manager for Wiedno Manufacturing. The plant manager has just asked you to come in to have a talk concerning what he considers an unacceptable rate of turnover in the plant. During the last year you have had approximately 60 percent of your new-hires leave within the first six months. The plant manager has asked you to find out the reason for this problem. When you return to your office, your secretary informs you that Adam Wright, an automobile lathe operator who was hired only two months ago, is scheduled for an exit interview in the next few minutes. You decide to do the exit interview yourself, rather than let the assistant personnel manager, Julie Rogers, do it as she usually does.

---

* Prepared by Jerry L. Wall. Copyright © 1982 by Business Publications, Inc. Reprinted by permission of Business Publications, Inc.

The information you gather is:

Adam reported for work the first as requested at 8:30 AM He met initially with your assistant personnel manager who started by giving him a "pep talk" that was aimed at convincing him the company was a good place to work. Next she read him the job description and gave a brief explanation of his new duties. He was told to get a cup of coffee at the coffee shop next door and return at 10:00 for a general orientation meeting, which he and several other employees would attend.

During this meeting the following subjects were covered:

1. Time-clock requirements.
2. Lunch hours, coffee breaks, and rest periods.
3. Overtime policies.
4. Pay.
5. Attendance, tardiness, and absenteeism.
6. Their immediate job hierarchy.
7. Insurance, pay, medical, and other administrative forms.

They were given a walking tour of the plant, covering all areas and facilities. As each new employee was taken through his or her respective department, each was introduced to the new supervisor. On completion of the tour, the group was met by each supervisor they had met earlier who escorted them back to their new departments.

The supervisor then explained the daily routine and showed Adam around the department. When possible on several occasions, co-workers were stopped for introductions but were not interrupted at their work. The supervisor then gave Adam some on-the-job training on the automatic lathe, observed his performance for a while, then was called away. Adam saw him again the next day for a few minutes when the supervisor slapped him on the back and asked how things were going. When Adam started to ask questions he was told, "Don't have time to talk now, have an appointment. Ask Joe over there." After Adam approached Joe with the question, Joe called over a group of other workers and the group teased Adam for his dumb question for almost an hour. This harassment and teasing has continued since. Adam now feels that he is out of place in the group, because they constantly ridicule him, and he simply wants to leave.

Although the information above is sketchy, you should be able to identify several things that went wrong with this orientation. What are these?

Discussions Questions

1. How do you believe that this orientation could be improved?
2. What should be covered and in what order?

92 Behaviorially Anchored Performance Evaluation*

INSTRUCTIONS

1. During the next two weeks, observe both your teachers' (all classes) and fellow students' performance.

Develop a list of critical incidents of college teacher performance and a list of critical incidents of student performance.

Each list should contain 20 behavioral examples; some of the examples should illustrate good performance and some poor performance. Each of the examples should describe actual behaviors you have observed.

2. Once you have your 20 examples, group the examples into 2–4 dimensions that appear to be key dimensions of student or teacher performance.

Hand in a list of the dimensions, a brief definition of each of the dimensions, and, under each dimension, list the critical incidents illustrating that dimension.

Assign each example to only one dimension.

List separately any critical incidents that don't seem to fit under any of your key dimensions.

Do the above steps separately for student performance and teacher performance.

3. Use the following five-point rating scale to rate each of your 40 critical incidents on the dimension to which you have assigned it.

5—Excellent performance on this dimension.
4
3—Average/adequate performance on this dimension.
2
1—Poor performance on this dimension.

List your incidents in order from excellent (**5**) to poor (**1**) under each dimension.

4. Rate yourself on each of your student dimensions and justify your rating. Use the incidents you have rated above to help you make your ratings.

93 A Field Study of Training†

Visit several industrial or nonprofit or governmental organizations in your locality that have several hundred employees. Try to obtain answers to the following questions and enter the information in the matrix below by check marks.

---

* Prepared by Vicki S. Kaman, Colorado State University.

† Prepared by Jerry L. Wall.

1. How long does the initial training period for your blue-collar (low-level) worker last?
2. How long does the initial training period for your technical and professional workers last?
3. How long does the initial training period for your supervisory and managerial workers last?

Length of Training Period

Check those which apply:

	Less than 2 Weeks	*2 Weeks to 1 Month*	*1 Month to 2 Months*	*2 Months to 3 Months*	*3 Months to 4 Months*	*More Than 4 Months*
Blue-collar						
Technical, Professional						
Supervisory, Management						

1. What types of training do you use for your blue-collar (low-level) employees?
2. What types of training do you use for your technical and professional workers?
3. What types of training do you use for your supervisory and managerial workers?

Types of Training Programs

Check those which apply:

	(Low-level) Blue-collar	*Professional, Technical*	*Supervisory, Management*
Apprenticeships			
Vestibule			
On-the-Job training	X	X	X
Coaching and counseling			
Transitory/anticipatory experiences			
Self-improvement programs			
Transfers, rotations			
Off-job training	X	X	X
Conference, discussions			
Programmed instruction			
Computer-assisted instruction			
Simulation approaches			

Types of Training Programs (concluded)

Check those which apply:

	(Low-level) Blue-Collar	*Professional, Technical*	*Supervisory, Management*
Management development	X	X	X
Training			
Role-playing			
Synectics			
In-basket techniques			
Management games			
Case methods			

Discussion Questions

Within your group and class, try to answer the following questions. Later these will be discussed by your teacher.

1. Did you notice any tendencies on the average length of blue-collar training as it compared to the other two?
   Technical and professional training as it compared to supervisory and managerial training.
   Why do you think these phenomena occurred?
2. What tendencies did you notice on the part of variety of training for blue-collar versus other employees?
   For technical and professional training versus supervisory and managerial employees?
3. Did you notice any differences by the type of company you went to? What were these.

94 A-1 Appliances, Inc.

The firm employs 1,500 persons. A-1 also has a plant in Phenix City, Alabama, and Sandusky, Ohio.

Recently, the firm has been trying to hire a new plant manager for the Sandusky plant. Because of the importance of the position, the firm has used multiple selection techniques. The techniques include: (1) interviews, (2) tests, (3) honesty tests, (4) graphology, and (5) references. A brief description of the candidates is given in Exhibit 1.

A-1 has had about an average profit and growth record for the industry. But Sandusky has been the real problem plant. Costs are high, and there has been a history of labor strife there.

Each of the applicants was interviewed by five executives at A-1. Then the executives were asked to rank the applicants in their order of preference. The results of these rankings are given in Table 1. The results of the intelligence tests are given in Table 2.

In terms of personality analysis drawn from interpretation of revised thematic apperception tests, the psychologists ranked the individuals as follows: (1) King, (2) Dappert, (3) Reddick, (4) Williams, and (5) Taylor. Once of the psychologist's comments was that "King and Dappert are quite competitive and ought to take charge well, especially when faced with a real challenge."

The honesty tests analyses indicated that most were thought to be honest, although the analyst had some questions about King. The analyst remarked "that he placed little faith in the paper-and-pencil honesty tests; he like the old-fashioned polygraphs when he wanted to get at the truth."

EXHIBIT 1 Biographical Data on the Candidates

1. **Charlie Reddick,** assistant plant manager at Sandusky. Age 48. Education: BS, BA, Kent State University; MBA, University of Akron. Has always worked for A-1 except during military service.
2. **Nathalee Williams,** assistant plant manager at Phenix city. Age 51 Education: A.A., Cuyahoga Community College. Has worked for A-1 for 10 years. prior to that, worked for two other appliance manufacturers (six and four years, repsectively), and before that a variety of other jobs.
3. **Ron Taylor,** assistant plant manager at Pomona. Age 41, Education: BA in political science, Yale University. has four years' military experience. Worked in appliance sales for competitors for three years and had production experience for competitor for five years. Has worked for A-1 for six years.
4. **George King,** plant manager of a small plant for a very aggressive competitor. Age 36. Education: BS in engineering, University of Central Florida. Has been employed at present company for 10 years, 3 as plant manager. Has four years' military experience.
5. **Mark Dappert,** former plant manager of electrical equipment firm which went bankrupt in Toledo. Age 58. Education: Attended University of Toledo's college of business; no degree. Worked for prior employer all of his working life. Ran a successful plant for this company, which failed for other reasons.

TABLE 1 Preferences for Candidates by Five A-1 Appliances Executives

	Candidates				
Interviewers' rankings	*Reddick*	*Williams*	*Taylor*	*King*	*Dappert*
President					
James Cox	5	3	1	2	4
Vice president—personnel					
Dale Young	3	2	1	5	4

TABLE 1 Preferences for Candidates by Five A-1 Appliances Executives *(concluded)*

	Candidates				
Interviewers' rankings	*Reddick*	*Williams*	*Taylor*	*King*	*Dappert*
Vice president—production Kenneth O'Connor	2	5	3	4	1
Plant manager, Sandusky Stanley Hale	4	3	5	1	2
Plant manager, Phenix city Ernest Butler	5	1	3	2	4

TABLE 2 Intelligence Tests Results at A-1 Applicances

Candidate	*Test (1) Score*	*Test (2) Score*
Reddick	127	133
Williams	118	121
Taylor	123	128
King	130	131
Dappert	110	115

Outstanding	King, Dappert, Williams
Acceptable	Taylor
Not acceptable	Reddick

Reference letters were favorable to all candidates.

95 Philadelphia Streets Department

The Philadelphia Streets Department, because of recent litigation filed against it, must find ways to dramatically increase the number of females in skilled and semiskilled classes. The department has maintained an antiwomen stance for at least the past 35 years. For example, the department has allowed female stereotypes to stand as the reason for refusing to hire women for the job of garbage collector. The belief was that the work was too dirty and that women could not do the heavy lifting required. In recent months, however, Elaine Taylor, an applicant who was turned down without an opportunity to attempt the physical lifting tests, has filed a class action suit.

The department would like to continue to refuse to hire women but it also knows that a token number of women can be hired at little cost to the department, thanks to a federal government grant and the lifting of a brief hiring freeze. At present, the department needs to hire 25 new employees. If past practice is followed, 50 employees will have to be hired to have 25 effective ones. The total training cost amounts to $2,250 per employee.

It has been proposed that testing might improve this employment record. For administering and using the test, the cost will be $77.50 per applicant. Table 1 presents data on the percentage of applicants who score various levels on the test and the percentage of applicants likely to be successful at various predictor-score levels.

TABLE 1 Employee Selection and Personnel Costs

							20					
	20						x					
	19						x					
	18						x					
	17					16	x	16				
	16					x	x	x				
	15					x	x	x				
	14					x	x	x				
	13				12	x	x	x	12			
	12				x	x	x	x	x			
	11				x	x	x	x	x			
Frequency	10				x	x	x	x	x			
	9				x	x	x	x	x			
	8				x	x	x	x	x			
	7			6	x	x	x	x	x	6		
	6			x		x	x	x	x	x		
	5		4	x	x	x	x	x	x	x	4	
	4		x	x	x	x	x	x	x	x	x	
	3	2	x	x	x	x	x	x	x	x	x	2
	2	x	x	x	x	x	x	x	x	x	x	x
	1	x	x	x	x	x	x	x	x	x	x	x
Score		10	20	30	40	50	60	70	80	90	100	110
Percent		2	6	12	24	40	60	76	88	94	98	100

TABLE 1 Employee Selection and Personnel Costs *(concluded)*

High							16	12	6	4	2	
							x	x	x	x	x	
						20	x	x	x	x	x	
						x	x	x	x	x		
						x	x	x	x	x		
						x	x	x	x			
						x	x	x	x			
						x	x	x				
					16	x	x	x				
					x	x	x	x				
					x	x	x	x				
					x	x	x	x				(50) successful
				12	x	x	x	x				
—	—	—	—	—	—	—	—	—	—	—	—	—
				x	x	x	x					
Criterion				x	x	x	x					50 unsuccessful
measure				x	x	x	x					
			6	x	x	x	x					
			x	x	x	x						
			x	x	x	x						
			x	x	x	x						
		4	x	x	x	x						
		x	x	x	x	x						
		x	x	x	x	x						
	2	x		x	x							
	x	x		x	x							
Low	x											
Percent	2	6	12	24	40	60	76	88	94	98	100	

Predictor

Requirements

Calculate the best predictor scores designed to minimize costs and maximize the number of best applicants to get 25 successful employees. Is the garbage collector's position only a "man's job?"

96 Training for Quality*

Your company has recently moved to a total quality management (TQM) philosophy. As part of the change, operative-level employees are going to be asked to participate more in decision making. Each work group will meet together periodically to discuss quality problems and propose possible solutions. Each group will be "co-facilitated" by the group's supervisor and by one operative-level employee. The co-facilitator role will be rotated through the work group every three to six months, so eventually each person in the group will have a chance to be co-facilitator. In addition, someone in each group will serve as the recorder for the group's minutes, and at least one other person will serve as liaison to other groups. The liaison person will be responsible for getting and sharing relevant information from other groups and individuals in the plant whose jobs have an impact on the group's ability to solve quality problems. The liaison person may interact with anyone from the plant manager to the director of purchasing to people in maintenance and engineering.

For many years, the company has followed a traditional approach to management from the top down. Employees are expected to do as they are told and not to concern themselves with anything except their own specific job assignments. Those jobs are all unskilled assembly line jobs. Most employees have a high school education and at least 10 years of seniority in the plant. About 10 percent of the workforce is functionally illiterate.

Within their work groups, which vary in size from 10 to 25 employees, people don't always cooperate or get along very well. Of course, some groups seem friendlier and more cooperative than others. But some groups also are composed of members who have long-standing grudges against one another. In addition, there is some racially oriented tension between blacks and whites. This becomes very apparent at lunchtime when blacks sit with blacks and whites with whites.

About half the supervisors at the plant were promoted from the rank and file. This group has, on average, two years of college education. The other group of supervisors was hired from outside, tend to be somewhat younger, and all have four-year college degrees. There is some tension between these two groups, with the older, promoted-from-within supervisors feeling one down to the younger group. The younger group sees themselves as destined for promotion to middle management and, therefore, superior to the others.

This change is scheduled to be implemented in about six months. The details of implementation are being left to each department head. Many of the supervisors have heard about it and are less than enthusiastic. Many operative-level employees also are complaining about the change and saying that quality problems should be solved by management.

---

*This exercise was prepared by Professors Arnon E. Reichers and John P. Wanous, The Ohio State University and Pennsylvania State University, respectively.

You work in the department of human resources and have a specialty in training and development. Recently, one of the department heads, in whose area the switch to TQM will soon be implemented, has contacted you for advice. He wants to run all his supervisors and one employee from each group through a half-day facilitator training session. At this time, he doesn't see the need for any other training.

Discussion Questions

1. For the move to TQM to be successful, do all employees and supervisors need training? Why or why not?
2. What knowledge, skills, and abilities do trainees need to function effectively as a problem-solving group?
3. What knowledge, skills, and abilities are especially important for:
   a. Facilitators.
   b. Recorders.
   c. Liaison people.
4. How should the training program(s) be designed to acknowledge varying levels of literacy and education?
5. What steps should you take to ensure that your recommendations are accepted by all department heads?

---

*97 Strengths, Weaknesses, Opportunities, Threats (SWOT) Application Exercise—Strategic Human Resource Management**

It does not surprise most students to learn that strategic planning is a critical part of an organization's survival and success processes. However, these same students may be surprised to realize the linkage between human resource management activities and strategic planning. An important part of strategic planning is identification of the organization's strengths, weaknesses, opportunities, and threats. To make any business strategy effective requires both a vision of what the organization should become, and effective execution of the plans to bring about that vision. To effectively execute strategic plans the organization must make sure that the financial and human resources are available to make the vision a reality. Some typical strengths, weaknesses, opportunities and threats are shown on the following page. In many of our classes, students have derived great benefit from applying concepts learned to their own organization. For example, in our projects-oriented total quality management

---

*This exercise was created by Kenneth M. York, Oakland University, with the assistance of George E. Stevens, Kent State University.

course, students may (with the instructor's permission) apply TQM concepts and analyses to a key process that occurs in their organization. A different approach may be to identify an organization that is or was at a critical juncture in its organizational life cycle. Your task is to work with your instructor to agree to do a SWOT analysis for any of the organizations listed below or others that he or she might assign:

- IBM in 1982, the year the IBM-PC was introduced.
- Exxon in 1972, the year of the OPEC oil embargo.
- Volkswagen in 1992, the first year of production in Mexico.
- Ernst & Young in 1990, after the merger of Arthur Young and Ernst & Whinney.
- Sears at the turn of the past century, before publishing its first catalog.
- Union Pacific Railroad in 1862, before the building of the transcontinental railroad.
- Major league baseball in 1992, before expansion.
- Du Pont in 1992, after discovery of ozone-fluorocarbon link.
- Westinghouse Nuclear, after the Three Mile Island incident.
- Johnson & Johnson, after the Tylenol tampering cases.
- AT&T, after the breakup into regional Bell companies.
- Toyota in the early 1970s, when American car companies made few small cars.

TABLE 1 SWOT Analysis—What to Look For

Potential Internal Strengths	*Potential Internal Weaknesses*
• Core competencies in key areas.	• No clear strategic direction.
• Adequate financial resources.	• Obsolete facilities.
• An acknowledged market leader.	• Subpar profitability because...
• Well-conceived functional area strategies.	• Lack of managerial depth and talent.
• Access to economies of scale.	• Missing some key skills or competencies.
• Insulated (at least somewhat) from strong competitive pressures.	• Poor track record in implementing strategy.
• Proprietary technology.	• Plagued with internal operation problems.
• Cost advantages.	• Falling behind in R & D.
• Better advertising campaigns.	• Too narrow a product line.
• Product innovation skills.	• Weak market image.
• Proven management.	• Weak distribution network.
• Ahead on experience curve.	• Below-average marketing skills.
• Better manufacturing capability.	• Unable to finance needed changes in strategy.
• Superior technological skills.	• Higher overall unit costs relative to key competitors.
• Other?	• Other?

TABLE 1 SWOT Analysis—What to Look For *(continued)*

Potential External Opportunities	*Potential External Threats*
• Serve additional customer groups. • Enter new markets or segments. • Expand product line to meet broader range of customer needs. • Diversify into related products. • Vertical integration (forward or backward). • Falling trade barriers in attractive foreign markets. • Complacency among rival firms. • Faster market growth. • Other?	• Entry of lower-cost foreign competitors. • Rising sales of substitute products. • Slower market growth. • Adverse shifts in foreign exchange rates and trade policies of foreign governments. • Costly regulatory requirements. • Vulnerability to recession and business cycle. • Growing bargaining power of customers or suppliers. • Changing buyer needs and tastes. • Adverse demographic changes. • Other?

Source: A. A. Thompson, Jr., and A. J. Strickland, III., (*Strategic Management: Concepts and Cases*, 6e. Homewood, IL: Richard D. Irwin, 1993).

Where to Read More

Strategic Planning and Human Resources Management

Van Dierdonck, R. (1992). "Success Strategies in a Service Economy." *European Management Journal*, 10(3), 365–373.

Schuler, R. S. (1992). "Strategic Human Resources Management: Linking the People with the Strategic Needs of the Business." *Organizational Dynamics*, 21(1), 18–32.

Samiee, S. (1990). "Productivity Planning and Strategy in Retailing." *California Management Review*, *32(2)*, 54–76.

Nicholson, N.; Rees; A.; and Brooks-Rooney, A. (1990). "Strategy, Innovation, and Performance." *Journal of Management Studies*, *27(5)*, 511–534.

Ball, L. P. (1990). "Take Charge: Be an Intrapreneur." *Personnel Journal*, *69(8)*, 40–44.

Ferris, G. R.; Russ, G. S.; Albanese, R.; and Martocchio, J. J. (1990). "Personnel/Human Resources Management, Unionization, and Strategy Determinants of Organizational Performance." *Human Resource Planning*, *13(3)*, 215–227.

Mission and Vision

Nathanson, C. (1993). "Three Ways to Prove HR's Value." *Personnel Journal*, *72(1)*, 19, 21.

Covey, S. R. (1991). "Seven Chronic Problems." *Modern Office Technology, 36(12),* 12, 14.

Ellig, B. R. (1991). Corporate Team Strategies: Do You Have the Right Stuff?" *HR Magazine, 36(10)*, 38–40.

Fusco, M. A. C. (1991). "Getting the Most from Teamwork." *Employment Relations Today, 18(2)*, 235–240.

Knowledge Workers

Copeland, K. (1993). "Infotech: Shaping Management to Come". *Business Quarterly, 57(3)*, 125–128.

Young, J. K. (1992). "Information Systems Help Knowledge Workers Work Even Harder at Productivity." *Computers in Healthcare, 13(7)*, 20-22.

Oliff, M. D., and Marchand, D. A. (1991). "Strategic Information Management in Global Manufacturing." *European Management Journal, 9(4)*, 361–372.

Harrigan, K. R., and Dalmia, G. (1991). "Knowledge Workers: The Last Bastion of Competitive Advantage." *Planning Review, 19(6)*, 4–9, 48.

Nolan, R. L. (1991). "The Strategic Potential of Information Technology." *Financial Executive, 7(4)*, 25–27.

Marchand, D. A. (1990). "Infotrends: A 1990s Outlook on Strategic Information Management." *Information Management Review, 5(4)*, 23–32.

Utility Analysis

Becker, B. E., and Huselid, M. A. (1992). "Direct Estimates of SD(subscript y) and the Implications for Utility Analysis." *Journal of Applied Psychology, 77(3)*, 227–233.

Raju, N. S.; Burke, M. J.; and Normand, J. (1990). "A new Approach for Utility Analysis." *Journal of Applied Psychology, 75(1)*, 3–12.

Becker, B. E. (1989). "The Influence of Labor Markets on Human Resources Utility Estimates." *Personnel Psychology, 42(3)*, 531–546.

McDaniel, M. A., and Schmidt, F. L. (1989). "Computer-assisted Staffing Systems: The Use of Computers in Implementing Meta-analysis and Utility Research in Personnel Selection." *Public Personnel Management, 18(1)*, 75–86.

Carr, A. F. (1988). "Utility Analysis and Human Resources Management." *Public Productivity Review, 12(2)*, 131–147.

Employee Commitment

Discenza, R., and Gardner, D. G. (1992). "Improving Productivity by Managing for Retention." *Information Strategy: The Executive's Journal, 8(3)*, 34–38.

Hope, V. (1990). "Our Most Valuable Asset Is People: Practising a Popular Philosophy in a Life Assurance Company." *Personnel Review, 19(5)*, 14–23.

Wisdom, B. L., and Denton, D. K. (1989). "Compensation Management in Practice: Using the Numbers to Communicate Corporate Vision." *Compensation & Benefits Review, 21(4)*, 15–19.

Fincham, R. (1989). "Natural Workgroups and the Process of Job Design." *Employee Relations, 11(6)*, 17–22.

Section B

Experiences in Human Resource Management

98 Scenarios: Is It Age Discrimination? (A)

THE OVERQUALIFIED APPLICANT*

Facts

National Bank announces that it is opening a new branch office and begins advertising for tellers. Denise Thomas, age 50 with 20 years of banking experience, applies for a position at the bank. The employment application asks for her age. Ms. Thomas answers the question truthfully.

The next week, Ms. Thomas receives a polite letter from the bank complimenting her on her qualifications but turning her down on the basis that she is overqualified. The applicant hired instead of Ms. Thomas is a 30-year-old with only 5 years of experience.

A QUESTION OF PERFORMANCE

Facts

Bob Johnson, age 50, was a manager with XYZ Paper Company. For the past 10 years he has received outstanding performance reviews. Two months after receiving a pay increase, he was fired for "poor performance." His replacement, age 35, started the day after he was fired.

---

*"How to Prove Age Discrimination," *Age Discrimination on the Job* (1994), case studies, American Association of Retired Persons, p. 12.

A REASON OTHER THAN AGE

Facts

Alfred Smith is a coordinator of labor relations for Ace Manufacturing Corporation. For the most part, he has performed his job well. His major problem is poor interpersonal skills, because he is often rude and uncooperative with his co-workers.

At a cocktail party given by the company president, Smith became loud and insulting to some of the guests. One year after the party, he applied for a promotion and seemed to be the only employee clearly eligible for the position. At the time of his application, he was 58 years old and for the past year had been making a determined effort to improve his interpersonal behavior. However, Smith was informed that, because of his poor interpersonal skills, the position would be given to employee benefits coordinator Harold Nyes, age 39.

---

*Scenarios: Is It Age Discrimination? (B)**

BENEFITS

Facts

In a meeting with your secretary concerning her performance appraisal, you both agree that it would be advantageous to your work if she took some college classes in management. However, she is doubtful that she will be able to afford the tuition on her secretary's salary. You reassure her that the company has an excellent tuition reimbursement program for job-related education. You approve her request for funds.

Two weeks later she comes to you with a memo from the human resources department explaining that the tuition reimbursement program is unavailable to employees age 35 or over. (Your secretary is 42.) What action should you take?

WAIVERS

Facts

Your company has suffered a decline in market demand and the CEO announces that an exit incentive will be offered to reduce the size of the workforce. Employees accepting the incentive will receive an extra six weeks of severance benefits. In similar situations in the past, the company has always asked employees accepting such an incentive to sign a waiver releasing the company from any legal claims against it in exchange for the additional benefits. Under current law, may your company still ask its employees to sign such a release?

---

*Age Discrimination on the Job. Copyright © (1994) American Association of Retired Persons.

THE BFOQ

Introduction

There are several exceptions or defenses contained in the ADEA. By including these exceptions, Congress recognized that some employer practices should be lawful. One of the exceptions is the bona fide occupational qualification (BFOQ).

You are the vice president of personnel for the Transamerica Bus Company. Over the years you have compiled comprehensive statistics on driver safety. By analyzing the data you learn that your drivers over age 45 have more accidents than your younger drivers. However, within the group of drivers over 45, a subgroup of drivers age 50 to 60 with 15 years of experience has the safest driving record in the company.

As a follow-up to your research, you consult several medical experts to determine whether accident proneness could be assessed by a medical examination. The experts inform you that except in extreme cases it would be very difficult to predict physiological changes 5 or 10 years in the future. They also note that degenerative changes begin around age 35 and that some of these changes could impair driving ability. They caution you that there is significant variation among individuals in how much change in reaction time they experience. Some individuals experience considerably slower reaction time as early as age 35 or 40, while others experience no change in their reaction time until a much older age. Finally, the experts point out there are tests available that can determine driver safety on an individual basis.

The company's president calls you into his office to tell you that he heard about your data and asks if they could be used to support a new policy he wants to implement—a mandatory retirement age of 60 for drivers.

How do you respond?

---

*99 Americans with Disabilities Act (ADA) Quiz**

Mark each statement as either true or false as it pertains to the ADA.

___1. An organization must hire all blind people who apply for a job.
___2. Only individuals with physical handicaps (in wheelchairs, blind, and the like) are covered by the ADA.
___3. The spouse of an individual with a disability is covered by ADA.
___4. All buildings with two or more stories must be equipped with an elevator.
___5. When Title I (the employment section) of the ADA is completely in effect, only employers with more than 15 employees will be covered.
___6. Gays and lesbians are covered by the ADA.
___7. A small company (25 employees) advertises for an individual with mechanical aptitude, the ability to lift 25 pounds repeatedly, and the problem-solving skills. A qualified individual with a disability applies for the job. However,

for the individual to be able to do the job, the company would have to pull up existing machinery and rearrange the manufacturing facility. The company must hire this qualified indvidual with a disability.

___ 8. Before hiring a job candidate, a company should ask whether the person has any disabilities.

___ 9. During a screening interview, an applicant discloses that he or she is a recovering alcoholic. An employer could not legally use that information in making a hiring decision.

___10. Individuals with AIDS cannot be discriminated against under the ADA.

___11. A company does not have to make reasonable accommodation for an individual with a disability if the person does not ask for the accommodation.

___12. The ADA outlaws the practice of drug testing.

___13. A pre-employment physical should only be given after extending a conditional offer of employment.

___14. Under the ADA, job descriptions must be rewritten to specify whether an individual with a disability could perform the job.

___15. A person with dyslexia is covered under the ADA.

___16. An applicant reveals that he was treated for depression in a mental hospital. The company is justified in using this information in a hiring decision.

___17. A person who is color-blind would be covered under ADA.

___18. A reasonable accommodation for a visually impaired applicant for a data entry position would be the purchase of a large-print monitor and a magnifying glass.

___19. All people whose fingertips were cut off would be covered under ADA.

___20. A person who frequently contracts colds and misses works is covered under the ADA.

100 Americans with Disabilities Act (ADA) Reasonable Accommodation Exercise*

The following exercise is intended to encourage people to think in creative ways about how to make reasonable accommodations for individuals with disabilities without causing the company undue hardship. Reasonable accommodation means modifying the work, workplace, or schedule so an individual with a disability could perform the essential functions of the job. The ADA requires companies to make reasonable accommodations for individuals with disabilities unless they present an undue hardship on the company. Undue hardship relates to the cost of the accommodation, given the size and resources of a company.

---

* This exercise was prepared by Professor Alice H. Walton, University of Detroit Mercy.

The following exercise can be completed with any job. List the job title where indicated. Individually or in small groups, devise accommodations that may be needed for the individual to perform the essential functions of the job. There are many sources in the library or from state rehabilitation services that may be useful. Decide whether the accommodation would be reasonable or whether it would cause undue hardship.

*Job Title:*__________________________

Qualified individuals with the following disabilities apply for the above job. What accommodations might be required? Would they be reasonable, in other words, not cause the company undue hardship in a small company with few resources? In a larger company with more resources?

	Reasonable	*Undue Hardship (Y/N)*	
Disability	*Accommodation*	*Small Co.*	*Large Co.*
1. Paraplegia			
2. Deaf			
3. Recovering alcoholic			
4. Right-arm amputee			
5. Left-leg amputee			
6. Blind			
7. Learning disabled			
8. Suffering from depression			
9. HIV positive			
10. Bad back			

101 Ryan Brook Assessment of Résumé Writing Skills*

DIRECTIONS: Read each item carefully and indicate your response by circling either the letter "T" or "F" in the response column.

T F 1. A résumé should never be longer than one page.

T F 2. A paragraph format is more desirable than an outline format in a résumé, since more information can be included in the same space.

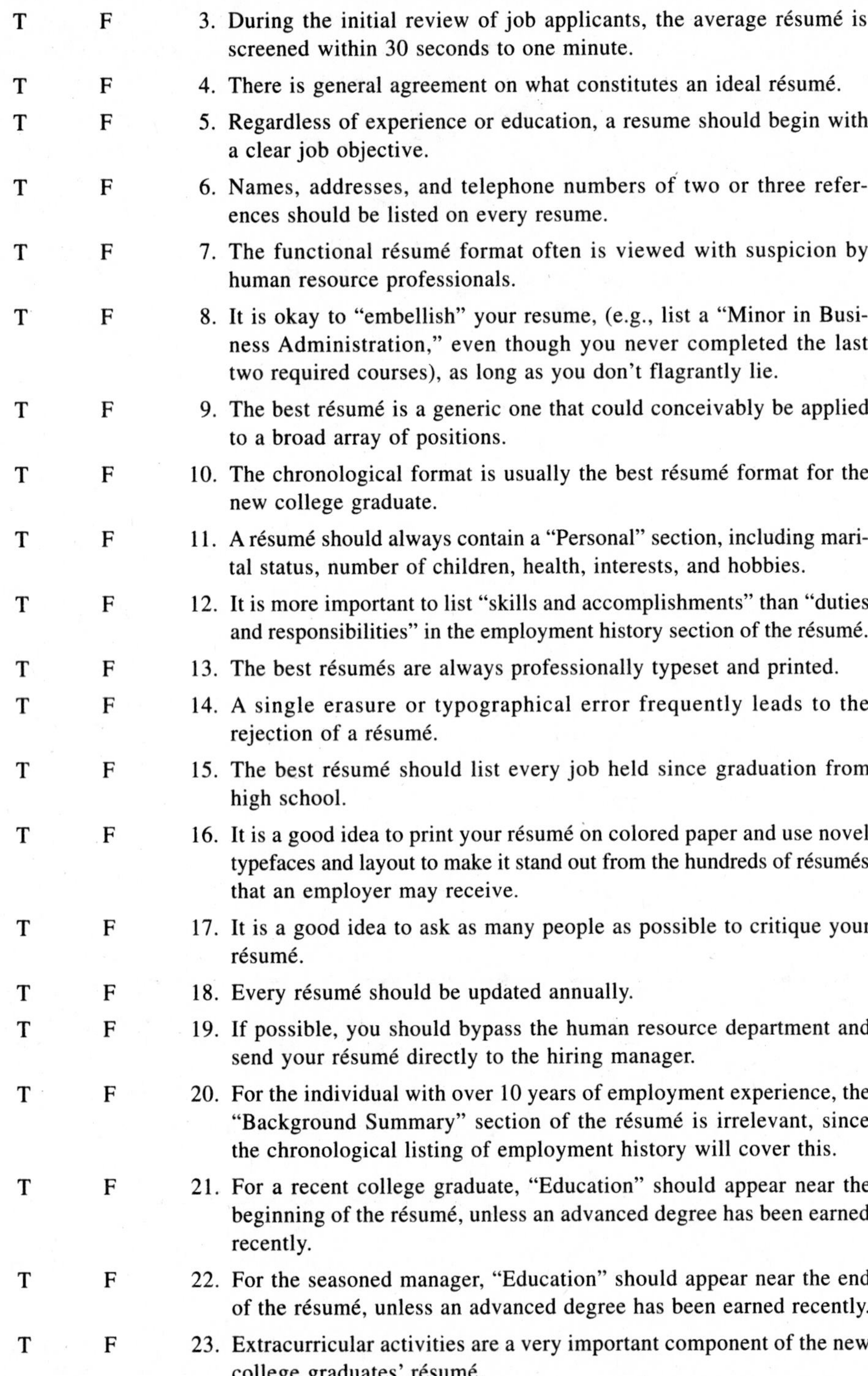

T F 3. During the initial review of job applicants, the average résumé is screened within 30 seconds to one minute.

T F 4. There is general agreement on what constitutes an ideal résumé.

T F 5. Regardless of experience or education, a resume should begin with a clear job objective.

T F 6. Names, addresses, and telephone numbers of two or three references should be listed on every resume.

T F 7. The functional résumé format often is viewed with suspicion by human resource professionals.

T F 8. It is okay to "embellish" your resume, (e.g., list a "Minor in Business Administration," even though you never completed the last two required courses), as long as you don't flagrantly lie.

T F 9. The best résumé is a generic one that could conceivably be applied to a broad array of positions.

T F 10. The chronological format is usually the best résumé format for the new college graduate.

T F 11. A résumé should always contain a "Personal" section, including marital status, number of children, health, interests, and hobbies.

T F 12. It is more important to list "skills and accomplishments" than "duties and responsibilities" in the employment history section of the résumé.

T F 13. The best résumés are always professionally typeset and printed.

T F 14. A single erasure or typographical error frequently leads to the rejection of a résumé.

T F 15. The best résumé should list every job held since graduation from high school.

T F 16. It is a good idea to print your résumé on colored paper and use novel typefaces and layout to make it stand out from the hundreds of résumés that an employer may receive.

T F 17. It is a good idea to ask as many people as possible to critique your résumé.

T F 18. Every résumé should be updated annually.

T F 19. If possible, you should bypass the human resource department and send your résumé directly to the hiring manager.

T F 20. For the individual with over 10 years of employment experience, the "Background Summary" section of the résumé is irrelevant, since the chronological listing of employment history will cover this.

T F 21. For a recent college graduate, "Education" should appear near the beginning of the résumé, unless an advanced degree has been earned recently.

T F 22. For the seasoned manager, "Education" should appear near the end of the résumé, unless an advanced degree has been earned recently.

T F 23. Extracurricular activities are a very important component of the new college graduates' résumé.

T F 24. There is neither a need nor a mechanism for respondents to "blind ads" to identify the advertising organization or the requirements of the job.

T F 25. The best résumé is "targeted"—that is, rewritten explicitly to match the requirements of the job and hiring organization.

102 The B.I.T.C.H. Test*

Black Intelligence Test of Cultural Homogeneity

Name________________________________ Age________ Date_____________
Grade__________________________

DIRECTIONS: Below are some words, terms, and expressions taken from the black experience. Select the correct answers and put a check mark in the space provided on the right of the test sheet. Remember, we want the correct definition as black people use the words and expressions. There is no time limit. Ten minutes should be sufficient time to complete the 20 items extracted from the full 100-item test. **Go ahead.**

a *b* *c* *d*

1. Bread
   (*a*) Something to eat (*c*) Religion 1. ____ ____ ____ ____
   (*b*) Weapons (*d*) Money
2. Crib
   (*a*) An apartment (*c*) A job 2. ____ ____ ____ ____
   (*b*) A game (*d*) Hot stuff
3. Deuce-and-a-quarter
   (*a*) Money (*c*) A house 3. ____ ____ ____ ____
   (*b*) A car (*d*) Dicey
4. Do rag
   (*a*) The hair (*c*) Washing 4. ____ ____ ____ ____
   (*b*) The shoes (*d*) Tablecloth
5. The eagle flies
   (*a*) The blahs (*c*) Payday 5. ____ ____ ____ ____
   (*b*) Movie (*d*) Deficit

* Prepared by Robert Williams, Washington University, St. Louis. Copyright © 1971 by Robert Williams.

			a *b* *c* *d*
6. Gig			
	(*a*) A job	(*c*) A car	6. ____ ____ ____ ____
	(*b*) Being discriminated against	(*d*) Jogging	
7. Gospel bird			
	(*a*) A pheasant	(*c*) A goose	7. ____ ____ ____ ____
	(*b*) A chicken	(*d*) A duck	
8. Hawk			
	(*a*) Rain	(*c*) Water	8. ____ ____ ____ ____
	(*b*) Sunshine	(*d*) Cold wind	
9. Heavy cat			
	(*a*) Fat	(*c*) Depressed	9. ____ ____ ____ ____
	(*b*) Arrogant	(*d*) Intelligent	
10. Hog			
	(*a*) Bad person	(*c*) Animal	10. ____ ____ ____ ____
	(*b*) A car	(*d*) A whiskey still	
11. Jaws are tight			
	(*a*) Hungry	(*c*) Angry	11. ____ ____ ____ ____
	(*b*) Excited	(*d*) Frightened	
12. Lay dead			
	(*a*) Do nothing	(*c*) To lose	12. ____ ____ ____ ____
	(*b*) Sneaky	(*d*) Deep	
13. Member			
	(*a*) Church-goer	(*c*) White	13. ____ ____ ____ ____
	(*b*) Black	(*d*) Foreigner	
14. Nose opened			
	(*a*) Flirting	(*c*) Deeply in love	14. ____ ____ ____ ____
	(*b*) Teed off	(*d*) Very angry	
15. On my case			
	(*a*) Sitting on my luggage	(*c*) Taking my money	15. ____ ____ ____ ____
	(*b*) My lawyer	(*d*) Criticizing me	
16. Rags			
	(*a*) Clothes	(*c*) Broke	16. ____ ____ ____ ____
	(*b*) Wornout	(*d*) Poor	
17. Sapphire			
	(*a*) Black preacher	(*c*) Dish of soul food	17. ____ ____ ____ ____
	(*b*) Black woman	(*d*) Hair style	

			a *b* *c* *d*
18. Stone fox			
	(a) Bitchy	(c) Sly	18. ____ ____ ____ ____
	(*b*) Pretty	(*d*) Uncanny	
19. T.C.B.			
	(*a*) That's cool, baby	(*c*) They couldn't breathe	19. ____ ____ ____ ____
	(*b*) Taking care of business	(*d*) Took careful behavior	
20. What had went down			
	(*a*) To throw someone off	(*c*) To say what is happening	20. ____ ____ ____ ____
	(*b*) Being confused	(*d*) To say someone had died	

103 Agronomics*

You are director of personnel for a small manufacturing company, Agronomics. Recently you have heard increasing complaints about pay in your organization. On investigation, you discover that most of the complaints deal with alleged internal inequities (i.e., with situations in which employees feel their salary is out of line in comparison with the amount of work that they do). You also have heard rumors that the blue-collar workers in your company are attempting to organize. They feel their wages are consistently lower than those of unionized workers in other companies. Finally, you've just received word from the Department of Labor that Sara Rynes, one of your more vocal feminists, has filed a complaint alleging that Agronomics is violating the Equal Pay Act. She claims that she is being underpaid for performing the same job as her co-workers because she is a woman.

In attempting to confront these problems, you have had your assistant collect the following data:

A. Job descriptions. (Your professor will give you directions on this. If you generated a job description during the job analysis exercise, you might use it here.)

B. A point evaluation system to determine the relative worth of these positions (Form A).

---

*Prepared by Vandra L. Huber. Copyright © 1984 by Vandra L. Huber, University of Washington.

C. A record sheet on which to record the point totals for the key organizational jobs (Form B).

D. A personnel inventory sheet which lists the names, age, sex, organizational and job tenure, performance rating, and current salary of all employees in the relevant job categories (Form C).

E. Wage and salary survey ranges for the positions (Form C).

F. Description of how to operate mini-tab.

PART I—JOB EVALUATION

5 pts 1. Calculate the point value of each job. The job descriptions are on file in the library. Record the results of your point evaluation on Form B. List the lowest point total and move to the highest.

5 pts. 2. Now that you have experience with the point evaluation system of job evaluation, briefly (one page or less) summarize the positive and negative aspects of this method. What problems did you encounter in using the system?

PART II—USING THE COMPUTER

Using the information discussed in class and the mini-tab handout, you are now ready to find out about the wage structure of Agronomics. After logging into the computer, enter the point totals into the mini-tab's memory. What you are doing is creating a new variable called "c9." Remember, when a job has more than one incumbent, you have to type in the point total for each person. If you run into trouble, type HELP.

Now you are ready to begin looking at the data.

5 pts. 3. Using the plot command, plot the relationship between point total and salary. Label this graph "Question 3—Job Evaluation."

Computer commands: height 20, plot 'salary' 'points'.

10 pts. 4. What does the graph tell you about the wage structure of Agronomics? Identify any problems you see with the wage structure.

5 pts. 5. To acquire an overview of the organization, calculate the means for each of the quantifiable variables.

Computer command: mean 'age'.

5 pts. 6. While the information in question 5 is useful, it does not tell you if there are differences between males and females. Because questions concerning the pay of males and females have been raised by Sara Rynes, it would be useful to determine if there are any male/female

differences. Therefore, you should calculate separate means for males and females. Label this output "Question 6—Male and Female means."

Computer command: Table 'sex';
mean 'salary';
mean 'age';
mean 'firm yrs';
mean 'job yrs';
mean 'rating';
mean 'points'.

This will make a table for you, listing the means on each variable by sex.

5 pts. 7. What do you now know about males and females in the organization? What are the key differences? If you found differences in salary point total, which variables (excluding sex) might be responsible for the differences? Summarize your findings (one page).

5 pts. 8. While this information is useful, it does not tell us how closely related or important these variables are. Therefore, the next step is to look at the correlation between the variables. Remember that a number closer to +1 means the two variables are highly related, and that a number closer to 0 means the relationship is weak. Positive correlations mean that, when one variable increases, the other variable also increases. When the correlation is negative, when one variable increases, the other decreases. Calculate the correlation between all of the quantifiable variables (c3-c9). Label this output "Question 8—Correlations."

Computer command: Correlation c3, c4, and so on.

5 pts. 9. Explain what the results tell you about the relationship between the variables. Which ones are strongly related and which ones are not? How do the results compare to what you think the relationship between salary and the other variables ought to be? Discuss (1–2 pages).

10 pts. 10. You now have available a great deal of usable information on which to make some decisions. In a professionally written and formatted memorandum (five pages or less), summarize your findings as they relate to the equity complaints detailed in the opening paragraph of the case. Be sure you detail key problems with the page structure and equity. Make specific recommendations in terms of what you would do to correct the problems. You have been given $20,000 to adjust *annual* salaries, should you have found any problems in the organization.

Extra credit:

10 pts. Compute a regression equation using age, organizational and job tenure, sex, and performance rating to predict salary. Label this output "Extra Credit." What does the regression equation tell you about the rela-

tionship between these variables? What happens to your salary if you are a male versus female? How does your age affect your salary? What effect does your performance rating have on salary? On other factors?

Now follow your recommendations that are detailed in Part III of the exercise. Create a new variable (c10), which will represent the new salaries after you have used the $20,000 to adjust individual salaries. Call the new variable "Newsal." Now calculate a regression equation where the other variables, age, tenure, sex, rating are used to predict these new salaries (c10). Label this output "Extra Credit with Adjustments." Do your proposed changes in the salary structure correct the problems you reported? Discuss (1–2 pages).

FORM A

Job Evaluation Manual

A. Education/Formal Training

This factor measures the extent of education or knowledge required by the worker to perform the job successfully. The education or knowledge may be the result of formal schooling or district-sponsored educational courses.

Degrees	Points
1. Non required	20
2. Grammar school (8th grade)	35
3. Two years high school or equivalent	50
4. Four years high school or equivalent	75
5. Partial college: One year	90
Two years	105
Three years	120
6. College graduate	150
7. Post graduate (master's level)	175
8. Postgraduate (PhD level)	200

B. Job Experience/Informal Training

This factor measures the time required by the worker to learn how to do the job, or the experience necessary to perform the job competently. Produced work should be of a quality and quantity to justify continuous work employment. Avoid confusing experience with formal education. Use same point scale for on-the-job training and apprenticeships.

One week	20	One year	90
One month	35	18 months	100
Two months	45	Two years	110
Three months	55	Three years	130
Six months	80	Four years	150
Nine months	85		

FORM A (continued)

C. Nonsupervisory Responsibility

These factors measure the degree of responsibility placed on the worker for materials, equipment, buildings, safety of others, money, confidential data, and so on. The activity may consist of transporting, stocking, loading, unloading, maintaining, cooking, and the like.

Great responsibility:	11–125
	10–115
	9–105
Moderate responsibility:	8–90
	7–80
	6–70
	5–60
Little responsibility:	4–40
	3–30
	2–20
	1–10

D. Supervisory Responsibility

These factors measure the responsibility to absorb and carry out policies, rules, and regulations, to understand worker psychology, and to maintain satisfactory human relations within the scope of the supervisor's jurisdiction.

Great responsibility:	11–70
	10–60
	9–50
Moderate responsibility:	8–40
	7–35
	6–30
	5–25
Little responsibility:	4–20
	3–15
	2–10
	1–5

E. Mental Effort

Measured here is the degree of intellectual attention and concentration required by the job.

Vital:	11–100
	10–90
	9–80
Important:	8–60
	7–50
	6–40

FORM A *(concluded)*

	5–30
Basic:	4–20
	3–15
	2–10
	1–5

F. Physical

Physical factors measure and compare endurance, fatigue, and strength under normal or abnormal conditions. Also relates to expenditure of physical exertion inherent in the job to be performed at a normal pace. Consideration must be given to muscular exertion required for material handling, use of tools, and operation of machines. Also, consider weights when the job requires pushing, pulling, or lifting; frequency of weight handling, speed, and time required to complete a job are equally important.

Vital:	11–200
	10–185
	9–170
Important	8–150
	7–135
	6–120
	5–105
Basic	4–185
	3–70
	2–55
	1–40

G. Working Conditions

These factors measure the environment and general conditions under which work is performed. Consider disagreeable features, such as cold, dampness, darkness, dirt, dust, fumes, grease, glare, heat, noise, oil, use of respirators, vibration, and other disagreeable conditions surrounding the job to which the worker is exposed.

Vital:	11–200
	10–185
	9–170
Important:	8–150
	7–135
	6–120
	5–105
Basic:	4–85
	3–170
	2–55
	1–40

FORM B

Job	*A* *Educational training*	*B* *Job experience*	*C* *Nonsupervisory responsibility*	*D* *Supervisory responsibility*	*E* *Mental effort*	*F* *Mental fatigue*	*G* *Physical effort*	*H* *Working conditions*			*Total points*

FORM C Agronomics: Personnel Inventory Sheet

Name *C1*	*Job Title* *C2*	*Age* *C3*	*Sex* *C4*	*Firm Yrs.* *C5*	*Job Yrs.* *C6*	*Rating* *C7*	*Monthly Salary* *C8*	*External Salary Range*	*Total Point* *C9*
1. Jimmy Jones	1. Janitor	24	0	2	3	5	2,500	1,000 to 2,000	
2. Henry Smith	1.	30	0	5	5	5	2,800		
3. Patsy Williams	1.	34	1	4	3	4	1,400		
4. Sara Jones	1.	22	1	2	3	5	1,200		
5. Walt Ratcliff	1.	50	0	12	8	1	1,800		
6. Henry "Hank" Sims	2. Pre-press supervisor	59	0	16	12	2	4,200	3,200 to 4,500	
7. Mike Rich	2.	36	0	20	16	4	3,400		
8. Chris Smith	3. Litigation associate	32	1	15	15	3	2,800	3,000 to 5,000	
9. Tom Selleck	3.	45	0	15	10	3	4,000		
10. Bruce Jenner	3.	34	0	5	5	4	3,000		
11. Chris Everett	3.	24	1	1	1	4	2,500		
12. Bob Sterns	4. Commercial advertising	44	0	10	8	3	3,500	2,500 to 3,500	
13. Denny Gioia	4. Director	40	0	10	10	2	4,000		
14. Ed Locke	4.	44	0	8	6	3	3,900		
15. Frederick Herzberg	4.	36	0	10	9	5	2,900		
16. Phil Podsakoff	5. Market research analyst	35	0	10	5	2	3,500	3,500 to 4,200	
17. Jo Churey	5.	36	1	15	8	3	2,800		
18. Pay Mayo	5.	25	1	5	3	4	2,900		
19. Henry Smith	5.	45	0	20	10	2	3,800		
20. Pat Kelley	5.	30	0	20	7	5	4,200		
21. John Boudreau	6. Process control engineer	38	0	8	8	1	3,600	3,400 4,200	
22. George Milkovich	6.	52	0	25	15	5	4,200		
23. Denny Organ	6.	35	0	19	16	4	3,600		
24. Lynn Johnson	6.	49	1	20	14	5	3,900		

FORM C Agronomics: Personnel Inventory Sheet (concluded)

Name *C1*	*Job Title* *C2*	*Age* *C3*	*Sex* *C4*	*Firm Yrs.* *C5*	*Job Yrs.* *C6*	*Rating* *C7*	*Monthly Salary* *C8*	*External Salary Range*	*Total Point* *C9*
25. Sara Smith	7. Internal development	28	1	8	4	3	1,800	1,500 to 3,000	
26. Harold Loew	7. Specialist	50	0	20	8	3	3,400		
27. Joan Benoit	7.	30	1	5	8	5	2,000		
28. Bob Risley	8. Senior financial analyst	52	0	22	12	3	3,200	2,400 to 3,600	
29. Fel Foltman	8.	66	0	25	10	3	3,200		
30. Susan Taylor	8.	38	1	8	3	4	2,800		
31. Janet Near	8.	25	1	2	1	5	2,400		
32. Henry Longfellow	9. CEO	47	0	10	10	2	6,000	4,000 to 10,000	
33. San Bacharach	10. Staffing specialist	30	0	2	2	4	1,800	1,400 to 1,800	
34. Pam Tolbert	10.	23	1	1	1	5	1,800		
35. Sara Rynes	10.	29	1	4	2	4	1,500		
36. Don Kane	10.	44	0	12	6	3	2,200		
37. Billy Lee	11. Shipping & receiving	42	0	10	6	3	2,400	1,500 to 2,200	
38. Janice Byer	11.	35	1	8	4	4	2,000		
39. Mike Krolewski	11.	40	0	15	10	3	2,200		
40. Bill Todor	11.	35	0	10	8	5	1,800		
41. Marcia Miceli	11.	22	1	2	2	4	1,200		

Sex codes —0 = Male; 1 = Female
Performance rating —1 = Low performance; 5 = High performance.

104 Women as Managers Scale*

Please give your personal opinion concerning attitudes toward women in business. The statements below cover many different and opposing points of view. You may find yourself agreeing strongly with some of the statements, disagreeing just as strongly with others, and perhaps uncertain about others.

Rating Scale

1	=	Strongly disagree	5	=	Slightly agree
2	=	Disagree	6	=	Agree
3	=	Slightly disagree	7	=	Strongly agree
4	=	Neither disagree nor agree			

To the left of each statement below is a blank space. Using the numbers from 1 to 7 on the above rating scale, mark your personal opinion about each statement in the blank that immediately precedes it. Remember, all that is wanted is *your* personal opinion. A rating of one (1) would mean that you *strongly disagree* with the statement, whereas a rating of seven (7) would mean you *strongly agree* with the statement. For example:

____ It is especially important that all workers be paid on the basis of their performance.

If you strongly agree with this statement, you should place the number 7 in the blank before the statement. In other words, the stronger your agreement with the statement, the higher the number you should select. Please respond to all 21 items.

______ 1. It is less desirable for women than men to have a job that requires responsibility.

______ 2. Women have the objectivity required to evaluate business situations properly.

______ 3. Challenging work is more important to men than it is to women.

______ 4. Men and women should be given equal opportunity for participation in management training programs.

______ 5. Women have the capability to acquire the necessary skills to be successful managers.

______ 6. On the average, women managers are less capable of contributing to an organization's overall goals than are men.

______ 7. It is not acceptable for women to assume leadership roles as often as men.

______ 8. The business community should someday accept women in key managerial positions.

---

* The WAMS was developed by Lawrence H. Peters of Texas Christian University, James R. Terborg of the University of Oregon, and Janet Taynor of Purdue University.

_____ 9. Society should regard work by female managers as valuable as work by male managers.
_____ 10. It is acceptable for women to compete with men for top executive positions.
_____ 11. The possibility of pregnancy does not make women less desirable employees than men.
_____ 12. Women would no more allow their emotions to influence their managerial behavior than would men.
_____ 13. Problems associated with menstruation should not make women less desirable than men as employees.
_____ 14. To be a successful executive, a woman does not have to sacrifice some of her femininity.
_____ 15. On the average, a woman who stays home all the time with her children is a better mother than a woman who works outside the home at least half-time.
_____ 16. Women are less capable of learning mathematical and mechanical skills than men.
_____ 17. Women are not ambitious enough to be successful in the business world.
_____ 18. Women cannot be assertive in business situations that demand it.
_____ 19. Women possess the self-confidence required of a good leader.
_____ 20. Women are not competitive enough to be successful in the business world.
_____ 21. Women cannot be aggressive in business situations that demand it.

Note: Directions for scoring the WAMS and an explanation of its meaning will be provided by your instructor.

---

*105 Myths and Realities: Statements about Mature and Older Workers**

MYTHS AND REALITIES OF AGING AND WORK*

The following is a list of statements about aging and work. Please mark each statement either true or false. After you have completed the exercise, each statement will be discussed to determine if it is myth or reality. Your responses will not be collected.

1. The percentage of the population over 65 has nearly tripled since 1900. True False
2. At age 65, on the average, women can expect to live 10 more years, men 5 more. True False

---

* "The Aging Workforce," *American Association of Retired Persons*.

3. A greater percentage of men over 55 were working in 1982 than in 1950.	True	False
4. Physical aging begins at age 39.	True	False
5. All five senses tend to decline in old age.	True	False
6. The majority of older people have no serious health problems that limit their activities, at least through their 60s.	True	False
7. Most old people will become senile if they live long enough.	True	False
8. The definition of "old" in the work place is 65 years.	True	False
9. There is a greater percentage of older workers in white-collar jobs than in blue-collar jobs.	True	False
10. Skill obsolescence is a problem for many older workers.	True	False
11. The ability to learn declines significantly by the age of 50.	True	False
12. Reaction time begins to slow at approximately age 25.	True	False
13. Older workers have more work-related accidents than younger workers.	True	False
14. Older workers have better attendance records than younger workers.	True	False
15. The number of age discrimination complaints filed with the government has increased approximately 20 percent since 1975.	True	False
16. In some cases, it is legal for employers to make employment decisions based on age.	True	False
17. Retirement is consistently the best solution for workers who "level out" or are nonpromotable.	True	False
18. As people age, they tend to become more alike.	True	False

*106 New Position Simulation**

You are the human resource manager of a rapidly growing high-tech firm in the local metropolitan area. One year ago, your firm had 45 employees; currently there are 225 full-time employees on the payroll, and the plans include expansion to 400 within the next 12 months. At the present time you have one subordinate: a

* Prepared by Alan Cabelly, Portland State University. Copyright © 1984; revised 1995 by Alan Cabelly.

recruitment/selection specialist. You have now been given authorization to hire a compensation analyst. Your objective is to develop appropriate support materials and to hire the proper person.

You have a bachelor's degree in business administration from the local state university and maintain close contact with the school. You are aware of the development of the human resource program in the university's business school, and you have been told by a faculty member whom you respect that a number of good candidates are available. Further, this professor has a strong background in compensation and has imparted a great deal of this knowledge to the students. Thus, you have decided to attempt to fill the position from among this year's crop of human resource management graduates. As a result of this decision, education, motivation, and intelligence will become more important selection criteria than experience.

This position provides an opportunity that rarely exists with old positions—all human resource tasks can be developed without having to correct past errors or worry about the incumbent's reaction. You seek to take advantage of this situation and to develop a comprehensive job manual for a compensation analyst before you make a hiring decision. Thus, your set of tasks includes the following:

1. Write a job analysis (description, specification, evaluation) for the compensa tion analyst job.
2. Develop a recruitment strategy (advertisements, posters, and the like) for the job.
3. Develop selection criteria for the position.
4. Produce an application blank.
5. Write a brochure for prospective candidates.
6. Develop an interview guide or other methods, or both, of selection (related to selection criteria).
7. Develop a compensation range for the position.
8. Produce a benefits package.
9. Develop performance appraisal criteria (related to the job description) and an appropriate appraisal format.
10. State how this person would be trained by you (remember—this is a person with academic learning and little experience).
11. Describe the career path for the successful applicant.
12. Interview applicants.
13. Make a selection decision, along with the associated compensation decision.
14. Write the appropriate letters of acceptance/rejection.

OTHER INFORMATION AND SUGGESTIONS

The pool of applicants includes all members of your class. Each student will interview with two companies; each team is to interview exactly two times as many applicants as it has team members (thus, a five-person team will interview 10 applicants). At each interview, at least two team members must be present. All interviews will be arranged by the instructor.

All students are to take the interviews *seriously*. This includes punctuality, appropriate dress, appropriate interview rooms, preparation, and so on. All students are required to give résumés to their prospective employers a few days before the interviews occur. In cases of borderline grades, being selected for a job will increase the course grade.

FINAL REPORT

A comprehensive professional report that describes the entire exercise and critically analyzes your efforts is expected. It should include all *relevant* appendixes (e.g., job description, blank interview guides, and the like). The truly outstanding report will be *comprehensive*, *analytical*, and *professional.*

1. *Comprehensive.* The report should show that the team went through all the steps discussed in the project description. Incomplete reports are unacceptable.
2. *Analytical.* Thorough analysis of all decisions is expected. Describe why and how you made your decisions. State what should have been done differently and why (it is better to analyze your errors than to ignore them and *hope* the instructor will not find them). Be certain to provide an overall analysis of the project. Reference to *academic* and professional journals, as well as to practitioners, is required.
3. *Professional.* Students at your stage of academic career should be able to present a truly professional report. Method of presentation is often as important as content. Your report should be structured appropriately (executive summary, main text, bibliography, appendixes, and so on) and be pleasing to the eye.

---

*107 Ryan Brook Assessment of Employment Awareness**

DIRECTIONS: Read each item carefully and consider whether the item is generally true or false for the average American middle manager or professional. Indicate your response by circling the letter "T" or "F" in the response column.

Section I: General Employment Outlook

T F 1. Job opportunities in certain industries are likely to be much better than those in other industries for some time to come.

T F 2. After a decade or more service, it relatively easy for an employee to switch industries.

T F 3. Accomplishments will be more important than titles during the 1990s.

T F 4. Middle managers are being replaced by computers.

T F 5. Employees have as much job security nowadays as they ever had.

T F 6. An unemployed worker may be more likely to find suitable employment by moving to another region of the country.

T F 7. Employers prefer to hire unemployed managers and professionals, since they are frequently willing to work for a lower salary.

T F 8. Moonlighting is likely to hurt your long-term employment prospects.

T F 9. Loyalty and long service to an organization are increasingly important nowadays.

T F 10. A job hunter is more likely to find employment in a small business than in a larger corporation.

Section II: Recruitment and Selection

T F 11. Résumés are becoming less important in the employment screening process.

T F 12. References from former employers are becoming more important in the employment screening process.

T F 13. It is a good idea to return to school at the mid-career stage (between the ages of 35 and 45).

T F 14. It is a good idea to participate actively in many professional organizations.

T F 15. Women are less likely than men to be promoted into middle-management positions.

T F 16. A bad credit record may hurt a person's chances for employment.

T F 17. It is not a good idea for an unemployed manager or professional to accept temporary employment.

T F 18. Networking is becoming more important to both employment and career development.

T F 19. One of the best job hunting strategies is to review the "Help Wanted" advertisements weekly in a regional newspaper, such as the *Boston Globe*.

T F 20. It is a good idea for an unemployed manager or professional to "cold call" potential hiring managers that they have never met and ask for advice on the job market.

Section III: The Employment Interview

T F 21. The hiring manager is likely to be the first to interview the job applicant.

T F 22. The applicant who has researched the potential employer has a significant competitive advantage over the applicant who has not.

T F 23. It is important for the job applicant to ask the interviewer questions about the position and the company.

T F 24. If the interviewer asks the applicant about salary requirements, it is important for the applicant to be honest about his or her desired salary.

T F 25. An interview by a human resource professional is likely to be more objective and systematic than one done by a hiring manager.

T F 26. If a firing or layoff was the result of a "personality conflict" with a boss who treated you badly or unfairly, it is a good idea to explain the circumstances in detail.

T F 27. A good strategy in any job interview is to "mirror" the interviewer's behavior.

T F 28. When asked about weaknesses, it is a good idea to say that you are a "workaholic."

T F 29. If the interviewer asks you an illegal question, (such as, "What is your religious affiliation?"), the best thing to do is to refuse to answer it on the grounds that it would be legally inappropriate for you to do so.

T F 30. While waiting to be called into the interviewer's office, it is a good idea to make small talk with the secretary or receptionist.

Part 4

In-Basket Exercises

Section A

In-Basket Exercises: A Discussion

*Introduction to the Use of In-Baskets**

This section introduces the last group of exercises: in-basket exercises. An in-basket is a series of such items as letters and telephone calls. This group of materials is designed to simulate the kind of material a supervisor or manager, such as a personnel manager, would receive in a workday.

As suggested by Terri Burchett in a *Personnel Journal* article of May 1987, supervisors, managers, personnel professionals, and others who are engaged in personnel decisions can make costly mistakes. Those mistakes having to do with personnel policies (e.g., lack of knowledge about disciplinary policies, the impact of setting precedents, understanding union–management relations, overtime policies, benefits, and the like.) can result in costly errors. The result may be grievances, improperly or inaccurately paid wages, and subsequent lawsuits.

It comes as no surprise, therefore, that most managers understand the importance of properly orienting those involved in personnel practices and procedures, whether in one-on-one meetings or by means of an organizationwide program.

Those who make personnel decisions are a diverse lot. The group may include experienced, long-tenured employees who, for the first time, have a supervisory role or those who are industry or corporate newcomers, team leaders, administrators, or executives. One tool that has proven invaluable in helping people understand the importance of personnel policies (without boring the learners to death or insulting

* Many thanks to Professor Walter A. Bogumil, Jr., University of Central Florida, for his discussion of the in-basket exercise grading (which appears in the *Instructor's Manual*) and his contribution of five in-baskets. Each of these in-baskets is 10 to 12 items in length. The intent of the smaller in-baskets is to provide the instructor with greater flexibility not normally provided by having to use 25–30 item in-baskets.

their intelligence) is the in-basket exercise. Trainers or other personnel professionals may create in-basket exercises of personnel issues in which trainees may work on simulated policy related concerns. "Reality" or relevance comes from the process of developing in-baskets which cover issues that the trainee is likely to find in his or her *own* in-basket.

The construction of an in-basket exercise is not very difficult. For each such exercise four basic steps must be followed: (1) define the general type of problem, (2) define the setting, (3) draft the appropriate materials, and (4) make the exercise realistic. I believe the in-basket contributors have properly followed each of these four crucial steps.

THE EXERCISES

The first part of the exercise consists of a description of the managerial setting and the role the participant will play. Next, the actual material waiting for the manager on his or her desk is provided.

These items are presented in the order in which they were received. It is your responsibility to sort out those which are the most pressing from those which can wait a bit. Typically, you will be given a time limit within which you must complete the work.

The professor will describe how he or she wants you to proceed with the data. In addition to the letters and phone calls provided, it is possible that during the exercise you will receive additional phone calls and memoranda. For, when you are on a job, no one hands you all your work for the day and then leaves you uninterrupted until you are finished.

Remember that you must place yourself in the situation described. When you have completed what you would do and in which order of importance, this can be compared with norms developed for the exercise. You should learn how you react to the time pressures and how well you make decisions in the usual less-than-full-information environment in which most managers work.

Section B

In-Basket Exercises

108 Ashland Regional Hospital*

The Ashland Regional Hospital is a nonprofit hospital that employs 600 employees. It was established by Kenneth Appleton, one of the current members of the board of directors. You are Scott Larson, the personnel director. You accepted this position six months ago. Rumor has it that there was a problem with the previous personnel director, which no one will discuss. You only recently have turned the department around and operations are now running on an even keel. However, at this time you must go on your first out-of-town meeting since you assumed command. You have only one hour in your office and must consider all of the items in your in-basket before departure. You will return to your office one week from today (Friday, January 30).

ITEM 1

To: Scott Larson
From: Madge Garrison, Selection Officer
Subject: Flunked Exam
Date: January 27

Mr. Jon Adams, who was applying for the job of lab tech, did not pass his physical exam. We explained to him that it was a condition of employment to pass the physical. Well, he became quite upset and wants to file for worker's compensation. He threatens that if he is not allowed to file for it he will go to the press. Please advise as to how to solve this problem. I need an answer as soon as possible.

* Prepared by Professor Walter A. Bogumil, Jr., University of Central Florida.

ITEM 2

To: Scott Larson
From: Lois Huners, Business Office Director
Subject: Pay Inequity
Date: January 26

One of the telephone operators, Donna Rebel, who worked for us for seven years, came to me to complain about one of the other telephone operators who was recently hired. The new employee earns only 15 cents less per hour than Donna. She is fuming mad. I told her I would get back to her after I talked with you. Please call me within a day. Thank you.

ITEM 3

To: Madge Garrison
From: Sandra Lockheed, Nursing Supervisor
Subject: Hiring of Nurses

Madge, you and I have talked on numerous occasions about the selection process for nurses. Obviously you were not listening. I am still getting people in my department who lack the experience we need. I will not stand for this any more. I am tired of training these people. If the problem is not corrected I will go over everybody's head.

ITEM 4

To: Scott Larson
From: Bonnie Alderman

Hope your trip is exciting. Have a good flight and learn lots of good ideas for us all.

ITEM 5

Phone message

Mr. Wilder, the administrator, called at 4:36 PM Wants you to call him back. Did not say what it is in reference to.

ITEM 6

To: Scott Larson
From: Andrew King, Controller
Subject: Upcoming Budget

ITEM 6 *(concluded)*

I thought I would take the opportunity to remind you that the annual budget time is approaching (February 15). Since this is your first budget here at ARH I might offer you some tips on our budget system. Give me a call.

ITEM 7

To: Scott Larson
From: Judith Spencer, RN
Subject: Supervisor

I am having a problem with my supervisor. I am afraid to say anything, especially since her mother-in-law is the department head. She does not treat me fairly and I don't know why. I have repeatedly asked for weekends off and I never get them. I was not hired to work every weekend. She did not give me a good performance appraisal a week ago, and when I refused to sign it she yelled at me and told me there were other people out there who wanted my job. Please help. I do not know what to do.

ITEM 8

To: Scott Larson
From: Sharon Newman, Personnel Assistant
Subject: *Employee Handbook*

The new revised editions of the *Employee Handbook* have just arrived. But, before we can hand them out, you are required to read it and make sure everything is in order. Mr. Wilder called and is anxious about getting them out to the employees. Come by and pick up a copy. I tried to drop one off yesterday afternoon, but you had already left.

ITEM 9

To: Scott Larson
From: Madge Garrison, Selection Officer
Subject: Sandra Lockheed

I know you are aware of the situation with Ms. Lockheed. I feel that I am between a rock and a hard place. I need to satisfy the employment requirements, but I also need to satisfy the minority hiring goals. I'm damned if I do and damned if I don't. I feel the real problem is Ms. Lockheed; I think she is prejudiced. I cannot prove it, but I think that is the real problem. Don't let her go over your head on this matter.

ITEM 10

To: Scott Larson
From: Joseph Wilder, Administrator
Subject: Personnel Convention

Scott, I would like very much for you to get together with me after you return from your convention. I am interested in what is going in the human resources field. I've never sent a personnel director to a conference before; you are the first. Good luck.

Item No.	*Priority*	*Action Information*

2 Sayers, Inc.

Sayers, Inc., is a retail department store located in the southeastern United States. It is a part of a large chain of stores that have a very centralized and bureaucratic structure. Advertising and marketing decisions and strategies are formed at headquarters. Recently, the accounting department was pared down and also centralized. Sayers, Inc., has more than 250 employees.

You are Larry Reed, the head of your store's personnel department. Having arrived early, you are in the process of clearing your in-basket before a day-long meeting.

INSTRUCTIONS

You have one hour to go through the items. Place a priority on each item and what action you would take for that item. Delegating is not a course of action you may take. The purpose of this in-basket is to test your abilities as a personnel manager in pressured and difficult situations.

ITEM 1

To: Larry Reed
From: Peter Roper
Re: Company Picnic

As you know, our company picnic will be in just three weeks. Please make the necessary arrangements for location, catering, activities, and decorations. We would also appreciate an extra effort in advertising this event to our employees so they will be able to attend. J. P. and I feel you will do an excellent job for our employees.

ITEM 2

To: Larry Reed
From: Marge Brown, Training Assistant

With the installation of courtesy cards at the registers we have found that customers are complaining about salesclerks not knowing where the merchandise is located in the store. I feel we should have all employees tour the store once every six months so they can be more helpful to our customers. I would appreciate any suggestions you might have in helping to correct this problem.

Thanks, Marge.

ITEM 3

To: Larry Reed
From: Mary Lawrence, Auditing Department

Once again part-time employees are working between 31 to 39 hours. If we let this continue, part-timers will be able to claim they should receive the benefits we give to full-time employees. Your personnel staff should add scheduled hours from the divisions to see if they are correct. Apparently the total hours shown for each employee are inconsistent with what they are actually working. I know you will appreciate this information. See you in the meeting.

ITEM 4

To: Larry Reed

From: Tracy Sinclair

I'm very concerned because I have heard rumors of a union organizing attempt. I can't believe that morale is so poor and conditions so bad that the employees would actually consider this. I just thought you should be aware of these rumors and would like to help if I can.

ITEM 5

Dear Mr. Reed:

I'm very upset that my raise was an increase of only $0.10 per hour. For an entire year of hard work I feel I was very unjustly treated. I also believe that it has something to do with the fact that I am a black woman. In any event, I am considering moving to another job.

Sincerely,
Cynthia A. Toth

ITEM 6

Hey, Larry,

Tina called you earlier and said please call her as soon as possible!

Jo

ITEM 7

To: Larry Reed

From: Bob Reyes, Personnel Assistant

Several employees have inquired about scheduling their vacations during our peak season. I have explained that our company policy specifies that vacations are to be taken in the off-season. I would also like to send out a companywide memo reminding employees of this policy. I made an exception for one employee and evidently the other employees are resentful of this exception, even though it was for a good reason. Just wanted to keep you informed of the situation.

ITEM 8

To: Larry Reed

From: Marion Hughes [Mr. Hopkins' secretary]

Mr. Hopkins would like for you to send out memos to all of the employees who are not taking their required meal periods and breaks. This needs to be expedited due to the Federal Wage and Hour Laws.

ITEM 9

To: All Divisions and Department Heads

From: J. P. Hopkins, Store Manager

I will be holding a general meeting on Friday, December 13. Please make the necessary arrangements in your schedule for that day as the meeting is expected to last the greater part of the day. The meeting will be centered around the previous quarter's sales data for our store. Come prepared.

ITEM 10

To: All Sayers, Inc., Personnel Managers

From: Mr. Charles Cross, Director of Personnel Relations

This is to advise you of a change in procedure concerning our profit-sharing plan for employees. As of January 1, 1990, all employees are required to reaffirm their decision to waive participation in the program. If at this time they decide to take advantage of this plan, they will be able to sign up. Forms to implement this new procedure will be arriving at your store in the coming weeks. In one week I will send a follow-up letter to advise you of specifics.

Item No.	*Priority*	*Action Information*

110 Happy Aircraft Company*

INSTRUCTIONS

Happy Aircraft Company is an aerospace subcontracting company located in Birmingham, Alabama. The company has 1,200 employees and manufactures various parts and components for large aerospace firms, such as Boeing and McDonnell Douglas.

Happy Aircraft was founded in 1979 by Maynard Jackson, a black entrepreneur, and has manufactured aircraft parts used in the construction of the DC-12 and the Boeing 757. Happy Aircraft was originally part of Boeing but was sold to a group of Boeing employees in hard economic times. The employees, headed by Mr. Maynard, used the plant assets as collateral and obtained financing for the buyout through the First Alabama Bank of Montgomery.

The company is currently developing new methods of manufacturing parts for the upcoming Boeing 777 project. The 777 is Boeing's first plane designed completely on computers—eight IBM mainframes. Happy Aircraft's Research and Development staff has been working with Boeing on the 777 project since 1990. The company also is working on improvements for existing parts for the Boeing 757 and the 737. However, orders for the 737 and 757 have fallen due to the decreased demand for these narrow-bodied jets. The market has shifted to wide-bodied jets, especially since the Japanese and other Asian carriers' demand for the Boeing wide-bodies has pushed Boeing's backlog of orders to a record $90.2 billion. Even so, the temporary slump in narrow-bodied aircraft orders will force cutbacks at Happy Aircraft Company.

Happy Aircraft is currently faced with layoffs due to decreased work orders from Boeing. The personnel director, Marla Hayes, quit after her fears were confirmed last week that another carrier would cancel more 737 and 757 orders from Boeing.

* This exercise was prepared by Byron Curtis and Professor Walter A. Bogumil, Jr., University of Central Florida.

Lloyd Marlin, a former assistant personnel director with Martin Marrietta in Florida, has been hired to replace her. After two weeks on the job, he has had the difficult task of laying off 60 people and must lay off another 100 within three months.

It is Friday, May 15, 12:00 noon. Mr. Martin must leave for the airport to catch a 2:00 flight to West Palm Beach. He will straighten out some problems with the moving company since his transfer to Birmingham necessitated his immediate transfer two weeks earlier. The following items were on his desk when he arrived at work—today at noon.

ITEM 1

HAPPY AIRCRAFT COMPANY

Interoffice Memorandum

To: Lloyd Marlin

From: Karrie Lamb

Date: May 15

Subject: Layoffs

Mr. Marlin, I know you don't know me—I work on sales staff. I have been with the company for about six months now. Recently, you laid off three salesmen in my department. Since I am so new to the company, I feel that I might be next. Please let me know soon so I will know whether or not to take a recent job offer from a company in Huntsville.

ITEM 2

HAPPY AIRCRAFT COMPANY

Interoffice Memorandum

To: Lloyd Marlin

From: Anwar Zaidi

Date: May 14

Subject: Proper layoff procedures

We agreed that all layoffs from the R & D Department would have to meet with my approval before actually sending out notices. Two of my staff, Ken Eirhart and Cindy Parkman, have been working with the Boeing people on the 777 project for almost two years. They have both come up with some outstanding innovations and Boeing is pleased. I have assured them that they are not being laid off and that I will clear up this mess for them.

I don't know what happened in your department that would cause such a tragic error but you'd better get on it right away. This is a very embarrassing situation for me. Amy Hannibal, whom we did agree would be let go, will surely question me on Monday when she gets her notice.

What's going on? Let's straighten this out as soon as possible!

ITEM 3

HAPPY AIRCRAFT COMPANY

Interoffice Memorandum

To: All Departments

From: Helen Vaughn (Personnel Assistant)

Date: May 18

Subject: Errors in Layoff Notices

Some errors were made in layoff notices. Notices were incorrectly sent to employees that weren't supposed to be laid off in the first place. Please check the personnel department if you have any questions.

ITEM 4

May 11

Birmingham Health Center
2224 Rocky Road
Birmingham, Alabama

Marla Hayes, Personnel Director
c/o Happy Aircraft Company
310 State Highway 39
Birmingham, Alabama

Dear Mrs. Hayes:

On May 8, Mr. Lloyd Martin talked to us about drug screening of your employees. We then proceeded to set up appointments for various employees. However, I feel that you should know that all but one of the 32 employees tested were black. Under normal circumstances, there should be a somewhat even distribution of races. I am not aware of the racial make-up of your employees, but I felt that there was some thing odd here. Please speak to Mr. Marlin about his selection of employees. The test results should be in on May 18.

Sincerely,

Kate Doherty, RN

ITEM 5

HAPPY AIRCRAFT COMPANY

Interoffice Memorandum

To: Lloyd Marlin

From: Annette Bishop

Date: Dinner

Lloyd, thank you for dinner last night. Call me before you leave town. Also: you left your ESOP notes at my place. I have them in my desk. Come over and see me if you want them.

ITEM 6

HAPPY AIRCRAFT COMPANY

Interoffice Memorandum

To: Helen Vaughn

From: John Woodard

Date: May 15

Subject: What's your problem?

There were over 40 people in manufacturing that were laid off this week, however; the date that their layoff will take effect is listed as May 30. Mr. Marlin told us that the employees would have a full month notice. Since your signature appears on all the notices, I am holding you responsible for this mistake. You will print up new notices with the correct dates as soon as possible.

ITEM 7

HAPPY AIRCRAFT COMPANY

Interoffice Memorandum

To: Lloyd Martin

From: Maynard Jackson

Date: May 14

Subject: Employee Stock Ownership Plan

I would like to let you know that your work laying off employees has been very much appreciated. Someone had to be the bad guy and you're it.

Currently, about half of the employees are owners here at Happy Aircraft Company. Perhaps we should look into additional stock options and stock awards and bonuses as a way to increase employee commitment throughout the company. I feel that as the number of employee owners increases, the company will benefit as more employees would be willing to work with us to get through this problem. My friend Jack Stack of the Springfield Remanufacturing Company in Missouri has been able to get through the toughest of times—and his company is 100 percent employee owned. I would like to discuss with you this option. So look into ESOPs further and tell me what you come up with. I should hear from you within the next two weeks.

ITEM 8

HAPPY AIRCRAFT COMPANY

Interoffice Memorandum

To: Lloyd Marlin

From: Jackie Stone

Date: May 14

Subject: Mr. Jackson's Birthday

ITEM 8 *(concluded)*

This is just to let you know that Mr. Jackson's 50th birthday is tomorrow. We're planning a surprise party for him in your office around lunchtime (1:00). Mrs. Jackson will drop by with the cake. The training and development room next to your office has plenty of room for the party. See you at the party.

ITEM 9

HOOVER BAPTIST FUNERAL HOME

May 12, 1992

Marla Hayes
310 State Highway 39
Birmingham, Alabama

Dear Mrs. Hayes,

The FAA has released the body of your husband. We are now making preparations for the funeral services. We attempted to reach you by telephone over the weekend. After such a difficult time, it is understandable that you might be staying with relatives.

Please respond as soon as possible so that we can begin preparations for the burial of Mr. Hayes. May God be with you.

Sincerely yours,
John Fairfield

ITEM 10

ACCIDENT REPORT

Date: ____/-____/-____ Time:_____________ Manager:_____________

Employee Name:_________________________________ ID#_______

Description of Accident:____

____

____

____

____

Location:____

Witness:________________ Employee Signature:_______________

Item No.	*Priority*	*Action Information*

111 Burton Electronics

Burton Electronics is a small manufacturing company located in Binghamton, New York. The company has 300 employees and manufactures electronic components for telephones, computers, aircraft, and appliances. Its customers include major manufacturers, both foreign and domestic. Burton's organization chart as it relates to this exercise is shown in Exhibit 1.

The company was founded in 1964 by Ken Burton and has developed a reputation for its high-quality products. Burton has shown a profit for the last 18 years. However, a financial analysis shows a downward trend in sales over the last three years. The company has not yet been successful in reversing this trend. The decline in sales has led to labor force problems, in that some employees have been overworked in efforts to complete projects on schedule while employees in other departments were idle because new projects were not started.

Richard Benson, the company personnel director, retired eight months ago after 16 years with Burton. Helen Wilcox, a bright and experienced personnel director, was hired to replace him. She immediately began to work on the uneven workload and developed a system of transferring or loaning employees interdepartmentally. Although the problem is not completely resolved, it has improved substantially.

Employee turnover is high in both the manufacturing and research and development departments. Helen suspects that the high turnover in R&D is directly related to the decreased sales. She feels that, if the R&D division were more productive and innovative, the salespeople would be more successful.

Helen's staff consists of her secretary, Ellen McKervey, and two assistants. The assistants, Anthony Cerratani and Kay Wallenberg, are both business students at the State University of New York at Binghamton. They work full-time during the summers and part-time during the school year. Mr. Burton is a strong believer in encouraging students to work while attending college and thinks that both the company and the students benefit from their experience with the company.

Today is Monday, December 2. Helen has just returned from a two-week vacation. Exhibit 2 shows the calendar for the month. The following items were in her in-basket when she arrived at work.

EXHIBIT 1 Burton Electronics

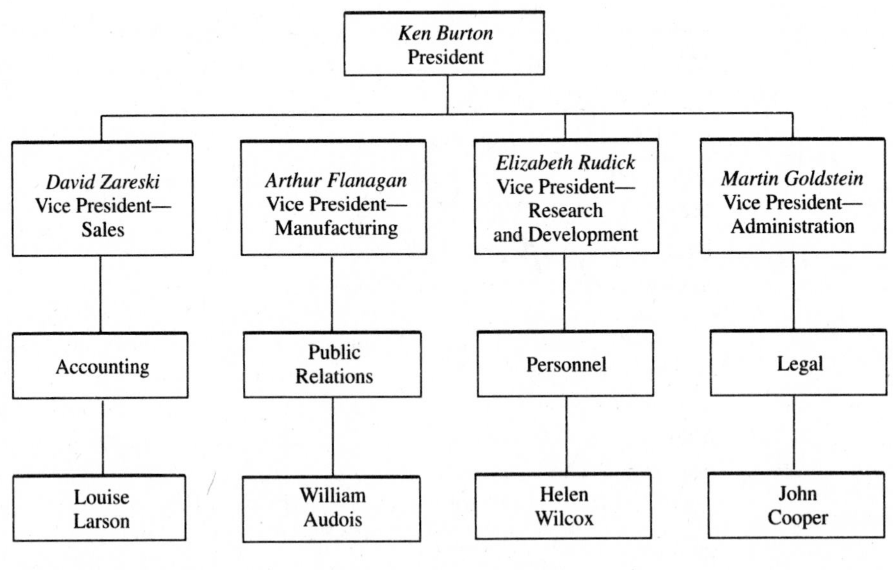

EXHIBIT 2 Calendar

December						
S	*M*	*T*	*W*	*T*	*F*	*S*
1	2	3	4	5	6	7
8	9	10	11	12	13	14
15	16	17	18	19	20	21
22	23	24	25	26	27	28
29	30	31				

ITEM 1

BURTON ELECTRONICS

Interoffice Memorandum

To: Helen Wilcox

From: Raymond Greenfield, Foreman (Manufacturing)

Date: November 22

Subject: Suggestion Plan

What's going on with your suggestion plan? In the last six months I've submitted eight very useful suggestions. I know that at least five of my men have also submitted suggestions. We haven't heard any response at all. It sure makes you feel like you're wasting your time. How about getting on the stick so we can improve the way this company operates.

ITEM 2

BURTON ELECTRONICS

Interoffice Memorandum

To: Helen Wilcox

From: Anthony Cerratani

Date: November 27

Subject: On-the-Job Accident Statistics

1989 Year-to-Date On-the-Job Accident Report

Dept.	*Jan.*	*Feb.*	*Mar.*	*Apr.*	*May*	*Jun.*	*Jul.*	*Aug.*	*Sep.*	*Oct.*
Sales	0	1	0	2	0	0	11	0	0	0
Manufacturing	9	11	12	16	13	15	17	23	16	19
R&D	2	1	1	0	0	1	0	0	1	1
Administration	0	0	0	1	0	0	0	0	0	0

I found the manufacturing accident rate startling and felt I should bring it to your attention.

Should I investigate further?

ITEM 3

BURTON ELECTRONICS

Interoffice Memorandum

To: Helen Wilcox

From: Lucy Koski

Date: November 29

ITEM 3 (concluded)

Subject: Unfair Working Hours

This is to inform you that I am planning to contact the local office of the Wage and Hour Division.

I have been required to work unpaid overtime by my boss, Mr. Flannigan, many times over the last six months. I worked the overtime without complaining because I thought I would be rewarded in other ways, such as a raise. No rewards have ever come.

Earlier this week I told Mr. Flannigan that I am no longer able to work 12-hour days without getting overtime pay. He responded by telling me, "You'll work the hours you need to in order to get the job done. And if you can't handle the job, there are other secretaries in the company who would love to have your job."

I have not taken a vacation this year because I was planning to take it the last two weeks of December. Now Mr. Flannigan tells me that there is too much work in the office for me to take a vacation.

I want you to be aware of the situation when you are contacted by the Wage and Hour Division office.

ITEM 4

BURTON ELECTRONICS

Interoffice Memorandum

To: Helen Wilcox

From: John Craig, Unit Manager, R&D

Subject: Salary Increase for Gary Wilson

Date: November 25

I am writing to request a policy waiver. Our policy states that the maximum annual salary increase is 10 percent. In my department, that is not always practical. With the shortage of engineers, we really have to compete with other companies in order to keep our good people.

Gary Wilson has been offered a job with another company here in Binghamton. It will take a substantial salary increase to keep him. He is one of our most motivated and creative engineers and we cannot afford to lose him. I am asking for a 15 percent raise for Gary in my 1990 budget.

Please send your okay as soon as possible so I can get back to Gary.

ITEM 5

BURTON ELECTRONICS

Interoffice Memorandum

To: Helen Wilcox

From: Ken Burton

Date: November 29

ITEM 5 (concluded)

Subject: Employee of the Month Program

I have heard that other companies have been very successful in motivating their employees by implementing employee recognition programs. These programs are said to increase employee commitment and morale.

I would like to see an "Employee of the Month" program instituted here at Burton Electronics. I have a few ideas and would like to discuss them with you.

Please see me the week of December 2 so we can begin setting up this program. We should aim to have it in effect by January 1.

ITEM 6

BINGHAMTON CENTRAL HIGH SCHOOL

November 22,
Ms. Helen Wilcox
c/o Burton Electronics
1386 Riverside Drive
Binghamton, NY 13905

Dear Ms. Wilcox:

The Future Business Leaders Club of Binghamton Central High School would like to invite you to be the guest speaker at our January meeting. The meeting will be held Thursday, January 23 at 3:30 PM at the school. We would like you to discuss "The Changing Role of the Professional Personnel Manager."

We believe that your presentation will be quite informative for us because our club members plan to either major in business in college or go into business for themselves.

We hope you will be able to accept this invitation. Our sponsor, Mrs. Mary Watson, will call you soon for confirmation.

Sincerely,

Kathryn Dahulich

ITEM 7

BURTON ELECTRONICS

Interoffice Memorandum

To: Helen Wilcox

From: Bill Sullivan

Date: November 25

Subject: Morale

I need your help with a morale problem.

I have a deadline of December 27 to finish my current project. In order to meet that deadline, I am having to ask my employees to work overtime. They just refuse, and seem to feel that if we don't finish the project on schedule it's not their problem. According to the Union Contract, I can schedule overtime if I don't get enough volunteers. But with the bad attitudes around here, I'm almost afraid to take that step.

What should I do?

ITEM 8

BURTON ELECTRONICS

Interoffice Memorandum

To: Helen Wilcox

From: Jack Day, Foreman (Manufacturing)

Date: November 21

Subject: Larry Smith

I have a serious problem with one of my employees. I would like you to help me if you can.

Larry Smith appears to have a serious drinking problem. He's been with the company 13 years and until the last 2 years he has been a satisfactory worker.

I have tried talking to him about his drinking, but he continues to deny he has a problem. I have even talked to his son who works in another department here at Burton. He told me that whenever it seems like his father is doing better, something happens to make him slip up. Larry has even come to work intoxicated a few times. I have sent him home, but I am concerned that he is becoming a bad influence on the other welders.

Is there anything more I can do or is it time to dismiss him?

ITEM 9

To Helen Wilcox

Date 11/27 Time 3:20 ☐ AM ☒ PM

WHILE YOU WERE OUT

M RS. Watson

of Binghamton Central H.S.

Phone ( ) 675-4001

Area Code Number Extension

TELEPHONED	✓	PLEASE CALL	
CALLED TO SEE YOU	✓	WILL CALL AGAIN	
WANTS TO SEE YOU		URGENT	

RETURNED YOUR CALL	

Message

EM

Operator

ITEM 10

BURTON ELECTRONICS

Interoffice Memorandum

To: Helen Wilcox

From: Dave Zareski

Date: November 20

Subject: Training Salespeople for the International Market

We are planning to expand our niche in the overseas market. I would like to have my salespeople trained in "dealing with the foreign customer."

We currently sell to West Germany, but I know my people are working at a disadvantage because they were never trained on the differences between a German and an American customer.

ITEM 10 *(concluded)*

We would like to expand our marketing territory to include Saudi Arabia and Japan. Can you pick a training package for me? Items I would like to see included are:

- Social and Business Customs.
- Key Words in the Language.
- Key Cities.
- General Orientation to the Country.

We are planning to send some of our people to a conference in Japan in April, so if you can have this ready by March 1, I would be most appreciative.

Call me if you have any questions.

ITEM 11

BURTON ELECTRONICS

Interoffice Memorandum

To: Helen Wilcox

From: Martin Goldstein

Date: November 27

Subject: 199x Budget

Our company's annual budget meeting will be held January 2. Since this will be your first budget for Burton Electronics, I would like to meet with you the week of December 16 to review your plans.

Please contact me to set up a meeting time.

Item No.	*Priority*	*Action Information*

112 Continental Parcel of America

INSTRUCTIONS

For the purpose of this exercise, you are to consider yourself to be Chris Barr. The company you work for is Continental Parcel of America, an air freight service specializing in rapid pickup and delivery of various immediate supply parcels between commercial companies throughout the United States. Central headquarters are located in Baltimore, Maryland, with four area headquarters over the United States, and districts falling within these areas.

Until this week, you have been the assistant manager in the Decatur, Georgia, area, Atlanta district. On Monday, January 7, you were notified that you were being immediately transferred to the position of city station manager in New Orleans, Louisiana, in charge of the eastern section. The present manager, Robert Morgan, suffered a sudden heart attack and is not expected to return to work. His assistant manager, Jeffrey Farnsworth, has not had enough experience to assume the position of manager. Because of this emergency situation, you have flown into New Orleans for the weekend on Saturday night, January 12, to familiarize yourself with the station. You must return to Decatur to complete some urgent final work in your present position and will not be able to return permanently to New Orleans until Thursday, January 17, at the earliest.

You are now in your new office. It is Sunday, January 13. You have been unable to contact your predecessor, Robert Morgan, because he is in the intensive care unit of the hospital. Your efforts to reach the district director, Patrick Bennett, were unsuccessful because he and the administrative manager, J. J. Stewart, have flown to Baltimore. You would like to take care of as much as possible before returning to Decatur. You will not be able to take any work back with you because of your heavy schedule, and your plane is due to leave in one and one-half hours.

Material has been left for you in your in-basket by the secretary, Doris Moses. This consists of letters, memoranda, reports, and so on. There is also a calendar, organizational chart, and policy manual. Your files are locked and the secretary has the key. You are unable to make any outgoing phone calls because the switchboard is closed.

Since you will be out of town, all actions should be handled in the form of written memos, letters, or notes to yourself or others. (You may want to use the in-basket memos to write on.)

Remember, all actions you deem necessary should be in writing. You now have one and one-half hours to complete all necessary work.

EXHIBIT 1

January						
Sunday	*Monday*	*Tuesday*	*Wednesday*	*Thursday*	*Friday*	*Saturday*
		1	2	3	4	5
6	7	8	9	10	11	12
13	14	15	16	17	18	19
20	21	22	23	24	25	26
27	28	29	30	31		

EXHIBIT 2

February						
Sunday	*Monday*	*Tuesday*	*Wednesday*	*Thursday*	*Friday*	*Saturday*
					1	2
3	4	5	6	7	8	9
10	11	12 Lincoln's Birthday	13	14	15	16
17	18	19 Mardi Gras	20 Ash Wednesday	21	22	23
24	25	26	27	28		

EXHIBIT 3 Eastern Section

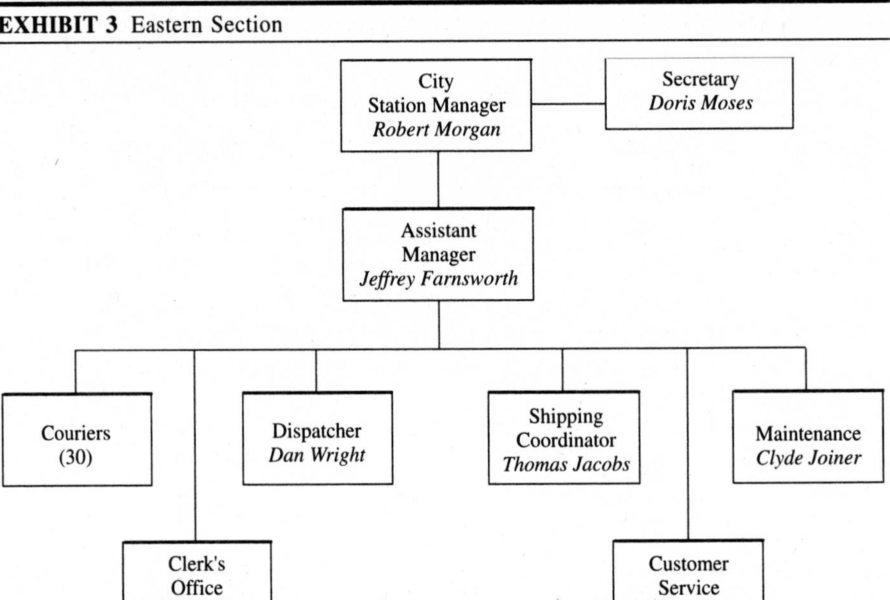

EXHIBIT 4 Continental Parcel of America, HQD Louisiana District, New Orleans

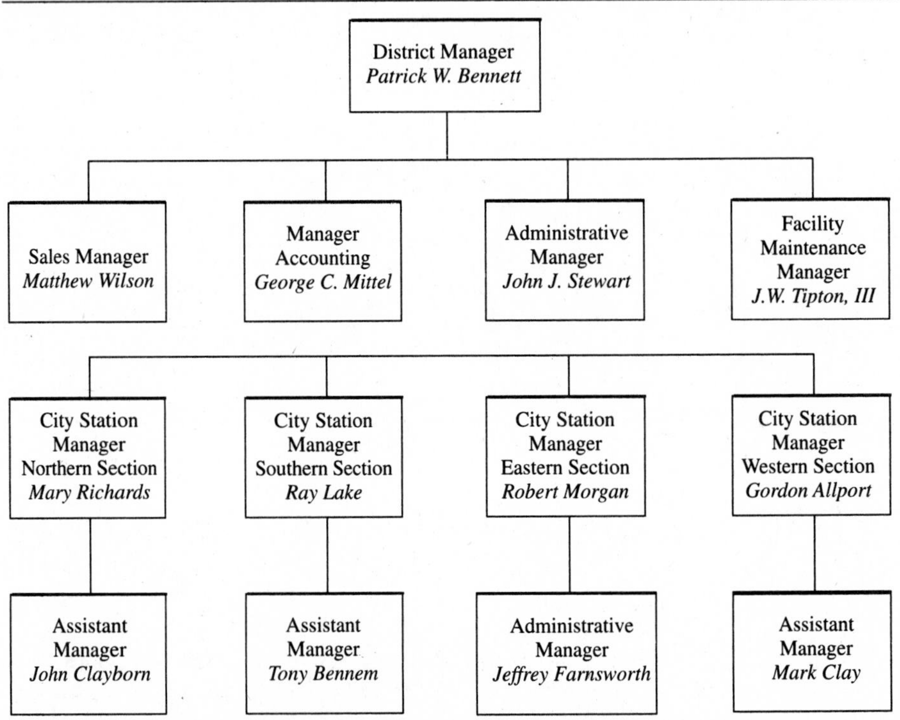

Continental Parcel of America

Policy Manual

Table of Contents

SECTION I Letter from the President

Dear Fellow Employees:

It is with great pleasure that I send this revised policy manual to you. The reason I say this is because the necessity of having to update our manual represents an important stage in the growth of our company. In addition, this reflects the vast amount of progress Continental Parcel of America has made since our first day of operation.

The main thought I wish to express, however, is that even though a policy manual is a set of rules, it is not a "set of don'ts." Instead, this manual serves as an extension of the genuine

SECTION I Letter from the President

interest CPA expresses for its employees.

One of our utmost concerns is that all of our employees are treated with the same fairness and equality. In order to accomplish that goal, it is imperative to have a framework by which day-to-day situations can be handled. With this framework and your cooperation CPA will remain a rewarding place to work.

Keeping your best interest in mind, I suggest that each of you become familiar with this new manual. Not only will it aid you in learning the benefits which CPA provides but it will also inform you of the changes in your job areas. While some of these changes will require a brief period of time for adjustment, the changes will result in less complicated job duties and a more efficient use of your time.

Finally, I would like to express my appreciation to everyone for their dedication and motivation in their work. Without these two factors CPA would not be experiencing the amount of success that we now have. Each employee of CPA can share with me the pride in our accomplishments to date. It is with the contributions of everyone that we can continue to proceed on the course of and determine the future progress of continental Parcel of America.

Alan C. Norton

President

SECTION II Employment

A. DETERMINATION OF EMPLOYEE NEEDS

The acquisition of all employees will first start with a determination from headquarters as to whether or not a need exists for a new employee.

Two alternatives are provided for this determination. First, a periodic check will be made at the headquarter's level and, if the need is determined, the appropriate manager will be notified. Second, at any time, and individual manager may request this determination. All requests will be handled through the Operations Division.

B. PROCEDURES FOR THE ACQUISITION OF NEW RECRUITS

There are three phases of processing new recruits. Phase one is conducted by company headquarters in determining and confirming the need of a recruit. Phase two is conducted by the Personnel Division at city headquarters. This phase includes the screening of initial applications for employment, checking references, verification of past employment and educational histories, and processing physical examination records.

Periodically, personnel will send lists of approved candidates to managers and, if necessary, managers may request approved candidate lists. The third phase is conducted by the manager who will be the immediate supervisor of the employee. This consists of personal interviews with approved candidates after review of the candidate data from personnel. The decision to hire rests with the manager.

C. NEPOTISM

The policy of hiring and promoting the best-qualified individuals shall extend to the relatives

SECTION II EMPLOYMENT *(concluded)*

of CPA employees, except that in no event may relatives report to each other, nor may husbands and wives have the same supervisor.

D. EEO

It is the policy of Continental Parcel of America to extend equal employment opportunities to all qualified persons, including handicapped individuals, disabled veterans, and veterans of the Vietnam era, without regard to race, color, sex, religion, age, or national origin. To deny one's contribution to our efforts because he or she is a member of a minority group is an injustice, not only to the individual but to the company. It is, therefore, the intent and desire of the company that equal employment opportunity be provided in employment, promotions, wages, benefits, and all other privileges, terms, and conditions of employment.

SECTION III Training and Evaluation

A. ORIENTATION

While continental Parcel makes every attempt to hire and promote the best-qualified individuals, it realizes that each job may have special and unique methods, language, and requirements to be learned. In order to facilitate this learning and to effect maximum productivity from all employees, each newly hired or promoted employee will complete a one-week training and orientation course.

B. FIELD TRAINING

After completion of the orientation program, all employees, each newly hired or promoted employee, will complete a minimum two-day training program at each respective individual's job location. It shall be the manager's responsibility to meet this requirement.

C. PROBATION AND EVALUATION

A probation period of one year is required for each newly hired or promoted employee. During this time, each individual will be evaluated, by a performance appraisal, on a quarterly basis. The performance appraisals shall be handled through the individual's immediate manager.

SECTION IV Benefits

A. VACATIONS

Continental Parcel of America provides vacations with pay for all eligible employees for the purpose of rest and recreation. CPA is convinced that both the employee and the company benefit thereby and employees are better prepared for the coming year. Each employee will be responsible for notifying his respective manager one month in advance of the preferred time period. No more than two employees from a work group, size 10 or more, may take vacation at the same time. No more than one employee from a work group, size 9 or less, make take vacation at the same time. Due to manpower needs, no employee shall be granted vacation during the time period of December 1 to January 15.

SECTION IV Benefits *(concluded)*

B. HOLIDAYS

Certain days of religious and historic importance are observed by the company as paid holidays in accordance with special eligibility rules.

The following holidays are observed by the company and eligible employees will receive holiday pay accordingly:

New Year's Day	Thanksgiving
Memorial Day	Christmas
Independence Day	Drifting holidays (three unscheduled drifting holidays)
Labor Day	

One drifting holiday will be designated by the manager and selected from among the following days:

Day after New Year's
Friday after Thanksgiving
Christmas Eve
Day after Christmas
New Year's Eve

C. OVERTIME

All overtime in any department or work group will be divided equally among all the respective employees unless the employee elects not to take the overtime.

D. HEALTH AND OTHER BENEFITS

Each full-time employee of CPA is entitled to certain insurance programs and retirement programs. These benefits are to aid the employee as well as CPA. The above programs are outlined in the *Employee Handbook.*

SECTION V Customer Service

A. CUSTOMER COMPLAINTS

All customer complaints received by telephone shall be directed to headquaters' complaint office via a toll-free number. However, any complaints which cannot be handled sufficiently at this office will be referred to either the respective city station complaint officer or the city station manager. All written communications regarding complaints will be handled by the appropriate city station and the respective manager or complaint officer.

B. CUSTOMER DELIVERIES

All customer pickups and deliveries are to be made or arranged to be made according to the dispatcher's daily workload. Under no circumstances should any delays occur for deliveries. All delays resulting in failure to meet TOP PRIORITY deadlines (the sender specifies all TOP PRIORITY deadlines) or failure to meet daily route completion deadlines shall be investigated thoroughly with the courier involved.

C. CUSTOMER DISCOUNTS

Customer discounts are provided to large-volume shippers. The rate for both TOP PRIORITY

SECTION V Customer Service *(concluded)*

and standard deliveries is 5 percent. Any requests for discounts must be referred to headquarters for approval. Under certain conditions, the discount rate may vary; however, changes in the discount rate occur only for exceptional occasions.

D. SPECIAL DELIVERY ARRANGEMENTS

Special arrangement considerations for pickups of packages are not the normal procedures for CPA. Only under exceptional circumstances of large volumes of parcels is this procedure changed. When under contract agreements, special arrangements are not considered unless an adjustment in the contract price occurs.

E. COLLECTION FOR SERVICES

Billing and collection for services is the responsibility of the city headquarters' accounting department. Any complaints or requests for information should be referred to that department. Pickups will be stopped within one month of a customer's nonpayment of account. The accounting department is responsible for notifying the customer and each station on the decision to discontinue customer service.

SECTION VI Operations Regulations

A. RESTRICTIONS OF PARCELS

1. *Weight Limits.* CPA restricts the weight of parcels it handles. Parcels can weigh no more than 50 pounds. No parcels exceeding 50 pounds will be accepted for delivery unless one week's prior notice is given. With prior notice given, a single parcel may exceed this limit by another 50 pounds. There are no limitations restricting the total weight of parcels from a single shipper, other than no single shipper may send over 300 pounds per day to a single consignee.

2. *Size Limits.* CPA also restricts the size of parcels it handles. Parcels can measure no more than 30 inches in width or height and 70 inches in length. No parcel exceeding these measurements will be accepted unless one week's prior notice is given. With prior notice given, a single parcel may measure up to 45 inches in width or height and 85 inches in length.

3. *Parcel Bundling.* Any parcels being shipped to a single consignee may be bundled for ease of handling. However, if parcel bundling occurs, the above weight and size limits are required.

4. *Parcel Shipping Costs.* The rate for shipping parcels is determined by two factors, distance of travel and weight. The rates for shipping parcels are listed in the *Customer Handbook.* Additional costs are required if a parcel exceeds the parcel restrictions.

5. *Parcel Acceptances.* All city stations are ultimately responsible for accepting only those parcels meeting the parcel restriction. Therefore, if any parcels exceeding these restrictions are accepted by a city station or courier, the proper overcharge will be deducted from a city station's budget.

B. VEHICLE SERVICING

All vehicle servicing is the responsibility of both the respective city stations and couriers.

SECTION VI Operations Regulations *(concluded)*

Therefore, regular maintenance shall adhere to the specifications stated in the *Owner's Manual* of the vehicle.

C. VEHICLE SAFETY

It is the responsibility of both the city station manager and the courier that company vehicles are safe to operate. Any problems which may endanger the welfare of a courier, the care of the vehicle, or the care of the shipment must be corrected, immediately, at the least possible cost.

D. ACCIDENT REPORTING

For insurance reasons, all accidents involving either employees, vehicles, or both must be reported to headquarters within 48 hours.

E. COURIER DELIVERY REPORTS

All courier delivery reports must be filled out properly and turned in by each courier, at the end of the day. After this, each city station's clerical staff shall transfer the appropriate data and send them to headquarters within the next 24 hours.

F. ALTERATION OF DELIVERY ROUTES

If at any time the need arises that requires a route to be changed, technical services at headquarters shall be notified. At no time should a city station manager arbitrarily change a delivery route without first receiving assistance from headquarters.

G. EMPLOYEE REPRIMANDS

If for any reason an employee does not uphold CPA's regulations, then that individual shall be issued a *written warning* upon the manager's discretion of the need of a warning. An employee who receives three *written warnings* within six months shall be subject to suspension.

ITEM 1

MEMORANDUM

To: Chris Barr, City Station Manager

From: Doris Moses

Date: January 9

Welcome to your new job. I have gathered some material that you may need to handle immediately. Since Mr. Morgan's untimely illness, things have gotten a little disorganized.

The letter to the staff was written by Mr. Morgan and he intended its submission to staff personnel immediately. If this, along with the tentative vacation schedules for January and February are satisfactory, please sign them. I will circulate the letter and inform the people that you have granted all vacation requests.

I will be glad to do anything I can to help. Just let me know. I am looking forward to meeting you.

Doris Moses

Doris Moses

Participant Action

1. How important is this item?

2. What should be done about this item?

ITEM 2

MEMORANDUM

To: All Personnel

From: R. Morgan, City Station Manager

Date: October 28

Subject: Policy Manual

As you may be aware, the company has recently published a new policy manual which apparently will be used to control all future operations.

This manual represents a departure from our previous methods of conducting business and I am required to have each member of the staff become familiar with the contents of the new manual. Therefore, I expect each of you to review the manual and take the necessary action to ensure compliance.

R. Morgan

Robert Morgan
Manger, New Orleans
Eastern Section

cc: Patrick Bennett

Participant Action

1. How important is this item?

2. What should be done about this item?

ITEM 3

MEMORANDUM

To: Robert Morgan, City Station manager

From: W. Pierre, Administrative Department

Date: December 18

Subject: Performance Appraisal Reviews

The period for the courier's quarterly performance evaluation is now over a month past due for several employees. the merit raise program, driver of the month, and driver of the quarter are seriously impeded without these reviews. Since part of company policy is to recognize those drivers with outstanding records, I do hope this information will be forthcoming.

The two reviews, which did arrive at my office, were turned in on the old review forms. As you are aware, the new policy changes within CPA included a new form. I am forwarding performance data, and will send you the new review forms if needed.

William Pierre

Participant Action

1. How important is this item?

____

____

____

2. What should be done about this item?

____

____

____

ITEM 3a Courier Quarterly Summary Report, 3d Quarter, 66 Work Days

Truck No.	*Route No.*	*Name of Driver-Courier*	*Total Days Absent*	*Total Times Tardy*	*Total Hours Over-time*	*Accidents per Million Miles*	*Average Pickup and Deliveries per Day*	*Avg. Miles per Day*	*Truck Maint. Cost (cents per mile)*
PA-4A	1	R. Sizemore	2	2	77	2.36	16	245	$0.29
PA-7X	5	C. Stark	3	1	76	1.50	19	265	0.41
PA-9S	6	R. Sullivan	1	0	74	1.32	21	290	0.30
PA-1A	10	O. Kimball	5	63	75	5.0	16	228	0.20
PA-9Q	11	J. Brown	8	2	80	6.80	19	242	0.18
PA-5R	13	II. Shrewsberry	10	8	69	4.61	13	220	0.50
PA-9R	15	C. Bedsole	2	0	75	4.15	19	265	0.28
PA-14R	16	O. Messick	8	4	78	5.61	18	250	0.22
PA-19S	18	G. Dillon	10	12	51	4.16	10	116	0.36
PA-1S	20	D. Stover	4	2	60	7.12	16	230	0.69
PA-2F	25	K. Nordan	3	3	74	4.10	19	261	0.30
PA-11A	30	J. Fincher	1	2	68	4.91	25	320	0.14
PA-6R	4	R. Rockey	4	1	40	1.65	18	260	0.68

ITEM 4

MEMORANDUM

To: R. Morgan

From: M. Hale

Date: January 7

Subject: Customer Satisfaction

Account #76–49244; Route #30

Recently I received a letter from Georgia Electronics regarding a number of TOP PRIORITY shipments, which have been arriving over the holiday period. They have been more than pleased with the service that CPA has extended them during this busy season. They stated that none of the sensitive equipment they received was damaged, and that the driver was very courteous during all transactions (even when he had to wait a few minutes for one package).

In connection with our recognition of drivers, I believe this kind of effort cannot go unnoticed.

M. Hale

M. Hale

Participant Action

1. How important is this item?

____

____

____

2. What should be done about this item?

____

____

____

ITEM 5a

VACATION REQUESTS
JANUARY–FEBRUARY

Name Dates	*Requested*
Doris Moses	Jan. 14–18
George Dillon	Jan. 28–Feb. 1
Art Johnson	Jan. 28–Feb. 1
Brian Ryals	Feb. 4–8
Dan Wright	Feb. 4–8

ITEM 5a (concluded)

VACATION REQUESTS
JANUARY–FEBRUARY

Name Dates	*Requested*
Carl Fristoe	Feb. 11–15
Jeffrey Farnsworth	Feb. 18–22

Participant Action

1. How important is this item?

2. What should be done about this item?

ITEM 5b

MEMORANDUM

To: All Personnel
From: R. Morgan, Station Manager
Date: January 3
Subject: Official Holiday Notice

Lincoln's birthday, Tuesday, February 12th, will be observed as one of the drifting holidays.

R. Morgan

R. Morgan
Station Manager
Eastern Section

Participant Action

1. How important is this item?

2. What should be done about this item?

ITEM 6

MEMORANDUM

To: M. Richards, C. Barr, R. Lake, G. Allport

From: Patrick Bennett

Date: January 8

Subject: Mardi Gras Rush Season

As we approach the Mardi Gras seasonal rush, please be aware that it is imperative for us to plan and coordinate all activities toward the increased service required.

Be prepared to present your project plans, suggestions, or problems on January 18 at 9:00 AM in the Charter Room, Central Office Building. At that time we will discuss and review all plans on a citywide basis.

Patrick Bennett

Patrick Bennett

Participant Action

1. How important is this item?

2. What should be done about this item?

ITEM 7

CONTINENTAL PARCEL OF AMERICA
Eastern Station, Jacksonville, Florida
CONSIGNEE COMPLAINT REPORT LOG
Monthly Report: October

Acct. No.	*Route No.*	*Date*	*Complaint*	*Action*
76–82560	11	10/3	Damaged content goods	Filed: C/dama

ITEM 7 *(concluded)*

75–29326	21	10/3	Broken carton; no content damages	
76–92501	12	10/3	Damaged carton; no content damages	
75–30256	3	10/4	Late pickup	
76–49244	25	10/5	Top priority item late; Ex 9/30	
74–92366	25	10/5	Late pickup	
74–90275	11	10/7	Damaged content goods	Filed: C/dama
76–50247	4	10/10	Damaged carton; slight content damage	
75–30256	3	10/11	Late delivery; Ex 10/17	
76–82560	11	10/11	Carton damaged	
76–49244	25	10/14	Top priority team late; Ex 10/11	
77–29260	8	10/17	Late pickup	
74–92856	10	10/19	Late delivery; 10/17	
77–29260	3	10/21	Damaged content goods	Filed: C/dama
74–86027	3	10/21	Carton damaged	
76–07250	13	10/25	Late delivery; Ex 10/20	
76–08200	11	10/25	Damaged content good	
74–92301	13	10/26	Late pickup	
74–96666	18	10/26	Late delivery; Ex 10/21	
74–82596	11	10/27	Damaged content goods	Filed: C/dama
75–92506	9	10/27	Late Delivery; Ex 10/24	

Participant Action

1. How important is this item?

____

____

____

2. What should be done about this item?

____

____

____

ITEM 8

MEMORANDUM

To: All Station Managers

From: Patrick W. Bennett

Date: December 17

Subject: Compliance with Company Policy

The new company policy manual has been in effect for two (2) months. This manual contains many needed revisions to standard operating procedures in all phases of our operations. It is apparent from a review of our customer complaints and operating data that we are not complying with these new policies.

Therefore, it is imperative that each of you meet with your staff members by December 28, review these policies, and specify what corrective action is required. I also expect you to inform me as to what date these meetings took place, staff reaction, problems encountered, and what further action(s) you plan to undertake for the full and complete compliance with the new standards.

Patrick Bennett

Patrick W. Bennett

CC: Assistant Managers

Participant Action

1. How important is this item?

2. What should be done about this item?

ITEM 8A

MEMORANDUM

To: Jeffrey Farnsworth

From: Robert Morgan

Date: December 21

Subject: December 17 Memo from Patrick Bennett

In accordance with our previous agreement (i.e., that you will handle all matters dealing with company policy changes), please follow up on Patrick Bennett's requests. Keep me informed on what action is being taken and what progress is being made.

Participant Action

1. How important is this item?

2. What should be done about this item?

ITEM 9

MEMORANDUM

January 1

Dear Mr. Morgan:

I do not understand the policy for assigning overtime to the couriers. It seems to me it should be fairly and evenly distributed, but it obviously is not. I have talked to Wright several times but he continues to have other drivers work overtime delivering in areas that I am supposed to cover on my route. I think something should be done about this situation.

Sincerely,

C. Stover

C. Stover
Courier, Route #20

Participant Action

1. How important is this item?

2. What should be done about this item?

ITEM 10

MEMORANDUM

To: Chris Barr

From: J. Farnsworth

Date: January 9

When I recently assumed the position of assistant manager, I was told that I would be allowed to take a week off for vacation fairly soon. I put in my request and the dates were OK'd.

I have made plans for that week and I intend to take that time off. I believe I have a good grasp of the operating procedure and my taking this vacation will not interfere with my job responsibilities.

J. Farnsworth

J. Farnsworth

Participant Action

1. How important is this item?

____

____

____

2. What should be done about this item?

____

____

____

ITEM 11

MEMORANDUM

January 4

Mr. Morgan:

I'm very sorry about the recent late delivery from ABC Manufacturing to Georgia electronics. I had assigned this particular delivery to one driver, but Mr. Farnsworth interceded and gave it to C. Stover, whose route #20 was close to this delivery point. I hope this didn't cause any undue problems for those concerned.

Sincerely,

Dan Wright

Dan Wright

Participant Action

1. How important is this item?

2. What should be done about this item?

ITEM 12

Nevins Novelty Company
24 Revine Avenue
New Orleans, LA

January 8

Continental Parcel of America
Eastern Section
1476 Orange Street
New Orleans, LA

ATTENTION: Robert Morgan, City Station Manager

Gentlemen:

This is to inform you, per contract agreement, that we will need to increase daily shipping allotments beginning February 18th through the 25th. We anticipate, by present order requests, shipping more than 25 packages per day to different consignees. Packages should be no more than 45 pounds each. These will be TOP PRIORITY shipments, and we wish to avoid weekend overcharges if possible.

In view of this early request for increased service and being a long-term customer, we feel it appropriate that you grant us a special discount on this large consignment. Without a discount we may be forced to ship by rail. A decision by January 25th would be appreciated.

Sincerely,

B.S. Pully

B.S. Pully
Manager, Shipping Department
Account #75–95320

Participant Action

1. How important is this item?

2. What should be done about this item?

ITEM 13

MEMORANDUM

To: Chris Barr, City Station manager, Eastern Section

From: Ray Lake, City Station Manager, Southern Section

Date: January 8

Welcome to the New Orleans District! I wanted to alert you to a problem we share as soon as possible. For some time our two districts have overlapped in the southeast section. My route 20 overlaps with your route 18. Some shipments have been missed because we duplicate pickups for four (4) customers. I don't know where the problem really lies—with the dispatcher, couriers, or the routing. Morgan never got around to meeting with me to resolve this problem.

Bennett runs a tight district and does not like mixups. We really should take care of this, considering the fact that you and I have the most congested areas to cover, especially the upcoming Mardi Gras rush.

Could we meet, have lunch, and discuss our mutual problems on January 22?

Again—welcome aboard. Look forward to meeting you.

Ray Lake

Ray Lake

Participant Action

1. How important is this item?

2. What should be done about this item?

ITEM 14

MEMORANDUM

To: Chris Barr

From: J. Farnsworth

Date: January 8

We should meet as soon as possible to discuss the continuing policy of this station. Due to Mr. Morgan's untimely illness, a few items need to be cleared up.

At this time, I don't see any major problems as Mr. Morgan let me handle quite a number of the administrative and other details. Everything is running along smoothly. We'll be waiting for you to effect your transfer.

J. Farnsworth

J. Farnsworth

Participant Action

1. How important is this item?

2. What should be done about this item?

ITEM 15

December 10

Mr. Morgan:

I have a bit of a problem on my route. A customer of ours, whom we service almost every day, is the brother of my ex-wife. He tries his best to make life very hard for me every time I make a stop there. He is a manager at Jason's, LTD. I would like very much to stay

ITEM 15 *(concluded)*

at Continental, but if I am forced to continue servicing this route, I may have to look for another job. Hopefully, I can get another route or at least delete this customer from my present route. I talked to Mr. Wright and he said something might be worked out if I wrote you and explained the situation.

Thanks,

Charlie Badsole

Charlie Bledsole
Route #15

Participant Action

1. How important is this item?

____

____

____

2. What should be done about this item?

____

____

____

ITEM 16

Ormond Antiques
3211 Broad St.
New Orleans, LA

November 29

Continental Parcel of America
Eastern Section
1476 Orange St.
New Orleans, LA

REGARDING; Account #72–15460, Route #20

ATTENTION: M. Hale, Customer Service

Gentlemen:

On November 27th, we received a valuable shipment of antiques from Rockefeller Center in New York. Several very valuable ceramic figures were damaged beyond repair, and the

ITEM 16 *(concluded)*

carton was visibly damaged. The driver left before the receipt of delivery was signed. We consider this flagrant disregard of company policy. Obviously, we cannot tolerate any further reoccurrence of this nature.

Sincerely,

George Hardwell

George Hardwell
Manager

Mr. Morgan
I talked to Mr. Farnsworth, and he said he'd take care of it. That was over a month ago, and nothing has been done. They did not file for damages. What should I do?
M. Hall

Participant Action

1. How important is this item?

2. What should be done about this item?

ITEM 17

Bithlo Computers
119 Fountain Street
New Orleans, LA

January 3

Continental parcel of America
1476 Orange Street
New Orleans, LA

ITEM 17 *(concluded)*

ATTENTION: Manager, New Accounts

Gentlemen:

We have to ship 10 pieces of a computer to Saint Louis, Missouri, within the next 20 days. We usually ship by water, but because of the urgency of this delivery we require special handling and service. We normally send these in a box type 411, which is 43" x 75" x 24", 100 pounds.

We need to know the packing and shipping prices as soon as possible.

Sincerely,

Marlene Dubois

Marlene Dubois
453-9238

This is a possible new customer, but the measurements exceed our limits. I've talked to them and they could change the size, but I prefer the box they have now. Should I accept their boxes for shipping?

M. Hall

Participant Action

1. How important is this item?

2. What should be done about this item?

ITEM 18

MEMORANDUM

To: R. Morgan

From: J. Farnsworth

Date: January 7

Subject: Covering of Courier Routes

I have a problem with Dan Wright. It seems that the dispatcher, Dan Wright, doesn't want to have each courier cover his own route. I've talked to him about it, but all he says is that some couriers can handle more that others. I don't understand his reasoning.

J. Farnsworth

J. Farnsworth

Participant Action

1. How important is this item?

___

___

___

2. What should be done about this item?

___

___

___

ITEM 19

November 30

Mr. Morgan:

The change to the new radial tire has drastically cut down on the number of blow-outs that the courier trucks have received. However, the other change to a different type starter system has resulted in many operating difficulties and has negated any time savings that the tire change gave us.

We as a group have discussed this with Clyde Joiner, but he doesn't seem to realize the extra costs of maintenance and efficient customer service. It is making us have

ITEM 19 *(concluded)*

to hurry through our routes, not allowing us to serve the customers, and having to speed between points.

Sincerely,

Ron Rockey, Route #4

R. Sizemore, Route #1

Art Johnson, Route #7

Charlie Bedsole, Route #15

Steve Lucas, Route #24

Participant Action

1. How important is this item?

2. What should be done about this item?

ITEM 20

MEMORANDUM

To: R. Morgan

From: Dan Wright

Date: December 28

Subject: Continued Service for Overdue Account

ITEM 20 *(concluded)*

I thought some clarification of policy should be made, so that some things can be cleared up.

Recently, Ms. Hale sent me a letter concerning Account #76–32095, an overdue account, requesting a termination of service until further notice. I did this as per company policy, but Mr. Farnsworth came in and said to keep servicing the account, that it would be taken care of. I then received another letter from Ms. Hale wanting to know why I was still giving service to this client. I again asked Mr. Farnsworth, and he said not to worry about it.

The client is asking for a parcel to be picked up in three days, a special package. Should I continue giving service to them or not?

Dan Wright

Dan Wright

Participant Action

1. How important is this item?

____

____

____

2. What should be done about this item?

____

____

____

ITEM 21

MEMORANDUM

To: R. Morgan

From: Clyde Joiner

Date: January 3

The recent maintenance changes for our trucks seem to be having a generally positive effect on truck performance. Since changing to NEWYEAR tires and using Ben's Repairs Shop we have cut down on vehicle problems.

Clyde Joiner

Clyde Joiner

Participant Action

1. How important is this item?

2. What should be done about this item?

ITEM 22

December 27

Continental Parcel of America
Eastern Section
1476 Orange Street
New Orleans, LA

ATTENTION: Manager

A person whom I know, Clyde Joiner, works in your company and doesn't seem to represent the type of organization in which he works. He spends most of his time at the "Hole in the Wall" bar, day and night, and hangs out there with a rough crowd from Ben's Repairs Shop.

They are almost always causing problems in the neighborhood by instigating arguments and fights. I'm surprised a man like this is allowed to work for a company which uses the name of our country.

A Helpful Citizen

Participant Action

1. How important is this item?

2. What should be done about this item?

ITEM 23

MEMORANDUM

To: R. Morgan

From: J. J. Stewart

Date: December 31

We now have the new performance appraisal forms which, by new policy regulations, should be put to use immediately. Since we have not yet received your quarterly courier reports, I urge you to get the forms as soon as possible. They are more thorough than the ones formerly used, and will also make the reports much easier to complete.

As you are aware, we need these appraisals before we can compile any bonus and raise proposals. Please get to it as soon as possible.

J. J. Stewart

J. J. Stewart

Participant Action

1. How important is this item?

2. What should be done about this item?

ITEM 24

MEMORANDUM

To: R. Morgan, City Station Manager

From: J. J. Stewart, Administrative Department Manager

The following is a list of courier applicants who meet standard qualifications for hire on a regular or substitute basis. All will be available beginning January 3. Initial screening interviews have been conducted; it is up to you to interview and hire as station needs dictate after receiving the necessary operations department approval.

Jim C. Kilgallen
7283 West Real Street
423-9783

Ray Leecher
85 King Street
623-7908

Raymond Cortez
2209 39th Street, S.E.
Apt. 3225

ITEM 24 *(concluded)*

Edgar Redding
3954 5th Street
425-6203

Ny Simmons
119 West Haven
423-1892

Roberta Simon
69 Jules Avenue
623-9781

Jody Llewyn
1578 Spring Terrace
425-1782

Pat Beecker
36 River Street, Apt. 29
623-8025

Jimon Waraz
2209 30th Street, S.E.
Apt. 3112
425-4098

Alex Curry
SW 19th Street, Apt. 2
423-7860

Robert Lee
3429 Juniper Lane
623-1785

Mr. Morgan
Operations has approved the hiring of one more courier as of January 3rd. A few worked during the Christmas holidays. Robert Lee and Ny Simmons both worked well.

Doris

Participant Action

1. How important is this item?

2. What should be done about this item?

ITEM 25

MEMORANDUM

To: R. Morgan

From: Mark Clay, City Station Assistant Manager

ITEM 25 *(concluded)*

Western Section

Date: January 4

We have heard that your use of a new type and brand of tire has helped to reduce maintenance costs in that area, and increased customer service.

When you get a chance, please send the name and brand of tire you have switched to.

Mark Clay

Mark Clay

Participant Action

1. How important is this item?

____

____

____

2. What should be done about this item?

____

____

____

ITEM 26

MEMORANDUM

To: R. Morgan

From: Dan Wright

Date: January 3

Subject: Expected Increased Business

Just to remind you, with the Mardi Gras season beginning the day before Ash Wednesday, I've already started to receive inquiries concerning our ability to handle extra business during that period of time.

This period of time traditionally is one of excessive work loads, and the need for extra help will become imperative in the near future. I believe I can work out a schedule to help alleviate the burden, if we know what manpower will be available.

If I can be of any further assistance during this time, please feel free to call me.

Dan Wright

Dan Wright

Participant Action

1. How important is this item?

2. What should be done about this item?

ITEM 27

MEMORANDUM

To: R. Morgan
From: J. Farnsworth
Date: December 28

I have received several inquiries from the drivers as to when their reviews will be completed. They are pressing for raises and are curious to know how their performances have been rated.

If you sign the authorization I've typed up, I'll go ahead and complete the reviews and award merit raises.

I authorize the assistant manager, J. Farnsworth, to complete all reviews and take action as he sees fit.

Station Manager

Participant Action

1. How important is this item?

2. What should be done about this item?

ITEM 28

MEMORANDUM

To: R. Morgan, City Station Manager

From: J. J. Stewart, Administrative Department Manager

Date: January 2

Subject: Traffic Violation Report

Our office has received notification of a speeding and failure to yield right of way ticket to courier Jack Brown, while driving CPA vehicle 90 on December 7th, 2:36 PM To date the only confirmation we have received is from the New Orleans Police Department.

I'm sure I need not remind you of CPA regulations. Please handle this immediately or it may affect more than the driver's record.

J. J. Stewart

J. J. Stewart

Participant Action

1. How important is this item?

---

2. What should be done about this item?

Part 5

Appendixes

Appendix A

Glossary of Human Resource Management Terms

A

absentees Absentees are employees who are scheduled to be at work but are not present.

accident and sickness policies Accident and sickness policies usually provide a minimum-care stipend for several weeks up to six months to help employees defray the loss of income while they are sick or recovering from an accident.

accreditation Accreditation is a process of certifying the competence of a person in an area of capability. The Society for Human Resource Management operates an accreditation program for personnel professionals.

accrued benefit Accrued benefit is the total amount of a pension benefit that a person has earned and will receive on reaching the plan's normal retirement age. Accrued benefits cannot be reduced, directly or indirectly, by a plan amendment. Accrued benefits include early retirement benefits.

active listening Active listening requires the listener to stop talking, to remove distractions, to be patient, and to empathize with the talker.

adverse selection Adverse selection occurs when an insurance company has a disproportionately high percentage of insureds who will make claims in the future. Adverse selection often results when people are given a chance to buy insurance without prescreening, which often means that a higher than normal proportion have a condition that is likely to cause them to be frequent claimants.

affirmative action programs Affirmative action programs are detailed plans developed by employers to undo the results of past employment discrimination, or to ensure equal opportunity in the future.

Age Discrimination in Employment Act of 1967 (as amended) This act prohibits discrimination on employment because of age against those who are 40 and older.

Albemarle Paper Company* v. *Moody Supreme Court case in which it was ruled that the validity of job tests must be documented and that employee performance standards must be unambiguous.

American Federation of Labor and Congress of Industrial Organization (AFL-CIO) The AFL-CIO is a federation of most national unions. It exists to provide a unified focal point for the labor movement, to assist national unions, and to influence government policies that affect members and working people.

Americans with Disabilities Act (ADA) This act requires employers to make reasonable accommodations for disabled employees. It prohibits discrimination against disabled people.

applied research Applied research is a study of practical problems, the solutions of which will lead to improved performance.

arbitration Arbitration is the submission of a dispute to a neutral third party.

assessment centers Assessment centers are a standardized form of employee appraisal that relies on multiple types of evaluation and multiple raters.

associate membership Associate membership in a labor organization allows people who are not employed under a union contract to affiliate with a union by paying fees and dues in return for union-supported benefits.

attitude surveys Attitude surveys are systematic methods of determining what employees think about their organization. The surveys usually are done through questionnaires. Attitude survey feedback results when the information collected is reported back to the participants. This process then usually is followed by action planning to identify and resolve specific areas of employee concern.

attrition Attrition is the loss of employees who leave the organization's employment.

audit report The audit report is a comprehensive description of personnel activities. It includes both commendation for effective practices and recommendations for improving practices that are ineffective.

audit team An audit team consists of those people who are responsible for evaluating the performance of the personnel department.

authorization cards Authorization cards are forms signed by prospective union members. The cards indicate their wish to have an election to determine whether a labor organization will represent the workers in their dealings with management.

autonomous work groups Autonomous work groups are teams of workers, without a formal company-appointed leader, who decide among themselves most decisions traditionally handled by supervisors.

autonomy Autonomy is having control over one's work.

B

bargaining book A bargaining book is a compilation of the negotiation team's plans for collective bargaining with labor or management. Increasingly, the bargaining book is being replaced by information stored in a company or union computer.

bargaining committee The union bargaining committee consists of union officials and stewards who negotiate with management's representatives to determine wages, hours, and working conditions to be embodied in the labor agreement.

behaviorally anchored rating scales (BARS) BARS rate employees on a scale that has specific behavioral examples on it to guide the rater.

behavioral modeling Behavioral modeling relies on the initiation or emulation of a desired behavior. A repetition of behavior modeling helps to develop appropriate responses in specified situations.

behavior modification Behavior modification states that behavior depends on its consequences.

beneficiary Beneficiary is an individual designated by the plan participant to receive pension-benefits in the event of the death of the participant.

bias The tendency to allow individual differences, such as color, gender, age, race, or other factors (recency of certain behavior), to affect the appraisal ratings an employee receives.

blind ads Blind ads are want ads that do not identify the employer.

bona fide occupational qualifications (BFOQ) A BFOQ occurs when an employer has a justified business reason for discriminating against a member of a protected class. The burden of proving a BFOQ generally falls on the employer. The BFOQ is specified by the 1964 Civil Rights Act.

bottom-line test The bottom-line test is applied by the Equal Employment Opportunity Commission to determine if a firm's overall selection process is having an adverse impact on protected groups. Even though individual steps in the selection process might exhibit an adverse impact on a protected group, the firm will be considered in compliance if the overall process does not have an adverse effect.

Boulwarism Boulwarism is a negotiation strategy developed by General Electric. Using this approach the company made its "best" offer to the union at the beginning of negotiations. Then it remained firm unless the union could find where management had erred in the calculations used to arrive at the offer. This strategy has been ruled as an unfair labor practice by the National Labor Relations Board and by the federal courts.

brainstorming Brainstorming is a process by which participants provide their ideas on a stated problem during a freewheeling group session.

buddy system The buddy system of orientation exists when an experienced employee is asked to show a new worker around the job site, conduct introductions, and answer the newcomer's questions.

burnout Burnout is a condition of mental, emotional, and sometimes physical exhaustion that results from substantial prolonged stress.

business agent A business agent is a full-time employee of a local (usually craft) union. The business agent helps employees resolve their problems with management.

business necessity This means justification for an otherwise discriminatory employment practice, provided there is a compelling legitimate business purpose.

business unionism Business unionism describes unions that seek to improve the wages, hours, and working conditions of their members in a businesslike manner. (See **social unionism**.)

buy-back A buy-back occurs when an employee who attempts to resign is convinced to stay in the employment of the organization. Normally the person is "bought back" with an offer of increased wages or salary.

C

cafeteria benefit programs Cafeteria benefit programs allow employees to select the fringe benefits and services that answer their individual needs.

career A career is all the jobs that are held during one's working life.

career counseling Career counseling assists employees in finding appropriate career goals and paths.

career development Career development consists of those experiences and personal improvements that one undertakes to achieve a career plan.

career goals Career goals are the future positions that one strives to reach. These goals serve as benchmarks along one's career path.

career path A career path is the sequential pattern of jobs that form one's career.

career planning Career planning is the process by which one selects career goals and paths to those goals.

career plateau A career plateau occurs when an employee is in a position that he or she does well enough not to be demoted or fired but not well enough to be promoted.

change agents Change agents are people who have the role of stimulating change within a group.

checkoff A checkoff provision in a union-management labor agreement requires the employer to deduct union dues from employee paychecks and to remit those moneys to the union.

Civil Rights Act of 1964 This act was passed to make various forms of discrimination illegal.

Civil Rights Act of 1991 This act amends Title VII of the Civil Rights Act of 1964, Section 1981 of the Civil Rights Act of 1866, the Americans with Disabilities Act, and the Age Discrimination in Employment Act of 1967. Congress wrote this act in response to five 1989 Supreme Court case decisions. The cases were *Wards Cove* v. *Antonio, Martin* v. *Wilks, Hopkins* v. *Price Waterhouse, Patterson* v. *McClean Credit Union*, and *Lorance* v. *AT&T Technologies*. The decisions, in the view of civil rights activists, were to limit the legal rights of plaintiffs, change rules of evidence, or redefine coverage under previous case law or existing statutes. The burden of proof in these cases shifted from defendant back to the plaintiff. This law permits the plaintiff to pursue compensatory and punitive damages.

closed shop A closed shop is a workplace where all employees are required to be members of the union before they are hired. These arrangements are illegal under the National Labor Relations Act.

codetermination Codetermination is a form of industrial democracy first popularized in West Germany. It gives workers the right to have representatives vote on management decisions.

coinsurance clause A coinsurance clause is a provision in an insurance policy that requires the employee to pay a percentage of the insured's expenses.

communication Communication is the transfer of information and understanding from one person to another.

comparable worth Comparable worth is the idea that a job should be evaluated on its value to the organization and then paid accordingly. Thus, jobs of comparable worth would be paid equally. For example, two people with widely different jobs would both receive the same pay if the two jobs were of equal value to the employer.

comparative evaluation approaches Comparative evaluation approaches are a collection of different methods that compare one person's performance with that of co-workers.

compensation Compensation is what employees receive in exchange for their work.

Comprehensive Employment and Training Act of 1973 (CETA) CETA was a broad-ranging act designed to provide job training, employment, and job-hunting assistance to less-advantaged persons. It has since been replaced by the Job Partnership Training Act.

concentration in employment Concentration exists when an employer (or some subdivision, such as a department) has a higher proportion of employees from a protected class than is found in the employer's labor market. (See **underutilization**.)

concessionary bargaining Concessionary bargaining occurs when labor–management negotiations result in fewer employer-paid fringe benefits or wage concessions, such as a freeze or wage cut.

conciliation agreement A conciliation agreement is a negotiated settlement agreeable to the EEOC and to all parties involved. Its acceptance closes the case.

conditional employee A conditional employee is a person that is employed on a less than full-time basis. The employee may be employed on the basis of an individual contract or be leased from an organization.

Consolidated Omnibus Budget Reconciliation Act of 1985 (COBRA) This act was signed into law in 1986. COBRA requires employers that provide group benefits to employees through a group plan to also provide group benefits to qualified beneficiaries with the right to elect to continue their coverage for a certain time after their coverage would otherwise terminate, with a few exceptions.

constructs Constructs are substitutes for actual performance. For example, a score on a test is a construct for actual learning.

contract labor Contract labor consists of people who are hired (and often trained) by an independent agency that supplies companies with needed human resources for a fee.

contributory benefit plans Contributory benefit plans are fringe benefits that require both the employer and the employee to contribute to the cost of the insurance, retirement, or other employer benefit.

coordinated organizing Coordinated organizing occurs when two or more unions pool their resources to organize a targeted employer or group of employees.

corrective discipline Corrective discipline is an action that follows a rule infraction and seeks to so discourage further infractions that future acts are in compliance with standards.

counseling Counseling is the discussion of an employee problem with the general objective of helping the worker cope with it.

counseling functions Counseling functions are the activities performed by counselors. These include advice, reassurance, communication, release of emotional tension, clarified thinking, and reorientation.

craft unions Craft unions are labor organizations that seek to include all workers who have a common skill, such as carpenters or plumbers.

critical incident method The critical incident method requires the rater to report statements that describe extremely good or extremely bad employee behavior. These statements are called "critical incidents," and they are used as examples of good or bad performance in rating the employee.

D

decision-making authority (See **line authority**.)

deductible clause A deductible clause is a provision in an insurance policy that requires the insured to pay a specified amount of a claim before the insurer is obligated to pay.

deferral jurisdictions Deferral jurisdictions are areas in the United States where the EEOC will refer a case to another (usually a state or local) agency; for example, Florida Human Relations Commission.

deferred stock incentive systems These incentives award stock that becomes owned gradually by the executive over several years.

defined benefit plan A defined benefit plan is a plan that provides a specific benefit at retirement using a definite formula. Usually only the employer contributes to such a plan.

defined contribution plan A defined contribution plan is a plan that provides benefits depending on the amount in the individual's account at retirement. (Either the employer only, the employee only, or both may contribute to such a plan.)

delegation Delegation is the process of getting others to share a manager's work. It requires the manager to assign duties, grant authority, and create a sense of responsibility.

Delphi technique The Delphi technique solicits predictions from a panel of experts about some specified future development(s). The collective estimates then are reported back to the panel so the members may adjust their opinions. This process is repeated until a general agreement on future trends emerges.

demographics Demographics is the study of population characteristics.

demotions Demotions occur when an employee is moved from one job to another that is lower in pay, responsibility, and organizational level.

development Development represents those activities that prepare an employee for future responsibilities.

Dictionary of Occupational Titles (DOT) *The Dictionary of Occupational Titles* is a federal government publication that provides detailed job descriptions and job codes for most occupations in government and industry.

differential validity Differential validity is used to demonstrate that tests or other selection criteria are valid for different subgroups or protected classes.

directive counseling Directive counseling is the process of listening to an employee's emotional problems, deciding with the employee what should be done, and then telling and motivating the employee to do it. (See **nondirective counseling.**)

discipline Discipline is management action to encourage compliance with the organization's standards.

dismissal Dismissal is the ultimate disciplinary action, because it separates the employee from the employer for a cause.

disparate impact Disparate impact occurs when the results of an employer's actions have a different effect on one or more protected classes.

disparate treatment Disparate treatment occurs when members of a protected class receive unequal treatment.

downsizing Refers to the process of reducing the number of people employed by the organization. Term seen as one of several euphemisms for dramatic reductions in a company's workforce.

Drug-Free Workplace Act of 1988 This legislation requires that organizations applying for federal grants certify that they will make good-faith efforts to provide a drug-free workplace.

dual responsibility for human resource management Since both line and staff managers are responsible for employees, production, and quality of worklife, a dual responsibility for human resource management exists.

due process Due process means that established rules and procedures for disciplinary action are followed and that employees have an opportunity to respond to the charges made against them.

E

early retirement Early retirement occurs when a worker retires from an employer before the "normal" retirement age.

early retirement window A type of incentive package; special offering to induce employees to retire early. The offering typically provides for liberal pension benefits and may include a cash payment as well.

Employee Assistance Programs (EAPs) EAPs are company sponsored programs to help employees overcome their personal problems through direct company assistance, counseling, or outside referral.

employee handbook The employee handbook explains key benefits, policies, and general information about the employer.

employee leasing This involves a long-term arrangement where an employer dismisses its existing employees, who are then hired by a leasing company and leased back to the original employer.

The Employee Polygraph Protection Act The act prohibits the use of polygraphs in private industry by forbidding any employer engaged in commerce or in the production of goods for commerce from directly or indirectly requiring, requesting, or causing any employee or prospective employee to take or submit to a lie detector test. Restrictions also cover use of information regarding results of such a test and the taking of adverse employment action against any employee who refuses, declines, or fails to take a lie detector test.

Employee Retirement Income Security Act (ERISA) ERISA was passed by Congress to ensure that employer pension plans meet minimum participation, investing, and funding requirements.

employment freeze An employment freeze occurs when the organization curtails future hiring.

employment function The employment function is that aspect of HRM responsible for recruiting, selecting, and hiring new workers. This function is usually handled by the employment section or employment manager of a large HRM department.

employment references Employment references are evaluations of an employee's work performance. They are provided by past employers.

employment tests Employment tests are devices that assess the probable match between the applicants and the job requirements.

Equal Employment Act of 1972 This act strengthened the role of the Equal Employment Opportunity Commission by amending the Civil Rights Act of 1964. The 1972 law empowered the EEOC to initiate court action against noncomplying organizations.

equal employment opportunity Equal employment opportunity means giving people a fair chance to succeed without discrimination based on factors unrelated to job performance—such as age, race, or national origin.

Equal Employment Opportunity Commission (EEOC) The EEOC is the federal agency responsible for enforcing Title VII of the Civil Rights Act, as amended, and other laws, such as the Age Discrimination in Employment Act.

***Equal Employment Opportunity Commission* v. *Aramco*,** 1991 (55 FEP Cases 449) This U.S. Supreme Court ruling stated that coverage of federal job discrimination law was limited to the territorial jurisdiction of the U.S.

equal employment opportunity laws Equal employment opportunity laws are a family of federal and state acts that seek to ensure equal employment opportunities for members of protected groups.

Equal Pay Act of 1963 This act prohibits discrimination in pay because of a person's gender.

ergonomics Ergonomics is the study of biotechnical relationships between the physical attributes of workers and the physical demands of the jobs. The object is to reduce physical and mental strain in order to increase productivity and quality of worklife. Ergonomics helps adapt the job to fit the person, rather than force the person to fit the job.

error of central tendency The error of central tendency occurs when a rater evaluates employee performance as neither good nor poor, even when some employees perform exceptionally well or poorly. Instead, the rater rates everyone as average.

evaluation interviews Evaluation interviews are performance review sessions that give employees feedback about their past performance or about their future potential.

executive order Executive orders are presidential decrees that normally apply to government contractors or managers in the executive branches of the federal government.

exit interviews Exit interviews are conversations with departing employees to learn their views of the organization.

expedited arbitration Expedited arbitration is an attempt to speed up the arbitration process. It may include an arrangement with the arbitrator for him or her to be available on short notice (one or two days) and to render a quick decision at the conclusion of the hearings (sometimes an oral decision is used in these cases).

experience rating Experience rating is a practice whereby state unemployment offices determine an employer's unemployment compensation tax rate based on the employer's previous experience in providing stable employment.

experiential learning Experiential learning means that participants learn by experiencing in the training environment the kinds of problems they face on the job.

exposure Exposure means becoming known by those who decide on promotions, transfers, and other career opportunities.

extrapolation Extrapolation involves extending past rates of change into the future.

F

facilitator A facilitator is someone who assists quality circles and the quality circle leader in identifying and solving workplace problems.

factor comparison method The factor comparison method is a form of job evaluation that allocates a part of each job's wage to key factors of the job. The result is a relative evaluation of the job.

fair employment practices Fair employment practices are state and local laws that prohibit employer discrimination in employment against members of protected classes.

Fair Labor Standards Act of 1938 (FLSA) FLSA is a comprehensive federal law affecting compensation management. It sets minimum wage, overtime pay, equal pay, child labor, and recordkeeping requirements.

Family and Medical Leave Act of 1993 The employee may be entitled to a total of 12 workweeks of leave during any 12-month period for such reasons as the birth of a son or daughter, placement of such child with the employee for adoption or foster care, or as a result of the need to provide parental, child, or spousal care for seriously ill person.

Federal Mediation and Conciliation Service (FMCS) The FMCS was created by the Labor Management Relations Act of 1947 to help labor and management peacefully resolve negotiation impasses through mediation and conciliation without resort to a strike. The FMCS also is a course of qualified labor arbitrators.

feedback Feedback is information that helps evaluate the success or failure of an action or system.

fiduciary Fiduciary is any person who exercises discretionary authority or control respecting the management of a pension plan or management or disposition of its assets.

field experiment A field experiment is research that allows the researchers to study employees under realistic conditions to learn how experimental and control subjects react to new programs and to other changes.

field review method The field review method requires skilled representatives of the personnel department to go into the "field" and assist supervisors with their ratings. Often it is the personnel department's representative that actually fills out the evaluation form after interviewing the supervisor about employee performance.

flexiplace A flexible work arrangement in which employees are encouraged and supported in their effort to work at home or utilize a satellite office. Such employees may share an office with fellow employees who rotate through on various schedules.

flextime Flextime is a scheduling innovation that abolishes rigid starting and ending times for each day's work. Instead, employees are allowed to begin and end the workday at their discretion, usually within a range of hours.

flexyear Flexyear is an employee scheduling concept that allows workers to be off the job for part of the year. Employees usually work the normal work year in less than 12 months.

forced choice method The forced choice method of employee performance evaluation requires the rater to choose the most descriptive statement in each pair of statements about the employee being rated.

forecasts Forecasts predict the organization's future needs.

four-day workweek A work schedule in which employees are required to work during certain core hours (e.g., 10:00 to 2:00 PM) on each of four days but have the flexibility to motivate the remaining hours of their work schedule on a planned basis.

four-fifths rule The four-fifths rule is a test used by the EEOC. When the election ratio of protected-class applicants is less than 80 percent (or four-fifths) of the selection ratio for majority applicants, adverse impact is assumed.

fully insured workers Fully insured workers are employees who have contributed 40 quarters (10 years) to Social Security.

functional authority Functional authority allows staff experts to make decisions in specified circumstances that are usually reserved for line managers.

funded plan Funded plans require an employer to accumulate moneys in advance so the organization's contribution plans plus interest will cover its obligation.

funded retirement plans A funded retirement plan is one in which the employer sets aside sufficient money to meet the future payout requirements.

G

gainsharing Gainsharing matches an improvement (gain) in company performance to some distribution (sharing) of the benefits with employees.

golden offerings Financial incentives offered to current employees aimed at enticing them to retire early. Arrangement may include providing same pensions they would expect to receive if they did so at the usual (e.g., age 65) time.

golden parachutes Golden parachutes are agreements by the company to compensate executives with bonuses and benefits if they should be displaced by a merger or acquisition.

grapevine communication Grapevine communication is an informal word-of-mouth system that arises from the social interaction of people in the organization.

grievance procedure A grievance procedure is a multistep process that the employer and union jointly use to resolve disputes that arise under the terms of the labor agreement.

***Griggs* v. *Duke Power Company* (1971)** The U.S. Supreme Court case that held that, when an employment criterion disproportionately discriminates against a protected class, the employer is required to show how the criterion is job-related.

guaranteed annual wage A guaranteed annual wage that assures workers of receiving a minimum amount of work or pay during the course of a year.

H

halo effect The halo effect is a bias that occurs when a rater allows some information to disproportionately prejudice the final evaluation.

harassment Harassment occurs when a member of an organization treats an employee in a disparate manner because of the worker's sex, race, religion, age, or other protected classification.

health maintenance organizations (HMOs) HMOs are a form of health insurance whereby the insurer provides the professional staff and facilities needed to treat its insured policyholders for a predetermined monthly fee.

hot-stove rule The hot-stove rule states that disciplinary action should have the same characteristics as the penalty a person receives from touching a hot stove. That is, the discipline should be with warning, immediate, consistent, and impersonal.

house organs A house organ is any regularly published organizational magazine, newspaper, or bulletin directed to employees.

human resource forecasts Human resource forecasts predict the organization's future demand for employees.

human resource planning Human resource planning systematically forecasts an organization's future supply, and demand for, employees.

human resources Human resources are the people who are ready, willing, and able to contribute to organizational goals.

I

Immigration Reform and Control Act of 1986 Employers are required to screen out unauthorized aliens. The act requires an employment verification system, a good-faith effort, and specified recordkeeping procedures.

imminent danger An imminent danger is a situation that is likely to lead to death or serious injury if allowed to continue.

independent contractors Independent contractors are self-employed workers hired for a finite time, such as free-lance writers or professors acting as consultants. However, some firms, which have downsized, have hired back experienced former employees on an independent contractor basis.

incentive systems Incentive systems link compensation and performance by paying employees for actual results, not for seniority or hours worked.

indexation Indexation is a method of estimating future employment needs by matching employment growth with some index, such as sales growth.

industrial democracy Industrial democracy refers to giving employees a larger voice making the work-related decisions that affect them.

industrial unions Industrial unions are labor organizations that seek to include all of an employer's eligible workers regardless of whether they are skilled, semiskilled, or unskilled.

in-house complaint procedures In-house complaint procedures are organizationally developed methods for employees to register their complaints about various aspects of the organization.

J

job analysis Job analysis systematically collects, evaluates, and organizes information about jobs.

job analysis schedule Job analysis schedules are checklists or questionnaires that seek to collect information about jobs in a uniform manner. (They also are called "job analysis questionnaires.")

job banks Job banks exist in state employment offices. They are used to match applicants with job openings.

job code A job code uses numbers, letters, or both to provide a quick summary of the job and its content.

job description A job description is a written statement that explains the duties, working conditions, and other aspects of a specified job.

job enlargement Job enlargement means adding more tasks to a job to increase the job cycle.

job enrichment Job enrichment means adding more responsibilities, autonomy, and control to a job.

job evaluations Job evaluations are systematic procedures to determine the relative worth of jobs.

job families Job families are groups of different jobs that require similar skills.

Job-Flo *Job-Flo* is a monthly report of frequently listed openings from job banks throughout the country.

job grading Job grading is a form of job evaluation that assigns jobs to predetermined classifications according to the job's relative worth to the organization. This technique is also called the "job classification method."

jobholder reports Jobholder reports are reports to employees about the firm's economic performance.

Job Information Service The Job Information Service is a feature of state employment security agencies that enables job seekers to review job bank listings in their efforts to find employment.

job instruction training Job instruction training is training received directly on the job. It is also called "on-the-job-training."

job performance standards Job performance standards are the work requirements that are expected from an employee on a particular job.

job posting Job posting informs employees of unfilled job openings and the qualifications for these jobs.

job progression ladder A job progression ladder is a particular career path where some jobs have prerequisites.

job ranking Job ranking is one form of job evaluation that subjectively ranks jobs according to their overall worth to the organization.

job rotation Job rotation is the process of moving employees from one job to another to allow them more variety on their jobs and the opportunity to learn new skills.

job satisfaction Job satisfaction is the favorableness or unfavorableness with which employees view their work.

job sharing Job sharing is a scheduling innovation that allows two or more workers to share the same job, usually by each working part-time.

job specifications A job specification describes what a job demands of employees who do it and the human skills that are required.

Job Training Partnership Act of 1983 This act provides federal funds to authorized training contractors, often city or state government agencies. These moneys are used to train people in new, employable skills. (It replaces the Comprehensive Education and Training Act of 1973.)

joint and survivor annuity This form of annuity is the "default" payment form for married participants. The pension benefit is paid over the lifetime of the participant and over the lifetime of the spouse.

joint study committees Joint study committees include representatives from management and the union who meet away from the bargaining table to study some topic of mutual interest in the hope of finding a solution that is mutually satisfactory.

juniority Juniority provisions require that layoffs be first offered to senior workers who may accept or refuse them. If sufficient senior workers do not accept the layoffs, then management is free to lay off the least-senior workers.

K

key jobs Key jobs are those that are common in the organization and in its labor market.

L

labor agreement A labor agreement, which is also called a "labor contract," is a legal document that is negotiated between the union and the employer. It states the terms and conditions of employment.

laboratory training Laboratory training is a form of group training primarily used to enhance interpersonal skills.

Labor Management Relations Act of 1947 (LMRA) The LMRA, also known as the Taft-Hartley Act, amended the National Labor Relations Act of 1935 by designing specific union actions that were considered to be unfair labor practices. The act also created the Federal Mediation and Conciliation Service and enabled the President of the United States to call for injunctions in national emergency strikes.

Labor-Management Reporting and Disclosure Act of 1959 (LMRDA) The LMRDA, also called the "Landrum-Griffin Act," amended the National Labor Relations Act. It created the union members' "bill of rights" by giving union members certain rights in dealing with their union. The law also established detailed reporting requirements for those who handle union funds.

labor market The labor market is the area in which the employer recruits.

labor market analysis Labor market analysis is the study of the employee's labor market to evaluate the present or future availability of workers.

Landrum-Griffin Act (See **Labor-Management Reporting and Disclosure Act of 1959.)**

law of effect (Thorndike's law) The law of effect states that people learn to repeat behaviors that have favorable consequences, and they learn to avoid behaviors that have unfavorable consequences.

layoffs Layoffs are the separation of employees from the organization for economic or business reasons.

learning curve A learning curve is a visual representation of the rate at which one learns given material through time.

learning principles Learning principles are guidelines to the ways in which people learn most effectively.

legal insurance Legal insurance is usually a group insurance plan provided by the employer that reimburses the insureds when they have specified legal expenses or provides the insureds with access to legal assistance at predetermined (and usually low) rates.

leniency bias A leniency bias occurs when employees are rated higher than their performance justifies.

leveraging Leveraging refers to resigning to further one's career with another employer.

line authority Line authority allows managers to direct others and to make decisions about the organization's operations.

local unions Local unions are the smallest organizational unit of a union. They are responsible for representing the members at the worksite.

long-term disability Long-term disability insurance provides a proportion of a disabled employee's wage or salary. These policies typically have long waiting periods and seldom allow the employee to attain the same income level that existed before the disability.

Lorance* v. *AT&T, 1989 (49 FEP Cases 1656) The U.S. Supreme Court ruled that the period for challenging an allegedly discriminatory seniority rule begins when the rule is adopted, rather than when an employee is affected by the rule.

lost-time accidents These are severe job-related accidents that cause the employee to lose time from his or her job.

M

maintenance factors Maintenance factors are those elements in the work setting that lead to employee dissatisfaction when they are not adequately provided. These factors are also called "hygiene factors" or "dissatisfiers." They include working conditions and fringe benefits.

"make-whole" remedies When an individual is mistreated in violation of employment laws, the wrongdoer usually is required to make up the losses that were suffered by the employee because of the wrongdoing.

management by objectives (MBO) MBO requires an employee and superior to jointly establish performance goals for the future. Employees subsequently are evaluated on how well they have obtained these agreed-on objectives.

management inventories Management inventories summarize the skills and abilities of management personnel. (See **skills inventories**, which are used for nonmanagement employees.)

management rights Management rights are the rights and freedoms that an employer needs to manage the enterprise effectively. These areas of discretion usually are reserved by management in the labor agreement.

Martin* v. *Wilks, 1989 (49 FEP Cases 1641) The U.S. Supreme Court permitted white firefighters to challenge a consent decree years after it had been approved by a lower court.

maturity curves Maturity curves are used to compensate workers based on their seniority and performance. Normally, these compensation plans are limited to professional and technical workers.

mentor A mentor is someone who offers informal career advice.

merit-based promotions Merit-based promotions occur when an employee is promoted because of superior performance in the present job.

merit raises Merit raises are pay increases given to individual workers according to the evaluation of their performance.

Meritor Savings Bank, FSB* v. *Vinson U.S. Supreme Court decision on sexual harassment, which held that existence of a hostile environment even without economic hardship is sufficient to prove harassment, even if participation is voluntary.

motivation Motivation is a person's drive to take action because that person wants to do so.

multiemployer plan A multiemployer pension plan is a plan negotiated by a union with more than one employer.

multiple employer plan The multiple employer plan is a plan sponsored by more than one employer; commonly used for parent and subsidiary corporations.

N

National Institute of Occupational Safety and Health (NIOSH) NIOSH was created by the Occupational Safety and Heath Act to conduct research and to develop additional safety and health standards.

National Labor Relations Act of 1935 (NLRA) The NLRA, also known as the Wagner Act, was passed by Congress to ensure that covered employees could join (or refrain from joining) unions for the purpose of their own mutual aid and protection and for negotiating with employers. The act also created the National Labor Relations Board.

National Labor Relations Board (NLRB) The NLRB was created by the National Labor Relations Act to prevent unfair labor practices and to conduct union representation elections.

national unions National unions are those parent bodies that help organize, charter, guide, and assist their affiliated local unions.

needs assessment Needs assessment diagnoses present problems and future challenges that can be met through training and development.

net benefit Net benefit means that there will be a surplus of benefits after all costs are included.

noncontributory benefit plans Noncontributory benefit plans are fringe benefits that are paid entirely by the employer. (See **contributory benefit plans.**)

nondeferral jurisdiction Nondeferral jurisdictions are areas where the EEOC finds no qualified agency to which it may defer cases.

nondirective counseling Nondirective, (or client-centered) counseling is the process of skillfully listening to an employee and encouraging him or her to explain bothersome problems, to understand them, and to determine appropriate solutions.

nonverbal communication Nonverbal communication is action that communicates without spoken words.

normal retirement age Normal retirement age is the age at which a participant in a pension plan may retire under the pension plan with full benefit.

O

Occupational Outlook Handbook The *Occupational Outlook Handbook* is published by the U.S. Department of Labor. It indicates the future need for certain jobs.

Occupational Safety and Health Act of 1970 (OSHA) OSHA is a broad-ranging law that requires employers to provide a work environment that is free of recognized safety and health hazards.

Occupational Safety and Health Administration The Occupational Safety and Health Administration is located in the U.S. Department of Labor and is responsible for enforcing the Occupational Safety and Health Act.

Occupational Safety and Health Review Commission The Occupational Safety and Health Review Commission is the federal agency that reviews on appeal the fines given to employers by the Occupational Safety and Health Administration for safety and health violations.

open communication Open communication exists when people feel free to communicate all relevant messages.

open-door policy An open-door policy encourages employees to go to their manager or even higher management with any problem that concerns them.

organizational climate Organizational climate is the favorableness or unfavorableness of the environment for people in the organization.

organizational development (OD) OD is an intervention strategy that uses group processes to focus on the whole organization to bring about planned change.

organizing committee An organizing committee consists of employees who guide the efforts needed to organize their fellow workers into a labor organization.

orientation programs Orientation programs familiarize primarily new employees with their roles, the organization, its policies, and other employees.

outplacement Outplacement occurs when an organization assists its present employees in finding jobs with other employers.

P

Pareto analysis Pareto analysis is a means of collecting data about the types or causes of production problems in descending order of frequency.

participation rates Participation rates are the percentages of working-age men and women in the workforce.

participative counseling Participative counseling seeks to find a balance between directive and nondirective counseling techniques, with the counselor and the counselee participating in the discussion and solution of the problem.

part-time layoffs Part-time layoffs occur when an employer lays off workers without pay for a part of each week, such as each Friday.

paternalism Paternalisms exists when management assumes that it alone is the best judge of employee needs and, therefore, does not seek or act on employee suggestions.

path-goal personnel strategy The path-goal personnel strategy is used by the personnel department when it attempts to improve the path toward a goal (such as reducing red tape) and then tries to improve the outcomes at the end of the path (such as improving the amount of merit pay or other rewards).

pattern bargaining Pattern bargaining occurs when the same or essentially the same contract is used for several firms, often in the same industry.

patterns and practices When discrimination is found to exist against a large number of individuals who are in a protected class a pattern and practice case exists.

Patterson* v. *McLean Credit Union, 1989 (49 FEP Cases 1814) The U.S. Supreme Court held that protection against racial bias under a key state (42 USC #1981) was limited to hiring and some promotion decisions, but did not extend to harassment on the job, discriminatory firing, or other post-hiring conduct by the employer.

pay-for-knowledge compensation systems These incentives provide employees higher pay as an incentive for each new skill or job they learn.

payout standards Payout standards are the benchmarks or triggers that determine whether an incentive or gain-sharing award is earned.

performance appraisal Performance appraisal is the process by which organizations evaluate employee performance.

performance measures Performance measures are the ratings used to evaluate employee performance.

performance standards Performance standards are the benchmarks against which performance is measured.

personal leave days Personal leave days are normal workdays that an employee is entitled to take off. (In some firms, personal leave days are used instead of sick days.)

personnel audit A personnel audit evaluates the personnel activities used in an organization.

personnel barriers Personnel barriers are communication interferences arising from human emotions, values, and limitations.

personnel management Personnel management is the study of how employers obtain, develop, utilize, evaluate, maintain, and retain the right numbers and types of workers. Its purpose is to provide organizations with an effective workforce. The more common term used is *human resource management.*

Peter principle The Peter Principle states that, in a hierarchy, people tend to rise to their level of incompetence.

piecework Piecework is a type of incentive system that compensates workers for each unit of output.

placement Placement is the assignment of an employee to a new or different job.

point system The point system is a form of job evaluation that assesses the relative importance of the job's key factors to arrive at the relative worth of jobs.

political grievances Political grievances are filed or supported because of their political implications, not their merits.

portability clauses Portability clauses allow workers to transfer accumulated pension rights to their subsequent employer when they change jobs.

Position Analysis Questionnaire (PAQ) The PAQ is a standardized, preprinted form that collects specific information about jobs.

precedent A precedent is a new standard that arises from past practices of either the company or the union.

preferential quota systems Preferential quota systems exist when a proportion of the job openings, promotions, or other employment opportunities is reserved for members of a protected class who have been previously discriminated against.

Pregnancy Discrimination Act of 1978 This act prevents discrimination in employment against women who are pregnant and able to perform their jobs. The law amends the Civil Rights Act of 1964.

prevailing wage rates Prevailing wage rates are the rates most commonly paid for a given job in a specific geographical area. They are determined by a wage and salary survey.

preventive discipline Preventive discipline is action taken to encourage employees to follow standards and rules so infractions are prevented.

Price Waterhouse* v. *Hopkins, 1989 (49 FEP Cases 954) The U.S. Supreme Court held that an employer could avoid liability for intentional discrimination in "mixed motive" cases if the employer could demonstrate that the same action would have been taken without the discriminatory motive.

private placement agencies Private placement agencies are for-profit organizations that help job seekers find employment.

proactive management Proactive management exists when decision makers anticipate problems and take affirmative action steps to minimize those problems, rather than to wait until after a problem occurs before taking action.

problem-solving interviews These types of interviews rely on questions that are limited to hypothetical situations or problems. The applicant is evaluated on how well the problems are solved.

production bonuses Production bonuses are a type of incentive system that provides employees with additional compensation when they surpass stated production goals.

productivity Productivity is the ratio of a firm's output (goods and services) divided by its input (people, capital, materials, energy).

professional associations Professional associations are groups of workers who voluntarily join together to further their profession and their professional development. When these associates undertake to negotiate for their members, they are also labor organizations.

profit sharing Profit-sharing exists when an organization shares a proportion of its profits with the workers, usually on an annual basis.

profit-sharing plans Profit-sharing plans enable eligible employees to receive a proportion of the organization's profits.

progressive discipline Progressive discipline requires strong penalties for repeated offenses.

promotion A promotion occurs when an employee is moved from one job to another that is higher in pay, responsibility, and organizational level.

protected groups Protected groups are classes of people who are protected from discrimination under one or more laws.

psychic costs Psychic costs are the stresses, strains, and anxieties that affect a person's inner self during a period of change.

Pygmalion effect The Pygmalion effect occurs when people live up to the highest expectations others hold of them.

Q

qualifiable worker A qualifiable worker is one who does not currently possess all of the requirements, knowledge, skills, or abilities to do the job, but who will become qualified through additional training and experience.

qualified handicapped The qualified handicapped are those mentally or physically handicapped individuals who, with reasonable accommodations, perform successfully.

quality circles Quality circles are small groups of employees who meet regularly with a common leader to identify and solve work-related problems.

quality of worklife Quality of worklife means having good supervision, good working conditions, good pay and benefits, and an interesting, challenging, and rewarding job.

quality of worklife efforts Quality of worklife efforts are systematic attempts by an organization to give workers a greater opportunity to affect their jobs and their contributions to the organization's overall effectiveness.

R

rap sessions Rap sessions are meetings between managers and groups of employees to discuss complaints, suggestions, opinions, or questions.

rate ranges Rate ranges are pay ranges for each job class.

rating scale A rating scale requires the rater to provide a subjective evaluation of an individual's performance along a scale from low to high.

rational validity Rational validity exists when tests include reasonable samples of the skills needed to perform successfully or where there is an obvious relationship between performance and other characteristics that are assumed to be necessary for successful job performance.

reactive management Reactive management exists when decision makers respond to problems instead of anticipating problems before they occur. (See **proactive management**.)

realistic job preview (RJP) An RJP allows the job applicant to see the type of work, equipment, and working conditions involved in the job before the hiring decision is finalized.

recency effect The recency effect is a rater bias that occurs when a rater allows recent employee performance to sway the overall evaluation.

recruitment Recruitment is the process of find and attracting capable applicants for employment.

red-circle rates Red-circle rates are wages or salaries that are inappropriate for a given job according to the job evaluation plan.

refreezing Refreezing requires the integration of what has been learned into actual practice.

regulations Regulations are legally enforceable rules developed by government agencies to ensure compliance with laws that the agency interprets and administers.

Rehabilitation Act of 1973 This act prohibits discrimination against those who are handicapped but qualified to perform work. It applies to employees who receive federal moneys and to federal agencies.

reinforcement schedules Reinforcement schedules are the different ways that behavior reinforcement can be given.

relations by objectives Relations by objectives is a program created by the Federal Mediation and Conciliation Service to improve labor–management cooperation between participating parties.

reliability Reliability means that a selection device (usually a test) yields consistent results each time an individual takes it.

relocation programs Relocation programs are company sponsored fringe benefits that assist employees who must move in connection with their jobs.

repetition Repetition facilitates learning through repeated review of the material to be learned.

replacement charts Replacement charts are visual presentations of who will replace whom in the organization when a job opening occurs.

resistance to change Resistance to change arises from employee opposition to change.

résumé A résumé is a brief listing of an applicant's work experience, education, personal data, and other information relevant to the applicant's employment qualifications.

reverse discrimination Reverse discrimination occurs when an employer seeks to hire or to promote a member of a protected class over an equally (or better) qualified candidate who is not a member of a protected class.

S

sandwich model of discipline The sandwich model suggests that a corrective comment would be sandwiched between two positive comments to make the corrective comments more acceptable.

Scanlon plan The Scanlon plan is an incentive program that compensates eligible employees for improvements in labor costs that are better than the previously established company norms.

scatter plot A graphical method used to help identify the relationship between two variables.

School Board of Nassau County (FL)* v. *Arline The U.S. Supreme Court ruling that persons with contagious diseases (Arline had contracted tuberculosis) are covered by the Vocational Rehabilitation Act.

search firms Search firms are private for-profit organizations that exist to help employers locate hard-to-find applicants.

Section 89, Internal Revenue Code This controversial statute requires certain employee benefit plans to meet five qualification standards for benefits under the plans to be nontaxable to all covered employees. Almost all welfare benefit plans (i.e., group medical, group legal, group life, cafeteria, tuition reimbursement, fringe benefit plans) are subject to these rules.

selection interviews Selection interviews are a step in the selection process whereby the applicant and the employer's representative have a face-to-face meeting.

selection process The selection process is a series of specific steps used to decide which recruits should be hired.

selection ratio The selection ratio of the number of applicants hired to the total number of applicants.

self-funding Self-funding occurs when an organization agrees to meet its insurance obligations out of its own resources.

semantic barriers Semantic barriers are limitations that arise from the words with which we communicate.

seniority Seniority means the length of a worker's employment in relation to the other employees.

seniority-based promotions Seniority-based promotions result when the most senior employee is promoted into a new position.

severance pay Severance pay is a payment made to workers when they are dismissed from the company. Employees who are terminated because of their poor performance or behavior usually are not eligible.

shelf-sitters *Shelf-sitter* is a slang term for upwardly immobile managers who block promotion channels.

shorter workweeks Shorter workweeks are employee scheduling variations that allow full-time workers to complete their week's work in less than the traditional five days. One variation is 40 hours work in four days.

single employer plan A single employer plan is a pension plan sponsored by one employer.

skilled obsolescence Obsolescence is a reduction in an employee's competence, resulting from a lack of knowledge of new work processes, techniques, and technologies that have developed since the employee completed his training or education.

skills inventories Skills inventories are summaries of each employee's skills and abilities. (Skills inventories usually refer to nonmanagement workers. See **management inventories**.)

Social Security Act of 1935 This act established the Social Security program of the federal government, which taxes workers and employers to create a fund from which Medicare, retirement, disability, and death payments are made to covered workers and their survivors.

social unionism Social unionism describes unions that seek to further their members' interests by influencing the social, economic, and legal policies of government at all levels—city, county, state, and federal. (See **business unionism**.)

socialization Socialization is the ongoing process by which an employee adapts to an organization by understanding and accepting the values, norms, and belief held by others in the firm. Orientation programs—which familiarize primarily new employees with their role, the organization, its policies, and other employees—speed up the socialization process.

Society for Human Resource Management (SHRM) It is the major association for professional personnel specialists and administrators.

sociotechnical systems Sociotechnical systems are interventions in the work situation that restructure the work, the work groups, and the relationship between the workers and the technology they use to do their jobs.

specialization Specialization occurs when a very limited number of tasks are grouped into one job.

sponsor A sponsor is a person in an organization who can create career development opportunities for others.

staff authority Staff authority is the authority to advise, not direct, others.

staffing table A staffing table lists anticipated employment openings for each type of job.

state employment security agency A state employment security agency (or unemployment office) matches job seekers with employers who have job openings.

steering committee The steering committee is part of a quality circle or other employee involvement effort and usually includes the top manager of the worksite (such as a plant manager) and his or her direct staff.

steward A union steward is elected by workers (or appointed by local union leaders) to help covered employees present their problems to management.

stock options Stock options are fringe benefits that give the holder the right to purchase the company's stock at a predetermined price.

strategic plan A strategic plan identifies a firm's long-range objectives and proposals for achieving those objectives.

stress Stress is a condition of strain that affects one's emotions, thought processes, and physical condition.

stress interviews Stress interviews rely on a series of harsh, rapid-fire questions that are intended to upset the applicant and show how the applicant handles stress.

stressors Stressors are conditions that tend to cause stress.

stress-performance mode The stress-performance model shows the relationship between stress and job performance.

stress threshold A stress threshold is the level of stressors that a person can tolerate before feelings of distress begin.

strictness bias A strictness bias occurs when employees are rated lower than their performance justifies.

structural unemployment Structural unemployment occurs when people are ready, willing, and able to work, but their skills do not match the jobs available.

structured interviews Structured interviews use a predetermined checklist of questions that usually are asked of all applicants.

suggestion systems Suggestion systems are a formal method for generating, evaluating, and implementing useful employee ideas.

suitable employment Suitable employment means employment for which the person is suited as a result of education, training, or experience.

supplemental unemployment benefits (SUB) SUB is an employer-provided fringe benefit that supplements state unemployment insurance when an employee is laid off.

T

Taft-Hartley Act (See **Labor-Management Relations Act of 1947**.)

Taft-Hartley injunctions Taft-Hartley injunctions allow the President of the United States to seek a court order to delay a labor–management strike for 80 days. During this cooling off period, the government investigates the facts surrounding the dispute.

task identity Task identity means doing an identifiable piece of work, thus enabling the worker to have a sense of responsibility and pride.

task significance Task significance means knowing that the work one does is important to others inside and outside the organization.

temporary employees These are contingent or nonpermanent employees—people who are hired to fill short-term increases in labor demand. No longer are such employees used only for secretarial work or to meet vacation or seasonal needs.

time studies Time studies are measurements of how long a job takes to perform.

Title VII Title VII refers to the part of the Civil Rights Act of 1964 that requires equal employment opportunities without regard to race, color, religion, sex, pregnancy, or national origin.

training Training represents activities that teach employees how to perform their present jobs.

transference Transference refers to how applicable the training is to actual job situations, as evaluated by how readily the trainee transfers the learning to his or her job.

transfers Transfers occur when an employee is moved from one job to another that is relatively equal in pay, responsibility, and organizational level.

turnover Turnover is the loss of employees by the organization. It represents those employees who depart for a variety of reasons.

two-tiered orientation program A two-tiered orientation program exists when both the personnel department and the immediate supervisor provide an orientation for new employees.

two-tier wage structure This pay structure occurs when one group of employees (usually new hires) receives a different wage rate than other employees. The employer achieves lower labor costs by paying new workers less while previously hired union members usually are able to retain their existing wage rates.

type A people Type A people are those who are aggressive and competitive, set high standards, and put themselves under constant time pressures.

type B people Type B people are more relaxed and easygoing. They tend to accept situations and work within them, rather than fight them or put themselves under constant time pressures.

U

underutilization Underutilization occurs when a department or an entire organization has a smaller proportion of members of a protected class than is found in the firm's labor market. (See **concentration in employment**.)

unemployment compensation Unemployment compensation is payment to those who lose their jobs, are unemployed, are seeking new employment, and are willing and able to work.

unfair labor practices (ULPs) ULPs are violations of the National Labor Relations Act as amended. These unfair labor practices are specific activities that employers and labor organizations are prohibited from doing.

union–management agreement (See **labor agreement**.)

union members' bill of rights The union members' bill of rights refers to Title I of the Labor–Management Reporting and Disclosure Act of 1959, which established the specific rights of union members in dealing with their unions.

union organizers Union organizers are people who assist employees in forming a local union.

union shop A union shop is a workplace where all employees are required to join the local union as a condition of employment. New employees are usually given 30, 60, or 90 days in which to join.

unstructured interview An unstructured interview uses few, if any, planned questions to enable the interviewer to pursue, in depth, the applicant's responses.

upward communication Upward communication is communication that begins at some point in the organization and then proceeds up the hierarchy to inform or influence others.

V

validity Validity means that the selection device (usually a test) is related significantly to job performances or to some other relevant criterion.

vertical staff meetings Vertical staff meetings occur when managers meet with two or more levels of subordinates to learn of their concerns.

vestibule training Vestibule training occurs off the job on equipment or methods that are highly similar to those used on the job. This technique minimizes the disruption of operations caused by training activities.

vesting Vesting is a provision in retirement plans that gives workers rights to retirement benefits after a specified number of years of service, even if the employee quits before retirement.

Vietnam Era Veteran's Readjustment Act of 1974 This act prohibits certain government contractors from discriminating in employment against Vietnam era veterans.

W

wage and salary surveys Wage and salary surveys are studies made by an organization to discover what other employers in the same labor market are paying for specific key jobs.

wage compression Wage compression occurs when the difference between higher- and lower-paying jobs is reduced. This compression usually results from giving larger pay increases to lower-paying jobs.

Wagner Act (See **National Labor Relations Act of 1935**.)

walk-ins Walk-ins are job seekers who arrive at the personnel department in search of a job without any prior referrals and not in response to a specific ad or request.

want ads Want ads describe the job and its benefits, identify the employer, and tell those who are interested how to apply.

Wards Cove Packing Co.* v. *Atonios, 1989 (49 FEP Cases 1519) The U.S. Supreme Court decided that an employer did not have to prove "business necessity" to defend a case in which a complainant had shown the employer's practice(s) had a disparate impact on a protected group. The Court required only that an employer provide business justification for the challenged practice.

weighted checklist A weighted checklist requires the rater to select statements or words to describe an employee's performance or characteristics. After those selections are made, different responses are given different values or weights to determine a quantified total score.

weighted incentive systems These systems reward executives based on improvements in multiple areas of business performance. Depending on the weights used, part of the incentive bonus can be tied to improvements in market share, profit return on assets, cash flow, or other indexes.

welfare secretary The welfare secretary was a forerunner of the modern personnel specialist. Welfare secretaries existed to help workers meet their personal needs and to minimize any tendency of workers to join unions.

well pay Well pay is a fringe benefit, provided by some employers, that pays employees for unused sick leave.

West Virginia University Hospitals* v. *Casey, 1991 (55 FEP Cases 353) The U.S. Supreme Court ruled that expert witness fees are separate from attorney's fees and, thus, most costs of hiring expert witnesses could not be recovered by successful civil rights plaintiffs.

wildcat strikes Wildcat strikes are spontaneous work stoppages that take place in violation of the labor contract and are officially against the wishes of the union leaders.

work measurement techniques Work measurement techniques are methods for evaluating what a job's performance standards should be.

work practices Work practices are the set ways of performing work in an organization.

work sampling Work sampling means using a variety of observations on a particular job to measure the length of time devoted to certain aspects of the job.

work simplification Work simplification means simplifying jobs by eliminating unnecessary tasks or reducing the number of tasks by combining them.

Worker Adjustment and Retraining Act Employers with 100 or more employees must provide employees 60 days' advance written notice of plant closing or layoffs.

worker's compensation Worker's compensation is payment made to employees for work-related injuries or to their families in the event of the worker's job-caused death.

Work-family conflicts These conflicts occur when the demands of work and family interfere with each other. The conflicts may result in time demands, stress induced from work or home, or behavior in one setting that is counter to behavior in the other.

workflow Workflow is the sequence of jobs in an organization needed to produce the firm's goods or service.

write-ins Write-ins are those people who send in a written inquiry, often seeking a job application.

wrongful discharge It is an employee dismissal that fails to comply with the law or violates biding components of a (implied or stated) contractual arrangement. For example, an employee fired without cause but stated to have been a dismissal only "for cause."

Appendix B

State and Federal Statutes Applicable to the Employment Relationship

AUTHOR'S COMMENTS ON APPENDIX B—STATE AND FEDERAL LAWS

Students reading this appendix must remember that laws vary by city, state, and even federal district jurisdiction. The selected state laws of Florida and Michigan are illustrative of the types of HRM legislation that may exist. I used information from these two states because I am most familiar with them and because I have been employed over the past dozen years by universities located in those states.

The difference in state laws may be illustrated by two topical areas. The subject of wrongful discharge is an important and timely one. Whereas Florida permits virtually no exceptions to the employment-at-will doctrines of employers, Michigan is much more willing to limit such powers by considering public policy, good faith, implied contract, and other exceptions. As noted below, Michigan has a whistleblower's statute. Florida does not have such a statute. In fact, individuals who blew the whistle in cases of actual legal wrongdoing were unable to protect themselves from termination by the individual(s) alleged to have perpetrated crimes, such as embezzlement of company funds. Also, note that some states cover types of discrimination that may not be covered by most other states. The state of Iowa has protections to assure that individuals are not victims of what some experts define as genetic discrimination—bias based on the genes carried within a person's cells. (The genes determine everything from eye color to predisposition to such disorders as heart disease, diabetes, and some cancers.) How does this work? Let's say you are one of three children. Your brother and sister both have contracted colon cancer. You take a variety of tests at your company for some insurance purpose. The history provided reveals that the two others had contracted colon cancer. The insurer decides to exclude coverage for any procedures relating to your intestinal tract because of your brother and sisters' illnesses.

CLAIMS BASED ON DISCRIMINATION

Americans with Disabilities Act of 1992. [42 U.S.C. 12101]. Public Law 101-336. This legislation builds upon and extends protections granted under the Civil Rights Act of 1964 and Rehabilitation Act of 1973. The law prohibits discrimination on the basis of disability, and protects qualified applicants and employees with disabilities from discrimination in hiring, promotion, discharge, pay, job training, fringe benefits, and other aspects of employment. The law also requires covered entities provide qualified applicants and employees with disabilities with reasonable accommodations that do not impose undue hardship.

Civil Rights Act of 1991. [42 U.S.C. 1981 S1745]. Public Law 102-166. This legislation makes major revisions to Title VII, and overturns seven U.S. Supreme Court decisions that were decided in 1989 through 1991. The most significant change for victims of discrimination is that general damages for emotional distress and punitive damages are now permitted under Title VII, whereas previously only back pay was permitted to be recovered. There is, however, a cap based on the number of employees the employer has. This act extends coverage of Title VII to American-owned or controled companies that operate overseas.

Glass Ceiling Act of 1991. This legislation is contained in Title II of the Civil Rights Act of 1991. The purpose of Title II or "The Glass Ceiling Act" is the establishment of a Glass Ceiling Commission to examine issues raised by the Glass Ceiling Initiative (e.g., underrepresentation in line functions, lack of access for qualified women and minorities to critical career opportunities, and the elimination of artificial barriers to the advancement of women and minorities to management and decision-making positions in business.)

Title VII of the Civil Rights Act of 1964 [42 U.S.C. S2000e-2(a), et seq.cb]. It is an unlawful employment practice for an employer to refuse to hire or discharge any individual on the basis of race, color, religion, sex, or national origin. An employer is further prohibited from discriminating against an employee with respect to compensation, terms, conditions, or privileges of employment based on these factors.

The Florida Human Rights Act of 1977 [Chapter 760, Florida Statutes]. An employer is prohibited from discriminating with respect to compensation, terms, conditions, or privileges of employment based on race, color, religion, sex, national origin, age, handicap, or marital status.

The Civil Rights Act of 1866 [42 U.S.C. S1981 and S1983]. Enacted following the Civil War, the Civil Rights Act attempted to ensure racial equality and provide the full benefit of all laws to the emancipated slaves. Section 1981 applies to private employers, whereas 1983 prohibits public employers from depriving any citizen of the rights, privileges, or immunities secured by the Constitution and other laws.

Age Discrimination in Employment Act of 1967, as amended [29 U.S.C. S621, et seq.]. An employer is prohibited from refusing to hire or to discharge any individual because of such individual's age. The act covers employees 40 years of age or older. Any notice or advertisement relating to employment may not indicate a preference based on age unless certain narrow exceptions apply.

Discrimination Based on Religion [42 U.S.C. S2000e-(j)(cb)]. An employer may not discriminate on the basis of religion unless the employer is unable to reasonably accommodate an employee's religious observances, practices, or beliefs without undue hardship on the conduct of the employer's business.

Elliot-Larsen Civil Rights Act of 1976 (M.C.L.A. 37.2101 et seq.; amendments). Prohibits discriminatory practices, policies, and customs based on religion, race, color, national origin, age, sex, height, weight, or marital status, including sexual harassment in the workplace. This act also limits use of polygraph, psychological stress evaluation, or similar tests in employment situations (37.2205 a & b) based on those characteristics stated above.

Sex Discrimination [42 U.S.C. S2000e-2(a)(cb)]. It is an unlawful employment practice to classify a job as male or female unless sex is a bona fide occupational qualification for that particular job. Policies that restrict the employment of married women, without providing analogous limitations on married men, constitute discrimination based on sex.

The Pregnancy Discrimination Act of 1978 [ob]42 U.S.C. S2000e(k)(cb)]. The prohibition against sex discrimination in Title VII includes discrimination on the basis of pregnancy, childbirth, or related medical conditions. Pregnancy related disabilities should not be treated differently from other temporary disabilities.

Sexual Harassment [ob]42 U.S.C. S2000e-2(e)(cb)]. The prohibition against sex discrimination in Title VII includes unwelcomed sexual harassment in the form of sexual advances, requests for sexual favors, or other verbal or physical conduct of a sexual nature that has the effect of unreasonably interfering with work performance and creating an intimidating, hostile, or offensive work environment.

The Immigration Reform and Control Act of 1986 [8 U.S.C. S1324b(a)(cb)]. This act prohibits discrimination on the basis of national origin or citizenship status.

The Migrant and Seasonal Agricultural Worker Protection Act of 1983 [(42 U.S.C. S8101, et seq.).]. Congress enacted this law to provide certain protections for migrant and seasonal agricultural workers with respect to wages, housing conditions, transportation, health standards, and other conditions of employment.

The Farm Labor Registration Law [(S450.27, et seq., Florida Statutes)]. This state statute provides comparable protections for migrant and seasonal workers as the federal scheme. A number of federal and state statutes regulate the employment of migrant workers.

Michigan Handicappers' Civil Rights Act of 1976 (M.C.L.A. 37.1101 et seq.). Guarantees the opportunity to obtain employment, housing, public services, educational facilities and equal utilization of public accommodations without discrimination because of a handicap.

The Rehabilitation Act of 1973 [(29 U.S.C. S701, et seq.)]. The Rehabilitation Act of 1973 prohibits discrimination against handicapped individuals by employers who receive federal financial assistance or anticipate in contracts with the federal government in excess of $2,500. Affected employers must reasonably accommodate the needs of handicapped employees and take other affirmative action to advance such employees.

Whistleblowers Protection Act of 1990 (M.C.L.A. 15.361 et seq.) This act is an amendment to the Standards of Conduct for Public Officers and Employees Act of 1973 (M.C.L.A 15.341 et seq; amendments). It provides immunity for state public employees who report violations of the law.

Discrimination Based on AIDS. The definition of handicapped individual in both federal and state statutes includes any person with AIDS, since this disease constitutes a physical or mental impairment which substantially limits one or more major life activities.

Discrimination Based on Sickle Cell [(S448.075-076, Florida Statutes)]. An employer may not refuse to hire or discharge any person solely because such applicant or employee has the sickle cell trait. No employer may require testing for the sickle cell trait as a condition for employment.

The Bankruptcy Code [(11 U.S.C. S525)]. No private or public employer may discharge or discriminate against an employee who has filed for bankruptcy.

The National Labor Relations Act [29 U.S.C. S158(a)(cb)]. The National Labor Relations Act prohibits discharge or discrimination based upon union membership, union activity, or other protected concerted activity.

Award of Attorney's Fees [42 U.S.C. S1988 and 42 U.S.C.S2000e-5(k)]. The court may exercise discretion in awarding attorney's fees to a prevailing party in certain discrimination actions.

EMPLOYEE COMPENSATION AND BENEFITS

Attachment and Garnishment of Wages (Michigan Revised Judicature Act of 1961, M.C.L.A. 600.101 et seq; amendments). This act provides for attachment powers by the circuit courts, but also protects individuals from employment discharge or dismissal because their wages have been garnisheed. Reinstatement and reimbursement provisions also are included.

Fair Labor Standards Act of 1938 [29 U.S.C. S201, et seq.]. Employers must pay at least the minimum wage ($4.25 per hour) and in the event employees work more than 40 hours per week, the employee must be compensated at a rate not less than one and one-half times the regular wage rate. The law contains many other important provisions.

Family and Medical Leave Act of 1993 [29 U.S.C. 2601] Public Law 103-3. Employers of organizations having 50 or more employees for 20 or more calendar workweeks in the current or preceding calendar year must provide the equivalent of 12 workweeks of leave to eligible employees who wish to care for a key relation (e.g., son or daughter, spouse, or parent) in the event of childbirth, adoption or need of otherwise in need of care (mental or physical disability, illness, etc.)

State Law Regarding Minimum Wage and Hour Provisions [S448.01,Florida Statutes.] In Florida, 10 hours of labor is considered a legal day's work, and absent a written contract to the contrary, an employee is entitled to extra pay for work performed in excess of 10 hours per day.

Minimum Wage Law of 1964 (M.C.L.A. 403.381 et seq.; amendments). Establishes a minimum wage for all employers subject to the federal Fair Labor Standards Act, and provides for civil action by an employee to recover differences between amounts paid and those minimums established by this act. This act also prohibits an employer from discharging or discriminating against an employee because the employee filed a complaint (408.483) against the employer in an action covered by the act.

The Equal Pay Act of 1963 [29 U.S.C. S206(d)[cb]. The Equal Pay Act prohibits sex-based wage discrimination and mandates equal pay for equal work which is performed under similar working conditions and which requires equal skill, effort, and responsibility. Wage differentials are permitted when such payment is made pursuant to: (1) a seniority system, (2) a merit system, (3) a system which measures earnings by quantity or quality of production, or (4) a differential based on any reasonable factor other than sex.

Wage Rate Discrimination (S448.07, Florida Statutes). Wage rate discrimination based on sex is prohibited unless one of the exceptions to the Equal Pay Act is applicable.

The Employee Retirement Income Security Act of 1974 (ERISA)[(29 U.S.C. S1001)]. ERISA provides a comprehensive federal scheme for the design and operation of employee pension benefit plans and employee welfare benefit plans. Financial and fiduciary standards of conduct are imposed on plan administrators to ensure that beneficiaries are not denied retirement benefits or otherwise discriminated against in pursuit of their rights under ERISA.

Michigan Employment Security Act of 1936 (M.C.L.A. 421.1 et seq.; amendments). This act provides for economic security through an unemployment compensation insurance fund, paid to eligible unemployed workers.

Worker's Disability Compensation Act of 1969 (M.C.L.A. 418.101 et seq.;amendments). This act provides for compensation to qualifying employees injured on the job, or compensation to an employee's dependents in a case involving the death of an employee.

The Unemployment Compensation Law [Chapter 443, Florida Statutes]. This chapter is liberally construed to promote employment security by increasing opportunities for placement and mandating the compulsory setting aside of unemployment reserves. An employee discharged for misconduct connected with his work is disqualified from receiving benefits.

Workers' Compensation Law [Chapter 440, Florida Statutes]. This Florida statute provides for compensation to an employee if a disability or death results from injury arising out of and in the course of employment. No compensation shall be payable if the injury was occasioned primarily by the intoxication or drug use of the employee.

Attorney's Fees for Unpaid Wages (S448.08, Florida Statutes). The court may exercise discretion in awarding a reasonable attorney's fee and court costs to a prevailing party in an action for unpaid wages.

THE HIRING PROCESS

The Immigration Reform and Control Act of 1986 (8 U.S.C. S1324a). Employers must verify that every job applicant is either a U.S. citizen or authorized to be employed in the United States by examining certain documents specified in the statute.

The Employee Polygraph Protection Act of 1988 (29 U.S.C. S2001, et seq.). This statute prohibits most private employers from discharging or disciplining an employee based on the results of a polygraph test. The act provides for certain exceptions from employers engaged in national defense or other security operations. The state of Florida regulates the credentials of those licensed to administer polygraph tests (S493.561, Florida Statutes).

Michigan Full Employment Act of 1978 (M.C.L.A. 408.901 et seq.) This act establishes full employment as a state priority and provides for the formulation of an annual employment plan, which would coordinate the efforts of the agencies of the state government toward the goal of employment for "every person able and willing to work."

Serologic Testing (S775.083, Florida Statutes). It is unlawful for an employer to require an applicant or employee to submit to a serologic exam as a condition of employment.

Manipulation of Drug Tests (S817.565, Florida Statutes). It is unlawful for any person to willfully defraud any lawfully administered urine test designed to detect the presence of chemical or controlled substances.

The Racketeer Influenced and Corrupt Organizations Act (RICO) (28 U.S.C. S1961, et seq.). Where an employer offers employment through the mails or via an interstate telephone call, an employee may have a cause of action for treble damages if the employer engaged in fraud or deliberate misrepresentation in the offer.

Consolidated Omnibus Budget Reconciliation Act of 1985 (COBRA) (29 U.S.C. S1161, et seq.). Certain employers must make available continued health insurance coverage to discharged employees on a contributory basis for 18 months following termination. An employee terminated for gross misconduct is not entitled to the continuation of insurance coverage. The Florida legislature has enacted comparable provisions in S627.6675 of the Florida Statutes.

The Worker Adjustment and Retraining Act (WARN) (23 U.S.C. S2101, et seq.). Employers with 100 or more employees must provide employees 60 days' advance written notice of plant closings or layoffs that will result in the employment loss of 50 or more full-time employees.

SAFETY IN THE WORKPLACE

The Florida Clean Indoor Air Act (S386.201, et seq., Florida Statutes). The act expressly prohibits any person from smoking in a public place or a public meeting except in designated smoking areas. Although existing physical barriers and ventilation systems should be used to minimize smoke in adjacent nonsmoking areas, an employer is not required to physically modify an area. In a workplace that includes both smokers and nonsmokers, employers are required to develop, implement, and post a policy regarding designation of smoking and nonsmoking areas which takes into consideration the proportion of smokers and nonsmokers in the company.

Florida Right-to-Know Law (Chapter 442, Florida Statutes). Employers who manufacture, process, use, or store toxic or hazardous substances in the workplace must provide employees information about these substances.

The Occupational Safety and Health Act (OSHA). (29 U.S.C. S651, et seq.). OSHA regulates the safety and health of employees in the workplace and provides a comprehensive scheme of safety standards.

The Florida Occupational Health and Safety Act (Chapter 442, Florida Statutes). Employers shall educate and train employees with respect to the nature and effects of toxic substances present in the workplace within 30 days of employment and at least annually thereafter. Every employer who manufactures, produces, uses, applies, or stores toxic substances in the workplace must post a notice regarding employee rights under this chapter.

Michigan Occupational Safety and Health Act of 1974 (M.C.L.A.408.1001 et seq.; amendments). This act regulates working conditions in both public and private sector employment. It requires employers to provide a reasonably safe working environment, as well as protective equipment, worker safety education, and posted information regarding workplace safety.

The Hazardous Substances Release Act (42 U.S.C. S9610). No employer shall discharge or discriminate against any employee who provides information to the government or agrees to testify in any proceeding regarding hazardous substance violations.

The Control of Sexually Transmissible Disease Act (Chapter 384, Florida Statutes). Disclosure of confidential information relating to a sexually transmissible disease may be made only under the following circumstances: (1) with the consent of all persons to which the information applies; (2) for statistical purposes or epidemiological information which does not identify the names of the persons affected; (3) revelation to medical personnel, appropriate state agencies, or courts in medical emergencies; (4) disclosure pursuant to subpoena; and (5) in child or adult abuse investigations. Any person who maliciously disseminates any false information or report concerning the existence of any sexually transmissible disease is guilty of a misdemeanor of the second degree.

MISCELLANEOUS STATUTES AFFECTING THE WORKPLACE

Bullard-Plawecki Employee Right to Know Act of 1978 (M.C.L.A. 423.501 et seq.; amendments). This act provides an opportunity for employees to review their personnel records, obtain copies of information contained in the personnel record, and establishes procedures to resolve disagreements.

Michigan Indoor Clean Air Act of 1986 (M.C.L.A. 333.12601 et seq.; amendments). Smoking inside any public building is prohibited. Specific exemptions may be allowed for special events, but nonsmoking areas must be designated.

The Consumer Credit Protection Act (15 U.S.C. S1601, et seq.). No employer may discharge any employee by reason of the fact that his earnings have been subject to garnishment.

Public Employee Collective Bargaining (M.C.L.A. 423.209 et seq). The **Strikes By Public Employees Act of 1947** (M.C.L.A. 423.201 et seq; amendments) prohibits strikes by public employees, but guarantees employees' right to collectively bargain. Public employers are authorized and required to bargain collectively with employee representatives.

Compulsory Arbitration of Labor Disputes in Police and Fire Departments Act of 1969 (M.C.L.A. 423.231 et seq.) This act requires a binding arbitration procedure for dispute resolution in public police and fire departments. This act sought to avoid illegal strikes by essential services public employees, while providing for an expedient and fair procedure to resolve collective bargaining differences.

The Protection of Jurors Employment Act (28 U.S.C. S1875). This act expressly prohibits the discharge or intimidation of any permanent employee for serving on a federal jury.

Jury Service Duty (S40.271, Florida Statutes). An employer may not discharge an employee for accepting jury duty in the state of Florida because of the nature or length of service.

Child Labor Law (S450.081, Florida Statutes). No minor 17 years of age or younger shall be employed in any gainful occupation for more than six consecutive days in any week or more than 10 hours per day. A minor may not be employed for more than 30 hours per week.

Election Code (S104.081, Florida Statutes). It is an unlawful employment practice for an employer to discharge or intimidate any employee for voting or failing to vote in any state, county, or municipal election.

Employment of Unauthorized Aliens (S448.09, Florida Statutes). It is an unlawful employment practice for any employer to knowingly employ, hire, or recruit for private or public employment an unauthorized alien.

Open Meetings Act of 1976 (M.C.L.A. 15.261 et seq.; amendments). This Act, while requiring open public meetings, also provides for limited rights to privacy for individuals on employment issues (through closed sessions regarding performance evaluations, and confidentiality of application files).

Right to Work (S448.045, Florida Statutes). It is unlawful for two or more persons to conspire to discharge or intimidate any person from procuring work in a corporation.

Right to Strike (S447.13, Florida Statutes). An employer may not interfere or impede an employee's right to strike or right to work.

Michigan Closed Shop Act of 1939 (M.C.L.A. 423.14). This act allows for a closed shop collective bargaining arrangement, if agreed to by employer and an employee labor organization. This title is contained in the **Mediation of Labor Disputes Act of 1939** (M.C.L.A. 423.1 et seq; amendments).

Appendix C

Index of Cases and Exercises

G

H

I

J

K

L

M

N

P

R

S

T

W